P9-CCO-138

IMPORTANT:

HERE IS YOUR REGISTRATION CODE TO ACCESS

YOUR ... RESOURCES.

D0435358

For key premium online r ... e code is
entered, you will be able ... .

If your course is using We... access the
McGraw-Hill content within your instructor's online course.

Access is provided if you have purchased a new book. If the registration code is
missing from this book, the registration screen on our Website, and within your WebCT
or Blackboard course, will tell you how to obtain your new code.

Registering for McGraw-Hill Online Resources

To gain access to your McGraw-Hill web
resources simply follow the steps below:

USE YOUR WEB BROWSER TO GO TO: **www.mhhe.com/basics**

CLICK ON **FIRST TIME USER**.

ENTER THE REGISTRATION CODE* PRINTED ON THE TEAR-OFF BOOKMARK ON THE RIGHT.

AFTER YOU HAVE ENTERED YOUR REGISTRATION CODE, CLICK **REGISTER**.

FOLLOW THE INSTRUCTIONS TO SET-UP YOUR PERSONAL UserID AND PASSWORD.

WRITE YOUR UserID AND PASSWORD DOWN FOR FUTURE REFERENCE.
KEEP IT IN A SAFE PLACE.

TO GAIN ACCESS to the McGraw-Hill content in your instructor's **WebCT** or **Blackboard**
course simply log in to the course with the UserID and Password provided by your instructor.
Enter the registration code exactly as it appears in the box to the right when prompted by the
system. You will only need to use the code the first time you click on McGraw-Hill content.

Thank you, and welcome
to your McGraw-Hill
online Resources!

Mc Graw Hill **Higher Education**

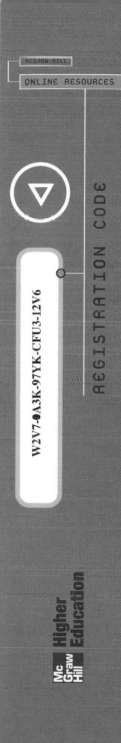

MCGRAW-HILL
ONLINE RESOURCES

REGISTRATION CODE

W2V7-0A3K-97YK-CFU3-12V6

Mc Graw Hill Higher Education

AAC
Taubman, C 201
Tel. (248)204-4120
Email: aac@ltu.edu

THE BASICS

4th Edition

A Rhetoric and Handbook

THE BASICS

4th Edition

A Rhetoric and Handbook

SANTI V. BUSCEMI
Middlesex County College

ALBERT H. NICOLAI
Middlesex County College

RICHARD STRUGALA
Middlesex County College

Boston   Burr Ridge, IL   Dubuque, IA   Madison, WI   New York
San Francisco   St. Louis   Bangkok   Bogotá   Caracas   Kuala Lumpur
Lisbon   London   Madrid   Mexico City   Milan   Montreal   New Delhi
Santiago   Seoul   Singapore   Sydney   Taipei   Toronto

For the Women in Our Lives:
Elaine Buscemi, Dorothy Polaski, and JoAnn Strugala

The McGraw·Hill Companies

Higher Education

THE BASICS: A RHETORIC AND HANDBOOK
Published by McGraw-Hill, a business unit of The McGraw-Hill Companies, Inc., 1221 Avenue of the Americas, New York, NY 10020. Copyright © 2005, 2000, 1998, 1995, by The McGraw-Hill Companies, Inc. All rights reserved. No part of this publication may be reproduced or distributed in any form or by any means, or stored in a database or retrieval system, without the prior written consent of The McGraw-Hill Companies, Inc., including, but not limited to, in any network or other electronic storage or transmission, or broadcast for distance learning. Some ancillaries, including electronic and print components, may not be available to customers outside the United States.

This book is printed on acid-free paper.

1 2 3 4 5 6 7 8 9 0 DOC/DOC 0 9 8 7 6 5 4 3

ISBN 0-07-249198-1

President of McGraw-Hill Humanities/
    Social Sciences: *Steve Debow*
Executive editor: *Lisa Moore*
Senior developmental editor: *Jane Carter*
Executive marketing manager:
    David S. Patterson
Senior media producer: *Todd Vaccaro*
Senior project manager: *Rebecca Nordbrock*
Production supervisor: *Carol A. Bielski*
Senior designer: *Gino Cieslik*

Lead supplement producer: *Marc Mattson*
Manager, photo research: *Brian J. Pecko*
Art director: *Jeanne Schreiber*
Permissions: *Marty Granahan*
Cover and interior design:
    Maureen McCutcheon
Typeface: *10/12 Minion*
Compositor: *Carlisle Communications, Ltd.*
Printer: *R.R. Donnelley and Sons Inc.*

Library of Congress Cataloging-in-Publication Data

Buscemi, Santi V.
    The basics : a rhetoric and handbook / Santi V. Buscemi, Albert H. Nicolai, Richard Strugala.--4th ed.
        p. cm.
    Includes index.
    ISBN 0-07-249198-1 (pbk. : alk. paper)
    1. English language--Rhetoric--Handbooks, manuals, etc. 2. English language--Grammar--Handbooks, manuals, etc. 3. Report writing--Handbooks, manuals, etc. I. Nicolai, Albert H. II. Strugala, Richard. III. Title.
    PE1408.B8852 2004
808'.042--dc22

                                        2003061624

www.mhhe.com

PREFACE

When we originally wrote *The Basics,* we had our own students in mind, many of whom had heavy responsibilities outside the classroom and struggled to compensate for inadequate preparation inside the classroom. Therefore, we set out to provide a handbook that was uniquely supportive of students with both varying levels of experience and varying educational needs. Because *The Basics* needed to be useful both as a classroom tool and as a reference for beginning writers to use independently, we made sure to include an introduction to important writing strategies and a thorough primer on research and documentation, as well as an easy-to-understand handbook on grammar and usage that uses a simple number-based reference system for easy navigation. And because students learn best when they practice skills as they learn them, we included many exercises to reinforce the lessons throughout the book. This edition of *The Basics* continues to do all these things and more.

WHAT'S NEW?

More Support for Students of Varying Abilities   This edition of *The Basics* offers more exercises integrated throughout the text to give students even more reinforcement for newly learned skills. These mini-lessons—from using adverbs correctly to writing effective introductions and editing paragraphs—ask students not just to make corrections to faulty sentences, but also to make the kinds of decisions that they will be called on to make in their own writing. Therefore, they don't just learn the rules; they learn how to apply the rules. The exercises can either be covered in class or assigned as homework to students who need extra help.

More Accessible Approach to Grammar, Punctuation, Spelling, and Mechanics   We continue to avoid jargon in our presentation of grammar, punctuation, spelling, and mechanics so that students can easily identify, understand, and apply the rules. In this new edition, we have made the material in these tabs even more accessible to students by presenting problems and their solutions in smaller, more easily digestible bites and by including checklists (in these tabs and throughout the text) so students will have a handy reminder of what they've learned.

> "The exercises . . . take a student through the ideas in the chapter in the same step-by-step way that the ideas themselves are developed. What is begun in one exercise is extended into others; we don't only get a list of unrelated tasks. Actually, the exercises serve to illustrate how well the ideas in the text progress."
>
> **Mike Cadden**
> Missouri Western
> State College

Demonstrating the Writing Process Through Student Samples   Because our own students don't come to college with an understanding of writing as a process, we cover the basics of the writing process up front, in Tab 1, "Reading, Writing, Arguing," as well as throughout the text. Because students new to college often don't know what's expected of them, we have tried to provide ample student samples to help students visualize what they should be doing at each stage of the writing and research processes. Through fourteen student samples (from single paragraphs to essays in multiple drafts), we *show* students how to write a summary and a critique, how to draft and revise an essay, how to develop an argument, and how to write (and document) a research paper using all the major documentation styles. In Tab 1, "Reading, Writing, Arguing," we include three drafts of a paper on Internet etiquette (or "netiquette"), as well as an argument essay on why we write. Tab 3, "The Research Process," references a paper on bilingual education that is then used as the model paper in Tab 4, "MLA Documentation." Tab 5, "APA Documentation," includes a complete student paper on Down syndrome. We also include two complete student papers, one on Walt Whitman and a new essay on Kate Chopin, in Chapter 18, "Writing About Literature" (in Tab 7, "Special Writing Situations").

> "I found the grammar much more direct and accessible than in any other handbook I have worked with."
>
> **Joyce Brotton**
> Northern Virginia
> Community College

Enhanced Coverage of Critical Thinking and Argument   In this edition of the text, we focus extensively on helping students become critical thinkers. We especially want students to learn to read and respond analytically to the writing of others and to be able to summarize college-level articles and essays accurately. To this end, we have added a new chapter, "Reading Critically" (Chapter 1), that prepares students to become active readers by teaching them how to engage with a text by taking notes, outlining, summarizing, critiquing, and synthesizing. We have expanded the chapter on developing arguments to cover purpose and audience, choosing a thesis statement, addressing opposing viewpoints, and avoiding logical fallacies. It also includes a sample student essay on why we write. By moving our coverage of argumentation into the first section of the book, we help ground students in the thinking processes that underlie so much of college writing.

More Attention to the Basics of Technology   In this edition, we recognize how much the computer has come to dominate college life, and we include a thorough introduction to using the computer. Special emphasis is placed on Internet research (including citing Internet sources and assessing their reliability) as well as the intricacies of using technology in the classroom and in the world of work—from word processing to creating resumés and Web sites to recognizing the differences among communicating with friends, fellow students, teachers, and prospective employers. Three succinct chapters in Tab 2, "Online Writing and Electronic Design," teach students the many ways they can use computers to enhance their college writing; Chapter 7, "Using Computers in College," gives students an overview of the benefits and pitfalls of using word-processing programs to organize and present information; Chapter 8, "Writing Online," offers a brief tutorial on communicating via the Internet—through e-mail, listservs, and newsgroups—and it includes "netiquette" guidelines to help students master the conventions of these new forms of communication; and Chapter 9, "Designing with Computers," includes advice on adding illustrations and graphics to a paper and covers the basics of Web site design. Chapter 20, "Communicating in Business" (in Tab 7, "Special Writing Situations") explains how students can format and post their resumés on the Internet to increase their chances of finding jobs during or after college. Finally, we have added "Basics of Technology" boxes and "basiclinks": "Basics of Technology" boxes support students who are new to using the computer for college writing, and "basiclinks" provide URLs for useful, reliable Web sites.

A Primer on Research   Because so many of our students are attracted to the Internet as a research tool but know little about problems Internet research can present to the unwary, we knew that adding a thorough guide to using the Internet for research was essential. We also knew that students need help finding sites that are not only authoritative but also relevant; that they must learn to use advanced search techniques (such as phrase searching, truncation, and Boolean operators); and that they should be able to differentiate between full texts and abstracts on databases like InfoTrac. Finally,

> "I think this is an excellent text—very thorough and helpful. The strengths include the examples of student writing, the section on paragraphs (Chapter 4), the number and variety of exercises, and the number of topics covered. This text could very well serve a student through all of his or her years in college."
>
> **Terry Craig**
> West Virginia Northern Community College

> "The beginning of the text feels like a course on College 101, which is a very good thing—first year composition courses often serve this function. . . ."
>
> **Anne Mills King**
> Prince George's Community College

we recognized a need to help students learn which online databases would best support their research. To address all these concerns and more, we reorganized and expanded the research section so that it thoroughly addresses not only traditional research and note-taking techniques but also the benefits and pitfalls of research in the electronic age. We include a brief new chapter that walks students through the process of writing a research paper and shows one student's journey from choosing a topic to writing her final research paper. This paper on bilingual education is then used as a model in Tab 4, "MLA Documentation." Finally, a new chapter—"Taking Notes and Avoiding Plagiarism" (Chapter 13)—highlights the potential for unintended plagiarism.

Three Documentation Styles   One of the major goals of the first-year writing course is to help students master documentation, so we have made sure to include the most up-to-date (2003) version of the MLA guidelines. We have also updated our APA guidelines to reflect changes that organization made in 2002. For easy reference, we offer individually tabbed sections on both MLA and APA styles, as well as complete sample student papers with marginal annotations pointing out MLA/APA requirements for layout and documentation. In a third tabbed section, we cover the new 2003 *Chicago Manual of Style (CMS)* documentation format. As students often have difficulty citing Web sites and online databases, we have made sure that the new MLA and APA guidelines on these types of citations are clear and complete.

New Coverage of Classroom Communication   Tab 7, "Special Writing Situations," follows the tabbed section on research and documentation. It begins with Chapter 18, "Writing About Literature," which continues to give students in literature classes special support by including material on topics from active reading to explication and critique. Included are two complete student essays—one on Walt Whitman and a new essay on Kate Chopin—as samples. A new chapter "Communicating in Class: Essay Examinations and Oral Presentations" (Chapter 19) follows, offering students support in two of their most anxiety-provoking classroom situations. Workplace writing, covered in Chapter 20, "Communicating in Business," has been expanded in this edition to include more coverage of writing online, with material on posting resumés to the Web via online employment services such as Monster.com and Hotjobs.com.

A Guide for ESL Writers Tab 12, "A Guide for ESL Writers," provides additional guidance to nonnative speakers. Multilingual students will find in-depth coverage of special usage issues, such as when to use articles; what is appropriate sentence structure in English; how to make subjects and verbs agree; and how to avoid common problems with verbs, adjectives, adverbs, and participles.

A New Design A bright, contemporary design reflects the thoroughness of this revision and will make *The Basics* easier to navigate and more appealing to students.

ANCILLARY PACKAGE

The Basics **Online Learning Center** On *The Basics* Online Learning Center (OLC) you will find Catalyst: A Tool for Writing and Research. Catalyst offers diagnostic pre- and post-tests to help assess students' strengths and weaknesses as well as over 3,000 exercises that provide question-by-question feedback to help students master aspects of the language with which they've had difficulty. Catalyst not only covers common problems with grammar and usage but also includes short (and funny!) animations to reinforce recognition of these problems. And because all scores can be e-mailed to instructors, teachers can make sure students have shown improvement in troublesome areas. Catalyst also offers: a guide to avoiding plagiarism; tutorials for evaluating sources and conducting Internet research; additional sample papers in MLA, APA, and *CMS* format; PowerPoint basics; an index of sound, print, and Internet research materials and sites; guides that provide step-by-step instruction for writing informative, argumentative, and interpretive essays (including literary analyses); a link to the *New York Times* that gives students access to articles on language; and Bibliomaker, a downloadable software program that automatically formats source information in APA, MLA, and *CMS* formats. In addition to Catalyst, *The Basics* OLC also provides additional coverage of "Special Writing Situations," including writing in the sciences, civic writing, and creating an organizational Web site.

Instructor's Manual The instructor's manual has been upgraded and expanded to offer more advice to teachers of writing. In addition, sample responses to all exercises are included.

ACKNOWLEDGMENTS We would like to express our gratitude to those colleagues across the country who reviewed *The Basics* and provided insight, criticism, and advice: Nancy H. Blattner, Southeast Missouri State University; James Brock, Florida Gulf Coast University; Joyce Brotton, Northern Virginia Community College;

Mike Cadden, Missouri Western State College; Shireen Campbell, Davidson College; Vaughn Copey, State University of New York—Cortland; Terry A. Craig, West Virginia Northern Community College; Cherie Post Fargan, Hawkeye Community College; Simone Gers, Pima Community College; Connie Gulick, Albuquerque TVI Community College; Kathleen Hagood, Howard Payne University; Amy Hawkins, University of Maryland; Lee Ann Hodges, Tri-County Community College; Susanna Hoeness-Krupsaw, University of Southern Indiana; Michael J. Hricik, Westmoreland County Community College; Deana Hueners, Dakota State University; Ellen Johnson, Berry College; Joseph P. Kenyon, Cumberland County College; Anne Mills King, Prince George's Community College; Deb Koelling, Northwest College; Kelly L. Krahwinkel, Pellissippi State Community College; Bonnie Kyburz, Utah Valley State College; Lisa J. McClure, University of Southern Illinois; Randall Pease, University of Southern Indiana; David Roberts, Samford University; Mary Peters Rodeback, University of Oregon; Rita Rogers, Halifax Community College; David A. Salomon, Black Hills State University; Lynn Saul, Pima Community College; Derek Soles, Wichita State University; Michael Strysick, Wake Forest University; Sally Wheeler, Georgia Perimeter College; Thomas L. Wiseman, Southern Polytechnic State University; Nancy Young, Curry College.

We are also indebted to several colleagues and friends at Middlesex County College who provided advice, assistance, and encouragement: David Crampton, Sallie DelVecchio, Andre Gitténs, Barry Glazer, James Keller, Jack Moskowitz, Elizabeth Oliu, Georgiana Planko, and Mathew Spano.

We would like to express our sincere gratitude to our McGraw-Hill family, which helped and inspired us during the development of this fourth edition: Rebecca Nordbrock, the project manager without whose efforts this book would still be a manuscript; Alice Jaggard, who patiently and carefully copyedited the manuscript; Gino Cieslik who oversaw the creation of the fabulous new design for *The Basics;* and Carol Bielski, the production supervisor who saw this project through to the end. We are also deeply indebted to Lisa Moore, our editor, for her nagging and pestering us until we got this edition right (we hope users will agree) and to Jane Carter, who oversaw the editorial development of this project. Finally, we extend special thanks to our development editor, Laura Barthule. Without her encouragement, vision, patience, and perseverance—not to mention all her hard work—we would never have completed this very ambitious revision.

We owe much to the women in our lives, to whom this book is dedicated. Their kind words and their example helped keep the spark of inspiration alive. Finally, we thank our students for teaching us so much about writing, learning, and working with others.

Santi V. Buscemi

Albert H. Nicolai

Richard Strugala

ABOUT THE AUTHORS

SANTI V. BUSCEMI is professor of English at Middlesex County College in Edison, New Jersey, where he teaches reading and writing. He received his BA from St. Bonaventure University and completed his doctoral studies at the University of Tennessee. He is the author of both *A Reader for Developing Writers* (McGraw-Hill), now in its sixth edition, and *An ESL Workbook* (McGraw-Hill), and coauthor with Charlotte Smith of *75 Readings Plus* (McGraw-Hill). He also authors McGraw-Hill's *AllWrite!,* an interactive computer software package in rhetoric, grammar, and research.

ALBERT H. NICOLAI is professor of English at Middlesex County College in Edison, New Jersey, where he teaches reading and writing. He received his BA from Hope College and his MA from Temple University.

RICHARD STRUGALA is professor of English at Middlesex County College in Edison, New Jersey, where he teaches reading and writing. Professor Strugala received his doctorate in composition and rhetoric from Rutgers University, where he was elected to Kappa Delta Pi. He is a certified trainer for the New Jersey affiliate of the National Writing Project. Additionally, Dr. Strugala has been selected as a regional scoring leader for the Online Scoring Network (OSN) at ETS in Princeton, New Jersey. The OSN coordinates the holistic scoring of the GMAT, GRE, CLEP, TOEFL, and TSE testing programs.

1

READING, WRITING, ARGUING

READING, WRITING, ARGUING

READING CRITICALLY

1.1 Become an active reader.

The more you read, the more fluent a writer you become. Reading and writing are interdependent—opposite sides of the same coin. In fact, some processes and techniques used in writing are also used in reading.

Like writing, reading is an active process. A curious mind, a questioning attitude, and a desire to engage the text in conversation will help you draw the full meaning from what you read. Effective readers digest, interpret, and evaluate what they read. They interact with the text by considering explicit and implied messages, questioning facts and assumptions, analyzing arguments and logical structures, evaluating evidence, asking questions, and applying their own insights and experiences.

Sometimes you might read an essay, poem, or other work without fully understanding it the first time through. This is normal. Not every text is fully understood the first time you read it, so read it a second or third time. Discuss it with friends and classmates, or put it aside for a few days to let ideas ferment. Doing these things is similar to writing multiple drafts of an essay, getting feedback from others, and putting the paper aside for a while before rewriting it. In short, give the text several chances before you give up on it.

Texts You Might Be Asked to Read in College

- Textbooks in specific disciplines
- Essays collected in anthologies
- Newspaper and magazine articles
- Articles in professional journals
- Monographs, which discuss one issue or question
- Scientific or technical reports
- Government pamphlets
- Literature—poems, plays, short stories, and novels
- Materials published on academic, professional, government, and corporate Web sites

1.2 Prepare to read: Preview.

Previewing, also called surveying, is an essential first step to reading. Previewing reveals much that helps you read more easily, effectively, and enjoyably.

- Begin by looking in the title for clues about what you will find, especially in essays or scholarly articles. Writers of such texts provide hints about content, purpose, and thesis in their titles.

- If a biographical or an introductory note precedes the essay or article—as in many essay collections used in composition classes—read this note before reading the essay itself. It may provide information about the education, writings, and other aspects of the author's life that will help you approach the text. It might also help you understand the cultural, historical, or political context in which the text was written, and it might provide clues to the author's purpose and point of view. If the note indicates the publication date or the title of the publication in which the text first appeared, you might be able to infer something about the author's purpose and intended audience.

- Read the first and last paragraphs carefully. An introductory paragraph is a good place to state a thesis, but depending on purpose and audience, a writer might place the thesis in the essay's body or conclusion. He or she might even choose not to state the thesis explicitly. Nonetheless, the introductory paragraph can provide clues about organization, purpose, and supporting ideas.

- Read subheadings or subtitles. They usually appear in boldface and can reveal much about the text's contents and direction. Then skim every paragraph for ideas that support the thesis. (You can draw an analogy between the human body and an essay: the thesis is the head or brain; supporting ideas are the skeleton; and details that develop those ideas are the flesh and blood.) Often, supporting ideas are expressed as conclusions. Look for words and phrases such as *therefore, thus, as such,* and *as a result.* They are often signals that the writer is stating an important conclusion or idea to support the thesis.

Preparing to Read

Read a chapter from a college textbook; an editorial from a national newspaper or major newsmagazine such as Newsweek, Time, *or* U.S. News & World Report; *or an article from a prominent publication such as* National Geographic, Harper's, *or* Atlantic Monthly *or from a magazine assigned by your instructor. Preview this text by following the advice provided above. If you want, try to find an article from an online version of one of the magazines mentioned.*

■ ■ ■ ■   ■ ■ ■ ■   **B A S I C L I N K**   ■ ■ ■ ■   ■ ■ ■ ■

WWW

Use the following addresses to access these publications online:

http://www.newsweek.com	**Newsweek**
http://www.usnews.com	**U.S. News & World Report**
http://time.com	**Time**
http://nationalgeographic.com/	**National Geographic**
http://www.harpers.org	**Harper's**
http://www.theatlantic.com	**Atlantic Monthly**

1.3 Read, take notes, and outline.

Some texts can be understood on the literal level. They mean exactly what they say, with little room for interpretation. Others require you to draw inferences (conclusions). In such cases, readers might come up with different interpretations of a statement or even of an entire essay that are equally valid. The more sophisticated a text— the richer its fabric of words and ideas—the more subject it is to varying interpretations. As you attempt your first reading, keep the following in mind:

- When you read a text for the first time, your aim is to comprehend the literal meaning.

- Reading with a pencil or highlighter in hand will allow you to underline words and phrases, make notes in the margins, and highlight sentences. However, a first reading will undergo revision. If you read the text a second time, you will have a clearer understanding, and you may want to change, delete, or clarify your notes. Therefore, use a pencil and eraser when you first read a text.

- If you come upon unfamiliar words, expressions, and historical or cultural references, don't be alarmed. Such encounters make reading a valuable process of discovery and growth. When this happens, underline or circle the items so you can look them up in a dictionary or encyclopedia later. Stopping immediately to look them up will break your concentration.

- Mark the thesis and important ideas that support the thesis.

- In the margins, write short questions about points that you don't fully understand, that you find interesting, or that simply trigger questions in your mind.

- To strengthen your grasp of the text, write an informal outline of its major points.

Outlining an Article, an Essay, or a Chapter in a Textbook

After your first reading, look over the words, phrases, and sentences you have underlined or marked. Then read the notes you made in the margins. Doing so should give you information you can use to make an informal outline of the text. Such an outline resembles the scratch outline you might make when writing an essay, as explained in Chapter 3.

1. Start by stating the essay's thesis.
2. Then list each of the major ideas the author uses to support that thesis.
3. Under each of those major ideas, list or summarize important details that illustrate, develop, or otherwise support each of the ideas.

Read "Uncle Sam Needs You," an essay by John Leo, as well as the marginal notes a student made as she first read this piece.

Uncle Sam Needs You
by John Leo
(A Student's First Reading)

John Leo has written for Time *and for the* New York Times, *has been an editor of* Commonweal, *and has worked as a columnist for* Society *and the* Village Voice. *Today he writes a column called "On Society" for* U.S. News & World Report, *a weekly newsmagazine. "Uncle Sam Needs You" appeared in the October 29, 2001, issue of that publication.*

1   During the go-go '90s, anybody who was anybody went into finance, entertainment, media, or law. <u>Those fields are</u>   *Thesis?*
<u>bloated with talent.</u> We will never run out of people eager to amuse us or to help us sue our neighbors. Other jobs, including just about everything in the public sector, were considered to be for those lower down the food chain. Now we must alter those priorities. We need our best young people to enter the fields that protect us from the threat of terrorism. <u>Those</u> fields are the ones looked on with
(indifference,) if not (disdain,) by our chattering and scribbling   *Meaning?*
classes: public service and national security, including the FBI, the CIA, and the military.

2   <u>Change is coming.</u> The president of Harvard said recently that a <u>career in the military is a "noble" calling.</u> Stop the presses. He   *Supporting ideas*
said this because his university's tradition of looking down its nose at the armed forces is under mild attack from alumni. Some 900 <u>Harvard graduates, including former Defense Secretary Caspar</u>   *Supporting ideas*
<u>Weinberger, want the university to allow the Reserve Officers'</u>
<u>Training Corps back on campus.</u> Like many elite universities, Harvard threw the ROTC off campus during the turmoil over

Vietnam. Students can join the ROTC, but they have to trek a mile or two over to the Massachusetts Institute of Technology to train. A crazed student group advocating the violent overthrow of the government would probably command space on campus, but the ROTC is different. It just wouldn't be right to have the grass of Harvard Yard (defiled) by the military boot. At Yale the trek is even longer and thus presumably more humiliating. To fulfill ROTC requirements, a student has to make a 150-mile round trip to the University of Connecticut for weekly training.

Meaning?

Supporting idea

3   **Mired in 1969.** The problem is obvious: On a great many campuses it is still 1969 and a generalized contempt for the armed forces is still fashionable. Americans of all classes and backgrounds including Jack Kennedy and George H. W. Bush, quickly signed up for World War II. The day after Pearl Harbor, according to the late columnist Rowland Evans, the line of Yale students waiting to enlist stretched around the block.

Subhead: signal to contents of paragraph

Supporting idea

Leo shows how things have changed

4   But the elites sat out Korea and Vietnam. Columnist James Pinkerton reports that Princeton lost 353 men in World War II but just 24 in Vietnam. This tradition continues: Princeton's Army ROTC graduated a grand total of two people last May. The elites think of the military as a source of (regimentation) and armed oppression. They don't serve and usually they don't even know anyone who does.

Restates an idea from paragraph 3; adds detail

Meaning?

5   A similar pattern holds at the CIA. The agency was created after World War II almost wholly by elites who felt the strong pull of patriotism. Most of the network that founded the agency came from Yale. The elites of the next generation felt differently. In recent years, the CIA recruited heavily among top collegians but had much more success at Big Ten and Big 12 schools than at places like Harvard, Yale, or Stanford. Even before the end of the Cold War, the elites came to see the CIA as a grubby cloak-and-dagger operation unworthy of a high-minded nation. And though they were reluctant to work for the CIA, they didn't leave it alone, either. One result of their meddling was that the CIA was effectively banned from recruiting unsavory characters to penetrate terrorist cells. That rule has now been repealed. The penetration no longer has to be accomplished solely by (choirboys,) but we still don't know how much damage the old ban inflicted.

Supporting idea

Which are?

Supporting idea

Meaning? What's he driving at?

6   The distancing of the elites from the people who protect us shows up in a lot of odd ways. Look at all the journalism about the more than 300 firefighters and police officers who lost their lives trying to save others at the World Trade Center. The praise was sincere, but much of it seemed drenched in astonishment, as if it had never occurred to the writers that these people might be worthy of great respect for what they do, that maybe they aren't

Leo implies lack of support for police—this is changing

Idea relates just a collection of <u>Archie Bunkers</u> who <u>can't seem to get jobs in</u>   *Allusion to*
well to Leo's <u>major corporations.</u>   *TV show*
thesis   7   America does not like to think of itself in terms of social
classes, but there are elites, and these elites sometimes seem to hold
themselves aloof from the work of defending the nation at time of
great peril. <u>The first step should be to shed the old Vietnam-era</u>   *Supporting*
<u>hostility toward the armed forces and security personnel in gen-</u>   *ideas*
<u>eral. The next step is to respond to the call.</u>
          8   <u>There are already good signs.</u> A CIA spokesman said the   *Supporting*
agency was getting 500 to 600 résumés a week from college stu-   *idea*
dents around the country before the September 11 attacks and is
Day after   now getting 10 times that number. At some colleges there were   ⌐ *Examples*
Pearl   even long lines waiting to see recruiters—a welcome echo of the | *that*
Harbor was | *illustrate*
attacked!   line of enlistees from Yale <u>on Dec. 8, 1941.</u>   ⌐ *the above*

THE BASICS OF TECHNOLOGY

USING A WORD PROCESSING HIGHLIGHTER

You can use your word processor's color highlighter to mark important
words and sentences in a document that is on the computer. This feature will
come in handy when you read a document for the first time. When you read
the document for a second or third time, you may want to eliminate some of
your original highlighting. You can do this easily by marking the text and then
clicking on the highlighter a second time. As you will realize, highlighting can
be useful as a tool for outlining as well. You can also add notes or questions
through your word processor's comments feature.

To get a document onto your computer screen, you will have to type it
yourself, import it through a scanner, or convert a document found on the
Internet into a word processing file. If you choose to use a scanner, remember that scanning technology is not perfect; you may have to revise and edit
the scanned document carefully.

Here's an example of an informal outline of Leo's essay:
Thesis: Bright young people needed to enter the military and other security
          services to fight against terrorism.

- In the past, talented graduates entered media, law, and other
  money-making fields, not public service.
  1. They wanted to get rich.
  2. They disliked the military during and after Vietnam, especially
     in the "elites."

3. Their interest in joining FBI and CIA decreased because "elites" hated these agencies.

4. For the same reason, image of the police tarnished.

- However, since attacks of September 11, 2001, talented young people showing renewed interest in protective services.

Taking Notes and Outlining

Use a pencil to make notes on the text you previewed in Exercise 1A. Underline the thesis and supporting ideas, and ask questions or make comments by writing brief notes in the margins. Then use this information to construct an informal outline. As an alternative, do this assignment on the computer, converting a magazine article found on the Web and using your word processor's highlighter feature to indicate the thesis and the supporting ideas.

:: EXERCISE 1B

1.4 Converse with the text: Read it again.

As you approach the text again, pretend you are having a conversation with the author. The text represents his or her part of the conversation. Your part of the conversation comes as you make marginal notes and underline important ideas to do the following:

- Add information that helps you understand a point, state agreement or disagreement, or express another point of view.
- Draw conclusions from the material presented and add insights, facts, and opinions taken from your own experiences, observations, or reading.
- Challenge facts, opinions, statistics, "expert" testimony, or other pieces of evidence.
- Challenge illogical conclusions. For example, if a writer indicated that because your hometown mayor is single she can't be family oriented, you would challenge that statement as illogical.
- Question the author's reference to undocumented sources. If your read that "a recent study proves eating chocolate softens the skin," you might ask: "Which study? Who conducted it? Where can I find a copy of the study?" and other legitimate questions.
- Comment on the author's tone and language. Is the essay fair and objective, or is it biased? Does it express a legitimate concern, complaint, or purpose, or is the author's position compromised by self-interest, personal feelings, or even ignorance? If the essay's purpose is to persuade, does the writer remain fair while appealing to the reader's emotions or self-interest, or is his or her approach excessive, one-sided, or even misleading?
- Make changes as appropriate in the notations (marginal notes, underscoring) you made during your first reading.

During this stage in the process, carry a healthy dose of skepticism. After all, even villains and liars have had their works published. So don't believe everything you read. Questioning, challenging, and demanding proof are the signs of an enlightened reader.

Reread the first five paragraphs of John Leo's essay, which follow. Notice the marginal and textual notes that the student has added as she read the essay for a second time. On what questions or matters has the student added information? Has she changed her mind on which statement is Leo's thesis? Has she identified any new supporting ideas or changed her mind about others?

Uncle Sam Needs You
by John Leo
(A Student's Second Reading)

1   During the go-go '90s, anybody who was anybody went into finance, entertainment, media, or law. Those fields are <u>bloated</u> with talent. We will never run out of people eager to amuse us or to <u>help us sue our neighbors</u>. Other jobs, including just about everything in the public sector, were considered to be for <u>those lower down the food chain. Now we must alter those priorities. We need our best young people to enter the fields that protect us from the threat of terrorism</u>. Those fields are the ones looked on with (indifference,) if not (disdain,) by our <u>chattering</u> and <u>scribbling</u> classes: public service and national security, including the FBI, the CIA, and the military.

Tone seems informal, relaxed

Strong word; negative implications?

Sarcasm

Thesis

Does he mean the media? unclear

Apathy/ scorn

2   <u>Change is coming. The president of Harvard said recently that a career in the military is a "noble" calling</u>. Stop the presses. He said this because his university's tradition of <u>looking down its nose</u> at the armed forces is under mild attack from alumni. Some 900 Harvard graduates, including former Defense Secretary Caspar Weinberger, want the university to allow the Reserve Officers' Training Corps back on campus. Like many elite universities, <u>Harvard threw the ROTC off campus during the turmoil over Vietnam</u>. Students can join the ROTC, but they have to trek a mile or two over to the Massachusetts Institute of Technology to train. A crazed student group advocating the violent overthrow of the government would probably command space on campus, but the ROTC is different. It just wouldn't be right to have the grass of Harvard Yard (defiled) by the military boot. <u>At Yale the trek is even longer and thus presumably more humiliating</u>. To fulfill ROTC requirements, a student has to make a 150-mile round trip to the University of Connecticut for weekly training.

Supporting idea

Leo uses direct quotation from an authority

Interesting image, but clichéd

Reference to historical/ political phenomenon

Supporting idea

Tone sarcastic

Soiled

Supporting idea

3   **Mired in 1969.** The problem is obvious: <u>On a great many campuses it is still 1969 and a generalized (contempt) for the armed forces is still fashionable</u>. Americans of all classes and backgrounds, including Jack Kennedy and George H. W. Bush, quickly signed up for World War II. The day after

Subheading: signals contents of paragraphs 3 & 4

Supporting idea

Strong noun

Appeals to authority on the subject

Pearl Harbor, according to the late columnist Rowland Evans, the line of Yale students waiting to enlist stretched around the block. | *Details show how things have changed*

Using "elite" sarcastically?

Appeals to authority and uses specific details as support

4   But the elites sat out Korea and Vietnam. Columnist James Pinkerton reports that Princeton lost 353 men in World War II but just 24 in Vietnam. This tradition continues: Princeton's Army ROTC graduated a grand total of two people last May. The elites think of the military as a source of (regimentation) and armed oppression. They don't serve and usually they don't even know anyone who does. | *More details like those in paragraph 2 Strict rules, little freedom*

5   A similar pattern holds at the CIA. The agency was created after World War II almost wholly by elites who felt the strong pull of patriotism. Most of the network that founded the agency came from Yale. The elites of the next generation felt differently. In recent years, the CIA recruited heavily among top collegians but had much more success at Big Ten and Big 12 schools than at places like Harvard, Yale, or Stanford. | *Supporting idea* *(Michigan, Ohio)*

Is this conclusion fair and logical? Is it substantiated?

Even before the end of the Cold War, the elites came to see the CIA as a grubby cloak-and-dagger operation unworthy of a high-minded nation. And though they were reluctant to work for the CIA, they didn't leave it alone, either. One result of their meddling was that the CIA was effectively banned from recruiting unsavory characters to penetrate terrorist cells. That rule has now been repealed. The penetration no longer has to be accomplished solely by choirboys, but we still don't know how much damage the old ban inflicted. | *Sarcasm?* *Supporting ideas*

Conversing with the Text

Reread the essay, article, or textbook chapter you took notes on for Exercise 1B. Make additional marginal notes and underline words and sentences to create a conversation with the text, as explained above. You might also revise or remove notes you made during your first reading. Then review and, if appropriate, revise the informal outline you made after your first reading. Again, you may want to do part of this on a computer by using your word processor's highlighter, printing out a hard copy, and then making marginal notes by hand.

EXERCISE 1C

1.5 Summarize: Make what you have read your own.

Summarizing is the restatement of the text's main and supporting ideas in your own words, thereby confirming your grasp of those ideas. Summarizing also requires you to manipulate someone else's language as you transform it into your own. Thus, it forces you to put into concrete form ideas and insights that otherwise would have remained abstract and vague. As such, summarizing always enhances comprehension.

Unlike a paraphrase, which simply restates the original in new words, a summary also condenses the original. Depending on its length and complexity, a chapter in a textbook or an article in a journal might be summarized in a few paragraphs. A summary of an essay of 1,500 to 2,000 words could be 150 to 200 words. Read the following tips on writing summaries. Then read the summary of Leo's essay, which follows.

- Before summarizing, read the text at least twice, make ample marginal notes, and mark important ideas.

- Review marginal notes and reread ideas you have marked.

- As a general rule, begin your summary by stating the essay's thesis, whether explicit (stated) or implied in the original. Also, consider stating the author's purpose and intended audience.

- Next, state each of the supporting ideas used to develop the thesis.

- Depending on the thoroughness required, include one or two examples of the details used to develop each supporting idea.

- If you believe it is necessary to use some of the author's own words, introduce them appropriately and place quotation marks around them (see Chapters 15–17).

- Don't summarize each of the essay's paragraphs in a sentence, one by one, in the order in which the paragraphs appear. Authors sometimes develop supporting ideas with details spread over more than one paragraph. Summarizing every paragraph in such cases is unnecessary. It is also misleading because it gives emphasis to minor aspects of the essay. (Remember that a summary is a condensation, not the restatement of every detail.) Finally, such an approach shows that the reader's grasp of the text's purpose and main idea is weak.

Here is a successful example of a student's summary of Leo's article:

Student Summary of John Leo's "Uncle Sam Needs You"

U.S. News & World Report columnist John Leo believes that talented people are needed in professions that protect us from terrorism. In "Uncle Sam Needs You," Leo charges that in the recent past, many talented young people shunned such professions for more lucrative careers in law and business. He traces the reason for lack of interest in the military to a "generalized contempt" for the armed services that developed during the Vietnam era. This is especially true at some Ivy League universities, which the author calls "elites." Students of Yale, Harvard, and Princeton were quick to enlist after the attack on Pearl Harbor, but no such commitment has been seen since then, claims Leo.

The same is true of interest in joining the CIA, whose power has been weakened, he implies, because of political influence exerted by the "elites." Even the image of the police has been unfairly affected. For Leo, the press's reporting on the dedication of the officers at the World Trade Center was tainted with astonishment—as if such heroism was unexpected. Despite such discouraging remarks, however, Leo offers evidence that respect for and interest in the protective services may now be on the rise.

Express a Unique Perspective: Avoid Plagiarism!

You can find out more about summarizing, paraphrasing, and quoting directly in Chapter 13, "Taking Notes and Avoiding Plagiarism." For now, make sure your summary is your original restatement of the text and that it contains no traces of plagiarism—do not repeat key words or phrases unless you put them in quotation marks, and do not rely on the author's sentence patterns.

The two summaries below are based on the first paragraph of John Leo's "Uncle Sam Needs You" (page 6). The first contains plagiarism—language is taken directly from the essay but not put in quotation marks; the second does not.

Summary with plagiarism: In the '90s, our best young people took jobs in high-paying areas such as finance, the media, and law. Today, however, public service and national security jobs need their talents.

More original summary: Today, the defense and well-being of the American people require that bright college graduates enter government service rather than more lucrative professions as they did a decade ago.

Note: The underlined words in the first example come directly from Leo. This version also seems to be modeled on the organization of Leo's work. The second example is a completely new rendering in both content and organization.

•••• •••• •••• THE BASICS OF TECHNOLOGY

••• •••USING THE SPLIT-SCREEN FUNCTION TO PARAPHRASE AND CHECK FOR PLAGIARISM

Most word processors offer a split-screen function, which can aid in both checking for plagiarism and summarizing material. With the split-screen function, you first type the original version of a text on the top half of the screen. You can then independently summarize that text on the bottom half of the screen. Each half of the screen can be scrolled separately, allowing you to compare specific sentences and paragraphs in detail to make your summary more accurate and to eliminate plagiarism.

:::: EXERCISE 1D

Summarizing

Using the notes you made for Exercise 1C, write a summary of the text you have been reading. Try to make use of your word processor's split-screen function to do this.

1.6 Critique: Evaluate what you have read.

A critique evaluates the validity (truth, accuracy) of a text's message and the effectiveness with which it is presented. An effective critique can identify both strengths and weaknesses.

A critique is usually longer than a summary. Depending on the assignment, it can even be a full-length essay. To write a critique, begin by reviewing your marginal notes and your summary. If necessary, go back to the text itself and reread it. Revise the notes you have already made in light of the criteria, or measuring sticks, you have decided to use to evaluate what you have read.

Criteria used to evaluate a text can differ from reader to reader. Below are only a few questions you might ask as you critique a text. Perhaps they will help you create some of your own criteria.

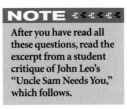

NOTE

After you have read all these questions, read the excerpt from a student critique of John Leo's "Uncle Sam Needs You," which follows.

Suggested Criteria for Evaluation

- What are the author's credentials? Is the source in which the essay was first published a reputable periodical, book, or other publication?
- Are the essay's thesis and purpose clear and reasonable? Does the author focus on a limited topic, or does he or she attempt to cover too much?
- Does the author use supporting ideas that are clear, credible, and logical? Do they relate directly to the thesis of the essay?
- Are supporting ideas developed in sufficient detail? Is that detail convincing?
- Does the author make unsubstantiated claims? Do these claims need support, or are they self-evident?
- Does the author use evidence from studies, experts, or other authorities to support his or her thesis without identifying these authorities by name? Is sufficient information provided to enable the reader to access these sources?

- Are these sources objective, complete, and trustworthy? Or are they biased? Is the research they contain reliable? (See pages 177 and 192–195, which cover evaluating Internet and other electronic sources; the same criteria can be used to evaluate print sources.)
- Is the author impartial, or does he or she use language intended to appeal to the reader's emotions and self-interest? If the latter, is this language simply strong and moving, or is it unfair, biased, or inappropriate in any way?
- Does the author use information that is incomplete or incorrect? If so, how much does this problem affect the essay's credibility?
- Does the essay lack important information that you know might contradict one of its supporting ideas or even its thesis? Has the author left this material out to mislead the reader?
- Does the author raise important questions and answer them adequately? Does he or she include opposing arguments and address them fairly and completely?
- Is the essay well organized and unified? Or does it contain material that is out of place or irrelevant?
- Is the language of the essay appropriate to the intended audience? Does it contain jargon and other language that is unnecessarily sophisticated?
- Does the essay keep your interest? What techniques—startling remarks and statistics, thought-provoking images, interesting examples, effective verbs and adjectives, and so on—does the author use to keep your attention?
- Is the author's tone appropriate to the intended audience and purpose? Should he or she have used less formal diction? Should he or she have used rhetorical questions or tried addressing the reader directly now and then? Or should the tone of the essay have been more formal or more objective?

The following two paragraphs have been excerpted from a complete essay. In them, student writer Vincent Terzo focuses on critiquing Leo's use of logic and of supportive details.

NOTE

If you believe it is important to include some of the author's own words, feel free to do so, but remember to use quotation marks.

Wisely, Leo does not feel the need to support his contention that more talented young people should enter careers that will protect us against terrorism, especially in light of the events on and after September 11, 2001. Instead, he focuses on the reasons young talents have stayed away from such careers in the last few decades, and he does an excellent job of explaining the role some Ivy League universities (he calls them the "elites") have played in discrediting the military. Citing facts and statistics from respected journalists, Leo paints a convincing picture. He also explains that the expulsion of ROTC cadres from the "elites" during the Vietnam era may have contributed to a "generalized contempt" of the military.

He is less convincing, however, when he discusses the CIA. Leo accuses the "elites" of weakening the CIA by "meddling" in its operations and supporting a ban on "recruiting unsavory characters to penetrate terrorist cells." However, he never explains the nature or extent of such meddling, nor does he substantiate the assertion. The same is true of his claim that the press's recent praise of the police for their heroism at the World Trade Center "seemed drenched in astonishment, as if it had never occurred to the writers that these people might be worthy of great respect." His argument might have been stronger had he quoted from an editorial or opinion column to illustrate such "astonishment."

EXERCISE 1E

Critiquing

Continue the process you have been working through in Exercises 1A through 1D by writing a critique of the essay, article, or textbook chapter you have been reading. Begin by reviewing the suggested criteria for evaluation, which appear above.

1.7 Synthesize: Bring ideas together in a new statement.

Learning to synthesize, or to bring ideas together from different sources, is a logical step in the development of critical reading skills. Synthesizing requires restating, combining, and reconciling ideas, opinions, and information from various sources in a logical and coherent way. Courses you take in college will ask you to evaluate one writer's position against another's, compare or contrast ideas on the same issue, and even create an entirely new perspective after reading several different discussions on a related issue. However, this new response should be more than a conglomeration of borrowed elements. It should also reflect your own ideas, perspectives, and experiences. Just as important, it should be developed and organized in a way you think suits your purpose.

A synthesis, then, is not simply a random mixture of ideas borrowed from others. It is a well-crafted and purposeful piece that uses the writer's ideas as well as

Crediting Your Sources

When you use other authors' materials in a synthesis, you must provide parenthetical citations (credits) that inform your reader that the material is not your own. You must do this whether you paraphrase, summarize, or quote directly. Follow standard guidelines such as those required by the Modern Language Association (see Chapter 15), the American Psychological Association (see Chapter 16), or the *Chicago Manual of Style* (see Chapter 17).

those of others to create a new statement or a new focus on the issue at hand. Indeed, the reason you write a synthesis and the thesis it develops may, in fact, be quite different from the purposes and theses of the resources from which you borrow information.

Read "A New Start for National Service," an essay by Senators John McCain and Evan Bayh, which appeared in the *New York Times*. It discusses a topic related to the one discussed in John Leo's "Uncle Sam Needs You," which appears on pages 6–8. After you complete "A New Start for National Service," read student Vincent Terzo's "Renewing Our Commitment," a synthesis of the pieces by Leo and by McCain and Bayh.

A New Start for National Service
by John McCain and Evan Bayh

1   Washington—Since Sept. 11, Americans have found a new spirit of national unity and purpose. Forty years ago, at the height of the cold war, President John F. Kennedy challenged Americans to enter into public service. Today, confronted with a challenge no less daunting than the cold war, Americans again are eager for ways to serve at home and abroad. Government should make it easier for them to do so.

2   That is why we are introducing legislation to revamp national service programs and dramatically expand opportunities for public service.

3   Many tasks lie ahead, both new and old. On the home front, there are new security and civil defense requirements, like increased police and border patrol needs. We will charge the Corporation for National Service, the federal office that oversees national volunteer programs, with the task of assembling a plan that would put civilians to work to assist the Office of Homeland Security. The military will need new recruits to confront the challenges abroad, so our bill will also improve benefits for our service members.

4   At the same time, because the society we defend needs increased services, from promoting literacy to caring for the elderly, we expand AmeriCorps and senior service programs to enlarge our national army of volunteers.

5   AmeriCorps' achievements have been impressive: thousands of homes have been built, hundreds of thousands of seniors given the care they need to live independently and millions of children tutored.

6   Since its inception in 1993, nearly 250,000 Americans have served stints of one or two years in AmeriCorps. But for all its concrete achievements, AmeriCorps has

been too small to rouse the nation's imagination. Under our bill, 250,000 volunteers each year would be able to answer the call—with half of them assisting in civil defense needs and half continuing the good work of AmeriCorps.

7 We must also ask our nation's colleges to promote service more aggressively. Currently, many colleges devote only a small fraction of federal work-study funds to community service, while the majority of federal resources are used to fill low-skill positions. This was not Congress's vision when it passed the Higher Education Act of 1965. Under our bill, universities will be required to promote student involvement in community activities more vigorously.

8 And for those who might consider serving their country in the armed forces, the benefits must keep pace with the times. While the volunteer military has been successful, our armed forces continue to suffer from significant recruitment challenges.

9 Our legislation encourages more young Americans to serve in the military by allowing the Defense Department to create a new, shorter-term enlistment option. This "18-18-18" plan would offer an $18,000 bonus—in addition to regular pay—for 18 months of active duty and 18 months of reserve duty. And we would significantly improve education payments made to service members under current law.

10 Public service is a virtue, and national service should one day be a rite of passage for young Americans. This is the right moment to issue a new call to service and give a new generation a way to claim the rewards and responsibilities of active citizenship.

1.8 Respond: Make your voice known.

There are times when your instructor will ask you to respond to an essay's thesis and supporting ideas as well as to critique the essay. These functions can be combined in a "critique and response" paper. In other cases, you might want simply to respond to the author's opinions or ideas. As with a critique, you can respond positively or negatively or both. Remember, however, that a response goes far beyond a simple summary. While you may find it necessary to restate the author's thesis and supporting ideas briefly, you should assume that your reader is as familiar with the text as you are and that he or she would find a summary unnecessary.

In a response, you must comment on the author's ideas by agreeing, disagreeing, drawing comparisons, adding evidence, presenting another point of view, raising questions, applying these ideas to other things you have read or observed, or doing all these things. Remember that you are still trying to engage the text as you did when you made notes in the margins or underlined important points. Now, however, your part of the conversation takes a more formal and organized shape. You are creating your own text, which might serve as a complement to, an addition to, or a rejection of the original text. In fact, it might serve all these purposes. The student paper that follows is an effective example of a response essay.

Terzo 1

Vincent Terzo

Professor Smith

English 201

27 June 2003

Renewing Our Commitment

Frames synthesis in
introductory
paragraph.

The events of September 11, 2001, have aroused a new patriotism in the American people. We have become aware that ensuring this country's welfare and safety is an enormous task requiring our vigilance and dedication. At the same time, many of us are calling for a renewed commitment to public service.

Uses signal phrase
(page 216) to refer
to Leo article.

In "Uncle Sam Needs You," syndicated columnist John Leo argues that the "protective services," including the military, the police, the FBI, and the CIA, need more young talent than ever before. In the recent past too many bright college gradu-

Summarizes Leo's
position.

ates—especially those from prestigious schools—have held such service in contempt and, instead, have opted for more lu-crative careers in law, business, and the media (pars. 1–2).

Cites relevant
paragraphs.

Summarizes
McCain/Bayh's
position.

U.S. Senators John McCain and Evan Bayh also see the need for an infusion of talent in the public sector. In "A New Start for National Service," they discuss legislation they have co-sponsored to increase interest in public service. For example, by invoking provisions of the 1965 Higher Education Act, the McCain/Bayh bill would require that colleges and universities en-courage students to engage in public service as part of their

Uses signal phrase to
refer to
McCain/Bayh article.

Terzo 2

academic requirements (par. 7). Such incentives are sorely

States own perspective.

needed. Currently, too few colleges make such activities attractive to students. My school is the only one of five in the state that offer public service courses for credit. We run a tutoring service for children at a nearby shelter, but only a few students participate.

Summarizes McCain/Bayh and student's own perspective.

The McCain/Bayh bill also includes incentives for joining the military: salary bonuses, shortened enlistment and reserve periods, and better educational benefits for veterans (pars. 8–9). While such support is needed, the government should also provide new incentives for service in the FBI and CIA; after all, given the recent terrorist attacks, including the anthrax problem, domestic security is a priority. Still, McCain/Bayh does propose expanding the mission of AmeriCorps to include "civil defense" as well as humanitarian services. Finally, there are incentives for volunteering in the work of the newly created Office of Homeland Security (pars. 3–6).

In his inaugural address, President Kennedy urged: "Ask not what your country can do for you. Ask what you can do for your country." In his "Thousand Points of Light" speech in 1988, George H. W. Bush, father of the current president, urged his fellow citizens to commit themselves to volunteerism. After so many years and so much tragedy, perhaps more of us will take the challenge of serving our neighbors, our community, and our country. Let us

Clearly restates thesis in conclusion.

hope that volunteerism becomes part of the American way of life.

Note difference between student's purpose and those of sources.

Terzo 3

Works Cited

Leo, John. "Uncle Sam Needs You." <u>US News & World Report</u>
29 Oct. 2001. 8 Nov. 2001 <http://www.usnews.com/
usnews/issue/011029/opinion/29john.htm>,

McCain, John, and Evan Bayh. "A New Start for National
Service." <u>The New York Times on the Web</u> 6 Nov. 2001.
11 Nov. 2001 <http://www.nytimes.com/2001/11/06/opin-
ion/ 06MCCA. html'?todaysheadlines>.

EXERCISE 1F

Synthesizing

Find another essay that relates directly to the topic or issue addressed in the essay you have been reading for Exercises 1A through 1E. Then write a short essay in which you synthesize ideas from what you have read with your own ideas.

Chapter Checklist

1 Like writing, reading is an active process. It requires intellectual curiosity, a questioning attitude, and a desire to engage the text in conversation.

2 Previewing is an essential first step in reading. As you skim, consider the title first; then read any subheadings used in the body of the text. Don't ignore introductory notes preceding the text, and pay close attention to introductions and conclusions.

3 Complete your first reading with a pencil in hand. Underline important elements, and make notes in the margins. Your aim at this stage is to understand the literal meaning, so if you come upon unfamiliar words or references, mark them and look them up later. Underline the thesis and important supporting ideas. Finally, make notes in the margins next to words or sentences that are unclear, that raise questions, or that arouse your curiosity.

4 To improve your grasp of the reading, write an informal outline using the notes and marks you have made during your first reading.

5 Read the text a second time. Erase old notes and add new ones that reflect your growing understanding. As you proceed, converse with the text: question the author, challenge his or her ideas, references, conclusions, sources, and so on. Also, draw your own conclusions from the text. Comment on the author's tone, language, and objectivity.

6 To solidify your understanding, write a summary of the text. Make sure you are expressing ideas in your own voice; avoid plagiarism.

7 Learn to pose evaluatory questions, which will help you frame a critique of the text's effectiveness and validity—its message, organization, and style.

8 A synthesis is not just a mixture of the ideas of others. Although it may use information from outside sources, it should contain your ideas and observations as well. More important, it should be informed by your unique perspective and direction.

9 When you respond to a text in writing, you are again engaging it in conversation; but you are also creating your own text, which might complement, add to, or reject all or part of what you have read.

PREWRITING

2

About now, you may be asking yourself: "Why do I need to take a writing course? After all, I took English in high school."

A college writing course sharpens the skills you need to continue your education or enter a career. At home, you will write notes and letters; at college, you will take essay tests and write essays; on the job, you will prepare memos and reports. The better your writing skills, the better readers will respond to you—and the better your chances for success!

2.1 See writing as a process of discovery.

The writing process involves several steps that build on one another. But don't get the idea that once you've completed the first step you should proceed to the second and third without ever looking back. You can and should stop often, review what you have done, and immediately make changes.

Say you decide to describe a city park. You begin by visiting the park and taking notes about what it looks like, sounds like, smells like, and so on (prewriting). You list details about the bench you sit on. You describe the graceful willow, the sound of newborn sparrows, and the smell of honeysuckle. When you get home, you read your notes and decide you have enough details to start drafting. As you write an outline and rough draft, you focus on the park's natural beauty, which you decide is its most important quality. Therefore, you cross out information about the bench and concentrate on the willow and the sparrows.

All of a sudden, however, you remember the park's most beautiful natural feature: a pond that is home to ducks and geese. So, before beginning the second draft, you start to record details about the pond and its inhabitants. You make a few sketchy notes. But your memory fails you, and you decide to return to the park to gather more details.

As you can see, writing does not always take you in a straight line from start to finish, from information gathering to final product. You may have to double back to gather more information, to eliminate facts and ideas that are no longer important to your project, or to focus on aspects of your subject that need clarifying.

Writing always involves discovery. That's what makes it exciting. The more you discover about a subject, the better you understand it and the more likely you are to change what you thought you wanted to say when you began. Don't mistake such changes as signs of indecision or confusion. They are important stages in any project, and they usually mean you are developing skill as a writer and as a thinker.

2.2 Learn four steps in the writing process.

Generally speaking, there are four steps in the writing process:

1. Prewriting is the stage in which you gather information (details) about your subject. It can take three forms:

- Recording what you already know through observation, reading, or experience.
- Interviewing people knowledgeable about your subject.
- Researching your subject in books, magazines, newspapers, journals, pamphlets, films, and electronic media such as CD-ROMs and the Internet.

2. Outlining and writing a rough draft begin when you read over your notes—the information you have collected in step 1. Then you can:

- Clarify your purpose and decide on a preliminary central idea—the idea that your paper will support, develop, defend, or prove.
- Determine your audience (readers) and their needs, and decide how best to approach them.
- Outline the structure of your essay, at least in preliminary form.
- Write your first draft, following the preliminary outline you just made and using the information you gathered in step 1.

3. Revising your first draft means rewriting, rewriting, and rewriting. As you proceed, each of your many drafts will become clearer, more detailed, better organized, and easier to follow.

4. Editing and proofreading, although often the last step in the process, are as important as the other steps. Editing means reading the best of your drafts and correcting grammar, punctuation, and other common errors discussed later in this text. It also means refining word choice, removing wordiness, and varying sentence structure to make your writing more concise and more interesting. Proofreading ends this process. Make sure that you have not left out words, that your spelling is correct, and that you have removed typographical errors.

2.3 Learn the basics of prewriting: Gathering information.

Ordinarily, you gather facts, opinions, ideas, statistics, and quotations at the start of a project, during the prewriting stage. However, you can continue to gather information at any point in the process whenever you need to add details. Basically, gathering information is done by

- Writing down what you already know about a subject.
- Recording what others say or have written about it.

2.3a Learn five ways to record information you already know.

Always begin by writing down what you already know about your subject. Doing so will help you gain self-confidence and overcome writer's block, the problem of staring at a blank page or computer screen without knowing how to begin. Five ways to gather information you may already know are listing, focused freewriting, brainstorming, clustering, and drawing a subject tree.

1. Listing is a quick way to record what is most important, startling, or obvious about your subject. Start with three or four broad details that first come to mind as you think about your subject. Here's how you might begin if you are describing your reaction to a serious auto accident:

Dizziness, nausea

Fear

Pain

My car, a lump of twisted steel

Sound of metal, glass breaking

Rough lists such as this one need not be precise or complete; their only purpose is to help you begin thinking about your subject. You can provide more exact details as you review each item and expand it. For example, you might expand "Fear" by writing

Thought I broke my leg

Was car about to explode?

Parents' reactions?

Heard police sirens/ambl'nce

Did brother get out of the wreck?

Don't know where I am

By going through the same process with the other four items in your rough list, you can continue adding details until you have enough to begin the first draft of a paragraph or an essay about this frightening event. Such a list might end up looking like this:

<u>Dizziness, nausea</u>

Disoreented

Forget where I am for a moment

Couldn't remember where I was going

Felt like vommiting

Trouble keeping my balance, head spining

Triped over the curb and fell on some wet grass

> **NOTE** ⟨⟨⟨⟨⟨
> **Do not worry about misspellings, repetition, and other errors at this point. You can correct them when you edit and proofread.**

<u>Fear</u>

Thought I broke my leg

Was car about to explode?

Parents' reactions?

Heard police sirens/ambl'nce

Did brother get out of the wreck?

Don't know where I am

<u>Pain</u>

Sharp, stabbing pains in arms and legs

Headache

Bruises on my face and elbow burned

Worried about my leg

<u>My car, a lump of twisted steel</u>

Camaro sandwiched between a light pole and the other car

Three cars wheels are off ground and spinning

Glass strewn across the street

I smell gasoline

Car leaking fluid

<u>Sound of metal, glass breaking</u>

Crunch of steel

Two loud thuds echoes in my mind

Glass tears into my coat an rip my forarm

Like the list above, yours may be a mixture of words, phrases, and complete sentences. It may also contain errors. *But these are unimportant at this point.* You can correct them later.

Always review any list of details you make—after, and only after, you think you have run out of things to say. Doing so will help you add other important details and make those you've already included clearer and more specific. After rereading the list above, for example, you might expand "Worried about my leg" to "My right leg had gone numb. I panicked and began to fear that I had lost it."

2. Focused freewriting is another good way to record what you know. It is the process of writing nonstop for five or ten minutes by recording facts and ideas as they pop into your mind. Focused freewriting requires you to concentrate on a chosen subject as you go along.

Details gathered through this method take the form of loosely constructed sentences and paragraphs. Here's what you might have written if you had used focused freewriting to gather details about the car wreck:

> I was disoreented, didn't remember where I was going. Felt like vommiting. For a minute, I had trouble keeping my balance, my head spining and I triped over the curb and fell on some wet grass. Was car about to exlode? Had I broken my leg? I thought about my parents, their reactions to all this. What happened? The police came. Heard their sirens screeching and the ambulance arrive—remembered brother. Was he out of the car? Where was he? How did I get here. Where is here? My legs and arms hurt—sharp, stabbing pains—head pounds. The Camaro was sandwiched between the light pole and the car that I hit (that hit me?) I became really worried about my leg. My head hurt badly, the brulses on my face and elbows burned, and my head pounded. No feeling in my leg. Is it there? Gas. 3 of wheels are off the ground and spinning.
>
> Glass tears through my coat an rips into my forarm. Gas stinks. There's glass across the street, gasoline leaking everywhere, antifreeze. Will this car explode? The crunch of steel and the two loud thuds still echo in my head.

Again, there's no need to worry about grammar and mechanical errors *at this time.*

3. Brainstorming by asking questions can result in the creation of a list, a paragraph, or even a group of loosely connected words and phrases spread across a sheet of paper. In some cases, what results from brainstorming looks like a big mess, a series of doodles with no meaning except, of course, to the writer who made them.

You can begin brainstorming in a variety of ways, but one of the best is to ask yourself the kinds of questions journalists ask to develop news stories: "What happened? Who was involved? When and where did it occur? How and why did it happen?"

Let's say you want to gather information for a paper on the irresponsible use of electronic devices. You might ask questions like these to get started:

What electronic devices do I use? For what purpose?

Where do people use electronic tools?

Where and when should such devices be banned?

Which devices cause the most annoyance?

Where and when can electronic devices constitute a danger?

What are the effects of microwave ovens on people with pacemakers?

Are wearing earphones and listening to a portable CD player really rude?

What dangers are associated with the use of car phones?

Should there be a penalty for disturbing the peace by blasting your car or portable radio?

What rights do bus and train passengers have? Do they have the right not to be disturbed by others talking on cell phones?

Why don't students turn off cell phones and beepers in class?

How can we convince advertisers not to turn up the volume when they air their TV commercials?

How can I stop unwanted sales calls at my home?

Why do people create computer viruses?

What damage can computer viruses cause?

Not every question will yield details that show how annoying or dangerous the abuse of electronic gadgets can be. However, one or two answers might provide enough information to begin a more complete discussion. Gathering details is a part of the writing process sometimes called invention, so invent as many questions as you need. Then, relying on your own experiences, answer these questions by recalling as much information as you can. If necessary, do some more brainstorming and get the opinions of others on this issue. For more demanding assignments, you might complete library or Internet research. (You can find out more about researching a topic in Chapters 10–12.)

Here is some information you might have put down in response to the preceding brainstorming questions:

Laptop computers, CD players,
cell phones and other electronic
devices can interfere with an airplane's
navigation system during takeoff and landing.

Cellular phones—on buses, trains, or
other crowded places—disturb others,
intrude on their privacy.

Car phones—can be dangerous.
Don't talk and drive!
Choose a designated caller!

Beepers that beep in class break my concentration.
Outlaw cell phones and beepers in class!

Blasting car radios distract drivers,
destroy their hearing;
Disturb our peace.

Computer viruses destroy
hours of work.

Using electronic devices
irresponsibly can annoy others
and be downright dangerous.

Viruses interfere with computer-controlled
equipment in hospitals, airports, etc.

■■■■   ■■■■   **BASICLINK**   ■■■■   ■■■■

WWW

Need more information on the value of brainstorming? Try
http://pratt.edu/~wtc/samplebrain.html
This Web site will provide you with a list of information gathered through
brainstorming as well as a link to the paper that resulted from it.

■■ ■■ ■■ ■■ ■■ ■■   ■■ ■■ ■■ ■■ ■■ ■■

Of course, you can always invent questions by yourself, but brainstorming can and should be shared with other writers. Together you may be able to find details that one person working alone might miss. Don't hesitate to join your classmates in asking and answering questions that will help each of you gather information on your topics.

4. Clustering, also called mapping and webbing, is a good way to shrink a broad subject into a limited topic that you can write about in a short essay. At the same time, it will help you gather details to use in your first draft.

Clustering works through free association, the same method used in focused freewriting. To cluster ideas, begin with a blank sheet of paper. In the middle, write

NOTE ⫷⫷⫷⫷⫷

As you will see in Chapter 3, in addition to helping you gather details, prewriting makes it easier to focus on a more defined topic. For example, in answering the brainstorming questions, the student has also focused on ideas related to "electronic communications devices," which is a more limited and focused topic than "electronic devices."

down and circle a word or phrase that names the general subject you want to write about. Let's say your general subject is "Violence in America." Think of ideas and details related to this subject. Write down whatever comes to mind. For example, you might think of subheadings such as "Domestic violence," "Rape," and "Street violence." Arrange these subheadings in circles around your general subject. Your paper might look something like this:

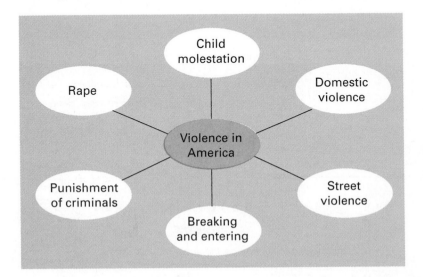

Next, write down ideas and details related to these subheadings; continue in this way until you run out of space or ideas. Circle each word and phrase, and draw lines between headings and the ideas and details that are directly related to them. The next page shows what your clustering might look like if you chose "Violence in America" as your general subject:

Notice that some subheadings receive greater attention than others. For example, the writer seems to have had more to say about punishment and child molestation than about street violence or breaking and entering. Clustering helps you focus on the aspect of your general subject that you know most about or are most interested in.

5. Drawing a subject tree is another good way to narrow a topic so that you can manage to cover or develop it adequately in a short essay. As with clustering, start with a broad subject. Then divide that subject into two or three branches, or subheadings. Next, subdivide each of those branches, and so on. Continue until you have narrowed your subject sufficiently and gathered enough detail to begin writing. On page 32 is an example that begins with "Diet and health" as the general subject.

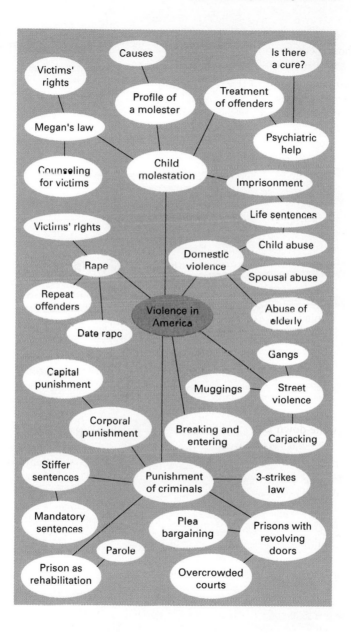

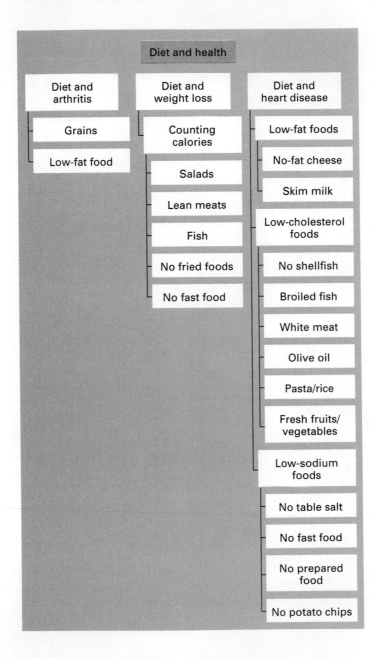

As you create a subject tree, you will almost naturally put down more details and ideas about subheadings that you know more about or have greater interest in. For example, the student who created the subject tree for "Diet and health" would probably be most comfortable writing an essay that focuses on the ways diet can reduce the chances of developing heart disease. Like clustering, creating a subject tree can help you discover the best and easiest topic to write about as you gather the details for a first draft.

Writing Down What You Know

EXERCISE 2A

Using a word processor or pen and paper, record details about one of the following subjects. Use one of the five methods just discussed: listing, focused freewriting, brainstorming, clustering, drawing a subject tree. If nothing on the list interests you, choose your own subject. Either way, pick a topic you know a lot about or have discussed with friends or classmates. Keep this information handy; you will find it useful when you complete the exercises in Chapter 3.

Using tax dollars to support private education
Illegal immigrants and public assistance
Random drug testing of transportation workers
Welfare reform
Your worst date
What you hate or like most about your school, job, or family
A favorite sport or pastime
Dieting
Penalties for drunk driving
Your hometown or neighborhood
Junk food: its effects on health
Juggling demands of school with those of work or family
Censorship of the Internet
Smoking
Why people join cults

2.3b Gather additional information if needed.

After recording what you know about a subject through listing, focused freewriting, brainstorming, clustering, or drawing a subject tree, you might find that you need even more information. Two ways to gather such material are summarizing what others have written about your subject and interviewing people who know a lot about it.

1. **Summarizing** is putting another writer's ideas into a few words of your own. A summary is shorter and more compact than the original; it includes only major points. (Chapters 1 and 13 contain more about summarizing.) Here is a paragraph from Gail Sheehy's "Jailbreak Marriage," followed by a student's summary:

SHEEHY

Although the most commonplace reason women marry young is to "complete themselves," a good many spirited young women gave another reason: "I did it to get away from my parents." Particularly for girls whose educations and privileges are limited, a jailbreak marriage is the usual thing.

STUDENT SUMMARY

According to Gail Sheehy many women marry young to escape their families. This is especially true of those who have few opportunities before marriage.

You can combine summarized information with what you already know about your subject or with details from other sources. Be careful to use your own words throughout the summary. Also, make sure your reader knows that the information you've summarized comes from someone else's work by giving that writer credit. For example, the student who summarized from "Jailbreak Marriage" used a signal phrase—"According to Gail Sheehy"—to alert the reader to the source of the ideas included.

Chapters 1 and 13 contain more about how to include information from someone else's work (through summaries, paraphrases, and direct quotations). Chapters 15, 16, and 17 explain how to cite (give credit to) the sources of such information. For more on summarizing, see Chapter 13.

···· ···· ···· THE BASICS OF TECHNOLOGY

⠒ ⠒ ⠒ SUMMARIZING

If you are summarizing a document that is in a Microsoft Word file, you can use the AutoSummarize tool found on Word's pull-down Tools menu. It will highlight key words and ideas and will even provide you with an executive summary. Keep in mind, however, that you will be able to use such material only as a guide to writing your own summary.

Another helpful device when summarizing is Word's highlighter tool, which appears on its formatting toolbar. It works just like a manual highlighter and comes in a variety of colors.

You can copy files from the Internet directly into Microsoft Word and then save them as electronic files. Of course, if the document you are summarizing is not in an electronic file, you will have to type or scan it in. In either case, make sure to read and edit this document carefully before you begin.

2. Interviewing is an excellent way to gather details from people who are more familiar with your subject than you are. Interviewing gives you at least one other perspective from which to view your subject and can yield information that otherwise you might not have learned.

Prepare for your interview carefully. Spend time thinking of questions that will draw useful information from the person you're interviewing. Questions you might ask during an interview are similar to those used in brainstorming.

···· ···· ···· THE BASICS OF TECHNOLOGY

USING E-MAIL TO INTERVIEW

Perhaps the person you want to interview is too far away or does not have the time to meet with you during business hours. You can try telephone interviewing, but that can get expensive. An alternative is e-mailing your subject a list of clear, precise questions that he or she can answer on that very e-mail. You may have to send several e-mails back and forth just to clarify points. This method provides an instant and automatic record of what is being discussed, and you can be sure that any quotations you get will be precise because they will have been written by the interviewee him- or herself.

Gathering Additional Information

Summarizing

Browse through a textbook you are using for another course and find two interesting paragraphs of about 100 words each. Summarize each of these paragraphs in a shorter paragraph of your own. Capture each writer's main idea in your own words.

Try doing this assignment on a computer. First, type or scan in the original paragraphs, converting them into electronic files. Then use your word processor's autosummarizing tool to help you identify main ideas. Rephrase each main idea in your own words. Remember, however, that this is your work, and you can reject information provided by the autosummarizing tool.

Interviewing

1. *Find someone, perhaps an instructor, who knows about the subject you considered in Exercise 2A. Schedule a twenty-minute interview with him or her, and state your subject when you make the appointment. Give your interviewee an idea of the kinds of questions you will ask so that he or she can prepare. Take notes by hand or via a laptop computer. You might want to conduct this interview through e-mail. At any rate, make an electronic record of the interview, which may mean transcribing your handwritten notes into an electronic file later on.*

2. *Gather information about the history of your hometown, campus, or family by interviewing someone who remembers important events in that history. People older than you would make the best subjects, but those your own age might also provide valuable information. Begin the process by choosing a topic that is focused. For example, start with a particular section of town or a particular family member.*

One or more of the ways to collect details explained in this chapter should help you gather plenty of information for projects you will be assigned in college. Keep these methods in mind, especially when you find yourself staring at a blank page or screen and having trouble deciding what you know about a subject or what you want to say about it.

Chapter Checklist

1. As you write, you will discover what you know about your subject (perhaps more than you thought), what you still need to find out, and what is important to you.

2. The writing process has four stages: prewriting, outlining and drafting, revising, and editing and proofreading.

3. In the **prewriting** stage, you gather information for your writing project by
   a. **Writing down** what you know about your subject.
   b. **Interviewing** people who know about your subject.
   c. **Researching** your subject in books, articles, and other materials.

4. The first version of your writing project is the **rough draft,** in which you begin to develop and organize your paper and decide on a central idea.

5. You then **revise** your draft several times, adding details and making your writing clearer and better organized.

6. In the **editing** process, you correct errors in grammar, spelling, punctuation, and so on, and you **proofread** your final version to make sure it is free of errors.

7. Begin the writing process by writing down what you already know about a subject. You might try
   a. **Listing** a few broad ideas that come quickly to mind.
   b. Recording information through **focused freewriting**, writing on a chosen subject nonstop for five or ten minutes.
   c. **Brainstorming** by asking questions that bring to mind details you can use.
   d. **Clustering** facts and ideas through free association.
   e. **Drawing a subject tree** to collect information and narrow a topic.

8. Gather any additional information you need by
   a. **Summarizing** another writer's ideas.
   b. **Interviewing** people who know about your subject.

OUTLINING AND DRAFTING AN ESSAY

3

In Chapter 2, you learned to gather details. Chapter 3 shows you how to consider both audience and purpose as you review your notes and design a working thesis statement. From there, you can write an outline—a blueprint for your essay—which can then help you write your rough (first) draft.

3.1 Consider your writing situation: Purpose and audience.

3.1a Determine your purpose.

Let's say you decide to write about your high school education. You might entertain the reader with a story about your history class, compare two schools you attended, or give reasons high schools should require foreign-language study.

Once you have determined your purpose, focusing on a main point will be easier, for you will have begun to decide which of the details you gathered in your notes will be useful and which will not. If you want to compare two high schools you attended, you can include details about their academic programs, athletic teams, students, or teachers. You might even compare the quality of their cafeteria food. But you wouldn't mention that you began guitar lessons a year before you left your old school or that you broke your leg a week after you transferred to your new one.

Determining Your Purpose

Turn back to Exercise 2A on page 33. If you responded to this exercise, read your notes about the subject you chose. (If you did not respond to Exercise 2A, do so now.) Next, write a sentence or two explaining what your purpose would be if you planned to write an essay on this subject. Record this information in an electronic file.

:: EXERCISE 3A

3.1b Consider your audience.

Before beginning your first draft, take a few moments to consider your audience, the people who will read your writing. Then consider the level of language you should use to communicate most effectively with these readers.

Consider the Needs of Your Audience

1. Assess your readers' level of education. In many academic situations, you will be addressing an instructor, and you can assume a high level of vocabulary and education. In other situations, you may be asked to write to fellow students, who may not have the same sophisticated command of language or educational background. In such cases, you may have to use language that, while accurate, forceful, and formal, is simpler and more universally understood.

2. Assess your readers' knowledge of your subject. If you are writing a review of a rock concert for your college newspaper, the majority of your readers will be students, who will probably understand much of the jargon and specialized vocabulary associated with contemporary rock music. They might even be fairly well grounded in the careers of particular artists or bands or in the development of particular styles of rock music. Therefore, you will not have to worry about avoiding or defining special rock-music terms or including a lot of background information when discussing musical history, styles, and techniques. But would the same be true if you were writing the review for a sixty-year-old professor whose vision of contemporary music extends no farther than Crosby, Stills, Nash, and Young (whoever they are!)?

The point here is that even highly educated people may have no knowledge of certain subjects, while people who may not be highly educated may be experts on certain subjects.

3. Assess your readers' interest in your subject. If you are writing to an environmental magazine advocating the preservation of wetlands in your state, you know that regular readers of that magazine will likely be interested in your topic. However, what if you are writing an essay to be distributed in your college writing class? Many students, and perhaps even your instructor, may have no interest in or knowledge of wetlands. In that situation, you will have to make an extra effort to get their full attention. To do this, you might use one of the techniques for writing effective introductions explained in Chapter 4. In the process, you might also explain the widespread effect of preserving those wetlands on the rest of the environment, even in places where no wetlands exist.

4. Assess your readers' position on your subject. Plunging directly into your argument by stating your thesis up front might work well with readers who are in complete agreement with your point of view, but what if your audience is undecided or even opposes your point of view? In such cases, you might first have to address opposing arguments and point out their weaknesses. Or you might acknowledge the validity of such arguments while proving that your position is more reasonable or represents a better alternative.

For example, say you are invited to write a guest editorial for your college newspaper arguing that all students, no matter what their national or ethnic backgrounds, should meet the same competencies in writing for graduation. Your audience is diverse, with 30 percent of the students being recent immigrants who speak English as a second language. You might begin such an editorial by acknowledging and praising the desire of such students to advance themselves through college study. You might also express your appreciation of how difficult it is to become an effective writer, even for native speakers. Only then might you go on to explain that English mastery is required for anyone who is to be successful in college and in the world of work.

5. Assess your relationship with the reader. As you will see in the next section, considering your relationship with the reader is extremely important when it comes to choosing the level of language you will use, as well as determining the value of specific pieces of information to include. You would certainly not think twice about using formal language when writing a business letter or an academic research paper. But would you use this level of formality when writing a letter to a former high school classmate? By the same token, you would not have to go into detail when, in a cover letter to a resumé, you explain that what you learned in organic chemistry will help you in your career as an environmental scientist. Explaining the importance of such a course to an entering college freshman, on the other hand, might take more effort.

Determine the Type of Language You Should Use

In general, there are three types of language:

1. Informal You can use informal language when writing to yourself and to friends and acquaintances. In such cases, your purpose might be simply to convey personal news. Such writing often includes slang (read more about slang on page 429), common household expressions, phonetic spellings, and even terms that only you and your readers understand. The tone or attitude expressed through such language is relaxed and easy. Often the writer uses contractions, such as "they're" for the more formal "they are."

Let's say you write to your best friend describing students you have met at college. Here is the kind of language you might use:

> Can you believe it? Some of the guys I hang with would remind you of the "Geek Cadets" we knew at Hoover High. They're intense. But they're cool because they know that hitting the books is key. And they're into some tough majors, so you got to admire them.

2. Familiar You might use familiar language when writing to relatives or to the editor of a local or college newspaper or when composing short business memos. Let's say you are writing a letter to your aunt on the subject described above. Here's what it might look like:

> My friends are pretty serious, but I admire them, even if they are trying to become eggheads. They're majoring in difficult subjects, and they know that burning the midnight oil is a must if you are going to do well.

This version is more formal than the first; it resembles everyday conversation among educated people. It does not contain slang or private language, but its tone is still a bit chatty, relaxed, and familiar. For example, the writer:

- Uses the colloquial expressions "pretty serious" for the formal "very serious," and "eggheads" for the formal "intellectuals." (You can read more about colloquial expressions in Chapter 31.)
- Includes the clichés "burning the midnight oil" and "is a must." (A cliché is a phrase the lacks originality; you can read more about clichés in Chapter 31.)
- Uses contractions.
- Addresses the reader directly (by using "you" rather than "they" or "one").

3. Formal This is the kind of language you should use when writing college essays; formal letters; or official business, technical, or government reports. Your audience for such writing will be instructors, classmates, business associates, and the like. Let's say you are describing fellow students in an essay for a college writing class. You might write the following paragraph:

People I call my friends are ambitious and studious. They have chosen challenging academic majors, know that working hard is essential to success, and are striving to become genuine intellectuals.

NOTE
You can read more about audience in Chapter 6, pages 98–99.

■■■■   ■■■■   **BASICLINK**   ■■■■   ■■■■
WWW
More on assessing and writing to an audience can be found at
http://www.dc.peachnet.edu/~shale/humanities/composition/handouts/
audience.html

■■ ■■ ■■ ■■ ■■ ■■   ■■ ■■ ■■ ■■ ■■ ■■

3.2 Make the central idea the focus of your writing.

The **central idea,** also known as the main idea, communicates your main point and purpose. It also determines the kind of detail a piece of writing contains.

The central idea can be expressed in an essay's **thesis statement.** This statement clearly expresses the point you wish to make, your reason for writing the essay in the first place. The central idea is the **focal point** to which all details in your essay point. Think of your writing as a photograph. Just as you focus your camera by aiming it at a fixed point, you can focus your writing by making every detail it contains relate directly to a central idea. In fact, every piece of information you include in your essay should help prove, illustrate, or support your central idea. You can also compare the central idea to an umbrella. Expressed as a thesis, it will be the broadest or most general statement in your essay, under which all other ideas and specific bits of information fit logically.

Writers often express the central idea in a thesis statement that appears at the beginning of a piece of writing in an introductory paragraph. (You will learn to write introductions in Chapter 4.) However, the thesis statement can come anywhere the writer thinks best. For example, if you need to give readers introductory details that will make the central idea easier to understand, you can place the thesis in the middle or even at the end of an essay. Doing so can also help build suspense. Finally, this technique lets you avoid offending readers who at first might oppose an opinion you are presenting.

3.3 Write a working thesis statement.

A working thesis statement is your first attempt to express your central idea formally. You will probably revise it many times as you draft your essay and discover exactly what you want to say about your subject. You will learn how to draft an essay later in this chapter. For now, remember that writing a working thesis involves two steps:

1. Choosing a subject to write about
2. Deciding what point to make about the subject

A subject—such as those you read about in Chapter 2—is abstract, general, and incomplete. A central idea, on the other hand, is concrete and specific; it has certainty and completeness. Compare a vague subject such as "cigarette smoking" with a central idea such as "Cigarette smoking is expensive, harmful, and offensive." Or consider how much more meaningful "poverty" becomes when you write "Signs of poverty are increasing in large cities." In general, the essays you write in college will be to make a point or to argue for a position.

Turning a subject into a central idea is easy, but you must decide why your subject is important or interesting to you and what you want your readers to know about it. In general, the more excited you are about your topic, the easier it will be to make your writing interesting to your readers.

Deciding on a central idea is called **focusing.** Begin focusing by reviewing the notes you made about a topic through listing, focused freewriting, brainstorming, clustering, or drawing a subject tree. Also, recall what you decided about your audience and purpose. Then, with that information fresh in your mind, ask yourself these questions:

1. What main point do I want to make about the topic?
2. What details should I include to develop or support that main point?
3. How do I limit the discussion to a manageable length?

3.3a Find your main point.

The next step in the process of focusing is to decide what to say about your subject. What is the most interesting or important point you want to make about the two high schools you are comparing? The answer will be your **main point,** the point that ties all the details of your essay together.

Once again, you turn an abstract subject into a central idea by stating a main point about that subject. If the main point of your comparison is that entering a new school improved your attitude toward education, your central idea might read (main point in italics): "Changing high schools *made me a more serious student.*"

Below, main points (in italics) have been added to subjects. Items on the right are clearer, more specific, and more complete than those on the left.

Subject	Working Thesis Statement
Uncle Theodore	Uncle Theodore *is a big spender.*
homelessness	Homelessness *has increased dramatically in my community over the last two years.*
sky diving	Sky diving *can be dangerous.*
strong math skills	Strong math skills *are required of engineers, computer programmers, and economists.*
heart disease	Heart disease *can be treated through exercise, diet, and medication.*

EXERCISE 3B

Finding Your Main Point

Turn back to Exercise 3A on page 37. Read the purpose statement you wrote about a subject you might discuss in an essay. You probably saved it in an electronic file. Now write a working thesis statement for that subject. Use the preceding examples as guides.

3.3b Select details.

Focusing will help when you start the first draft of an essay; a good working thesis statement will guide you in choosing details you should or should not include. Say your central idea is "Transferring from Lincoln to Buchanan High made me study harder." You might compare Buchanan's faculty with Lincoln's teachers, discuss the caliber of Buchanan's student body, or describe its excellent library and science labs. You might even explain that Buchanan's athletic program sparked your interest in school. But you probably wouldn't tell which school had the larger enrollment or discuss the cafeteria food.

Selecting Details

Reread the working thesis statement you wrote in Exercise 3B. Now turn back to the notes you took when you responded to Exercise 2A on page 33. Reread those notes and pick out items important to that working thesis statement. Explain why certain items you recorded during prewriting should not be included in an essay based on your working thesis.

_____

_____

_____

_____

_____

3.3c Limit the discussion to a manageable length.

Ordinarily, college students write short essays. That's why you should limit your working thesis statement and make it as specific as you can. Otherwise, you won't be able to develop it in enough detail to make your point clearly, completely, and persuasively.

Say you want to persuade someone to stop smoking. You know this person is impatient with lectures and won't read more than a couple of pages. Therefore, you limit yourself to three of the most convincing reasons to stop smoking: the health risks, the rising price of cigarettes, and the discomfort smoking causes others. Your working thesis is "Break the habit: it will ruin your health, empty your wallet, and annoy your friends."

You begin your rough draft by discussing several serious illnesses caused by smoking. After a few sentences, however, you realize that you can't cover all three reasons and keep the essay within two pages, so you decide to limit your thesis by writing on health risks alone. Your thesis statement thus becomes "Break the habit: smoking causes heart disease, emphysema, and cancer."

NOTE

Clustering and drawing a subject tree, which are explained in Chapter 2, are good ways to turn a broad subject into a shorter, more manageable topic while you gather details for your first draft.

More Advice on Writing a Thesis Statement

1. Make your thesis a complete sentence, which contains a subject and a verb and which expresses a complete idea.

    Not: Misusing popular electronic devices

    Not: How misusing popular electronic devices annoys others

    But: Misusing popular electronic devices annoys others.

2. Limit your focus.

    Not: Misusing electronic devices annoys others.

    Not: Using electronic devices annoys others.

    But: Misusing popular electronic devices annoys others.

3. State your main point directly; don't announce it.

    Not: In this paper I am going to discuss the fact that misusing popular electronic devices annoys others.

    Not: This essay will discuss how misusing popular electronic devices annoys others.

    But: Misusing popular electronic devices annoys others.

4. Don't explain that your thesis represents your own opinion. Readers can assume that for themselves.

    Not: I believe that misusing popular electronic devices annoys others.

    Not: In my opinion, misusing popular electronic devices annoys others.

    But: Misusing popular electronic devices annoys others.

5. Make your point clearly.

    Not: Misusing popular electronic devices affects others.

    But: Misusing popular electronic devices annoys others.

6. Be straightforward; try not to hedge.

    Not: At times, misusing popular electronic devices annoys others.

    Not: Misusing popular electronic devices can annoy others.

    But: Misusing popular electronic devices annoys others.

NOTE ⚞⚞⚞⚞⚞⚞

You can find more on writing a thesis in Chapter 6, "Developing Arguments."

. . . .   BASICLINK   . . . .
WWW

If you need more help in creating a thesis, go to
http://leo.stcloudstate.edu/acadwrite/thesistatement.html

3.4 Review information and check the working thesis.

Before you start outlining, review the details you want to use in your essay. Make sure they are appropriate to your audience and relate to your purpose and working thesis. Discard material that does not relate to them, and add new material that seems necessary. Keep your notes handy; they will help you as you construct an outline and write a first draft. Next, check your thesis to make sure it's clear. Let's say you start with the following:

Topic: Electronic communications

Purpose: To discuss the misuse of electronic devices

Main point about topic: It causes problems.

Working thesis: The misuse of electronic devices causes problems.

As you review your working thesis, you realize that your main point isn't clear and that your topic should be more limited: "In what ways are electronic devices being misused? What problems does this cause? What kinds of electronic devices do you want to discuss?" The answers come when you reread the information you already gathered about this topic through brainstorming (see Chapter 2, pages 28–29). This information is repeated on the next page.

After rereading these notes, you decide that your chief interest lies in electronic *communications* devices, and you are especially concerned with how annoying the misuse of these gadgets can be. So you refine your working thesis as follows:

The misuse of electronic communications devices is annoying.

This working thesis can be the starting point for an outline.

> **NOTE**
>
> This chapter recommends that you write a preliminary thesis, then an outline, and then a rough draft. This method works well for many students. However, you may want to approach this process in a different order. For example, you might choose to write the thesis statement after completing the first draft. Also, you can repeat steps as often as you like. For example, you might want to rewrite your outline after completing your rough draft, or you might want to rework your thesis after completing an outline.

Laptop computers, CD players,
cell phones, and other electronic
devices can interfere with an airplane's
navigation system during takeoff and landing.

Cellular phones—on buses, trains,
other crowded places—disturb others,
intrude on their privacy.

Car phones—can be dangerous.
Don't talk and drive!
Choose a designated caller!

Beepers that beep in class break my concentration.
Outlaw cell phones and beepers in class!

Blasting car radios distract drivers,
destroy their hearing;
disturb our peace.

Computer viruses destroy
hours of work.

Using electronic devices
irresponsibly can annoy others
and be downright dangerous.

Viruses interfere with computer-controlled
equipment in hospitals, airports, etc.

Checking Your Working Thesis

1. *Write a working thesis statement about a limited topic such as one of those listed below.*

Limited Topics to Choose From
The three best things about your campus
The three worst things about your campus
The reasons you decided to attend college
The reasons you decided to attend your particular college
Three things to do if you want to flunk out of college
Three good ways to lose weight
The reasons to begin a regular exercise program
The qualities that make a particular relative interesting or fun to be with
How to wash a car, paint a wall, bathe a baby, or complete any common household
   task

Use an outline like this:

Topic: _____

_____

Purpose: _____

_____

Main point about topic: _____

_____

Working thesis: _____

_____

Record this information in an electronic file.

2. On a separate piece of paper or in an electronic file, write two or three more thesis statements about other topics. Then review these statements and try to make them even clearer and more specific.

3.5 Write a scratch or formal outline.

3.5a Write a scratch outline.

Some writers make a detailed outline before they start drafting. However, a rough, or scratch, outline often provides enough of a blueprint for your first draft.

Make your working thesis the starting point for a scratch outline. The following outline was drawn from the working thesis about the misuse of electronic communications devices. It begins with introductory or background material, including the working thesis. Then it lists four major headings that cover various types of devices the writer has chosen to discuss. Each heading groups related details and, therefore, helps organize the body of the essay. The information under each heading comes from the notes made during prewriting (see the brainstorming section on pages 28–29). The outline ends with a conclusion, which explores possible remedies for the problem.

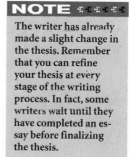

NOTE The writer has already made a slight change in the thesis. Remember that you can refine your thesis at every stage of the writing process. In fact, some writers wait until they have completed an essay before finalizing the thesis.

ANNOYING CONVENIENCES

1. Introduction
   a. Increases in number and kinds of electronic devices
   b. Usefulness of cell phones, beepers, computers
   c. Abuse of cell phones, beepers, computers, portable CD players
   d. Starting example from recent personal experience
   e. **Working thesis:** Misusing electronic communications devices annoys others.
2. Playing car stereos at blast levels
   a. Adds to noise pollution
   b. Endangers user's hearing
   c. Distracts driver

3. Computer viruses
   a. Ultimate horror
   b. Frustrates personal communication
   c. Destroys important work—academic, business, and professional
   d. Costs people and businesses tons of time and money
   e. Interferes with computer-controlled systems at airports, hospitals, military bases, railroads
4. Beepers and cell phones
   a. Disturbing beeps and rings at inappropriate times and places—in class, in church, at funerals
   b. Loud talking into cell phone while on a bus, train, or plane disturbs others around you
   c. Driving while holding or dialing a cell phone causes accidents
5. Portable CD players with earphones
   a. Annoy people who are trying to speak with you
   b. Insulting to teachers and other students when worn in class
6. Conclusion—What can be done?
   a. Restatement of idea in introduction
   b. Outlaw cell phones in class, cars
   c. Punish virus creators

···· ···· ···· THE BASICS OF TECHNOLOGY

⠿ ⠿ ⠿ USING A WORD PROCESSOR TO CREATE OUTLINES

Many word processors can help you prepare an outline for a document you are creating. They can also help you create an outline for a document you are reading, thereby making it easier for you to analyze it. For example, the Outline utility under Microsoft Word's View menu allows you to insert headings and subheadings in an easy-to-follow manner. You can also analyze a document by working with it in outline view or through Document Map, which you can access on the standard toolbar or under the View menu.

3.5b Write a formal outline.

A scratch outline, such as the one above, might be just the thing to get you started on a short paper. However, if you are attempting a more detailed discussion, you might make a more complete, formal outline. Let's say you decide to write an extended essay on the academic uses of computers. As you gather information, you limit this broad topic to the uses of computers for students, specifically college students. After writing a scratch outline, you realize that you need a specific and formal blueprint to guide you through the writing of this long paper. Here's what such an outline might look like:

COMPUTERS AND THE COLLEGE STUDENT

I. Introduction
  A. In the past two decades, computers have revolutionized education at all levels.
  B. Colleges and universities use computers for a variety of tasks.
  C. Professors use computers for class work and scholarly research.
  D. **Thesis:** *Computers are also essential tools for college students.*
II. Computers are indispensable to writing papers.
  A. The Internet can be used to gather valuable information.
  B. Word processors make it easier than ever to compose and revise.
      1. Some programs offer outlining templates.
      2. Text can be manipulated with a few keystrokes.
      3. Some word processors have built-in revision functions.
  C. Specialized writing software helps students organize, draft, and revise papers.
  D. Word processors also help students edit their work.
      1. Important tools include spell checkers and thesauruses.
      2. Online handbooks and grammar and rhetoric software programs are useful.
III. The Internet has opened a new world of communication.
  A. Researching paper topics or finding more information about classroom topics is now easier.
  B. Distance learning offers several possibilities.
      1. Students unable to come to campus can have greater access to course offerings by registering for online courses.
      2. Online course materials—lectures, exams, even class discussions—can be accessed at the individual student's convenience.
      3. Distance learning can save travel time and money for community college and other commuting students.
  C. E-mailing over the Internet increases communication among students, their instructors, and their fellow students.
IV. Computers make excellent tools in a variety of classes.
  A. Accounting classes use electronic spreadsheets.
  B. Drafting tables in engineering classes have been replaced by CAD/CAM software.
  C. Specialized software in foreign languages, mathematics, and the physical sciences provides additional learning possibilities.
V. What higher education can expect from the electronic revolution in the near future.
  A. Multimedia approaches promise to make learning more interesting and teaching more effective.
  B. Computers help teachers address differences in student learning styles.

EXERCISE 3E

Writing Outlines

Do some brainstorming, focused freewriting, clustering, or other prewriting activity to gather information about the working thesis statement you wrote in Exercise 3D on page 46. Then write both a scratch outline and a formal outline based on that thesis and the information you gathered. Try to write your outlines on a word processor. Save them for later reference. You will need them when you are completing Exercise 3F, which requires shifting blocks of text.

3.6 Write a rough draft.

One way to complete a rough draft is to write as much information as you can about each section of your outline. Sometimes it helps to put the information for each section in its own paragraph. If any one paragraph becomes too long, you can divide it when you revise your rough draft.

Some people write the introduction first; others start with the body paragraphs. The choice is yours. Just keep moving. If you run out of things to say in one paragraph, go to the next section of your outline. You can go back and fill in blank spots later.

Here are some other points to remember about writing a rough draft:

1. Stick to your outline, but don't be afraid to add information as it pops into your mind. Creating a first draft will help you understand your subject better, so feel free to add information not mentioned in your outline as long as it clearly relates to your thesis.

2. Don't worry about paragraph structure and development. You can add details and reorganize paragraphs when you rewrite the draft.

3. Don't be concerned about errors in spelling, grammar, or sentence structure, either. You can correct them later, when you edit your rewritten draft.

Chapter 5 shows you how to revise, edit, and proofread your work. Before you get to that chapter, read the following rough draft. It provides a good idea of the kind of essay an outline can help you write.

Annoying Conveniences (First Draft)

1   In the last fifteen years the world went thru a true revalation in the communications industry. Computers help us send long e-mail messages quick, cheaply and without much effort. Fax machines allow us to transmit long documents in a flash. But, like with all things, there is a down side to this. They forget that using

devices like these require using the same etiquette and good sense that you would use when communicating using any other media. This morning, example, I noticed that the man in the next car was driving, drinking coffee, and trying to dial the office from a cell phone all at the same time. This rather dangerous site made me very frightened, especially when he almost swerved into my lane. After all we could have had a dangerous wreck. But cell phones are not the only abusers, in fact, using electronic communications devices irresponsbtly can annoy others.

2   How often have you been scared out of your wits by a car that goes by with it's stereo Blasting? Besldes adding to the noise pollution problem, such behavior can add to the pollution problem, which is a major problem in our large, overcrowded cities where screaming police and fire sirens and the roar of traffic grate on our nerves and eardrums. However, it can also destroy the driver's hearing or cause him or her a dangerous distraction. Which could result in a car accident.

3   Misusing computers, especially by that new menace—the virus maker   is yet another insult we must endure. But viruses can be dangerous, too. Think of the damage they can do if they attack hospital computers that control sensitive machinery, airport control systems, or defense bases.

4   Beepers and cell phones—too often people forget to turn off their beepers and phones when they walk into classrooms and movie theaters. Beeps and rings cause others who are deeply into what is going on a great disturbance. Cell phones can be dangerous. This morning i saw a woman driving to work while talking on a hand-held phone and putting on makeup! I suppose she was steering with her feet. That's why so many big cities are outlawing cell phones in taxis these days. Too many accidents have been caused when the cab drivers try to talk on the phone while navigating in thick traffic at the same time.

5   Listening to a portable CD player while wearing earphones is another annoyance. This really gets you when you are trying communicate with someone who is wearing this contraption. Even worse, students walk into class wearing these gagdets, and insulting the teacher and their fellow students, who have come to class prepared to discuss important ideas and learn something. Do they have such little regard for the school and thier fellow students that they want to shut them out. Certainly electronic tools have made communicating a lot easier these days. But we need to use them in a common sense way. Maybe we need a new set of laws or rules that would apply to our new toys. Like western desperados who checked their guns at the tavern door, we might have to check our cell phones before entering class. We might have to stop making calls from our cars, at least when the car is moving. And we should punish those virus makers, who shut done important computer applications just for fun.

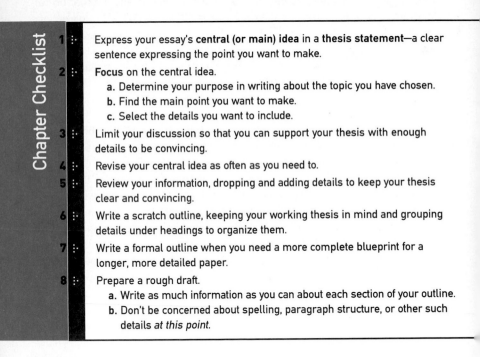

EXERCISE 3F

Writing the Rough Draft

Use the scratch or formal outline you created in Exercise 3E on page 50 as a blueprint for the rough draft of an essay. Before you begin drafting, however, review your thesis; make sure it is clear and focused. In addition, remember to think about the audience you will address and the kind of language you might use with that audience. Next, review your outline. Add, remove, or rearrange information as needed. Finally, write your draft. Use a word processor to draft your essay, and save it in an electronic file. Or, if you are more comfortable working with pen and paper, draft your essay longhand and then type it before handing it in.

Chapter Checklist

1. :· Express your essay's **central (or main) idea** in a **thesis statement**—a clear sentence expressing the point you want to make.

2. :· **Focus on the central idea.**
   a. Determine your purpose in writing about the topic you have chosen.
   b. Find the main point you want to make.
   c. Select the details you want to include.

3. :· Limit your discussion so that you can support your thesis with enough details to be convincing.

4. :· Revise your central idea as often as you need to.

5. :· Review your information, dropping and adding details to keep your thesis clear and convincing.

6. :· Write a scratch outline, keeping your working thesis in mind and grouping details under headings to organize them.

7. :· Write a formal outline when you need a more complete blueprint for a longer, more detailed paper.

8. :· Prepare a rough draft.
   a. Write as much information as you can about each section of your outline.
   b. Don't be concerned about spelling, paragraph structure, or other such details *at this point.*

DEVELOPING PARAGRAPHS FOR THE BODY, INTRODUCTION, AND CONCLUSION OF AN ESSAY

4

A paragraph discusses one limited idea. In an essay, there are three types of paragraphs, each of which serves a different purpose. Introductory paragraphs begin an essay and often contain the thesis statement. Body paragraphs contain information that develops, supports, or explains the thesis. Concluding paragraphs end the essay in a logical and memorable way.

4.1 Decide when to start a new paragraph.

A paragraph is a unit of thought that discusses a very limited idea. When it comes time to draft paragraphs of your essay, follow this rule: Use one full paragraph to discuss each idea or point that relates to the central idea of your essay. In fact, you can think of a paragraph as a mini-essay. Like an essay, a paragraph uses information to develop a central idea. In other words, it makes one main point about a subject and then uses details to support or prove that point. However, a paragraph's focus is much more limited than an essay's.

In the following paragraph, student Gail Shapiro focuses on only one aspect of her dog's "personality"—her attitude toward strangers:

> *Our dog Fawn despised strangers, particularly if they appeared to threaten me or members of my family.* Her temperament was such that a stranger using his hands or arms to speak would quickly feel her jowls wrapped around his trousers, and in a few instances on his legs, arms, or derriere. She literally "left her mark" on three visitors and had to be quarantined for a one-month stretch per bite. (From "Fawn My Dear")

If you were to put this paragraph into a full-length essay arguing that Fawn has a distinct "personality," you might also discuss her undying loyalty to the family and her intelligence, but each of these points would be developed in its *own* paragraph.

A paragraph's central idea is expressed in a topic sentence, as in the sentence that is italicized in the paragraph about Fawn. As you can see, a paragraph is a fairly short unit; for beginning writers, 70 to 120 words is a good range. Of course, a paragraph can be shorter or longer, depending on your purpose. Most paragraphs, however, contain at least two sentences. One-sentence paragraphs can be useful, but they can make your writing choppy, disconnected, and confusing. Try to avoid them.

4.2 Limit the paragraph's focus.

The most important thing to remember about a paragraph is that its central idea is limited, far more limited than the central idea of an essay. Let's say you plan an essay with this thesis: "Pregnant women should get regular medical checkups, avoid alcohol, and eat nutritious meals." This thesis makes three main points. It is limited enough for an essay, but not for a paragraph. In fact, if you wrote an essay with this thesis, each body paragraph might cover only one point. An outline for such an essay might look like this, with the central ideas for the body paragraphs (2, 3, and 4) stated in topic sentences:

Paragraph 1:   Introduction with thesis

Paragraph 2:   Regular medical checkups during pregnancy increase the chances for a safe delivery.

Paragraph 3:   Birth defects are less likely if an expectant mother avoids alcohol.

Paragraph 4:   The baby's health depends greatly on the mother's eating habits.

Paragraph 5:   Conclusion

In this example, it's easy to see where to start a new paragraph. The thesis statement contains three main points, so the writer can simply cover each point in a separate paragraph.

But not all thesis statements break down so neatly. Let's say you want to argue that "some television programs use violence to attract viewers." This thesis does not suggest any single way to divide your essay into separate paragraphs. You have to decide for yourself. For instance, if you decide to discuss why you find three or four popular shows violent, you might devote a separate paragraph to each show. On the other hand, if you want to discuss three *types* of programs that often feature violence, you could divide the body of your paper into three paragraphs, each of which discusses a different type of violent show. Here's what the outline for such an essay might look like; the central idea of each body paragraph is expressed as a topic sentence.

Paragraph 1:   Introduction with thesis

Paragraph 2:   TV cartoons often use violence as a source of comedy.

Paragraph 3:   Televised sports, such as boxing and hockey, can be brutal, yet fans applaud this violence.

Paragraph 4:   Some television adventure movies glorify violent characters.

Paragraph 5:   Conclusion

4.3 State the paragraph's central idea in a topic sentence.

As a beginning writer, you should always express a paragraph's central idea formally in a topic sentence. Doing so will help you organize and develop your work. You should know, however, that not all experienced writers reveal their central ideas in sentences readers can point to. In fact, in some cases, the central idea of a paragraph might be so obvious that the writer chooses not to state it.

Read the two paragraphs below. In the first, the topic sentence is in italics. The second has no topic sentence; the writer lets readers determine the central idea for themselves.

Leaving children and pets in locked cars even when outside temperatures are not high is dangerous. Temperatures in cars exposed to direct sunlight can rise quickly. Last year on a September day, several people in my town returned to their parked cars only to find their dogs near death. In one case, a baby left in a car for only a few moments was rescued by a passer-by who saw her gasping for air and broke the window.

There I was in the Supreme Market's parking lot when I noticed a baby gasping for air in a Toyota with the windows closed. I had heard stories about pets and children suffocating in hot cars during the summer, but this was September. The car was locked, so I picked up the nearest rock and cracked the window. The inside temperature must have been over 90 degrees as the hot sun beat down on the baby. As I pulled her out, I saw her father running to me and screaming that he had been gone only five minutes.

As you can see, then, *experienced* writers sometimes choose not to state their central ideas formally. As a developing writer, however, you should put central ideas into topic sentences. That's the best and easiest way to create a strong focus in your paragraphs. To maintain that focus, you will also need to make your paragraphs unified and coherent.

4.4 Maintain unity.

When you draft a paragraph, begin with a working topic sentence, which you can revise when you complete the paragraph. Use your working topic sentence as a guide to determine whether your writing is unified. A piece of writing is unified when all the details it contains relate directly to its central idea.

In the next paragraph, the student writer maintains unity by relating all information to the topic sentence, which is in italics.

(1) *"Run-on," a common way to waste energy and water in America, is the habit of leaving machines and appliances running when they don't have to be.* (2) Many people in this country routinely forget to turn off lights, televisions, and radios when they leave a room. (3) Some take half-hour showers day after day, when they know that a five-minute scrubbing will get them just as clean. (4) And too many of us leave the car running as we wait outside a store for a friend to finish shopping. (Michael Pulsinelle, "Run-On")

Notice how unity works in the preceding paragraph:

1. The idea of wasting energy, expressed in sentence 1, appears in sentence 2 when the writer mentions that people "forget to turn off lights, televisions, and radios."

2. Wasting water pops up in sentence 3, where we learn about people who "take half-hour showers."

3. The writer again refers to wasting energy in sentence 4 when he says that "too many of us leave the car running as we wait outside a store."

4. The idea that "run-on" is a "habit" (sentence 1) is developed by "routinely" (sentence 2), "day after day" (sentence 3), and "too many of us" (sentence 4).

Always ask yourself if all your information has to do with the central idea. If it does not, you can either (1) remove the irrelevant information or (2) broaden the central idea to include it.

4.4a Remove irrelevant information.

Look for irrelevant information—information that does not relate to the central idea—in the following paragraph:

(1) *International students at my college are having problems adjusting to the United States.* (2) They can't find part-time jobs to support themselves while they attend college because their visas do not permit them to work. (3) Finding part-time jobs isn't a problem for American students. (4) Many international students have left families behind and have no emotional support system to rely on. (5) All find English composition a challenging course. (6) None likes the food in the college cafeteria. (7) Native-born students feel the same way about the cafeteria.

The paragraph lacks unity. Sentences 2, 4, 5, and 6 are about international students, as called for in the topic sentence. But sentences 3 and 7 are about American students. To unify the paragraph, the writer might eliminate sentences 3 and 7.

(1) *International students at my college are having problems adjusting to the United States.* (2) They can't find part-time jobs to support themselves while they attend college because their visas do not permit them to work. (3) Many have left their families behind and have no emotional support system to rely on. (4) All find English composition a challenging course. (5) None likes the food in the college cafeteria.

4.4b Broaden your central idea.

Broadening the central idea works well if you have included information that suits your purpose but does not relate to your topic sentence. Here's a revision of the preceding paragraph. The topic sentence has been rewritten to include "American students."

(1) *Many problems facing international students at my college are different from those of American students, but many are the same.* (2) For example, international students can't take part-time jobs to support themselves while they attend college because their visas do not permit them to work. (3) On the other hand, finding part-time jobs isn't a problem for American students. (4) In addition, many foreign students have left their families behind and, unlike native-born classmates, have no emotional support system to rely on. (5) However, both groups find English composition a challenging course. (6) And neither group likes the food in the college cafeteria.

The purpose of this version is different from that of the earlier one. It discusses problems of both groups, not just those of international students.

Maintaining Unity

EXERCISE 4A

1. *Rewrite the following paragraphs by using one or both of the methods for creating unity that you just learned: (1) eliminate information that is irrelevant to the central idea or (2) broaden the central idea. Save this assignment in an electronic file for future reference. Before you begin rewriting, read each paragraph thoroughly and underline its topic sentence.*

  a. A year after leaving high school, I found myself working for a landscaping company. Though physically demanding, the job built character. I got it through a cousin of mine who knew the owner's son. After about a month, I noticed that my hands had become calloused and that the skin on my neck, back, and legs had grown rough and weathered. I didn't like my boss very much, for he often got gruff and cranky after a hard day's work. The customers complained a lot, too, especially when we failed to plant a tree or trim a bush just to their liking. They were a real nuisance. However, this was my first steady job, and it taught me that I could get satisfaction from simple things, like coming to work on time each morning, co-operating with my co-workers, and working hard to earn the money I needed to support myself. The job also introduced me to my current girlfriend, who was one of our customers.

b. Many people dread November in the Northeast. The weather is often gray and cold, but usually not cold enough for ponds and lakes to freeze over, so you can't even enjoy ice skating. What's more, it rains a lot in November, and our part of Rhode Island always seems to get the heaviest storms. Thanksgiving comes in November, bringing with it cheer and goodwill, not to mention a long weekend. In the early part of the month, newly fallen leaves that have been soaked by the rains pose a real danger to motorists and pedestrians alike. Of course, people who don't like extremes of heat and cold prefer November to months like August or January. And if November's here, can the winter holidays be far beyond? Then again, November means having to wear woolen pants rather than cutoffs, bulky sweaters rather than T-shirts, and heavy boots rather than sneakers or sandals.

2. *Write two short paragraphs, each of which uses one of the following topic sentences:*

College textbooks are expensive.
My parents work hard.
Large cities are dangerous (fun, dirty, noisy, etc.).
Swimming is good exercise.
I enjoy walks in the woods (mountains, city, etc.) during autumn (spring, the early morning, etc.).
Working in a restaurant (factory, store, etc.) is exhausting.
My dog (cat, goldfish, etc.) is intelligent (lovable, faithful, nervous, etc.).
Living on campus (commuting to school each day) takes a lot of adjusting.
The effects of drinking too much coffee (cola, beer, etc.) are . . .
The easiest way to gain weight is to . . .

Make sure each paragraph is unified by providing only details that relate to the topic sentence. Rely on your own experiences for those details. Use a word processor to write this assignment, and save your work in an electronic file.

4.5 Create coherence.

A paragraph is *coherent* if all its sentences are connected logically so that they are easy to follow. An essay is coherent if its paragraphs are connected logically.

You can create connections in and between sentences and between paragraphs by (1) using transitions and (2) referring to words and ideas you have mentioned earlier.

4.5a Create coherence by using transitions.

Transitions, also called **connectives,** are words, phrases, and even sentences that make a clear connection between one idea and another, between one sentence and another, or between one paragraph and another. Let's say you are composing a speech honoring your sister's college achievements. You write the following sentences:

> My sister began college by enrolling in remedial math courses. She graduated at the top of her class in engineering.

Using a transition to connect these ideas will make your writing smoother.

> My sister began college by enrolling in remedial math courses. *However,* she graduated at the top of her class in engineering.

Transitions for Many Purposes

1. Use transitions to indicate time.

> The students rushed into the classroom chattering. *After a few minutes,* they became silent and settled down to work.
> Miriam entered college on September 1, 2003. *Before* that date, she had served in the U.S. Navy.

Other Transitions That Relate to Time

after a short while	at that time	in those days	thereafter
afterward	by that time	meanwhile	thereupon
all of a sudden	by then	since	until then
all the while	during	soon	when
a short time later	in a few hours	suddenly	whenever
as soon as	in the meantime	then	while

2. Use transitions to show similarities and differences.

> Jason takes after his grandmother in some ways. *Like* her, he appreciates fine antiques. *Unlike* her, *however,* he doesn't have the money to buy them.

Other Transitions That Show Similarities and Differences

Similarities	Differences
similarly	although
in the same way	even though
likewise	though
as	in contrast
as if	on the contrary
as though	on the other hand

3. Use transitions to add information.

Phoenix was a natural woman. She lived off the land, growing her own potatoes and collard greens. *What's more,* she hunted rabbit and woodchuck.

Other Transitions Used to Add Information

also	in addition
and	furthermore
as well	moreover
besides	too
further	

4. Use transitions to introduce information that contradicts, changes, or qualifies what you have said.

The thief claimed he had nothing to do with the break-in. *But* Columbo knew better! Professor Eng told us to turn in our tests. I had not finished, *however,* so I kept writing.

Other Transitions Used to Contradict, Change, or Qualify

although	otherwise
even so	still
even though	then again
in contrast	though
nevertheless	while
nonetheless	yet
on the other hand	

5. Use transitions to introduce examples, repeat information, or emphasize a point.

Example: My father worked extra jobs to provide for his family. One year, *for example,* he spent his days off selling dry goods to pay for my college tuition.

Repetition: When Mom had her first child and became a full-time homemaker, Dad took a part-time job three nights a week at a supermarket. This was *another* sign of his devotion to us.

Emphasis: Hard work was nothing new to Dad. *In fact,* he had to quit school when he was sixteen and got a job in a barbershop.

Other Transitions Used to Introduce Examples, Repeat Information, or Emphasize a Point

Introduce Examples	Repeat Information	Emphasize a Point
as an example	again	as a matter of fact
for instance	once again	indeed
specifically	once more	more important
such as		to be sure

6. Use transitions to show cause and effect.

Abe Lincoln had a habit of sitting on the ground, grabbing his legs, and rocking back and forth as he told funny stories. *Consequently,* his trousers got baggy at the knees.

Other Transitions That Show Cause and Effect

as a result	so that
because	then
hence	therefore
since	thus

7. Use transitions to show condition.

I'd better pay the bill soon. *If* I don't, the power company will shut off my electricity.

Other Transitions That Show Condition

as long as	provided that
as soon as	unless
in case	when
in order to	

Creating Coherence by Using Transitions

Transitions have been removed from the paragraphs that follow. Rewrite the paragraphs, creating coherence by inserting transitions from the lists in section 4.5a wherever you think they are needed. Record your work in an electronic file.

1. I learned a great deal about our community and our family from the stories my grandmother told me. The most fascinating—and the most valuable—were those she told about herself. Several of these illustrated the importance of education. My grandmother had always wanted a high school education. Her parents were very old-fashioned. They encouraged her brothers to finish high school. They believed a girl should be married quickly. She was sixteen. Her parents arranged a marriage for her and made it known that they expected her to begin raising a family right away. She thought she might continue her schooling after the wedding. Her education remained an illusion. Her husband had other plans. A year after her marriage, my grandmother was blessed with the first of her two children. She realized the marriage was doomed to failure. It lasted three years. My grandfather and grandmother divorced. Being a single mother was a disgrace. My grandmother was left to raise her children in a hostile environment without the education she knew she needed. (Gwendolin Gravesande, "My Grandmother")

2. The New York Rangers hockey team has an unparalleled record of losing. The Rangers have not won a championship in over forty years. Their fans are the most frustrated and disappointed partisans in all of American professional sports. They are among the most loyal and vocal in the country. The Rangers play their home games in Madison Square Garden. Faithful fans come out in droves to attend. For twenty years, every single home game has been sold out. A night at a Ranger game is unlike a night at any other sporting event. I have attended New York Ranger hockey games only four times in my life. I have sat in the blue seats, more commonly known as "The Blues," which are no more than ten rows from the roof. I am amazed to see that most of the people up there know each other from past games. The atmosphere is more like that of a neighborhood bar than of a sporting event. The playing surface is distant. It is difficult to make out the numbers on the players' uniforms. The fans in "The Blues" couldn't care less.

   The game starts. The level of excitement in "The Blues" is incredible. The puck is in play. The fans remain riveted to the action below, as if their lives depend on the outcome. The Rangers score a goal; a celebration erupts. The fans throw their hands up in unison and scream as loudly as they can. An opponent's goal is greeted by a collective groan of disgust, a thundering chorus of boos, intense profanity, an occasional shower of beer cups on those unlucky to be sitting below. (Dan Roland, "French Yuppies, The Blues, and Hoboken, New Jersey")

4.5b Create coherence by referring to material that came earlier.

As noted earlier, using transitions is only one way of creating coherence within and between paragraphs. Another way is by referring to material you have mentioned earlier. You can refer to earlier material by using pronouns and by restating details and ideas.

Pronouns That Link Details and Ideas

Linking pronouns point to details mentioned earlier; they direct readers' attention to nouns called **antecedents.** These pronouns connect ideas and help you avoid repeating the same noun. Patricia Irons uses them in the introduction to her essay "Heaven."

> Several months ago, my son, *who* is only six years old, came home from school with an unusual drawing. What made *this* picture different from *his* others was *its* brilliant array of colors. Ordinarily, Christopher's drawings consist of a fast dash of pencil or marker with the scribble of a single color to fill in the outline. *This* time Christopher had been careful with lines and borders. *Each* was clear and distinct. Obviously, something had intrigued *him* enough to make him sit still longer than *his* normal thirty seconds; I wanted to know what *it* was. "What is *this?*" I asked. *He* answered matter-of-factly, and suddenly I found myself listening to a six-year-old lecture me on "heaven," *which* he discussed slowly, seriously, and confidently.

The paragraph above contains only a few of the pronouns you might consider to make your writing coherent. Here are several types of pronouns you can use:

1. Personal pronouns refer to people.

   Personal Pronouns

you (your, yours)	we (us, our, ours)
he, she, it (him, his, her, hers, its)	they (them, their, theirs)

2. Relative pronouns describe nouns by connecting them with clauses (groups of words that contain subjects and verbs).

   Relative Pronouns

who (whom, whose)	that	which

3. Demonstrative pronouns usually precede the nouns they refer to or stand for nouns they refer to. Sentences like "*Those* are the best seats in the house" and "*That* is my worst subject" use demonstrative pronouns.

   Demonstrative Pronouns

this	these
that	those

4. Indefinite pronouns make general, not specific, reference. Use them if you are sure readers can spot their antecedents easily: "Both Sylvia and Andrew were in an accident. *Neither* was hurt." The antecedents of *neither* are "Sylvia" and "Andrew."

Indefinite Pronouns

all	each	everyone	none	some
another	either	neither	no one	somebody
any	everybody	nobody	several	someone

Restating Important Details and Ideas

Another way to refer to material mentioned earlier is to repeat words and phrases or to use **synonyms,** terms that have the same meaning as those words or phrases. William Zinsser uses repetition in this paragraph from his book *On Writing Well*:

> *Some people* write by day, *others* by night. *Some people* need silence, *others* turn on the radio. *Some* write by hand, *some* by typewriter or word processor, *some* by talking into a tape recorder. *Some people* write their first draft in one long burst and then revise: *others* can't write the second paragraph until they have fiddled endlessly with the first.

Ellen Goodman uses synonyms to tell us about the temptation of wild raspberries in Casco Bay, Maine. She also repeats *I* and *bush* to create coherence between paragraphs.

> The dirt road by the cottage leads me almost daily into the *bushes.* I seem unable to pass the raspberries that hang like bright ornaments, *final gifts* from *branches* that have turned brown.
>
> I reach out for one small handful, easing the fragile *fruit* from its core. And then I am caught, following the *crop,* migrating from one *bush* to another, deep again in the middle of the field.

higher in the winter months when windows are kept closed. The amount that accumulates also depends on how tightly the home is insulated. Therefore, with the increased use of insulation materials to conserve energy, radon contamination has become a serious concern. Indeed, people who had never heard of radon only a few years ago are now forced to install venting systems to remove the gas from their homes. (Carole A. Leppig, "Radon")

4.6 Learn to develop body paragraphs of various types.

When writing in college, you will often be asked to write essays or papers, but your teachers may not tell you specifically that they want you to write a comparison-and-contrast essay or a definition essay. (This is especially true in courses other than composition.) Instead, they will expect you to choose the appropriate structure to fit your ideas. If, for example, you want to persuade your reader that a democratic form of government has distinct advantages for the electorate, you might compare a democratic society with a totaliarian one. Thus, your essay would take the shape of comparison and contrast. If, on the other hand, you want to persuade your reader that your grandfather is the best cook in your family, you might use description to convey the delicious, mouthwatering scents that come from your grandfather's kitchen. Of course, description can be combined with comparison and contrast. You could compare the scents from Grandpa's kitchen with those that emanate from your Aunt Martha's. Whatever the subject, you should think about how your topic would best be conveyed and use the structure(s) appropriate to your topic.

4.6a Learn to develop narrative paragraphs.

Use narration when you want to recall an event or explain a process. A narrative is a story. It arranges pieces of information in chronological order, as they occurred in time. One event in a story or one step in a process follows another just as it happened.

Narratives contain action verbs, which move the story or process along. They also use transitions such as *first, then, soon, after,* and *suddenly,* which maintain coherence and show movement from one event to the next.

The following narrative paragraphs by Jill Warnock, a student nurse, recall her first experience with a dying patient. Action verbs are underlined; transitions are in italics.

I <u>placed</u> my clipboard down and <u>moved</u> nearer her face. I <u>felt</u> her breath on my cheek. "Can you hear me, Rose?" I <u>asked.</u> *Suddenly* her eyes <u>flickered</u> and her dry mouth <u>puckered</u> slightly in a weak attempt to answer. I <u>stroked</u> her wrinkled forehead and, *for a moment,* her eyes <u>opened, closed,</u> and <u>opened</u> again. They were clear, crystal blue. As I <u>looked</u> into them, I <u>noticed</u> a deep sadness, which I have never forgotten. These eyes, which <u>had witnessed</u> a lifetime, *now* <u>strained</u> to see my image before them. *At that moment,* I was Rose's anchor, her only link to life.

For a While, she <u>held</u> my hand tightly, afraid to let go. *When* she <u>began to tremble,</u> I <u>covered</u> her, carefully avoiding the IV lines that <u>grew</u> from her arms. I <u>sat</u> with Rose for what seemed like hours, <u>talking</u> softly to her. I knew that she wanted to answer but could not. I <u>told</u> her about my daughter, about the rain and mud I went through to get to the hospital that night, about my new rosebush. *Occasionally,* a weak smile or nod <u>told</u> me she <u>was listening.</u> *When* she <u>drifted</u> off to sleep, I <u>watched</u> her chest straining <u>to breathe,</u> waiting for its next rise. I <u>could see</u> her slipping away without a fight. Rose was prepared for her journey: no tears, no panic. *For the first time,* I <u>saw</u> death as a path, not as an obstacle.

I could not leave her. No one, not even the brave, should die alone. *When* her final breath was gone. I <u>sat</u> holding her hand in the darkness. *And* I <u>said</u> good-bye. ("The Dying Stranger").

EXERCISE 4D

Narrating an Experience

Using a word processor or pen and paper, write two or three paragraphs that narrate a dangerous, sad, embarrassing, or exciting experience you remember well. Use action verbs and transitions to move your story along and to make it interesting. Here are some suggested topics:

My first day on a college campus (at a job, in a new town, etc.)
The first time I saw a dead person
The first time I cooked a meal (built a fire, changed the oil in my car, etc.)
An auto accident
The time I got a bad case of poison ivy (sunburn, chicken pox, etc.)

4.6b Learn to develop descriptive paragraphs.

If you want to discuss the nature or character of a person, place, or thing, you can start with physical **description.** Rely on your five senses to gather details about what your subject looks, sounds, feels, smells, or even tastes like.

Unlike narration, which presents information from beginning to end, description can be arranged in any paragraph pattern you think best. Usually, that pattern is spatial; it presents things as they appear in space. But each writer chooses his or her own perspective—the position from which to view the subject. And each decides where to begin and where to end.

If you were to describe a beach, you might begin with what you see in the north and then move south. To describe a tall oak, on the other hand, you might move from the top of the tree to the bottom. You could start by describing its highest branches. Then, moving down the trunk, you could discuss its limbs and bark. The tree's huge root system, bulging from the earth, would come last. If you were describing a painting of a farm, you might begin with the red barn that is at the center and acts as the picture's focal point. You could then mention the trees, silos, and livestock around the barn and, finally, the fields, sky, clouds, and sun that appear at the painting's edges.

Each of these patterns will work well. However, another writer might want to describe the beach from south to north, the oak from bottom to top, and the painting from the edges to the center. In the next example, student writer Nancy Boemo approaches her subject from the outside and then moves inward.

> The road into Saladsburg, Pennsylvania, takes several twists and turns until it comes to a small steel bridge and crosses on to Main Street in this sleepy village with a population of 250. In the center of town is Saladsburg's landmark: Cohick's Trading Post, home of Cohick's famous ice cream. The building is approximately 50 3 75 feet, or a total of about 3,750 square feet. Outside are two gas pumps and a reassuring sign: "If you treat your customers well, they will always come back." Once you get inside, you are confronted with a magnificent potpourri. On the front counter sits a wheel of aged sharp cheddar, from which customers may cut their own portions. As you stroll over the creaking old pine boards and down the narrow aisles, you encounter everything from buckshot to butter pecan ice cream. Other items range from hardware and agricultural supplies to dry goods, from sporting goods and hunting licenses to locally grown produce. The walls of the store are lined with animals that were shot or trapped and later stuffed: a porcupine, squirrels, several possum, a moose, and a rattlesnake. At the rear is a huge black bear mounted in a ferocious pose. ("The Trading Post Is a Survivor")

Describing a Scene

On a separate piece of paper or in an electronic file, write a paragraph that captures the character of a place you recall vividly. Describe a place that is relatively small: your room, the inside of a neighborhood store, your family's backyard, or the reading room in a college library. Before you begin, decide on your perspective, the position from which you will view your subject. Then decide how to arrange details—where to begin, where to end, and so on.

EXERCISE 4E

4.6c Learn to develop explanatory and persuasive paragraphs.

Narration and description can also be used to explain an idea or statement, to convince readers that an opinion is correct, or to persuade them to do something. But such purposes also lend themselves to other methods of development. The method of development you choose determines the kinds of details you will use in a paragraph. Depending on your purpose—on what you want to accomplish—you can choose one or more of the following methods to develop your paragraph's central idea:

Illustration	Offers examples
Comparison or contrast	Explains similarities or differences
Definition	Explains what a term means
Classification	Distinguishes among types or classes
Cause and effect	Explains why something happens
Conclusion and support	Presents facts or statistics to clarify an idea or support an opinion or assumption

Each of the following paragraphs uses one of these methods of development to explain, convince, and persuade.

Illustration

The following paragraph uses five examples to **illustrate** how important computers have become to business:

> Personal computers have many uses, but they are especially important to running a successful business. For example, creating memos, letters, and reports on a word processor saves time over using a standard typewriter. Electronic spreadsheets are used to keep track of inventories, costs, and profits. Computer tax packages can help a business owner file income and sales tax returns quickly and accurately. Databases store millions of bits of information, which can then be presented and analyzed systematically. Finally, desktop publishing software can help create and print eye-catching brochures, manuals, and pamphlets that attract and keep customers. (Pam Trico, "Computers on the Job")

Comparison or Contrast

Comparison explains similarities; **contrast** explains differences. Read the next two paragraphs, from Marie Winn's book *Childhood Without Children*. The first compares playing marbles and playing video games; the second contrasts these two pastimes.

> Is there really any great difference . . . between . . . playing video games by the hour . . . and spending equal amounts of time playing marbles? It is easy to see a similarity between the two activities: each requires a certain amount of manual dexterity [skill], each is almost as much fun to watch as to play, each is simple and yet challenging enough for that middle-childhood age group for whom time can be so oppressive [burdensome] if unfilled.
>
> One significant difference between the modern preteen fad of video games and the once popular . . . pastime of marbles is economic; playing video games costs twenty-five cents for approximately three minutes of play; playing marbles, after a small initial

investment, is free. The children who frequent video-game machines require a significant outlay of quarters to subsidize their fun; two, three, or four dollars is not an unusual expenditure [cost] for an eight- or nine-year-old spending an hour or two with his friends playing Asteroids or Pac-Man or Space Invaders.

Definition

To **define** is to explain what a term means. Defining helps readers see a word, thing, or idea for what it is. In some cases, defining helps introduce readers to a subject that is new to them; in others, it helps change or clarify their opinions about a subject. Here's an example from Robert Fulghum's best-seller *All I Really Need to Know I Learned in Kindergarten:*

> Ever seen an abacus? You know, those centipedelike things with wooden beads in rows. They're sold mostly in knickknack import shops, for wall decoration. But, in fact, an abacus is an adding machine, calculator, and computer. On second thought, that's not quite true. The abacus is just a visual record of the computations going on in the person using it.

Classification

When writers **classify,** they organize related bits of information about a subject into separate types or groups, also known as categories, so that the subject can be discussed logically and systematically. For example, Linda Beck discusses husbands by dividing them into three different groups. Using this classification, she is able to organize her information in a manner that is easy to understand and to remember.

> Although there are as many types of husbands as there are married men, most husbands can be classified into three general categories. In the first are men who see themselves as the heads of households. They believe wives should not work outside the home and that the primary responsibility of married women is to care for husbands and children. The second group consists of men who consider themselves "liberated." For them, marriage is a partnership in which each spouse shares equally. They are likely to be cooking dinner while their wives change the oil in the car. However, the majority of men are more realistic than those in either group. They realize that most women must work outside the home, and they share many household chores. At the same time, they continue to take on tasks that have traditionally been done by men. ("Husbands")

Cause and Effect

A paragraph developed through the **cause-and-effect** method explains *why* something happens. This type of writing is especially useful to scientists, who must explain natural events, but it can be used for a variety of other purposes. In the next paragraph, Charles Sorrentino relies on cause and effect to persuade his fellow students to attend class regularly.

Never miss class. At the end of the term, instructors look more kindly on students who came to class regularly than on those who skipped a lot. Besides, being absent deprives you of information useful in preparing for tests or in doing homework. In fact, missing class may mean missing important quizzes or exams, which will hurt your final grade. ("Get to Class")

Conclusion and Support

This method of developing a paragraph uses facts, statistics (numbers), or opinions to **support** or clarify an idea or defend an opinion. The idea being supported—the **conclusion**—is often expressed in the paragraph's topic sentence. In the following paragraph, a student writer, who wishes to remain anonymous, starts with the idea that living with an alcoholic parent is very difficult. This is her conclusion and the paragraph's topic sentence (in italics). She then supports her conclusion by providing details that show how difficult this problem is.

The nights my mother was home were nightmares. She sat on the living room couch with a case of Budweiser, just drinking, listening to music, and talking to herself. On many occasions, she turned up the record player so high that the police stopped by our house late at night to ask that she lower the volume. I spent those evenings sitting up with my crying sister, reassuring her that everything would be all right, while the sounds of Paul Anka vibrated into her bedroom. My brother went for long walks and sometimes didn't return until school was dismissed the next afternoon. The day after, I would find my mother sitting on the couch surrounded by beer cans and slumped over one corner of the couch. The record player would still be running, with the needle in the center of the record, playing nothing. ("Mom")

EXERCISE 4F

Writing Paragraphs That Explain, Convince, and Persuade

On a separate piece of paper or using a word processor, write three paragraphs of between 50 and 75 words, each of which uses a different method of development. Below are topic sentences you can use as guides to the kinds of central ideas you should develop in your paragraphs:

Topic Sentences That Can Be Developed Through *Illustration*
My boss is a slave driver.
Some TV comedies depict men as stupid.
Music videos contain too much sexual material.
Sometimes I believe my dog can communicate.
The cafeteria offers many low-calorie foods.
Marni is a dedicated mother.

Topic Sentences That Can Be Developed Through *Comparison or Contrast*
Packing a lunch every day is much less expensive than eating in the cafeteria.
My parents' views on education (money, sex, marriage, careers, etc.) differ from mine.

My plans after college are not at all like my sister's.

My grandfather and I have a lot in common when it comes to cars (politics, the outdoors, model trains, gardening, music, etc.).

Computers and TVs are similar in some ways.

Topic Sentences That Can Be Developed Through *Definition*

A good shopper is someone who can . . .

A snob (racist, bigot, etc.) thinks that . . .

My cousin is a perfectionist, a person who . . .

To be a genuine slob, one has to . . .

Have you ever seen a . . . ?

Topic Sentences That Can Be Developed Through *Classification*

There are three types of students in my English (chemistry, accounting, algebra, etc.) class.

Four types of restaurants can be found downtown.

We learned about several families of instruments in the history of music course.

The gym I go to recommends three types of aerobic exercise.

American colleges are becoming diversified; students of various religions (races, ethnic groups, ages, family-income brackets, etc.) now attend my school.

Topic Sentences That Can Be Developed Through *Cause and Effect*

Heavy traffic on Highway I made me late for my eight o'clock class.

Coming to class late can affect your grade.

Clipping discount coupons from a newspaper will save you money at the supermarket.

Running three miles a day can help you lose weight.

Students who arrive late disturb the class.

Topic Sentences That Can Be Developed Through *Conclusion and Support*

Drugs kill.

A computer can make writing easier.

My parents are understanding (supportive, caring, good at listening, etc.).

Noise pollution is becoming a problem on campus.

Smoking can be an expensive habit.

Registering for class last semester was a nightmare.

4.7 Learn four patterns of arrangement.

Earlier you learned that details in descriptive writing can be arranged in various patterns, depending on your purpose. The same is true of writing developed through illustration, comparison or contrast, definition, classification, cause and effect, and conclusion and support. As you know, the method of development you choose determines the kind of details you use in a paragraph. The pattern of arrangement determines the order in which details are presented or organized in a paragraph. Here are four patterns to practice:

General to specific	Begin the paragraph with a broad statement (the topic sentence); develop the rest of the paragraph or essay with supporting details.
Specific to general	Begin the paragraph with supporting details that lead to a broad concluding statement (the topic sentence).
Question to answer	Begin the paragraph with a question to which the details that follow provide an answer.
Order of importance	Begin the paragraph with the least important detail; end it with the most important detail.

4.7a Write paragraphs that go from general to specific.

Beginning the paragraph with a general statement followed by specific details that support it is a good way to argue a point or make an abstract idea convincing. The information in the next two paragraphs is arranged this way. The topic sentences are in italics. (In both paragraphs, the main method of development is contrast, but Suzanne Britt, the author, also uses illustration to develop her central ideas.)

> . . . *thin people aren't fun.* They don't know how to goof off, at least in the best fat sense of the word. They've always got to be adoing. Give them a coffee break, and they'll jog around the block. Supply them with a quiet evening at home, and they'll fix the screen door and lick S&H green stamps. They say things like "There aren't enough hours in the day." Fat people never say that. Fat people think the day is too damn long already.
>
> *Thin people make me tired.* They've got speedy little metabolisms that cause them to bustle briskly. They're forever rubbing their bony hands together and eyeing new problems to "tackle." I like to surround myself with sluggish, inert, easygoing fat people, the kind who believe that if you clean up today, it'll just get dirty again tomorrow. ("That Lean and Hungry Look")

EXERCISE 4G

Arranging Material from General to Specific

Write a paragraph in which you use comparison or contrast as your main method of development and in which you arrange your material from general to specific. Begin with a topic sentence that expresses a major similarity or difference between two people, places, or objects you know well. Then provide details to support your main point. As you did with other exercises, try saving your work in an electronic file.

Say you decide to explain how different you and your brother are about spending money. Your topic sentence might read: "My brother says I'm cheap, but he spends money like a wealthy land baron." In the rest of the paragraph, you explain that by bringing your lunch to work, carpooling with neighbors, and buying clothes on sale, you were able to pay for your books this term. You conclude by stating that eating in expensive restaurants, treating friends to movies, and buying designer clothes have forced your brother to borrow money to pay for his books. Here are other topic sentences you can use as models:

My boyfriend (girlfriend, spouse, roommate, etc.) and I never agree on restaurants.
Most dogs are friendly and faithful; the cats I know seem cold and independent.
Goldfish need less care and attention than cats or dogs do and thus make better pets.
Watching a rented videotape at home is (is not) better than going to the movies.
Studying for a test with friends has advantages over studying alone.
My best friend and I have different career goals.

4.7b Write paragraphs that go from specific to general.

Arranging material from specific to general is a good way to create suspense or build to an emotional high point. In the following paragraph, student writer Bill McGlynn tells what happened when his car's locks froze on a cold February night. He sums up his frustration over this situation in a topic sentence, which is in italics, at the end of the paragraph.

I was too cold now. My teeth were chattering, my feet frozen like lifeless stumps. I looked up to the heavens and screamed in agony, damning the fates. I lit another cigarette and expressed my dismay over the two friends who had accompanied me on this pilgrimage. Suddenly, I spotted them walking back to the car, their heads down, shoulders hunched, and hands buried deep within their coat pockets. I knew there was no need to talk. I understood immediately that they had found no help. I handed the keys and the lighter to Jason. He fumbled with them for a few minutes, but with no luck. Robert walked to the park bench and sat down. I looked away from them. My own frustration was compounded by the pain in their eyes. I felt another surge of self-pity. The dull agony of the cold, the biting pain of the wind, the guilt of endangering the lives of my friends: *it was all too much to bear.* ("Taking the Blame")

In the next three paragraphs, from *Rachel and Her Children,* Jonathan Kozol illustrates the public's attitude toward homelessness. His examples lead directly to a conclusion (Kozol's central idea) in the last sentence.

In several cities, it is a crime to sleep in public; in some, arm rests have been installed in the middle of park benches to make it impossible for people to lie down. In others, trash has been defined as "public property," to make it a felony for the poor to forage [search] in the rotted food.

Some grocers in Santa Barbara have sprinkled bleach on food that they discarded in their dumpsters. In Portland, Oregon, owners of some shops in the redeveloped Old Town have designed slow-dripping gutters (they are known as "drip lines") to prevent the homeless from attempting to take shelter under their awnings.

In Fort Lauderdale, harsher tactics have been recommended. A member of the City Council offered a proposal to spray trash containers with rat poison to discourage foraging by homeless families. The way to get rid of vermin, he remarked, is to cut their food supply. Some of these policies have been defeated, but *the inclination to sequester [segregate, cut off], punish, and conceal the homeless has attracted wide support.*

EXERCISE 4H

Arranging Material from Specific to General

Write a paragraph in which you use illustration (examples) as your main method of development and in which you arrange your material from specific to general. Begin with examples that support a central idea, which you express in your last sentence. Say you want to show how harsh winter in your city can be. To develop this idea, you might write that temperatures in February rarely get above 10° F, blizzards closed the schools four times last winter, and the snow seldom melts until May. You can then use your topic sentence to conclude as follows: "Winters in my town are harsh." Again, save your work in an electronic file.

Here are other topic sentences you might use to end paragraphs you have developed through illustration and arranged from specific to general:

People around here are kind to strangers.
Eating at fast-food restaurants will ruin your diet.
My family takes pride in its garden.
Getting to class on time is never easy.
Elderly people can learn new skills.
My cousin doesn't take criticism well.

4.7c Write paragraphs that go from question to answer.

You can capture readers' attention by beginning with a question. This pattern is also an easy way to arrange information. After asking a question, fill the rest of the paragraph with examples or other details that answer or discuss it. Consider this example from student writer Nicholas Cannino's essay "The Junk-Food Junkie":

What's so bad about junk food? A great deal. For example, it usually contains artificial colors, flavors, and preservatives, the kinds of additives that pose serious health hazards and, over the long run, may even cause cancer. In addition, much junk food is packed with sugar, fats, or cholesterol. It adds inches to our waistlines, clogs our arteries, and disturbs our metabolism. Most important, junk food contains few nutrients. Eating cotton candy, potato chips, and chocolate bars may satisfy our hunger, but for that very reason it keeps us from eating the foods we need to stay healthy.

Arranging Material from Question to Answer

Write a paragraph in which you arrange your material from question to answer. Use classification, definition, illustration, or narration as your main method of development. If you wish, you may build your paragraph as Nicholas Cannino did in his paragraph on junk food. Open with an interesting question; then summarize the answer in a short phrase or sentence that expresses your main point. Finally, develop your paragraph by using details that support your answer. Here are sample questions you might use as models to begin your paragraph:

When are the best times to buy textbooks?
Is studying in the cafeteria a good idea?
Why is eating a good breakfast so important?
Can love be dangerous?
Should all classes use a pass-fail grading system?
What's wrong with missing class now and again?
Are good class notes really important?
What kind of men (women) make the best husbands (wives)?
What are the best kinds of aerobic exercise?
Do I have more responsibilities today than I had five years ago?

4.7d Arrange information in order of importance.

Writers of fiction often save the most important or startling information for last. Doing so helps them maintain suspense or create emphasis. You can use this pattern whether your purpose is to tell a story, describe a scene, explain an idea, or defend an opinion. Here's an example by student writer Lena Schmidt:

> I am divorced now, free and alone, a woman of 45 with children who have gone off to spin out lives of their own. I married at 19. Back then, some young people got married because they were genuinely in love, but *too many of those I knew tied the knot for the wrong reasons.* Some sought security: some, companionship, romance, or sex. A few even "had to" get married. But the most compelling reason to wed in those days was that everyone else was doing it, and nobody wanted to be left behind. ("Time to Grow Up")

Arranging Material by Order of Importance

Write a paragraph on paper or in an electronic file in which you arrange your material by order of importance. Use any method of development discussed in this chapter. End your paragraph on a high note; save the most important information for last. Use

(continued)

the following sentences as models for the topic sentence on which you will base your paragraph:

I came to school for three reasons.
Each math (history, English, science, etc.) course I take gets harder and harder.
I like eating at Joe's Truck Stop for three reasons.
Several people helped me when I came to campus.
Blind dates can be classified as bad, worse, and worst.
Unsafe sex can have several bad effects, some of which are worse than others.

4.8 Write effective introductions.

Most effective essays begin with a formal introduction. A good introduction captures the readers' attention and makes them want to read on. Moreover, an introductory paragraph is a good place to state your thesis and prepare readers for what follows.

Before deciding what to put into an introductory paragraph, ask yourself if your essay needs a formal introduction. Many essays do not. If you're writing a narrative, you can simply start with the first event in your story. Of course, you should include interesting details, vocabulary, or ideas to spark your readers' interest. But you may not need to include background information before you begin your story. If you find that you need to express your central idea in a formal thesis, you can always do so later, in the body of the essay or even in your conclusion.

4.8a Learn four uses of a formal introduction.

If you or your instructor decide that your essay should have a formal introduction, remember that the most important function of an introductory paragraph is to capture readers' attention. But that is not its only use.

A formal introduction can also:

1. Capture your reader's attention
2. Express a central idea in a formal thesis statement
3. Prepare your reader for important points you will make in the body of the essay
4. Provide background information to help your reader understand your thesis and the details you will use to develop it

4.8b Master several ways to write an introduction.

Sometimes the easiest way to write an introductory paragraph is simply to state your thesis and explain in general terms what you mean by it. (You can spend the rest of your essay developing that statement with specific details or examples.)

Richard Marius uses this method in "Writing and Its Rewards." Here is his introduction; the thesis statement is in italics.

> *Writing is hard work, and although it may become easier with practice, it is seldom easy.* Most of us have to write and rewrite to write anything well. We try to write well so that people will read our work. Readers nowadays will seldom struggle to understand difficult writing unless someone—a teacher perhaps—forces them to do so. Samuel Johnson, the great eighteenth-century writer . . . said, "What is written without effort is in general read without pleasure." Today what is written without effort is seldom read at all.

You can write your introduction in a variety of other ways. Here are seven of them:

1. Present an interesting example of your thesis.
2. Use startling remarks or statistics.
3. Create a vivid image to prepare readers for what follows.
4. Ask a question
5. State a problem.
6. Make a comparison or contrast.
7. Cite an expert or define a term.

Read the following examples of these various other ways to write introductory paragraphs. The thesis statements are in italics, except, of course, where the author chose not to express the central idea.

Presenting an Interesting Example

John Naisbitt and Patricia Aburdene believe the world is getting smaller, for we are sharing in each other's cultures. They begin discussing this idea in *Megatrends 2000* by describing a new food that combines tastes from around the world.

> West Los Angeles is the home of Gurume, a Japanese-run restaurant whose specialty—Gurume chicken—is oriental chopped chicken and green beans in an Italian marinara sauce, served over spaghetti, with Japanese cabbage salad, Texas toast, and Louisiana Tabasco sauce. *It is a symbol of what is happening to world lifestyle and cuisine.*

Using Startling Remarks or Statistics

Like interesting examples, startling remarks and statistics (numbers) stir readers' interest and provide a natural lead-in. The first paragraph below uses startling remarks, the second—startling statistics. Whichever you use, make sure your details are accurate and appropriate to the thesis.

> The Cyclone [Coney Island roller coaster] is art, sex, God, the greatest. It is the most fun you can have without risking bad ethics. I rode the Cyclone seven times one afternoon

last summer, and I am here to tell everybody that *it is fun for fun's sake, the pure abstract heart of the human capacity for getting a kick out of anything.* (Peter Schjeldahl, "Cyclone! Rising to the Fall")

In a new study published in the [April 2003] *New England Journal of Medicine* . . . researchers Eugenia Calle, Ph.D., and colleagues determined that [being] overweight . . . may account for 20% of all cancer deaths in U.S. women and 14% in U.S. men. That means 90,000 cancer deaths could be prevented each year if Americans could only maintain a normal, healthy body weight. (American Cancer Society News Center)

Creating a Vivid Image to Prepare Readers for What Follows

Michael S. Serrill begins "Famine," a cover story for *Time*, with a frightening picture of the victims of the Ethiopian famine.

They look like the scrawny camp followers of a medieval army as they gather under a huge bluff. . . . The earth is boiled beige, with hardly a blade of green. There are nearly 7,000 of them and they began assembling here long before dawn. Dressed in ragged homespun cotton and wrapped in long shawls called "netela," they come in entire families, grandfathers and grandchildren. The men hold herding sticks; the women carry babies bound to their backs with cloth. And then there are the youngsters, some of them naked and with their heads shaved except for a single tuft in front. They are strangely silent.

Asking a Question

If you begin with a question, you can devote the rest of your essay to discussing it and perhaps to providing answers. George R. Stewart asks an intriguing question in the first paragraph of an essay that defines our notion of junk and later explains why this problem is becoming a crisis.

A typical American city now displays—like a fair-sized hill or modern mountain—its heap of discarded automobile hulks. The effect upon the American public of these heaps has been profound, curious, and out of all proportion to reality. "Shocking!" is a common reaction. But why, in the face of such gargantuan problems as those of sewage and garbage, should people be so concerned about some piles of metal? ("Not So Rich as You Think")

Stating a Problem

Stating a problem is similar to asking a question. If you state a serious problem in your introduction, you can use the paragraphs that follow to discuss its effects and tell how it was (or was not) solved. Consider this example from student Irina Groza's "Growing Up in Rumania":

I was in the third grade when our beloved president, Gheorghe Gheorghiu-Dej, died. He was succeeded by Nicolae Ceausescu, a young and ambitious general who promised us a bright future. At his election, no one was able to see the magnitude of his egomania, ruthlessness, and incompetence. *The tyranny that followed nearly destroyed Rumania and inflicted widespread suffering on its people for many years.*

Making a Comparison or Contrast

Comparison points out similarities: contrast points out differences. Both methods can be used to introduce your subject, emphasize a point, and catch readers' attention. In the first paragraph below, John Graig compares the Y in his town to a castle; in the second, student Jessie Sullivan uses contrast to explain the truth about her neighborhood that outsiders never see.

> The Y.M.C.A. in our town, like Y.M.C.A.'s of that period the world over, was a red brick, military-looking building, with Gothic towers at the corners. You had the feeling that, with a moat around its stone base, it could have repelled legions of infidels almost indefinitely. (*How Far Back Can You Get?*)

> A look of genuine surprise comes over my classmates when I mention where I live. My neighborhood has a reputation that goes before it. People who have never been there tend to hold preconceived notions about the place, most of which are negative and many of which are true. Those who actually visit my neighborhood usually notice only the filth, the deterioration of buildings and grounds, and the crime. *What they fail to see isn't as apparent, but it is there also. It is hope for the future.* ("If at First You Do Not See . . .")

Citing an Expert or Defining a Term

When you cite an expert, you use information supplied by someone who is knowledgeable about your subject. You can cite experts by presenting their ideas in your own words or by quoting them directly. For example, in "Writing and Its Rewards," which appeared earlier, Richard Marius quotes Samuel Johnson, the famous English writer and authority on language.

By defining an important term, you can explain aspects about your subject that make it easier for your readers to understand and agree with your central idea. But avoid dictionary definitions; they are often limited and can make your writing flat. Instead, rely on your own knowledge to create definitions that are interesting and appropriate to your discussion. That's what student Elena Santayana did in her paper on alcoholism.

> *Alcoholism is a disease whose horrible consequences go beyond the patient.* Families of alcoholics often become dysfunctional; spouses and children are abandoned or endure physical or emotional abuse. Co-workers suffer too. Alcoholics have high rates of absenteeism, and their work is often unreliable, thereby decreasing office or factory productivity. Indeed, alcoholics endanger the whole community. One in every two automobile fatalities is alcohol related, and alcoholism is a major cause of violent crime. ("Everybody's Problem")

Making Introductions Interesting and Effective

Practice any two of the methods for creating effective introductions by writing introductory paragraphs for two essays on a separate piece of paper. Try to record your work in an electronic file. You might write on topics such as the following:

The differences between you and your brother (sister)
High school and college responsibilities
Working in the fast-food business (or at any other job)
Why people should practice safe sex
The effects of drug or alcohol abuse
Waking up after a wild night of partying
Watching a house burning down (or witnessing any other disaster)
Why you decided to quit smoking
What we should do about date rape

4.9 Write effective conclusions.

A good conclusion brings your discussion to a timely and natural end. Spend as much effort on your conclusion as you do on other parts of your essay. Leave readers with something to remember! The conclusion's length will depend on your purpose and thesis. In some cases, one sentence may be enough to bring your discussion to a logical and timely conclusion. In others, you might try one of these five methods:

1. Recall your thesis and introduction.
2. Ask a question.
3. Offer advice or call for action.
4. Look to the future.
5. Explain how the problem was resolved.

Recalling Your Thesis and Introduction
Notice how well Jessie Sullivan's conclusion recalls the thesis of "If at First You Do Not See . . . ," the essay whose introduction you read on page 79.

> When friends visit me in my apartment for the first time, they frequently ask in awe and bewilderment, "How can you live in such a bad place?" I always give them the same reply: "It isn't where you live, but how you live and what you live for."

Asking a Question
A concluding question allows readers to participate in your essay. It also helps make your writing memorable. Readers find it hard to forget an essay that ends

with the question to which they have considered answers. Remember George R. Stewart's introduction to his essay about junk (page 78)? Questions in Stewart's conclusion invite us to imagine the consequences of a problem he has described in his essay, and they make his message vivid.

> In this modern world strange stories circulate. One of them recently was of an urban family with three TV sets. Unusual affluence [wealth] was not the cause; perhaps, rather, the reverse. The family frugally picked up its sets from discount houses or other stores where there was no trade-in for the old set. But what, eventually, is this family going to do? Will they pay someone to cart the old sets away? Or will they themselves take them to a dump? Or will they take them out and dump them by the side of the road somewhere, as some people abandon an old car? ("Not So Rich as You Think")

Offering Advice or Calling for Action

A conclusion that both offers advice and calls for action appears in Elena Santayana's "Everybody's Problem," the introduction of which appears on page 79.

> If you have alcoholic friends, relatives, or co-workers, the worst thing you can do is to look the other way. Try persuading them to seek counseling. Describe the extent to which their illness is hurting their families, co-workers, and neighbors. Explain that their alcoholism endangers the entire community. Above all, don't pretend not to notice. Alcoholism is everybody's problem.

Looking to the Future

Sometimes you can look beyond your essay and predict the outcome of events, questions, or issues you have discussed. To make your conclusions convincing, base your predictions on evidence from your essay. In "Famine," the introduction of which you read on page 78, Michael S. Serrill tells what starving Ethiopians can expect once they finish the last of their relief rations.

> "They won't be laughing in a couple of weeks' time," says an Ethiopian official with tears in his eyes. "Now they smile even on half rations because today they can exist." His gloomy prediction seems true. The road between Mekele and Wukro remains closed most of the time. And nobody knows just when the next food convoy will come.

Explaining How a Problem Was Resolved

If you have introduced your essay by presenting a problem, you can devote the body paragraphs to explaining its effects. The conclusion then becomes the logical place to explain how the problem was resolved. This is the way Irina Groza organized "Growing Up in Rumania," an essay about the tyranny that "nearly destroyed" her homeland. Groza's introduction appears on page 78.

> In 1977 . . . I had the opportunity to leave [Rumania]. The day I emigrated, the course of my life changed for the better though my heart broke for those I left behind.

Now, however, new hope blossoms for Rumania. In December 1990, as part of the overthrow of corrupt Communist governments across Eastern Europe, the people deposed the Ceausescu regime and established a democracy.

EXERCISE 4L

Writing Effective Conclusions

Assume you have just written an essay about one of the topics listed in Exercise 4K. (If necessary, jot down a few of the major points that you might have covered in this essay.) Then, using any of the methods described in section 4.9, write a paragraph that would make a good conclusion to such an essay. If none of the topics in Exercise 4K work for you, choose one of your own or try one of the following:

The rising costs of attending college
Reasons people should exercise regularly
The challenge of working part-time (full-time) while going to school
Reasons people should contribute to your favorite charity
Reasons you chose to major in . . .
Advice about making good grades
The dangers of abusing drugs (alcohol, sex, etc.)
The importance of having fun

■■■■   ■■■■   **BASICLINK**   ■■■■   ■■■■
WWW

You can find out more about effective introductions and conclusions at
http://www.gmu.edu/departments/writingcenter/handouts/introcon.html

Chapter Checklist

1. A paragraph focuses on a limited idea. Its central idea should be stated clearly and completely in a topic sentence.

2. All supporting ideas and details in the paragraph should relate to or help explain your topic sentence. Remove those that do not, or broaden your central idea to include them.

3. If connections between sentences are not clear and logical, add transitions and linking pronouns, repeat vocabulary, or use synonyms that will improve coherence.

4. Narration can be used in paragraphs that recall events or explain a process.

5. Description can be used to paint a verbal picture of and discuss the nature of people, places, or things.

6. Some techniques can be used to explain or convince: illustration, comparison or contrast, definition, classification, cause and effect, and conclusion and support.

7. The material in a paragraph may be arranged
    a. From general to specific.
    b. From specific to general.
    c. From question to answer.
    d. By order of importance.

8. A good introduction can capture readers' interest, express your central idea, prepare readers for points you will develop later, and provide background information.

9. You can make your introduction effective by
    a. Stating your thesis and explaining what you mean by it in general terms.
    b. Giving an interesting example of your thesis.
    c. Using startling remarks or statistics.
    d. Creating a vivid image.
    e. Asking a question.
    f. Explaining a problem.
    g. Making a comparison or contrast.
    h. Citing an expert or defining a term.

10. You can bring your essay to an effective conclusion by
    a. Recalling your thesis and introduction.
    b. Asking a question.
    c. Offering advice or calling for action.
    d. Looking to the future.
    e. Explaining how a problem was resolved.

5

REVISING, EDITING, AND PROOFREADING

5.1 Ask questions for revision.
5.2 Make important changes.
5.3 Learn to revise on a computer.
5.4 Edit the final draft.
5.5 Prepare the manuscript.
5.6 Proofread the manuscript.
CHAPTER CHECKLIST

The first draft of an essay, such as the one you saw in Chapter 3, is certainly not the end product of the writing process! Anything worth reading must go through many careful revisions. Before you begin rewriting, however, take a break. If possible, put the draft away for a day or two. When you are ready to rewrite, complete at least three or four additional drafts—one rewrite is rarely enough. Then edit your best draft carefully, and proofread the final manuscript.

5.1 Ask questions for revision.

Begin the process of rewriting by reading your rough draft carefully, two or three times. Then ask the following questions:

1. Has my main point about my subject changed over the course of my essay? Should I revise my thesis statement to make it clearer or more accurate?
2. Is my writing unified? Have I included details that are unrelated to my thesis or are unnecessary?
3. Should I reorganize my essay by rearranging paragraphs?
4. Is each paragraph unified? Should some details be shifted from one paragraph to another?
5. Is each paragraph adequately developed, or do I need to add more detail?
6. Are my paragraphs coherent, or do I need to add transitions and linking pronouns?
7. Have I written an interesting introduction and conclusion?

You might even want to share your rough draft with some of your classmates. Ask them the questions you have asked yourself. Keep your responses and theirs in mind as you write additional drafts.

5.2 Make important changes.

The paper that appears on pages 85–86 is the second draft of the essay in Chapter 3. This second draft shows that the main point made about *electronic communications devices* has changed. In fact, writing the second draft helped the student discover what she really wanted to say.

Revised thesis: Using any electronic communications device irresponsibly can annoy and even endanger others.

Look for other important changes in the paper as you read the second draft, complete with errors, which follows:

> **NOTE**
> Added material has been underlined. Deleted material appears with a line drawn through it.

Electronic Etiquette
(Second Draft)

1   In the last fifteen years the world <u>has gone</u> ~~went~~ thru a ~~true~~ <u>revolution</u> ~~revalation~~ in the communications industry. Computers <u>enable</u> ~~help~~ us <u>to</u> send long e-mail messages <u>quickly</u>, cheaply, and <u>easily</u> ~~without much effort. Fax machines allow us to transmit long documents in a flash. But, like with all things, there is a down side to this.~~ <u>However, there have been some disadvantages to this progress.</u> They forget that using devices like these require using the same etiquette and good sense that you would use when communicating using any other media. This morning, example, I noticed that the man in the next car was driving, drinking coffee, <u>eating a donut,</u> and trying to dial the office from a cell phone all at the same time. <u>I suppose he was steering with his feet!</u> ~~This rather dangerous site made me very frightened, especially when he almost swerved into my lane. After all we could have had a dangerous wreck.~~ But cell ~~phones~~ <u>callers</u> are not the only abusers, in fact, using <u>any</u> electronic communications devices irresponsiblty can annoy <u>and even endanger</u> others.

2   ~~How often have you~~ <u>I have often</u> been scared out of ~~your~~ <u>my</u> wits by a car that goes by with it's stereo Blasting. ~~Besides adding to the noise pollution problem, such behavior can add to the pollution problem~~ <u>Such behavior adds to noise pollution,</u> ~~which is~~ a major problem in our large, overcrowded cities. ~~where screaming police and fire sirens and the roar of traffic grate on our nerves and eardrums. However,~~ It can also destroy the driver's hearing or ~~cause~~ <u>create</u> ~~him or her~~ a dangerous distraction. Which could result in a car accident. <u>A similar annoyance is</u>

caused by the use of CD players at inappropriate times. Students listening to music through earphones while sitting in class insult both the teacher and thier fellow students, who have come prepared to discuss important ideas and learn something. Do such "headphone freaks" have such little regard for the school and their fellow students that they want to shut them out.

3   Computer viruses are ~~Misusing computers, especially by that new menace—the virus maker—is~~ yet another insult imposed on us by the abuse of electronics ~~we must endure.~~ These vicious mini-programs create chaos with the work done on comuters, such as those used by students who spend hours collecting data and writing long reports only to have them snatched away into the darkness of cyberspace by some fool computer clown. However, ~~But~~ viruses can be dangerous as well as annoying, ~~too. Think of~~ The damage they can do if they attack hospital computers that control sensitive machinery, airport control systems, or defence bases can be monumental and can even endanger people's safety and lives.

4   ~~Beepers and cellphones—~~Too often people forget to turn off their beepers and phones when they walk into classrooms and movie theaters. In no time, beeps ~~Beeps~~ and rings cause others who are deeply into what is going on a great disturbance. Cell phones even have a habit of ringing during weddings, religious ceremonies, and even funerals. ~~Cellphones can be dangerous.~~ And they too can even pose a serious traffic hazard. ~~This morning i saw a woman driving to work while talking on a hand-held phone and putting on makeup! I suppose she was steering with her feet.~~ That's why so many big cities are outlawing cell phones in taxis these days. Too many accidents have been caused when the cab drivers try to talk on the phone while navigating in thick traffic at the same time.

5   ~~Listening to a portable CD player while wearing earphones is another annoyance. This really gets you when you are trying to communicate with someone who is wearing this contraption. Even worse, students walk into class wearing these gagdets and insulting the teacher and their fellow students, who have come to class prepared to discuss important ideas and learn something. Do they have such little regard for the school and their fellow students that they want to shut them out.~~ Certainly electronic tools have made communicating a lot easier these days, but we need to use them judiciously. But we need to use them in a common sense way. ~~Maybe we need a new set of laws or rules that would apply to our new toys.~~ Like western desperados who checked their guns at the tavern door, we ~~might have to~~ students should check ~~our~~ their cell phones before entering class. ~~We~~ Drivers might have to stop making calls from their ~~our~~ cars, at least when they are in motion, ~~the car is moving.~~ Most important, the courts should punish, ~~And we should punish those~~ virus makers, who shut done important computer applications just for fun.

5.2a Compare the second draft with the first.

1. The title has been changed to reflect the topic of the paper more accurately.

2. The thesis has been revised. In revising the rough draft, the writer discovered that misusing electronic communications devices can be dangerous as well as simply annoying.

3. Paragraph 5 has been divided. The second half has become the paper's conclusion. Information from the first half, which has been rewritten, has been combined with related ideas in paragraph 2. Discussing the annoyance of portable CD players earlier in the paper allows the writer to end with a discussion of a more serious topic: the dangers of using cell phones while driving. Thus, the paper saves the most startling information for the end, allowing the writer to create emphasis as the paper develops.

4. Paragraph and essay unity has been improved. You learned about unity in Chapter 4. Remember that all the details in a paragraph should relate to its topic sentence (main idea). In paragraph 2, for example, information about urban noise pollution—which is irrelevant to the paragraph's topic and the essay's thesis—has been removed.

5. Paragraphs 2, 3, 4, and 5 have been expanded with information that makes them more vivid and convincing.

6. Unnecessary words and ideas have been removed. In paragraph 4, the example of the woman driving while using a cell phone has been removed because it is nearly identical to the example used in the introduction.

7. Sentence structure has been improved. For example, the essay's second sentence has been rewritten to correct for parallel structure.

8. Coherence in and between paragraphs has been improved through the use of transitions, such as "similar" in paragraph 2 and "In no time" in paragraph 4.

9. The conclusion has been revised. It is now smoother, clearer, and less wordy.

5.3 Learn to revise on a computer.

Word processing software has made revising more convenient and efficient than ever before. You can use a computer to create multiple drafts of a paper without typing each draft in its entirety. Two of the most common revision methods are explained here:

1. Revise on a printed copy; then type in your handwritten changes.
   - Type the first draft of your paper, and save it under a file name that includes the number 1 (*Etiquette1* or *Etiquette1.doc,* for example).

NOTE

Revising can be a lengthy job; you may have to rewrite a paper several times before you get to a version like the one in section 5.2. Remember that problems with spelling, grammar, and so on can wait until you edit and proofread. For now, make sure your writing is focused, well developed, and well organized.

Print out a hard (paper) copy of this draft, and revise it using pen or pencil.

• Using your word processor's copy/paste function, copy your first draft and paste it onto a blank screen. Save it under a file name that includes the number 2 (*Etiquette2* or *Etiquette2.doc,* for example). Then type the revisions you made on the hard copy into this file. Save the new version again.

• Continue revising draft after draft in this way until you are satisfied that you have finished making major changes in the content and structure of your work.

2. Use the word processor's revising tool.

• Type the first draft of your paper, and save it under a file name that includes the number 1 (*Etiquette1* or *Etiquette1.doc,* for example).

• Activate your word processor's revising tool (in Microsoft Word, for example, choose Tools and then choose Track Changes). Then delete unwanted text and add new text as needed. At the same time, use the copy/paste function to move phrases, sentences, or paragraphs. These changes will be tracked on the screen in a color that is different from that of the original text. Once you have revised the first draft, save it under a new file name (*Etiquette2* or *Etiquette2.doc,* for example).

• You may want to print out a hard copy of your draft for easier reading. If you are using a color printer, the changes in your manuscript will appear in a second color. If you are using a standard printer, deletions will have lines drawn through them and additions will be underlined. Drafts that have been revised using this method appear on pages 85–86 and 89–91.

• Continue revising draft after draft in this way until you are satisfied that you have finished making major changes in the content and structure of your work.

EXERCISE 5A

Rewriting the Rough Draft

Rewrite the rough draft you wrote in response to Exercise 3F on page 52. Begin by reading your rough draft carefully. Ask yourself again the questions listed in section 5.1. Then revise your paper again and again until you are satisfied that you have written a focused, well-developed, and well-organized essay.

5.4 Edit the final draft.

Editing means carefully rereading your work and correcting distracting problems. Among the most important are wordiness and mistakes in subject-verb
agreement, verb tenses, sentence structure, punctuation, word choice, spelling,
and capitalization. While editing your final draft, you might also want to revise
your title or even fine-tune your thesis.

Become familiar with the chapters on revising and editing (Tabs 8 through
11). Use a dictionary to check spelling and word definitions and a thesaurus to
find synonyms that will help you vary your vocabulary.

Below is a list of tips to help you edit your work most effectively:

1. Put the paper away for a short time so that you can give it a fresh look when
   you begin to edit.
2. Check every sentence individually to make sure it is complete. Correct run-
   ons and comma splices (see Chapter 22).
3. Find the subject of every sentence, and make sure its verb agrees with it in
   number (see Chapter 35).
4. Read your essay aloud at all stages, and listen for errors in grammar and
   punctuation (see Tabs 10 and 11).
5. Read every word carefully. Eliminate unnecessary words and redundancies
   (see Chapter 32). Make sure every word is used according to its correct
   meaning (see Chapter 30). If you have doubts, refer to a dictionary. Check
   spelling (see Chapter 46).
6. Check pronouns to see whether you have switched illogically from one person to another: first person (I/we); second person (you); third person (he,
   she, it/they) (see Chapter 37).
7. Make sure that you have not switched verb tenses without reason (see
   Chapter 34).
8. Make certain each sentence is related to the one that comes before and to the
   paragraph's topic sentence (see Chapter 4).

Here is the third draft—complete with editing
changes—of "Electronic Etiquette," the paper that was
revised in section 5.2.

NOTE
Added material has
been underlined.
Deleted material ap-
pears with a line drawn
through it.

Electronic Etiquette
(Third Draft)

rects spelling.

s more specific
'ds, smoother
asing.

1   In the last fifteen years the world has gone <u>through</u> ~~thru~~ a
revolution in the communications industry. Computers enable
us to send long e-mail messages quickly. cheaply, and easily.
However, <u>progress does not come without costs</u> ~~there have~~

Corrects pronoun problem by replacing "they".

~~been some disadvantages to this progress.~~ <u>Sometimes people</u> ~~They~~ forget that using <u>electronic communications</u> devices ~~like these~~ requires ~~using~~ the same etiquette and good sense that <u>one</u> ~~you would~~ uses when communicating <u>in</u> ~~using~~ any other

Replaces "you" with more formal "one".

media. This morning, example, I noticed that the man in the next car was driving, drinking coffee, eating a donut, and trying to dial the office from a cell phone all at the same time. ~~I suppose he was steering with his feet!~~ <u>However,</u> ~~But~~ cell phone

Removes unneeded statement.

callers are not the only abusers.~~-In~~ in fact, using any electronic communication device <u>irresponsibly</u> ~~irresponsiblty~~ can annoy <u>and insult others, disrupt business, and even endanger life,</u> ~~and even endanger others.~~

Corrects comma splice.

Revises thesis to reflect paper's content.

Uses more formal language and avoids cliché.

2   I have often been ~~scared out of you're my wits~~ <u>startled</u> by a car that goes by with <u>its</u> ~~it's~~ stereo Blasting. Such behavior adds to noise pollution, a major problem in our large, overcrowded cities It can also destroy the driver's hearing or create a dangerous distraction<u>, which.</u> ~~Which~~ <u>can</u> ~~could~~ result in a car accident. A similar annoyance is caused by the use of CD players at inappropriate times. Students listening to music through earphones while sitting in class insult both the teacher and thier fellow students, who have come prepared to discuss important ideas and learn something. Do such "headphone <u>devotees</u>"

Corrects spelling.

Corrects sentence fragment.

Replaces slang with more formal language.

~~freaks~~" have such little regard for the school and their fellow students that they want to shut them out.

3   Computer viruses are yet another insult imposed on us by the abuse of electronics. These vicious mini-programs create chaos ~~with work done on computers, such as those used by students who spend~~ <u>by destroying the work of people who have spent</u> hours collecting data and writing long reports only to have them snatched away into the darkness of cyberspace. ~~by some fool computer clown.~~ However, viruses can be dangerous as well as annoying. The damage they can do if they attack ~~hospital~~ computers that control sensitive <u>hospital</u> machinery, airport control systems, or defencese bases can be ~~monumental~~ <u>catastrophic</u> and can even endanger people's ~~safety and~~ lives.

Makes phrasing smoother; uses fewer words.

Deletes phrase to make tone more formal.

Corrects problem in sentence logic by changing word order.

4   Too often people forget to turn off their ~~beepers~~ <u>pagers</u> and phones when they walk into classrooms and movie theaters. In no time, beeps and rings <u>begin disturbing</u> ~~cause~~ others who are <u>listening intently and trying hard to concentrate.</u> ~~deeply into what is going on a great disturbance.~~ Cell phones even have a habit of ringing during weddings, religious ceremonies, and ~~even~~ funerals. <u>In addition,</u> ~~And~~ they ~~too~~ can even pose a serious traffic

Makes phrasing smoother and more concise.

Changes "beepers" the more formal "pagers".

Corrects repetition "even".

hazard. That's why so many big cities are out-lawling cell phones in taxis ~~these days.~~ Too many accidents have been caused when the cab drivers try to talk on the phone while navigating in ~~thick~~ heavy traffic. ~~at the same time.~~

5   Certainly electronic tools have made communicating a lot easier these days, but we need

to use them judiciously. ~~But we need to use them in a common sense way.~~ Like western desperadoes who checked their guns at the

tavern door, we students should check ~~their~~ our cell phones before entering class. Drivers should be required to stop their cars before using their cell phones ~~might have to stop making calls from their cars, at least when they are in motion~~. Most impor-tant, the courts should sentence the creators of computer

viruses to long jail sentence. That will send an important message to would-be pranksters who believe destroying important data and endangering lives is just another computer game. ~~punish virus makers, who shut done important computer applications just for fun.~~

> **NOTE**
>
> As you can see in this third draft, editing and revising are not always separate. As you edit, you will come upon sentences and paragraphs you might want to rewrite, not just edit for grammar, punctuation, and mechanics.

5.5 Prepare the manuscript.

Depending on your instructor's preference, you may have to type the edited draft on 8½-by-11-inch white bond paper or copy it legibly and clearly on lined paper in blue or black ink. In either case, follow your teacher's instructions carefully, and present a paper that is neat and easy to read. Note that if you are printing out a version of an electronic file, you may want to print out a copy that shows changes, as in the preceding sample.

Some Tips for Preparing a Manuscript

1. Write your name, course number, and date on the paper. Your teacher may ask you to put this information on a cover sheet.

2. Leave margins of 1 inch at the top and bottom and on the right and left sides of each page.

3. Give your essay a title, which you center at the top of the first page. Skip 1 line between the title and the first paragraph.

> **CAUTION!**
>
> If using a computer to write your essay, use your word processor's spell checker. However, remember that a spell checker is no substitute for a writer's good judgment and careful use of a dictionary. A spell checker is simply a list of words. As it scans a document, it stops at words it does not recognize, that is, words not in its database. Whether the word is spelled incorrectly is up to you to determine; if it is, you must choose a correct alternative. Spell checkers have special difficulty with proper nouns. Let's say you were writing a paper on John Donne, the
>
> *(continued)*

English poet. Your spell checker would question "Donne," and you would have to override it. However, before you did, you would have to be sure that "Donne" was the correct spelling.

In addition, a spell checker can't distinguish homonyms, words that sound alike but are spelled differently. Thus, if you write "two" when you mean "to" or "principal" when you mean "principle," your spell checker will not pick up the error, for the words *two* and *principal* are in its database.

4. Double-space all text.

5. Begin each paragraph by tabbing over half an inch. (Most word-processing programs will let you create an automatic indent; see the Help feature for instructions.) Capitalize the first word in each sentence.

6. Number the pages.

(If your teacher requires you to follow MLA, APA, or *Chicago* style, consult Chapters 15, 16, or 17 as appropriate.)

5.6 Proofread the manuscript.

Proofreading means carefully reading your manuscript to correct typing errors, eliminate repeated words, add missing words and punctuation, or fix other minor problems. You can often do this by neatly making corrections in your own handwriting. Once again, check with your teacher for instructions, and become familiar with the appropriate chapters in Tabs 8 through 11.

The proofreading tips below can help you to correct careless errors:

1. Read each word aloud and listen carefully. Correct all typographical errors.

2. Check for punctuation problems, especially missing apostrophes, commas, and periods.

3. Make sure you have capitalized proper nouns, the word that begins each sentence, and other words that require capitals.

Here are some proofreading corrections made by the writer in the first two paragraphs of "Electronic Etiquette." Comments in the margins explain the reasons for the changes.

Electronic Etiquette
(Fourth Draft)

1   In the last fifteen years the world has gone through a revolution in the communications industry. Computers enable us to

Replaces period with a comma.

send long e-mail messages quickly, cheaply., and easily. However, progress does not come without costs. Sometimes people forget that using electronic communications devices requires the same etiquette and good sense that one uses when

Adds missing word.

communicating in any other media. This morning, <u>for</u> example, I noticed that the man in the next car was driving, drinking coffee, eating a donut, and trying to dial the office from a cell phone all at the same time. However, cell phone callers are not the only abusers. In fact, using any electronic communication device irresponsibly can annoy and insult others, disrupt business, and even endanger life.

2 I have often been startled by a car that goes by with its stereo bBlasting. Such behavior adds to noise pollution, a major problem in our large, overcrowded cities. It can also destroy the driver's hearing or create a dangerous distraction, which can result in a car accident. A similar annoyance is caused by the use of CD players at inappropriate times. Students listening to music through earphones while sitting in a class insults both the teacher and thier their fellow students, who have come prepared to discuss important ideas and learn something. Do such "headphone devotees" have such little regard for the school and their fellow students that they want to shut them out?_

Adds period.

Corrects capitalization.

Corrects spelling.

Corrects agreement problem.

Replaces period with question mark.

···· ···· ···· THE BASICS OF TECHNOLOGY

USE SPELL CHECKERS AND GRAMMAR CHECKERS CAUTIOUSLY

Spell checkers and grammar checkers can provide useful feedback. However, there is no substitute for a human editor and proofreader. So rely on yourself to edit and proofread your own work. For example, a spell checker might not be able to catch misspellings of proper nouns, and it can't distinguish between homonyms such as *their* and *there*. Grammar checkers sometimes provide misleading advice on the length of sentences or the inadvisability of using the passive voice. In short, you may want to use such tools as guides, but in the end, you must rely on your own judgment. After all, it's your paper.

▪▪▪▪   ▪▪▪▪   **B A S I C L I N K** ▪▪▪▪   ▪▪▪▪

WWW

Online Reference Works

http://www.bartleby.com/61/   bartleby.com includes links to *The American Heritage Dictionary of the English Language,* Fourth Edition, as well as the *Columbia Encyclopedia, Roget's Thesaurus,* and reliable reference works on English usage.

http://www.m-w.com/home.htm   The Merriam-Webster homepage includes links to a dictionary (both the collegiate and the unabridged) and a thesaurus.

http://humanities.uchicago.edu/   You can also find the 1911 edition of *Roget's* forms_unrest/ROGET.html   *Thesaurus* at this site.

Proofreading Techniques

http://www.unc.edu/depts/wcweb/   This site offers useful tips on how to handouts/proofread.html   proofread effectively; it also offers helpful information about the editing process.

▪▪ ▪▪ ▪▪ ▪▪ ▪▪ ▪▪   ▪▪ ▪▪ ▪▪ ▪▪ ▪▪ ▪▪

Chapter Checklist

1 As you review your rough draft, ask yourself these questions:
   a. Does my thesis statement still express my main point?
   b. Are all the details I have included necessary?
   c. Should I rearrange paragraphs?
   d. Should I move material from one paragraph to another?
   e. Does any paragraph need more detail?
   f. Are my introduction and conclusion interesting?

2 Revise your rough draft, using your answers as a guide.

3 Now ask those questions again, and revise, revise, revise.

4 Edit your final draft. Check all sentences individually, and correct them using the tips for editing a final draft in section 5.4.

5 Type your edited version double-spaced, or write it clearly and neatly on lined paper (as your teacher requires).

6 Proofread your manuscript, and make the necessary corrections.

DEVELOPING ARGUMENTS

In terms of effective writing and speaking, the term *argument* does not mean a loud and heated discussion. An argument is simply an attempt to prove a point or support an opinion through logic and concrete evidence. Sometimes argument is used as the basis of a paper or speech whose object is not only to prove a point but also to persuade others to take a specified action or adopt a particular behavior. Frequently, the essays you write in college will take the form of an argument.

6.1 Choose a thesis that is debatable, supportable, and focused.

In all types of writing, a good argument is based on an effective thesis. The thesis for an argumentative essay is often referred to as the claim because it is the idea or opinion the writer wishes to prove, defend, or support.

Start with a preliminary thesis. As you collect information for, outline, and draft your essay, you may find that you need to revise your thesis more than once; the very process of writing will give you a clearer understanding of what you want to say.

Unless your instructor assigns you a specific topic, consider writing your argumentative essay on a serious issue or question you already know something about or are concerned about. Many of us have very strong opinions having to do with health care, animal rights, economic fairness, national defense, affirmative action, school choice, protection of the environment, and many other subjects. Those ideas can lead you to frame a thesis—at least a preliminary thesis—for an argumentative essay.

That doesn't mean, of course, that you shouldn't learn more about your topic through research or that you cannot radically change your position on an issue once you have learned more about it. However, writing about something you believe is important tends to provide the intellectual energy and commitment you need to complete an effective argumentative essay.

In addition, as you begin your essay, keep in mind the following three criteria for framing an effective claim or thesis:

1. An effective claim is debatable. It is something more than a simple statement of fact or personal preference. A reader might respond to a fact or statement of preference with "So what?" because facts and preferences are not debatable and will not yield sustained discussion. A debatable thesis, on the other hand, raises a question or issue that can be discussed at length, whatever your position. Compare the following:

Statement of fact:	My college's Code of Student Conduct contains eighteen different provisions.
Debatable thesis:	My college's Code of Student Conduct unfairly restricts students' right to free speech.

The first item cannot be debated. Either the code contains eighteen provisions or it doesn't. The second item, on the other hand, can yield sustained discussion by defining *unfairly,* examining specific provisions of the code, and citing evidence (examples) showing how the application of those provisions restricts freedom of speech.

Personal preference:	Being overweight makes a person less attractive to the opposite sex.
Debatable thesis:	Being overweight makes a person more susceptible to diabetes or heart disease.

The first item is based on personal taste, a slippery criterion, to say the least. (Indeed, in the past, "full-figured" was often the preferred look.) The second item, on the other hand, is debatable because it can be discussed in the light of objective medical research.

NOTE

You need not take one or the other side of an issue exclusively when writing a thesis. For example, you can argue that illegal immigration needs to be stopped while still expressing concern over the plight of those desperate enough to risk imprisonment, deportation, or worse to enter this country.

2. An effective claim is defensible. Before you decide to take a position, think it through, or collect concrete evidence to defend your thesis by using one of the prewriting strategies discussed in Chapter 2. If you have difficulty gathering appropriate evidence, you may need to change your thesis. For example, it would be hard to gather evidence that abusing children and spouses is not a serious offense. It would be easier to gather evidence that some people who abuse their spouses or children can be rehabilitated through psychological counseling. Compare these two items as well:

Indefensible:	To reduce fat in your diet, you must become a vegetarian.
Defensible:	Eating less meat and more fruits and vegetables can help you reduce fat in your diet.

The first example argues that there is only one way to reduce fat intake, a claim that can be dismissed easily, given the fact that there are many varieties of meat and fish that are low in fat. The second claim is far more reasonable and defensible.

3. **An effective claim is focused.** As indicated above, once you have drafted your essay, you may want to revise your preliminary claim or thesis to make it more specific or to fit a change in your position, which you came to after researching the question thoroughly. In any event, your thesis must also be focused enough to be argued effectively in a short essay.

Too general:	The college does not maintain up-to-date equipment.
Focused:	The college must replace its computers with current models if it is to support classes requiring the latest business and engineering software.

The first item could result in an essay whose length might greatly exceed what was assigned. To prove that thesis, you would need to discuss a wide range of equipment. Writing an essay on the second item would be much easier. First, you would need to discuss only computers, not all equipment. Second, you would need to discuss only those computers used in business and engineering classes, not those used in all disciplines.

■ ■ ■ ■   ■ ■ ■ ■   BASICLINK ■ ■ ■ ■   ■ ■ ■ ■

WWW

For more on writing thesis statements for argumentative essays, visit these sites:
http://www.humboldt.edu/~act/about.html
http://owl.english.purdue.edu/handouts/general/gl_argpers.html

Writing a Thesis That Is Debatable, Supportable, and Focused

The following thesis statements lack focus, are indefensible, or are not debatable. Revise them.

1. The major that I have chosen requires me to take twelve credits in modern language.
2. Many poor people are not covered by health insurance.
3. All workers, regardless of ability or effort, should receive the same bonus awards this year.

EXERCISE 6A

4. The environment must be kept wild.
5. There are many definitions of *sexual harassment.*
6. The depiction of violence on television influences people to act violently.
7. Nothing good can come from research into cloning.
8. The government should punish white-collar crimes as severely as it punishes rape and murder.

NOTE

As you consider your audience, keep the following in mind:

- Use the motivational approach, as explained on p. 106, only if you are knowledgeable about the nature of your audience, their needs, and their opinions.
- Assess the readers' familiarity with the issue. Provide the necessary background information to help readers new to the issue understand it fully. However, include only enough explanatory information and data to make your claims clear and convincing. Don't include three illustrations and six sets of statistics when only one of each will do.
- Express yourself clearly and simply. Don't use highly sophisticated or technical vocabulary unless you are sure your readers will understand it. Otherwise, they might suspect you are trying to confuse them or cloud the issue.

6.2 Establish your interest and credibility.

Generally speaking, the best place to state a thesis is in your introduction. This is also the place to establish your interest in the subject and your credibility as an advocate for a particular position. For example, you might begin your essay by describing your frustration when trying to work with the college's outdated software. You might mention that you have taken courses in history and government to establish some authority on the issue of free speech. You might even explain that you have personally witnessed the effects of spousal abuse. Indeed, the very experiences, knowledge, and opinions that led you to choose a particular topic can help you establish your credibility.

6.3 Consider your purpose and audience.

As you just learned, a claim or thesis supported by concrete evidence is the heart of an argument. If your purpose is to convince your audience that your stand on an issue has merit, that a conclusion you have drawn is defensible, or that your hypothesis is correct, a well-supported, logical argument will suffice. In fact, an effective argument can be developed logically solely through the use of expert testimony—direct quotations from scholars or other authorities in the field—and concrete evidence in the form of data, statistics, and illustrations.

For example, say you argue that adults should engage in regular aerobic exercise. Taking an authoritative approach, you might refer to statistical evidence from a study in the *New England Journal of Medicine* or quote a noted cardiologist to the effect that aerobic exercise promotes cardiovascular health. Combining this with other data and concrete illustrations, you might also explain the effects of such exercise on the reduction of cholesterol levels.

On the other hand, sometimes logic, expert testimony, and concrete evidence alone are not enough to persuade readers. While remaining clearheaded and fair, you might also want to appeal to your audience's pride, values, and even self-interest. This is sometimes called the motivational approach.

For example, say you are addressing an audience of people between fifty and sixty years old on the advisability of their joining a community-sponsored aerobic exercise program. Your purpose now is to persuade your readers to take action, not simply to convince them of something. Therefore, you might appeal to their desire to stay healthy in order to enjoy their children and grandchildren for many years. You might also point out the opportunities for travel offered by an active retirement. You might even suggest that, regardless of a person's age, regular aerobic exercise improves sex.

Considering Your Purpose and Appealing to Your Audience

Read each of the following statements, which describe a purpose and an audience. Then in an electronic file or on a separate piece of paper, write a short paragraph explaining how you might appeal to that particular audience.

1. You are writing a letter to the editor trying to persuade your fellow students not to mark up, make notes on, fold, or in other ways damage printed material in the college library.
2. You are writing to the president of your college and to members of its board of trustees to designate a place in the middle of campus where anyone can speak freely on any issue, at any time.
3. You are writing to the owner of a major recording studio to place warning labels on CDs containing materials that espouse violence or that are sexually explicit.
4. You are writing to your fellow students asking them to contribute money to a worthy charity—money they would otherwise spend on a dinner out, a beer blast, or some other form of entertainment.

EXERCISE 6B

6.4 Gather concrete evidence to support your thesis.

Many of the ways used to develop paragraphs in an essay, as explained in Chapter 4, can also be used to approach an argument. For example, to argue that the college's Code of Student Conduct restricts a student's freedom of speech, you might first define the right of free speech and reveal the source of that right. If you argue that the college's computers need to be replaced, you might use cause and effect to explain the difficulties engineering and business students experience completing assignments with the old software. Whatever approach you take, remember that you must use enough concrete evidence to make your position convincing.

The most convincing types of evidence to support an argument are documented data, facts, and statistics; expert testimony; and illustrations.

NOTE ⋯⋯⋯

Use statistics sparingly. Too many statistics can overwhelm your readers, bore them, or even make them question your intentions.

1. Use documented data, facts, and statistics. To prove that being overweight is a health hazard, you might quote research data published in scientific journals. You might also use statistics taken from medical studies or insurance actuarial tables to show that obese people suffer higher rates of mortality from coronary disease than do those who are not obese.

2. Use expert testimony. Begin by explaining why the expert you are quoting or referring to is an expert. In other words, mention academic credentials, professional experience, published works, awards, and other information to convince readers of your source's expertise. You might use expert testimony in the form of statements from college faculty, staff, and students to prove that the college's computers are outdated. You might quote constitutional lawyers, judges, or government experts to support your claim that the college's Code of Student Conduct restricts freedom of speech.

NOTE ⋯⋯⋯

Cite sources of data, statistics, and expert testimony by using an acceptable format for documentation, such as one of those explained in Chapters 15 through 17.

⋯⋯ ⋯⋯ ⋯⋯ THE BASICS OF TECHNOLOGY

⋮⋮ ⋮⋮ ⋮⋮ REVIEWING AND RESPONDING

Want to make your voice known? Try reviewing, critiquing, or simply responding to an editorial, column, novel, CD, or movie. Then submit your work to your college newspaper or literary magazine. Such publications are always looking for interesting response pieces. Or try writing a review of a book, CD, or DVD for Amazon.com (www.amazon.com) and Barnes & Noble (www.bn.com) online. You might even offer your services as a reviewer to Sharp Writer (www.sharpwriter.com), which publishes e-books. Finally, if you're interested in reviewing movies, try the Online Film Critics Society (http://ofcs. rottentomatoes.com).

3. Use illustrations. Illustrations are factual examples or instances of the idea you are trying to support. You would be using illustrations if you discussed specific cases in which the Code of Student Conduct was used to punish or silence students who had expressed their opinions on controversial campus issues. Always make sure your examples are concrete and well developed. Mention names of the people involved, include statements of the charges and punishments, explain the "offense," summarize arguments, quote testimony, and cite specific parts of the code. Finally, choose examples that are directly relevant to your claim and that appeal to your audience. For example, in discussing an alleged violation of the Code of Student Conduct, you would need to do more than claim that Jennifer Forthright spoke out against the Math Department. You might add that she did so in a polite, well-reasoned letter to the college newspaper, which calls itself "the student's voice." You might even quote directly from that letter.

Of course, most argumentative essays use a combination of these kinds of evidence. For example, to strengthen your claim that the Code of Student Conduct violates students' rights of free speech, you might include the testimony of legal experts when you cite examples. Again, the important thing is that you use enough concrete evidence to be convincing.

6.5   Present evidence logically: Use induction, deduction, and claims and warrants.

6.5a   Reason inductively: From specific to general.

One of the most popular ways to present a reasoned argument is to develop it through the **conclusion-and-support method,** which you learned about in Chapter 4. The conclusion-and-support method is **inductive;** that is, it offers specific details to support a general conclusion. The conclusion or position such an essay expresses is its thesis or claim. The support, or evidence, comes in the form of specific details. The following paragraph uses inductive reasoning; its conclusion is in italics.

The college's Code of Student Conduct illegally restricts freedom of speech. In the past two years, fifty students (3 percent of all enrolled) have appeared before the Student Court to answer charges that they engaged in "offensive" speech. This week, two students who had written letters to the college newspaper poking fun at the president's end-of-semester address received letters of reprimand from the Office of the Academic Dean, and the editor was banned from serving on the paper for a year. Another student was expelled for using an obscenity in a speech criticizing Senator Anderson's support for Arctic oil drilling. All four students have appealed, basing their cases on a recent Indiana Supreme Court ruling: *Hagstrom* v. *Langley State University* (July 2002), which affirms the right of students to use college-funded publications and college property to express their opinions. Indeed, Arlene Smith, faculty advisor to the newspaper, and Joseph S. Choir, head of the Legal Studies Department, have co-signed an open letter to the college president in which they explain that because the college is publicly funded, "enforcing the Code of Student Conduct ban on 'speech that offends members of the community or that polarizes the community' violates the First Amendment right to free speech."

The writer uses concrete evidence, as explained above, in the form of statistics, illustrations, and expert testimony to support her argument. She begins by including statistics that reveal the seriousness and extent of the problem. She then includes three recent incidents (illustrations) in which students were punished for speaking their minds. Finally, she appeals to authority by referring to a recent court case and by quoting experts in journalism and law. Note that the quotation from Professors Smith and Choir contains a direct quotation of the provision that violates the students' rights.

■■■■   ■■■■   **BASICLINK**   ■■■■   ■■■■
WWW

For more on induction, visit this site:
http://trochim.human.cornell.edu/kb/dedind.htm

■■   ■■   ■■   ■■   ■■   ■■   ■■   ■■   ■■   ■■   ■■   ■■

EXERCISE 6C

Reasoning Inductively: From Specific to General

Read the following sets of specific details. Then, reasoning from specific to general, draw a conclusion from each set. Use your own words to express that conclusion in a complete sentence. Next, on a separate sheet of paper or in an electronic file, write a paragraph based on each set of specific details. In each case, make the conclusion you have drawn the topic sentence of the paragraph. Add details of your own if you like. Make sure your paragraph is well organized, unified, and coherent.

My Town
Three new restaurants open on Main Street.
The Bijou movie house is remodeled and expanded.
The city hospital adds a new wing.
An abandoned factory on Spring Avenue is converted to an indoor shopping center.
Construction workers break ground for a new ten-home subdivision just outside of town.

Conclusion/topic sentence:_____

_____

_____

Noise Pollution

Tractor trailers roar down the street.

Buses and cars honk their horns.

Their whistles blowing loudly, trains clank over old tracks.

Police and fire sirens can be heard in the distance.

Children scream.

Enormous radios blast rock music from every open window.

Conclusion/topic sentence:_____

_____

_____

6.5b Reason deductively: From general to specific.

Using the **deductive method,** writers start with a general statement they believe readers will agree with. Next, they apply a specific case or example to that statement. Finally, they draw a conclusion from the two. You would be reasoning from general to specific if you wrote

General statement:	The college's computers cannot run the latest generation of business software.
Specific case or example:	Accreditation requirements for several business programs stipulate that students learn the latest generation of software.
Conclusion:	The college's computers must be replaced with models that can run this software.

This type of structure is called a **syllogism,** with the general statement being the major premise and the specific case being the minor premise. As such, the three statements above could serve as the skeleton of an argumentative essay, with the conclusion being placed in the introduction. Of course, you would have to support both the major and minor premises with concrete evidence, the same kind of evidence you would use in an essay that argued from specific to general.

■■■■   ■■■■   **B A S I C L I N K**   ■■■■   ■■■■

WWW

Reasoning deductively—from general to specific—as a method of scientific investigation is most commonly attributed to the ancient Greek biologist and philosopher Aristotle (384–322 B.C.). Aristotle was one of Plato's students. He was also the founder of the Lyceum (a school in Athens) and the tutor of Alexander the Great. You can find more on Aristotle and deductive reasoning on the World Wide Web at http://www. utm.edu/research/iep/a/aristotl.htm

■■ ■■ ■■ ■■ ■■ ■■   ■■ ■■ ■■ ■■ ■■ ■■

Although the specific-to-general and general-to-specific methods are different, they almost always complement each other. In fact, logical and well-supported arguments often contain both types of thinking. The most important thing to remember about an effective argument is that it is *both* logical and well supported. You can reason from specific to general or from general to specific. You can use illustrations, documented facts, statistics, or expert testimony as evidence. You can define terms, create contrasts, and even create analogies if they are logical and relevant. In short, you have the responsibility to choose the best ways to make your writing convincing and easily understood.

EXERCISE 6D

Reasoning Deductively: From General to Specific

Read the four general statements that follow. Then make up a specific case or example that would apply to each. Finally, draw a conclusion from each pair of statements.

1. Students majoring in liberal arts must complete a foreign language.

Specific case or example:_____

_____

Conclusion:_____

2. The government offers scholarships for nursing students.

Specific case or example:_____

_____

Conclusion:_____

3. Fire destroyed all the homes on Laredo Street.

Specific case or example:_____

_____

Conclusion:_____

4. Only people with tickets will be let into the concert hall.

Specific case or example:_____

_____

Conclusion:_____

6.5c Reason using claims and warrants.

In 1963, Steven Toulmin, a British rhetorician, devised a method for argumentation based on formal logic and concrete evidence, which is closer, he believed, to the way ordinary people debate than to the syllogistic method (see page 103) used for centuries. Published in 1963, Toulmin's "Layout of Argumentation" is applicable to any discipline, issue, or question. As you read about Toulmin's method, you may decide to incorporate parts of it into your own brand of argumentation. The method contains six major components:

1. **Data.** Information that leads the writer or speaker to take a position on a question or an issue.
2. **Claim.** A statement of the position being defended, the thesis.
3. **Warrants.** Major ideas used to support a claim. The three types of warrants are authoritative, substantive, and motivational. Warrants must relate directly and logically to the claim.
4. **Backing.** Evidence used to support or prove a warrant. Backing comes in three forms: expert testimony, data and statistics, and concrete illustrations.
5. **Reservation.** A statement anticipating an opposing argument before it decreases your argument's credibility.
6. **Qualifier.** A statement or phrase that restricts the scope of the claim.

As noted above, Toulmin uses the word *claim* for the thesis of an argument, the point you are trying to prove. Toulmin also uses *warrants* in his "Layout of Argumentation." These are major ideas that relate directly to and support the claim. In some ways, warrants resemble topic sentences, ideas that support a thesis. They, in turn, are developed via concrete evidence, which Toulmin calls backing.

An **authoritative warrant** relies on the theories, opinions, and studies of experts. Such information may be paraphrased, summarized, or quoted directly. For example, if you claim that listening regularly to classical music increases IQs in children, you might quote experts in child development, psychologists, and testing specialists. You might also make reference to scientific studies conducted by universities, professional organizations, or government agencies to support your claim.

A **substantive warrant** uses a variety of rhetorical modes or techniques—especially the conclusion-and-support, comparison-and-contrast, cause-and-effect, and process analysis methods—to present concrete facts, data, and illustrations that support the claim. For example, you might explain how (process analysis) listening to classical music affects the human brain in its formative stages. You might compare (comparison and contrast) those effects with the effects of listening to other kinds of music or of being exposed to no musical stimulation. In addition, you might cite statistics from professional studies (conclusion and support) to help develop this warrant. Or you might describe the effects of classical music documented in case studies (illustration) of children who were exposed regularly to the works of Mozart and Beethoven.

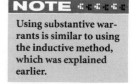

NOTE

Using substantive warrants is similar to using the inductive method, which was explained earlier.

A **motivational warrant** can be used if you know your audience, including their needs and opinions. In such cases, you might appeal to their personal and professional beliefs, their values, their pride, or even their self-interest. As you might assume, the motivational warrant is particularly useful when writing persuasive essay. For example, if you know that you are writing to the parents of school-age children, you might want to link exposure to classical music to the child's performance on standardized mathematics tests in elementary school and high school. You might also point out that, later on, such scores will surely help the student's chances of being admitted to a prestigious college and even of being awarded an academic scholarship.

■ ■ ■ ■   ■ ■ ■ ■   **B A S I C L I N K**   ■ ■ ■ ■   ■ ■ ■ ■
WWW
For more on the Toulmin method, visit this site:
http://writing.colostate.edu/references/reading/ toulmin

■ ■ ■ ■ ■ ■ ■ ■ ■ ■ ■ ■   ■ ■ ■ ■ ■ ■ ■ ■ ■ ■ ■ ■

6.6 Address contrary opinions.

Another way to ensure the persuasiveness of an argument is to anticipate and address opinions different from your own. Indeed, as discussed above, Toulmin recommends that you include a reservation in an argument to head off opposing arguments before they affect the credibility of your position. For example, an argument supporting regular aerobic exercise for people between the ages of fifty and sixty might acknowledge the fact that some people overexercise and, consequently, might do themselves more harm than good.

Since arguments are rarely absolute, Toulmin suggests including a qualifier, a statement that limits the claim. For example, you might qualify the claim made above by rephrasing it in either of these two ways:

Most people between the ages of fifty and sixty will benefit from regular aerobic exercise.

People over the age of fifty should engage in regular aerobic exercise unless advised otherwise by their doctors.

In general, you can follow three steps to avoid having your credibility or the strength of your argument affected by the doubts, skepticism, or opposing arguments harbored by members of your audience:

1. Anticipate the opposition. Let's say you believe that local property taxes should be raised to increase teachers' salaries, install a computer lab, and provide extra tutoring at your town's high school. You could take a straightforward approach that the average taxpayer might accept. For example, you might argue that faculty salaries don't compare with those paid by other school districts, that a computer lab will teach students job skills, and that tutoring will help raise grades. That might be enough to convince the taxpayer who has three school-age children, but what about members of the audience who have no school-age children? You need to anticipate their concerns as well as their arguments against a tax increase. For example, such people might see no *direct* benefit to themselves in your proposal. Indeed, they might focus only on the fact that they will be paying higher taxes.

2. Recognize the validity of different points of view. To begin with, you must consider whether there is some validity in an opposing point of view. If there isn't, you have to explain what is wrong with that position and dismiss it convincingly.

On the other hand, if you find some validity in the opposing argument, the wisest thing to do is to acknowledge it immediately. For example, a better-paid high school faculty, a new computer lab, and an after-school tutoring program will provide little direct benefit to people without school-age children. Pretending that they will benefit directly is futile and counterproductive. The worst thing to do is to ignore opposing arguments; doing so only weakens your credibility and strengthens the opposition's resolve.

3. Address opposing arguments. To convince people without school-age children, you might have to show that funding the changes you describe will bring them long-term, if *indirect*, benefits. For example, the changes you advocate will improve the school system, thereby making your community a more desirable place to live, which in turn will raise property values for everyone. In addition, after-school tutoring might help reduce teenage crime, which affects all members of the community, not just people with school-age children.

Addressing Opinions Different from Your Own

Think of a serious issue affecting your campus, neighborhood, hometown, state, or country. Choose a topic you know well. Then write a letter to your college or local newspaper arguing for a way to respond to the issue. Use logic and factual evidence to make your letter convincing, but appeal to your readers' pride, values, or self-interest as well. In addition, address opinions that differ from your own if doing so will strengthen your case. Here are some topics you might use:

    Should public funding of AIDS research be increased?
    Should everyone be required to recycle newspapers, glass bottles, and metal cans?
    Should an evening curfew be established for high-crime areas of a city?

EXERCISE 6E

Should people sentenced to jail terms be required to work for their food and medical care?

Should students be required to take courses not directly related to their majors?

Should tuition be eliminated in all public colleges?

Should everyone be guaranteed free health care?

Should college students learn basic computer applications such as word processing and spreadsheet programs?

Should all cars except taxis, police cars, and emergency vehicles be banned in large cities?

Should the college raise tuition and fees to improve the library, the computer center, or another important area?

Should letter grades be replaced with a pass-fail or other system?

6.7 Learn to develop ideas in an argumentative essay.

Let's say you have decided to write an essay on the benefits of aerobic exercise. Here's what an outline for that essay might look like:

Working thesis/introduction: Regular aerobic exercise, such as jogging, swimming, and walking, promotes both physical and mental well-being.

Topic sentence/paragraph 2:   Aerobic exercise is a proven method of weight control.

Topic sentence/paragraph 3:   Jogging, swimming, or walking at least three hours per week increases stamina and promotes clearer thinking.

Topic sentence/paragraph 4:   Aerobic exercise also helps prevent heart disease and thus prolongs life.

Topic sentence/conclusion: Aerobic exercise even reduces tension and, some people claim, improves one's sex life.

The body paragraphs of this essay can be developed in several ways. Here are a few suggestions:

Paragraph 2 might use the specific-to-general form of reasoning (the conclusion-and-support method) to present illustrations from your own experiences and observations. For example, you could explain that you lost twenty pounds in four months by walking briskly for two miles three times a week. You might include examples of friends who have achieved similar results by walking or jogging. Finally, you could explain that your chronically overweight uncle has shed thirty-five pounds this year by swimming twenty laps every day in the community pool.

Paragraph 3 can be developed through the expert testimony of doctors, medical researchers, trainers, and psychologists through the specific-to-general method. You might quote directly from articles published in reputable journals, magazines, and newspapers. You might also include information gathered in an interview with your psychology or health professor. This evidence can then be combined with what you learned in anatomy and physiology class: aerobic exercise causes an increased flow of oxygen to the brain, thereby improving the thinking process.

Paragraph 4 provides an opportunity to reason from general to specific. You might argue as follows:

a. Since aerobic exercise helps prevent heart disease; and

b. Since heart disease is a leading killer of adults;

c. Therefore, aerobic exercise promotes longevity.

Of course, you will want to back up ideas (*a*) and (*b*) with statistics, quotations from doctors, the findings of medical studies, and so on. Nonetheless, the way you present your evidence and think through your argument would be an example of reasoning from general to specific.

The most important thing to remember about an effective argument is that it is *both* logical and well supported. You can reason from specific to general or from general to specific, or you can do both. Just make your arguments clear and easy to follow. Then, whatever type of reasoning you have used to reach your conclusions, support those conclusions fully with details in the form of examples, statistics, expert opinions, analogies, comparisons, firsthand observations, and the like. In short, make sure your writing contains enough detail to be convincing and easily understood.

Developing Ideas in an Argument

Write a short essay that uses logic and convincing detail to argue that adopting a particular behavior makes sense. Using the outline on page 108 as your guide, try to put two or three reasons for adopting that behavior in your thesis statement. Then use those reasons as the basis of topic sentences that control the paragraphs in the body of the essay. Pick a topic you know a lot about. Here are some topics you might use:

Giving up smoking

Jogging regularly

Eliminating fats and cholesterol from your diet

Adopting a particular method of studying

Making your own clothes

EXERCISE 6F

(continued)

Joining a political party
Joining a gym
Practicing safe sex
Learning a foreign language
Learning how to maintain your car

Develop each paragraph as you see fit. But remember that you are trying to explain why a particular action is beneficial, not how you go about doing it. Turn to Chapter 4 if you want to review ways to write a good introduction and conclusion for this essay.

6.8 Avoid ten logical fallacies.

Errors in logic, though sometimes subtle and hard to detect, appear in political speeches and advertisements, in television commercials, in newspaper editorials, and even in the well-written and sincere arguments of bright college students. Learn to recognize the most common logical fallacies in the work of others, and avoid them in your own writing.

6.8a Avoid generalizations supported with insufficient evidence.

Using induction, writers sometimes draw conclusions that are not justified by the amount of information they have gathered. Failing to consider enough examples can lead to faulty generalizations such as these:

My Uncle Randolph never attended college, yet he has a net worth of more than $2 million. Therefore, the claim that college graduates have greater earning power than those who are not college graduates is a myth.

The governor vetoed the new crime bill. She must be soft on criminals.

The clerk at the perfume counter did not know whether the store carried stereo speakers. Mallrat's Department Store doesn't hire competent salespeople.

Arthur Miller's *A View from the Bridge* is about a New York dockworker's incestuous desires for his wife's niece. Miller's plays reveal an obsession with sexuality.

6.8b Avoid the straw man fallacy.

As the name implies, the straw man is an argument that is easy to knock down. When writers use a straw man, they falsely attribute an indefensible argument to their opponents in order to refute it and thereby cast their opponents in a bad light. The straw man is a pretense; it has little to do with the point at hand and does not accurately reflect the opponent's views. In most cases, it is created only to distract the audience from valid arguments the opposition advances. Here's an example:

Your position: You argue that we should create a plan to reform welfare to break the cycle of poverty and help people find jobs so that they can support themselves. You propose that mandatory vocational training programs be set up for welfare recipients who are physically and mentally capable of working. You also ask that public child care centers be established so that the children of welfare recipients can be cared for while their parents work. Finally, you propose that able-bodied people accept jobs paying a living wage or forgo all welfare benefits after six months of being offered employment.

Your opponent's position: Using the straw man, your opponent argues that you are antifamily because you propose that children spend time away from their parents. Your opponent also accuses you of advocating forced labor since you want people to submit to government intimidation and take jobs no one else wants.

6.8c   Avoid the ad hominem argument fallacy.

Ad hominem is Latin for "to the person." When writers engage in this unethical practice, they attack the person rather than his or her position, logic, facts, or opinions.

For example, when John F. Kennedy ran for president in 1962, some unscrupulous people attacked him because he was a Roman Catholic. Of course, they ignored the fact that Kennedy had on numerous occasions affirmed his commitment to the separation of church and state.

Another example concerns Ronald Reagan. When he ran for governor in California in the 1970s and again when he ran for president, Reagan's critics attacked him for his experience as a Hollywood actor, often ignoring the issues he advocated.

6.8d   Avoid begging the question.

This fallacy has particular relevance to deduction. It occurs when the writer shortcuts the syllogism by allowing the major premise (general statement) alone to determine the conclusion. Here's an example:

Major premise:	Members of the Honor Society do not cheat on tests.
Minor premise:	Eileen is a member of the Honor Society.
Conclusion:	Therefore, Eileen could not have cheated on the test.

After having read this syllogism, we still can't be sure that Eileen did not cheat. The major premise equates being a member of the Honor Society and not being able to cheat. But there is no necessary correlation between the two. In other words, the writer has not proved the major premise, so the syllogism begs the question: "Did Eileen cheat on the test?"

6.8e Avoid red herrings.

The red herring is a technique used to distract the audience from the real issue at hand. It gets its name from a practice used by farmers to protect their planted fields from fox hunters and their hounds. The farmers would drag a red herring along the edge of their fields, where it would leave a scent that would distract the hounds and keep them and the horsemen that followed from trampling the young crops.

Today, advertisers often use red herrings. For example, automobile commercials often picture luxury cars being driven along scenic mountain highways where the driver—usually suave, sophisticated, and daring—can escape the mundane world of work and responsibility. In one commercial, a shiny, new four-wheel-drive vehicle is pictured as an adult toy. All these ads ignore the fact that most people buy cars for one practical reason—transportation. More important, they distract from the reality that to pay for these "toys," we will have to work extra hard and, in most cases, tie ourselves to an all-too-real auto loan that takes three, four, or five years to pay off.

6.8f Avoid non sequiturs.

A Latin term, *non sequitur* translates roughly as "does not follow." A non sequitur occurs when a statement does not proceed logically from the previous statement. Here are two examples:

> My ninety-year-old grandfather smokes a pack of cigarettes a day. Therefore, smoking can't be bad for one's health.
>
> Gina finds accounting a challenging course. She will never succeed in business.

In both examples, the second statement does not follow directly from the first. The fact that one man who smokes heavily has reached the age of ninety in no way contradicts the massive research proving that, for the vast majority of people, smoking is a health hazard. Similarly, although Gina finds accounting challenging, the time and effort she puts into studying this subject may enable her to master it. On the other hand, a mastery of sophisticated accounting principles may not be necessary for success in the kind of business she plans to pursue.

6.8g Avoid false analogies.

An argument based on a false analogy incorrectly assumes that because two situations may be alike in some respects, the same rules, principles, or approaches apply to both or the same conclusions can be drawn about both. You would be guilty of false analogy if you wrote:

> Jason's father had a heart attack at fifty. Jason will suffer from heart disease, too.

The analogy presumes that the only cause for heart disease is heredity. But what if Jason has a healthy lifestyle, while his father smoked heavily, failed to exercise, and ate a high-fat diet?

Before the United States invaded Afghanistan in the fall of 2001, many political commentators predicted a long, drawn-out conflict with thousands of casualties. Their prediction was based on a false analogy between the United States's involvement and the former Soviet Union's disastrous military occupation of Afghanistan in the 1980s. But there were significant differences in the goals and preparedness of the two armies. Moreover, the Afghani political situation in 2001 had changed from what it was in the 1980s.

6.8h   Avoid the either-or fallacy.

Failing to see all the aspects or all the choices associated with a problem or situation can result in an either-or fallacy. You would create such a fallacy if you wrote:

> The only way students get through Professor Wilson's history class is to cheat on their exams or resign themselves to a D.

Of course, no matter how demanding the instructors, there is a third alternative: to study hard.

6.8i   Avoid the erroneous-cause fallacy.

In Latin, this fallacy is called *post hoc, ergo propter hoc* ("after this, therefore because of this"). It occurs when the writer assumes that because one thing follows another, it must necessarily have resulted from (been caused by) the other. Here's an example:

> The college restricted student parking to Lots A and B last semester, so Rachel got more parking tickets than ever.

The reason Rachel got more parking tickets was not that the college decided to restrict student parking. After all, Lots A and B might be sufficient to hold all student cars. Rachel's getting more tickets is a direct result of her choosing to park where she shouldn't.

6.8j   Avoid the going-along, or bandwagon, fallacy.

This fallacy assumes that an idea, action, or proposal must be valid if a great many people support or believe in it. Recall that in some primitive cultures the vast majority of people believed in the practice of human sacrifice to appease their gods. You would be falling into this logical error if you wrote:

> Overwhelming popular support for the new mayor shows she can achieve greatness.

■ ■ ■ ■   ■ ■ ■ ■   **BASICLINK**   ■ ■ ■ ■   ■ ■ ■ ■
WWW

More on logical fallacies can be found at these sites:
http://www.datanation.com/fallacies/
http://www.carmen.artsci.washington.edu/propaganda/logic.htm

6.9 Analyze a sample persuasive essay.

As a review of what you have learned about developing arguments, read the following persuasive essay, "Why Learn to Write?" by Carrie Hill. Pay attention to the logic and supporting evidence in this essay, and read the comments in the margins to understand the techniques the writer used.

Why Learn to Write?

Writing well is not easy. For a few people, it is a simple process, with words flowing easily from a pen or across a computer screen. But for most, especially for beginning writers, it is a long, laborious, and nerve-racking process. So why should we learn to write? Why should we learn a process that so fills us with self-doubt that it often leads to panic attacks and a blank page? The answer is simple: We should learn to write to communicate.

> Begins with comparison and question—both effective ways to write an introduction; Chapter 4 describes others.

> Essay's thesis appears at end of introduction.

First, we should learn to write to communicate with the world at large and to pass our ideas on to those who follow. The spoken word dies, but the written word lives on. Thomas Jefferson wrote the Declaration of Independence so that all people—not just his fellow revolutionaries—would know why the colonies rebelled. If Lincoln had not written down the Gettysburg Address, none but those present would have heard his stirring words, and they would soon have been forgotten. Today, however, Lincoln still challenges our minds and stirs our hearts. Of course, one could argue that times have changed and that electronic technology lets us hear, record, and rehear words of famous people. However, technology is not always available, and the only sure way to capture important events and ideas is through writing.

> The word *communicate* ties topic sentence directly to essay's thesis.

> Two examples develop paragraph's topic sentence.

> Writer addresses an opposing view.

Second, we should learn to write to communicate with our personal worlds, whether in the classroom or on the job. In college we use writing to communicate with instructors and other students in a variety of classes, no matter what our majors. Some students will claim that good writing is important only in English classes. On the contrary, the need to write well runs across the curriculum. No longer are biology, history, and economics tests purely short-answer. Exams in many courses require essays, and teachers of subjects other than English are assigning papers. On the job, we communicate with employers, customers, and fellow workers. In fact, a major requirement for getting any good job is the ability to write effective letters, memos, reports, and summaries. A glance through the want ads shows that "good communication skills" are essential to high-paying jobs.

> Topic sentence relate directly to essay's thesis.

> Paragraph uses specific details to support topic sentence—good example of reasoning from specific to general.

> Writer addresses an opposing argument.

> Writer appeals to reader's self-intere

Writer reasons from general to specific.

Third, but by no means least, we should learn to write to communicate with ourselves. Writing is a process of discovery, and putting ideas on paper gives us new perspectives—new ways of seeing. As a result, it helps us look at our world and make sense of it. It helps us create order out of chaos. It helps us understand ourselves. At times, what we write makes us cry; at others, it makes us laugh. No matter, writing helps us survive by acting as the key to unlock the doors behind which lie our innermost hopes and dreams.

Writer appeals to reader's values and self-interest.

Yes, writing is not easy. But we can make it easier by remembering why we should write. We can also make it easier by remembering that we control the writing process; it does not control us. As with anything worth doing, writing involves work, lots of it. When we write, the essayist Jonathan Swift tells us, we must "Blot out, correct, insert, refine, / Enlarge, diminish, interline." Sometimes this process seems endless, but the effort is always worthwhile. So, whenever you have doubts about your writing, take courage and follow the advice of the poet Philip Sidney: "Look in thy heart and write."

Conclusion recalls introduction and contains two memorable quotations; Chapter 4 describes other effective ways to conclude an essay.

Chapter Checklist

1. Argument is the attempt to prove a point. Persuasion uses but goes beyond argument to get readers to act.

2. To write an effective argument, start with a thesis that is debatable, supportable, and focused.

3. To strengthen your position, establish your credibility early in the essay.

4. Consider your intended readers, their needs, and their attitudes as you plan your approach. At the same time, clarify your purpose and adopt an approach appropriate to it.

5. Rely on a variety of concrete evidence to support the thesis of an argument, especially documented data, facts, and statistics; expert testimony; and illustrations. Evaluate your evidence carefully; make sure it is convincing and that it relates directly to the thesis. In addition, try to gauge its effect on your readers before you decide to use it.

6. Present your evidence logically. Make use of the specific-to-general method (induction), the general-to-specific method (deduction), or the claim-and-warrants method of reasoning.

7. To change your readers' attitudes or to persuade them to act, appeal to their pride, personal values, or self-interest. Depending on your audience, address different or even opposing opinions before you begin to argue for your own.

8. Learn to spot common logical fallacies in what you read, and avoid them in what you write.

2
ONLINE WRITING AND ELECTRONIC DESIGN

2

ONLINE WRITING AND ELECTRONIC DESIGN

7

USING COMPUTERS IN COLLEGE

In the 1980s, the computer came into its own as a powerful academic tool. In addition to helping with student service functions—registering students, maintaining academic transcripts, classifying library holdings, and the like—computers are used as tools for learning in almost every discipline, including the liberal arts, which was never before seen as a study demanding technical expertise. In addition, distance education via the Internet has become a standard instructional delivery method at most colleges and universities. In short, the computer has revolutionized higher education.

7.1 Write essays, reports, and other documents.

As you have seen in Chapters 1 through 6, word processing software can be used as a powerful tool for writing. One can argue that since the introduction of computers, writing has become easier. For example, while freewriting, you can simply turn off the monitor and start typing. Doing so will allow you to gather and record raw information without having to be distracted by grammatical and mechanical errors that appear on the screen. You also can gather information about a topic by reading about it on the Internet. Or you can interview experts via e-mail. Keep in mind that these techniques, while providing a richer base on which to build a piece of writing, may also require more work from you.

Computer software also provides ways to create outlines, check spelling, and even correct minor grammatical problems. Perhaps the most useful function offered by word processors, however, is the

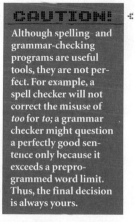

CAUTION!

Although spelling- and grammar-checking programs are useful tools, they are not perfect. For example, a spell checker will not correct the misuse of *too* for *to*; a grammar checker might question a perfectly good sentence only because it exceeds a preprogrammed word limit. Thus, the final decision is always yours.

ability to revise and rewrite easily. In the past, revision would require the writer to retype the entire document. Today, because documents can be stored electronically and revised selectively, multiple revisions can be completed with much less effort.

Many writers store multiple drafts of their work in separate electronic files just to keep track of how extensively they have changed and developed a document from the first to the last draft. In fact, some word processors provide a split-screen function, which allows the writer to revise one copy of a document on the bottom half of a screen and compare it with the original version on the top half. Another tool allows the writer to record, see on-screen, and print out revisions. Typically, such revisions appear in red or another color (see Figure 7.1).

In the last fifteen years the world ~~went~~ has gone ~~thru~~ through a ~~true revalation~~ revolution in the communications industry. Computers ~~help~~ enable us to send long e-mail messages quickly, cheaply, and- easily ~~without much effort~~. ~~Fax machines allow us to transmit long documents in a flash. But like with all things there is a downside to this.~~ However, there have been some disadvantages to this progress.

Figure 7.1   Using the Track Changes Tool in Microsoft Word

···· ···· ···· THE BASICS OF TECHNOLOGY

USING THE SPLIT-SCREEN FUNCTION

To use the split-screen function in Microsoft Word, open the document you want to revise. Then select the entire text of that document and click on the Copy icon in the toolbar at the top of the screen. Next, open a new document, and click on the Paste icon to insert the text of the original document into the new document. Finally, go to Window in the toolbar of the new document and click on Arrange All. You will now be able to work on the copy you want to revise (the new document) while still being able to view your original text. (Saving the documents with a 1 and a 2 at the end of the file name [and so on, as you revise further] will help you keep track of which document is the original and which is the revision.)

EXERCISE 7A

Using a Computer to Revise

Learn to use the split-screen or revision tools your word processor offers. The easiest way to do this is to read the on-screen tutorials offered by your program (usually clicking on a Help icon will do the trick). To test your skills, try revising a paper you are now completing or have recently completed.

7.2 Create tables, charts, and graphs.

Most word processing programs provide templates that enable you to create and modify tables you can place directly into a document. This is an important function, for a table can convey a mass of data in a way that is quicker and easier to read than if the same information were presented in a sentence or paragraph. Indeed, well-constructed tables are essential to writing business, scientific, and technical reports, and they can be used effectively in papers written for history, art, psychology, and other nontechnical courses. Easy-to-use spreadsheets such as Microsoft's Excel allow you to represent large amounts of data in pie and bar charts, line graphs, and other graphic elements, thereby enabling you to express important informational relationships and comparisons in a way that makes them easy to understand. Such tools are invaluable in papers written in the sciences, mathematics, engineering, and the technologies. However, business writers, journalists, and people writing in the social sciences can use these tools to advantage as well. You can read more about using a computer to design documents in Chapter 9.

EXERCISE 7B

Creating Tables of Information

Create a table of information by using a word processor or an electronic spreadsheet. Then incorporate that table in a document created on your word processor. You can choose any subject or kind of information you like; one of the most useful might be a weekly schedule of class periods, study hours, work hours, and rest and recreation times.

7.3 Organize and present data.

You just learned that spreadsheets can help you create charts and other graphics. As you might expect, such tools are essential in organizing the kinds of data used by accountants, retailers, economists, and insurance specialists. However, a spreadsheet also can be used to organize information about exotic plant species observed and collected by field botanists. Environmental engineers can use a spreadsheet to discuss levels of toxicity found in different areas of a chemical spill. Statisticians can use spreadsheets to organize data that lead to the creation of demographic portraits important to education, urban planning, the use of natural resources, economic forecasting, and the delivery of social services.

Even more effective in terms of their presentation value are electronic slide programs such as Microsoft's PowerPoint. This versatile tool will allow you to record lists of important information on electronic slides in clear, easy-to-read formats, which can then be printed out or projected on-screen for presentation before large audiences. Colors as well as typefaces and sizes can be manipulated easily to enhance the presentation. PowerPoint also enables you to add graphics, illustrations, and photographs. You can even add motion, fade-ins and fade-outs, and sound to add emphasis and interest.

Both PowerPoint and Excel come with on-screen instruction; additionally, some colleges offer noncredit and even credit courses in powerful computing tools such as these. In any case, it is a good idea to learn about and use a variety of such tools throughout your college career. In fact, you would be wise to indicate your mastery of them on your employment resumé. Employers are always on the lookout for people who are computer versatile, not just computer literate.

EXERCISE 7C

Learning to Use Spreadsheets and Presentation Programs

Explore the possibilities of using an electronic spreadsheet or a presentation program in your course work. Begin by going to the online tutorials offered by such programs. You can find out more about using such tools at these sites:

http://www.fgcu.edu/support/office2000/ppt/
http://www.usd.edu/trio/tut/excel

7.4 Learn more about class work.

Have you ever sat in a class following the discussion easily when, all of a sudden, a question arises that takes you into material that is totally new, unfamiliar, or even confusing? You can always raise your hand and ask for an explanation, or you can stop by your instructor's office after class to get things cleared up. However, asking such questions is not always possible. Class time is sometimes limited, and your instructor might not always be able to stay after class.

Of course, you can always seek help in the college's tutoring center or do some library research. However, a good way to find out more about a subject is through the Internet. Information taken from reputable Web sites such as those sponsored by colleges, universities, and government or scholarly organizations can clear up confusion, add to your store of knowledge, and help you keep up with the rest of the class. (See Chapter 12 for ways to evaluate Web sites.) Indeed, you can supplement what you read in your assigned textbook by regularly investigating two or three academic Web sites on a subject. For example, let's say your Introduction to Psychology syllabus indicates that your instructor will discuss the significance of dreams as explained by Jung and Freud. If your textbook mentions their theories only in passing, you might want to spend an hour or two reading about dream theory on the Internet. Doing so will prepare you to follow the class more easily. It may even help you add information or ask intelligent questions that will both enrich the discussion and impress your professor.

Other good sources of information are books published on CD-ROM and DVD-ROM. Many of these are essentially encyclopedias, so they provide only general knowledge. Although such information might not be suitable for inclusion in a research paper, it can improve your grasp of a particular subject. Among the most useful of such tools is the *Encyclopaedia Britannica* on CD-ROM. Of course, more specialized resources are also available. For instance, *The Eyes of the Nation,* by Vincent Virga and the curators of the Library of Congress, traces the history of the United States through illustrations and photographs.

■ ■ ■ ■   ■ ■ ■ ■   **BASICLINK**   ■ ■ ■ ■   ■ ■ ■ ■
WWW

To read more about Virga's book, visit
http://lcweb.loc.gov/loc/lcib/9711/eyes.html

■ ■ ■ ■ ■ ■ ■ ■ ■ ■ ■ ■   ■ ■   ■ ■   ■ ■   ■ ■   ■ ■   ■ ■

7.5 Research information for papers and reports.

Before the computer revolution, students writing research papers were limited essentially to printed resources available in their libraries. As valuable as printed resources—books, journals, newspapers—are and will continue to be, electronic resources also have an important role. Today, a variety of electronic resources are making available information previously unavailable or at least not easily accessible to most students.

The first of these resources is, of course, the Internet, which, as indicated above, contains academic, government, and professional Web sites that provide information on an unlimited number of subjects. Finding such Web sites is relatively easy. However, you must have access to a Web browser such as Netscape or Microsoft Explorer, and you need to learn how to use AltaVista, Google, or another comprehensive search engine such as those discussed in Chapter 12.

Remember that Web sites found by one search engine might not appear in a list generated by another, so don't get discouraged if your search on one engine is not as successful as you had hoped. Try it again on another search engine.

Generally speaking, the most reliable information can be obtained from Web sites sponsored by colleges and universities, the government, or professional organizations such as the American Medical Association **(http://www.ama-assn.org)** or the American Chemical Society **(http://www. chemistry.org)**. URLs for college and university sites usually end in *.edu;* those for government sites usually end in *.gov;* those for sites sponsored by professional organizations usually end in *.org* or *.net.*

As you will learn in Chapter 12, there are several ways to evaluate the validity and objectiveness of information on a particular Web site. Be especially careful with sites whose URLs end in *.com,* the abbreviation for *commercial.* Sponsored by corporate entities, these sites are often designed to enhance company images and increase sales, not to provide objective information. Also be careful with Web sites whose URLs end in *org,* for *organization.* Some organizations, such as the League of Women Voters **(www.lwv.org)**, the American Psychological Association **(www.apa.org)**, the American Red Cross **(www. redcross.org)**, and the National Model Railroad Association **(www.nmra.org)**, can be trusted to provide unbiased data. Others, such as the AARP, formerly known as the American Association of Retired Persons **(www.aarp.org)**, and Amnesty International **(www.amnesty.org)**, while reputable organizations, exist to advance particular points of view or to protect the rights of particular groups. Keep this in mind when you consider using information from such groups. Finally, there are Web sites sponsored by organizations whose only function is to advance a particular political or social point of view. Many organizations of this type are extremely biased and present distorted and misleading information. Some, in fact, are racist, sexist, or bigoted in other ways. Of course, you will want to avoid such Web sites. But be careful; such organizations often masquerade as public service or mainstream religious or political groups to make their message seem more respectable.

In addition to finding information on Web sites, you can also find information on periodical databases, to which most college libraries subscribe. These can usually be accessed on or off campus. Some databases provide bibliographical information, which helps you locate printed copies of newspaper, magazine, and journal articles. Others also include abstracts, or summaries, of those articles to help you decide whether trying to find the full article is worth your time. Finally, more and more databases are providing full texts, so you can print out the complete version right from the computer you used to find the article.

You can read more about these databases in Chapter 12, but among some of the most used are JSTOR, which provides access to back issues of important scholarly journals, and ProQuest, which contains newspaper articles. To access such information, you must usually provide a college identification number. However, other periodical databases can be accessed directly from the Internet for free. Included in this list are Agricola, which covers agriculture and related disciplines; RNdex, which is especially useful to nursing students; PsycINFO, which contains full texts of articles, books, dissertations, and technical reports in psychology; and the Oxford English Dictionary, an online version of the famous dictionary that traces word origins and uses to Anglo-Saxon times. Ask your librarian for a complete list of free databases, noting those to which your college subscribes.

You can get copies of articles that have been published in popular magazines online. The Internet also makes available a number of e-zines, magazines published solely on the Web. Finally, many full-length books, usually those for which the copyright protection has expired, are available online.

Finding Information to Use in Class Discussion and Academic Papers

Use the Internet or other electronic means to locate at least three reliable sources of information you might use in class discussion or in a paper for any course you are taking.

EXERCISE 7D

7.6 Access college and class information.

Almost every college and university now has a Web site, which is essentially a virtual college catalogue. Such sites can be huge, providing information on student services; degree offerings and requirements; academic majors and departments; tuition, fees, and financial aid; and a number of other important topics. Many announce upcoming concerts, plays, lectures, and athletic events. Nearly all include a catalogue of courses as well as a class schedule for the current term. Finally, faculty and staff information, including academic credentials, office locations, and e-mail addresses, is provided. Often, users of such sites can simply click on an instructor's e-mail address to send a message.

Figure 7.2 shows the home page of the University of Tennessee at Martin. You can click on Academics if you want to find out more about an academic major or department and that school. You can click on Library if you want to learn about the library's holdings. If you are a student at UT Martin, you can even access one of the databases to which the college subscribes.

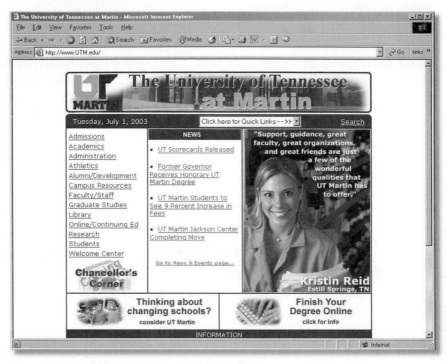

Figure 7.2   Sample Home Page of a University

Figure 7.3 shows the home page for the Geological Sciences Department at Indiana University at Bloomington. Note that you can click on Faculty to get a listing of department members, or you can click on Research Areas to learn more about subfields in this discipline.

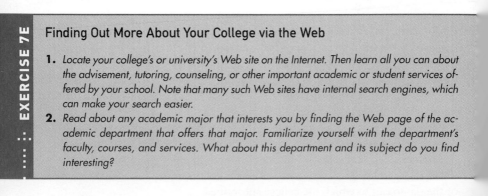

EXERCISE 7E :: ......

Finding Out More About Your College via the Web

1. *Locate your college's or university's Web site on the Internet. Then learn all you can about the advisement, tutoring, counseling, or other important academic or student services offered by your school. Note that many such Web sites have internal search engines, which can make your search easier.*

2. *Read about any academic major that interests you by finding the Web page of the academic department that offers that major. Familiarize yourself with the department's faculty, courses, and services. What about this department and its subject do you find interesting?*

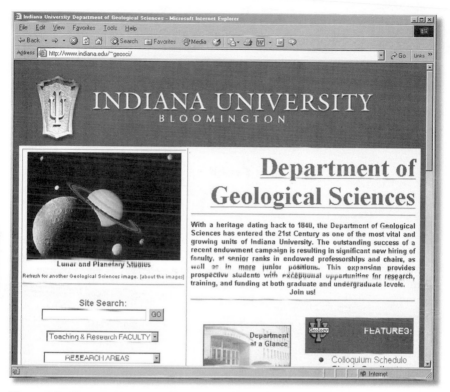

Figure 7.3   Sample University Department Home Page

7.7 Communicate with faculty and with other students.

Figure 7.4 (on the next page) lists faculty in the Department of Art History at the University of Wisconsin. To e-mail a faculty member, you need only to click on the e-mail icon. Biographical information and the instructor's telephone number are also provided.

More and more faculty are creating their own Web pages, by which to provide learning materials, remind students of dates and assignments, recommend readings or Web sites, or provide other important information. Indeed, many colleges are now offering credit courses completely online. Such offerings typically do not require regular class attendance, but they often ask you to participate in discussion via an Internet forum set up by the instructor to facilitate class discussion. Don't be fooled, however, into thinking that not having to attend a regularly scheduled class makes passing such courses easier. Indeed, online courses often require a great deal more work than traditional classes.

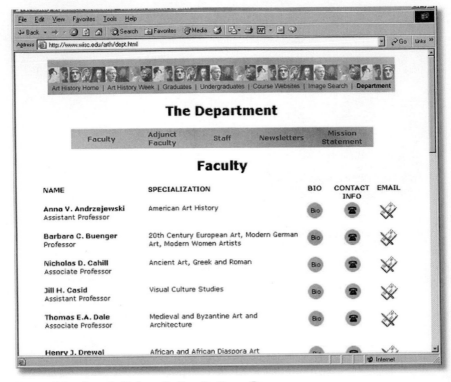

Figure 7.4   Sample University Faculty Home Page

If you are thinking about taking an online (also called a distance education or distance learning) course, you should consider whether the class is right for you. To do well in an online course, you need to be self-motivated. There will be no one in class twice a week to remind you of homework assignments and upcoming tests. If you are having problems, you will have to be the one to seek help. You will also need to be comfortable communicating in writing: all your contact—with the teacher and with other students—will take place over the Internet or through e-mail. Finally, you will need a computer with a good deal of memory and a fast modem (check with the school you are considering to find out what the minimum requirements are). Otherwise, the time it will take you to get and send information will be daunting, and completing your assignments on time will be highly frustrating.

Figure 7.5 is the home page of a Web site of Dr. Robert Roth, an English professor who teaches both online and traditional composition and literature

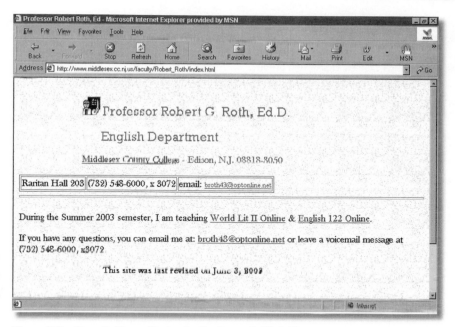

Figure 7.5 **Sample Home Page of a Professor's Web Site**

classes. Notice that it includes ample contact information and offers links to course syllabi and to Dr. Roth's e-mail address.

In years past, students often created study groups, meeting periodically to review material presented in classes they had in common. At the very least, they exchanged telephone numbers so that a student who missed a class could contact a classmate to get notes and learn about important assignment or test announcements. Today, both of those functions can also be done via the Internet and e-mail. Indeed, many instructors—even those teaching traditional classes—require students to join online study groups conducted as online chat rooms or forums. (You can learn more about forums and chat rooms in Chapter 8.) In addition, it is important to add the e-mail addresses of your instructor and of several fellow students to your e-mail address book.

If you don't have a computer or don't have access to e-mail, your college may have a service that provides computer access and e-mail free of charge. In addition, there are several free e-mail services, including Hotmail.com and Mail.com, which allow you to set up and access your e-mail account from any computer.

Chapter Checklist

1 :· Use a computer to plan, compose, and revise.

2 :· Learn to incorporate data in written assignments via computer-generated tables, charts, and graphs.

3 :· Begin to use spreadsheets and presentation programs to complete academic assignments.

4 :· Use information gathered from electronic sources in class discussions and academic papers.

5 :· Learn more about your college and your major online.

6 :· Use a computer to communicate with faculty and fellow students.

WRITING ONLINE

8

8.1 Learn to communicate with e-mail.

Electronic mail (e-mail) is a way to send messages, memos, letters, and even longer documents to others through the Internet. To send and receive e-mail, you need an e-mail address, which can be obtained from an Internet service provider such as America Online (AOL), Microsoft Network (MSN), Netscape, or CompuServe. You can also use specific e-mail services such as Hotmail. Most colleges and universities also make e-mail accounts available to faculty and students through institutional service providers.

8.1a Compose and send e-mail messages.

E-mail is a convenient and rapid way of sending and receiving information. Generally, e-mail is considered less formal than a letter, but you should still be aware of the needs and expectations of your audience when sending an e-mail, and concentrate on clear and effective writing. The first step in composing an e-mail is to locate the e-mail address of the recipient. Although there is not yet an e-mail directory akin to the telephone book, e-mail addresses are usually readily available. For example, most colleges and universities include e-mail addresses in their faculty and staff directories. Also, individual professors often include e-mail addresses as part of the introductory information given to students during the first week of classes, along with office hours, office location, and telephone numbers. Communicating through e-mail has become so commonplace that e-mail addresses are included in advertisements, on business cards, in newspaper and magazine articles, and in television and radio commercials. Your Internet service provider (ISP) usually provides a mechanism for you to store e-mail addresses in an online address book to facilitate e-mail communication.

To compose and send e-mail messages, follow these steps:

1. Find the e-mail section on your e-mail service provider's home page.
2. Click on the icon labeled To Mail, Create Mail, Compose, or other appropriate title. You will see a screen that displays the To, Subject, Cc, Bcc, and

Elements of an E-mail Address

- The name of the person or organization holding the account followed by @, the symbol for "at"
- The domain name—the name of the e-mail service provider followed by a three-letter abbreviation indicating the type of organization hosting the account

.edu = educational

.gov = government

.org = nonprofit

.com = commercial

.net = network service

For example, *Bbaccala@Sgenaro.edu* is the e-mail address for Barbara Baccala at St. Genaro University.

Attachments fields or spaces. In some cases, fields for other types of information will also appear.

3. In the To field, type the e-mail address of the person or organization to which you are writing. Make sure the address is accurate to the last character; otherwise, your message will not be delivered.

4. In the Subject field, type a short phrase describing the subject or nature of your message.

5. If you would like to send a copy of your message to someone other than your principal correspondent, in the Cc ("carbon" copy) field, type the e-mail address of the other recipient. If necessary, you can also send a copy of your message to another reader without informing your principal correspondent that you have done so. This type of message is called a blind carbon copy (Bcc). In the Bcc field, type the name of the recipient to whom the blind carbon copy will go.

6. In the Attachments field, type the drive/directory/file name of any document you wish to send with your primary e-mail message. Let's say you have saved a file called *Etiquette2* in a directory called *Essays* on a disk. After writing your primary e-mail message, you need only click on the Attachments icon or button and then locate the *Etiquette2* file in the *Essays* directory of the appropriate drive. From this point, simply follow the on-screen directions for attaching the file.

7. Compose your message in the space provided.

8. After writing and proofreading your message, click the Send icon to send the message and any indicated attachments to the recipient(s).

Composing and Sending E Mail Messages

After reading an editorial or op-ed column in a newspaper or magazine, locate the e-mail address of the editorial writer or columnist. Compose and send an e-mail to the author explaining why you agree or disagree with the opinion expressed in the article.

8.2 Follow netiquette guidelines.

Generally, writing online follows the basic, common-sense conventions that apply to all clear and effective communication. Suggestions that pertain particularly to writing online have been grouped into a set of guidelines known as **netiquette** (Inter*net* etiquette).

CAUTION!

The same rules of good writing and courtesy apply to both e-mail and paper correspondence. Remember that another person will receive this message—be polite. And avoid using all capital letters, an annoying practice that makes your message hard to read and is considered rude.

Netiquette Guidelines

- Plan your message carefully. Once transmitted, the accessibility to your message cannot be controlled. Be careful of the tone that a brief message conveys. Always proofread all messages before sending them.
- Include your name and e-mail address.
- Include a brief subject heading that accurately describes the content of your message.
- Follow reasonable norms for mechanics, punctuation, and spelling. While, e-mail is more informal than most other written communication, you should refrain from practices that might offend or irritate a reader. For example, writing in ALL CAPS, which indicates shouting, is considered rude and is therefore unacceptable.
- Always cite the source of all quoted information that you find on the Internet.
- Follow the norms and policies of the computer labs of your college or university, or those established by the Internet service provider.
- Respect your audience. Be as considerate of the individuals receiving your message as you would want them to be of you.

Occasionally, writers use symbols or abbreviations in online writing to personalize certain messages or because they assume the communications are informal.

Some common emoticons: :-) (happy) :-((sad) :-/ (ambivalent) ;-) (sly)
Some common abbreviations: FYI   for your information
                            FAQ   frequently asked questions
                            BTW   by the way
                            FWIW   for what it's worth

The use of **emoticons** (emotion + icons) and **abbreviations** is discouraged in academic and professional writing.

These netiquette guidelines are appropriate for all online activities that may require written contributions and responses. Your participation in listservs, newsgroups, Web-based forums, and chat rooms, discussed in the following sections, should reflect your desire to transmit clear and essential information.

■■■■   ■■■■   **BASICLINK** ■■■■   ■■■■
WWW

To learn more about netiquette, visit this site devoted to the subject:
http://www.albion.com/ netiquette/

■■ ■■ ■■ ■■ ■■ ■■   ■■ ■■ ■■ ■■ ■■   ■■

8.3 Learn to post messages to Internet forums and newsgroups.

In ancient Rome, the forum was an open place where business and government affairs could be transacted and where people could assemble. When Rome was still a republic, speakers could address their fellow citizens and debate the issues of the day. Today, such forums still exist. Hyde Park, in London, for example, still offers Speaker's Corner, where anyone can speak his or her mind to anyone else who cares to listen.

8.3a Identify appropriate Internet forums and newsgroups.

Today, Internet forums and newsgroups provide virtual places in which people can discuss or debate common concerns or express their views on a specified subject. Forums and newsgroups are nearly identical: **forums** are housed on a server to which the host or moderator of the forum has access; **newsgroup** messages, on the other hand, are not housed on a single server, but rather they can be duplicated and stored on many servers throughout the world.

Forums and newsgroups are useful if you are interested in communicating with people who share a common interest or concern, academic or not (such as the Crime Forum shown in Figure 8.1). Any organization—private or public, professional or amateur, business, industrial, or academic—can host a forum. Many are sponsored and moderated by professional organizations, ISPs, or online newspapers. Figure 8.2 shows a listing of forums sponsored and moderated

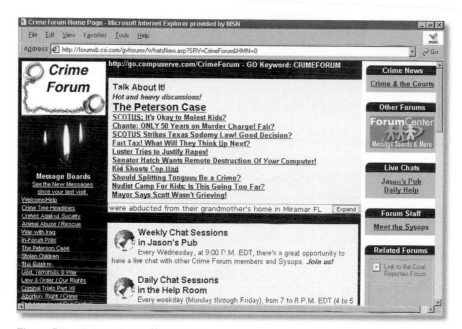

Figure 8.1   Crime Forum Home Page

Figure 8.2   *New York Times* Internet Forums

by the *New York Times*. Forums can be sources of reliable information. However, unlike chat rooms and message boards (discussed in the next section), they do not provide immediate responses to questions or comments. The common characteristics of all forums are that they focus on a specific subject and that they require participants to post messages relevant to the subject only.

▪ ▪ ▪ ▪   ▪ ▪ ▪ ▪   B A S I C L I N K   ▪ ▪ ▪ ▪   ▪ ▪ ▪ ▪

WWW

To search for a newsgroup or listserv on a topic of interest to you, visit
www.tile.net

▪ ▪   ▪ ▪   ▪ ▪   ▪ ▪   ▪ ▪   ▪ ▪   ▪ ▪   ▪ ▪   ▪ ▪   ▪ ▪   ▪ ▪   ▪ ▪

Each forum is conducted according to rules set down by the host. Some hosts require you to provide information about yourself; to subscribe to a newspaper, magazine, or Internet service; or to become a member of an organization. Before you join and begin to participate in a forum, make sure you understand how that forum is run. (Figure 8.3 shows the first item in a list of guidelines for participation in usnews.com forums.)

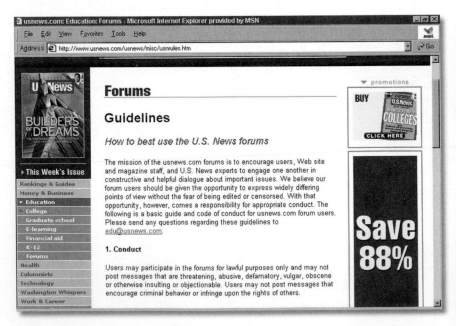

Figure 8.3   Guidelines for usnews.com Forums

Most forums have a manager. This person is usually an expert in the subject area. He or she is responsible for posting the question or questions that members of the forum are expected to discuss or debate. Responses can be made to the stated question or to responses posted by other participants. The written conversation that develops is called the thread. Having a focused question to write about prevents the forum from becoming a chat room, in which a conversation can take on a life of its own and move from subject to subject at the whim of the participants. After all, people join forums because they want to learn more about and to express themselves on a specific topic, not simply to talk to others on random subjects. (Figure 8.4 illustrates a discussion about e-learning college degree programs, including a response from the *U.S. News* e-learning advisor.)

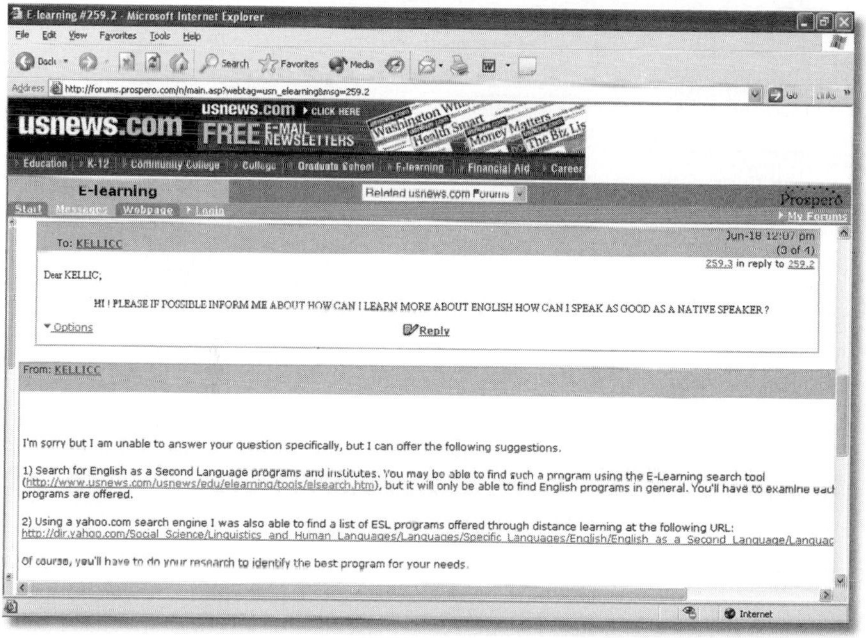

Figure 8.4   Online Discussion: E-Learning

8.3b Write messages for Internet forums and newsgroups.

Because forums are essentially conversations, you can generally adopt a familiar style when posting messages. However, take your lead from the style used by others in the group. For example, the style used in postings to a model railroad forum might be fairly relaxed, even informal at times. The style used by members of a professional academic organization, on the other hand, might be more formal.

FINDING A FORUM

You can find a forum through your Internet service provider or through search engines such as Yahoo! or Google. Simply go to the home page of the search engine (for example, www.google.com); then type in "forum" and your topic in the search box. See Figure 8.5 for a sample of forums dealing with alternative medicine that were located through a Google search.

Figure 8.5 Forums Located Through a Search Engine

Writing for the Internet is no different from writing an essay. To make a valid contribution to any forum or newsgroup and to make others respect your opinion, you must think about, prepare, and post your message carefully. As much as possible, adhere to the same steps you use in the process of writing any other important document:

1. Gather enough information to make your message credible.
2. Organize and develop your ideas carefully. You might even write a rough draft on paper or in a word processing file before posting it.
3. Revise your draft—on paper or online.

4. Edit—on paper or online.

5. Proofread—online.

Some people use all lowercase letters when writing online. Others forget about proper punctuation, use abbreviations or jargon unnecessarily, and, in general, violate grammar and other rules that make for clear and effective communication. Avoid making these mistakes. Keep in mind that writing for a forum or newsgroup is essentially no different from writing an essay exam you hope will earn a good grade.

Posting Messages to Internet Forums or Newsgroups

Using your Internet service provider (ISP), locate a forum based on a subject that interests you. Familiarize yourself with the forum guidelines. Then take the plunge and participate in an online "thread."

EXERCISE 8B

8.4 Learn to post messages on listservs and in chat rooms.

Chat rooms and listservs are similar to forums and newsgroups because they communicate messages to a large group of people, with each person in the "room" or each member of the list receiving the message simultaneously.

8.4a Learn to post messages on listservs.

A **listserv** is essentially an e-mail database used to send multiple copies of a message electronically. Most Internet browsers enable users to create listservs through functions associated with e-mailing. Many corporations, colleges, and other large organizations use listservs to communicate with large groups of their employees, students, or members all at once. Once a listserv is established, the writer composes a message and, with one keystroke, e-mails that message to as many readers as the list contains. Think of a listserv as a faster and far less expensive alternative to bulk mailing.

Unlike forums and newsgroups, listservs are not interactive, so using them to create a continuous conversation or debate is somewhat difficult. Because most listservs are used by organized groups such as the types mentioned above, the writing rules that apply to forums and newsgroups also apply to listservs. Whether you are a company president or a member of a small study group for History 101, remember that any e-mail you send should be effective and easy to read. Your style can vary from familiar to formal depending on the audience and the occasion (see Chapter 31), but your grammar, punctuation, and mechanics must be correct, and your message must be clear and complete.

8.4b Learn to post messages in chat rooms and on message boards.

In **chat rooms,** conversations can occur in real time, with different people posting messages simultaneously. Therefore, the exchange of information can be instantaneous. Most chat messages are short and informal. Indeed, many chat rooms have been established simply to provide social interaction or entertainment. However, chat rooms can be established for a variety of other purposes. A list of chat room topics located in the MSN Chat section of the MSN.com Web site is presented in Figure 8.6. **Message boards** are similar to chat rooms in that the topics can range widely, and multiple topics can be addressed by anyone at any time. Messages posted on message boards often reflect the style and interests of the participants. Figure 8.7 lists a range of message board topics that are accessible to AOL subscribers when they access the International Community section of AOL's PeopleConnection link.

One of the most common uses of chat rooms is for instruction via the Internet. Although many online classes use college-sponsored forums, there are times when instructors want to conduct real-time discussions in chat rooms. If you are enrolled in such a class, remember that comments made in a virtual classroom should approximate those made in a real classroom. An academic chat

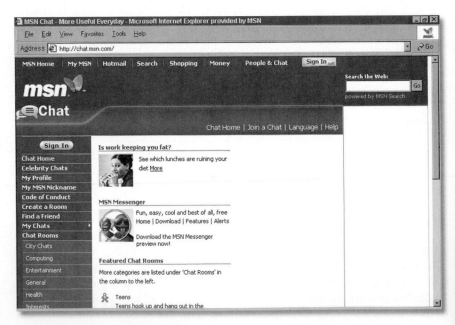

Figure 8.6   MSN.com Chat Topics

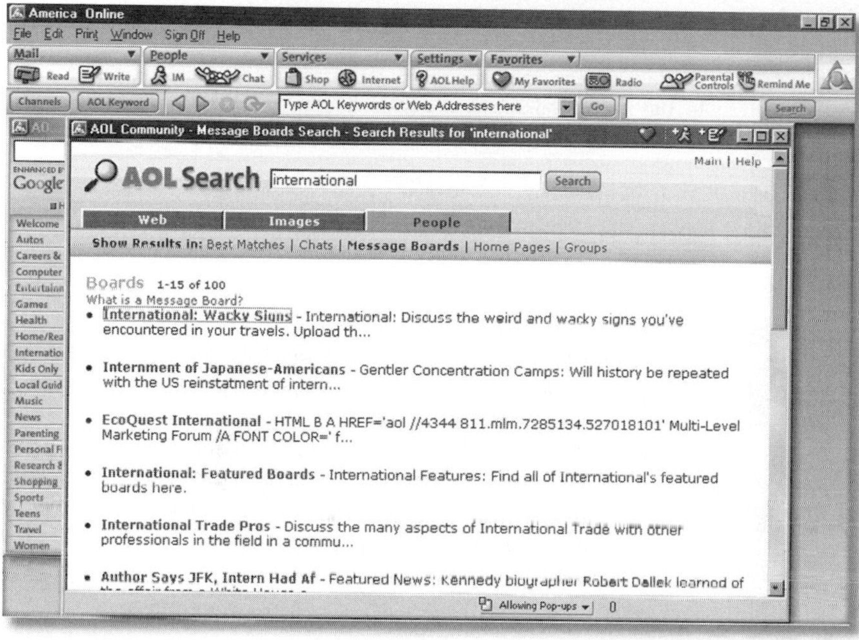

Figure 8.7 AOL International Message Boards

room is as much a community of learners as is any physical classroom. Therefore, while you can adopt a less than formal tone and style, remember that you are talking to an entire class—not just to the instructor or to one other student. Moreover, you must focus on the question at hand and make sure that your comments are articulated clearly. In short, remember that you have a responsibility to the rest of the class to help enrich and advance the learning process.

Posting Messages on Listservs or in Chat Rooms

Access the International Community section of AOL's PeopleConnection or a similar section offered through your ISP; then locate a message board that reflects your family's cultural or ethnic heritage. Following the message board guidelines, identify individuals with interests similar to your own. Begin to post messages, and enjoy the conversations!

EXERCISE 8C

Chapter Checklist

1 ⋮ When composing e-mail messages:
   a. Make sure you type the correspondent's address correctly.
   b. Use the Cc and Bcc functions as needed.
   c. Learn to attach files to your primary e-mail messages by using the Attachments function.
   d. Apply the same rules of good writing and courtesy as you would with any other kind of correspondence.

2 ⋮ When writing any online communication, follow the netiquette guidelines for content and form when posting messages to Internet forums, to newsgroups, on listservs, in chat rooms, and on message boards.

3 ⋮ When posting messages to Internet forums and newsgroups:
   a. Follow the standards set by the forum sponsor and write in the style used in other posted messages.
   b. Follow the directions from the forum manager since the focused question-and-answer format helps participants learn more about a specific subject.

4 ⋮ When posting messages on listservs and in chat rooms:
   a. Remember to use clear and effective writing in your messages.
   b. Keep in mind the purpose of the chat room. For a social or entertainment chat room, communication can be relaxed and informal. For an academic or professional chat room, the conventions for an in-class or formal group discussion usually apply.

DESIGNING WITH COMPUTERS

This chapter focuses on the general design of papers written for college classes. The design of your document depends on your academic situation and includes elements such as size of margins; spacing between lines; justification of right margins; and use of tables, graphs, charts, and other visual enhancements. The following suggestions are standard for most college-level writing. However, requirements can vary by department or assignment, and individual instructors may have personal preferences, so before writing your paper, be sure to review the requirements with your instructor.

9.1 Choose the most effective format options for your purpose.

Before you begin to write your paper, make sure that the margins, line spacing, and justification discussed below meet the requirements set for the course or the specific assignment.

9.1a Set standard margins, line spacing, and justification.

Most of your assignments should be printed on 8½-by-11-inch white paper. Always leave a margin of between 1 and 1½ inches on all sides of the paper (leave a 2-inch margin on the left side if the paper is to be bound). These margins provide space for you to make corrections on your early drafts and for your instructor to make comments and corrections on your final drafts.

Generally, you will be asked to double-space all your final drafts since doing so makes for easier reading than does single-spacing. Double-spacing your early drafts also allows for easier editing as it provides more room in which to revise your work.

Word processing programs allow you to justify (align) your right margin, as are the right-hand margins of this text. However, in justified text the word processor will automatically add or delete spaces between words and between words and punctuation in a line to make the lines the width of the text area. For example, justified lines might sometimes come out like this:

The   card   catalog   consists   of   an   alphabetical   listing
of   books   according   to   author's   name,   title   of   book,   and

Further, such justified margins may create the need for the overuse of hyphenation at the end of lines. Keep this in mind when deciding whether to use justification or a "ragged" right margin.

9.1b Choose an appropriate size and style of font.

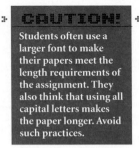

CAUTION!

Students often use a larger font to make their papers meet the length requirements of the assignment. They also think that using all capital letters makes the paper longer. Avoid such practices.

If you are working with a word processor, you can set font size. The normal size font for a college paper is from 10 to 12 points. Anything smaller is too small to be easily read, and anything larger (unless used for a specific purpose) can be overwhelming.

Standard font style should also be used. Unusual styles, such as those that simulate handwriting, can be distracting and hard to read. Among the most popular styles are Courier and Times Roman.

9.2 Use appropriate headings.

Short papers rarely need to be divided into sections preceded by headings. Topic sentences and paragraph divisions are sufficient. However, longer papers, such as research papers, might be more effective if appropriate headings are used to differentiate sections and make the basic organization of the paper clear to the reader.

Whenever you use headings, make sure to use parallel structure (see Chapter 24) throughout the paper. Here are four basic types of headings that you can use:

1. **Imperative sentence headings**
    Begin with prewriting.
    Write a rough draft.
    Revise the rough draft.
    Edit the work.
    Proofread the work.

2. ***-ing* headings**
    Deciding when to start a new paragraph
    Limiting the paragraph's focus
    Maintaining unity
    Creating coherence

3. **Noun phrase headings**

The elements of narration

The characteristics of description

The four patterns of arrangement

4. **Question headings**

How can I eliminate sentence fragments?

How can I correct fused sentences?

How can I avoid comma splices?

The most important thing to remember when using headings is consistency, not only in form but also in placement and style. The headings you use can be either first-level or second-level. Make sure all first-level headings are set alike; the same goes for second-level headings. As an example, you might always center and print in **boldface** your first-level headings. Then you might place your second-level headings flush with the left margin and underline them. Such a design would look like this:

First-level heading

Second-level heading

Other placements and styles may be used, but again, the key word to remember is consistency. Variations within a pattern break up the visual design and can be distracting to the reader.

9.3 Use a displayed list to enumerate items.

Displayed lists catch the reader's eye and are easier to read (as in the previous list of types of headings) than are lists that run on as part of your text. Displayed lists may also serve as a quick introduction to what you are about to discuss.

Your list should be introduced by a sentence (an independent clause—see Chapter 21) followed by a colon. The individual items in the list are not followed by punctuation unless they are complete sentences or unless they complete the thought begun in the introductory sentence.

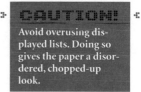

CAUTION!

Avoid overusing displayed lists. Doing so gives the paper a disordered, chopped-up look.

The items in the list can be set off in some way. The standard methods are to precede each item with a bullet (usually dots), a dash, or an Arabic numeral followed by a period. A list and its introductory sentence might look like this:

The Fujita (or F) scale, which was created by T. Theodore Fujita, is used to classify tornadoes:

•F-0 (40–72 mph)

•F-1 (73–112 mph)

- F-2 (113–157 mph)
- F-3 (158–206 mph)
- F-4 (207–260 mph)
- F-5 (>261 mph)

Source: *The World Almanac and Book of Facts* (1999).

EXERCISE 9A

Using a Displayed List

Write a list of steps you would recommend that a fellow student follow to complete a process with which you are familiar. Remember to introduce your list with a sentence and use the imperative (command form) for each item in the list. Here are some sample topics:

Writing a research paper
Studying for a test in a particular subject
Summarizing an essay
Preparing an oral presentation
Writing a laboratory report
Registering for college classes

Appealing to an instructor for a grade change
Persuading a police officer not to give you a traffic ticket
Preparing for a job interview

9.4 Add other visual aids such as charts, graphs, and tables.

Adding visual aids helps you convey information in a clear, concise, and vivid manner. In a paper written for a class, you can use "borrowed" visuals as long as you indicate the source of your information. Or you can use your computer to create your own visuals.

9.4a Create pie charts.

The following pie chart shows an annual budget allocation for Monro Township, indicating percentages of the total budget allocated for the four major budget categories. Pie charts are useful for depicting such percentage differences and showing the relationships of parts to wholes.

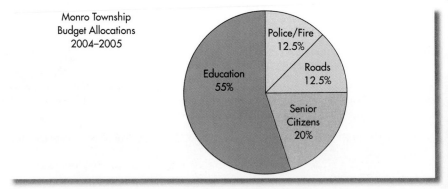

Monro Township
Budget Allocations
2004–2005

Police/Fire 12.5%
Roads 12.5%
Education 55%
Senior Citizens 20%

9.4b Create line graphs.

Line graphs are effective for pointing out changes in degrees, amounts, percentages, and so on over time or across groups. The first of the following line graphs (a **single-line graph**) shows the progression in the Dow Jones Industrial Average for a ten-year period.

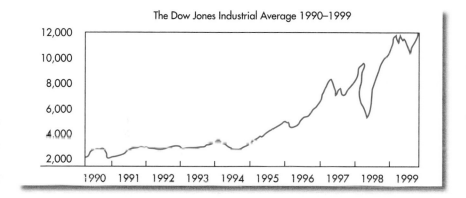

The following **multiple-line graph** provides a comparison at a glance of the normal monthly temperatures over a 30-year period in three cities from different parts of the country.

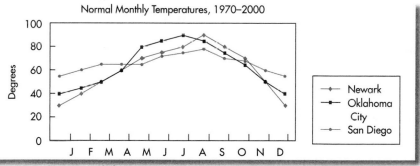

Source: *The World Almanac Book of Facts* (2001).

9.4c Create bar graphs.

The first **bar graph** depicts the increase in the number (in millions) of asthma attacks in the United States between 1980 and 1998.

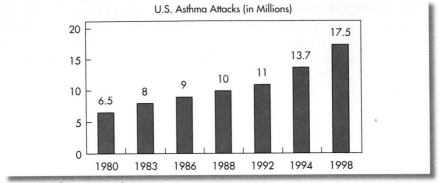

U.S. Asthma Attacks (in Millions)

Source: Centers for Disease Control.

The second bar graph shows the number of lives lost (by passenger class) when the *Titanic* sank in 1912 after hitting an iceberg on its maiden voyage.

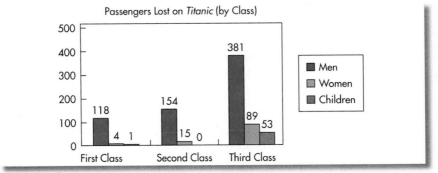

Passengers Lost on *Titanic* (by Class)

Source: *New York Times*

Bar graphs, like line graphs, show a change in degree, amount, percentage, and the like over time or, as above, by some other group or category; they are most effective when the change or difference is dramatic.

9.4d Create tables.

NOTE

The use of charts and graphs allows for the use of color, which can add visual interest to your paper.

Although tables might not be as visually attractive as charts and graphs, they provide a means of listing numerical data in a limited amount of space. The following table provides 100 years of statistics in a concentrated, easy-to-read format.

Total Population of the World by Decade, 1950–2050
(Historical and Projected)

Year	Total world population (mid-year figures)	Ten-year growth rate (%)
1950	2,556,000,053	18.9%
1960	3,039,451,023	22.0
1970	3,706,618,163	20.2
1980	4,453,831,714	18.5
1990	5,278,639,789	15.2
2000	6,082,966,429	12.6
2010	6,848,932,929	10.7
2020	7,584,821,144	8.7
2030	8,246,619,341	7.3
2040	8,850,045,889	5.6
2050	9,346,399,468	

Source: U.S. Census Bureau, International Database.

Creating Charts, Graphs, and Tables

Using Microsoft Word or Excel or another software program, create

1. *A pie chart that shows in percentages the amount of time you spend on the following five activities: studying, attending class, socializing, working, and participating in all other activities.*
2. *A line graph, bar chart, or table that traces the increases in income you plan to achieve in the first five years after completing your education.*

9.5 Design a World Wide Web site.

Perhaps the easiest way to create a Web site is to use a template (pattern) found in many word processing programs, such as Microsoft Word, as well as in many commercial browsers, such as Netscape. All you need to do is fill in certain outlined areas with your own text, graphics, e-mail address, and hotlinks (URLs that take the user to other relevant Web sites or to other pages on your Web site). For example, Microsoft Word provides several Web page formats and styles on which to pattern your own. Netscape offers Webpage Designer, a tool for people with some experience, as well as Instant Webpage, a tool for beginners.

:::: :::: :::: T H E   B A S I C S   O F   T E C H N O L O G Y

:. :. :.TO FIND MICROSOFT WORD'S WEB PAGE WIZARD

1. Open Word.
2. With the mouse, click on File at the top of the page.
3. At the top of the menu, click on New.
4. In the screen that appears, click on the Web Pages tab at the top of the box; then click on Web Page Wizard.
5. Follow the on-screen instructions for choosing and using a template.

Jeremy Jobseeker used Microsoft's Personal Web Page template to create a personal Web site to advertise his academic preparation, experience, and employment skills. (You will learn to write resumés and cover letters like Jeremy Jobseeker's in Chapter 20).

To publish your site on the World Wide Web, you will have to find an Internet service provider (ISP), such as America Online (AOL), EarthLink, or Netscape, that rents space on its server to individuals or institutions for this purpose. Many of the major providers offer this service, so start your search with your own ISP. In some cases, however, you might be able to publish your Web site on your college or university server. In any event, always check with your ISP or the appropriate college office for information and any special instructions on how to design and post your Web site.

9.5a Design a Web page: General suggestions.

1. Start with a home page that is simply but attractively laid out and that contains clearly marked hotlinks to other pages on your Web site or to other sites. Like the introduction to an essay, a home page should pique visitors' interest and get them to explore other pages on your site.

2. Don't overload your home page with text. Doing so will discourage visitors from exploring your site. At the same time, don't include too many large graphic files, which can be difficult to load and can frustrate visitors.

3. For subsequent pages, use a layout similar to that of the home page. In fact, you might simply rely on the same template provided by your Web page design software for all pages.

4. Be concise. Keep each of your pages to no more than three screens. If you need to provide additional information about a particular subject, add links to that page.

5. Make sure that links to other pages stand out. You can list such links in the margins or in any text that appears on your page.

6. Label the Web site with a clear and attractive title. Title your linked pages as well, and make sure each includes a link back to the home page.

7. Use attractive colors to set off different aspects of a page, but don't overdo it. Too many colors can result in sensory overload for site visitors.

8. Make sure you have a clear purpose. Are you trying to sell your talents and professional skills? Are you designing a Web site for a company that needs to define itself and publicize its products and services? Are you building a site to display information about student services and athletics at your college? Keep your purpose in mind as you decide what to include.

9. Know your audience. What are their needs and educational level? Can you assume that your typical user has accessed other Web sites? Is the user likely to be conversant with the Internet? Are you writing in an appropriate style and using vocabulary that is accessible to your audience? Or is your text too technical for the intended user?

10. Ask yourself what your user will need to navigate the Web site. Design your page's layouts with this user in mind. Position and label links, graphics, and other materials so that they are easy to access.

9.5b Choose appropriate content.
Using Web Sites in Job Searches

1. Your home page should list your full name and address, telephone and fax numbers, and e-mail address. As an alternative, you might take your lead from Jeremy Jobseeker (see pages 152–154) and simply use a Contact Information page linked to your home page. In any event, note that by including this information, you make it available to anyone—prospective employer or not—who has access to the Internet. In some cases, you may wish to indicate your name and e-mail address only.

2. Your home page should contain links to your resumé, to documents you have written, to descriptions of major projects completed, or to other information—personal, academic, or professional—that will help a prospective employer learn more about you and your potential value as an employee. You might also post letters of recommendation, your college transcript, and any other official documents that speak to your abilities. All these items should be on separate pages.

3. You might include digital portfolios on your Web site. For example, if you are applying for a job as a technical writer, why not include a link that takes the visitor to three or four of the best technical reports you wrote in college? If you are a photographer or other type of artist, you can include a digital gallery of your work.

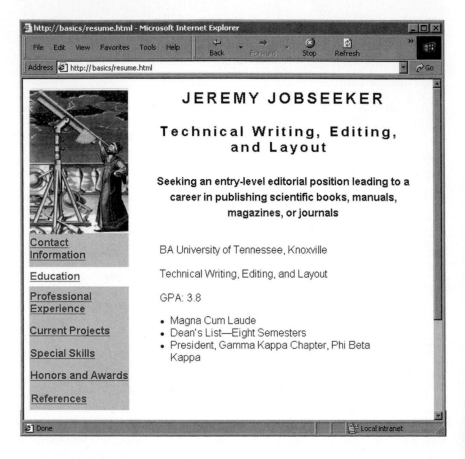

4. If you include textual or graphic materials (photographs, diagrams, charts, or other visual elements) not of your own making, cite the source. If you use materials that are copyrighted, ask permission before using them. Check the Web or print sources from which you got the material; they usually explain how to secure permission for reproduction.

Study the sample personal Web site pages prepared by the fictional Jeremy Jobseeker to advertise his employment skills.

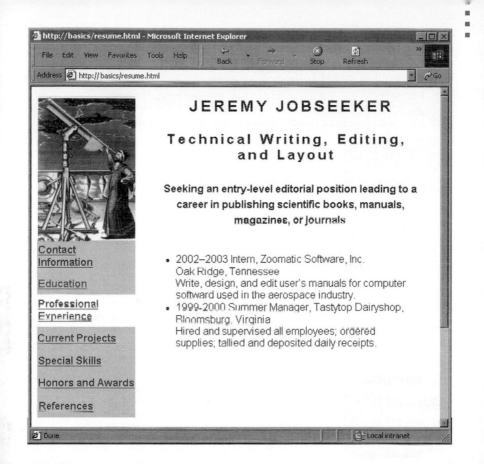

Designing a Personal Web Site

Using Microsoft's Personal Web Page template, Netscape's Webpage Designer, or another Web page design tool, create a personal Web site that displays information about your education, employment history, and employment qualifications. Use the Web site of Jeremy Jobseeker as an example. Include a home page and at least two other pages linked to the home page.

••••   ••••   BASICLINK   ••••   ••••
WWW

To read a list of guidelines for creating effective Web pages, visit
http://www.engr.psu.edu/ www/spt/faq/wordtips.htm

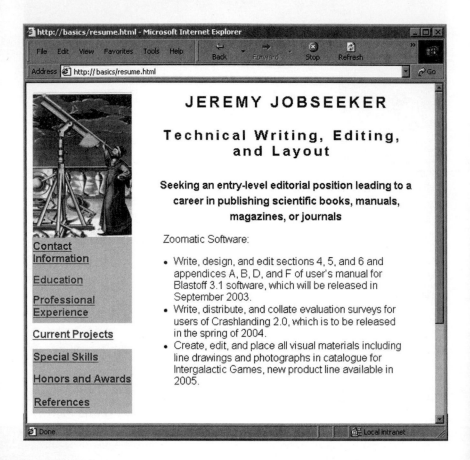

1 :: Design your document according to the academic requirements of your class.

2 :: Set standard margins, line spacing, and justification unless directed to do otherwise.

3 :: Use the most appropriate size and style of font.

4 :: Add visual aids such as charts, graphs, and tables.

5 :: Create your own personal Web site.

  a. List all pertinent personal information, including telephone and fax numbers and e-mail address.

  b. Link the home page to your resumé and other documents.

  c. Include a link to a digital portfolio of your work, if appropriate.

  d. Cite sources of any textual or graphic materials you borrow.

3

THE RESEARCH PROCESS

CREATING A RESEARCH STRATEGY

In this chapter, you will see how Suzanne Mastronardo, the student author of the research paper on bilingual education, which is reproduced in Chapter 15, went about planning her project, choosing her topic, and focusing on a particular question.

10.1 Plan a schedule.

During the fourth week of the term, Suzanne Mastronardo's composition class was given the assignment to write a research paper of no less than 1,500 words, using at least eight sources (both print and electronic). The students were to have eight weeks to complete the assignment. Suzanne realized immediately that this paper would be a major undertaking. Unlike many students who wait until the last week to attempt to write such a paper, she knew that it would be impossible to research, write, and revise it in such a short time, especially if she needed material that she could only get through interlibrary loan, a process that could take weeks. Therefore, she created an eight-week schedule, which she vowed to follow closely:

Week 1
Choose a working topic, clear it with the instructor, and do background reading. Pose a research question, and write a preliminary or working thesis statement.

Weeks 2/3
Locate sources and develop a working bibliography. Preview sources. Then, focusing on those that seem most promising, start taking notes.

Week 4
Continue taking notes. Decide on a tentative thesis and plan of development.

Weeks 5/6
Begin drafting the paper and, if necessary, complete additional research to answer questions that arise during the drafting stage, to provide more information, and to make the paper more convincing.

Week 7
Finish writing the draft and prepare a works-cited page.

Week 8
Revise the draft at least twice, edit the final draft, and double-check all internal citations and works-cited page items.

Note that the plan devotes about three weeks to drafting and revising the paper.

Like Suzanne, you will want to plan your work. You need not follow her model; the kind of plan you choose is up to you. The time you put aside to work on your paper depends on the scope and length of the paper assigned, the due date, and other factors particular to your situation. However, allow yourself sufficient time to complete your project. To increase your chances of success, always make a plan. If possible, show this plan to your instructor and get his or her approval before you launch your project. Being guided by such a blueprint, you will become more confident and experience less stress.

10.2 Choose a general topic and complete background reading.

Suzanne decided early that her topic would be bilingual education. She was an education major, and she had come from a high school with many students whose first language was Spanish. Many of them had been required to take some bilingual-education classes, in which academic subjects, such as mathematics and history, were taught in their native language until the students were ready to be instructed in English.

Suzanne got her topic approved by her instructor, but she was cautioned to limit the topic significantly and to focus on a specific research question and thesis. Suzanne began doing some background reading on bilingual education on the Internet. (Interestingly, she printed and kept copies of some of these materials for future reference.) She also discussed the issue with a few instructors on campus. Combined with the knowledge she had gained about the subject by talking to students and teachers when in high school, Suzanne felt confident that she could deal with this topic.

If your instructor allows you to decide on your own topic, choose one about which you have at least a little knowledge. Even more important, like Suzanne, pick a topic that interests you or that relates to your college or career goals.

EXERCISE 10A

Choosing Your Topic

Once your instructor has explained the parameters of your research paper, such as length, submit two general topics on which you would like to do research. Try to present narrow enough topics for each to be dealt with in the requested number of pages. (If you're not sure, ask your instructor for advice.) Here's an example:

Not: The causes and treatments of eating disorders.

But: The causes and treatments of *anorexia nervosa*.

10.3 Limit the topic and pose a research question.

As she did her background reading, Suzanne realized that several of the same questions about bilingual education kept popping up as she read information on numerous Web sites. Here is a list of the most common:

Possible Research Questions

- What kind of credentials should a teacher of bilingual education have?
- Does teaching subjects such as math and history in the students' own language cost taxpayers more than placing such students in English-speaking classes?
- What effect does placing second-language students into bilingual classes have on their integration into the social life of the student body as a whole?
- Do second-language students learning mathematics, history, and other subjects in their native languages learn the material better than students who take those classes in English?
- What are the advantages of trying to teach students English via bilingual education?
- Is bilingual education more or less effective at teaching language-minority students (LMS) English than the immersion method, in which such students take their academic classes in English?

Suzanne remembered that her instructor had cautioned her to limit her topic. After all, her paper was going to be relatively short—about eight pages. If a topic is to be covered adequately in such a limited space, it must be limited as well. Therefore, she decided to focus on the last of the questions in this list. She would channel her research efforts into finding information that would relate to it and it alone. This would be her **research question**—the question she would later answer in her preliminary or working thesis.

Note that one important reason Suzanne chose this question was that many of the Web sites she looked at addressed it in some detail. As a result, she felt secure that she could find sufficient information on her topic to write a fully developed college paper. Again, it would be this question that her preliminary thesis statement would answer.

At the same time, she remembered what her instructor had said about a general topic and research question: Both are simply tools to keep you going on your research project. As you go along, you are free to change the focus and direction of your research. Indeed, students sometimes choose to address research questions different from those they first posed once they have begun their research in earnest. In some cases, another aspect of a topic emerges as more interesting than the original question. In other cases, the student finds that another aspect of a topic is simply easier to research.

As you complete background reading for your project, look for recurring topics and questions in the material. You might be able to use one of these as your research question or at least to fashion your own research question from them. Doing so will enable you to focus your topic so that it can be covered adequately in a relatively short paper.

EXERCISE 10B

Posing a Research Question

After having done some preliminary reading on your topic, narrow it even more, and write a research question that might help guide you as you attempt further research. For example, if you were writing on anorexia nervosa, you might decide to consider only the treatments of anorexia nervosa. Then, you could focus on a question such as one of the following:

What are the medical treatments for the disease?
What psychological treatments are available?
To which treatments do patients respond best?
Does the treatment for anorexia nervosa vary with cause?

10.4 Decide on a working or preliminary thesis statement.

As indicated earlier, Suzanne had kept copies of various materials she had found on the Internet, which revealed important statistics on the extent and variety of bilingual-education programs in Arizona, Texas, California, Oregon, and New York. She had also read about and kept information on California's Proposition 227 (passed in 1998), which restricted bilingual-education programs and endorsed immersion programs.

Reviewing this information and additional material (the Web sites she had browsed contained references to additional sources both on the Internet and in print), Suzanne was able to narrow her topic even more. You will remember that she had decided to concentrate her reading on materials that related to the following research question:

> Is bilingual education more or less effective at teaching language-minority students (LMS) English than the immersion method, in which such students take their academic classes in English?

It was time to answer this question in a preliminary thesis statement.

As she continued to read, she began to favor arguments for the immersion method, and she decided on the following as her preliminary or working thesis:

> The immersion method of teaching LMS English is more effective than the bilingual-education approach.

She would use this statement as a guide to further research, but she remained open to revising it at any time depending on where her research led her. In addition, to focus her search even more, she decided to concentrate on just two states: California and New York.

Like Suzanne, you should remember to write a preliminary thesis statement. However, keep in mind that this is only a tool to help direct your research and give your work a sense of order. You may want to change this statement as you learn more about your topic through research.

Writing a Preliminary Thesis Statement

After reviewing materials you have read on your limited topic and on the question you posed in Exercise 10B, write a preliminary thesis statement for your research paper.

EXERCISE 10C

10.5 Collect keyword search terms before beginning to research.

In addition to the term "bilingual education," Suzanne wanted to see if there were other terms she could use when researching. Therefore, she went to the *Library of Congress Subject Headings* (a five-volume set of red-bound books in the reference section of her college library) to look for related terms. She ignored some subject headings (such as "bilingual authors") and focused on those she believed would lead to information related to her paper. Part of what she found is listed below.

Bilingual education
    USE Education, Bilingual
Bilingual method (Language teaching)
    USE Language and languages—Study and
        Teaching—Bilingual method

Using these terms as well as "bilingual education" would increase her ability to find relevant materials as she looked for books, periodical articles, online information, and other sources.

EXERCISE 10D

Finding Research (Keyword) Terms

Once you have determined your topic, begin your research by finding research (keyword) terms. Refer to the Library of Congress Subject Headings to find other terms you can use when researching your topic.

Chapter Checklist

1 ⋮ It takes several weeks to complete a college research paper. Make a work schedule for this project, and stick to it.

2 ⋮ Begin by choosing a general topic, which you have cleared with your instructor. Then do some preparatory reading.

3 ⋮ Limit your topic by focusing on one aspect. Based on your preparatory reading, pose a research question that will help direct your research.

4 ⋮ Write a preliminary thesis statement based on your research question, but keep yourself open to changing this statement.

5 ⋮ Remember to be flexible; after all, writing is a process of discovery. Your focus can change as you continue through the process.

6 ⋮ Gather a number of keyword search terms before you begin researching in earnest.

11

RESEARCHING AND EVALUATING
TRADITIONAL SOURCES

Suzanne Mastronardo, the student whose paper appears in Chapter 15, knew from experience that research papers require the use of outside sources. She could not base this paper solely on her own observations and knowledge. She would need to use **traditional print** sources such as books; articles found in magazines, newspapers, and scholarly journals; pamphlets; and doctoral dissertations. **Traditional nonprint** sources she might need to consider include audio and video recordings, lectures, personal and telephone interviews, and works of art. All of these sources are called "traditional" because they were in existence prior to the electronic revolution and the Internet. Today, however, students like Suzanne also have electronic tools to help them. They include online databases, CD-ROMs, and, of course, the Internet. (You can find out more about electronic sources in Chapter 12.)

Suzanne realized that, whatever sources she used, she would have three responsibilities when researching materials: 1) To locate source materials, evaluate their usefulness and reliability, and take notes on important information in them in an efficient way (Chapters 11–13); 2) to organize and present information in a form accessible to readers (Chapter 14); and 3) to acknowledge or document the sources of that information (Chapters 15–17).

The second and third week of Suzanne Mastronardo's research plan (see Chapter 10) required that she locate sources, develop a working bibliography, and begin to take notes. In preparation for this stage, read this chapter and the two that follow. This chapter includes advice about finding traditional sources (print and nonprint). Chapter 12 discusses research techniques using electronic sources. Chapter 13, which covers taking notes and avoiding plagiarism, explains in depth the process Suzanne used to gather materials for "Educating Language Minority Students: Bilingual Education vs. Immersion," a paper reproduced in its entirety in Chapter 15. (Another student paper, on Down syndrome, the subject of much of the research in this chapter, appears in Chapter 16. Both essays are the type you might be asked to write in a college class.)

11.1 Locate traditional sources for research.

11.1a Record source information.

Whenever you use outside sources—whether traditional or electronic—you are responsible for documenting that information, so make sure to create a working bibliography as you research. You may not end up using information from all the sources you include in your working bibliography, and you may end up adding sources as well, but keeping careful track now of the sources you find will help you avoid the frustration of trying to track your sources down again later. (Remember that the book you need may be checked out when you return to the library to look for it.) It is important to recognize that not documenting your sources—whether traditional or electronic—is plagiarism, a serious offense! The information you will need to create a working bibliography (and information on how to avoid plagiarism) is discussed in Chapter 13; guidelines on how to document print and Internet sources are provided in Chapters 15, 16, and 17.

11.1b Locate appropriate books.

You can search the **card catalog**—traditional or computerized—of your college library for books by using the author's name, the title of the book, or the subject. Using the author's name or the title of the book is easy, but using the subject can prove to be a problem if you do not use the right terms. For that information, you have to go to the five-volume manual called simply *Library of Congress Subject Headings (LCSH)*, often referred to as "the big red books." These volumes provide you with the correct terms to use in your search. The following is a sample entry:

Down syndrome (*May Subd Geog*) ————————	May Subdivide Geographically
[*RC571 (General)*] ————————————	Class numbers, which generally represent the most common aspect of a subject, and an explanatory term to indicate a specific discipline (not always present)
[*RG629.D68 (Fetal medicine)*]	
[*RJ506.D68 (Pediatrics)*]	

UF 21 trisomy ————————————	UF: used for (unauthorized headings—do not use)
Down's syndrome [*Former heading*]	
Mongolism [*Former heading*]	
Mongolism (Disease)	
Trisomy 21	
BT Human chromosome abnormalities	BT: broader topic (associated headings)
Mental retardation	
Syndromes	
RT Human chromosome 21	RT: related topic (associated headings)

Here are other notations you might find:

— —   two dashes indicate subdivisions

USE   refers to the appropriate heading

Traditionally, the information about the books in a library has been arranged in a file of index cards, but most college catalogs are now computerized. Computerized catalogs provide the bibliographic information one used to find in a card catalog, such as author, title, subject, edition, call number, and number of copies in the library. Some computerized systems also include status messages such as "in," "checked out," and "not on shelf." If a computerized card catalog is part of a network, it will also display a list of local or regional libraries where a book can be found.

The author of the paper on Down syndrome (in Chapter 16) began his search for materials on his topic by going to his college's computerized catalog. In this case, the library was part of a network, which, if necessary, would allow him to search several (up to six) designated library collections at one time or to search the combined catalogs of all the libraries in the network. He elected to search only his college's library, a search that produced a list of 5 possible sources (see Figure 11.1). The first pages of his search are reproduced in Figures 11.1, 11.2, and 11.3.

After looking over the list of books his search generated (Figure 11.2), he decided he wanted to examine one of them, the one by Cliff Cunningham (number 1 on the list). However, before looking for it on the shelf, he wanted to know a little more about the book, so he went to another screen of the catalog and called up information on it (by selecting the box to the left of the number and hitting "Display checked records from this page"). Among other things, he found that the book was currently available (Status: Not Checked Out) and could be found in the open stacks (Location: CIRC) (see Figure 11.3).

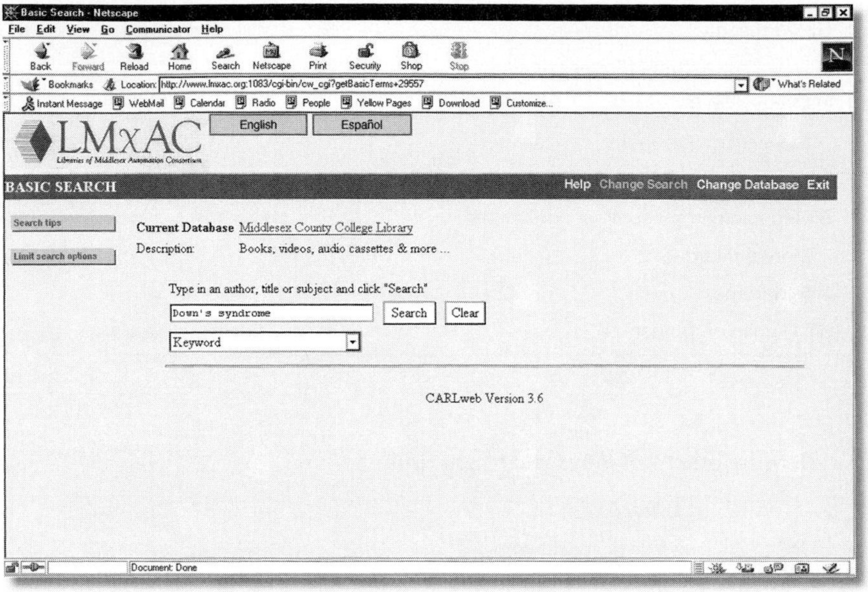

Figure 11.1   Basic Search Screen of a Computerized Catalog

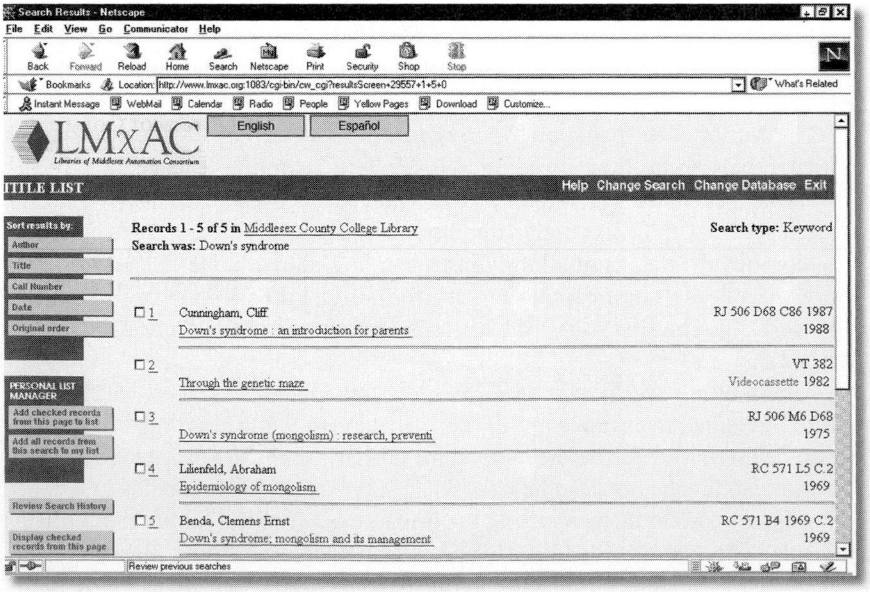

Figure 11.2   Title List Screen of a Computerized Catalog

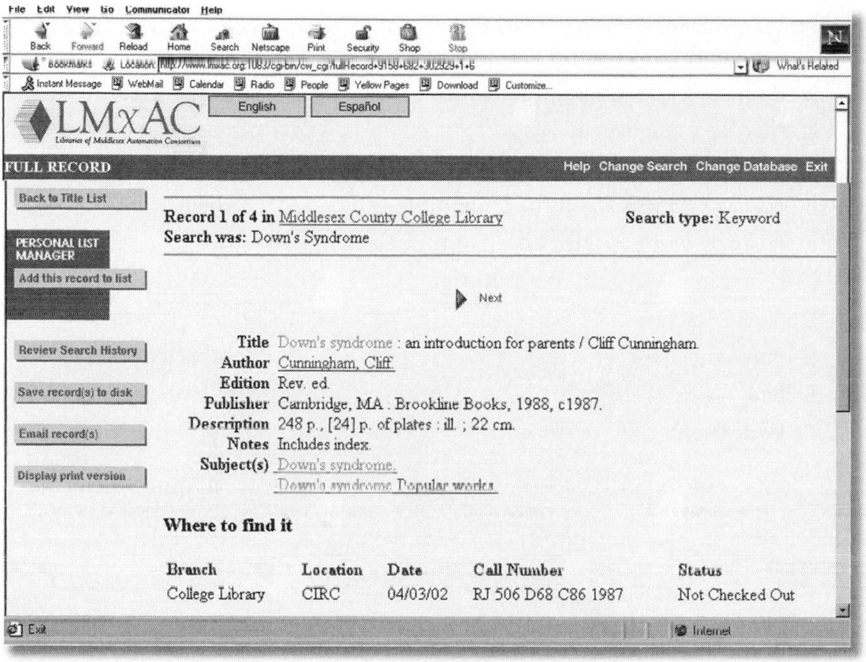

Figure 11.3   Full Record Screen of a Computerized Catalog

The screen in Figure 11.3 also contained the call number of the book (RJ 506 D68 C86 1987), the number assigned to the book by the Library of Congress, a library that contains almost every book published in the United States. The Library of Congress (LC) Classification system is used in most large public, college, and university libraries today. A Library of Congress number contains three parts: a letter or letters at the left (RJ), a number in the middle (506), and a letter-number combination at the right (D68 C86 1987). Overall, the Library of Congress places books into one of twenty-one classes, with each class designated by a letter of the alphabet.

The stacks and shelves in the library the student used are organized according to this classification system, similar to the way supermarket aisles are numbered, so he could find what he needed quickly. The call number for the book by Cliff Cunningham (RJ 506 D68 C86 1987) directs you to the stack and shelf where the book is located. You can begin your search by looking for the two letters (RJ) in the call number; these call letters are posted at the end of each library stack where books are stored. The call number also appears on the spine of the book, so train your eye to scan the call numbers as you glance along the shelf.

Library of Congress Classification System

A General Works	M Music
B Philosophy. Psychology, Religion	N Fine Arts
C Auxiliary Sciences of History	P Language and Literature
D History: General and Old World	Q Science
E History: America and the United States	R Medicine
F History: United States Local and America	S Agriculture
G Geography, Anthropology, Recreation	T Technology
H Social Science	U Military Science
J Political Science	V Naval Science
K Law	Z Library Science
L Education	

■ ■ ■ ■   ■ ■ ■ ■   **BASICLINK**   ■ ■ ■ ■   ■ ■ ■ ■
WWW

For more information on the Library of Congress Classification system, visit
http://www.loc.gov/catdir/cpso/lcco/lcco.html

Some libraries may use the Dewey Decimal Classification system, which uses numbers rather than numbers and letters. As with the Library of Congress system, the first portion of these call numbers will normally be posted at the end of each stack. Once you reach the correct stack, you simply scan the shelves for the book you're seeking.

Dewey Decimal Classification System

000–009 General Works	500–599 Natural Sciences
100–199 Philosophy	600–699 Applied Sciences
200–299 Religion	700–799 Fine and Decorative Arts
300–399 Social Sciences, Government, Customs	800–899 Literature
400–499 Language	900–999 History, Travel, Biography

EXERCISE 11A

Locating Books for Research

Select a topic (subject area or person) you wish to learn more about, and use the online card catalog in your library to find three books that relate to your topic. Copy the information, and locate these books in the library by using their call numbers.

···· ···· ···· THE BASICS OF TECHNOLOGY

···ACCESSING YOUR COLLEGE LIBRARY CATALOG FROM HOME

If you own a computer, you will most likely be able to access your college library's electronic catalog from home. Most colleges have links to their library Web sites on their home pages. (If you aren't sure about the URL for your college, just type the name of the college into a search engine [see Chapter 12], and it should pop right up.) The library Web site might also include helpful information on interlibrary loan, as well as links to access databases of journal and newspaper articles, although you might need a password from your college to access some of these features.

11.1b Locate appropriate articles in periodicals.

Magazines, journals, and newspapers are important sources of information for research projects. They are called **periodicals** because they are published periodically—daily, weekly, biweekly, monthly, quarterly, and so on. You can find periodicals listed alphabetically by author and subject in various print and electronic indexes in your library's reference section.

As a rule, **magazines,** such as *American History, Audubon, Esquire, Business Week, Film Comment, Forbes, Fortune, Newsweek, New York, Outdoor Life, Time, U.S. News & World Report, Working Woman,* and *Vanity Fair* contain articles that appeal to a broad readership. The best-known magazine index is the *Readers' Guide to Periodical Literature.* You can use this tool to find articles published in more than 100 magazines of interest to the general public. The print form of the *Readers' Guide* is bound annually. The listings are also available in a variety of electronic forms, including CD-ROM. The following is an entry from the *Readers' Guide:*

Down Syndrome

Going strong [C. Burke, former cast member on television program Life goes on]
    S. Horsburgh por *People Weekly* v56 no23 p125–6 D 3 2001

The various elements of the entry above and what they indicate are listed below:

Down Syndrome	Topic of article
Going strong [C. Burke, former cast member on television program Life goes on]	Article title and short description (in brackets)
S. Horsburgh	Article author
por	Notation that the article contains a portrait
People Weekly	Name of periodical in which the article appears
v56	Volume number of the periodical
no23	Issue number
p125–6	Page numbers on which the article appears
D 3 2001	Publication date of the periodical (December 3, 2001)

EXERCISE 11B

Understanding Entries in the *Readers' Guide to Periodical Literature*

Using the Readers' Guide *entry below, determine what each piece of information in the entry indicates. If you are unsure of the meaning of any abbreviations or symbols used in this entry, check the first few pages of the* Readers' Guide *for an explanation.*

Two against the odds [battling poachers in Zambia's Luangua National Park]
    M Owens and D Owens. il pors *International Wildlife* 22:13–14 S/O '92

Journals contain articles appropriate to a particular discipline or field of interest. They are published monthly, quarterly, semiannually, or annually. Although the articles published in journals are written primarily by professionals for professionals and are peer reviewed (that is, screened by a panel of experts—the author's peers), they can be useful to college students as well. One of the most widely known professional journals is the *Journal of the American*

Medical Association (JAMA), which reports on breakthroughs in medical treatments and pharmaceutical research.

Some journals, such as *American Indian Culture and Research Journal, American Journal of Psychoanalysis,* and *Journal of Learning Disabilities,* contain the word *Journal* in their titles. However, you can't always rely on the title to identify the periodical as a journal. Some titles, such as *American Anthropologist, Lancet,* and *Harvard Business Review,* are journals but don't include that word in the title, while others contain the word *journal* but are actually something else. For example, the *Wall Street Journal* isn't a journal but a newspaper.

You can find journal articles in a variety of library indexes. Like the journals they index or refer you to, each of these tools focuses on a specific discipline or field of interest. For example, the *Index Medicus* (Medical Index) lists titles of articles published in over 3,700 national and international medical journals, such as *American Journal of Health Behavior, Annals of Noninvasive Electrocardiology, Frontiers in Bioscience,* the *Indian Journal of Gastroenterology, News in Physiological Sciences,* and *Respiratory Care.* The listings appear in four sections: (1) alphabetically by abbreviated title, followed by the full title; (2) alphabetically by full title, followed by the abbreviated title; (3) alphabetically by subject field; and (4) alphabetically by country of publication. (Each entry provides all publication dates as well as volume and page numbers to help you locate the articles easily.) Other indexes that might help you find journal articles on a specific subject are the *Applied Science and Technology Index, Business Periodicals Index, Education Index,* Educational Resources Information Center (ERIC), *Engineering Index, Guide to Nursing and Allied Health,* and *Social Sciences Citation Index.*

Large-circulation **newspapers** often put out guides, or indexes, to their own articles. The *New York Times Index,* for example, lists articles that have appeared only in that newspaper. However, because of the increasing computerization of information, more comprehensive listings of material are also available. *ProQuest,* a computerized index for newspapers and periodicals, enables researchers to combine search terms and to search multiple sources and years with one search strategy; it also provides abstracts (brief summaries) for each article indexed. The *Newspaper Abstracts—National Edition* of this database contains abstracts and indexes articles from the *New York Times,* the *Wall Street Journal,* the *Washington Post,* the *Christian Science Monitor,* and the *Los Angeles Times.* Other sources for news and columns are the *American Journalism Review,* which can be accessed at http://ajr.org, and *NewsLink,* which can be accessed at http://newslink.org.

Almost all indexes provide explanatory guides to their use. Usually, this guide appears at the beginning of the volume. Read it carefully; it will help you conduct systematic searches for articles on your subject. Keep in mind that in addition to printed versions, newspaper indexes are often available on CD-ROM or on the Internet, or on commercial sites that are available by subscription (your college library may have one). In some cases, you can access an electronic index only from a computer workstation in your library. In other cases, indexes may be available on your campus network or over the Internet. In addition, you can access some of the sites from home by using an assigned student number (often the number in the bar code of your student identification card). (For more on electronic databases, see Chapter 12.)

11.2 Learn to cross-reference.

Many students get frustrated when they look up a topic and find only one or two articles. If you encounter this problem, try **cross-referencing;** that is, look through the list of related topics to identify parts of your primary topic, and then search for articles about each of them. For example, after looking for articles under "Elephants," the student author of a paper called "Saving the Elephants" (the first two pages of which appear in Chapter 17) looked up a related topic, "Ivory industry." Here is what she found in the *Readers' Guide* under "Ivory industry":

IVORY INDUSTRY ———————————————————— (A subtopic that was referenced second)

  Revival for ivory poaching? C. Holden il *Science* 255:407 Ja 24 '92

The title of the article, "Revival for Ivory Poaching?" suggested another related topic. While checking for entries in the *Readers' Guide* under "Ivory poaching," the student found the following:

IVORY POACHING

  (See Poaching) ——————————————— (Another topic area found through cross-referencing)

Continuing the process of cross-referencing by looking under "Poaching" in the *Readers' Guide,* the student found these two additional articles on her topic:

POACHING

  The ivory war [battling poachers in North Luangua National Park; Condensed from The

    eye of the elephant] D. Owens and M. Owens il *Reader's Digest* 141:185-8+ O '92

  Shameful harvest C.J. Poten il *Reader's Digest* 140:70-4 F '92

Although both of these articles were condensed versions, she now had specific titles and names of authors to look up so she could read the original articles.

Locating Magazine, Newspaper, and Journal Articles

1. *Using the same topic you used in Exercise 11A, go to the Readers' Guide and locate* **three** *articles that provide additional information about the topic; then accurately copy the information from the Guide. Next, cross-reference your primary topic to identify subtopics. Find* **two** *additional entries listed under these subtopics and accurately copy the information from the Guide. Then locate these articles in your library, photocopy the first page of each article, and submit them to your instructor along with the information about the five sources you copied from the Guide.*

2. *Follow the process in exercise 1 (above) to find newspaper articles that relate to your topic. Instead of the Readers' Guide, use the New York Times Index (or another specialized index that lists only newspaper articles). Locate* **three** *entries relevant to your topic or subtopic and accurately copy the information. Then find the articles and copy the opening of each article (in most cases, you will have to use a microfilm or microfiche reader to read these articles). Submit the list of articles and the copied paragraphs to your instructor.*

3. *Use a special index to locate articles about your topic in professional journals. Follow the same procedures you used to locate magazine and newspaper articles and find* **two** *articles that relate to your topic or subtopic.*

If you have trouble completing these assignments, do not hesitate to ask the librarian for help.

11.3 Use special print and nonprint sources.

So far, this chapter has focused on books and articles found in periodicals. However, effective research is often based on a variety of sources. Do not overlook additional print sources of information such as encyclopedias, biographies, bibliographies, atlases, government documents, pamphlets, personal interviews, films, videos, transcripts, radio and television programs, dramatic performances, recordings, and lectures. A partial list of sources in some of these areas appears in the next four sections. Sources like these are usually located in the reference section of your library. (Many of the printed sources listed below are also available electronically on CD-ROM or on the Internet.) Remember, however, that while general reference works are a good place to start your research, you should not rely on these sources exclusively.

CAUTION!

You can use these references to begin your research, for they can provide background information or lead you to more in-depth information about your topic. However, don't rely solely on them for materials that you put into your paper. An effective research paper requires you to go far beyond these basic sources when gathering information.

11.3a Use general reference dictionaries and encyclopedias.

Dictionaries

The American Heritage Dictionary of the English Language (4th ed., 2000)

The Oxford English Dictionary (OED) (20 vols.)

The Random House Dictionary of the English Language (2nd ed., unabridged, 1987)

Random House Historical Dictionary of American Slang (2 vols. published to date covering A–O)

Webster's Third New International Dictonary (unabridged, 2002)

Encyclopedias

The Canadian Encyclopedia (*L'Encyclopédie canadienne;* 2000)

Columbia Encyclopedia (6th ed., 2001)

Compton's Encyclopedia (2001)

Encyclopedia Americana (30 vols., 2001)

Encyclopaedia Britannica (12th ed., 1994)

11.3b Use specialized encyclopedias.

History

The Cambridge Ancient History (12 vols., 3rd. ed., 2000)

Cambridge History of Africa (8 vols., 1986)

The New Cambridge Medieval History (7 vols. published to date, 1998–)

The Encyclopedia of African-American Civil Rights (1992)

Encyclopedia of African-American Culture and History (5 vols., 1996)

Encyclopedia of American History (7th ed., 1996)

Encyclopedia of American Social History (3 vols., 1993)

Encyclopedia of Asian History (1989)

Encyclopedia of North American Indians (1996)

Encyclopedia of the Renaissance (6 vols., 2000)

Gale Encyclopedia of Multicultural America (2 vols., 2nd ed., 2000)

Harper Encyclopedia of the Modern World (2 vols., 1970)

Harvard Encyclopedia of American Ethnic Groups (1980)

The Latino Encyclopedia (1996)

The New Cambridge Modern History (14 vols., 1957)

Humanities and Social Sciences

The Cambridge History of English and American Literature (18 vols., 2000)

Concise Oxford Companion to the Theater (1992)

Contemporary Literary Criticism (1997)

Dictionary of Literary Biography (1996)

Encyclopedia Mythica: An Encyclopedia on Mythology, Folklore, and Legend (2003)

Encyclopedia of American Architecture (1995)

Encyclopedia of Architecture (1986)

Encyclopedia of Religion (1993)

Grove Dictionary of Art (34 vols., 1996)

Grove Dictionary of Music and Musicians (29 vols., 2001)

Grove Encyclopedia of American Art Before 1914 (1999)

Grove Encyclopedia of Italian Renaissance and Mannerist Art (1999)

Grove Encyclopedia of Latin American and Caribbean Art (1999)

Handbook of North American Indians (17 vols. published to date, 2001)

Native American Writers (1998)

The New Oxford History of Music (11 vols., 2nd ed., 2001)

The New Princeton Encyclopedia of Poetry and Poetics (1993)

Routledge Encyclopedia of Philosophy (10 vols., 1998)

Women's Studies Encyclopedia (3 vols., 1999)

Sciences

CRC Handbook of Chemistry and Physics (81st ed., 2000)

Encyclopedia of AIDS: A Social, Political, Cultural, and Scientific Record of the HIV Epidemic (1998)

Encyclopedia of Astronomy and Astrophysics (4 vols., 2001)

Encyclopedia of Biodiversity (5 vols., 2001)

Encyclopedia of Bioethics (5 vols., 1995)

Encyclopedia of Computer Science (4th ed., 2000)

Encyclopedia of Computer Science and Technology (45 vols., 2002)

Encyclopedia of Human Biology (9 vols., 1997)

Encyclopedia of Physical Science and Technology (10 vols., 3rd ed., 2001)

Encyclopedia of Physics (2nd ed., 1993)

Macmillan Encyclopedia of Earth Sciences (2 vols., 1996)

McGraw-Hill Concise Encyclopedia of Science and Technology (4th ed., 1998)

McGraw-Hill Encyclopedia of Environmental Science and Engineering (3rd ed., 1993)

McGraw-Hill Encyclopedia of the Geological Sciences (1988)

Social Sciences and Education

Companion Encyclopedia of Anthropology (1997)

Encyclopedia of Bilingualism and Bilingual Education (1998)
Encyclopedia of Education (2nd ed., 2002)
Encyclopedia of Psychology (8 vols., 2000)
Encyclopedia of Social and Cultural Anthropology (1996)
Encyclopedia of Sociology (4 vols., 1992)
Encyclopedia of World Cultures (10 vols.)
International Encyclopedia of Communication (4 vols., 1989)
International Encyclopedia of the Social Sciences (11 vols., 1977)

11.3c Use atlases.

NOTE

Keep in mind that geographical boundaries change with historical and political events, so be sure that the atlas you are consulting matches the time period you are researching.

Hammond Atlas of the World (2nd ed., 1998)
Historical Atlas of the World (1999)
National Geographic Atlas of the World (1999)
National Geographic Satellite Atlas of the World (1998)
The New York Times Atlas of the World: Comprehensive Edition (9th ed., 1992)
Rand McNally Premier World Atlas (1997)

11.3d Use biographical guides.

American National Biography (ANB) (24 vols., 1999)
Biography Index (updated yearly)
Chamber's Biographical Dictionary (6th ed., 1997)
Contemporary Authors (updated regularly)
Current Biography (updated regularly)
Dictionary of American Biography (DAB) (covers deceased Americans; 1994)
Dictionary of Canadian Biography (covers deceased Canadians; 14 vols., 1998)
International Who's Who
New Dictionary of National Biography (NewDNB) (covers Britain, 2000)
Notable American Women, 1607–1950: A Biographical Dictionary (1974)
Who Was Who in America (14 vols., 2002)
Who's Who in America (published yearly)
Who's Who in Canada
Who's Who in 20th Century America
Who's Who in the World

11.3e Use almanacs, yearbooks, and other sources.

The Facts on File Dictionary of Cultural and Historical Allusions (2000)

FedStats (provides links to statistics and to statistical agencies: http://www.fedstats.gov)

Information Please Almanac (published yearly)

The New York Times Almanac (published yearly)

11.4 Learn to evaluate print sources.

Once you have located source material that will be useful in completing your research project, it is important to evaluate the material for accuracy, timeliness, objectivity, and the like. The following suggestions will help you determine the appropriateness of the research information you have collected:

1. Is the source **thorough?** Is there significant detail and background information? Does the source explain the topic, issue, or related concepts in depth?

2. What are the author's or authors' credentials? You might evaluate an author's credentials by looking up his or her name in *Who's Who in America* or another biographical index. You might also search for the name on the Internet. If your Internet search reveals that the author is a professor at a prestigious university who has published widely on the topic you have chosen, you can feel confident that the work is reliable. If, however, you find that the author's expertise is in a completely different area or that this author has no obvious credentials, you should be wary of using this article as one of your sources.

Another way of ascertaining an author's importance in a field is to find out whether her or his work is referred to in other academic or professional articles. The following indexes allow you to see how frequently, if at all, the author is mentioned: *Science Citation Expanded, Social Sciences Citation Index,* and *Arts & Humanities Index.* (For further information on these useful sources, which are available in electronic form, see Chapter 12.)

3. From what **point of view** is the information presented? Is there an obvious bias or slant to the material? Does the author deal with the opposing viewpoints in a fair and objective manner? Is the publisher of the book or document reputable? Is the information published in a well-respected newspaper, magazine, or journal?

4. Is the source **timely and current?** Does the source reflect state-of-the-art information? Does the source provide an appropriate historical context?

5. Does the source contain **references to other information** about the topic? Has the author included a bibliography to indicate the academic or professional nature of the information?

■ ■ ■ ■   ■ ■ ■ ■   **BASICLINK**   ■ ■ ■   ■ ■ ■ ■

WWW

For more information on evaluating sources, visit:
http://owl.english.purdue.edu/handouts/research/r_evalsource.html

■ ■   ■ ■   ■ ■   ■ ■   ■ ■   ■ ■   ■ ■   ■ ■   ■ ■   ■ ■   ■ ■   ■ ■

Chapter Checklist

1 ∷ Start researching with a keyword search of the card or electronic catalog for books and of various library indexes for periodicals.

2 ∷ Search for related topics as you cross-reference to find additional sources on your topic.

3 ∷ Don't overlook government documents, pamphlets, personal interviews, specialized encyclopedias, atlases, and other special sources in your research. Consider using standard reference texts such as general encyclopedias **to start** your research, but don't rely on them exclusively. Instead, find more specific sources for the information you put into your paper.

4 ∷ Take the time to evaluate the validity and usefulness of print sources. Don't accept what is written just because it is written. Consider:
   a. thoroughness of the source
   b. reputation of the author
   c. point of view of the material
   d. currency of the information
   e. references to other information about the topic

RESEARCHING AND EVALUATING ELECTRONIC SOURCES

Suzanne Mastronardo, whose plan for a research project you read about in Chapter 10 and whose research paper appears in Chapter 15, found a number of valuable traditional print and nonprint sources, as discussed in Chapter 11. However, she realized that she could also find a great deal of additional information by using electronic sources. These include portable databases, some of which can be found on CD-ROM (Compact Disc–Read-Only Memory), online databases, and the Internet, which she could access through Internet service providers such as America Online, CompuServe, Worldnet, and EarthLink.

THE BASICS OF TECHNOLOGY

THE POWER OF THE INTERNET

The Internet is a dynamic tool that assists students in completing research. It can provide access to a vast collection of databases that include books, articles, essays, reports, statistical information, and government documents.

12.1 Use the Internet to research.

Virtually every library in the world is computerizing and making its resources accessible through the Internet. In addition to searching card catalogs, you can use the Internet for locating periodicals, electronic journals and newsletters, and various resources listing newspaper articles and government documents, as well as specialized subject databases.

The scope of research has changed and will continue to change drastically, thanks to the vast resources of the Internet. Both the ways you seek information and the types of information you find will surprise and challenge you at the same time.

12.1a Document electronic sources.

Just as when you use traditional print sources, you are responsible for documenting the information you locate through the Internet and then use in your research papers. You may not end up using all the information you find online, and you will likely end up adding sources as well, but keeping careful track now of the sources you find will help you avoid the frustration of trying to track your sources down again later. (Remember that online providers regularly update and delete materials from their sites, so it may be impossible for you to find again the Web page you want desperately to quote in your reasearch paper.) It is important to recognize that not documenting your sources—whether traditional or electronic—is plagiarism, a serious offense! The information you will need to create a working bibliography (and avoid plagiarism) is discussed in Chapter 13; guidelines on how to document print and Internet sources are provided in Chapters 15, 16, and 17.

12.1b Use uniform resource locators (URLs).

The easiest way to search the Internet is through the World Wide Web. One way you can search the Web for information on a particular topic is by using a specific uniform resource locator (URL). A URL is a unique series of characters separated by dots (.) and slashes (/) that are used to identify and find each page on the World Wide Web. In short, the URL is a Web site's address.

If you know a Web site's URL, you can type it in the Web browser's address box (sometimes called Go To or Location or Netsite). For example, if you want to access the Web site for the division of McGraw-Hill that published this book, you type in

http://www.mhhe.com/socscience/english

The protocol is http://, the domain name is www.mhhe.com/, and the file path is socscience/english. The last part of the domain name indicates the type of site; in this case, .com indicates that it is a commercial site. Here are other types of sites:

.aero (aviation)	.museum (museums)
.biz (businesses)	.name (individuals)
.coop (business cooperatives such as credit unions)	.net (network)
.gov (government)	.org (organizations, usually nonprofit)
.info (informational)	.pro (professionals)
.mil (military)	

In some instances, the type of site will be followed by another abbreviation that tells you the country the site is located in, for example

.au (Australia)	.jp (Japan)
.ca (Canada)	.nz (New Zealand)
.de (Germany)	.uk (United Kingdom)
.fr (France)	.us (United States)

12.1c Use search engines.

If you are trying to find information on a specific topic from a variety of sources, you will need to use a search engine. A **search engine** is a commercial service that accesses thousands of databases to find information related to keywords that you provide. Any Web browser you use can provide easy access to several search engines.

Lists of search engines often appear on a college or university's home page, and you need only click the engine's name to call it up. You can also access a search engine by typing its URL in the Web browser's address box. A list of search engines along with a brief description of each appears below:

AltaVista <http://www.altavista.com>   One of the largest and most useful of all the search engines for academic purposes, it provides access to more than 30 million pages of electronic information. It provides an advanced search, which will help limit responses to those containing just the right combination of keywords.

Excite <http://www.excite.com>   This search engine is capable of completing concept searches, so if you type in the phrase *spousal abuse,* Excite also searches for *wife abuse* and *domestic violence.*

Google <http://www.google.com>   This search engine provides both comprehensive coverage of the Web and relevancy. It examines over 2 billion Web pages to find the most relevant pages for any query and typically returns those results in under a second. According to reports, no other search engine accesses more of the Internet than Google.

HotBot <http://www.hotbot.lycos.com>   Now a part of the Lycos system, HotBot, which debuted in May 1996, has an index of about 500 million pages. When Lycos acquired HotBot in 1998, it failed to make search a priority, but it is now in the process of refocusing on search.

Lycos <http://www.lycos.com>   Launched in 1994, Lycos is one of the oldest search engines on the Web and provides relevancy and comprehensiveness. It stopped searching the Web for its own listings in April 1999 and now uses results provided by FAST

Figure 12.1   Homepage of the AltaVista Search Engine

The Search box is to the left of the Find button at the top of the screen.

<http://www.alltheweb.com>. Its entire database is updated every month, and new pages are added weekly.

Yahoo! <http://www.yahoo.com> Yahoo! is a powerful search engine that allows users to browse predetermined categories—both popular and academic— and then search for more specific topics within those subjects.

Once you get to the home page of the search engine of your choice, simply type an appropriate keyword in the search box and press Enter on the keyboard or Click the Find (or Search or Go) button on the screen.

12.1d Use multisearch engines.

Multisearch engines access other search engines such as those listed above. Thus, they are useful because they can expand your search significantly. However, before they can respond, they have to wait for the other search engines to respond. So multi-search engines are much slower than other electronic search tools. In addition, their responses include only the top ten or fifteen sites found by the engines they have searched. Nonetheless, they can be useful. Here are two of the most popular:

Dogpile <http://www.dogpile.com>

MetaCrawler <http://www.metacrawler.com>

12.1e Use archives.

Archives contain the texts of books and speeches, as well as historical documents. Because of copyright laws, they are limited primarily to older works in the public domain, but they can still be a good source of research materials. Below is a list of several very useful archive sites and a description of the kinds of material they contain:

American Memory <http://memory.loc.gov> A source of primary material related to the culture and history of the United States.

Electronic Text Center <http://etext.lib.virginia.edu> An Internet-accessible collection of SGML (Standard Generalized Markup Language) texts and images, including classic British and American fiction, major authors, children's literature, American history, African-American documents, and Shakespeare at the Electronic Text Center at the University of Virginia Library.

Eurodocs <http://library.byu.edu/~rdh/eurodocs> Links to Western European (mainly primary) historical documents that are transcribed, reproduced in facsimile, or translated.

Internet History Sourcebooks <http://www.fordham.edu/halsall/index.html> Collections of public domain and copy-permitted historical documents.

12.1f Use directories.

Information specialists create **directories** by arranging sites based on such topics as education, health, and public issues. The sites below can help you find an array of specific sites that might be useful in researching your topic:

Argus Clearinghouse <http://www.clearinghouse.net> The current site is still running but no longer actively maintained. The directories that are posted should be helpful, but make sure the materials you consult aren't too outdated to be useful.

Infomine <http://infomine.ucr.edu> This site allows users to search and browse by database (agricultural, biological, and medical sciences; business and economics; electronic journals; social sciences and humanities; visual and performing arts; and so on).

Internet Scout Project <http://www.scout.cs.wisc.edu/archives> This is a searchable and browsable database that contains 11,711 critical annotations (overall analysis including general content, attribution, currency, availability, and accessibility) of selected Internet sites and mailing lists.

Librarian's Index to the Internet <http://www.lii.org> This is a searchable database of material related to government and law, health and medicine, news media and magazines, people, society and social issues, and so on.

World Wide Web Virtual Library <http://www.vlib.org>   This is a database covering agriculture, computing, education, engineering, humanities, law, recreation, regional studies, science, society, and so on.

12.1g Use government and news sites.

Numerous government agencies at all levels provide online material, including legal texts, facts and statistics, government reports, and searchable reference databases. Here are the URLs for a few such sites:

Census Bureau <http://www.census.gov>

Fedstats <http://www.fedstats.gov>

Thomas Legislative Information <http://thomas.loc.gov>

United Nations <http://www.un.org>

U.S. Federal Government Agencies Directory <http://www.lib.lsu.edu/gov/ fedgov/html>

News organizations offer current information on the Web. Older (archived) information may be obtained only for a fee, although many libraries subscribe to news archives so that library users can access them for free. Here is a list of a few such sites:

CNN <http://www.cnn.com>

Kidon Media-Link <http://www.kidon.com/media-link/index.html>

Los Angeles Times <http://www.latimes.com>

New York Times <http://www.nytimes.com>

Washington Post <http://www.washingtonpost.com>

12.2 Use electronic databases.

The way a researcher seeks information has changed dramatically because of the increasing sophistication of computer technology. Two primary sources of computer-generated material are portable databases (available primarily on CD-ROMs) and online databases.

12.2a Use portable databases.

In addition to the more traditional sources of information discussed in Chapter 11, most libraries offer portable databases such as *Periodical Abstracts, Wilson Business Abstracts, PsycLit,* and *General Science Index.*

Generally, on-screen instructions will assist you in searching for relevant articles on CD-ROM databases. For example, Jillian Polaski used several databases as she began the research for her paper about the illegal trade in ivory, part of which appears in Chapter 17.

Using **ProQuest,** a database of newspaper abstracts stored on CDs, she found these two entries on the topic of ivory:

Access No:	01666402	Number of the CD that contains article
Title:	Ivory Ban Reconsidered	
Source:	Christian Science Monitor (CSM) ISSN: 0882-7729	Title and location code of newspaper that contains article
	Date: Feb 28, 1992 **p:** 8 **col:** 1 **Type:** News **Length:** Short	Date article was published; page and column in which article is located
Companies:	New York Zoological Society	Organizations or agencies mentioned in article
Subjects:	Hunting; Ivory; Trade policy; International relations; Africa	Subjects mentioned in article; may also be used as subjects for cross-referencing
Abstract:	Several African nations are expected to ask a multinational trade conference to rescind the 1989 prohibition of the international trade of ivory. The New York Zoological Society is expected to argue that the ban led to declines in poaching and ivory prices.	Short summary of article.

Access No:	01657005
Title:	"Culling" Ivory, Saving Elephants
Authors:	Littell, Richard
Source:	Washington Post (WP) ISSN: 0190-8286
	Date: Feb 23, 1992 **Sec:** C **p:** 5 **col:** 4 **Type:** Commentary **Length:** Long **Illus:** Illustration
Companies:	Convention on International Trade in Endangered Species
Subjects:	Ivory; Endangered & extinct species; International trade; Poaching; South Africa
Abstract:	Richard Littell comments that although the Convention on International Trade in Endangered Species of Wild Fauna and Flora banned world trade in ivory after being faced with the wholesale slaughter of elephants, it will be asked to allow the resumption of the ivory trade under a South Africa plan.

Using the **Academic Index** database, the student found these two articles:

Subject:	poaching	
	Save the elephants! (Zimbabwe)	
	Forbes Sept 14, 1992 v150 n6 p338(5)	Title of magazine; date of publication; volume, number, and page on which article appeared; total number of pages (in parentheses)
Author:	Richard C. Morais	

Abstract:	The people of small villages in Zimbabwe are selling the rights for hunters to shoot elephants and other wild game as a source of revenue for the townspeople. The idea allows the townspeople to profit from the elephants, while at the same time managing the numbers of elephants.
Subjects:	elephants—economic aspects
	poaching—prevention
	game-laws—economic aspects
	Zimbabwe—business and industry
Locations:	Zimbabwe
Features:	illustration; photograph

Subject:	ivory industry
	Running for their lives. (Rapid diminution of African elephant population because of poaching) *International Wildlife* May–June 1990 v20 n3 p4(10)
Author:	Virginia Morell
Subjects:	ivory industry—laws, regulations, etc.
	poaching—laws, regulations, etc.
	African elephant—protection
Locations:	Africa
Features:	illustration; photograph; map

12.2b Use online databases.

Unlike their portable counterparts, online databases can be accessed only through the Internet or through a service such as the Dow Jones News Retrieval Service, Dialog, InfoTrac, or LexisNexis. Most college and university libraries provide such online computer search services. To access these services, you will probably need to work with a reference librarian who will help you identify appropriate keywords that the computerized service will track to give you a list of relevant articles.

Jillian Polaski also made use of online databases; one result of her search using the **Magazine Database** accessed through **Dialog** is shown below:

Subject:	elephants, endangered	
	Are elephants protected to death?	
	World Press Review April, 1995 v42 n4 p41 (2)	Title of magazine; date of publication; volume number, and page on which article begins; total number of pages (in parentheses)
Authors:	Kai Hermann and Mihaly Moldvay	

Abstract: The 600,000 elephants living in Africa are deforesting the game parks, impacting the other animals there, damaging villages, and killing villagers. Africans in countries such as Zimbabwe and Kenya are more and more taking the view that people are more important than the elephants.

"Key" Words: wildlife conservation—social aspects

elephants—protection

Africa—environmental aspects

Locations: Zimbabwe, Kenya

Features: illustration, photograph

Many online databases contain whole articles that you can print directly from the computer. For example, many people subscribe to the *New York Times* Online to get up-to-the-minute news. They simply select those articles that they want to read. While the current day's *New York Times* Online is free, you must subscribe to access archived articles. In fact, most online databases require subscriptions paid for by the individual user or by a college or university library.

The *New York Times* Online can be used to retrieve whole articles published only in that paper; other databases will lead you to whole articles from a variety of popular and professional publications. For example, EBSCOhost, to which your college or university library may subscribe, is a huge online database accessed through the Internet that provides complete copies of many articles. Figures 12.2 and 12.3 show pages produced by a student's search using EBSCOhost at her college library for articles related to her subject, "child abuse".

Note that this database contains articles that appeared in a variety of publications. Although most college and university libraries in the United States and Canada will have print copies of the *Christian Science Monitor* and *Newsweek,* few will subscribe to the *Journal of Transcultural Nursing,* the source of the second article in the EBSCOhost search (Figure 12.3). Thus, the strength of such a database lies in its ability to provide immediate access to entire articles that might have been accessible only through interlibrary loan, which can take days to get you the materials you need.

Both portable and online database services have streamlined the research process and drastically reduced the time required for the collection of information. Many indexes and other sources traditionally available only in print form can now be conveniently accessed through electronic means. For example, *Business Abstracts, General Science Abstracts, Humanities Index, Social Sciences Abstracts, Applied Science & Technology Abstracts,* and the *Art Index* are all available through the Wilson Database. Some databases are mounted on a local area network (LAN) so that several students can access the databases from any computer in a library that is part of the network.

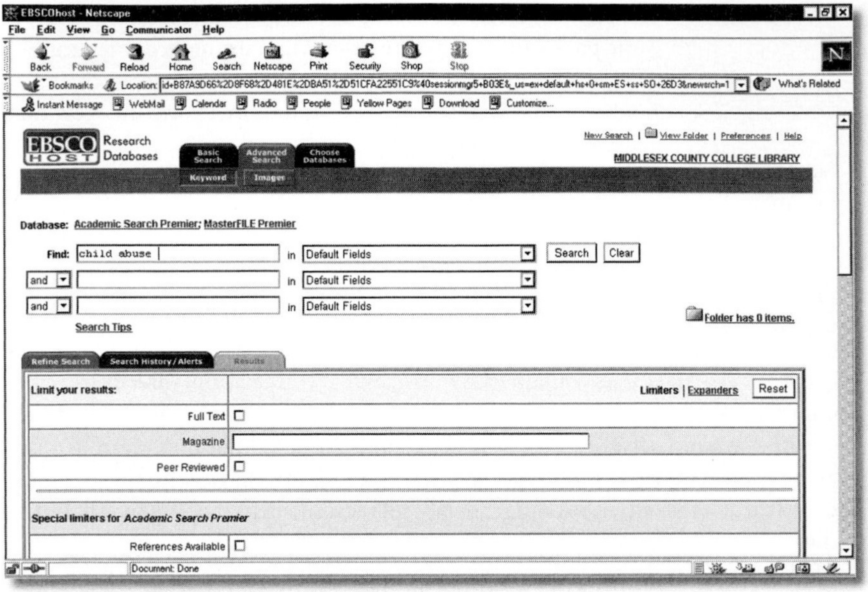

Figure 12.2   EBSCOhost's Basic Search Page

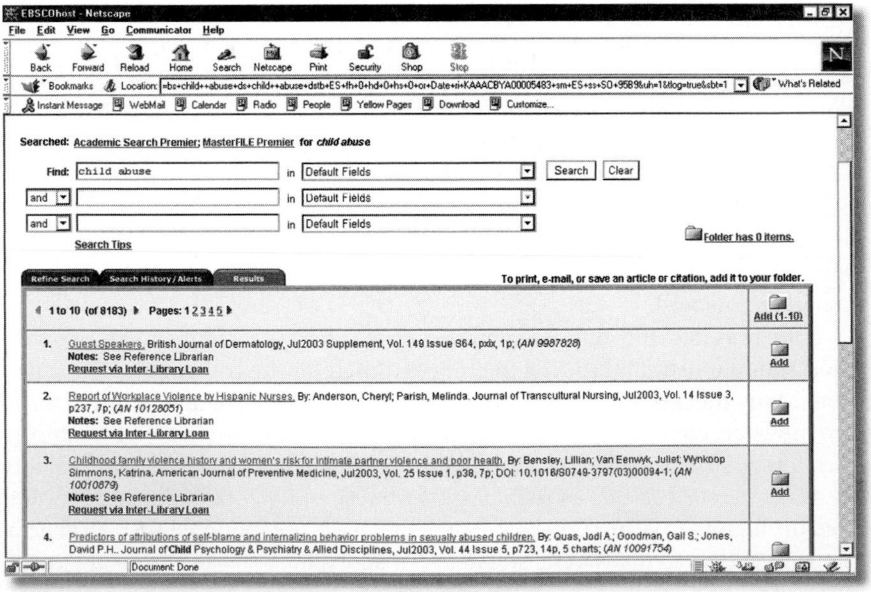

Figure 12.3   EBSCOhost's Search Results Page

Useful Online Databases

Here is a list of some of the most useful online databases to which your college library might provide you access.

Academic Search Premier. A large, scholarly, multidisciplinary, full-text database designed for academic institutions. As of July 2002, the total number of periodicals indexed and abstracted was 4,425, of which 3,280 were peer-reviewed (screened by a panel of fellow specialists). The total number of periodicals in full text was 3,467, of which 2,591 were peer-reviewed. The database covers such areas as social sciences, humanities, education, engineering, language and linguistics, medical sciences, and computer sciences.

Alt-Health Watch. A full-text database that focuses on health care and wellness. It is a source for nearly 50,000 articles from over 160 international, peer-reviewed professional journals, magazines, and research reports, as well as hundreds of pamphlets, booklets, consumer newsletters, and newspapers. The database covers primarily the period from 1990 to the present, with some journals indexed and abstracted as far back as 1984.

ERIC. A full-text database for the U.S. Department of Educational Resources Information Center. It contains more than 1 million abstracts of documents and journal articles on education research and practice. It provides abstracts of journal articles and documents for free, but you may be charged a fee for full-text articles. (For more information, go to <http://www.askeric.org/Eric/>.)

JSTOR. Provides access to back issues of core journals in the humanities, social sciences, and sciences.

LexisNexis Academic Universe. A full-text database that provides access to a range of news, legal, and reference information.

MLA International Bibliography. A database that covers international scholarly materials on language, literature, linguistics, and folklore. It includes over 1.4 million citations from over 3,000 journals and series, as well as monographs, working papers, and conference proceedings, and represents all national literatures.

PsycINFO. A database that provides abstracts of psychological literature from 1887 to the present. It covers journal articles, book chapters, books, dissertations, and technical reports in the field of psychology, as well as the psychological aspects of such related disciplines as education, linguistics, medicine, and sociology. (For more information, go to <http://www.apa.org/psycinfo/about/>.)

▪▪▪▪   ▪▪▪▪   B A S I C L I N K   ▪▪▪▪   ▪▪▪▪
WWW

Over 1,000 academic and public libraries make their online catalogs available via the Internet to individuals around the world. To check out these online public access catalogs (OPACs), go to
http://www.metronet.lib.mn.us/lc/lca.cfm

12.3 Narrow your search.

The Internet is an indispensable resource, but the amount of material available online can sometimes be overwhelming. There are some ways to use search engines and online databases to help you find the specific information you need for your research paper without wading through thousands of Web sites. You can refine your searches and narrow your search results by using some of the following techniques. Keep in mind that not all search engines use the same command terms and characters to refine searches. The following tips, which were used by the student authors of the sample research papers in Chapters 15, 16, and 17 list the most common ways to narrow your search:

NOTE

You can also combine the exact phrase (in quotation marks) with other terms by using the Boolean command AND.

1. **By inserting the word AND or a + (plus sign),** you are able to search for more than one word at a time, finding those items in which both terms appear. For example, in a paper (part of which appears in Chapter 17) about the ivory trade in Africa, a student using AltaVista kept narrowing her search by adding words in the keyword box until she limited the number of matches to a reasonable number.

Keywords	Number of Matches
Elephants	184,772
Elephants AND Africa	81,313
"African elephants" AND endangered species	43,702
"African elephants" AND endangered species AND ivory	548
"African elephants" AND endangered species AND ivory trade	307
"African elephants" AND endangered species AND illegal ivory trade	39

Using the same search engine, another student doing a paper about art restoration entered the following keywords to narrow his search:

Keywords	Number of Matches
Sistine Chapel ceiling	1,238,233
Sistine Chapel ceiling AND Michelangelo	232,414
Sistine Chapel ceiling AND Restoration	202

2. Suzanne Mastronardo, the student who wrote the paper on bilingual education that appears in Chapter 15, used the same search engine to begin research. **By inserting a − (minus sign),** she eliminated those sources that focused on ESL (English as a Second Language).

Keywords	Number of Matches
"Bilingual education" +NJ	2,265
"Bilingual education" +NJ −ESL	1,340
"Bilingual education" +NJ +secondary grades −ESL	115

3. By inserting the words NOT or AND NOT or a − (minus sign), you can search for sources that contain one of the words but not the other.

Keywords	Number of Matches
Hannibal Barca AND NOT Hannibal Lechter	234
William Schwenk Gilbert AND NOT Sullivan	23

4. By inserting the word OR, you can expand your search; doing so will allow you to find all the sources that contain material related to either term.

Keywords	Number of Matches
Shakespeare's Falstaff OR Verdi's Falstaff	2,645

5. By inserting the word NEAR, you can focus your search on the words as they appear in close proximity to each other, as did a student writing a paper for his political science class.

Keywords	Number of Matches
Unemployment NEAR immigration	2,301
"US unemployment" NEAR immigration	267
"US unemployment" NEAR "illegal immigration"	48
"loss of jobs" NEAR immigration	4

6. Some search engines also allow you to **use symbols in place of Boolean commands.** You have already seen how a + (plus sign) or a − (minus sign) can be used. Other symbols that can be used are & (AND), [(OR), ! (NOT), and ∼ (NEAR).

7. You can also **use truncation (also called wildcarding)** in your search. **Truncation** means asking the search engine to look for variants of a keyword by using the symbol * (asterisk) in place of the word ending or some letter within the word. For example, you can type *kidnap** and come up with matches for *kidnapping, kidnappers,* and *kidnapped* all in the same search. This search generated 626,426 matches!

It is important to note that not all search engines and databases use the asterisk (*) to indicate truncation. For example, ProQuest uses a question mark (?), while LexisNexis uses an exclamation point (!). Most search engines and databases have an advanced search link that will give you some pointers if you're not sure which symbol to use.

EXERCISE 12A

Research Using Keywords

Using the same keyword, conduct searches using three of the Internet search engines listed in section 12.1C (pp. 181–182). Focusing on the differences, note how each works and give an oral report to the class in which you explain your findings.

12.4 Learn to evaluate Internet sources.

Like all other materials you use, those found on the Internet need to be evaluated for accuracy and timeliness. The Internet is a wonderful tool, which allows everyone to publish his or her ideas and opinions on a system that reaches hundreds of millions of people. Be aware, however, that not everyone who publishes on the Internet is an expert on the topic he or she discusses. Also be aware that many people who publish electronically—even more so than those who publish on paper—may not have an unbiased view on an issue, may have done faulty research, or may simply be inaccurate. The risks can be greater with some Internet sources, because, unlike books or periodicals, Internet sources do not always have a publisher or editorial board acting as a gatekeeper. Since the cost of posting material on the Internet is low, *anyone* can make his or her voice heard. This is both a strength and a weakness of the Internet.

Here are some questions you can ask to help you evaluate Internet sources:

1. Who is the author, and what are his or her credentials? Can you tell whether the person has worked in the field about which he or she is writing? Is he or she connected with a university, a prominent think tank, a government agency, or a professional journal?

Let's say you have been asked to research the political and economic theory of St. Thomas More as explained in his sixteenth-century work *Utopia*. More was executed on the orders of King Henry VIII of England in 1535 for refusing to recognize the king as the head of the Church of England.

When you search for "Thomas + More" on AltaVista, you find the following Web site: http://www.r3.org/bookcase/more/mariuo1.html. The site contains an online chapter from Richard Marius's biography of Thomas More, which was published in 1984 by Alfred A. Knopf. You notice that the site displays information about Marius's life: he is a Harvard University professor who was editor of the *Complete Works of Thomas More*. He is also the author of a biography of Martin Luther. To double-check Marius's credentials, you search the Internet for "Richard +Marius," and you find confirming information on an unrelated Web site. You also check the *Arts & Humanities Citation Index* to see whether other historians of this period have referred to his work and find that Marius is widely cited on this topic. (If you were researching a topic in the sciences or social sciences, you would check out the author in *Science Citation Expanded* or *Social Sciences Citation Index*.) Thus, you decide the online chapter from Marius's book is appropriate, and you add it to your preliminary list of sources.

On the other hand, when you continue to search, you find an online essay entitled "Socialism in the Utopia of Sir Thomas More," posted in 1993. This essay looks promising. However, under the author's name, you notice the following subheading: "Introduction to English Literature 110–200A." You suspect that this might be a student's research paper, and you decide you should rely on the work of more experienced scholars.

2. Who is the Web site's sponsor? Is it an educational institution, an arm of government, a business, or a professional organization? Or is it just a personal Web site?

Let's say you are writing a paper on gun control. You come upon an online essay entitled "Gun Control" by Timothy Baimbridge. After reading it, you decide that it relates to your topic, but you realize that this is a personal Web site, not endorsed by any professional organization or group that you know to be authoritative. Thus, you choose not to list this source in your preliminary bibliography.

On the other hand, you find materials sponsored by the American Civil Liberties Union of Florida at http://www.aclufl.org and by the U.S. Department of Justice's Bureau of Justice Statistics at http://www.ojp.usdoj.gov/bjs/cvict.htm.

These, you realize, are reputable organizations, so you add these materials to your preliminary list of sources.

3. Are the Web site's author and sponsor unbiased?

In your search for materials on gun control, you come upon the Web site of Canada's National Firearms Association at http://www.nfa.ca, which calls itself the "United Voice of Canadian Firearm Owners." You suspect that this organization is not impartial on this issue, for its stated purpose is solely to advance the rights of firearms owners; as its opening Web page states, it "is an alliance of Canadians dedicated to preserving our firearms heritage."

Your search also turns up Michael Grunwald's "Experts Disagree on Schoolyard Shooting," an article in the *Boston Globe*'s newspaper archives. The article supports gun control, but it is published in a national newspaper, which can be considered impartial. In fact, as you search the *Boston Globe*'s online archives further, you find an article entitled "The Constitution Doesn't Prevent Us from Asserting Our Will on Gun Control," which opposes gun control. Thus, you decide to add both.

4. Is there any overt bias in the material you have read? Does the author make claims that are unsubstantiated or unconvincing? Does the author contradict himself or herself?

Let's say you find a Web site entitled "Facts About Gun Control," which argues that Hitler and Stalin were able to kill millions in the 1930s and 1940s because they had first banned private ownership of guns. The author claims that the United States nearly fell under such tyranny in 1932, when U.S. troops broke up a demonstration of World War I veterans who had marched on Washington, D.C., to demand their military bonuses early. However, the author never explains the government's side of the story (the veterans rioted) so that readers might evaluate his example fairly. His argument becomes even less valid when he likens the U.S. government's response in 1932 to the atrocities committed by Hitler and Stalin. Clearly, this site is biased, so you decide not to add it to your preliminary bibliography.

5. Has the author provided a list of sources from which he or she has taken information? Are these sources reputable and unbiased? Are there hyperlinks to other sites? Do the materials on these sites seem reasonable, unbiased, and accurate? Who are the authors and sponsors of these sites?

In researching Thomas More, you come upon an online book, *The Story of Thomas More,* by John Farrows, at http://www.cin.org/farmor.html. In his foreword, Farrows names specific people who helped him gather information at the Huntington Library and British Museum. This acknowledgment is a good indication that his work is based on reliable scholarly sources. Checking further, you find that the book has a bibliography of printed sources the author researched. So you decide to add Farrows's book to your preliminary bibliography.

Next, you find an online essay on Thomas More's life by Geraldine Wickerhof, which contains information that seems authoritative and is relevant to your topic. Unfortunately, Wickerhof neither lists sources for her article nor includes links to other sites. Although this essay might be reliable, you have found no assurances that it is, so you do not include it in your preliminary list of sources.

6. Can you tell whether the site is updated regularly? Does the author rely on current data? Are links to other pages and sites current?

When you check the dates of publication for the two *Boston Globe* articles on gun control, you find that they were posted on April 6, 1998, and June 1, 1998. Although the articles are not current, when you read them, you find that they contain enough valid background information to be useful in the writing of your paper.

7. Is the material well written, or are there grammatical and spelling errors? Does the author rely heavily on flashy graphics rather than on hard data and convincing prose?

As you read a 450-word online article entitled "Facts About Gun Control," you find misspellings, comma splices, and other errors, as in these two examples:

> Gun control is not only takeing away our guns but also our Freedom!

> And then there's Joseph Stalin who, while he ruled Russia, used guncontrol to kill millions of men, women, and children. Now you may be thinking that this would or could not happen in America, well you're wrong, it almost did.

The frequency of errors makes you question the usefulness of this essay to your project, so you decide not to include it in your preliminary bibliography.

8. Was the document published in a print version as well as on the Web? If not, could it have been?

Several works already mentioned exist in print as well as online. Marius's biography of Thomas More was originally published in 1984 by Alfred A. Knopf. Farrows's *The Story of Thomas More* was originally published by Sheed and Ward. The two *Boston Globe* articles on gun control originally appeared in that newspaper's print edition. This information should make you more confident about the reliability of these sources.

Evaluating Internet Sources

Look for one Internet article related to your research topic (if determined) or some other topic your teacher finds acceptable. Answer the eight questions in section 12.4 about evaluating Internet sources.

EXERCISE 12B

Chapter Checklist

1. Become familiar with the terms associated with electronic research.
2. Use electronic sources to help you research your topic.
3. Learn the advantages various search engines offer.
4. Learn the advantages various databases (portable and online) offer.
5. Learn the parameters of Boolean keyword searches.
6. Evaluate your Internet sources carefully. Look for
   a. credentials of the author
   b. sponsor of the Web site
   c. bias of the Web site's sponsor
   d. bias of the author of the material
   e. references to other sources or hyperlinks to other sites
   f. currency of the information and updating of the site
   g. careful editing and professional presentation of the content
   h. publication of the document in a print version.

TAKING NOTES AND AVOIDING PLAGIARISM

After finding a number of sources she thought might be valuable, Suzanne Mastronardo, the writer of the paper that appears in its entirety in Chapter 15, decided it was time to start recording information that would eventually find its way into her research paper. The following chapter explains the kinds of methods and techniques that Suzanne used to record information in note form, to avoid plagiarism, and to decide which information in her paper would have to be cited.

13.1 Make a working bibliography.

As you locate sources you think might be important to your research, make a working bibliography, which contains information you will need when it comes time to write the works-cited list (Modern Language Association style) or the references list (American Psychological Association style) of your research paper. Of course, you might not include information from all the sources on your working bibliography in the final draft of your paper. Also keep in mind that you might want to add sources to this bibliography as you work your way through the research process. Nonetheless, a working bibliography provides order to your research, and it will help you maintain confidence and direction.

Your working bibliography does not have to follow any particular style or form. However, make sure that it contains all the information you will need to write your research paper's works-cited or references list. Also, make sure to include information appropriate to the kind of source you are researching. Use the following lists as guidelines for the types of information you should include:

Books
- Name of author(s)
- Title and subtitle of book

- Publisher, place of publication, date of publication
- Edition (if second or later)
- Name(s) of editor(s) or translator(s), if appropriate

Magazine, Journal, Newspaper Articles
- Name of author(s)
- Title and subtitle of article
- Title of magazine, journal, or newspaper
- Date of publication
- Volume and issue number, if appropriate
- Page number(s) on which article is found

⌐ CAUTION!

Online providers update (and delete) computer-published materials daily, so it is important that you always record the date on which you accessed a particular story or article and that you include this date when you record the source in your works-cited (MLA style) or reference (APA style) list.

Electronic Sources
- Internet source
- Name of author
- Title and subtitle of source
- Title and subtitle of Web site, online magazine, journal, newspaper, discussion group, or other entity in which the source appears
- Relevant page or paragraph numbers, if available
- Publication data if the source appeared originally in print form
- College, university, company, professional organization, or other group sponsoring the site
- Date the information was published or last updated on the Internet, if available
- Date you accessed the site

13.2 Preview sources.

13.2a Preview books.

Not everything in a book may be useful, and at times nothing will. To save time, you can do the following:

1. Check the publication date to see if the book is out-of-date or can provide only background information.
2. Check the author's background to see if she or he is an accepted specialist in the field, including checking the *Social Sciences Citation Index* and the *Arts & Humanities Citation Index* to see if the author's works are cited in other publications.

3. Look at the table of contents to see if anything relates to the specific focus of your paper.

4. Skim the preface to see what the author's purpose was for writing the book.

5. Look up specific keywords in the index to see if there is anything that relates to your topic.

6. Read the opening and closing paragraphs of any section that might help you with your topic.

7. Ask yourself if the tone of the writing is scholarly and if the author's approach seems unbiased.

Previewing Books in Your Library

Using a keyword search, find two books related to your topic in your library's collection. On the basis of the seven steps listed above, write a preview of each book. Then, in a small group discussion, compare your responses with those of your classmates.

EXERCISE 13A

13.2b Preview articles.

Several of the same approaches used to preview a book can be used to preview an article.

1. Check the publication date.

2. Check the author's background.

3. Consider the reputation of the magazine or journal in which the article appears.

4. Look for an abstract at the beginning of the article and read it.

5. Examine the headline and read the lead paragraph of newspaper articles.

6. Examine any photographs, charts, and diagrams that appear in the article to determine the article's range and focus.

13.2c Preview Internet sources.

The same steps you used to evaluate Internet sources (see pages 192–195) can be used to preview them:

1. Check to make sure the Web site is updated regularly and that the links are current.

2. Check the author's background.

3. Consider the type of organization that has created the Web site and check its reputation.
4. Ask yourself whether the tone of the writing is unbiased and scholarly.
5. Look for a list of sources from which the author has obtained information and assess those.
6. Consider whether the material on the site is carefully written and well argued.
7. Find out whether the material on the Web site is also available in printed form.

13.3 Take notes.

Taking notes on your reading is probably one of the most important elements of writing a research paper because the accuracy and reliability of the information in your paper depend on the notes you have taken. If the facts are incorrect, so too is your paper.

After deciding which sources will provide the material you will need to write the paper, begin reading them and taking careful notes. These will become the building blocks for your paper. They are what you will use to support your thesis, the main element of the blueprint or structure of the paper.

Many people choose to print out or photocopy material they may want to use in their papers. This is particularly important for Web sites, which remove or revise material frequently.

While there are many different ways to take notes, such as with a word processor or on sheets of paper or as annotations on printouts and photocopies, the most effective is to write your notes on **note cards.** It is far easier to arrange and rearrange note cards as you narrow your topic and revise your thesis than it is to arrange and rearrange sheets of paper or many paragraphs compiled on a word processor. So stick with note cards.

When you are ready to take notes, use one note card per idea. Again, doing so lets you organize ideas easily. Below is a sample note card Suzanne Mastronardo wrote. It contains information from an Internet article on language immersion, the topic of her paper, which appears in Chapter 15:

Chavez

Statistics—Oceanside, California—"Immersion"

Before "immersion" (1988): 2nd grade reading scores for
      Limited English Proficient (LEP) students—12th
      percentile

After "immersion" (1990): 2nd grade reading scores for
      LEP—32nd percentile

What makes this an effective note card is that it is thorough. Don't trust your memory, for when it comes time to put everything together, you don't want to have to retrace your research on the Internet or in the library to get information from a source you had called up or returned to the library weeks before.

For each new source, create a works-cited card (or reference card if you are using American Psychological Association style—see Chapter 16) with all the necessary publication information taken from your working bibliography. Then set that card aside. Doing so will make it easier to write a works-cited (or references) page, since you can then simply alphabetize the cards and copy the information. You can also make a list in a document saved on a word processor and then sort the items alphabetically as long as each item has been entered as a separate paragraph. (For MLA works-cited formats, see Chapter 15; for APA reference formats, see Chapter 16.)

Below is the works-cited card Suzanne Mastronardo made for the Chavez article:

> Chavez, Linda. "Uneducated Bilingualism: Why Latinos
> Should Oppose Bilingual Education."
> _Hispanic Magazine_ 2 Feb. 2001 2pp. 3 Apr. 2001 http://
> www.hispaniconline.com/pol&opi/opinion/conbil.html

However you decide to take notes, make sure you write down the complete citation for any information you take from other sources. Be sure, too, to put in quotation marks any material taken word for word from a source so that you won't mistakenly take credit for work that is not your own. Taking credit for another's work by not attributing words or ideas to their rightful source is plagiarism, an extremely serious offense that can put a blot on your entire college career and sometimes beyond. (See section 13.4 on avoiding plagiarism.)

One thing you will have to determine for yourself is when to stop researching. After a while, you will begin to read the same information over and over in different sources. At that point, you are probably ready to stop researching one aspect or idea and go on to another. When you feel you have enough information to cover all the ideas you want to, start outlining and drafting your paper. You can always do more research later on if, while drafting, you realize that you don't have enough information to cover a particular point adequately.

> **CAUTION!**
>
> Never tear pages out of a book or journal, or mark up the pages of a source to make note-taking easier. Doing so prevents others from using these valuable, expensive, and sometimes irreplaceable sources of information. Instead, use photocopies or just take careful notes.

13.4 Learn to avoid plagiarism while taking notes.

Remember that effective note-taking techniques will enable you to keep plagiarism out of your paper. Plagiarism is the use of someone else's words or ideas without telling your reader their source. In essence, plagiarism is intellectual theft.

Intentional plagiarism occurs when you

1. Copy something from a source, usually word for word, and put it into your writing as if it were your own, that is, without enclosing it in quotation marks or acknowledging the source of the material.
2. Paraphrase or summarize someone else's material without acknowledging the source.
3. Submit someone else's work as your own—whether you bought a paper, printed one from the Internet, copied one from someone else, or had someone else write one for you.

Unintentional plagiarism occurs when you

1. Forget to put quotation marks around information you record on your note cards—the result of careless note taking.
2. Neglect to include a source for material you summarized or paraphrased from that source—again, the result of careless note-taking.

To avoid unintentional plagiarism, make sure you always put quotation marks around material taken from other sources, note source information carefully and completely, and paraphrase and summarize carefully to avoid mimicking the sentence patterns of your source. (See sections 13.4b and 13.4c below.) Taking notes carefully is the first step in gathering the kind of information that will make your research paper a success. You can take notes in three forms: as **direct quotations,** as **paraphrases,** and as **summaries.** Examples of each method appear below.

> **NOTE** ✦✦✦✦✦
>
> To keep track of sources easily, write the author's name on the note card, followed by the page number(s) from which you took the information or quotation. If no author is given or if you use more than one book or article by the same author, include a shortened form of the title as well. And be sure to note the complete bibliographic information on a works-cited (or reference) card.

13.4a Use a direct quotation.

You will sometimes come upon information expressed in words so precise, clear, or moving that you will want to use it in your paper exactly as it appears in the original. In that case, you will have to use a **direct quotation,** an exact, word-for-word copy of the original phrase, sentence, or paragraph. Be sure to place quotation marks ("/") around such material as you take notes. Doing so will remind you that the material has been copied word for word and that you will have to enclose it in quotation marks when you put it into your paper. After taking the note, double-check to make sure that you have copied both the words and the punctuation correctly.

Here are examples of note cards that record direct quotations:

Morell 10

"The plight of Kenya's animals is only part of the elephant story. Across the continent— from the savannas of Tanzania to the forests of Zaire—an estimated 700,000 tuskers (more than half of Africa's elephants) have fallen to poachers' guns just within the past decade."

Chavez 106

"Bilingual education was supposed to help such students—largely Hispanics—by teaching most lessons in Spanish while the children slowly learned English. But instead of helping these children, many bilingual programs often devoted so little instruction time to English that the children languished in bilingual classrooms for years on end."

"No More Jokes" 4

"Ex-White House speechwriter David Frum reveals that President Bush has met with most families of 9/11 victims, and it's taken a toll. . . . 'He doesn't tell goofy jokes anymore,' says Frum, author of the Bush book The Right Man. And, he adds, 'Bush has trouble putting on a happy face. He cannot fake emotion.'"

The last of these cards contains a quotation from a source for which no author was indicated. Therefore, the student simply used the title of the article, "No More Jokes," to identify the source. Note that a direct quotation of the words of David Frum appears inside this direct quotation, so Frum's words appear within single quotation marks.

13.4b Use a paraphrase.

When you **paraphrase** information, you put it into your own words. Generally, a paraphrase is as long as the original. Remember that paraphrasing does not mean simply replacing a few words here and there. It means recasting the original in your own words. Moreover, paraphrasing requires you to abandon sentence patterns used in the original and to come up with new ones of your own. Failing to do these things is considered plagiarism. Consider this unacceptable paraphrase of the material quoted from Morell, which appears in section 13.4a.

PARAPHRASE CONTAINING PLAGIARISM

> Morell 10
>
> The problem facing <u>Kenya's animals</u> is just one <u>part</u> of the problem facing elephants. Throughout <u>Africa,</u> <u>more than half</u> of the <u>elephants</u> have been killed by <u>poachers within the past decade.</u>

Note that the underlined words are copied directly from the original and that the paraphrase uses sentence structure that is too close to that of the source.

Of course, some words or phrases cannot be paraphrased. So, if you include them, be sure to put quotation marks around them to help you identify them as quoted when you draft your paper. The paraphrase below is acceptable because, other than for the material placed in quotation marks, it uses new language and sentence structure.

ACCEPTABLE PARAPHRASE

> Morell 10
>
> The fate of the elephants in Kenya is not unusual. "From the savannas of Tanzania to the forest of Zaire," poachers killed over 50% of Africa's estimated 1.3 million elephants during the 1980s.

Now, compare the following examples of plagiarized and acceptable paraphrases based on the original quotation from Chavez, which appears in section 13.4a.

PARAPHRASE CONTAINING PLAGIARISM

> Chavez 106
>
> Bilingual education was developed to help limited-English-proficient students—largely Hispanics—by providing instruction in Spanish while the students slowly learned English. However, so little English was used that the students remained in bilingual classrooms for years on end.

This version contains obvious evidence of plagiarism. First, the sentence structure mirrors that of the original. Second, the writer has lifted words and phrases without placing them within quotation marks.

PARAPHRASE CONTAINING PLAGIARISM

This version avoids using words and phrases from the original, but the sentence structure is patterned on that of the source.

> Chavez 106
>
> Bilingual education was developed to help Hispanic students by providing instruction in Spanish while the students began to acquire English. However, so little English was used that the students remained in Spanish-speaking classes for much of their schooling.

ACCEPTABLE PARAPHRASE

> Chavez 106
>
> Because too much of the teaching is done in Spanish and not English, bilingual education retards the progress of Hispanic students who need to master English. Indeed, instead of learning English quickly, they spend years in a system that provides them minimal exposure to the language.

This version is acceptable because it uses both orginal language and orginal sentence patterns.

13.4c Use a summary.

When you **summarize** information, you condense it into one or two short sentences in your own words. Here are summaries of the material from Morell and Chavez that was quoted in section 13.4a:

Morell 10
    During the 1980s, more than half of Africa's estimated
    1.3 million elephants were killed.

Chavez 106
    Bilingual education programs fail to produce their
    intended objective, which is to help Hispanic
    speakers learn English in an efficient and timely
    manner.

EXERCISE 13B

Learning to Take Notes

Photocopy one page from a source you might use in a research paper and highlight one or two paragraphs (at least twelve lines). Then copy, paraphrase, and summarize that material on note cards. Make sure to list your source and the page(s) from which you took the information.

13.5 Determine which information needs a citation.

As you learned above, you need to provide citations for material taken from other sources. However, there are exceptions to this rule (unless you are quoting directly). Generally, you must judge for yourself whether a piece of information (summarized or paraphrased) needs to be cited. Here are some guidelines and examples to help you make an appropriate determination. Additional examples are listed below.

1. You don't need to mention the sources of facts and ideas that you have discovered firsthand through observations or experiences.

2. You don't need to cite sources of common knowledge. You would not need to explain, for example, where you learned that smoking causes lung disease. Nor would you need to explain where you read that the musical *West Side Story* is based on Shakespeare's *Romeo and Juliet.*

Additional Examples of Information You Do Not Need to Cite

P. J. O'Rourke has written several best-selling satires, including *All the Trouble in the World* and *Parliament of Whores.*

Andrew Johnson and Bill Clinton were the only U.S. presidents impeached by the Senate.

The last emperor of Rome was Romulus Augustus, who took his first name from Rome's legendary founder and his second name from its first emperor.

3. You must cite opinions, ideas, or information that you took from others, that has been discovered through their research, and that is not considered common knowledge. For example, you must cite the source of statistics that show a rise in lung cancer deaths over the past two decades. Also, you must cite an article from a Shakespeare scholar that shows how much the author of *West Side Story* borrowed from Romeo and Juliet.

Additional Examples of Opinions, Ideas, or Information You Must Cite

According to P. J. O'Rourke, during the 1990s, the U.S. government spent enough money in agricultural subsidies to buy most of the farms in this country.

The real motivation behind the impeachment of President Andrew Johnson had to do with his opposition to the Senate's wish to impose harsh economic and political penalties on the South as part of the plan for Reconstruction.

The fall of the Roman Empire can in some ways be traced to the adoption of Christianity as the state religion.

Chapter Checklist

1 ⋮ Compile a working bibliography to give your research direction and to help you proceed in an orderly and confident way.

2 ⋮ Preview your sources to determine their applicability to your project.

3 ⋮ Give the sources for all facts, ideas, and opinions that are not common knowledge whether you quote them directly, paraphrase them, or summarize them. Failure to identify a source is plagiarism.

4 ⋮ Write each piece of information you find in a source on a note card so that you can arrange and rearrange the cards in any order you like as you organize and start to write your paper.

   a. Use a direct quotation for material that is particularly well expressed. Enclose the words in quotation marks.

   b. Paraphrase material by putting it into your own words and sentence patterns.

   c. Summarize material by condensing it into one or two sentences of your own.

   In all three cases, be sure to note the source, including the page number.

5 ⋮ Be able to distinguish between the kinds of materials that need citations and those that don't.

   a. No citations are needed for information taken from personal experience or observation.

   b. No citations are needed for information that is common knowledge.

   c. Citations are needed for information that is not common knowledge and that has been taken from someone else.

WRITING THE RESEARCH PAPER

As soon as Suzanne Mastronardo (her paper appears in Chapter 15) completed as much research as she thought she needed, she decided to begin writing right away. If she waited a few weeks or even a few days, her grasp of the material might weaken. Of course, she knew she would not need to complete the paper in one or two sittings. She wanted to take her time and move from outline to final draft slowly and carefully over two to three weeks.

This chapter describes steps like those Suzanne took to complete her paper. In fact, her outline and thesis statements, both preliminary and final, appear in what you will read below.

14.1 Establish a setting and strategy.

Consider the following as you establish the setting and strategy for writing a paper.

1. Settle yourself at a large, flat space so you can spread out your materials. A desk or a kitchen table is good, but any flat, clean surface will do.

2. Work in a fairly quiet place, with minimal distractions. Putting together an effective research paper takes a great deal of concentration.

3. Make sure you have all your note and your works-cited (or reference) cards with you (see Chapter 13 on taking notes).

14.2 Review your research and revise the preliminary thesis.

1. Start the process by recalling and writing down your research question and your preliminary thesis. Suzanne Mastronardo's (from Chapter 10) appear below:

Research question: Is bilingual education more or less effective at teaching language-minority students (LMS) English than the immersion method, in which such students take their academic classes in English?

Preliminary thesis: The immersion method of teaching LMS students English is more effective than the bilingual-education approach.

2. Read your note cards again. You will find that a number of major themes, concerns, and ideas keep popping up. Record these major concepts on a piece of paper or in a computer file; you will be able to use them in your outline. Also, arrange your note cards into piles that correspond to each of the major concepts you have listed. Doing so will make it easier to put down relevant information in an organized way as you turn your outline into a fleshed-out rough draft.

3. Review your preliminary thesis. Has your opinion changed since you did your research? If so, revise your preliminary thesis statement now. Here's how Suzanne revised hers:

Revised thesis: The challenge is to teach language-minority students (LMS) English while maintaining the integrity of the student's native language.

14.3 Make a rough outline and draft the paper.

You just learned that, as you reread your note cards, a number of ideas or points will recur. If you write them down as you go along, you will have a good rough outline on which to base your draft. Here's Suzanne Mastronardo's outline:

- **Introduction:** Background of the bilingual-education debate; need for softer rhetoric. **Statement of revised thesis.**
- Definitions of bilingual education and immersion method.
- California's Proposition 227 and its effects.
- The immersion method: advantages and disadvantages.
- Bilingual education: advantages and disadvantages.
- **Conclusion**—the need to listen to parents of students, need for common sense approach.

Once you have arranged your note cards into piles that correspond to each of the major concepts listed in your outline, you can start writing your paper. Flesh out each section by using both your own ideas and information found in each pile of cards. If gaps appear, you still have time to do some more research.

Of course, different writers work differently. However, whether you draft your paper on a computer or on a legal pad, the approach outlined above is straightforward and will keep you working in a directed and confident manner.

14.4 Revise and edit the paper.

As mentioned often, writing effective papers involves rewriting and rewriting and rewriting. As with any paper, you must ask yourself a series of questions:

Have I focused on my central idea?
- Is it stated clearly?
- Does it tell the reader the main point and the purpose of my paper?
- Are all body paragraphs directly related to the thesis?
- Do they help develop the thesis in detail?

Is the content of my paper strong?
- Have I included enough evidence from my research to support my thesis and convince my readers?
- Is all of this information directly relevant to the thesis? Has that relevance been made plain to the reader?
- Are my arguments logical and well supported?
- Have I eliminated material that is redundant or irrelevant to the thesis?

Have I organized my paper well?
- Are ideas developed in a logical, easy-to-follow order from the beginning of the paper to the end?
- Are paragraphs unified and coherent? And, by extension, is the entire paper unified and coherent?
- Have I included transitions between paragraphs to make reading easier?
- Have I introduced and concluded the paper effectively?

Have I included and documented all researched material well?
- Is all researched material, whether directly quoted, paraphrased, or summarized, cited properly? (See Chapters 15, 16, and 17.)
- Are all quotations accurate? Are they placed in quotation marks or indented within the text?
- Have I integrated research into my paper effectively by using signal phrases rather than just dropping the material into the paper? (See Chapters 15 and 16 on using MLA and APA style.)

- Can my readers easily judge where researched materials begin and end? Are my own ideas easily distinguishable from those that I have taken from others?
- For every source cited in the text of the paper, is there a corresponding entry in the works-cited or references list? For every entry in the works-cited or references list, is there a corresponding citation in the body of the paper?

Have I edited and proofread the paper well?

- Is my writing concise? (See Chapter 32.)
- Have I used language that is correct, concrete, and vivid? (See Chapters 30–31.)
- Have I varied vocabulary and sentence structure? (See Chapter 27.)
- Have I corrected major errors in sentence structure (fragments, comma splices, misplaced modifiers, and the like)? (See Chapters 22–26.)
- Have I corrected errors in grammar, punctuation, and mechanics? (See Chapters 33–46.)

Once Suzanne had written a rough draft, these questions helped her revise and polish her essay before handing it in.

Chapter Checklist

1. Find a quiet comfortable place to work, and don't rush the writing of the paper.

2. Review your note cards, and revise your preliminary thesis statement.

3. Use the major ideas that emerge when you reread your note cards as the basis for a rough outline. Arrange your note cards in piles that correspond to the major ideas in your outline.

4. Follow your outline as you take information from your note cards to prepare your first draft.

5. Revise, edit, and proofread your draft as with any other paper.

4

4

15

WRITING THE RESEARCH PAPER USING MLA FORMAT

In Chapters 11 and 12, you learned how to use the library and electronic sources to find information. In this chapter, you will learn how to incorporate research into your written paper and how to set up a works-cited list using Modern Language Association (MLA) style.

15.1 Learn how to reference all researched material.

15.2 Learn how to place researched material into a paper.

15.3 Learn how to prepare a works-cited list.

15.4 Study a student's research paper.

CHAPTER CHECKLIST

15.1 Learn how to reference all researched material.

As you know, you must always tell your readers the sources of all material you have researched every time you use that material in your paper. This process is known as citing your sources or referencing your research, and it applies to paraphrases and summaries as well as direct quotations.

One way to reference researched material is by introducing it with a **signal phrase,** which includes the author's name and a verb such as *argues, asserts, claims, contends, implies, maintains, notes, points out, suggests, thinks,* or *writes,* and by following the signal phrase with a parenthetical citation (usually just a page number). Another way is to use a parenthetical citation alone. Parenthetical citations include information about the source of the material. They are called parenthetical because they display this information in parentheses. Usually, the information includes the author's last name, or a short title if the author is unknown, and the number of the page in the source (unless it is an unpaginated source from the Internet) from which you have summarized, paraphrased, or quoted the material. As you will soon see, however, what actually appears in a parenthetical citation can vary depending on the source and on the way you incorporate the researched material into your paper. In any case, your readers will be able to use this information to find out more about the source by looking it up in your works-cited list (another important part of a research paper), which contains complete publication information about your sources. Putting together a works-cited list is discussed later in this chapter.

216

· · · ·   · · · ·   B A S I C L I N K   · · · ·   · · · ·

WWW

For the latest updates on MLA style and a list of frequently
asked questions about the style, visit
www.mla.org

15.2 Learn how to place researched material into a paper.

The information you provide in parenthetical citations depends on the way you incorporate or place researched materials into your paper. Here are a number of ways to do this using MLA formats. The formats given here are found in the sixth edition of the *MLA Handbook for Writers of Research Papers* (New York: MLA, 2003). If your instructor asks you to use American Psychological Association (APA) formats, follow the instructions in Chapter 16. For the format used in *The Chicago Manual of Style,* see Chapter 17.

1. SUMMARIZED OR PARAPHRASED MATERIAL

Remember that you must cite the source of material that you summarize and paraphrase, as well as material that you quote. Often the easiest way to cite your source is to put the last name of the author and the page number of the source in parentheses after the summarized or paraphrased material. In the following example, a student who wrote a paper about the decimation of elephant herds by poachers who were after their ivory put into her own words information taken from page 3 of a book by Douglas H. Chadwick:

> In the nineteenth century, Africa contained an estimated 5 million elephants, a number that had slowly decreased to an estimated 3 million by 1970 (Chadwick 3).

Note that no punctuation separates the author's last name and the page number. Nor is the abbreviation *p.* (for "page") used. The period that ends the sentence appears *after* the closing parenthesis.

2. DIRECT QUOTATION WITH THE AUTHOR'S LAST NAME IN THE TEXT OF YOUR PAPER

Sometimes it is a good idea to name the author of the direct quotation in your text. In the following example, the student has directly quoted a sentence from an article by Christopher Dickey and introduces it with a signal phrase. Since the quotation is a complete sentence, the student has chosen to set it off from her own writing with a colon. And because the student uses the author's last name to introduce the quotation, only the number of the page in the source from which the quotation is taken appears in the parenthetical citation.

In relation to the problem of poaching, Dickey has written: "In the African badlands the quickest way to make money with a gun has always been to take ivory" (101).

3. DIRECT QUOTATION WITHOUT MENTIONING THE AUTHOR'S LAST NAME IN THE TEXT OF YOUR PAPER

You can introduce a direct quotation without mentioning the author's name in the text of your paper. In that case, put the author's last name and the page from which the quotation was taken in parentheses at the end, just as you would do if you had paraphrased the author's words.

Ivory had, in essence, replaced money. As one commentator has pointed out, "After decades of chaos and corruption, ivory had become in effect one of Africa's few hard currencies" (Dickey 101).

4. DIRECT QUOTATION AS PART OF YOUR OWN SENTENCE

NOTE

When quoting a source, capitalize the first word of a quoted sentence, but do not capitalize the first word of a quoted phrase, especially if you are using the quotation as part of your own sentence.

If you want to make a direct quotation part of your own sentence, the only punctuation you need is quotation marks. Just combine the quoted passage with your own words naturally, as in the following sentence. But don't forget the quotation marks.

It is hard to believe that within the past two decades poachers have killed almost "80 percent of Kenya's elephants, reducing their numbers from 130,000 to around 16,000" (Morell 6).

5. DIRECT QUOTATION OF MORE THAN FOUR LINES

If you are including a direct quotation of more than four lines, you must double-space it and indent it ten spaces or one inch from the left margin (called a **block quotation**). In such cases, no quotation marks are used since the indentation tells your reader that you are quoting directly from a source, as in the following example:

As Underwood points out, there is a natural substitute for ivory, a substance called tagua, which grows on trees:

> Tagua, or vegetable ivory, is made from the dried and polished nuts of several South American palms. "It is remarkably similar to animal ivory in both looks and feel," says Marlene Kanas. . . . Tagua is durable and easily carved and it even mimics the porosity of animal ivory. "Evidently, those similarities were not lost on early botanists, who named the palm genus Phytelephas—'elephant plant.'" (29)

Note that, in this block quotation, the author includes a direct quotation from another author, Marlene Kanas, whose work she researched. Also, note that when you use a block quotation, the parenthetical citation goes after the punctuation mark that ends the quotation.

6. SOURCE WITH NO AUTHOR GIVEN

If no author's name appears in the source from which you took information, place the title of the source in the parentheses; follow the title with the page number. The source will appear in your works-cited list in alphabetical order by its title.

> Still another problem facing those who would protect the animals is their growing numbers in certain areas, such as Zimbabwe, which has not participated in the ban on hunting ("Poacher's Pause" 42).

7. INDIRECT SOURCE

When using material quoted in your source, type *qtd. in,* for "quoted in," before your source's name in the parenthetical citation.

> In assessing the importance of language, William James said that without words our world would become "a spiritual sand-heap" (qtd. in Allport 294).

8. SELECTION IN AN ANTHOLOGY

When referencing the material in such a selection, use the name of the selection's author, not the name of the anthology's editor.

> In "Shopping and Other Spiritual Adventures in America," Phyllis Rose defines shopping as a "form of therapy" that provides a "feeling of power" (114).

9. TWO OR MORE WORKS BY THE SAME AUTHOR

If you are using two or more works by the same author, introduce the material by including the author's name in your signal phrase. Then write the name of the work (in an abbreviated form, if necessary) in the parenthetical citation, along with the page number.

> Jonathan Kozol claims that the cause of homelessness in the United States is not the "deinstitutionalization" of mental patients but the lack of affordable housing for the poor ("Distancing the Homeless" 1).

> In his critically acclaimed full-length study of homelessness in America, Kozol points out that "early death or stunted cognitive development" as well as severe "emotional damage" are common in homeless children in the United States (Rachel and Her Children 83).

If you must include both the author and title in the citation, it should look like this:

> The cause of homelessness in the United States is the lack of affordable housing for the poor (Kozol, "Distancing the Homeless" 1).

10. SOURCE BY TWO OR THREE AUTHORS

If your source has two or three authors, give the last name of all the authors in your signal phrase or in your parenthetical citation.

In their article discussing the Supported Education Initiative in Great Britain, Isenwater, Lanham, and Thornhill explain that "the typical structure of these programs aims to support students who attend mainstream courses both practically and psychologically" (43).

11. SOURCE BY FOUR OR MORE AUTHORS

With a source that has four or more authors, MLA gives you two choices: (1) give the first author's last name followed by *et al.* (meaning "and others"—with no punctuation between the name and *et al.*) in the signal phrase or the parenthetical citation, or (2) give all the last names.

According to the authors, "the landscape of Supported Employment (SE) services for people with psychiatric disabilities living in the community is changing" (Furlong et al. 13).

12. THE BIBLE

Indicate the edition of the Bible, the book, the chapter, and the verse number(s) when you are referencing the Bible. You can do so in the body of the text or in a parenthetical citation. You can abbreviate chapters of the Bible when necessary in your parenthetical citation.

The end of the flood is explained in the Bible in a way no modern meteorologist would dare: ". . . God made a wind pass over the earth, and the waters assuaged. The fountains also of the deep and the windows of heaven were stopped. . . ." (<u>King James Bible</u>, Gen. 8:1–2).

13. CORPORATE AUTHOR

If authorship is claimed by an organization, use the name of the organization to introduce the information or include its name in the parenthetical citation.

President Herbert Hoover personally supervised the removal of important government documents from the Oval Office during a fire on Christmas Eve in 1929 (White House Historical Assn. 147)

Note that it is appropriate to shorten words that are commonly abbreviated, such as "Assn."

14. IDEAS FROM AN ENTIRE WORK

To include information from an entire work, simply include the name(s) of the author(s) in the text or in the parenthetical citation. Obviously, no page number(s) can be indicated.

Animals, some scientists now believe, actually experience distress, joy, anger, jealousy, and other primal emotions once thought to be exclusively human (Masson and McCarthy).

15. SOURCE THAT IS NOT PAGINATED

You might run across a source that is not paginated, particularly when you are working with online or electronic sources. Although printouts of electronic materials may show page numbers, these are the numbers assigned by the printer, and different printers may indicate different page numbers. So, instead of trying to assign page numbers arbitrarily to this material, simply cite the work in its entirety by using the author's last name (if an author is indicated), by using the title, or by using both. If the material is divided into sections or numbered paragraphs, also include these in your parenthetical citation.

> In an article entitled "Shock Therapy," Dennis Cauchon maintains that many patients are often not made aware of the many dangers associated with shock therapy and discusses a four-month investigation conducted by USA Today (pars. 3-5)

In the example above, the writer mentions the title of the article ("Shock Therapy"), names the author, and then follows up with a parenthetical citation that includes the paragraphs (pars. 3–5) from which this information was summarized.

16. TWO DIFFERENT AUTHORS WITH THE SAME LAST NAME

If you cite material by two authors with the same last name, make sure to use both authors' first as well as last names when you include information from their work.

> As one author has remarked, "the endless struggle between the flesh and the spirit found an end in Greek art" (Edith Hamilton 65).

17. INFORMATION FROM TWO DIFFERENT WORKS IN THE SAME SENTENCE

Use a semicolon to separate the author and page number(s) of each work in the parenthetical citation.

> It's no wonder poachers went on a rampage. During the 1980s, the elephant population in Kenya alone decreased from around 130,000 to 16,000 (Contreras 87; Morell 6).

18. SOURCE WHOSE AUTHOR IS UNKNOWN

If the author's name is not available, use the title of the work to introduce the information or include the title in the parenthetical citation. If you choose the latter, you may shorten the title.

> The National Women's Conference held in Houston, Texas, in 1977 produced a "25-point, revised national Plan of Action," which was to set the agenda for the Woman's Rights Movement for the next decade (70 Years in Review).

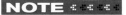

NOTE

This publication is not paginated in the usual way. Instead, it presents major events from 1923 to 1993 In chronological order, with each page covering a specific year. Therefore, no page number is required in the citation.

19. MULTIVOLUME WORK

If you take information from more than one volume in a multivolume work, indicate the volume number you used in the parenthetical citation. Separate the volume and page number(s) with a colon.

> In <u>A History of Philosophy</u>, Frederick Copleston explains that the British chemist and physicist Michael Faraday (1791-1867) became interested in science while he was apprenticed to a bookbinder (8:18).

However, if you cite only one volume of a multivolume work, you need not include the volume number in your parenthetical citation. In the parenthetical citation, simply state the author's last name followed by the page number, and include the volume number in your works-cited entry.

> <u>A History of Philosophy</u> discusses the scientific theories and discoveries of Michael Faraday (Copleston 251).

20. ENCYCLOPEDIA OR DICTIONARY

When referencing an encyclopedia or dictionary entry, use the entry word itself in the parenthetical reference, not the title (or author, if there is one) of the reference work. If you wish to reference a specific definition in the dictionary, give the relevant information (such as the number or number and letter) after the abbreviation *def.*

> As a law term, <u>purge</u> means "to clear (a person) of a charge or imputation" and is "often used with respect to contempt of court" ("Purge," def. 3).

21. LITERARY WORK

If the editions of a literary work are numerous, your works-cited list will tell your reader which edition you are using. You will normally reference a prose work by page number. If you are referencing a play, use act, scene, and line numbers (using arabic, not roman, numerals). If you are referencing a poem, reference the part (if the poem is divided into parts) and line numbers (again, in arabic numerals).

NOTE
Use arabic numerals, and separate them with periods only, no space.

NOTE
If the poem is not divided into parts, use line numbers. For the first reference, use the word *lines* to let the reader know to what you are referring (lines 72-83). After that, use just the numbers (91-94).

> Early in the play, Lear announces his purpose:
>> Give me the map there. Know that we have divided
>
> In three our kingdom; and 'tis our fast intent
> To shake all cares and business from our age,
> Conferring them on younger strengths, while we
> Unburdened crawl toward death. (<u>King Lear</u> 1.1.36-40)

> At the end of <u>Paradise Lost</u>, Milton describes our "first parents'" exit from the Garden of Eden in very poignant lines: "They hand in hand with wandering steps and slow / Through Eden took their solitary way" (12.648-49).

22. QUOTATION TO WHICH YOU HAVE ADDED MATERIAL OR FROM WHICH YOU HAVE DELETED MATERIAL

If you insert something into a direct quotation for whatever reason, put the inserted material in brackets. If you delete something from the quoted material, indicate it by using ellipsis points (three spaced periods).

As Chadwick has pointed out,

> [the] poachers resembled the field forces of drug operations in the Golden Triangle and Columbia: They traveled in large, well-armed, paramilitary groups supported by vehicles, radios, an occasional spotting plane, and a network of informants that sometimes reached to the highest level of government. Their weapon of choice was the semiautomatic rifle or machine gun. Few . . . stopped to take so much as one steak from the tons of meat left lying to rot after the tusks were hacked out of the animals with an ax or chain saw. (43)

15.2a Use notes with parenthetical documentation.

You may use two kinds of notes with parenthetical documentation: (1) notes that provide the reader with information, explanations, and comments that cannot be included in the text, and (2) bibliographic notes that list other sources or provide evaluative comments.

To indicate these notes, place a superscript arabic numeral at the appropriate place in your text and write the information after a matching numeral either at the bottom of the page (a footnote) or at the end of the text (an endnote).

15.3 Learn how to prepare a works-cited list.

A works-cited list, at the very end of your paper, is an *alphabetical list* of all the sources—books, articles, book reviews, interviews, and so on—from which you obtained the information you used in your paper.

15.3a Start by making bibliography cards or using your computer to record sources.

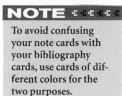

NOTE To avoid confusing your note cards with your bibliography cards, use cards of different colors for the two purposes.

Before you start taking notes, prepare a separate bibliography card for each of your possible sources. On this card, record the publication information that must appear in your works-cited list so that readers can identify your sources. For each reference, also include the catalog call number if your source is a book or the URL for an electronic source. Later on, you will have to put your sources in alphabetical order, and rearranging cards is much easier than changing the order of items on a sheet of paper.

The information you put on a bibliography card depends on the source. For example, a bibliography card for a book would mention the author, the title, the publisher, and the place and date of publication. One for an article in a magazine or journal would include the author, the title of the article, and the title of the magazine or journal in which it was published. It would also include the volume number (if any),

NOTE ⸭⸭⸭⸭⸭

You must include a separate entry in your works-cited list for every source that appears in your paper's parenthetical citations.

the issue date, and the numbers of the pages on which the article appears. Electronic sources require the author's name; the title of the item; the title of the Web site, online magazine, or similar; the relevant page or paragraph numbers (if provided on the site); the group sponsoring the site; the date the site was published or updated; the date you accessed the site; and the URL. Here is a sample bibliography card for a journal article considered as a possible source by the author of the student paper that appears on pages 241–253 of this chapter:

CHAVEZ, LINDA

"Uneducated Bilingualism: Why Latinos Should Oppose
Bilingual Education," Hispanic Magazine, 2/2/01, 2pp.

Found 4/3/01

www.hispaniconline.com/pol&opi/opinion/conbil.html

If you prefer, you can record your sources on your computer. Many software programs will help you document a paper or create a bibliography. In fact, most word processors have automatic footnote and endnote features. Just be sure that the software you use provides the documentation style called for by your project. Up-to-date software can format footnotes or endnotes even for material found on Web pages. One such program is offered on the Web site that accompanies this book: **http://www.mhhe.com/basics**.

An *annotated bibliography* is a list of sources used in a research paper that includes for each entry an explanatory note identifying the focus of the information and providing a brief description or evaluation of the source.

15.3b Prepare a works-cited list.

The works-cited style explained here is the one created by the Modern Language Association (MLA). To learn how to prepare a reference list for a paper using the American Psychological Association (APA) format, turn to Chapter 16. *Chicago Manual of Style (CMS)* format is discussed in Chapter 17.

The last section of a research paper, the works-cited list, is an alphabetical list of complete publication information about each source referenced in your paper's parenthetical citations. Although the format of the individual entries (sources) in a works-cited list and the information they supply vary according to the type of source, the list as a whole is arranged in the pattern described in the next section.

15.3c Learn the pattern of a works-cited list.

1. Entries are listed alphabetically by the last name of the author or by the first major word of the title if no author is given. If a source has more than one author, it is alphabetized by the last name of the author whose name appears first. The entries are not numbered.

2. Entries are double-spaced.

3. The first line of each entry begins at the left margin. If more than one line is needed to complete the entry, additional lines are indented five spaces or half an inch (called a **hanging indent**).

The exact information you include for each source in your works-cited list depends on the source. Thus, a works-cited-list entry for a book is different from an entry for a magazine or journal article and both are different from an entry for an electronic source. You can use the following sample entries as models for those in your own list of works cited. (You should refer to these samples when you write bibliography cards as well, since it will save you time when you compose your works-cited list.)

15.3d Review sample entries for a works-cited list.

Books

1. BOOK BY A SINGLE AUTHOR

Chadwick, Douglas. <u>The Fate of the Elephant</u>. San Francisco: Sierra Club, 1992.

Elements of the Preceding Entry

Chadwick, Douglas.	The author's name (last name first), followed by a period.
<u>The Fate of the Elephant</u>.	The title of the book (underlined), followed by a period.
San Francisco:	The city (not the state) in which the book was published, followed by a colon.
Sierra Club,	The publisher of the book, followed by a comma.
1992.	The year the book was published, followed by a period.

MLA style calls for shortening a publisher's name as long as doing so does not create confusion or leave out information that the reader will need to identify the publisher. For example, you can shorten *McGraw-Hill* to *McGraw*.

2. BOOK WITH A SUBTITLE, BY A SINGLE AUTHOR

Moss, Cynthia. <u>Elephant Memories: Thirteen Years in the Life of an Elephant Family</u>. New York: Morrow, 1988.

3. BOOK BY TWO AUTHORS

Bynum, Jack E., and William E. Thompson. <u>Juvenile Delinquency: A Sociological</u>
<u>Approach</u>. 5th ed. Boston: Allyn, 2002.

4. BOOK BY THREE AUTHORS

Laws, Richard M., I. S. C. Parker, and R. C. B. Johnstone. <u>Elephants and Their</u>
<u>Habitats: The Ecology of Elephants in Northern Bunyora, Uganda</u>. Oxford:
Clarendon, 1975.

5. BOOK BY FOUR OR MORE AUTHORS

Jencks, C[hristopher], et al. <u>Inequality: A Reassessment of the Effect of Family and</u>
<u>Schooling in America</u>. New York: Basic, 1972.

Often, only the initial of the author's first name is given on the title page. If you
know or can find the full first name, insert the rest of the name in brackets. For
example, a computer search using the title of the above-mentioned book produced the author's first name. However, it is not necessary to spell out the author's full first name (see number 4 above).

The Latin abbreviation *et al.* means "and others." It is used in place of the
names of all authors except the first when there are four or more authors.
Another option is to list all of the authors' names.

6. BOOK BY AN UNKNOWN AUTHOR

If the author's name is not given, begin with the title. Place the book in the works-
cited list by alphabetizing according to the first letter of the first major word in
the title. The following entry would appear under "W" for "Way."

<u>The Way to Eternity: Egyptian Myth</u>. London: Baird, 1997.

7. TWO OR MORE BOOKS BY THE SAME AUTHOR

List the items in alphabetical order according to the first major word in the title.
Place the author's name in the first item only. In the item(s) that follow, type
three hyphens and a period in place of the author's name:

Bloom, Harold. <u>Book of J</u>. New York: Random, 1991.
---. <u>How to Read and Why</u>. New York: Scribner's, 2000.
---. <u>Shakespeare: The Invention of the Human</u>. New York: Riverhead-Penguin, 1998.

Some publishers use **imprints,** or special names, for certain lists of their books.
If an imprint appears on the title page, give the name of the imprint, then a hyphen, and then the name of the publisher, as in the third example here.

8. BOOK WITH AN EDITOR OR EDITORS

Updike, John, and Katrina Kenison, eds. <u>The Best American Short Stories of the</u>
<u>Century</u>. Boston: Houghton, 1999.

9. BOOK IN A SERIES

Type the series name and the series number, if any, between the editor's name and the publication information. Do not underline or use quotation marks around the name of the series.

> Dickens, Charles. <u>Great Expectations</u>. Ed. Janise Carlisle. Case Studies in
> Contomporary Criticism 4. Boston: Bedford-St. Martin's, 1996.

10. BOOK CONTAINING THE TITLE OF ANOTHER WORK WITHIN ITS TITLE

If the title of another work appears within the title of the book you are citing, ask yourself if that other work would be underlined if it stood alone. If the answer is yes, *do not* underline it.

> Alexander, Nigel. <u>Poison, Play, and Duel: A Study in</u> Hamlet. Lincoln: U of Nebraska P,
> 1971.

The abbreviations *U* and *P* stand for "University" and "Press."

On the other hand, if the title of that other work would appear in quotation marks if it stood alone, place quotation marks around it and underline the entire title of the book in which the other title appears.

> Patrides, C. A., ed. <u>"Lycidas": The Tradition and the Poem</u>. New York: Holt, 1961.

11. EDITION OTHER THAN THE FIRST

If you are listing a work that has been republished in a later edition or editions, indicate the number of the edition you are using.

> Gibaldi, Joseph. <u>MLA Handbook for Writers of Research Papers</u>. 6th ed. New York:
> MLA, 2003.

12. MULTIVOLUME WORK

> Anderson, Theodore, and Mildred Boyer. <u>Bilingual Schooling in the United States</u>. 2
> vols. Washington: GPO, 1970.

If your paper cites only one of the volumes, indicate the volume number before the city and note the number of volumes in the work after the date:

> Anderson, Theodore, and Mildred Boyer. <u>Bilingual Schooling in the United States</u>. Vol. 1.
> Washington: GPO, 1970. 2 vols.

The abbreviation *GPO* stands for "Government Printing Office."

13. SELECTION FROM AN ANTHOLOGY

> Orwell, George. "A Hanging." 1931. <u>75 Readings Plus</u>. 6th ed. Ed. Santi V. Buscemi
> and Charlotte Smith. New York: McGraw, 2002. 2-6.

If the selection in the anthology was previously published, you may give the date when the selection first appeared by placing it after the title, followed by a period. The abbreviation *Ed.* means "Edited by."

14. ANTHOLOGY WITH AN EMPHASIS ON THE EDITOR OR EDITORS

Buscemi, Santi V., and Caroline Smith, eds. 75 Readings Plus. 6th ed. New York:
    McGraw, 2002.

15. TWO SELECTIONS FROM THE SAME ANTHOLOGY

Sontag, Susan. "Women's Beauty: Put-Down or Power Source." 1975. 75 Readings Plus.
    6th ed. Ed. Santi V. Buscemi and Charlotte Smith. New York: McGraw, 2002. 122-24.
Steinem, Gloria. "Erotica and Pornography." 1978. 75 Readings Plus. 6th ed. Ed. Santi
    V. Buscemi and Charlotte Smith. New York: McGraw, 2002. 138-42.

16. THREE OR MORE SELECTIONS FROM THE SAME ANTHOLOGY

Cohen, Andrew D. "The Case for Partial or Total Immersion Education." Simoes 65-89.
Fishman, Joshua A. "Bilingual Education and the Future of Language Teaching and
    Language Learning in the United States." Simoes 229-35.
Simoes, Antonio, ed. The Bilingual Child. New York: Academic, 1976.
Zinkel, Perry A., and John F. Greene. "Cultural Attitude Scales: A Step toward
    Determining Whether the Programs Are Bicultural or Bilingual." Simoes 3-16.

Alphabetically, list the anthology with the full publishing information. Then list each
of the articles separately with the name of the author, the title of the article (in quotation marks), the last name of the editor, and the page numbers of the article. No
punctuation appears between the editor's name and the page numbers of the article.

17. TRANSLATION—FOCUS ON THE ORIGINAL AUTHOR

Begin with the author's name (last name first). Follow with the title, the transla-
tor's name, and the publication information.

Barthes, Roland. The Fashion System. Trans. Matthew Ward and Richard Howard.
    Berkeley: U of California P, 1990.

18. TRANSLATION—FOCUS ON THE TRANSLATOR

Begin with the name(s) of the translator(s). Follow with the title, the author's
name, and the publication information.

Ward, Matthew, and Richard Howard, trans. The Fashion System. By Roland Barthes.
    Berkeley: U of California P, 1990.

19. FOREWORD, INTRODUCTION, PREFACE, AFTERWORD, OR EPILOGUE

Franklin, Phyllis. Foreword. MLA Handbook for Writers of Research Papers. 6th ed. By
    Joseph Gibaldi. New York: MLA, 2003. xv-xvii.
Callan, Edward. Introduction. Cry, the Beloved Country. By Alan Paton. New York:
    Scribner Paperback, 1995. 19-30.
Page, Norman. Preface. Jude the Obscure. By Thomas Hardy. New York: Norton,
    1978. ix-xii.
Norwich, John Julius. Epilogue. A Short History of Byzantium. By Norwich. New York:
    Knopf, 1997. 382-83.

20. PUBLISHED BY AN ORGANIZATION OR A CORPORATION

List the corporate author first, followed by the title. Then list the publisher, even if the author and the publisher are the same.

Appalachian Trail Conference. Appalachian Trail Guide to Tennessee-North Carolina. Harper's Ferry: Appalachian Trail Conference, 1998.

21. REPUBLISHED BOOK

When citing a republished book—for example, a paperback version of a book originally published in a clothbound version—give the original publication date, followed by a period, before the publication information for the book you are citing.

Graham, Katharine. Personal History. 1997. New York: Vintage-Random, 1998.

22. ENCYCLOPEDIA OR DICTIONARY

"Elephant." The Encyclopaedia Britannica: Micropedia. 15th ed. 1991.
"Aquaculture." The American Heritage College Dictionary. 3rd ed. 1993.

23. BIBLE OR OTHER SACRED TEXT

King James Version. Holy Bible. Nashville: Nelson, 1976.

Articles in Periodicals

24. ARTICLE IN A MAGAZINE—SIGNED AND UNSIGNED

Signed
Rose, David. "Iraq's Arsenal of Terror." Vanity Fair May 2002: 120-31.

Elements of the Preceding Entry

Rose, David.	The author's name (last name first), followed by a period.
"Iraq's Arsenal of Terror."	The title of the article in quotation marks, followed by a period within the closing quotation marks.
Vanity Fair	The title of the magazine (underlined).
May 2002:	The date of publication, followed by a colon. (No punctuation appears between the title of the magazine and the date of publication.) Note that most months, such as Nov. and Dec., are abbreviated. Only May, June, and July are not abbreviated.
120-31.	The pages (inclusive) of the magazine on which the article appears, followed by a period.

Unsigned
"Poacher's Pause." Economist 2 Mar. 1991: 42.

25. ARTICLE IN A SCHOLARLY JOURNAL, PAGINATED BY VOLUME—SIGNED AND UNSIGNED

Signed

Morell, Virginia. "Running for Their Lives." International Wildlife 20 (1990): 4-13.

The number 20 in the above example refers to volume 20 of *International Wildlife*. Generally, libraries bind together in one volume all the issues of a journal published in one year (or half-year) if the page numbers of each issue run consecutively, starting with the first issue and ending with the last. If such is the case, you need not include the issue number or the month or season in your works-cited list.

> Ferris, Dana. "Students' Views of Academic Aural/Oral Skills: A Comparative Needs Analysis." TESOL Quarterly 32 (1998): 289-318.

Unsigned

"Elephantine Contraception." Lancet (North American Edition) 340 (1992): 583-84.

26. ARTICLE IN A SCHOLARLY JOURNAL, PAGINATED BY ISSUE

Jisi, Wang. "The Price of America Going It Alone." New Perspectives Quarterly 19.3 (2002): 48-49.

A journal's title page may also include an issue number. The example above included just such an issue number (Number 3). The title page may also include a month or season before the year (April 2002, Summer 2002), but you need not include this information unless there is no issue number provided.

27. ARTICLE IN A SCHOLARLY JOURNAL, BY MULTIPLE AUTHORS

Bailey, Kathleen M., Andy Curtis, and David Nunan. "Undeniable Insights: The Collaborative Use of Three Professional Development Practices." TESOL Quarterly 32 (1998): 546-68.

Bailey, Francis, et al. "Language Teacher Educators Collaborative Conversations." TESOL Quarterly 32 (1998): 536-46.

28. ARTICLE IN A NEWSPAPER—SIGNED AND UNSIGNED

Signed

Hargrove, Thomas. "Bilingual Charter Schools Stir Heated Debate among Experts." Star-Ledger [Newark, NJ] 11 Nov. 2001. sec. 10:9.

For newspapers, the date (given as day, month, year) replaces the volume and issue number. You may also need to supply section numbers or letters in addition to page numbers. Note that if the newspaper is not widely known, you should include the city in which it is published unless the city appears in the title.

Unsigned

"Ivory Ban Reconsidered." Christian Science Monitor 28 Feb. 1992: 8.

29. EDITORIAL IN A NEWSPAPER

Use the same format for an editorial as for an unsigned article, but type the word *Editorial* immediately after the title of the editorial.

"The Need to Test Drugs on Children." Editorial. <u>New York Times</u> 7 Apr. 2002: A14.

30. LETTER TO THE EDITOR

Lecocq, Yves. Letter. <u>Wildlife Society Bulletin</u> 25 (1997): 215.

31. BOOK REVIEW

Graham, Loren. "From the H-Bomb to Human Rights." Rev. of <u>Sakharov: A Biography</u>, by Richard Lourie. <u>New York Times Book Review</u> 7 Apr. 2002: 9.

Electronic Sources

The material in this section is based on the most recent edition of the *MLA Handbook,* published in 2003. For the most up-to-date information on citing electronic sources, visit www.mla.org

Because electronic works are not as fixed and stable as print works, they require more citation information than references to printed documents. Often, however, electronic sources do not supply all the needed information, such as page or paragraph numbers, so you just have to cite whatever information you can find. Many times, for instance, an online document will not have been published in a print version; obviously, in that case, you cannot include information about the print publication. The following example of a common type of citation (an article in an online publication) shows all the information you *should* include in a citation if the information is available.

32. ARTICLE IN AN ONLINE PUBLICATION

Lemonick, Michael D. "The Ivory Wars." <u>Time</u> 16 June 1997: 53-54. <u>Time Online Edition</u>. 16 Apr. 2002. Time Inc. 12 Jan. 2003 <http://www.time.com/time/magazine/1997/dom/970616/environ.the_ivory_war_html>.

Elements of the Preceding Entry

Lemonick, Michael D.	The author's name (last name first), followed by a period. If there is no author's name, begin the entry with the title of the document.
"The Ivory Wars."	The title of the document, in quotation marks, followed by a period inside the closing quotation mark.
Time 16 June 1997: 53-54.	Information about the print publication, if available. If this information is not available, cite only the electronic publication, following the author's name and title of the document.

<u>Time Online Edition.</u> 16 Apr. 2002. Time Inc.	Information about the electronic publication. This usually includes the title of the site (underlined), the date of electronic publication or the latest update, and the name of the institution or organization that sponsors the site.
12 Jan. 2003	Date of access. The date on which you viewed the document or, if you viewed the document more than once, the most recent date on which you viewed the document. Note that no punctuation follows the access date.
<http://www.time.com/ time/magazine/1997/ dom/970616/environ. the_ivory_war_html>.	The URL (network address) at which the document can be found. Enclose the URL in angled brackets. If a URL must be divided into two or more lines, break it only after a slash or a dot; do not use a hyphen at the break. Use the exact URL for the document whenever possible; however, if the URL is so long that it will be cumbersome to use or transcribe, you can give the URL for the site's search page (if the site has a search page).

33. INTERNET SITE

<u>Rain Taxi: Review of Books</u>. Ed. Eric Lorberer. Winter 2002/2003. 26 Feb. 2003
    <www.raintaxi.com>.

Elements of the Preceding Entry

<u>**Rain Taxi: Review of Books.**</u>	Title of the site (underlined).
Ed. Eric Lorberer.	Name of the editor of the site (if given).
Winter 2002/2003.	Electronic publication information, which may include version number, date of electronic publication or latest update, and name of any sponsoring institution or organization.
26 Feb. 2003	Date of access.
<www.raintaxi.com>.	URL (network address).

34. HOME PAGE FOR A COURSE

Begin the entry with the name of the course instructor (last name first); then list the title of the course followed by the description *Course home page* (do not underline or use quotation marks). Include the dates of the course, the names of the department and institution, the date of access, and the URL.

Mooney, Jennifer. Studies in Women Writers. Course home page. Aug.-Dec. 2002. English Dept., Virginia Tech. 26 Sept. 2002 <http://athena.english.vt.edu/~jmooney/wwpages/wwsyllabus.html>.

35. HOME PAGE FOR AN ACADEMIC DEPARTMENT

English. Dept. Home page. Virginia Tech. 26 Feb. 2003 <http://athena.english.vt.edu>.

36. ONLINE BOOK

Follow the directions on pages 225–229 for citing a printed book, modifying them where necessary for an electronic source. For example, you may need to add the electronic publication information, date of electronic publication, date of access, and URL for the book.

Anderson, Sherwood. Winesburg, Ohio. 1919. Bartleby.com: Great Books Online 2003 26 Feb. 2003 <http://www.bartleby.com/fiction>.

> **NOTE**
>
> If a site does not assign a URL to each document, and if you cannot list a search page, give the URL of the site's home page, followed by the word *Path* and a colon; then list the sequence of links a reader can use to find the document. For example:
> Furtado, Antonio, and Paolo A. S. Veloso. "Folklore and Myth in The Knight of the Cart," Arthuriana 6.2 (1996): 18–43. 6 June 2003 <http://www.smu.edu/arthuriana/> (Path: Access; Articles).

37. PART OF AN ONLINE BOOK

To cite part of an online book, list the title or name of the part after the author's name and before the title of the book. If the part is an introduction, preface, foreword, or afterword, do not enclose it in quotation marks. If it is an article, a titled chapter, or (as here) a poem, however, do place it in quotation marks.

Dickinson, Emily. "Success is counted sweetest." The Complete Poems. Boston: Little, 1924. Bartleby.com: Great Books Online. 2000. 26 Feb. 2003 <http://www.bartleby.com/113/index1.html>.

38. ARTICLE IN AN ONLINE SCHOLARLY JOURNAL

Hill, Kevin A. "Conflicts over Developmental Values: The International Ivory Trade in Zimbabwe's Historical Context." Environment and History 1.3 (1995): 10 pars. 16 Apr. 1999 <http://www.fiv.edu/~khill/elephant.htm>.

Scholarly journals can be found online independently or as part of a database. If you are citing a journal that is part of a database, follow the print information for the article with the name of the database, the date of access, and the URL of the article within the database.

Online databases are accessed through a computer service or network. If you locate research material from a printed source through an online database, the entry for the works-cited list should contain additional information: the name of the database used, the name of the service, the name of the library, the date of access, and the URL of the service's home page, if known.

> Eastgate, Jan. "The Case against Electroshock Treatment." <u>USA Today Magazine</u> Nov.
> 1998: 5 pp. <u>Master FILE Premier</u>. EBSCOhost. Middlesex County College
> Library, Edison, NJ. 8 Mar. 2001 <http://search.epnet.com>.

Elements of the Preceding Entry

Eastgate, Jan.	The name of the author (last name first), followed by a period.
"The Case against Electroshock Treatment."	The title of the article, in quotation marks, followed by a period inside the quotation marks. (NOTE: Do not capitalize prepositions when they appear in the middle of a title.)
<u>USA Today Magazine</u>	The title of the magazine (underlined), followed by no punctuation.
(Nov. 1998).	The date of publication of the article, in parentheses, followed by a period.
5 pp.	Page numbers or the number of pages, paragraphs, or other numbered sections (if they are given), followed by a period.
<u>Master FILE Premier.</u>	The name of the database, underlined, followed by a period.
EBSCOhost.	The name of the service, followed by a period.
Middlesex County College Library, Edison, NJ.	The name and the location of the library, followed by a period.
8 Mar. 2001	The date of access, followed by no punctuation.
<http://search.epnet.com>.	The URL of the service's home page, in angled brackets, followed by a period.

39. ARTICLE IN AN ONLINE NEWSPAPER OR FROM A NEWSWIRE

Radler, Melissa. "US Closer to Posting Rewards for Capture of Palestinian Terrorists."
<u>Jerusalem Post Internet Edition</u> 10 Aug. 2001. 15 Apr. 2002 <http://
www.jpost. com/Editions/2001/08/10/News.32328.html>.

40. REVIEW

Orr, David. " 'Springing': What's Not a Poem Has Been Discarded." Rev. of <u>Springing:
New and Selected Poems</u>, by Marie Ponsot. <u>New York Times on the Web.</u> 21
Apr. 2002. 26 Apr. 2002 <http://www.nytimes.com/2002/04/21/books/
review/21ORRLT.html>.

41. ARTICLE IN AN ONLINE MAGAZINE

Sundman, John. "Artificial Stupidity." Salon.com 26 Feb. 2003. 28 Feb. 2003
    <http://www.salon.com/tech/feature/2003/02/26/loebner_part_one/index.html>.

42. ANONYMOUS ARTICLE

"Saudi Ambassador to UK Praises Suicide Bombers." Toronto Star 15 Apr. 2002. 15
    Apr. 2002 <http://www.thestar.com>.

43. EDITORIAL

"Amtrak's Future." Editorial. New York Times on the Web 27 Feb. 2003. 27 Feb. 2003
    <http://www.nytimes.com/2003/02/27/opinion/27THU3.html>.

44. LETTER TO THE EDITOR

Heilbronner, Michael. Letter. New York Times on the Web 27 Feb. 2003. 20 Feb. 2003
    <http://www.nytimes.com/2003/02/27/opinion/L27PROT.html>.

45. NONPERIODICAL PUBLICATION ON CD-ROM, DISKETTE, OR MAGNETIC TAPE

This source should be cited the same way you would cite a book source, but with an indication of the medium of publication (CD-ROM, Diskette, Magnetic tape). Usually, only one publication date and one vendor's name are given because the information provider and publisher are almost always the same for this type of source.

McGraw-Hill Encyclopedia of Science and Technology. CD-ROM. New York:
    McGraw-Hill, 1999.

46. MATERIAL FROM A PERIODICALLY PUBLISHED DATABASE ON CD-ROM

CD-ROM databases are added to or updated periodically to provide users with up-to-date resources. Treat an article in a CD-ROM database the same way you would treat a printed version. However, add the name of the database underlined (SIRS Government Reporter, for example), the medium (CD-ROM), the name of the vendor, and the electronic publication date.

Gilreath, James. "History of a Book: Madison Council Told of First Book Printed in
    America." Library of Congress Information Bulletin 1 May 1995: 200-02. SIRS
    Government Reporter. CD-ROM. SIRS, Inc. Fall 1998.

47. WORK FROM A LIBRARY SUBSCRIPTION SERVICE

Eastgate, Jan. "The Case against Electroshock Treatment." USA Today Magazine 27
    Nov. 1998: 22-34. Master FILE Premier. EBSCOhost. Middlesex County College
    Library, Edison, NJ. 8 Mar. 2001 <http://search.epnet.com>.

48. WORK FROM A PERSONAL SUBSCRIPTION SERVICE

When you are citing a source from a personal subscription service such as AOL, and if you have used a keyword to find your sources, indicate *keyword:* at the end, followed by the word itself.

Hutson, James H. "Benjamin Franklin." <u>World Book Online</u>. 2003. America Online. 6
June 2003. Keyword: Benjamin Franklin.

49. E-MAIL COMMUNICATION

Saunders, Nicholas. "Re: Questionnaire for Doctoral Dissertation." E-mail to the
author. 10 Feb. 2002.

50. ONLINE POSTING

Kwazi, Leo. "Migratory Patterns of Elephants in Southwest Africa." Online posting. 18
May 1999. Wildlife News. 19 May 1999 <http://www.wildlife.org/>.

51. SYNCHRONOUS COMMUNICATION

Saunders, Nicholas. Online debate. "What Price Ivory?" 27 May 1999. U Town MOO.
27 May 1999 <telnet://next.vs.pth.edu.6541>.

52. DOWNLOADED COMPUTER SOFTWARE

<u>McGraw-Hill Bibliomaker</u>. Vers. 1. 27 Feb. 2003 <http://novella.mhhe.com/sites/
0070400555/student_view0/research-999/bibliomaker.html>.

Other Sources: Print and Nonprint (Includes Online Versions)

This section includes examples of traditional print sources, as well as multimedia sources not covered elsewhere in this chapter. If you find one of the sources
in this section online, follow the model for the source, giving whatever additional
information is available for the online source. Be sure to end all your citations for
online material with the date of access and the URL.

53. ADVERTISEMENT

When citing an advertisement, give the name of the product, company, or institution. Follow it with *Advertisement* (not in quotation marks or underlined).
Finish the citation with the usual publication information.

Cartier. Advertisement. <u>Vanity Fair</u> May 2000: 45.

54. CARTOON OR COMIC STRIP

State the name of the cartoonist or comic strip artist. Follow the name with the
title of the cartoon or comic strip (if any), in quotation marks, and either *Cartoon*
or *Comic strip* (not in quotation marks or underlined). Finish the citation with
the usual publication information.

Johnston, Lynn. "For Better or for Worse." Comic strip. <u>Star-Ledger</u> [Newark, NJ] 16
Apr. 2002: 44.
Litton, Drew. "Forsberg's All Over the Map." Cartoon. <u>Rocky Mountain News</u> 13 Feb.
2003. 26 Feb. 2003 <http://cfapp.rockymountainnews.com/drew/
index.cfm?Month=2&ID=262&year=2003>.

Note that you should include the city of publication for locally published newspapers unless the location appears in the title.

55. DISSERTATION—ABSTRACT

Begin with the author's name, followed by the title of the dissertation in quotation marks. Then type the abbreviation *Diss.* and the name of the university at which the dissertation was written, followed by the date of its completion. End with the abbreviation, *DA* or *DAI* (*Dissertation Abstracts* or *Dissertation Abstracts International*), followed by the volume, the year of publication, and the page number.

> O'Brien, Jeremiah J., II. "Community College Chief Instructional Officers: An
> Exploratory Study." Diss. U of Oregon, 1996. <u>DAI</u> 57/09 (1996): 3790A.

56. DISSERTATION—PUBLISHED

Treat a published dissertation as a book. However, add the abbreviation *Diss.* after the title, as well as the name of the university that granted the doctorate and the year the dissertation was completed. End with the publication information as usual.

> Edwards, Flora Mancuso. <u>The Theater of the Black
> Diaspora: A Comparative Study of Black Drama in
> Brazil, Cuba, and the United States</u>. Diss. New York
> U, 1975. Ann Arbor: Xerox U Microfilms, 1987.

NOTE
The year the dissertation was accepted is 1975; the year it was published in book form is 1987.

To cite a master's thesis, substitute *MA thesis* or *MS thesis* for *Diss.*

57. DISSERTATION—UNPUBLISHED

Begin with the author's name, followed by the title of the dissertation, in quotation marks. Then type the abbreviation *Diss.* as well as the name of the university that granted the doctorate and the year that the dissertation was completed.

> Dann, Emily. "An Experimental Pre-Statistics Curriculum for Two-Year College
> Students." Diss. Rutgers U, 1976.

58. GOVERNMENT PUBLICATION

Ordinarily, the government (whether federal, state, or municipal) is considered the author of such works. After typing the name of the government, type the name of the specific agency that published the work.

> New Jersey. Div. of Youth and Family Services. <u>Children at Risk 1995-96</u>. Trenton: NJ
> Div. of Youth and Family Services, 1998.
> United States. Bureau of the Census. <u>Historical Statistics of the United States:
> Colonial Times to 1970</u>. Bicentennial ed. Washington: GPO, 1975.

59. LECTURE OR ADDRESS

Begin with the speaker's name, followed by the title of the presentation, in quotation marks, and the name of the sponsoring organization. End with the place and date of the presentation.

Partopillo, Alessandro. "Giotto and the Dawn of the Italian Renaissance." Art League
of Madison, Madison, OR. 8 May 1999.

60. PLAY—LIVE PERFORMANCE

Begin with the title of the play, followed by the name of its author. Next, indicate
the names of the director and the principal performers. End with the name of the
theater, its location, and the date of the performance you saw.

The Iceman Cometh. By Eugene O'Neill. Dir. Howard Davies. Perf. Kevin Spacey and
Tony Danza. Brooks Atkinson Theater, New York. 22 June 1999.

61. MAP OR CHART

When citing a map or chart, treat it as you would an anonymous book, but add
the label *Map* or *Chart*.

The Inca: An Empire and Its Ancestors. Map. Washington: National Geographic, 2002.
"Denver, Colorado." Map. Mapquest. 27 Feb. 2003 <http://www.mapquest.com>.

62. A MOTION PICTURE, DVD, OR VIDEOCASSETTE

Moulin Rouge. Dir. Baz Luhrmann. Perf. Nicole Kidman, Ewan McGregor, John
Leguizamo, and Jim Broadbent. 20th Century Fox, 2001.

Cite a DVD or videocassette as you would a film, but include the original release
date and the medium, each followed by a period.

Billy Elliot. Dir. Stephen Daldry. Perf. Julie Walters and Jamie Bell. DVD. Universal, 2000.
Grand Hotel. Dir. Edmund Goulding. Perf. Greta Garbo, John Barrymore, Joan Crawford,
Wallace Beery, and Lionel Barrymore. 1932. Videocassette. Turner, 1989.

63. PAMPHLET

As with a book, begin the entry with the author's name, if known. If the author
is unknown, begin with the title of the pamphlet.

Webrogan, Signe I. Projections of the Population of States by Age, Sex, and Race:
1989-2010. Washington: GPO, 1990.

64. PERSONAL INTERVIEW

Morgan, James. Personal interview. 17 Jan 2002.

65. PERSONAL LETTER

Begin with the writer's name, followed by *Letter to the author* and the date.

Christian, David. Letter to the author. 2 May 2002.

66. PUBLISHED INTERVIEW

Begin with the name of the person interviewed. Follow with the title of the interview, if any, in quotation marks. If the title of the interview does not include

the word *interview* or if the interview has no title, simply type the word *Interview* after the subject's name.

Johnson, Paul. "Live with TAE: Interview with Paul Johnson." <u>American Enterprise</u> Sept./Oct. 1998: 20-23.

67. RADIO OR TELEVISION INTERVIEW

Begin with the name of the person interviewed, followed by the word *Interview*. Then include the title of the program (underlined). End with the name of the network and city, and the date the program was aired.

Bush, George W. Interview. <u>Hardball</u>. NBC. WNBC, New York. 29 June 1999.

Sills, Beverly Interview. <u>Charlie Rose</u>. PBS. WNET, New York. 26 Apr. 2002.

68. RADIO OR TELEVISION PROGRAM

If you are drawing information from a titled episode of a program, begin with the title of that episode, in quotation marks. If not, begin with the name of the program (underlined). Then indicate the name of the host, narrator, or director, if available. Next, type the name of the network, the local station and city (if any), and the date of the broadcast.

"The Great Chain." <u>The American Revolution</u>. Host William Curtis. History Channel. 3 July 1999.

"Bush Grows Impatient on Iraq Issue." <u>Crossfire</u> CNN. 18 Feb. 2003. Transcript. 26 Feb. 2003 <http://www.cnn.com/TRANSCRIPTS/0302/18/cf.00.html>.

69. SONG LYRIC

Midler, Bette, and Marc Shaiman. "Nobody Else but You." <u>Bette</u>. Warner Bros., 2000.

70. SOUND RECORDING

Abbado, Claudio, cond. Symphony no. 9 in D minor, op. 125. By Ludwig van Beethoven. Vienna Philharmonic. Deutsche Grammophon, 1987.

NOTE

For recordings, the person you list first depends on which one you wish to emphasize.

Callas, Maria. "La mamma morta." By Umberto Giordano. Rec. 1955. <u>La Divina 3</u>. EMI, 1994.

Eaglen, Jane. "Un bel di vedremo." By Giacomo Puccini. <u>Jane Eaglen: Italian Opera Arias</u>. Sony, 2001.

Flaherty, Stephen, and Lynn Aherns. <u>Ragtime: The Musical</u>. Orch. William David Brohn. Perf. Brian Stokes Mitchell, Marin Mazzie, and Audra McDonald. Cond. David Loud. BMG, 1998.

Slatkin, Leonard, cond. Symphony no. 1. By John Corigliano. National Symphony Orchestra. RCA Victor, 1996.

Verdi, Giuseppe. <u>La Traviata</u>. Perf. Ileana Cotrubas, Placido Domingo, and Sherrill Milnes. Bayerisches Staatsorchester. Cond. Carlos Kleiber. Deutsche Grammophon, 1977.

71. WORK OF ART

Begin with the artist's name, if known, followed by the title of the work (underlined). Next, type the name of the institution and the city in which the work is housed. To indicate when the work was created, add the date immediately after the title.

Hopper, Edward. <u>Nighthawks</u>. Art Institute, Chicago.

Hockney, David. <u>A Bigger Splash</u>. 1967. Tate Gallery, London. <u>Sister Wendy's 1000 Masterpieces</u>. By Sister Wendy Beckett. New York: DK, 1999. 207.

Rousseau, Henri. <u>The Dream</u>. 1910. Museum of Mod. Art, New York. 27 Feb. 2003 <http://www.moma.org/collection/depts/paint_sculpt/blowups/paint_sculpt_010.html>.

EXERCISE 15A

Preparing a Works-Cited List

Using the source information given below, prepare a properly formatted works-cited list:

1. A book entitled *Dreams of a Final Theory* written by Steven Weinberg. The book was published in 1992 by Pantheon in New York.

2. An article written by Charles Krauthammer entitled "A Social Conservative Credo." The article appeared on pages 274–280 in a collection of articles called *Reading and Writing across the Curriculum,* edited by Laurence Behrens and Lincoln J. Rosen. The book, currently in its seventh edition, was published in 2000 in New York by Longman.

3. An article written by Mary Louise Pratt entitled "Humanities for the Future: Reflections on the Western Cultural Debate at Stanford." The article appeared on pages. 7–25 of the journal *South Atlantic Quarterly,* volume 89, published in 1990.

4. An article that appeared in the April 8, 2002, issue of *Newsweek*. The article, entitled "Israel and the Bush Doctrine," was written by George F. Will and appeared on page 64.

5. An article by Laurence K. Altman entitled "New Ideas to Help AIDS Orphans," which appeared on page A15 of the February 5, 2001 issue of the *New York Times.*

6. An article by Francis L. Jackson entitled "Mexican Freedom: The Idea of an Indigenous State." The article appeared in the 1997 issue of the journal *Animus,* volume 2, issue 3. The article was retrieved on April 4, 2002, from the Internet at <http://www.mun.ca/animus/1997vol2/jackson2.htm>.

7. An unsigned article that appeared on page A3 of the August 20, 1984, issue of the *Philadelphia Inquirer,* entitled "Report Says Crisis in Teaching Looms."

8. A book entitled *The Rhetoric of Laughter: The Best and Worst of Humor Night* written by Hans P. Guth, Gabriele L. Rico, John Ruszkiewicz, and Bill Bridges. The book was published in 1996 by Harcourt in Fort Worth.

15.4 Study a student's research paper.

The following is a research paper written by Suzanne Mastronardo, a student in a first-year composition class. Review it carefully.

↑
1″
↓

Suzanne Mastronardo

Professor Nicolai

English 122

June 5, 2003

Educating Language-Minority Students:

Bilingual Education vs. Immersion

←1/2″→Over the past several decades, there has been consider-

able debate over the subject of bilingual education. In fact,

the word *lingual* has been joined with so many prefixes that it

is difficult to remember what the initial debate was all about.

Individuals on both sides of the issue claim their argument to

be on the side of "right," with those in favor of bilingual educa-

tion at times referring to their opponents as "anti-immigrant" or

"racially insensitive" (Steinberg). If we truly desire to provide

the best possible education for all of our students, then we

must be willing to soften the rhetoric and to put aside agendas

and look at results. Indeed, the challenge is to teach

language-minority students (LMS) English while at the same

time maintaining the integrity of the students' native language.

In the United States, bilingual education dates back to be-

fore the middle of the nineteenth century. As Lopez points out:

In the public schools of many states between

1839 and 1880--including Ohio, Louisiana, and

New Mexico--German, French, and Spanish were

↑
1″
↓

Margin annotations:

Essay double-spaced throughout.

← 1″ →

← 1″ →

Source unpaginated, so no page numbers included.

Thesis stated at end of introduction.

Signal phrase used to introduce quotation.

Quotations longer than 4 lines indented 1″ from left margin.

← 1″ →

Mastronardo 2

used for instruction. Between 1880 and 1917,

German-English bilingual schools, in which both

languages were used for instruction, operated in

Ohio, Minnesota, and Maryland.

However, bilingual education was brought to the fore in 1968,

when Congress passed the Bilingual Education Act, ruling

that language-minority students must be given the opportunity

for an education equal to that of their English-speaking peers.

As Ryan and Cooper point out, in 1974, the US Supreme

Court, in Lau v. Nichols, found "that there is no equality of

treatment merely by providing students with the same facili-

ties, textbooks, teachers, and curriculum; for students who are

effectively foreclosed from any meaningful education (96)."

Subsequently, the US Office of Civil Rights developed guide-

lines for bilingual education, which stated that LMS should be

taught academics in their first language until they could effec-

tively benefit from English-language instruction. In contrast,

the immersion method of educating LMS initially places the

priority on teaching the students English by "immersing" them

in English, with a teacher who understands their first lan-

guage but instructs them mostly in English (94-96).

California passed Proposition 227 in 1998, placing

severe restrictions on bilingual education programs. In sharp

contrast to the previously established guidelines, the new

Source unpaginated, so no page numbers included.

Historical overview provided using narrative method of paragraph development (see pp. 65–66).

Mastronardo 3

California legislation stated that "all children in California

Material quoted in
Gandara et al.
indicated in citation.
public schools shall be taught English by being taught in

English" (qtd. in Gandara et al.). Proposition 227 blazed a

unique trail in education reform, as it was "the first time that

the public had been asked to vote on a specific pedagogical

strategy for educating children" (Gandara et al.). A resulting

debate has raged regarding the best way to educate LMS.

The US Census projected that by the year 2000, there

would be 39.5 million non-English-language-background

(NELB) individuals in the United States, and the rate of in-

crease for NELB groups is expected to rise by 96% between

1995 and 2020 (Snetzler and Qualls 564). And some experts

Deleted material
indicated by ellipsis
("...") to show
student responsible
for cut.
say that "by the 2030s . . . English-Language-Learners (ELLs)

will account for approximately 40% of the entire school-aged

population in the United States" (Roseberry-McKibbin and

Brice). Presently, NELB students make up approximately 25%

of California's total student population (Mora 345), and New

York City's bilingual program "educates nearly one in six pub-

lic school students" (Steinberg).

California's abrupt switch from bilingual to immersion

forms of education was passed by an overwhelming vote. The

new law required that instruction must be "overwhelmingly in

English" (McMahon and Watson-Gegeo), but it allowed for the

use of students' native language "when a student had trouble

Mastronardo 4

understanding a concept or was emotionally distressed and
needed comforting or counseling" (Chavez)

The years since Proposition 227 was passed have
proved to be interesting, especially for Proposition 227's proponents, as California's test scores have shown substantial increases in all subject areas. The most dramatic increases can
be seen when comparing individual districts. For example, in
Oceanside, reading scores for limited-English-proficient students in the second grade went from the 12th percentile to the
32nd percentile, while math scores went from the 18th percentile to the 47th percentile. In Santa Barbara, the reading
scores for the same age group went from the "14th to the 39th
percentile, math scores from the 19th to the 40th percentile,
and language scores from the 13th to the 34th percentile." In
comparison, in Santa Ana, where officials "refused to imple-
ment the program," the reading and language scores for the
second-graders "went up only slightly from the 17th and 16th
percentiles, respectively, to the 22nd percentile" (Chavez).

However, the primary method of administering tests in
English to determine academic progress seems unfair to
many. For example, Kenji Hakuta, a professor at Stanford and
"one of the most prominent proponents of bilingual education
in the nation, told reporters that the scores were meaningless
because the tests themselves were designed for native

Facts, quotations used to support topic sentence (see p. 100).

Mastronardo 5

English speakers" (Chavez). If such is the case, as Chavez points out, "that should make Oceanside's [and] Santa Barbara's . . . impressive gains even more compelling."

Word added included in brackets ("[and]").

Comparison-contrast method of paragraph development used to support claim that immersion more effective than bilingual ed. (see pp. 68–69).

As California seems to be making some progress in teaching English to NELB students, New York City's bilingual program has come under close scrutiny due to grim statistics. In his article entitled "The Secret to Becoming Bilingual," John Tierney points out that "most kindergartners who start in a bilingual program are still there in second grade. After four years of bilingual education, a third still aren't ready for main stream classes. After nine years, 17 percent are still stuck."

One could look to the story of Elva Alvarez for a comparison of bilingual education and immersion. Alvarez came to the United States as a third-grader from the Dominican Republic and was placed in a bilingual program at the public school near where she lived.

Illustration method of paragraph development used here (see p. 68).

Direct quotation within block quotation indicated by quotation marks.

> "They taught reading in English, but the rest of the classes were all in Spanish," she said. "My parents were really worried because I wasn't learning English." After two years in the public school, her parents moved her to St. Rose of Lima [a Roman Catholic grammar school on West 164th Street]. What was her English like at that point, after two years of bilingual education in the public schools? . . .

Identifying comments by student author in brackets.

Ellipsis used in block quotation to show deletion.

Mastronardo 6

"At first, I couldn't understand what the teacher was saying. I was, like, really confused. By the end of the year, my English was a million times better than at the start, but it still wasn't perfect. But then the next year it got a lot better. Now I feel I know more words in English than Spanish." (Tierney)

Note period at end of block quotation comes before reference (in parentheses).

St. Rose of Lima still uses the traditional immersion technique. Joyce Oberthal, who has taught there for fourteen years, "begins each school year with a kindergarten class composed mainly of children who cannot speak English (qtd. in Tierney)." But she says the students learn quickly.

Short quotation (less than 4 lines) integrated into paragraph.

"We haven't been in school quite six weeks, but already the kids can carry on a limited conversation and follow fairly complicated directions." By the end of a typical year, Miss Oberthal said, virtually all the kindergartners are able to converse. "There might be one or two who are struggling to speak English, but even they can understand a lot. They just haven't made the leap to speaking it yet. They do that the next year. By the end of the first year it's very difficult to tell who came in speaking Spanish and who didn't." (qtd. in Tierney)

Authoritative quotation used to support claim that children learn English more quickly through immersion (see p. 100).

On the West Coast, a similar story is being told. Christian Dominguez, a seven-year-old boy from Mexico,

Mastronardo 7

enrolled in a public school in Oceanside, California. According
to Chavez, in just nine months, he "went from speaking not a
word of English to being able to read whole books about dinosaurs, all in English."

Problems with
immersion method
acknowledged here
and below (see
pp. 106–107).

    Some would argue that Alvarez and Dominguez are ac-
tually at a disadvantage. Indeed, acculturation, in which "im-
migrant students acquire the culture of their host country
without being forced to give up their affinity with their home
culture" is at the heart of the philosophy of bilingual education. Supporters feel that bilingual programs not only provide
language support but also provide bilingual role models and
"send a message that cultural diversity is honored and val-
ued in American society" (Mora 350). A California bilingual
teacher expressed her concern that "most teachers want to
Anglicize the kids as rapidly as possible, replacing Spanish
with English." In addition, many fear that immersing children
in English delegitimizes students' native languages, as well
as their heritages, and thereby harms their self-identity and
self-esteem (McMahon and Watson-Gegeo).

    Bilingual teachers play a key role in relation to the social
messages NELB students may receive in the classroom.
California's bilingual teachers have had to make enormous
changes in their teaching styles since the passage of
Proposition 227. Many have reported feeling "frustrated by not

Mastronardo 8

being able to use the full range of skills they possessed to in-
struct their English learners" (Gandara et al.), and teaching

Facts, statistics,
quotations used
to support topic
sentence (see
p. 100).

staffs have suffered low morale (McMahon and Watson-
Gegeo). However, a study conducted in a rural California
school with 45% Spanish-speaking students during the first
year of Proposition 227 implementation painted a more trou-
bling picture. Several teachers reported psychological strain,
and one expressed that limiting the use of the Spanish language in the classroom left her feeling "immoral, unprofes-
sional, and even cruel" (qtd. in McMahon and Watson-
Gegeo). Teachers experienced great stress and strain as they
spent a much greater amount of time preparing lessons to
satisfy the new requirements. And possibly the most significant effect on the teaching staff was the fear of using
Spanish, which may have been unconsciously communicated
to students, thereby sending a negative message about the
students' native language. In fact, McMahon and Watson-
Gegeo write that "studies have demonstrated the negative impact on language-minority children's self-esteem and academic success when their primary language and culture are
treated as inferior or prohibited in the classroom."

McMahon and Watson-Gegeo further point out that researchers recognize the fact that immersion is effectively
teaching English to California's NELB students, but of con-

Mastronardo 9

cern is the "cost of acquiring these language skills, and the long-term educational outcomes for students." The teachers in the above-mentioned study reported that although students were learning "a great deal of English," they were also losing their Spanish. This illustrates a possibly negative effect of immersion: subtractive bilingualism, in which the student learns English but does not enhance his or her native language in the process. Ironically, the study mentions the fact that parents expressed a desire to see their children achieve English fluency more quickly than the bilingual program had done but later complained that their children were not developing their Spanish in the immersion program.

Another danger of immersion is semi-lingualism, in which a child acquires both his native language and English inadequately (Marsh, Hau, and Kong). In 1994, a study of New York City public school bilingual students found that semi-lingualism was occurring, and children were learning neither English nor their native languages well (Steinberg). Researchers have found that semi-lingualism is a result of an individual's having no positive identification with any culture (Marsh, Hau, and Kong).

Preserving one's native language is vital, researchers argue, for cognitive, psychological, and social reasons. For example, New York's Board of Education statistics show:

Mastronardo 10

that those students who do manage to successfully complete bilingual or English-as-a-second-
language programs do better on English Regents
exams, for example, than all other students.
Students who pass bilingual programs also have
a higher graduation rate (77.4 percent) than all
other students who receive a mainstream education (66.1 percent), though critics say that those
who exit bilingual programs fastest are high
achieving to begin with. (Steinberg)

Another study showed that "when bilingual education is done
well, children who develop literacy and other cognitive skills in
their first language before being required to learn a second
language do much better in school than children submerged
in a second language" (McMahon and Watson-Gegeo).

Opposition addressed
(see pp. 106–107).

Unfortunately, bilingual education is not always "done
well." Finding certified bilingual teachers has been a nation-
wide problem. In New York City, only one in three bilingual
teachers at the junior high school level is certified (Holloway).
According to 1999 National Center for Education statistics, although 54% of public school teachers had LEP students, only
20% felt well prepared to teach them (Mora 356).

Page number not
included because
source only one page
long.

As McMahon and Watson-Gegeo have pointed out,
"there is a very strong belief that linguistic rights are a funda-

Mastronardo 11

mental human right." In fact, some have even dared to compare California's bilingual education limitations to Hitler's "ethnic cleansing" strategy of limiting the use of the Yiddish language. Further, some advocates for bilingual education view the issue as an attempt by "socially powerful, mainstream white American groups" to exert their power over the weaker classes, for "whoever controls the language in which the children must learn also controls who the children become, and may control as well, for good or ill, whether children can succeed at school." On the other hand, predictions about the effects of immersion techniques range from higher drop-out rates to higher crime rates for NELB people.

As complicated a political issue as this may be, most people simply want to provide the education that is ultimately going to have the greatest benefits for NELB students. Unfortunately, disentangling authoritative studies from common sense, as well as special-interest groups' agendas from the true desires of parents, is one of the biggest challenges ahead for education decision makers.

Introduction recalled in concluding paragraph (see p. 80).

↑
1"
↓

Mastronardo 12

Works Cited

← 1" → Chavez, Linda. "Uneducated Bilingualism: Why Latinos Should

←1/2"→ Oppose Bilingual Education." <u>Hispanic Magazine</u> 2 Feb.

2001. 2 pp. 3 Apr. 2001 <http://www.hispaniconline.

com/pol&opi/opinion/conbil.html>.

Gandara, Patricia, et al. "The Initial Impact of Proposition 227

on the Instruction of English Learners." <u>UC LMRI</u>. UC

Linguistic Minority Research Institute, Education Policy

Center, U of California, Davis. Apr. 2000. 38 pp. 4 Apr.

2001 <http://www.usc.edu/dept/education/CMMR/227/

lmri227report.pdf>.

Holloway, Lynette. "Immersion Promoted as an Alternative to

Bilingual Education." <u>New York Times</u> 17 Oct. 2000: B1.

Lopez, Richard V. "Bilingual Education: Separating Fact from

Fiction." <u>NABE Report</u> 18 Sept. 1995. 6 pp.

<http://www.ncbe.gwu.edu/miscpubs/nabe/fact.htm>.

Marsh, Herbert W., Kit-Tai Hau, and Chit-Kwong Kong. "Late   ← 1"   →

Immersion and Language of Instruction in Hong Kong

Schools: Achievement Growth in Language and

Nonlanguage Subjects." <u>Harvard Educational Review</u>

70.3 (2000). 7 pp. 5 Mar. 2001 <http://

edweb.macarthur. uws.edu.au/self/f00marsh.htm>.

McMahon, Maureen, and Karen A. Watson-Gegeo. "Research

on the Initial Implementation of Proposition 227." UC

↑
1"
↓

Mastronardo 13

LMRI Publications: Final Grant Reports. 31 May 2000.

19 pp. 6 Mar 2001 <http://www.lmrinet.ucsb.edu/

researchactivities/mcmahon.htm>.

Mora, Jill Kerper. "Staying the Course in Times of Change:

Preparing Teachers for Language Minority Education."

Journal of Teacher Education 51 (2000): 345–57.

Roseberry-McKibbin, Celeste, and Alejandro Brice. "Acquiring

English as a Second Language." ASHA Leader 5.12

(2000): 4 pp. Academic Search Premier. EBSCOhost.

Middlesex County College Library, Edison, N.J. 24 Nov.

2001 <http://search.epnet.com>.

Ryan, Kevin, and James M. Cooper. Those Who Can, Teach.

8th ed. New York: Houghton, 1998.

Snetzler, Suzi, and Audrey L. Qualls. "Examination of

Differential Item Functioning on a Standardized

Achievement Battery with Limited English Proficient

Students." Educational and Psychological Measurement

60 (2000): 564-77.

Steinberg, Jacques. "Answers to an English Question." New

York Times on the Web 22 Oct. 2000. 4 pp. 5 Mar. 2001

<http://www.nytimescom/2000/10/22/answers.html>.

Tierney, John. "The Secret to Becoming Bilingual." New York

Times on the Web 17 Oct. 2000. 2 pp. 5 Mar. 2001 <http://

www.nytimes.com/2000/10/17/nyregion/secret.html>.

Total length of work indicated when work unpaginated.

Name of database, service, and host library provided for items from library subscription service.

Book titles underlined.

All works cited included in list.

Title of Web site included.

Date posted, total number of pages, date accessed, and URL given.

URL included; note URLs can be broken at slashes or dots.

Chapter Checklist

1 ⋮· **Reference** your research material usually by placing the last name of the author and the page number in parentheses after a quotation, summary, or paraphrase. If the author is unknown, use the full title or a shortened version of the title of the source and the page number in parentheses.

2 ⋮· **Prepare** a bibliography card, listing all the necessary information for each source from which you have taken information.

3 ⋮· **Arrange** the bibliography cards in alphabetical order by the last name of the author or by the first major word of the title if no author is named. Use these cards as the basis of your list of works cited, which follows the conclusion of your essay.

4 ⋮· **Check** to be sure that every source mentioned in your paper appears in your works-cited list and that every source that appears in your works-cited list is mentioned in your paper.

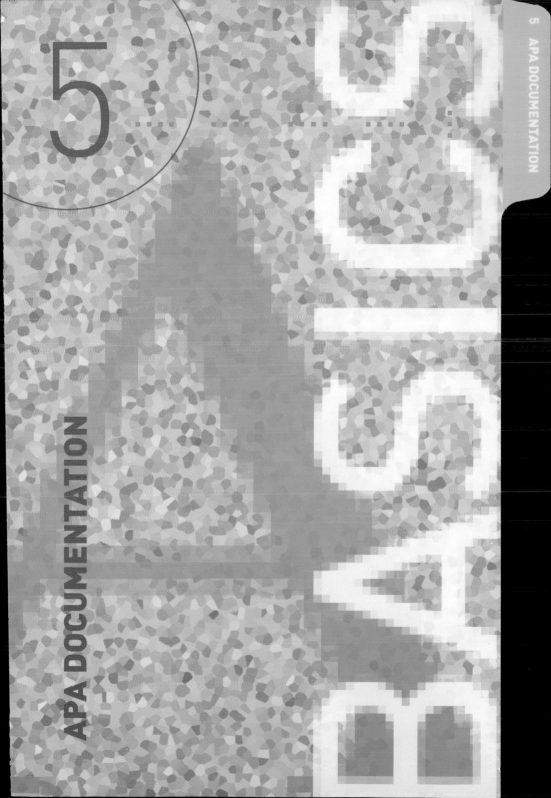

5

APA DOCUMENTATION

5

16

WRITING THE RESEARCH PAPER USING APA FORMAT

In Chapter 15, you learned the documentation style of the Modern Language Association. This chapter describes the documentation style of the American Psychological Association (APA). The formats described here come from the fifth edition of the *Publication Manual of the American Psychological Association,* published in 2001.

These formats are used primarily in the social sciences and related courses, such as anthropology, education, political science, psychology, sociology, and various business courses. The basic difference between the MLA and APA styles is that the APA style places the date of publication in the parenthetical citation so that the reader can tell at a glance how current the information is.

■■■■   ■■■■   **BASICLINK** ■■■■   ■■■■
WWW

To learn more about using APA format, visit:
http://owl.english.purdue.edu/handouts/research/r_apa.html

■■   ■■   ■■   ■■   ■■   ■■   ■■   ■■   ■■   ■■   ■■   ■■

16.1 Learn how to place researched material into a paper.

1. SUMMARIZED OR PARAPHRASED MATERIAL

In most cases, the easiest way to cite summarized or paraphrased material is with a parenthetical citation that contains the last name of the author and the year of publication of the source from which you took the information. In the following example, the student has paraphrased information from an article written by S. I. Hayakawa:

In relation to their son Mark, who was afflicted with Down syndrome, the Hayakawas were told the best thing they could do was to place him in an institution where he could be cared for properly (Hayakawa, 1995).

Note that a comma separates the author's last name and the year of publication. The period that ends the sentence appears *after* the closing parenthesis.

2. DIRECT QUOTATION WITH THE AUTHOR'S LAST NAME IN THE TEXT OF YOUR PAPER

It is a good idea to introduce the material, including a direct quotation, with the author's last name. In the following example, the direct quotation from an article by S. I. Hayakawa has been placed into the text. Since the quotation from Hayakawa is a complete sentence, the student has set it off from his own writing with a colon.

In response to the generally accepted advice that children born with Down syndrome be institutionalized, Hayakawa (1995) has written: "Fortunately Mark was born at a time when a whole generation of parents of retarded children had begun to question the accepted dogmas about retardation" (p. 106).

The year of publication appears in parentheses after the author's name in the **signal phrase** (see Chapter 15, page 216, for a discussion of signal phrases). Because the passage contains a direct quotation, the abbreviation *p.* (for "page") and the page number of the quotation follow in parentheses.

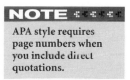

NOTE
APA style requires page numbers when you include direct quotations.

3. DIRECT QUOTATION WITHOUT THE AUTHOR'S LAST NAME IN THE TEXT OF YOUR PAPER

You can introduce a direct quotation without mentioning the author's name. If you do that, however, remember to put the author's last name, the year of publication, and the page number from which the quotation was taken in parentheses at the end of the quotation.

As one writer has pointed out, "today, genetic counseling is available to guide parents as to the probability of recurrence on a scientific basis" (Hayakawa, 1995, p. 108).

In the original quotation, the word *today* was capitalized; however, APA format allows you to change the first letter of the first word of a quotation to an uppercase or a lowercase letter. Note that commas separate the elements of the citation.

4. DIRECT QUOTATION AS PART OF YOUR OWN SENTENCE

To make a direct quotation part of your own sentence, you don't have to set off the quotation with punctuation. Just combine it with your own words naturally, as in the next example. But don't forget the quotation marks.

After all, as in many other areas, the "one-size-fits-all approach" will not prove effective in the classroom (McKeon, 1998, p. 498).

5. DIRECT QUOTATION OF FORTY OR MORE WORDS

If you are including a direct quotation of forty or more words, indent it five spaces or half an inch from the left margin. This format is called a **block quotation.**

> In "Our Son Mark," Hayakawa (1995) discusses the problems the family faced in dealing with their son's mental retardation:
>
>> There are different degrees of retardation, just as there are different kinds of brain damage. No two retarded children are exactly alike in all respects. Institutional care *does* turn out to be the best answer for some kinds of retarded children or some family situations. The point is that one observes and reacts to the *specific* case and circumstances rather than to the generalization. (p. 106)

Note that in the preceding example no quotation marks are used because the indented format tells the readers that you are quoting directly from a source. (Quotation marks would be used only around quoted material that appears within the block quotation.) Note, too, that the page number appears in parentheses *after* the end punctuation.

6. SOURCE WITH NO AUTHOR GIVEN

If no author is given for a source from which you took information, place a shortened title of the source, followed by a comma and the year of publication, in the parentheses.

> According to one source, political beliefs can have an influence even on theories concerning mental retardation ("Mental Retardation," 1996).

7. SELECTION IN AN ANTHOLOGY

When referring to a selection in an anthology, reference the author, not the editor of the anthology.

> According to Frappier (1959), the source of Chretien de Troyes's understanding of courtly love came from the troubadours.

8. MATERIAL FROM TWO OR MORE WORKS AT THE SAME TIME

When naming two or more works *by different authors* in the same parentheses, list them in the order in which they appear in the reference list, separated by a semicolon.

> Two studies (Frampton, 1997; Lapidus, 1998) examined the placement of Down syndrome children in the traditional classroom.

When naming two or more works *by the same author,* list them according to the year of publication. Use the author's last name with only the first reference; for each of the subsequent ones, give only the date.

A number of more recent studies (Hollister, 1999, 2000) continued to examine the placement of Down syndrome children in the traditional classroom.

When naming two or more works *by the same author published in the same year,* list them by using the letters *a, b, c,* and so on after the year. These letters are also attached to the works in the reference list, where the works are listed alphabetically according to the first major word in the title (see page 265).

Several studies (Polaski, 2001a, 2001b, 2001c; Guaranino, 2002a, 2002b) have indicated that mainstreaming Down syndrome students has been extremely effective.

9. INTERNET SOURCE

When naming an Internet source, use the author's last name or a short title if no author is given. Include the date of publication or update of the source. If no date is indicated in the source, use *n.d.* ("no date").

In a rather tongue-in-cheek opening to his review, Orr (2003) maintains that, in a democracy, one has the right to dislike poetry for any reason whatsoever without being condemned.

10. WORK WITH TWO AUTHORS

When referencing a source that has two authors, use the last names of both authors joined by an ampersand (&) if the names are used in a parenthetical reference or by *and* if they are used in a signal phrase.

Parenthetical Reference

In their introduction, the authors (Bynum & Thompson, 2002) posit that many will be able to relate to the text because "the book is about young people . . . not much younger than most of the college students who will be reading the book" (p. 1).

Signal Phrase

In the introduction, Bynum and Thompson (2002) posit that many will be able to relate to the text because "the book is about young people . . . not much younger than most of the college students who will be reading the book" (p. 1).

11. WORK WITH THREE TO FIVE AUTHORS

When referencing for the first time a source that has three to five authors, use the last names of all the authors. In a parenthetical reference, use an ampersand; in a signal phrase, use *and* before the final name.

Parenthetical Reference

As a result of their study, the authors maintain that teachers still need a greater understanding of learning disabilities (Winn, Umphlett, Lane, & Bruno, 2003).

Signal Phrase

Winn, Umphlett, Lane, and Bruno (2003) maintain that teachers still need a greater understanding of learning disabilities.

In subsequent references, use the first author's last name followed by *et al.* (meaning "and others") in either the signal phrase or the parenthetical reference. No comma follows the author's last name.

12. WORK WITH SIX OR MORE AUTHORS

When you reference a work by six or more authors, use only the first author's last name followed by *et al.* in the signal phrase or in the parenthetical citation.

The study proved to be a long and exhausting one, since there were over 400 taped interviews with individuals who survived the attack on the World Trade Center, and they had to be catalogued before they could be analyzed (O'Brien et al., 2002).

13. QUOTATION TO WHICH YOU HAVE ADDED MATERIAL OR FROM WHICH YOU HAVE DELETED MATERIAL

When you delete something from a quotation, indicate you have done so by inserting ellipsis points (three spaced periods), with a space before and after. When you add something to a quotation, place the addition in brackets.

As Gorman (2002) has pointed out:

The initial shock of Sept. 11 has worn off . . . but millions of Americans continue to share a kind of generalized mass anxiety. A recent Time/CNN poll found that eight months after the event [May 2002], nearly two-thirds of Americans think about the terror attack at least several times a week. (p. 46)

14. PERSONAL COMMUNICATION

A personal communication can be a letter, a memorandum, an e-mail, an interview, a telephone conversation, and the like. Because such communications usually cannot be recovered, they are not included in the reference list. Rather, they are cited only in the text of the paper. When you do so, provide the initials as well as the last name of the communicator, the phrase *personal communication,* and as exact a date as possible.

Needless to say, he was as surprised as anyone at the progress his brother made when he was mainstreamed, since they had all been told there was a chance that his brother would encounter even more difficulties (L. M. Doll, personal communication, November 29, 2003).

16.1a Use notes with parenthetical documentation.

Content footnotes can be used as an addition to the essay, providing details that can make your essay stronger. However, they should be short and used sparingly.

To indicate these notes, place a superscript (small, raised) arabic numeral at the appropriate place in your text, and write the information after a matching numeral at the end of the text. Type these notes double-spaced on a separate page before the reference list. Indent the first line of each numbered note five spaces or half an inch. Center the title *Footnotes* at the top of the page.

16.2   Learn how to prepare a reference list.

To make sure information in a reference list is accurate, refer to your bibliography cards or computerized reference list (see section 15.3a).

16.2a   Learn the pattern of a reference list.

1. Entries are listed alphabetically by the last name of the author or by the first major word of the title if there is no author named. If there is more than one work by the same author, the entries are arranged by date, with the earliest appearing first. If works by the same author appeared in the same year, the entries are arranged alphabetically by title, with the lowercase letters *a*, *b*, and so forth after the year within the parentheses, for example (2002a).

2. As in MLA style, the author's last name appears first. However, unlike MLA style, initials rather than full first names are used. When you have more than one author for an entry, use an ampersand (&) before the last name rather than the word *and*. Invert the names of all authors.

3. Separate the names with commas (unless there are only two). If there are more than six authors, list the first six authors and follow the last name with *et al.* to indicate that there are more authors.

4. Begin the first line of each entry flush with the left margin, indent subsequent lines five spaces or half an inch (called a **hanging indent**), and double-space throughout.

5. Italicize (APA style preference) or underline the titles and subtitles of books. Capitalize only the first word of titles and subtitles and any proper nouns. Use upper- and lowercase for the names of periodicals, and italicize them. Do not use quotation marks around the titles of articles.

16.2b   Review sample entries for a reference list.

Books

1. BOOK BY A SINGLE AUTHOR

> Preston, R. (2002). *The demon in the freezer: A true story.* New York: Random.

NOTE

Use *n.d.*, the abbreviation for "no date" for works with no available publication date.

Elements of the Preceding Entry

Preston, R.   The author's last name, a comma, the initial of the author's first name, and a period.

(2002).	The year of publication, in parentheses, followed by a period.
The demon in the freezer: A true story.	The title of the book, italicized, followed by a period. Only the first word of the title, the word after a colon, and proper nouns are capitalized.
New York:	The place of publication, followed by a colon.
Random (House).	The publisher of the book, followed by a period. Note that you can shorten the name of a commercial—not an academic— publisher as long as it is easily identifiable by the reader.

2. BOOK BY TWO AUTHORS

Bynum, J. E., & Thompson, W. E. (2002). *Juvenile delinquency: A sociological approach* (5th ed.). Boston: Allyn & Bacon.

3. BOOK BY THREE TO SIX AUTHORS

Miller, B., Lord, B., & Dorney, J. (1994). *Staff development for teachers.* Newton, MA: Education Development Center.

Unless the city is a major one (for example, New York), identify the city's location by following it with the name of the state using the two-letter abbreviations of the U.S. Postal Service. Separate the city and state with a comma. The same is true for foreign cities: if they are not well-known (for example, Manchester, England), identify the province or country.

4. SELECTION FROM AN ANTHOLOGY

One Author

Share, J. B. (1975). Developmental progress in Down's syndrome. In R. Koch & F. F. de la Cruz (Eds.), *Down's syndrome (mongoloidism): Research, prevention and management* (pp. 78–86). New York: Brunner/Mazel.

More Than Six Authors

Bailey, K. M., Bergthold, B., Braunstein, B., Jagodzinski-Fleischman, N., Holbrook, M. P., Tuman, J., et al. (1996). The language learner's autobiography: Examining the "apprenticeship of observation." In D. Freeman & J. C. Richards (Eds.), *Teacher learning in language teaching* (pp. 111–129). Cambridge, England: Cambridge University Press.

Note that APA requires the use of entire numbers in inclusive pages.

5. BOOK WITH AN EDITOR OR EDITORS

Nadel, L. & Rosenthal, D. (Eds.). (1995). *Down syndrome: Living and learning in the community.* New York: Wiley-Liss.

6. BOOK IN MORE THAN ONE VOLUME

Ceci, S. J. (Ed.). (1986). *Handbook of cognitive, social, and neuropsychological aspects of learning disabilities* (Vols. 1–2). Hillsdale, NJ: Erlbaum.

7. BOOK BY A CORPORATE AUTHOR

If the author is an organization, the organization is usually the publisher. In that case, use *Author* as the publisher's name.

American Psychiatric Association. (2003). *Evidence-based practices in mental healthcare.* Washington, D.C.: Author.

8. LATER EDITION

Anastasi, A. (1982). *Psychological testing* (5th ed.). New York: Macmillan.

9. REVISED EDITION

Pueschel, S. M. (2001). *A parent's guide to Down syndrome: Toward a brighter future* (Rev. ed.). Baltimore, MD: Paul H. Brooks.

10. TRANSLATION

Wunderlich, C. (1977). *The mongoloid child: Recognition and care* (R. L. Tinsley, Jr, T. R. Harris, & D. I. Marquart, Trans.). Tucson: University of Arizona Press. (Original work published 1973.)

11. TWO OR MORE BOOKS BY THE SAME AUTHOR

Alphabetize by the author's last name, arranging the entries by date with the earliest first.

Anderson, J. R. (1980). *Cognitive psychology and its implications.* San Francisco: Freeman.

Anderson, J. R. (1983). *The architecture of cognition.* Cambridge, MA: Harvard University Press.

12. TWO OR MORE BOOKS BY THE SAME AUTHOR, PUBLISHED IN THE SAME YEAR

List the works as usual, but arrange them alphabetically according to the first major word in the title, rather than by date. To the date in parentheses add the lowercase letters *a, b,* and so on.

Evanovich, J. (2002a). *Hard eight.* New York: St. Martin's.

Evanovich, J. (2002b). *Visions of sugar plums.* New York: St. Martin's.

Articles in Periodicals

13. ARTICLE IN A MAGAZINE—SIGNED AND UNSIGNED

Signed

Gorman, C. (2001, June 10). The science of anxiety. *Time, 159,* 46–54.

Elements of the Preceding Entry

Gorman, C.	The author's name (last name first, with initial of first name), followed by a period.
(2001, June 10).	The date of issue—month spelled out, in parentheses, followed by a period.
The science of anxiety.	The title of the article, with no quotation marks and only the first word capitalized, followed by a period.
Time, 159,	The title of the magazine and the volume number, both followed by a comma, both italicized.
46–54.	The page numbers of the article, followed by a period.

Unsigned

Calling for kids with Down syndrome. (1994, November). *Parents, 69,* 25.

14. ARTICLE IN A SCHOLARLY JOURNAL PAGINATED BY VOLUME

Knott, F., Lewis, C., & Williams, T. I. (1995). Sibling interaction of children with learning disabilities: A comparison of autism and Down's syndrome. *Journal of Child Psychology and Psychiatry and Allied Disciplines, 36,* 965–976.

15. ARTICLE IN A SCHOLARLY JOURNAL PAGINATED BY ISSUE

Leonard, H. S. (2003). Leadership development for the postindustrial, postmodern information age. *Consulting Psychology Journal: Practice and Research, 55*(1), 3–14.

Include the month or season with the year only if the journal does not have a volume number. Include the issue number (not italicized) in parentheses immediately after the volume number (with no space between the volume number and opening parenthesis of the issue number) only if each issue starts at page 1.

16. ARTICLE IN A NEWSPAPER

Labaton, S. (2003, June 5). Senators move to restore F.C.C. limits on the media. *The New York Times,* pp. C1, C8.

With a newspaper article, the abbreviation *p.* (for "page") or *pp.* (for "pages") is used. The page number is preceded by the section number in which the article appears. If the article referred to appears on discontinuous pages, all pages are listed, separated by commas.

Electronic Sources

17. ARTICLE IN AN ONLINE JOURNAL

Coleman, M. (1997). Vitamins and Down syndrome [Electronic version]. *Down Syndrome Quarterly, 2*(2). Retrieved April 16, 2003, from http://www.denison.edu/collaborations/dsq/_vitamin.html

NOTE
No period follows the URL. Following the name of the publication, the italicized *2* is the volume number, and the 2 in parentheses is the issue number.

Dick, P. T., & Canadian Task Force on the Periodic Health Examination. (1996). Periodic health examination, 1996 update: Prenatal screening for and diagnosis of Down syndrome. *Canadian Medical Association Journal, 154,* 465–479. Retrieved April 16, 2003, from http://www.cma.ca/cmaj/vol-154/0465e.htm

Doman, R. J., Jr. (1999). Down syndrome perspectives. *Journal of the National Academy for Child Development, 12*(2). Retrieved April 16, 2003, from http://www.nacd.org/articles/newds.html

18. ARTICLE FROM AN ONLINE DATABASE

Lopez, F. G., Melendez, M. C., Sauer, E. M., Berger, E., & Wyssmann, J. (1998). Internal working models, self-reported problems, and help-seeking attitudes among college students. *Journal of Counseling Psychology, 45,* 79–83. Retrieved June 9, 2002, from PsycARTICLES database.

Strauss, E. (1997). The tissue issue. *Science News, 152*(12), 190. Retrieved March 5, 2002, from Academic Search Premier database.

19. ARTICLE IN AN INTERNET-ONLY JOURNAL

Kirsch, I., & Sapirstain, G. (1998, June 26). Listening to Prozac but hearing placebo: A meta-analysis of antidepressant medication. *Prevention & Treatment, 1,* Article 0002a. Retrieved June 4, 2002, from http://journals.apa.org/prevention/ volume1/pre0010002a.html

NOTE
If a URL runs over to another line, break it after a slash or before a period.

20. ARTICLE IN AN INTERNET-ONLY JOURNAL, RETRIEVED VIA FILE TRANSFER PROTOCOL (FTP)

Harnad, S. (1990). Scholarly skywriting and the prepublication continuum of scientific inquiry. *Psychological Science, 1.* Retrieved April 12, 2003, from ftp://ftp.princeton.edu/pub/harnad/Harnad/harnad90.skywriting

21. ARTICLE IN AN INTERNET-ONLY NEWSLETTER

Some steps in helping children following disaster. (2002, January 11). *Rocky Mountain Region Disaster Mental Health Newsletter, 5*(1). Retrieved April 8, 2003, from http://www.angelfire.com/biz3/news/mhm71.html

If no author is indicated, move the title to the author position.

22. ARTICLE AVAILABLE ON A UNIVERSITY PROGRAM OR DEPARTMENT WEB SITE

Black, J. B., McClintock, R., & Hill, C. (1994). *Assessing student understanding and learning in constructivist environments.* Retrieved June 12, 2003, from Columbia University, Institute for Learning Technologies Web site: http://www.ilt.columbia .cdu/publications/asulcse.html

23. ONLINE NEWSPAPER ARTICLE

Lehmann, A. L. (2001, August 21). A long night in dark land of autism. *New York Times.* Retrieved May 19, 2002, from http://www.nytimes.com

24. E-MAIL COMMUNICATION

An e-mail message is not included in the reference list, since it is a personal communication not available to other researchers. However, the e-mail should be mentioned in the body of the paper in a parenthetical note.

According to J. Domino's theory (personal communication, June 18, 2002) . . .

25. DOCUMENT FROM A WORLD WIDE WEB SITE

Zigman, W. (n.d.) *Aging and Down syndrome.* Retrieved April 16, 2002, form National Down Syndrome Society Web site: http://ndss.org/content .cfm?fuseaction=ResearchCurrStdyArticle&article=504

Note that if you are citing an entire Web site and not a specific document on that site, you give the address of the Web site in the text only. An entry in the reference list is not required.

26. GOVERNMENT REPORT FROM THE INTERNET

United States Department of the Interior, Bureau of Indian Affairs. (2002, June 3). *Interior department report addresses strategy for managing Indian trust money accounts.* Retrieved October 12, 2002, from http://www.doi.gov/news/ 07032002.htm

27. MESSAGE POSTED TO A NEWSGROUP

Duvall, D. (2001, June 5). Negative definition of Down syndrome— comments? Message posted to http://groups.google.com/ groups?hl=en&1r=&ie=UTF-8&selm=e.ddc36c2.284eefde%40cs.com

28. MESSAGE POSTED TO AN ELECTRONIC MAILING LIST

Arms, W. Y. (2000, October 2). Economic effects of link-based search engines on e-journals. Message posted to Ref-Links electronic mailing list, archived at http://www.doi.org/mail-archive/ref-link/msg00087.html

29. DOCUMENT FROM A WEBLOG ("BLOG")

Marshall, J. M. (2003, August 11). [Commentary on Frank Foer's article regarding the attachment conservatives feel toward exiled "'opposition leaders'" in August 18,

2003, issue of *The New Republic*]. Talking Points Memo. Retrieved August 13, 2003, from http://www.talkingpointsmemo.com/aug0302.html

If individual segments of the Weblog (or "Blog") are untitled, provide a description of the article in brackets in place of the article title. Be sure to provide enough information so that someone looking for the article can identify it.

30. COMPUTER PROGRAM OR SOFTWARE

Norton Antivirus (2003). [Computer software]. Cupertino, CA: Symantec.

Other Sources: Print and Nonprint

31. ABSTRACT

Rudolph, M., & Destexhe, A. (2002). Models of neocortical pyramidal neurons in the presence of correlated synaptic background activity: High discharge variability, enhanced responsiveness and independence of input location [Abstract]. *Society for Neuroscience Abstracts, 26,* 1623.

32. BOOK REVIEW

Teresi, D. (2002, April 14). Flesh and machines [Review of the book *Flesh and machines: How robots will change us*]. *New York Times Book Review,* p. 16.

33. DISSERTATION—ABSTRACT

Adamie, K. N. (2001). Social interaction in hospice work: A study of humor (Doctoral dissertation, Kent State University, 2001). *Dissertation Abstracts International, 62,* 779.

34. DISSERTATION—UNPUBLISHED

Blalock, J. (1997). *A study of conceptualization and related abilities in learning disabled and normal preschool children.* Unpublished doctoral dissertation, Northwestern University, Evanston, Illinois.

35. ENCYCLOPEDIA ARTICLE

Autism. (2002). In *The new encyclopaedia Britannica* (Vol. 1, p. 722). Chicago: Encyclopaedia Britannica.

36. GOVERNMENT DOCUMENT

U.S. Census Bureau. (2001). *Statistical abstract of the United States.* Washington, DC: U.S. Government Printing Office.

37. LETTER TO THE EDITOR

Coleman, A. L. (1999, July 2). The use and misuse of test scores [Letter to the editor]. *The Chronicle of Higher Education,* p. B13.

38. MOTION PICTURE (IN ANY FORMAT)

Green, S. (Director), & Siegel, B. (Director). (2003). *The weather underground.* [Motion picture]. United States: Independent Television Service/KQED, San Francisco.

39. SOUND RECORDING

Jenkins, S. (2003). Crystal baller [Recorded by Third Eye Blind]. On *Out of the Vein* [CD]. New York: Elektra.

40. TELEVISION SERIES

Bruckheimer, J. (Producer). (2003). *CSI: Crime scene investigation* [Television series]. New York: CBS.

Preparing a Reference List

EXERCISE 16A

Using the source information given in Exercise 15A on p. 240, prepare a properly formatted reference list.

16.3 Study a student's research paper.

The following is a research paper written by Steven Hoebel, a student in a first-year composition class. Study it carefully.

Title page required.

Full (explanatory) title, centered, set on top half of title page.

Down Syndrome Children:

From the Institution to the Classroom

Steven Hoebel

English 121: English Composition

Professor Nicolai

June 15, 2003

Writer's name, course title, professor's name, and date included on title page.

Shortened title and page number at top right of every page.

Full title (centered) at top of page.

Paragraphs indented ½-inch or 5 spaces.

In-text citation includes authors' names (with "&" not "and") and date; no page numbers here because source unpaginated.

Double citation. Second includes title and date only because no author or page numbers in citation.

↑
½"
↓

1"   Down Syndrome Children   1 ←   1"   →
↓

Down Syndrome Children:

From the Institution to the Classroom

←½"→About 3% of the population is born with Down syn-   1" margins on all sides.

drome, "the most frequently identified cause of mental retar-

dation" (Quanhe, Rasmussen, & Friedman, 2002). Just a few

decades ago, nearly all of these individuals spent their lives in ←   1"   →

institutions, without any hope for the future or enjoyment of

the present. However, the culture of the late 1960s and 1970s

reached into this area as well, as the new generation of par-

ents of retarded children began to question the inevitability of

institutionalization and the disastrous effects on families who

failed to commit their retarded children to these places. These

parents discovered that not only could their disabled children

get along just fine when placed in everyday situations, but

they also exhibited a special sort of love which deeply af-   Paragraph prepares reader for subject of essay using comparison-contrast method (see p. 79).

fected their parents and their siblings (Hayakawa, 1995;

"Dealing with Down syndrome," 2001).

However, not all of the credit can go to the parents.

During this time, researchers had started thinking the same

and had begun conducting studies to prove their hypotheses.

They produced hard evidence which suggested that retarded

children respond better to love and communication than to in-

stitutional routine and Thorazine (Nirje, 1976).

↑
1"
↓

Down Syndrome Children   2

Early Treatments and Attitudes

Primary heading (centered) identifies main idea of section.

These were not the first researchers to study the mentally retarded. Those who came before them also put forth
quite convincing arguments about the worthlessness of the
retarded in society and the futility of trying to teach them anything. They had no learning potential, the old researchers
said, and the best that could be done for them was to make
existence as painless as possible, which meant the constant
administration of heavy sedatives (Wolfensberger, 1976).

Summary provides historical perspective for reader

Up until the early 1980s, being born with Down syndrome was like being condemned to Hell. Institutionalization
was considered the only course of action; many felt that the
retarded could never make it in mainstream society and that
their presence there would have a negative effect upon others
around them (Blatt, 1993). Unfortunately, even today, some
supposedly educated people express doubts about the effi-
cacy of mainstreaming (O'Neill, 2001). Others believed that
the retarded were indifferent to physical extremes, such as
heat, cold, and restraint. Therefore, it was common for them
to be kept like dogs, often left naked, tied up, and/or covered
in their own filth for hours on end. In addition, many felt that
the retarded were unable to appreciate aesthetics. The patients in each ward slept in cavernous rooms without parti-
tions or any other measures of privacy (Wolfensberger, 1976).

Down Syndrome Children   3

Perhaps Farber (1991) best captured the true attitude of
the era in his book. In a section depicting the mentally ill as a
"surplus population," he wrote:

$\leftarrow$1/2"$\rightarrow$This book regards the mentally retarded as constituting

a segment of the organizationally surplus population

both by being labeled as deviants and by their incom-

petence. As deviants, they are stigmatized and treated

differently from others; as incompetents, they generally

fail to perform roles adequately in the basic institutions

of the society. (p. 19)

Farber also goes on to point out that impoverished and unsta-
ble families tend to produce more retarded children than do
middle-class families. He theorizes that this disorder may actually serve to fill a need for unskilled and semiskilled laborers
at a low pay rate. Such cold, disparaging views of the mentally handicapped are perfect examples of how they were
viewed just 30 years ago.

Changes in Treatment and Attitudes

Around the mid-1970s, everything began to change.
The peace-and-love generation had graduated from college,
and a new breed of health professional was born. These
new arrivals found the old way of treating the mentally disabled shockingly harsh and inhuman. They set about creating a new system that would give some dignity back to and

---

Signal phrase used to introduce quotation.

Quotations longer than 40 words indented ½" or five spaces from left margin.

Parenthetical page reference appears after the closing period.

Down Syndrome Children   4

create avenues of growth for retarded individuals

(Wolfensberger, 1976). This included a bill of rights for

these individuals that basically guaranteed their protection

from abuse, neglect, and inhumane forms of restraint and

therapy (Blatt, 1993). The goal of the new wave of care-

givers was to let the retarded children live as much like nor-

mal children as possible, a plan they called *mainstreaming.*

Normalization Approach

Secundary heading used to identify significant subsection.

In an essay, Nirje (1976) describes what he calls "the nor-

malization principle": "The normalization principle means mak-

Quotation shorter than 40 words in quotation marks, not indented.

ing available to all mentally retarded people patterns of life and

conditions of everyday living which are as close as possible to

the regular circumstances and ways of life of society" (p. 231).

Summary and quotation used to explain "normaliza-tion principle."

Nirje's point is that a normal life is the best therapy anyone can

get. He points out that mental retardation is not one handicap

but three: the actual retardation, the imposed retardation

springing from others' perception of their retardation, and the

awareness of their own retardation. The end result, Nirje says,

is a lack of ability based as much on the actual retardation as

on the individuals' negative self-concept and lack of faith in

their originally diminished ability. When the normalization princi-

ple is in full effect, the hustle and bustle of a daily routine can

take the children's minds off what they cannot do and allow

them to make progress towards their potential, whatever it may

Down Syndrome Children   5

be. In an institution, on the other hand, people barely notice the passage of the seasons; the perception of some milestone is essential to their development as individuals, claims Nirje. At home, the children have opportunities to pass through progressive steps, which do not exist inside an institution.

Developmental Approach

Along the same lines is the developmental approach to mental retardation, originally proposed by Zigler in 1969. This school of thought "is predicated on the idea that retarded children, while they develop at a slower rate and stop developing at lower levels, otherwise develop in the same way nonretarded children do" (Zigler & Hodapp, 1991, p. 37). In a study, Truesdell and Abramson (1992) prove Zigler's hypothesis, at least in the classroom. While the grades of the retarded were always lower than normal as a whole, she noted that not one of the students failed, unlike their average peers. When treated as people with struggles and futures like anyone else, the retarded are raised out of subhuman status into human, if not mainstream, society.

Then and Now

In 1966, the average Down syndrome children spent their days in the sterile dayroom of an institution, too heavily drugged to be unhappy. They could expect to flounder this way until perhaps the age of 30, when people with this

"And" not ampersand ("&") used in signal phrase.

Summary of Truesdell and Abramson article used to support contention made in Zigler and Hodapp.

Comparison-contrast used to highlight change in treatment and attitude.

condition usually died. By 1996, the parents of Down syndrome children were treating their children like any others. As a result, the children began to reap as much benefit as they were able from their homes and families. Everything else was left to genetics.

In 1966, if one were to walk down the street and see children with mongoloid features, one would likely think: "What are children like that doing out in public?" Mongolism was something that people did not like to talk about, and its victims were hidden from sight. Today, the faces of retarded children are not such an unfamiliar sight, and most people are not repulsed by them. Down syndrome children are much more likely to be accepted in any given community, especially if they attend school with normal peers. The newfound understanding and acceptance of the mentally retarded manifest themselves in the community but originated in clinical settings. If it had not been for those new researchers in the 1970s who thought alternative treatments deserved a chance, Down syndrome children would still be looked upon as subhuman freaks—and then they would have no chance for happiness at all.

Thesis restated in conclusion.

↑
1″   Down Syndrome Children   7
↓

References

Blatt, B. (1993). *Souls in extremis: An anthology on victims and victimizers.* Boston: Allyn & Bacon.

Dealing with Down syndrome. (2001, October/November). *Australian Parents,* 48–49. Retrieved May 19, 2003, from EBSCOhost database (Academic Search Premier).

Farber, B. (1991). *Mental retardation: Its social context and social consequences.* Boston: Houghton Mifflin.

Hayakawa, S. I. (1995). Our son Mark. In P. Eschholz & A. Rosa (Eds.), *Outlooks and insights: A reader for college writers* (4th ed. pp. 105–111). New York: St. Martin's.

Nirje, B. (1976). The normalization principle. In R. B. Kugel & A. Shearer (Eds.), *Changing patterns in residential services for the mentally retarded* (pp. 231–240) (DHEW Publication No. OHD 76-21015). Washington, DC: U.S. Government Printing Office.

O'Neill, T. (2001, August 20). On to college. *Report/Newsmagazine (Alberta Edition), 28,* 57. Retrieved May 19, 2003, from EBSCOhost database (Academic Search Premier).

Quanhe, Y., Rasmussen, S. A., & Friedman, J. M. (2002). Mortality associated with Down's syndrome in the USA from 1983 to 1997: A population-based study. *Lancet,*

↑
1″
↓

Margin notes:
Heading centered.
Reference list starts on new page.
Entries alphabetized by last name (or title if no author listed).
Year (in parentheses) follows author's name.
Only first word and proper nouns (names) capitalized in titles.
Shortened form of publisher's name used.
For entries longer than one line, ½″ hanging indent used. ←1/2″→
← 1″ →
Date retrieved indicated for works from Internet or database.
Article titles set in regular type, no quotation marks.

359, 1019–1025. Retrieved May 19, 2003, from

EBSCOhost database (Academic Search Premier).

Truesdell, L. A., & Abramson, T. (1992). Academic behavior

and grades of mainstreamed students with mild

disabilities. *Exceptional Children, 58,* 392–398.

Wolfensberger, W. (1976). The origin and nature of our

institutional models. In R. B. Kugel & A. Shearer (Eds.),

Changing patterns in residential services for the

mentally retarded (DHEW Publication No. OHD 76-

21015, pp. 35–82). Washington, DC: U.S. Government

Printing Office.

Zigler, E., & Hodapp, R. M. (1991). Behavioral functioning in

individuals with mild retardation. *Annual Review of*

Psychology, 42, 29–50.

Ampersand ("&")
used between
authors' names.

Book and journal
titles set in italics.

Chapter Checklist

1 ⁑ Reference your researched material by placing the author's last name and the date of publication of the work, separated by a comma, within parentheses after the referenced material.

2 ⁑ When you introduce the researched material with the author's name in a signal phrase, use only the date of publication in parentheses after the material.

3 ⁑ Direct quotations must include the page number or numbers, preceded by p. or pp.

4 ⁑ Check to be sure that every source mentioned in your paper appears in your reference list and that every source that appears in your reference list is cited in the paper.

6

CMS DOCUMENTATION

6

17

WRITING THE RESEARCH PAPER USING *CHICAGO MANUAL OF STYLE* FORMAT

17.1 Learn *CMS* format.

The Chicago Manual of Style (CMS) was originally prepared by the University of Chicago Press to serve as a guide for its own editors and authors. However, it is now used also by many writers in the humanities and social sciences. The following discussion is based on the fifteenth edition of *The Chicago Manual of Style,* published in 2003.

■■■■   ■■■■   **BASICLINK** ■■■■   ■■■■
WWW

To learn more about CMS format, visit
http://www.wisc.edu/writing/Handbook/DocChicago.html

■■ ■■ ■■ ■■ ■■ ■■   ■■ ■■ ■■ ■■ ■■ ■■

The *CMS* allows two methods of documentation for quotations, paraphrases, or summaries of researched material in an essay:

1. An author-date parenthetical style, similar to that of the APA (recommended for use in the natural and most social sciences)
2. A documentary-note (footnote or endnote) system.

This chapter describes and presents examples for using the note system. With this system, each reference to a particular source in the research paper is followed by a superscript (small, raised) arabic numeral. The numbers are sequential throughout the paper and generally appear at the end of the sentence, after the punctuation. The publishing information that goes with the reference number then appears at the bottom of the page on which the citation appears (footnotes) or, in the style preferred by the *CMS*, on a separate page after the last page of text (endnotes) under the heading "Notes" (centered at the top of the page).

17.2 Learn how to prepare a notes list and a bibliography.

If you include all your citations in footnotes or endnotes, you may not need to supply a bibliography as well. However, should you use the author-date system of citation or should your instructor require a bibliography, the format for those references is included below the (numbered) note example. In the *CMS* system, you may list in the bibliography only the works cited in the research paper or other works you also consulted. Check with your instructor about what he or she expects.

To make sure information in a bibliography is accurate, refer to your bibliography cards (or computer file of sources). For more on making bibliography cards, see section 15.3a.

17.2a Learn patterns of a notes list and a bibliography.

1. **Notes.** Number the notes sequentially. Indent the first line of the note five spaces or half an inch from the left margin. Place any subsequent lines flush with the left margin. Double-space both within and between notes. Type the name(s) of the author(s) in normal order (first name first). Use italics for the titles of books and periodicals. In general, commas separate elements within notes.

2. **Bibliography.** List entries alphabetically by the last name of the author or by the first major word of the title if no author is indicated. Invert the name of the first author only. Place the first line of the entry flush with the left margin. Indent any subsequent lines three or four spaces from the left margin (a **hanging indent**). Double-space within and between entries. Use italics for book and periodical titles. In general, periods separate elements within bibliography entries.

17.2b Review sample entries for a notes list and a bibliography.

In the following samples of note and bibliographic entries using *CMS* style, the note format is given first.

Books

1. BOOK BY A SINGLE AUTHOR

The publishing information, in parentheses, follows the italicized book title. The note ends with the page number(s) from which the material was taken.

> 1. Douglas H. Chadwick, *The Fate of the Elephants* (San Francisco: Sierra Club, 1992), 98.

A bibliography entry for a book puts the author's last name first and does not include page numbers.

Chadwick, Douglas H. *The Fate of the Elephants.* San Francisco: Sierra Club, 1992.

2. BOOK BY TWO AUTHORS

When a book has two authors, the names are joined by *and,* with no comma.

2. Derek Wilson and Peter Averst, *White Gold* (London: Heinemann, 1976), 71.

With two authors, the second name in a bibliographic citation goes in normal order. A comma follows the first name of the first author; the names are joined by *and.*

Wilson, Derek, and Peter Ayerst. *White Gold.* London: Heinemann, 1976.

3. BOOK BY THREE AUTHORS

Although not preferred in MLA format, using the author's initials is acceptable in *CMS* format, and all author names in a note go in normal order. Further, *CMS* prefers that the word *Press* be spelled out, not abbreviated as *P* (as in MLA style).

3. Richard M. Laws, I. S. C. Parker, and R. C. B. Johnstone, *Elephants and Their Habitats: The Ecology of Elephants in Northern Bunyora, Uganda* (Oxford: Clarendon Press, 1975), 103.

Laws, Richard M., I. S. C. Parker, and R. C. B. Johnstone. *Elephants and Their Habitats: The Ecology of Elephants in Northern Bunyora, Uganda.* Oxford: Clarendon Press, 1975.

4. BOOK BY MORE THAN THREE AUTHORS

In the note, rather than listing the names of all the authors, use *et al.* or *and others.* No punctuation follows the first author's name in a note.

4. C. Jencks et al., *Inequality: A Reassessment of the Effect of Family and Schooling in America* (New York: Basic Books, 1972), 42.

Jencks, C., Marshall Smith, Henry Acland, and Mary Jo Bane. *Inequality: A Reassessment of the Effect of Family and Schooling in America.* New York: Basic Books, 1972.

5. BOOK WITH AUTHOR UNKNOWN

If the name of the author is unknown, both the note and the bibliography entry should begin with the title of the work; avoid using *Anonymous* or *Anon.*

5. *The Way to Eternity: Egyptian Myth* (London: Duncan Baird, 1997), 16.

The Way to Eternity: Egyptian Myth. London: Duncan Baird, 1997.

6. TWO OR MORE BOOKS BY THE SAME AUTHOR

6. Jonathan Franzen, *The Corrections* (New York: Farrar, Straus and Giroux, 2001), 17.

7. Jonathan Franzen, *How to Be Alone: Essays* (New York: Farrar, Straus and Giroux, 2002), 47.

In a bibliographic citation, instead of repeating the author's name, use a long dash (six typed hyphens) in all entires after the first.

Franzen, Jonathan. *The Corrections.* New York: Farrar, Straus and Giroux, 2001.

————. *How to Be Alone: Essays.* New York: Farrar, Straus and Giroux, 2002.

7. BOOK IN MORE THAN ONE VOLUME

The Work as a Whole

7. Marcel Proust, *Remembrance of Things Past,* trans. C. K. Scott Moncrief, Terence Kilmartin, and Andreas Mayor, 3 vols. (New York: Random House, 1982).

Proust, Marcel. *Remembrance of Things Past.* Translated by C. K. Scott Moncrief, Terence Kilmartin, and Andreas Mayor. 3 vols. New York: Random House, 1982.

A Particular Volume

7. Marcel Proust, *Remembrance of Things Past,* trans. C. K. Scott Moncrief, Terence Kilmartin, and Andreas Mayor (New York: Random House, 1982), 2: 127–29.

Proust, Marcel. *Remembrance of Things Past.* Translated by C. K. Scott Moncrief, Terence Kilmartin, and Andreas Mayor. Vol. 2. New York: Random House, 1982.

Note that in *CMS* style, inclusive numbers are shortened. Therefore, 127–129 becomes 127–29.

8. LATER EDITION

8. Jack E. Bynum and William E. Thompson, *Juvenile Delinquency: A Sociological Approach,* 5th ed. (Boston: Allyn and Bacon, 2002), 242.

Bynum, Jack E., and William E. Thompson. *Juvenile Delinquency: A Sociological Approach.* 5th ed. Boston: Allyn and Bacon, 2002.

9. REPRINT

9. Wilkie Collins, *The Haunted Hotel,* in *Three Supernatural Novels of the Victorian Period,* ed. E. F. Bleiler (1889; reprint, New York: Dover Publications, 1975), 75.

Collins, Wilkie. *The Haunted Hotel.* In *Three Supernatural Novels of the Victorian Period,* ed. E. F. Bleiler. 1889. Reprint, New York: Dover Publications, 1975.

10. SELECTION FROM AN ANTHOLOGY

10. Richard Schechner, "Who's Afraid of Edward Albee?" in *Edward Albee: A Collection of Critical Essays,* ed. C. W. E. Bigsby (Englewood Cliffs, N.J.: Prentice-Hall, 1975), 62–65.

Although it is not necessary to cite the original publication date of the source in the note, that information should be given in the bibliography entry.

Schechner, Richard. "Who's Afraid of Edward Albee?" In *Edward Albee: A Collection of Critical Essays,* edited by C. W. E. Digsby. Englewood Cliffs, N.J.: Prentice-Hall, 1975. First published in *Tulane Drama Review* 7, no. 3 (1963): 7–10.

11. TRANSLATION

11. Roland Barthes, *The Fashion System,* trans. Matthew Ward and Richard Howard (Berkeley and Los Angeles: University of California Press, 1990), 82.

NOTE

The abbreviation *trans.* (meaning "translated by") may also be used.

Barthes, Roland. *The Fashion System.* Translated by Matthew Ward and Richard Howard. Berkeley and Los Angeles: University of California Press, 1990.

12. BOOK PUBLISHED BY AN ORGANIZATION OR A CORPORATION

12. American Psychiatric Association, *Diagnostic and Statistical Manual of Mental Disorders,* 4th ed. (Washington, D.C.: American Psychiatric Association, 1994), 112.

American Psychiatric Association. *Diagnostic and Statistical Manual of Mental Disorders.* 4th ed. Washington, D.C.: American Psychiatric Association, 1994.

13. BOOK WITH AN EDITOR OR EDITORS

13. John Updike and Katrina Kenison, eds., *The Best American Short Stories of the Century* (Boston: Houghton Mifflin, 1999).

Updike, John, and Katrina Kenison, eds. *The Best American Short Stories of the Century.* Boston: Houghton Mifflin, 1999.

14. BOOK WITH AN AUTHOR AND EDITOR

14. Charlotte Brontë, *Jane Eyre,* ed. Richard J. Dunn (New York: W. W. Norton and Company, 2000), 176.

Brontë, Charlotte. *Jane Eyre.* Edited by Richard J. Dunn. New York: W. W. Norton and Company, 2000.

15. BOOK IN A SERIES

15. Grant M. Farr, *Modern Iran,* Comparative Societies Series (New York: McGraw-Hill, 1998), 98.

Farr, Grant M. *Modern Iran.* Comparative Societies Series. New York: McGraw-Hill, 1998.

16. ENCYCLOPEDIA OR DICTIONARY

Well-known reference works are generally not listed in a bibliography. When they appear in notes, do not give the publication information, but give the edition if it is not the first. In a reference to a work arranged alphabetically, cite the item preceded by *s.v.* (*sub verbo,* meaning "under the word"). Do not give the volume number or the page number.

16. *Encyclopaedia Britannica,* 15th ed., s.v. "elephant."

Articles in Periodicals

17. ARTICLE IN A MAGAZINE—SIGNED AND UNSIGNED

Signed

> 17. Mary Wells Lawrence, "The Lady Was an Adman," *Vanity Fair,* May 2002, 208.

Lawrence, Mary Wells. "The Lady Was an Adman." *Vanity Fair,* May 2002, 206–17.

Unsigned

> 17. "Poachers' Pause," *Economist,* March 2, 1991, 42.

"Poachers' Pause." *Economist,* March 2, 1991, 42.

18. ARTICLE IN A SCHOLARLY JOURNAL, PAGINATED BY VOLUME—SIGNED AND UNSIGNED

Signed

> 18. Dana Ferris, "Students' Views of Academic Aural/Oral Skills: A Comparative Needs Analysis," *TESOL Quarterly* 32 (1998): 311.

Ferris, Dana. "Students' Views of Academic Aural/Oral Skills: A Comparative Needs Analysis." *TESOL Quarterly* 32 (1998): 289–318.

Unsigned

> 18. "Elephantine Contraception," *Lancet* (North American Edition) 340 (1992): 583.

"Elephantine Contraception." *Lancet* (North American Edition) 340 (1992): 583–84.

19. ARTICLE IN A SCHOLARLY JOURNAL, PAGINATED BY ISSUE

> 19. Jisi Wang, "The Price of America Going It Alone," *New Perspectives Quarterly* 19 (Summer 2002): 49.

Wang, Jisi. "The Price of America Going It Alone." *New Perspectives Quarterly* 19 (Summer 2002): 48–49.

In both note and bibliographic citations, use season or month and year if no issue number is available.

20. ARTICLE IN A NEWSPAPER

If the city is not part of the newspaper's name, add it at the beginning of the name and italicize it along with the official name of the newspaper. Insert the name of the state, italicized and in parentheses, after a city name that is not well known. Page numbers are not usually included in citations of daily newspapers.

> 20. Laurence Hall, "Facing Big Trouble, Elephants Aren't Ready to Turn Tail Yet," *Newark (NJ) Star-Ledger,* April 2, 1999.

Hall, Laurence. "Facing Big Trouble, Elephants Aren't Ready to Turn Tail Yet," *Newark (NJ) Star-Ledger,* April 2, 1999.

21. BOOK REVIEW

21. Chris Petrakos, "Battling the Ivory Trade to Save Africa's Elephants," review of *Battle of the Elephants,* by Iain Douglas-Hamilton and Oria Douglas-Hamilton, *Chicago Tribune,* May 20, 1992, sec. 5, p. 3.

Petrakos, Chris. "Battling the Ivory Trade to Save Africa's Elephants." Review of *Battle of the Elephants,* by Iain Douglas-Hamilton and Oria Douglas-Hamilton. *Chicago Tribune,* 22 May 1992, sec. 5, p. 3.

Electronic Sources

The Chicago Manual of Style (2003) has updated its formats for electronic sources. In general, in referencing electronic sources, always include as much information as possible to enable your reader to access the material, including the URL and the date you accessed the site (in parentheses following the URL). Whichever variation you choose, be consistent throughout your paper.

Another source for formatting information is the *Columbia Guide to Online Style* by Janice R. Walker and Todd Taylor (New York, Columbia University Press, 1998).

22. ARTICLE IN AN ONLINE MAGAZINE

22. Michael D. Lemonick, "The Ivory Wars," *Time,* June 16, 1997, http://www.pathfinder.com/time/magazine/1997/dom/970616 (accessed May 3, 1998).

Lemonick, Michael D. "The Ivory Wars." *Time,* June 16, 1997. http://www.pathfinder.com/time/magazine/1997/dom/070616 (accessed May 3, 1998).

23. ARTICLE IN AN ONLINE JOURNAL

23. Kevin A. Hill, "Conflicts over Developmental Values: The International Ivory Trade in Zimbabwe's Historical Context," *Environment and History* 1 (October 1995), http://www.fiv.edu/~khill/elephant.htm (accessed April 16, 1999).

Hill, Kevin A. "Conflicts over Developmental Values: The International Ivory Trade in Zimbabwe's Historical Context." *Environment and History* 1 (October 1995). http://www.fiv.edu/~khill/elephant.htm (accessed April 16, 1999).

24. ARTICLE IN AN ONLINE NEWSPAPER

24. Melissa Radler, "US Closer to Posting Rewards for Capture of Palestinian Terrorists," *Jerusalem Post on the Web,* August 10, 2001, http://www.jpost.com/Editions/2001/08/10/News.32328.html (accessed April 15, 2002).

Radler, Melissa. "US Closer to Posting Rewards for Capture of Palestinian Terrorists." *Jerusalem Post on the Web,* 10 August 2001. http://www.jpost.com/Editions/2001/08/10/News.32328.html (accessed April 15, 2002).

25. ARTICLE IN AN ONLINE DATABASE

25. Amado M. Padilla, "English Only vs. Bilingual Education: Ensuring a Language-Competent Society," *Journal of Education* 173, no. 2 (1991), Academic Search Premier, EBSCOhost database (accessed May 4, 2002).

Padilla, Amado M. "English Only vs. Bilingual Education: Ensuring a Language-Competent Society." *Journal of Education* 173, no. 2 (1991). Academic Search Premier, EBSCOhost database (accessed May 4, 2002).

26. BOOK REVIEW IN AN ONLINE NEWSPAPER

26. David Orr, review of *Springing: New and Selected Poems,* by Marie Ponsot, *New York Times on the Web,* April 21, 2002, http://www.nytimes.com/2002/04/21/books (accessed April 26, 2002).

Orr, David. Review of *Springing: New and Selected Poems,* by Marie Ponsot. *New York Times on the Web,* April 21, 2002. http://www.nytimes.com/2002/04/21/books (accessed April 26, 2002).

27. CD-ROM ISSUED PERIODICALLY

27. James Gilreath, "History of a Book: Madison Council Told of First Book Printed in America," *Library of Congress Information Bulletin* CD-ROM (May 1, 1995): 200–202.

Gilreath, James. "History of a Book: Madison Council Told of First Book Printed in America." *Library of Congress Information Bulletin* CD-ROM (May 1, 1995): 200–202.

28. DOCUMENT FROM A DATABASE

28. Marguerite Holloway, "On the Trail of Wild Elephants," *Scientific American,* December 1994: 48–50, Expanded Academic ASAP [CD-ROM], Information Access Company (accessed April 12, 1995).

Holloway, Marguerite. "On the Trail of Wild Elephants." *Scientific American,* December 1994, 48–50. Expanded Academic ASAP [CD-ROM]. Information Access Company (accessed April 12, 1995).

NOTE ✸✸✸✸✸✸

E-mail communications are not listed in a bibliography.

29. E-MAIL COMMUNICATION

29. Kevin F. O'Brien, "Survivors Project," e-mail to author June 18, 2002, (accessed June 19, 2002).

30. ONLINE BOOK

30. Kate Chopin, *The Awakening and Selected Short Stories,* 1994, http://digital.library.upenn.edu/webbin/gutbook/lookup?num=160 (accessed August 5, 2002).

Chopin, Kate. *The Awakening and Selected Short Stories.* 1994. http://digital.library.upenn.edu/webbin/gutbook/lookup?num=160 (accessed August 5, 2002).

Other Sources: Print and Nonprint

31. DISSERTATION—ABSTRACT

31. Kathleen Kieran Edwards Bennett, The Effects of Syntax and Verbal Mediation on Learning Disabled Students' Verbal Mathematical Problem Scores (Ph.D. diss., Northern Arizona University, 1981). Abstract in *Dissertation Abstracts International* 42/03-A (1981): 1093.

Bennett, Kathleen Kieran Edwards. "The Effects of Syntax and Verbal Mediation on
Learning Disabled Students' Verbal Mathematical Problem Scores." Ph.D. diss.,
Northern Arizona University, 1981. Abstract in *Dissertation Abstracts
International* 42/03-A (1981): 1093.

32. DISSERTATION—UNPUBLISHED

32. John Thomas Kelly, "Studies in *Beowulf* Criticism" (Ph.D. diss., University of
Oklahoma, 1969), 36–38.

Kelly, John Thomas. "Studies in *Beowulf* Criticism." Ph.D. diss., University of
Oklahoma, 1969.

33. GOVERNMENT DOCUMENT

33. New Jersey Division of Youth and Family Services, *Children at Risk 1995–96*
(Trenton, N.J., 1998), 17.

New Jersey Division of Youth and Family Services. *Children at Risk 1995–96*. Trenton,
N.J., 1998.

34. VIDEORECORDING

34. *Love! Valour! Compassion!* Videocassette, directed by Joe Mantello
(New Line Home Video, 1997).

Love! Valour! Compassion! Videocassette. Directed by Joe Mantello. New Line Home
Video, 1997.

35. PERSONAL INTERVIEW

35. Thomas Polaski. Interview by author, Washington, D.C., February 3, 2002.

Personal interviews are not listed in a bibliography.

36. SCRIPTURAL REFERENCE

References to the Judeo-Christian scriptures are, for the most part, confined to
the text or notes. You should include the version you are using.

36. John 3:16 (Revised Standard Version).

37. SOUND RECORDING

37. Johann Sebastian Bach, *The Violin Concertos,* The Chamber Orchestra of
Europe, Salvatore Accardo, Philips compact disc 416 413-2.

Bach, Johann Sebastian. *The Violin Concertos.* The Chamber Orchestra of Europe.
Salvatore Accardo. Philips compact disc 416 413-2.

17.3 Study samples from a student's research paper.

↑
1/2″
↓
1″
Polaski   2
↓

← 1″ →

In the nineteenth century, Africa contained an estimated 5 million elephants, a number that had slowly decreased to an estimated 3 million by 1970.[1] But then something started to happen. The numbers began to decrease at an alarming rate. By 1979, the number had decreased to an estimated 1.3 million, and by 1990, to an estimated 609,000.[2] The cause of this sudden decrease is not hard to determine. It was "M-O-N-E-Y. Easy M-O-N-E-Y. Almost unimaginable amounts of M-O-N-E-Y."[3]

The money came from the sale of ivory, or "white gold." The demand for ivory was unending. It was used to produce everything from rings, necklaces, and earrings to musical instruments and elaborately carved sculptures of all sizes. And it was in demand everywhere—from Germany, Italy, France, and the United States to India, Southeast Asia, China, and Japan, ← 1″ → the "world's largest consumer of ivory."[4] This demand "sent the price of ivory skyrocketing into the rarefied realm where the likes of gold, rhinoceros horn, diamonds, and hard drugs

Superscript numbers used to indicate notes.

Numbers written out for one to ninety-nine and round numbers; numerals used for large numbers.

Notes used to cite sources of information and quotations.

Preparing the Manuscript for a Paper Using CMS Style

CMS style requires 1-inch margins at the top, bottom, and sides of the page. While *CMS* style does not require a title page, it is a good idea to include one. Indicate title, author, date, course number, professor's name, and any other information required by your instructor. Paginate your paper by starting on the first page of the manuscript.

Polaski   3

around 130,000 to around 16,000.[7] As the slaughter continued,
the poachers' methods became more and more sophisticated
and destructive. As one commentator has pointed out,

> [the] poachers resembled the field forces of drug opera-
> tions in the Golden Triangle and Colombia: They traveled
> in large, well-armed, paramilitary groups supported by
> vehicles, an occasional spotting plane, and a network of
> informants that sometimes reached to the highest level
> of government. Their weapon of choice was the semiau-
> tomatic rifle or machine gun. Few ever stopped to take so
> much as one steak from the tons of meat lying to rot af-
> ter the tusks were hacked out of the animals with an ax
> or chain saw.[8]

In 1989, in an effort to combat the poaching and to end the
slaughter, the Convention on International Trade in Endangered
Species (CITES) issued "a moratorium on international trade in
ivory," a temporary ban that went into effect in 1990.[9] Although
there was some opposition to the original moratorium, CITES
voted to retain it at a meeting in March 1992.[10]

Overall, the moratorium seems to have worked. Indeed,
David Western, the director of Wildlife Conservation International,
has stated that "the ivory ban has done an enormous amount of
good for elephants all over Africa."[11]

Block quotations—
longer than 8 to 10
lines indented.

All text, even
quotations,
double spaced.

↑
1″   Polaski   8
↓

Heading centered.

Notes

1. Douglas H. Chadwick, *The Fate of the Elephants* (San Francisco: Sierra Club, 1992), 3.

2. Virginia Morell, "Running for Their Lives," *International Wildlife* 20 (May/June 1990): 10.

Use only author's last name and page in subsequent notes.

3. Chadwick, 39.

4. Anne Underwood, "The Good Fake," *International Wildlife* 21 (July/August 1991): 29.

Notes double-spaced.

5. Chadwick, 41.

6. Morell, 11.

7. Joseph Contreras, "The Killing Fields," *Newsweek,* November 18, 1991, 86–88; Morell, 6.

8. Chadwick, 43.

9. "Poachers' Pause," *Economist,* on March 2, 1991, 42.

Notes longer than 1 line set paragraph style.

10. "When Is Culling the Animal Not Killing the Animal?" *Africa Report,* May/June 1992, 10.

11. Contreras, 87.

Polaski   9

Bibliography

Chadwick, Douglas H. *The Fate of the Elephants.* San

Francisco: Sierra Club, 1992.

Contreras, Joseph. "The Killing Fields." *Newsweek,*

November 18, 1991, 86–88.

Entries listed in alphabetical order by author's last name (or title, if no author given).

"The Elephants' Telltale Tusks." *Futurist,* March/April

1990, 51.

Entries double-spaced.

Morell, Virginia. "Running for Their Lives." *International*

Wildlife 20 (May/June 1990): 4–13.

"Poachers' Pause." *Economist,* March 2, 1991, 42.

Hanging indent used for entries longer than 1 line.

Tattersall, Ian. "The Elephant Wars." Review of *At the*

Hand of Man: Peril and Hope for Africa's Wildlife, by

Raymond Bonner. *New York Times Book Review,*

May 2, 1993.

Underwood, Anne. "The Good Fake." *International Wildlife*

21 (July/August 1991): 29.

"When Is Culling the Animal Not Killing the Animal?" *Africa*

Report, May/June 1992, 10.

17.4 Learn resources for other styles.

CHEMISTRY

Dodd, Janet S., ed. *The ACS Style Guide: A Manual for Authors and Editors* 2nd ed. Washington: American Chemical Society, 1997.

ENGINEERING

Institute of Electrical and Electronics Engineers. *IEEE Standards Style Manual.* Rev. ed. New York: IEEE, 2001.

GEOLOGY

Bates, Robert L., Rex Buchanan, and Maria Adkins-Heljeson, eds. *Geowriting: A Guide to Writing, Editing, and Printing in Earth Science.* 5th ed. Alexandria: American Geological Institute, 1995.

GOVERNMENT DOCUMENTS

Garner, Diane L. *The Complete Guide to Citing Government Information Resources: A Manual for Writers and Librarians.* Rev. ed. Bethesda: Congressional Information Service, 1993.

United States Government Printing Office. *Style Manual.* Washington: GPO, 2000.

JOURNALISM

Goldstein, Norm, ed. *Associated Press Stylebook and Briefing on Media Law.* 35th ed. New York: Associated Press, 2000.

LAW

Harvard Law Review et al. *The Bluebook: A Uniform System of Citation.* 17th ed. Cambridge: Harvard Law Rev. Assn., 2000.

MATHEMATICS

American Mathematical Society. *The AMS Author Handbook: General Instructions for Preparing Manuscripts.* Rev. ed. Providence: AMS, 1998.

MEDICINE

Iverson, Cheryl. *American Medical Association Manual of Style: A Guide for Authors and Editors.* 9th ed. Baltimore: Williams, 1998.

MUSIC

Holoman, D. Kern, ed. *Writing about Music: A Style Sheet from the Editors of* 19th-Century Music. Berkeley: University of California Press, 1988.

PHYSICS

American Institute of Physics. *Style Manual: Instructions to Authors and Volume Editors for the Preparation of AIP Book Manuscripts.* 5th ed. New York: AIP, 1995.

POLITICAL SCIENCE

American Political Science Association. *Style Manual for Political Science.* Rev. ed. Washington: APSA, 1993.

SCIENCE: NATURAL AND APPLIED

Huth, Edward J. *Scientific Style and Format: The CBE Manual for Authors, Editors, and Publishers.* 6th ed. New York: Cambridge University Press, 1994.

For a fuller explanation of Council of Science Editors' format (formerly CBE format), see <http://www.councilscienceeditors.org> and <http://www.mhhe.com/basics>.

SCIENCE AND TECHNICAL WRITING

American National Standard for the Preparation of Scientific Papers for Written and Oral Presentation. New York: American National Standards Institute, 1979.

Rubens, Philip, ed. *Science and Technical Writing: A Manual of Style.* 2nd ed. New York: Routledge, 2001.

SOCIAL WORK

National Association of Social Workers. *Writing for NASW Press: Information for Authors.* Rev. ed. Washington: NASW Press, 1995.

Chapter Checklist

1 ·:· **Reference** your material with the format appropriate for the course you are taking. Not all instructors require the use of MLA or APA formats. Some may require *CMS* or another format.

2 ·:· **Learn** *CMS* and other formats.

7

SPECIAL WRITING SITUATIONS

7

SPECIAL WRITING SITUATIONS

7 SPECIAL WRITING
SITUATIONS

WRITING ABOUT LITERATURE

18

In college literature courses, you will read, discuss, and write about literary texts (poems, plays, novels, short stories) to discover meaning and to give shape to your own experiences. The focus of this critical work of reading and writing is on what the author is saying and on the meaning of what is being said. By interacting with literary texts, you enlarge your understanding of life and the challenges and rewards that it offers.

18.1 Learn to read closely and actively.

When you read a literary text, finding a way to get inside of it becomes a crucial aspect of your reading. If you read closely and actively, you will engage in a process of analysis and interpretation. This concentrated effort is what makes the reading active, and it requires more than simply scanning the words with your eyes. The purpose of this close, active reading is to see possible patterns, connections, and meanings that emerge from the text. To read and understand a text as completely as possible, follow the guidelines discussed below.

18.1a Focus on an author's words.

To focus on an author's words, you must have the necessary tools, one of which is a high-quality dictionary. More important than a dictionary, however, are the patience and discipline needed to discover the meaning of words with which you may be unfamiliar. Remember that one of your goals in reading critically is to understand as fully as possible what an author is saying, so a logical first step is to understand the language an author is using to communicate. (See Chapter 1 for additional strategies for reading critically.)

18.1b Complete multiple readings of a text.

Completing multiple readings of a text is a sign of an intelligent reader. Sometimes a text is difficult to understand after one reading. This complexity may be the result of the author's language and writing style, the sophistication of the thematic elements, or the inclusion of technical devices and elements such as dialect. Multiple readings will result in a greater awareness of what the writer is saying and how it is being said. Just as you notice additional meanings and symbols when you see a movie more than once or hear additional sounds and nuances when you listen to a song again and again, you also will discover additional levels of meaning and understanding by reading a text more than once.

18.1c Annotate a text and keep a reading journal.

Annotating a text is a technique to help you probe the elements of a literary work. During your second or even third reading, jot notes, questions, and reactions to what you are reading. Whether you circle, underline, highlight, or place notes in the margin, develop a system to remind yourself of elements that caught your attention, puzzled or surprised you, or caused some other reaction. Your goal is to explore the literary elements as they unfold before your eyes. Below are some questions to ask as you read and reread a literary work:

> **What** is occurring? What is the action? What is the plot? Are there subplots?
>
> **Who** is involved? How do the characters behave? How do they interact?
>
> **When** and **where** is the action occurring?
>
> What is the **point of view?** Who is speaking to the audience?
>
> What is the **main idea?** What is at the heart of the matter?
>
> What is the **mood** or **emotional tone** of the work?
>
> How effective and powerful is the writer's **language** and **imagery?**
>
> What **type of work** is it? What are the obvious characteristics of the work?

Using these questions to guide your reading and annotation of a text will help you find ways to get inside—and that, after all, is the key to a fuller and richer experience.

An excellent way to think through your initial reactions to a text is by recording your thoughts and making connections among them in a journal. Thoughts and ideas you record in a journal can prepare you for class discussion and may provide fertile ground for essay ideas. Also, keeping a journal can give you practice with writing that will increase your confidence when you are confronted by a blank sheet of paper.

18.1d Study a student's annotations and journal entry.

Following are sample annotations and a journal entry completed while Marilyn Manzer was reading Walt Whitman's "When Lilacs Last in the Dooryard Bloom'd":

Annotated Text

When Lilacs Last in the Dooryard Bloom'd

1

Gentle image— reminder of previous spring

When lilacs last in the dooryard bloom'd,
And the great star early droop'd in the western sky in the
    night,

Sorrow/Grief

I mourn'd, and yet shall mourn with ever-returning
    spring.

Lilac is a beautiful flower and is sweet-smelling. All the sorrow will return each spring.

Ever-returning spring, trinity sure to me you bring,
Lilac blooming perennial and drooping star in the west,
And thought of him I love.

2

O powerful western fallen star!

These images indicate sadness, sorrow, and despair.

O shades of night—O moody, tearful night!
O great star disappear'd—O the black murk that hides the
    star!

Powerless and overpowered by grief

O cruel hands that hold me powerless—O helpless soul
    of me!
O harsh surrounding cloud that will not free my soul.

Repetition

3

In the dooryard fronting an old farm-house near the
    white-wash'd palings,
Stands the lilac-bush tall-growing with heart-shaped
    leaves of rich green,
With many a pointed blossom rising delicate, with
    the perfume strong I love,

Whitman begins to carefully select images from nature— lilac and thrush.

With every leaf a miracle—and from this bush in the
    dooryard,
With delicate-color'd blossoms and heart-shaped leaves of
    rich green,
A sprig with its flower I break.

4

In the swamp in secluded recesses,
A shy and hidden bird is warbling a song.

Solitary the thrush,
The hermit withdrawn to himself, avoiding the
    settlements,
Sings by himself a song.

Is this the expression of grief?

Song of the <u>bleeding throat,</u>
<u>Death's outlet song of life,</u> (for well dear brother I know,
If thou wast not granted to sing thou would'st surely die.)

5

Over the breast of the spring, the land, amid cities,
Amid lanes and through old woods, where lately the
   violets peep'd from the ground, spotting the gray debris,

Series of vital signs of spring and life

Amid the grass in the fields each side of the lanes, passing
   the endless grass,
Passing the yellow-spear'd wheat, every grain from its
   shroud in the dark-brown fields uprisen,
Passing the apple-tree blows of white and pink in the
   orchards,
Carrying a <u>corpse</u> to where it shall rest in the grave,
Night and day journeys a <u>coffin.</u>

Counters with negatives of corpse and coffin

6

Coffin that passes through lanes and streets,
Through day and night with the great cloud darkening the
   land,
With the pomp of the inloop'd flags with the cities draped
   in black,
With the show of the States themselves as of crape-veil'd
   women standing,

All the vibrant colors are overwhelmed by black.

With processions long and winding and the flambeaus of
   the night,
With the countless torches lit, with the <u>silent sea of faces</u>
   and the unbared heads,
With the waiting depot, the arriving coffin, and the
   sombre faces,

Feels like a slow-motion sequence in a movie.

With <u>dirges through the night,</u> with the thousand voices
   rising strong and solemn,
With all the <u>mournful voices of the dirges</u> pour'd around
   the coffin,
The <u>dim-lit churches and the shuddering organs</u>—where
   amid these you journey,
With the <u>tolling tolling bells' perpetual clang,</u>
Here, coffin that slowly passes,
I give you my sprig of lilac.

Journal Entry

> STANZA 1
>
> The mentioning of lilacs blooming as a marker of time passing is interesting and unique. But immediately it is coupled with the darker image of the "great star early droop'd." It seems with every spring, the poet will mourn.
>
> STANZA 2
>
> Multiples of sorrow ("moody, tearful night!" "black murk that hides the star!"). The feeling of sorrow fills the poet's soul—his soul is imprisoned by his grief.
>
> STANZA 4
>
> Another important image from nature—the bird/thrush. Have to spend more time on these two phrases: "Song of the bleeding throat" and "Death's outlet song of life." Not quite sure what they mean, but they are powerful images.
>
> STANZA 5
>
> Whitman seems to catalog a series of images that signify life and vitality—violets, grass, wheat, apple blossoms—but then he includes the stark image of the coffin on its journey.

As you can see, this journal entry contains the beginnings of connections that the writer discovered in Whitman's poem. Continuing to annotate the poem and completing additional journal entries enabled the student to develop much of the material for the explication essay in section 18.3a.

Annotating a Literary Text

Using the example of Marilyn Manzer's annotations of sections of Walt Whitman's "When Lilacs Last in the Dooryard Bloom'd" as a model, annotate a poem by your favorite poet. Use highlighting, underlining, circling, and the like to mark the text of the poem, and then add margin notes to record your reactions. After annotating the poem, compose a journal entry in which you expand the marginal notes to discover threads that you can connect into patterns of understanding.

EXERCISE 18A

18.2 Learn to discover and explore complexities in literary texts.

Discovering and exploring complexities in a literary text require an organized and focused examination of that work. The elements for effective essay writing are common to writing about literature as well. The process of developing an essay (see Chapters 3 and 4) and the methods for constructing an argument (see Chapter 6) that you studied earlier in this book will assist you in presenting your interpretation and analysis of a literary text. As you begin, you need to state the **central premise** that is a result of your critical reading of and reaction to a literary text. This premise can be seen as a provable assertion that you will develop through an examination of related claims. (The central premise and related claims are similar to the claim and warrants in Toulmin's layout of argumentation, which was discussed in Chapter 6.) In a logical discussion, you will move from one aspect of the literary work to another while keeping the essay focused and structured.

It is also necessary to illustrate the accuracy of your claims by including textual evidence from the literary work that you are analyzing. As you continue to blend your comments with textual evidence, your essay will reveal additional and more complex insights. Through a continuous process of drafting and revising, you have the opportunity to produce an enhanced and more thoughtful interpretation.

NOTE

Any type of literary analysis should include **textual evidence** to illustrate your analytical comments. This evidence should be quoted directly from the selection under consideration and should follow the conventions for use of signal phrases, quotation marks, and proper citation format according to the instructions provided by your professor. (See Chapter 15 for information on how to include direct quotations in your essay; see Chapter 44 for information on the use of quotation marks.)

Responses to literature can follow a number of approaches. Three primary formats for literary analysis are summary and response, explication, and literary critique. It is customary to follow the Modern Language Association (MLA) format for citing textual evidence (see Chapter 15 for more information) when writing these types of essays.

18.2a Summary and response.

This type of literary analysis requires a writer *to summarize the most important information that an author presents and then to compose a reaction to the literary text.* In completing a **summary and response** assignment, you must first demonstrate an understanding of the essential points in a text. The response forms the second part of the assignment, and here you can agree or disagree with the author's premise and conclusions, or you can describe what you thought about and how you felt as you read the work. Also, you may discuss what impact the reading had on you. Rereading individual passages or the entire text will make your summary more accurate and thorough and your response more certain and complete.

Summary and response assignments are often used as the basis for class discussion, as a supplement to close reading of a literary text, and as the starting point for more elaborate methods of literary analysis, like explication and critique, which are discussed in the following sections.

■ ■ ■ ■　　■ ■ ■ ■　　**B A S I C L I N K**　■ ■ ■ ■　　　■ ■ ■ ■

WWW

To read more on writing about literature, visit
http://owl.english.purdue.edu/handouts/general/gl_lit.html

18.3 Learn to explicate.

This type of literary analysis requires a writer *to review a literary text in a systematic manner* and generally includes *combining a thematic analysis with observations about the technical elements of a text.* An **explication** often involves a line-by-line review of a short poem, a section from a longer poem, or a brief passage from a short story or novel. For example, in explicating a poem, you would combine an analysis of what the poet is writing about with comments about how the poet's intentions were accomplished through the poem's structure and components. In addition to commenting about the theme, you would describe the word choices, images, line length, meter, beat, rhyme, and other noteworthy technical features in the poem. You would explore how the elements work individually and together to help the poet achieve a specific effect or a particular purpose.

18.3a Analyze a sample explication.

The following essay grew out of the annotations and journal entry illustrated earlier in this chapter (see sections 18.1d and e).

Student's/professor's name, course title, date in upper-left corner.

Marilyn J. Manzer

Professor Strugala

English 243-IS

20 July 2003

"When Lilacs Last in the Dooryard Bloom'd,"   *Title centered.*

by Walt Whitman

All poets manifest passion for the natural world and uni-

verse, and Walt Whitman reflects this philosophy in his poem

"When Lilacs Last in the Dooryard Bloom'd," written immedi-

ately following Lincoln's death as his body was taken by train

in a long procession through American cities back to his home

in Springfield, Illinois. In "Lilacs," Whitman illustrates his in-

tense grief over Lincoln's death through masterful imagery: *Central premise stated.*

lilac, star, bird, song, wind, and trees. Whitman's writing style

is pensive and meditative, and his thoughts spring forth as

seeds blooming into a poignant harmonizing of his grief.

The lilac is symbolic of Whitman's love for Lincoln, and

since this fragrant flower is perennial, Whitman's love and

memories of Lincoln will be immortal, eternal, deathless. He

speaks of the lilac bush "in the dooryard fronting an old farm-

house," which has "heart-shaped leaves" and a "delicate . . .   *Ellipsis used to indicate omission.*

perfume strong I love" (lines 12-14). Breaking a sprig from the

early green flower, yet to experience its lavender bloom, he

says: "Here, coffin that slowly passes, / I give you my sprig of   *Slash used to indicate line division.*

Historical back-ground given in introduction to help reader understand poem.

Quotations used as support.

Word lines used with first quotation.

Writer's last name and page number in upper-right corner of all pages.

Word *lines* omitted from subsequent references.

lilac" (44-45). Further, he writes: "The lilac that blooms first, / copious I break . . . the sprigs from the bushes, / With loaded arms I come, pouring for you" (51-53). The symbol of the lilac also carries sorrow in that Lincoln's life was cut short in mid-bloom. Whitman refers to a "trinity," which includes the "lilac," a "drooping star," and the "thought of him I love."

Short quotations integrated into text.

Poem analyzed line by line; organized by symbols used.

Whitman elaborates on this "drooping star," lamenting: "O powerful western fallen star! / O shades of night—O moody, tearful night! / O great star disappear'd—O the black murk that hides the star!" (7-9) and "O western orb sailing the heavens" (55). The star symbolizes Lincoln. Just as stars and planets hold eternal, fixed positions in the heavens, the star fittingly symbolizes Lincoln's steadfast leadership of the nation. The star now <u>droops</u> as Lincoln lies in death. In his grief, Whitman describes hearing the song of a bird in the swamp, but "the lustrous star has detain'd me, / The star my departing comrade holds me" (69-70), and he writes: "O comrade lustrous with silver face in the night" (197).

Lincoln's body, carried by train through the night, in a coffin draped in black, is symbolized as a star concealed by clouds, veiled as "the black murk that hides the star!" (9). The image of death and sorrow represented by veils and clouds <u>hiding</u> the star is consistent in Whitman's references to the "Coffin that passes through lanes and streets, / . . . with the great cloud

Manzer 3

darkening the land" (33-34), and "the flags with the cities draped in black," and "crape-vell'd women standing" (35-36).

Lincoln's persona is represented not only by the <u>star</u>, but also by the <u>bird</u> and his <u>song</u>. Whitman writes: "In the swamp in secluded recesses, / A shy and hidden bird is warbling a song. / Solitary the thrush . . . Sings by himself a song" (18-22). This bird is Lincoln, as his life pours out in song, passing through the fields, swamps, and woods by train en route to his home in Illinois. His dying message is a "Song of the bleeding throat, / Death's outlet song of life" (23-24); thus Whitman writes: "Sing on there in the swamp, / O singer bashful and tender" (66-67), and "Sing on, sing on you gray-brown bird, / Sing from the swamps" (99-100). Also, the lines "Sing on dearest brother, warble your reedy song, / Loud human song, with voice of uttermost woe" (102-03), connect the persona of the bird to Lincoln. The bird is called a "brother" who sings a "human song," and the star is his "comrade," his friend.

Analysis of structure combined with list of symbols used.

The lilac, star and clouds, bird, song, and trees are referenced in a circular pattern, one to the next and back again, and gradually all are brought together. The last verse begins: "I cease from my song for thee" (195), as Whitman's grief subsides in the gray-brown bird's song of comfort, and he finds solace in the beauty of the memories of his beloved President. He writes: ". . . memory ever to keep, for the dead I loved so well, /

Manzer 4

For the sweetest, wisest soul of all my days and lands . . ." (203-4). Whitman conveys harmony as the images come together in the last two lines of the poem, and he concludes: "Lilac and star and bird twined with the chant of my soul, / There in the fragrant pines and the cedars dusk and dim" (205-6).

Whitman's writing style in "Lilacs" is appropriate to the mood and theme. Symbolic images and new thoughts are introduced in short lines, just as thoughts, memories, or observations might dart into one's mind or be recalled in a gentle simplicity, e.g., "O powerful western fallen star" (7), "Solitary the thrush" (20), "Song of the bleeding throat" (23), "I give you my sprig of lilac" (45), "Sing on there in the swamp" (66), "Lo, body and soul—this land" (89), or "From deep secluded recesses" (129), "Come lovely and soothing death" (135), "To the tally of my soul" (163), and "I cease from my song for thee" (195).

Following these introductions, the lines become longer and more elaborate. For example, after "Song of the bleeding throat," Whitman writes: "Death's outlet song of life, (for well dear brother I know, / If thou wast not granted to sing thou would'st surely die.)" (24-25). Also, after "Sing on there in the swamp," he writes: "O singer bashful and tender, I hear your notes, I hear your call, / I hear, I come presently, I understand you" (67-68). Most exemplary of this style are the lines which follow "Sea winds blown from east and west" (74), as Whitman

Observations about technical aspect of poem used to further thematic analysis.

Manzer 5

engages in a detailed description of the landscape along "the long black trail." He describes details of "Pictures of growing spring and farms and homes" (81), "pale green leaves of the trees prolific" (84), "ranging hills on the banks" (86), "scenes of life and the workshops, and the workmen homeward returning" (88), and "varied and ample land, the South and the North in the light" (96), "spires, . . . tides, and the ships" (90), "scenery of my land with its lakes and forests" (110), "fields all busy with labor" (114), and "summer approaching with richness" (114). It is as though Whitman sets readers on the train alongside Lincoln, viewing the American countryside as it passes by the solemn windows. Just as "winds that blow east and west" meet at the prairie, joining the nation together, likewise Lincoln is the symbolic wind unifying the nation in the Civil War. Appropriately, just as human thoughts spring forth extemporaneously, and the human mind ponders in an ordinary exposition, Whitman's "Lilacs" is free of a rhyme scheme.

"When Lilacs Last in the Dooryard Bloom'd" expresses Whitman's intense grief over the loss of Abraham Lincoln, a man whom he revered. As Whitman's emotions heighten, he turns to the natural world and universe in an introspective quest for death's meaning; then his sorrow lifts, and he acknowledges beauty in this mysterious cycle, which ushers in a peaceful serenity in the final realization that life and death

Central premise restated in conclusion.

Manzer 6

share splendor. The lilac, star, bird, song, and trees all come

together in one place, as if one's tense hand spread in a full

span might have its five fingers gently knitted together in

repose.

This analysis explores Walt Whitman's use of poetic imagery as a vehicle to express his intense grief over Abraham Lincoln's death. The introductory paragraph presents an overview that explains how Whitman's use of natural images throughout the poem contributes to his purpose. The student carefully analyzes each image in succession and integrates quotations from the poem to illustrate her comments. The quoted lines and passages are exactly as they appear in the poem. A slash is used to indicate line divisions. This explication contains a reasonably effective balance of analysis and textual evidence from the poem.

Developing an Explication

Building on the annotations and journal entry that you completed in Exercise 18A, compose an explication of the poem that you have chosen for review. Remember to combine the essential elements of a thematic analysis with observations about the poet's use of technical elements. Include specific evidence from the poem to illustrate the explication.

EXERCISE 18B

18.4 Learn to critique.

A **literary critique** focuses primarily on how writers use language to express their ideas and perceptions in unique styles. Such critiques may require the student writer *to look at an individual text from a specific critical stance.* Each stance is based on specific assumptions and requires the student writer to approach a literary text from a particular perspective. Below is a list of stances students of literature may be called upon to adopt.

Formalist stance: Focuses on the language and structure of a work. Emphasis is placed on how the form and content of a work express the author's meaning. Traditional elements (plot, setting, narrative technique) and unique elements (diction, metaphor, symbol) receive special consideration.

Biographical stance: Focuses on the author's life through autobiography, biography, letters, diaries, interviews, and other works to inform and enrich this perspective on the text.

Psychological stance: Focuses on psychoanalytical concepts (for example, Freud's theories about the unconscious) to understand motivations and symbolic meanings in a text. These theoretical concepts can also be applied to the author or to a reader's personal reaction to a text.

Mythological stance: Focuses on elements (archetypes) in a work that speak to universal hopes, fears, perceptions, and the need for meaning in the lives of individuals and cultures. Some common archetypes include quests, initiations, and death-rebirth cycles.

Cultural stance: Focuses on individual and group relationships as they exist in a literary work; the notion of social forces and the impact on groups or classes of people.

Feminist stance: Focuses on representations of women, analyzed from a female-consciousness perspective, with attention to gender issues such as image and equality.

Deconstructionist stance: Focuses on the language of a text analyzed closely to demonstrate its instability in contributing to a single meaning. This critical theory holds that all literary texts have contradictory meanings and no unified, or "fixed," meanings.

Reader-response stance: Focuses on the reader's process of reading and reacting to a text, particularly what a reader experiences intellectually and emotionally when interacting with a text. A reader, in fact, is re-creating the work, and this interpretation informs the critique.

18.4a Analyze a sample literary critique.

The student essay on the following pages provides a useful example of a literary critique.

Sara Murphy

Professor Strugala

English 244

21 March 2003

The American Novel: Kate Chopin's <u>The Awakening</u>

Throughout the centuries, women have had a difficult journey in order to become full persons. Women's feelings and
wants were often unnoticed or disregarded by their husbands,
as well as the society in which they lived. They were forced to
fight hard in order to develop themselves as individuals capable
of communicating their desires. Women had to struggle to free
their sexual wishes and passions. Kate Chopin's novel <u>The
Awakening</u> gives its readers insight into a woman's exploration
of both her emotional freedom and her sexual awareness.

Women must become sensitive to their own needs and
shed their concern for others' opinions before they can feel
true freedom. Kate Chopin allows her readers to walk through
the steps of Edna Pontellier's slow unfolding of herself. Edna
buds slowly throughout the novel and blooms over time, ex-
posing her exotic colors. The more she discovers about herself, the freer she allows herself to become.

Women at the turn of the century often felt repressed
by the men within their communities. Edna Pontellier is no

Central premise stated.

Writer's interpretation linked to Chopin's novel.

Flower metaphor (buds, blooms) used here for main character's process of self-discovery.

Murphy 2

Textual evidence (direct quote from novel) used to illustrate theme.

different from these women. Chopin writes, "An indescribable oppression, which seemed to generate in some unfamiliar part of her consciousness, filled her whole being with a vague anguish" (6). Edna recognizes that something stands in her way. She knows that a wall exists between the women and men within her society; Edna senses this boundary in her own life. She even feels it while in a place associated with the greatest peace, as well as the greatest sexism—church. Chopin explains, "A feeling of oppression and drowsiness overcame Edna during the service . . . her one thought was to quit the stifling atmosphere of the church and reach the open air" (38). New feelings begin to stir within her and as a result she begins to see the manacles of oppression which possess her freedom.

Edna's process of discontent and discovery tracked.

Edna's first brief glance of freedom is compared to a child's first realization that he or she is capable of maneuvering on his or her own. Chopin illustrates this by writing, "that night she was like the little tottering, stumbling, clutching child, who all of a sudden realizes its powers, and walks for the first time alone, boldly and with over-confidence" (29). Little by little Edna allows the heavy chains that hold her down to loosen themselves. She, like the newly developing child, begins to take small steps in the direction of self-reliance and liberation from both society and herself. Chopin paints Edna's aroused

Murphy 3

feelings by explaining, "A feeling of exultation overtook her, as if some power of significant import had been given her to control the working of her body and her soul. She grew daring. . . . She wanted to swim far out, where no woman had swum before . . . she swam out alone" (29-30). Even though she is invigorated by this feeling, Edna becomes afraid of the vastness that lies before her. She tells her husband, "I thought I should have perished out there alone" (30). Like a child, she regresses to old behavior because of fear of the unknown. Edna returns to the traditional beliefs of society; she longs to be free yet is afraid of standing alone.

Sophisticated understanding of focal character's behavior shown here.

As Edna becomes more aware of her need to free herself from the puppet strings that determine her every move, she begins to take in and appreciate newly arisen sensations. She begins to slowly shed her old self and expose her soul, her true identity, to the world. Chopin explains, ". . . Edna felt as if she were being borne away from some anchorage which had held her fast, whose chains had been loosening—had snapped the night before when the mystic spirit was abroad, leaving her free to drift whithersoever she chose to set her sails" (37). Chopin illustrates this breaking through with a metaphor of a clothed body slowly revealing its nakedness to nature. She writes:

Powerful quote from novel used to illustrate theme—dramatic sundering of character's previous identity.

> Edna . . . loosened her clothes, removing the
> greater part of them. . . . She ran her fingers

Murphy 4

> through her loosened hair for a while. She looked
> at her round arms as she held them straight up and
> rubbed them one after the other, observing closely,
> as if for the first time, the fine, firm quality and tex-
> ture of her flesh. (39)

Edna begins to capture the essence of who she is; she gets to know herself in the most intimate of ways. Chopin explains:

> She could only realize that she herself—her present
> self—was in some way different from the other self.
> That she was seeing with different eyes and making
> the aquaintance of new conditions in herself that
> colored and changed her environment, she did not
> yet suspect. (43)

Edna is aware that changes are taking place, but she is un-aware of how deeply rooted these changes are. She knows that unseasoned sensations are being stimulated, but due to her in-experience with them, Edna in unsure of how to deal with them.

Edna cautiously seeks out her true identity, careful not to fully expose herself all at once. She slowly lets this new self's ideas and beliefs seep out into her daily life. Chopin reveals that Edna, "remained in the drawing-room the entire afternoon re-ceiving her visitors. . . . This had been the programme which Mrs. Pontellier had religiously followed since her marriage six years before" (54). To illustrate Edna's change, Chopin writes,

Murphy 5

"Mrs. Pontellier did not wear her usual Tuesday reception gown; she was in ordinary house dress" (54). Not only does Edna disregard her established rituals, but she also gives no explanation as to why she has ignored her expected arrangements. She becomes unconcerned with the beliefs and thoughts of others.

Over time, Edna does not concern herself with what other people say about her. She asks her husband, "Why are you taking the thing so seriously and making such a fuss over it?" (55). Her husband explains, "I'm not making any fuss over it. But it's such seeming trifles that we've got to take seriously; such things count" (55). Edna becomes less concerned with her social standing as she begins to unlock her heart's chains and allows her desires to go free. She harmonizes only with her needs and her aspirations. Chopin states, "She began to do as she liked and to feel as she liked" (61). Her sole concern is her own happiness, which she has previously put on hold in order to please the other people in her life. Edna begins to live for herself and to disassociate from guilty feelings due to her newfound freedom.

As part of Edna's unveiling, she slowly peels away her former self and discards it from her life. She permits this new personality to shine through. Chopin paints this picture by writing, "she was becoming herself and daily casting aside that fictitious self which we assume like a garment with which to appear be-

Murphy 6

fore the world" (62). Edna treats her emotions like items, which can be removed with no sense of loss; she is glad to rid herself of the familiar. In addition, she encompasses the ideal of freedom. Part of her yearns for escape from the societal traditions she faces. Edna states, "I know I shall like it, like the feeling of freedom and independence" (86). Chopin explains that Edna "had resolved never again to belong to another than herself" (86). She only wants to listen to the stimulating and steady song found within her heart.

Edna Pontellier becomes aware not only of her freedom but of her budding sexuality as a result of her self-exploration. She cannot help but expel the stifled and systematic "love" that she experiences with her husband. Edna opens herself to the sting of true love. For the first time, she is haunted by intense passions for Robert. Chopin reveals Edna's awareness by writing, "No multitude of words could have been more significant than those moments of silence, or more pregnant with the first-felt throbbings of desire" (32). These feelings allow Edna the freedom to welcome the sparks needed to turn her heart's kindling into a blaze.

Her passion enables her to fully shed her concern for others' opinions: "Every step . . . toward relieving herself from obligations added to her strength and expansion as an individual. . . . No longer was she content to 'feed upon

Textual evidence used to track deepening of Edna's self-awareness.

Metaphorical language (sparks, heart's kindling, blaze) used to demonstrate student writer's understanding of Edna's embrace of sensual and carnal desires.

Murphy 7

opinion' when her own soul had invited her" (101). Edna wants control over her life; she now feels she is capable of bringing her feelings to the surface and expressing them as she sees fit.

Similarly, Edna awakens to latent feelings of love once she realizes that she is free to act upon her desires. Chopin illustrates, "When he [Robert] leaned forward and kissed her, she clasped his head, holding his lips to hers. It was the first kiss of her life to which her nature had really responded. It was a flaming torch that kindled desire" (90). Her insides burn with desire, but she does not want the fire to be extinguished. Edna wants this passion to continually flame. Once she releases herself and reveals her needs to herself, she tells Robert, "I love you . . . only you; no one but you. It was you who awoke me last summer out of a life-long, stupid dream" (117). By speaking her true emotions, Edna comes to the understanding that it takes only a simple act of love to unfasten rusted shackles put in place to hold human emotion. Just as quickly as she realizes this, Edna learns that love can only fill the heart's void; love cannot fill the emptiness of the soul when it is too strong.

Claim that Edna's emotional upheaval comes with psychological turmoil is presented and supported with textual evidence.

Edna tastes the bittersweetness of love when she realizes that she cannot be with Robert; he had not yet shed the shackles of social opinion. Chopin reveals, "The house was

Murphy 8

empty. But he [Robert] had scrawled on a piece of paper

that lay in the lamplight: 'I love you. Good-by—because I

love you'" (121). Because Robert and Edna love each other

"too well," they cannot execute the action. Edna brings forth

love in Robert, and he awakens her senses. As she realizes

that the two of them will never be together, all her freshly

awakened emotions leave her open to pain and deep

thought. Chopin writes, "Edna grew faint when she read the

words. . . . She did not sleep. She did not go to bed" (121).

She is unable to put newly arisen sentiments to bed and, in

turn, begins to experience the anguish that often results

form forbidden, perfect love.

    The first experience of heartbreak leaves Edna deeply

hurt. Chopin compares her to a wounded bird. She writes, "A

bird with a broken wing was beating the air above, reeling, flut-

tering, circling disabled down, down to the water" (124). But

through this pain Edna achieves freedom. Like a bird, she can

now shed the earth and soar alone. Chopin demonstrates this

by bringing Edna back to the sea. Edna exposes herself to the

elements and this time embraces the solitude that comes with

complete freedom:

        . . . for the first time in her life she stood there naked

        in the open air, at the mercy of the sun, the breeze

        that beat upon her, and the waves that invited

Writer's comments
successfully
interwoven with
appropriate textual
evidence to justify
interpretation.

Murphy 8

her. . . . She remembered the night she swam far

out, and recalled the terror that seized her at the

fear of being unable to regain the shore. She did not

look back now, but went on. (124)

Kate Chopin paints a picture of a young woman coming

to terms with who she is, as well as her ability to make her life

what she wants it to be. Despite the trials and pain that go

along with gaining ultimate freedom, it is all worth it in order to

break free from the binding chains of the male-dominated so-

ciety. Through Chopin's description of Edna Pontellier's

"awakening," it is possible to understand the need for individu-

ality. When women take the initiative to liberate themselves

from binding situations, they gain the greatest freedom ever

found: self-knowledge.

Essay concludes by discussing result of Edna's gaining emotional freedom and sexual awareness.

This literary critique explores the themes of emotional freedom and sexual awareness in Kate Chopin's *The Awakening*. To delineate her interpretation, Sara Murphy effectively explores her central premise that "Chopin allows her readers to walk through the steps of Edna Pontellier's unfolding of herself." In her essay, Murphy evidences a very sensitive reading of the novel that leads to her perceptive analysis of Edna's evolving self-recognition and self-discovery. Her commentary is quite successful in its structured review of relevant themes and the inclusion of appropriate textual evidence as illustration.

EXERCISE 18C

Developing a Literary Critique

Select one of the critical stances explained in section 18.4, and develop a literary critique of a short story of your choice. Remember to feature the specific perspective of the critical stance you have selected and illustrate the analysis with textual evidence from the story.

Chapter Checklist

1 ∷ Learn to read closely and actively by focusing on an author's words, completing multiple readings of a literary text, annotating the text thoroughly and carefully, and keeping a journal.

2 ∷ Learn to discover and explore complexities in literary texts by understanding different types of literary formats, such as summary and response, explication, and literary critique.

3 ∷ Remember to include evidence from the text (short story, novel, poem, play, autobiography, biography, memoir, or letter) to illustrate your analytical comments.

4 ∷ Be certain to document properly all textual evidence according to the directions provided by your instructor.

COMMUNICATING IN CLASS:
Essay Examinations and Oral Presentations

19.1 **Develop a technique for writing essay examinations.**

19.2 **Understand the elements of oral presentations.**

CHAPTER CHECKLIST

19.1 Develop a technique for writing essay examinations.

Examinations that require you to write an essay in response to a question or topic are becoming more prevalent in college courses. These essay examinations provide you with an opportunity to demonstrate that you understand the material, concepts, and knowledge from a specific course or discipline. They may also allow you to show you can apply the information to a specific situation or set of theoretical constructs.

19.1a Apply the writing process.

In an essay examination, you will write in a timed situation on a topic or in response to a question that may be unknown to you in advance. To compose an effective essay in a timed situation, you can apply the stages of the writing process, discussed in Chapters 2, 3, and 5. Although time is of the essence, if you manage the situation wisely, you can use the examination time to plan, draft, and edit your response.

Although the time allowed for the exam may not be as much time as you would like or need, you can control how it is used. Breaking it down into segments (according to your needs for planning, drafting, and editing) and determining the portion of time needed for each stage will give you the best results. For example, in a one-hour essay exam, student A may allot ten minutes for planning, forty minutes for drafting, and ten minutes for editing; student B may alter that plan and use five minutes for planning, fifty minutes for drafting, and five minutes for editing. Again, the variable that you control is how you divide the time allotted for completing the response. By becoming familiar with your own writing process, you can divide the examination time into the most effective segments to meet your individual needs as a writer.

19.1b Decode the directions.

Successful essay writing in a testing situation requires that you understand what is expected of you. An essay exam topic usually includes a **core word** that indicates the primary academic activity the examination is set up to test. This core word provides directions to the examinee about the response that is expected. Here are some core words often found in essay exam topics, along with brief definitions:

Analyze	Separate into parts and discuss the parts and their meanings
Argue	Present a claim and provide reasons supporting it
Clarify	Make clear and understandable
Classify	Organize into groups
Compare and contrast	Identify similarities and differences
Define	State the meaning of
Describe	Depict in words
Discuss	Consider or comment upon
Evaluate	Determine the significance or value of
Explain	Make clear or intelligible
Identify	Explain the origin or nature of
Interpret	Provide the meaning of
Relate	Demonstrate connections
Summarize	Show the major points

Often, additional words, called **modifiers,** are used in the directions to help you focus your response to the topic. For example, adjectives or adverbs, such as *most significant, primary, briefly, comprehensively,* will be used to limit or qualify the primary direction.

Sample Topics for Essay Examinations

Identify the most significant problem facing world leaders in the twenty-first century.

In this example, *identify* is the core word and *most significant* is the modifier. A successful response to this topic would name a critical problem facing world leaders and explain why it is the most critical problem.

Describe the primary function of the pituitary gland.

In this example, *describe* is the core word and *primary* is the modifier. A successful response would present details of the most essential action of the pituitary gland.

Discuss the principal effect of Ralph Nader's campaign on the 2000 presidential election.

Here, *discuss* is the core word and *principal* is the modifier. An effective response would consider the impact Nader's campaign had on the campaigns of his opponents, Al Gore and George W. Bush, and explain its key role in the election.

Explore how John Steinbeck's *The Winter of Our Discontent* can be seen as a metaphor for American society at the time it was written.

In this example, *explore* is the core word. An effective response would explain how the narrative action of the novel and the moral dilemmas faced by the characters reflect social upheaval in American society.

19.1c Prepare well and maintain a good attitude.

As with other written assignments, a successful essay-exam response depends on the amount of preparation you have completed. Reviewing the material that will be the focus of the examination (chapters from a textbook, lecture or class notes, discussion group activities) will give you a degree of certainty about the course material.

This preparation will, in turn, increase your self-confidence about performing well on the exam. Also, when drafting the essay, remember to support your comments with examples and illustrations. Often these examples will be specific evidence quoted directly from the texts that are the basis for the exam. If you prepare well and follow this process, you can be confident about demonstrating your mastery of the course content.

19.2 Understand the elements of oral presentations.

Even though our world is becoming more technologically advanced in the realm of written communications, businesses as well as graduate and professional schools are emphasizing competence in the oral communication skills of undergraduate students. Recently, a major state university in the eastern United States instituted an oral proficiency requirement throughout its expository writing program. The requirement resulted from requests by business and industry for improved oral presentation skills in recently hired employees. As part of the writing curriculum, students will now receive instruction in reporting results of group work, providing status reports on individual writing projects, and developing techniques for formal presentations of research findings. Another example involves the owner of a local real estate agency who contacted our college for assistance in enhancing the oral presentation skills of his agency's sales representatives.

Oral presentations, much like essays, can range from explaining something to encouraging a specific action on the part of your listeners. Along with reading and writing, being able to express yourself orally is an ability that will pay lifelong benefits. Focusing on the following elements will help you become a successful oral presenter: purpose, audience, message, and preparation. Note that sample student notes are included to illustrate what these four elements entail.

19.2a Decide on your purpose.

The first element is deciding on a purpose for your presentation. Are you trying to explain an idea, reaction, or concept? Are you reporting on something that has occurred, or are you providing a status report on the current state of a process, project, or problem? Are you trying to persuade your audience to change its opinion or to follow a specific course of action? Spending some time thinking about and refining your purpose will provide a workable blueprint for the presentation.

Sample Student Notes: Purpose of the Presentation

Assignment for Composition 101: Oral presentation of documented essay research results
1. *Purpose is to present holistic treatments of pets (especially dogs).*
2. *Specific focus will be on use of acupuncture to treat arthritis in older dogs.*
3. *Will also work to persuade audience that acupuncture for treatment of arthritis in*
dogs is improvement over conventional treatments.

19.2b Identify your audience.

An important element is assessing the audience for your presentation. Conventional demographic information (age, gender, etc.) about the audience is useful, as is a determination of the audience's level of familiarity with and knowledge of the topic of the presentation. This information will help you decide on the amount and level of details and definitions you need to include. Your goal is to strike a balance of providing enough specifics to explain clearly without losing the audience in a sea of details.

Sample Student Notes: Planning the Appeal to the Target Audience

Audience: professor, eighteen students in Composition 101 class
1. *Professor is about age fifty; knowledgeable (obviously?) about many areas.*
2. *Students are approximately in late teens to early twenties; equal number of males and females; three or four students seem to be older (thirties?).*
3. *No knowledge if any are pet owners or dog owners; might be a good opening to poll audience by show of hands to see if any are pet/dog owners; ask if any have heard of alternative treatments in vet medicine.*
4. *Will need to define terms in holistic veterinary medicine and briefly describe traditional veterinary treatments such as medication and surgery.*

19.2c Make your message clear.

Obviously, the message is the reason for the presentation. Having determined your purpose and characterized your audience, you can customize the material of your message to develop the most appropriate and effective presentation. The language of your message should be clear and concise. The organization should be easy to follow, so type out an outline (see Chapter 3) to work from; make sure you cover your key points in a logical order. You will also need to provide oral clues or prompts so that the audience can follow your line of reasoning. (Review the material on transitions in Chapter 4.) The oral directions that you provide will work as signals to guide your audience through complicated information. Remember, whatever your purpose, you certainly want your audience to understand the message.

Sample Student Outline: Planning the Content of the Presentation

A. **Background and context**

1. Background of personal interest (my dog Buddy).
2. Overview of holistic veterinary medicine: acupuncture, chiropractic, herbal medicine, homeopathy, nutrition counseling, and complementary modalities.
3. Specific focus: treatment of arthritis in older dogs through the use of acupuncture.
4. Arthritis affects dogs similar to the ways it affects humans: discomfort and stiffness in joints; difficulty rising, standing, and walking. Certain breeds are more prone to suffer arthritis than others; size and weight of breed are also factors.
5. Traditional treatments: anti-inflammatory medications such as aspirin and cortisone-like drugs; nutritional supplements such as glucosamine sulfate, glucosamine hydrochloride, and chondroitin.
6. Acupuncture is an effective treatment because it increases blood flow, decreases inflammation, improves movement, and relieves pain.

B. **Explanation of acupuncture**

1. Acupuncture has a history of thousands of years as medical treatment.
2. Practice founded in China; Chinese concept of "qi," or "ch'i," involves energy meridians along the body. Sterilized needles are inserted at acupuncture points to correct an imbalance with or interruption of the flow of energy.
3. Practitioner needs to be skilled in needle insertion techniques.

C. **Application of acupuncture to veterinary medicine**

1. Types of problems that can be treated with acupuncture: musculoskeletal, respiratory, urogenital, as well as problems related to the nervous and digestive systems.
2. Breed of dog for my example is golden retriever; age is twelve years; symptoms are stiffness in hip joints and some difficulty in rising, standing, and walking.
3. Treating veterinarian must be licensed in acupuncture therapy; suggests treatment that will stimulate acupuncture points; prescribed treatment requires insertion of needles at specific points around neck, along spine, in hip region, and in lower rear legs. [Refer audience to slides of acupuncture points.]

4. Schedule of treatments will be twice a week for three weeks, followed by a maintenance schedule of one treatment every other week.
5. Treatment involves insertion of needles at acupuncture points; needles remain in place for twenty minutes.
6. Treatments result in gradual sedating effect on animal following insertion of needles. Bounce-back effect, with increased energy and feeling of well-being, occurs within twenty-four hours of treatment.

D. Wrap-up and final comments
1. Positive, minimally invasive treatment; does not involve drugs or surgery.
2. I have observed dogs receiving treatment; no evidence of pain or discomfort from insertion of needles. Sedative effect noticed in dog's relaxed demeanor and breathing.
3. Treatment is not curative; cannot reverse osteoarthritis or joint instability.
4. Treatment does relieve pain, increase joint mobility, enhance movement, and improve quality of life.
5. Additional promising work being conducted with the use of a laser instead of the needles.
6. Provide audience with Web sites for more information.
   a. www.alternativevet.org
   b. www.altvetmed.com
   c. www.wbvc.bc.ca

19.2d Prepare to give the presentation.

The initial impression on an audience is critical, so you want to plan the introduction of the presentation very carefully. Briefly acknowledging the invitation to speak or mentioning the setting or purpose establishes a positive link to the audience. The tone of the message should be appropriate to your purpose and audience as well. In general, a friendly, conversational tone of voice works well in most situations; the degree of formality or informality can be adjusted during the presentation. Similarly, the closing of the presentation requires careful thought. Depending on your purpose, you will need to determine if a repetition of the most significant points is essential, or if a humorous or inspiring comment would be more appropriate. The presentation should have a definite conclusion. If time is available, you might allow questions from the audience as a way of tying up loose ends and reminding the audience of key points.

Audio and Visual Aids

Many presenters include audio and/or visual aids to highlight or reinforce key points in their presentations. These materials can be charts, graphs, photographs, slides, videos, audiotapes, flip charts, and PowerPoint presentations. You need to be judicious in the use of such aids. For instance, if you distribute a handout, avoid providing a written text of the presentation. You do not want the audience to be reading while you are trying to engage them. Also, when using visual aids such as PowerPoint slides, be certain that everyone in the audience can see the information. A visual aid that cannot be seen or read is useless. Test the effectiveness of any visual aid that you plan to use. Imagine sitting in the audience; ask yourself whether the audio or visual aid would add to or detract from the presentation. For more information on how to design visual aids, see Chapter 9.

Sample Student Notes: Show slides of canine point outline to indicate acupuncture points for insertion of needles during treatment.

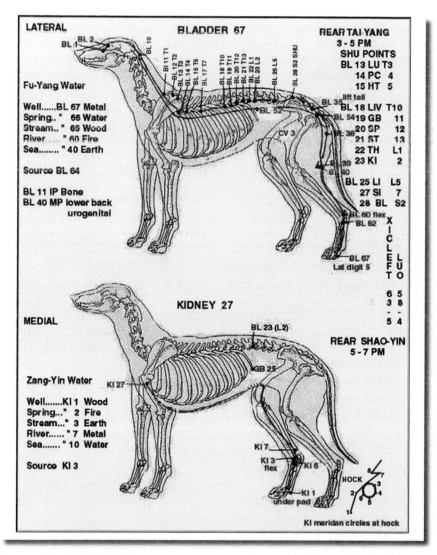

Acupuncture Point Outline

Practice

Always make sure you practice your presentation until you are comfortable with your material and comfortable in front of an audience. Remember that good presenters do not read from a prepared script or memorize their presentations word for word. Instead, they practice until they are comfortable working from brief notes or lists of key topics, and speaking directly to the audience.

When first starting to rehearse your presentation, work in front of a mirror. Then tape your presentation (on video or audio tape) and lip synch to the tape. This will help you perfect your timing and allow you to concentrate on making sure your gestures are appropriate and that you make eye contact. Finally, try to gather a real audience to practice in front of; you will feel more comfortable before your target audience if you practice in front of a live audience.

Sample Student Notes: Planning the Rehearsals

1. I want to rehearse in front of a full-length mirror and tape-record the presentation.

2. When I play back the tape, I want to lip-synch the words and concentrate on gestures and eye contact.

3. If I have time, maybe I'll get some friends or family members to sit in as a "real" audience and provide feedback on the clarity of the message and evaluate the overall presentation.

Tips for Oral Presentations

1. Decide whether your purpose is to explain, report, or persuade, and keep this purpose in mind as you craft your presentation.

2. Identify your audience and tailor your presentation to them.

3. Make sure you have a clear message and prepare a simple, easy-to-follow outline of essential words and phrases to guide you.

4. Practice the presentation—first in front of a mirror and later in front of a live audience (if possible)—so that you can make any necessary adjustments. Practice until you are so comfortable with your material that you can speak directly to your audience without depending heavily on your notes or becoming unduly nervous.

All these elements can enhance a presentation and produce a more satisfying result.

Developing an Oral Presentation

EXERCISE 19A

Following the steps explained in sections 19.2a through 19.2d, develop an informative oral presentation on a subject of your choice.

- *Design an audience profile based on your classmates from a current course.*
- *Organize a formal outline of the information.*
- *Select appropriate audio and/or visual materials to illustrate the presentation.*
- *Rehearse the presentation until you are comfortable with your oral skills, gestures, body language, and timing.*

Chapter Checklist

1 To be successful in essay-examination situations, you need to manage the time allotted for the exam so that you have the opportunity to plan, write, and edit your response. Also, become aware of the primary direction (pay special attention to core words), which will provide a clue to responding in the best way possible. In your essay, include examples that illustrate your commentary.

2 Preparation for essay examinations is crucial. Develop a strategy for reviewing important concepts and course material that will be covered on the test. Review notes taken during lectures and class discussions and reread significant passages from the textbook.

3 In oral presentations, you need to understand your purpose, audience, and message. Decide whether your primary purpose for making the presentation is to explain, to report, or to persuade. Become familiar with your audience, so you can tailor your presentation to make it most effective. Also, you might include audio and/or visual aids to illustrate complicated information or ideas. Finally, plan and practice the presentation to achieve the best results.

20

COMMUNICATING IN BUSINESS

All students will have to write business correspondence—letters and memoranda—during and after college. In fact, among the most common forms of business writing are resumés and cover letters, used when applying for jobs. Writing for work is not very different from writing in college. Both require completeness, clarity, and correctness. However, letters and memoranda written for businesses and professional groups require techniques you might not have practiced in academic papers.

20.1 Learn to write business letters.

Business letters take many forms and serve many purposes: marketers compose sales letters; customers write order letters and letters of complaint; business executives write letters of inquiry, thanks, and recommendation. Every business letter should observe important conventions of style and format. The most popular format is the block letter, in which the major parts of the letter are set flush with the left margin and paragraphs are single-spaced and not indented with one line space between each. In modified block format, the return address, date, and closing all start near the center. On page 335 is a business letter in modified block format.

NOTE

Many word processors contain templates, or patterns, and sample documents that will help you compose letters, memoranda, and resumés. For example, if you are using Microsoft Word, click on File and then click on New to find templates and samples you can use to design and compose a variety of documents.

Elements of a Business Letter

LETTERHEAD

Most business letters are written on preprinted stationery that displays the company's or organization's logo, name, address, and phone number. The letterhead

Letterhead/return
address

ROSALIE'S ROSES

5 Gardenhouse Lane
Gardenia, Illinois 08776-0430
Flowers for All Occasions

Date

January 5, 2004

↑
1 line space
↓

Inside
address

Dr. Marie Anderson
123 Sunset Road
Magnolia, IL 08765
↑
1 line space
↓

Salutation Dear Dr. Anderson:
↑
1 line space
↓

Thank you for your letter of December 27 inquiring about our ability to provide floral arrangements for your wedding on June 15 at the Highbrow Club in Megabucks,
Indiana. I would like to meet with you to discuss ways we can help you create the
← 1" → perfect floral arrangements for both ceremony and reception. We can meet in our
nearby Gardenia office or, if you prefer, in your home.
↑
1 line space
↓

Body

Enclosed is a brochure of standard wedding arrangements with an accompanying
price list. However, we can also design new creations exclusively for your affair.
While our individually designed packages are a bit more expensive than our standard arrangements, they are sure to make your special day even more memorable.
↑
1 line space
↓

I will contact you to schedule an appointment convenient for you. When we meet,
I can show you additional samples and explain more about the possibilities of creating a unique floral package for your wedding.
↑
1 line space
↓

Closing

Sincerely,
↑
1 line space
↓

Rosalie Bloom ↑
4 line spaces
↓

Rosalie Bloom,
General Manager

Enc.
Phone 800-555-2567
Fax 800-655-3567
Rroses@email.com

NOTE ◄◄ ◄ ◄ ◄ ◄

If you are not representing a company or organization, you may not have a letterhead. In that case, just use quality 8½-by-11-inch bond paper, and be sure to include a return address. If you are using a word processor, you might even create your own logo from available clip art, and type your name, address, and other information in a special typeface and style so that they stand out from the body of the letter. At any rate, be sure to include information that will enable your reader to respond.

may also include the fax number, e-mail address, and Web site address. However quite often, some of this information appears at the foot of the letter simply to avoid cluttering the letterhead.

DATE

Always include the date on which you wrote the letter. It will help you and your reader keep track of correspondence.

INSIDE ADDRESS

On the first line, type the name and, if appropriate, the title of the addressee. However, if the title is lengthy, type it on the second line. Then, as needed, type the department and institution or company name, the office or room number, and the building name or number. Follow with the street address or post office box, the city, state, and ZIP code. Here are two versions of the same inside address:

Belissario Begonia, Editor
Home Gardening and Horticulture
The Do-It-Yourself Press
333 Octavo Lane
Burbank, Wyoming 45678

Belissario Begonia
Editor, Home Gardening and Horticulture
The Do-It-Yourself Press
333 Octavo Lane
Burbank, Wyoming 45678

■ ■ ■ ■   ■ ■ ■ ■   **BASICLINK**   ■ ■ ■ ■   ■ ■ ■ ■

WWW

For more information on writing business letters, visit

http://writing.colostate.edu/references/documents/bletter/

SALUTATION

Always begin the salutation of a business letter with *Dear* and end it with a colon.

Not:	Greetings!
Not:	Dear Dr. Anderson,
Not:	My Dear Dr. Anderson;
But:	Dear Dr. Anderson:

As a rule, try to learn the first and last names of your correspondents. If doing so is impossible, however, use a salutation similar to one of these:

Dear Sir: Dear Customer Service
             Representative:

Dear Madam: Dear Admissions Director:

Dear Adjustor:

Skip one line after the salutation. Then begin the first paragraph.

BODY

Remember not to indent paragraphs if you are using block or modified block format. Instead, skip a line between paragraphs, and keep them relatively short. Doing so allows you to take advantage of white space, thereby making your letter attractive and easy to read.

Business letters are written to accomplish a specific purpose, and readers of such letters are usually very busy. So state your purpose and main point—or thesis—as early as you can. If you are responding to a request for information, as in the preceding sample letter, refer to that inquiry and then make your purpose clear, for example, to schedule a meeting in which to discuss your services with the customer. Similarly, if you want your reader to act on or respond to a question or request for information, state your purpose in the first paragraph.

> **CAUTION!**
>
> Do not abbreviate titles that come after a name.
>
> **Not:** Sylvia Fernandez, Pres.
>
> **But:** Sylvia Fernandez, President
>
> However, you may abbreviate titles that come before a name, for example, *Dr. Salgado, Prof. Mai.*

> **NOTE**
>
> The only exception to stating your purpose in the first paragraph applies to making a request of a reader who you know will not be disposed to your point of view and might even toss your letter aside before reading the reasons behind your request. For example, sales letters typically list a number of the product's advantages and uses *before* asking the reader to buy. Letters denying a customer's request for an adjustment never begin with the bad news. Instead, they explain company policy and present reasons that lead up to a statement, which, while positive, makes it clear that the adjustment cannot be approved.

> Dear Dean Hentoff:
>
> Can you spare a few minutes to respond to five important questions? Our college is trying to improve services for part-time students, and your insight and suggestions would be invaluable to us. You can return your comments in the enclosed postage-paid envelope.

You might follow this paragraph by discussing deficiencies in the number or nature of current services for part-time students to give Dean Hentoff a better idea of your situation and needs. However, you will have given the dean a clear indication of your purpose at the very outset.

LAST PARAGRAPH

What you put in your last paragraph depends on the purpose of your letter. If you are answering a customer's complaint, you might explain how to return the product or where to send it for repair. If you are thanking customers for their patronage, you might invite them to call whenever they need additional service. In all cases—even when you must deny a person's request or communicate bad news—close on a positive note. Whenever possible, leave the door open to continued correspondence or invite readers to continue doing business with you.

CLOSING

The most widely accepted closing consists of the word *Sincerely* followed by a comma. However, *Yours truly, Sincerely yours,* and *Respectfully yours,* can also be used. Follow this with your signature (leave four lines of space to accommodate it), your typed name, and, if appropriate, your title.

ENCLOSURES OR COPIES

Indicate after your signature and title that an enclosure is included or that you have sent copies to other interested parties. *Enc.* or *cc:* (meaning carbon copies) followed by a list of additional recipients should be typed flush left, leaving one line space between your typed name and the additional information. If both are included, *cc.* should be typed one line space below *Enc.*

Addressing Business Letter Envelopes

When addressing an envelope, use the exact mailing address that appears in the letter. Center the address on the envelope. If you are not using a preprinted corporate or organizational envelope, type a return address in the upper left corner. After typing your name, use the exact return address that appears in the letter.

Rosalie Bloom
Rosalie's Roses
5 Gardenhouse Lane
Gardenia, Illinois 08776-0430

Dr. Marie Anderson
123 Sunset Road
Magnolia, IL 08765

20.2 Compose special-purpose letters.

The letter by Rosalie Bloom, of Rosalie's Roses (page 335) responds to a request. Later in this chapter, you will read a resumé cover letter. Although they follow the same general rules of writing, these letters address different purposes and are focused and developed differently. Other common types of business letters are those that request information, sales letters, and letters that say "no."

20.2a Letters requesting information

Letters that request information contain the following three major components:

> **NOTE** ▪ ▪ ◂ ◂ ◂ ◂
>
> If you are sending multiple copies, personalize each letter by addressing the correspondent by name rather than by an anonymous salutation such as "Dear Madam" or "Dear Club President." Also, increase the incentive for responding by including a self addressed, stamped envelope.

1. In the first paragraph, an explanation of the reason(s) the information is needed. If appropriate, offer readers an incentive for responding. In the sample letter on p. 340, the incentive is that the Downhill Club will share the information it gathers.

2. In the body, a list of specific questions readers can answer easily. Number or bullet the questions, and leave two or three blank lines between questions so that readers can respond easily by writing their comments directly on your letter.

3. In the last paragraph, an indication of the date by which you need a response and an expression of your gratitude.

The Downhill Club
Icehaven Community College
Slopesville, PA 10987

November 12, 2004

Paula Powder, President
State University Student Ski Club
Collegevale, PA 19453

Dear Ms. Powder:

States reason
information is
needed; offers
incentive to reply.

Our ski club plans to ski the Rocky Top Preserve, which caters to college groups, during the semester break. If your club has ever visited Rocky Top, we hope you can provide advice on bus transportation. We are writing to ten other ski clubs as well and will send you a summary of the information we collect. You can write your responses directly on this letter and return it in the enclosed stamped envelope.

1. Our group includes eighty or more skiers. What companies, if any, rent buses with a capacity of forty or greater?

Lists specific
questions with spaces
for responses.

2. Which bus companies offer the most reasonable rental prices?

3. Which company or companies have you found to be the safest and most reliable?

4. Is there any bus company you would not recommend?

Tactfully informs
reader of deadline.

Thank you for taking the time to consider this request. We hope you can respond by November 30.

Sincerely,

Samuel Skilodge

Samuel Skilodge, Vice President
The Downhill Club

20.2b Sales letters

Sales letters, which generate new business or maintain good relations with existing accounts, are usually sent to targeted customers, readers identified as having a potential interest in or need for the product or service.

In sales letters, you should:

1. Keep the first paragraph brief; begin by stating the benefits the reader will gain from your product or service. If possible, add an endorsement from a satisfied customer and find a way to compliment the reader. In the letter on page 342, the reader is reminded that she is attending "Oregon's best university."

2. In the next paragraph(s), expand on the benefits mentioned in the first paragraph. If necessary, use a numbered or bulleted list to organize this section. Next, explain what makes your company's products or services better than those of its competitors. Repeat the name of your company and/or product as much as possible without becoming tiresome. Whenever possible, enhance your image. The Pasquale's Pizzeria letter that follows attracts clients by including positive words such as *fresh, homemade,* and *family.*

3. Close by explaining what you want the reader to do: telephone your office? mail an enclosed postcard for more information? stop by your showroom? If possible, include an incentive.

Pasquale's Pizzeria
661 Raguza Road
Renfield, OR 07901

February 22, 2004

Ms. Deborah Allen
Murphy Hall
Pinetree University
Renfield, OR 07902

Dear Ms. Allen:

Briefly describes product; includes endorsements; congratulates reader on attending "Oregon's best university."

Welcome to Pinetree University! For over twenty-five years, our family has served the best Italian food in Renfield to students of Oregon's best university. According to finance major Salvatore Marino (2003), "Pasquale's deep-dish pizza is as good as any I've eaten back in Chicago." "The vegetable lasagna melts in your mouth," says Angela Diaz (2002) of Brooklyn, New York.

We use only <u>fresh</u> ingredients, <u>never canned</u> vegetables or herbs. We roll <u>our own</u> bread and pizza dough every day, and we are famous for our <u>homemade</u> pasta. <u>Pasquale's</u> pizzas and breads are baked in <u>wood-burning, brick ovens</u>, and our sauces are prepared fresh daily. What's more, all our cheeses are <u>imported</u> from Italy, as is our olive oil. Of course, we stuff <u>our own</u> sausages and prepare our meatballs <u>right on the premises</u>.

Supports claim in paragraph 1 with specifics about quality.

Underlined words enhance restaurant's image.

Renfield offers several other good Italian restaurants, but only Pasquale's delivers directly to your dorm.

Explains why Pasquale's is better than the competition.

Closes with an invitation and incentive.

Please use the enclosed 30 percent-off coupon to enjoy your first lunch or dinner at Pasquale's, in our lovely and quiet dining room. Or have your meal delivered piping hot to your dorm room at no extra charge. We know you will want to eat with our family again.

Sincerely,

Pasquale di Norfrio

Pasquale di Norfrio,
Head Chef and Proprietor

20.2c Letters that say "no"

"No" letters refuse requests that are unreasonable or impossible to fulfill. Unfortunately, people who must deny such requests run the risk of damaging a long-standing business or professional relationship or of doing harm to the image of their organization, so "no" letters must be carefully crafted. Such a letter appears on page 344.

1. Never begin a "no" letter by denying the request outright. Instead, thank the reader for his or her request and express your understanding of the problem. Refer to the date of his or her correspondence, whether it was a letter, an e-mail, or a telephone call.
2. In the body of the letter, state why you cannot meet the reader's request. If necessary, refer to official policy, but don't leave it at that. Explain the reason the policy was instituted in the first place.
3. Near the end of the letter, offer another solution to the reader's problem if you can. If none is possible, express your hope that the reader will understand the reasons for your decision. Then state your concern for the reader and express your desire to keep your professional or business relationship intact.

Composing Special-Purpose Letters

EXERCISE 20A

1. *Write a letter asking for information about college scholarships and/or financial aid. Address your letter to a service organization, such as the Knights of Columbus, the Elks, or the Lions Club; to a labor union, such as the Teamsters or AFL-CIO; to a religious organization; to your local chamber of commerce; or to a government agency. Ask for information and an application. Include information about your major, courses you are taking or have taken, and the college you are now attending or to which you plan to transfer. Also, describe your professional goals and explain why you need financial assistance. These Web sites might provide insight:*

   www.finaid.org/
   www.collegeboard.com/paying/
   www.ed.gov/offices/OSFAP/Students

2. *Write a sales letter advertising a commercial product or service with which you have been very satisfied. Address the letter to the student body at your school.*
3. *Pretend you are a customer service representative for a shoe manufacturer and have received a letter requesting that you replace a pair of hiking boots ruined when the wearer walked through a swamp. New boots come with instructions on how to apply SuperProof, a waterproofing agent that must be bought separately if customers wish to waterproof their boots. The customer indicated that he had not waterproofed his boots because he thought that having to pay extra for SuperProof was unfair. Write a letter refusing the request.*

Division of Humanities
Bivalve College
Clambake, MA 02166

July 30, 2003

Sara Schooner
234 Skipjack Ave.
Westmore, MA 03211

Dear Ms. Schooner:

Thank you for your letter of July 25. I am pleased to hear that you have transferred to Bivalve College. As you know, the Registrar's Office has accepted twenty-four credits in science and mathematics from Blowfish Institute of Technology. Therefore, I certainly understand your concern about our not accepting your three remaining credits, for English 200: Technical Writing, in transfer for Bivalve's English 101: English Composition.

Thanks reader for contacting him and makes specific reference to her letter; does not begin by saying "no."

Blowfish Institute's catalog description for Technical Writing indicates this is a challenging course. However, the skills for which it demands mastery are different from those required by Bivalve's English 101. Specifically, English 200 does not require students to write argumentative essays or complete documented library/Internet research papers. At Bivalve, the skills needed to complete such assignments are important in general education courses and thus are required for graduation.

States reason for denial; explains rationale behind college policy.

To facilitate your transfer, let me suggest that you try earning the credits for English 101 through our credit-by-exam program. You can make an appointment with our Testing Department in Nautilus Hall 105. If you decide to take this advice, I will be happy to waive the $50 testing fee.

Offers another solution.

Welcome to Bivalve, Ms. Schooner. I wish you the best of luck with your studies, and I hope you will call on me if you need further assistance.

Tries to reestablish good relations by closing on a positive note.

Sincerely,

Bernard Barnacle

Bernard Barnacle,
Dean of Humanities

20.3 Learn to write memoranda.

Memoranda, or memos, are short pieces of correspondence that organizations use internally to make announcements, explain procedures, outline steps in a process, distribute progress reports, and complete many other essential office tasks. Electronic and paper memos are handy for keeping an ongoing log or history of the development of a policy or procedure or for detailing the ways an organization has addressed a particular problem or taken advantage of an opportunity.

In some ways, a memo is like a letter. However, a memo is usually less formal. In addition, a memo can be addressed to a number of people—sometimes to every member of the organization—while a letter is usually addressed to only one or two people. A typical business memo appears on page 346.

Elements of a Memorandum

INFORMATIONAL HEADING

The informational heading of any memo is extremely important. In the TO line, list the recipients as specifically as possible; include titles as appropriate. In the FROM line, include your name and title, and (in printed memos) initial this item. In the DATE line, spell out the month and use cardinal (not ordinal) numbers:

Not: Jan. 8th, 2004

But: January 8, 2004

In the SUBJECT line, include a brief description or title.

BODY

Skip two lines between the SUBJECT line and the body of the memo. Align all text flush left, and leave one line space between paragraphs. Use bullets or numbers with all listed items. Include the reason you are writing (in the first sentence) followed by any supporting information. All information should be written concisely and in a businesslike tone. Memoranda should be brief—ideally, one page. If you must include additional pages, repeat the information in the TO and FROM lines (in an abbreviated form) and include a page number at the top of each subsequent page: *Katz to Groomers and Trainers—p. 2.*

CLOSING

NOTE

No formal closing is necessary in memos. The writer simply writes his or her initials at the end of the FROM line.

No closing is necessary in a memo. However, as with business letters, if additional materials are enclosed with the memo, skip one line after the body and type *Enc.* If additional copies are sent to anyone not included in the TO line, skip another line, type *cc:* (for *carbon copy*), and list the additional recipients. Additional recipients would include anyone who you want to make aware of the memo's contents but who does not need to act on your information or instructions (for example, your boss or the heads of departments whose personnel are affected).

Letterhead

Photogenic Felines

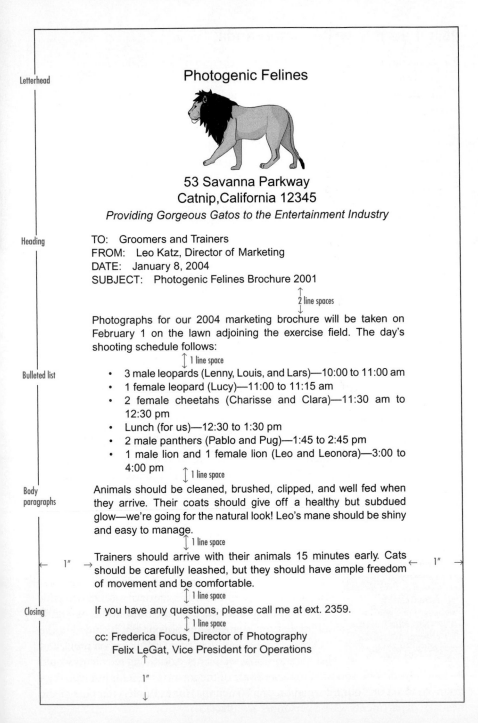

53 Savanna Parkway
Catnip,California 12345
Providing Gorgeous Gatos to the Entertainment Industry

Heading

TO: Groomers and Trainers
FROM: Leo Katz, Director of Marketing
DATE: January 8, 2004
SUBJECT: Photogenic Felines Brochure 2001

↑
2 line spaces
↓

Photographs for our 2004 marketing brochure will be taken on February 1 on the lawn adjoining the exercise field. The day's shooting schedule follows:

↑ 1 line space

Bulleted list

- 3 male leopards (Lenny, Louis, and Lars)—10:00 to 11:00 am
- 1 female leopard (Lucy)—11:00 to 11:15 am
- 2 female cheetahs (Charisse and Clara)—11:30 am to 12:30 pm
- Lunch (for us)—12:30 to 1:30 pm
- 2 male panthers (Pablo and Pug)—1:45 to 2:45 pm
- 1 male lion and 1 female lion (Leo and Leonora)—3:00 to 4:00 pm

↑ 1 line space

Body paragraphs

Animals should be cleaned, brushed, clipped, and well fed when they arrive. Their coats should give off a healthy but subdued glow—we're going for the natural look! Leo's mane should be shiny and easy to manage.

↑ 1 line space

Trainers should arrive with their animals 15 minutes early. Cats should be carefully leashed, but they should have ample freedom of movement and be comfortable.

← 1″ →

← 1″ →

↑ 1 line space

Closing

If you have any questions, please call me at ext. 2359.

↑ 1 line space

cc: Frederica Focus, Director of Photography
    Felix LeGat, Vice President for Operations

↑
1″
↓

EXERCISE 20B

Composing Memoranda

1. *Pretend you have been made the leader of a four-member student group appointed by the president of your college to gather student suggestions about a particular campus problem, such as student parking, the quality of food in the cafeteria, a shortage of campus housing, or the need to expand library holdings. Write a memorandum to your group assigning each member (make up their names, if you like) a particular task in the information-gathering process. You might ask one member to put together a student questionnaire, another to schedule student gripe sessions, and so on.*

2. *Pretend you have been asked to run a campus blood drive. Write a memorandum to college faculty asking them to announce in their classes an appeal for blood donors. When explaining how students can schedule appointments, include information such as times and locations. Also explain the reasons that donors are needed. At the same time, invite the faculty to participate.*

20.4 Learn to write resumés and cover letters.

Finding a great job often involves a long and careful search, which begins with writing a resumé. Because employers usually receive more resumés than the number of positions available, you must make your resumé stand out from the rest. An effective resumé includes an accurate summary of your education, your experience, and, especially, your qualifications for a particular job. It may also list personal strengths such as your ability to communicate and cooperate with others, to work hard and to learn, and to solve problems. Remember, however, that a good resumé is just the beginning; its purpose is to get you a job interview.

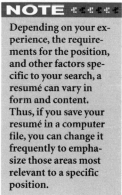

NOTE

Depending on your experience, the requirements for the position, and other factors specific to your search, a resumé can vary in form and content. Thus, if you save your resumé in a computer file, you can change it frequently to emphasize those areas most relevant to a specific position.

The following pages explain what a resumé should contain, and they provide examples of two common types of resumé formats: chronological and functional. Chronological resumés can be used in all situations, but they are especially popular with people who are just entering the job market. They present the applicant's work history by listing jobs he or she has held in chronological (time) order. Functional resumés, often used by applicants who are changing jobs, highlight skills the applicant has attained throughout his or her career.

20.4a Elements of a resumé.

While the particular form your resumé takes will depend on your experience, number of years out of college, and other variables, most resumés include the following:

1. Personal information. Include your name, address (with ZIP code), telephone number, e-mail address, and fax number (if you have one). If you are writing from college, include both that address and your home address.

2. Career objective. Explain the kind of position you are seeking now, but indicate your long-term plans as well.

3. Statement of special skills or summary of qualifications. List skills or talents that qualify you for the position. Be concrete but brief. If possible, match the skills and qualities you are describing to the qualifications in the job listing or advertisement.

4. Education. Begin with your most recent educational experience and work back in time. If you have just completed a college degree, go back no further than high school. (There is no need to include high school information if you have a master's or other advanced degree or if you have several years of relevant work experience.)

> **NOTE**
>
> If you are entering the job market while in college or soon after graduation, list your education information before the employment section. Otherwise, list your employment information first.

List dates of attendance for each school, degrees earned, academic major(s), and honors awarded. Include grade point average (GPA) if it is strong. List specific college courses or training seminars you have completed if they are relevant to the position.

5. Experience. The setup of this section depends on the resumé format you choose. In a **chronological resumé,** list the jobs or other experience you have had, in reverse chronological order; indicate your title, the company or organization name, and the city or state in which you worked. Next, briefly describe your responsibilities and accomplishments by using strong, active verbs, as in this example:

September 2003-Present: Technical Writing Intern, Zoomatic Software, Oak Ridge, TN

Intern with Martha Modem, Director of Documentation. *Write, design,* and *edit* sections of instructional manuals for Blastoff 4.1, software used in the aerospace industry. *Write, distribute,* and *collate* evaluation surveys for users of Crashlanding 5.2, which is currently being upgraded.

In a **functional resumé,** your current work history appears in two sections: professional experience and employment history.

- Under **professional experience,** discuss the responsibilities you have had and the skills you have used in your career. Try to group responsibilities and skills under categories relating directly to those of the job for which you are applying. In the example on pages 352–353, Josephine Jobseeker chose the headings *Management, Development,* and *Sales and Marketing.*

- Under employment history, list the names and addresses of current and past employers. Indicate the title(s) of position(s) held, but don't describe your duties in each job (you have already provided that information in the professional experience subsection).

Begin each item in your employment history with an active verb, using parallel structure for ease of reading.

Hired staff of twenty full-time and part-time servers

Ordered food, cleaning, and linen supplies

Inspected and maintained food-processing machines for cleanliness and efficiency

The items above are parallel in structure because each begins with a verb (or verbs) followed by a direct object.

Whichever format you choose, use active verbs to describe your responsibilities. Note the verbs in the previous example and in the following list:

Other Active Verbs

achieve	coordinate	hire	lead	produce
analyze	create	implement	manage	research
arrange	develop	improve	measure	supervise
assess	establish	increase	monitor	support
compile	evaluate	initiate	organize	train
contribute	expand	institute	perform	troubleshoot
control	generate	investigate	plan	

Combine similar responsibilities in the same item.

Not: Hired and supervised ten full-time servers

Hired and supervised ten part-time servers

Hired and supervised three full-time cooks

But: Hired and supervised twenty full-time and part-time servers, three full-time cooks

Give yourself credit; describe your accomplishments briefly but in detail. Include items such as:

- Major projects or activities you have led or worked on, with an emphasis on collaborative work experiences
- Important reports, proposals, and other major documents you have designed or written
- Products or procedures for which you have received patents or that you have helped develop
- Major problems you have helped solve

- Awards you have won
- Improvements you have made in production, employee relations, safety, or other important areas
- Amounts of money you helped the company earn or save; other savings or profits you helped achieve

In the process, mention personal strengths, such as your ability to communicate and work with others in a team, plan effectively, adhere to deadlines, set priorities, and accomplish a great deal with little supervision. Whenever possible, relate your skills and experience to the employer's needs as stated in the job listing. If you store your resumé electronically, you can revise it easily to emphasize different aspects of your profile to address different job requirements.

6. **Special interests, skills, and other information.** This is *your* resumé; you can include any information you feel is pertinent. For example, you might indicate a willingness to travel or to relocate to another state or even another country. Or you might mention special interests or skills not mentioned earlier that might be relevant to the job you seek. In any case, keep this section brief.

7. **References.** At one time, most resumés listed references. Today, it is more appropriate to devote this space to information that will help you get an interview. You can present a typed list of references at the interview, or you can attach a separate list of references. Either way, make sure you get permission from those listed to use them as references and include all their contact information— telephone number, address, e-mail address.

20.4b Sample resumés

The two sample resumés on pages 351–353 should give you ideas about how to build your own. The first is a chronological resumé for someone recently out of college. The second is a functional resumé from a more experienced candidate.

20.4c Write a cover letter.

A cover letter should accompany every resumé you send. Such a letter gives you an opportunity to expand on the information presented in your resumé. It also allows you to explain how your qualifications and experiences relate to the needs of the organization to which you are applying. If you type your letter using a word processing program, you can easily tailor each letter to the specific requirements described in the job posting or advertisement.

For example, if the position requires the writing of instruction manuals and safety procedures, your cover letter might point out that a set of instructions you wrote for one of your college classes now appears in a college textbook as a sample of effective technical writing.

Jeremy Jobseeker
125 Eager Lane
Careerville, Tennessee 30444
789-675-8908
Jjobseeker@email.com

Career objective: Entry-level editorial position leading to career in publishing scientific books, manuals, or journals

Special skills: Proficient in Microsoft Word, Publisher, PowerPoint, and Photo Editor

provides overview of skills.

Education: University of Tennessee at Knoxville, BA in Technical Writing (May 2004). GPA 3.75/4.00; dean's list eight semesters _Uses reverse chronological order._

Major courses: Writing for the Sciences; Business and Professional Writing; Technical and Scientific Layout and Design; Magazine Reporting and Editing

mentions relevant coursework.

Garfield Senior High School, Gatlinburg, Tennessee, H.S. degree (May 2000)

Experience:

Fall 2003– Present: Technical Writing Internship with Zoomatic Software, Inc., Oak Ridge, Tennessee. Intern with Martha Modem, Director of Documentation. Write, design, and edit sections of instructional manuals for Blastoff 4.1, software used in the aerospace industry. Write, distribute, and collate evaluation surveys for users of Crashlanding 5.2, which is currently being upgraded. _Provides brief but specific description of duties._

shows he is hardworking and responsible.

Summers 1997–2003: Manager, Tastytop Dairy Shop, Bloomsburg, Virginia. Under Terence Tastytop, owner, hired and supervised twelve full-time and part-time employees. Ordered all food supplies, inspected and maintained three ice-cream makers, opened and closed the business seven days per week, tallied and deposited daily receipts.

Josephine Jobseeker
722 Old Hand Road, Apt. 2B
Dunlooking, GA 30336-3618
Jobseeker@Internet.com

Objective: Executive position in corporate training and employee development

Summary of Qualifications

- History of designing and delivering successful training programs for IT personnel in large corporations.
- Ability to assess client needs and solve complex training and staffing problems.
- Facility for anticipating technology trends and preparing for future needs.
- Record of successful proposal writing that has secured new business.
- Team-building skills used to help manage four successful national training groups.
- Working knowledge of Microsoft Office, Publisher, Project, ACT, and Lotus Notes.

Lists types of skills mentioned in job posting.

PROFESSIONAL EXPERIENCE

Management

- Assisted in directing a team of four national training managers who solicited accounts for instructor-led training, e-learning, and help-desk services.
- Staffed, scheduled, and evaluated on-site training for more than 250 clients in software and IT industries.
- Coordinated work of three curriculum designers in program that in 2002 offered over sixty-five distinct training modules.
- Hired and evaluated more than forty outside instructors per year.

Begins each item with a verb; uses parallel structure.

Supports claims with specifics.

Development

- Created and managed new distance-learning modules, including online instruction and videoconferencing, which increased client enrollments by 15 percent in 2002 and 27 percent in 2003.
- Recommended and helped create three new product lines that added over $150,000 to gross revenues.
- Streamlined and improved communication among sales, design, and instructional personnel by creating and piloting self-contained instructional teams assigned to specific accounts.

Uses accurate but exciting language.

Sales and Marketing

* Wrote proposals resulting in signing of $3 million in new business in 2002–2003.
* Developed and revised all cost models, resulting in projects' coming in at or below budget 100 percent of the time.
* Improved customer retention by 22 percent by authoring new needs-assessment model and instructor-evaluation tools.
* Helped develop and institute year-end review of advances and developments in IT to anticipate training needs of current and potential clients.

Details ways she improved earnings and savings.

EMPLOYMENT HISTORY

1999-Present: Assistant Director of Training
Training and E-Learning Division
Peachtree Computer Services
Atlanta, GA 30325

1996–1999: Training Manager/Proposal Writer
Erudite Professional Development Services
Blue Bell, PA 19422

1994–1996: Human Relations/Training Associate
Oakland Industries
Philadelphia, PA 19106

EDUCATION AND AFFILIATIONS

2002-Present: Pursuing MS in Instructional Design (online),
Fairhaven University, Fairhaven, FL 33334

1994: BA Communications/Computer Design
Western Maryland College, Westminster, MD
3.6/4.0 GPA

Member and vice president, Atlanta chapter of
MetroSet; member, National Association of
Instructional Designers

SPECIAL SKILLS/ASSETS

Speak, read, and write Spanish. Willing to travel internationally. Willing to relocate anywhere in the United States or Latin America.

····   ····   ···· **THE BASICS OF TECHNOLOGY**

E-MAILING RESUMÉS AND COVER LETTERS

Many companies and organizations allow job applicants to e-mail their resumés and cover letters. If you choose this method, be sure to attach your resumé and cover letter as plain text or ASCII files so that your prospective employer will be able to access them easily.

■■■■   ■■■■   **BASICLINK**   ■■■■   ■■■■
WWW

For additional tips on writing resumés and cover letters, visit
http://www.indiana.edu/~wts/wts/resumes.html

A cover letter to accompany Jeremy Jobseeker's chronological resumé appears on page 355. The letter addresses the following job advertisement:

Technical writer proficient in the design and writing of safety and instructional manuals for a growing company that creates software for use by the chemical and pharmaceutical industries. Write Personnel Director, Sensational Software, P.O. Box 222, Saratoga Springs, NY 10002.

125 Eager Lane
Careerville, TN 30444

May 1, 2004

Personnel Director
Sensational Software
P.O. Box 222
Saratoga Springs, NY 10002

Dear Sir or Madam:

I would like to apply for the technical writing position that Sensational Software advertised in last Sunday's *Careerville Reporter.* As you will see from my resumé, my bachelor's degree in technical writing and my work with Zoomatic Software have given me the skills and experience to make a valuable contribution to your organization.

I am particularly interested in the fact that you are seeking someone who can write both software instructional manuals and safety procedures. These are the kinds of writing at which I excel. In college, I completed three courses—all with A's—in which writing effective safety and evacuation procedures was required. In addition, I have prepared several instructional manuals, one of which appears in a college textbook—*Writing for the Sciences and Technologies* by John Q. Professor (McGraw-Hill, 2003)—as a sample of effective student writing.

For my senior internship, I am working with the publications director of Zoomatic Software to write, design, and edit sections of a technical manual used by professionals in the aerospace industry. I also have a good grounding in computer science, having completed eighteen credits for a minor in this subject.

Finally, I am a hard worker. As my resumé indicates, I earned my college tuition by managing an ice-cream store, a job I began when I was only nineteen.

I would be happy to discuss employment at Sensational Software with you at your convenience. Please call me if you would like to know more about my qualifications. Of course, I can travel to Saratoga Springs for a personal interview.

Sincerely,

Jeremy Jobseeker

Jeremy Jobseeker
789-675-8908
Jjobseeker@email.com
Enc.

Writing a Resume and Cover Letter

Look in the newspaper for job advertisements relevant to your interests and academic preparation. Then write a chronological resumé and a cover letter that address one of those advertisements. To provide details for these documents, look ahead and consider the kinds of college courses you might take and the experiences you might have as you work toward a degree in your major.

20.5 Post your resumé on the Web.

In addition to responding to specific job advertisements, you might mail your resumé broadcast-style to various employers, whether or not they are advertising a position for which you are qualified. One way of doing this is to mail out hundreds of generic resumés and cover letters, but this is often expensive and time-consuming. Another way is to post your resumé on the Web. You can do this by subscribing to one of many online employment services, which thousands of employers access each day. Several of these employment services are free. Among the easiest to use are:

Monster.com

Hotjobs.com

USJobboard.com

Thingamajob.com

Some online employment sites ask you to provide information that will be used to generate an electronic resumé. Others allow you to paste your own resumé electronically onto a blank page. Most provide advice on how to write resumés and cover letters and to prepare for a job interview. Some will even post your cover letter. (For more information on creating an electronic resumé, see Chapter 9.)

In any case, you will also be asked to become a member of the service and to provide pertinent information such as your career objective, telephone number, e-mail address, location preferences, and willingness to relocate or to travel on the job. Once you have provided all required information, your resumé will be posted on the service's Web site.

Chapter Checklist

1. Block and modified block are the most commonly used business letter formats. Make sure your business letters
   a. Use letterhead or show a return address.
   b. Include the date and inside address as well as a salutation, which must be followed by a colon.
   c. Use paragraphs that are concise and relatively short.
   d. Avoid clichés.
   e. End with an appropriate closing, followed by an indication that you have included attachments or enclosures or sent additional copies.

2. When addressing the envelope for a business letter
   a. Use the same mailing address that appears in the letter.
   b. If you are not using a preprinted envelope, type a return address in the upper left corner.

3. In addition to standard format requirements, special letters call for the use of other techniques to accomplish their purpose.
   a. Letters requesting information should explain why the information is needed, list specific questions the reader can answer easily, and indicate a date by which a response is needed.
   b. Sales letters should describe the benefits of the product or service to the customer, discuss advantages of the product or service over that of the competitors, and urge the customer to buy.
   c. Letters that say "no" should never begin negatively, should state why the writer cannot meet the reader's request, and should offer another solution, if possible.

4. When writing memoranda,
   a. Begin with a heading that includes TO, FROM, DATE, and SUBJECT lines.
   b. Use block format for the body of the memo.
   c. Use bullets or numbers to separate items in a list.
   d. Ideally, limit the length to one page.

5. When writing a resumé
   a. Begin with your name, address, and telephone number. Include an e-mail address and/or fax number if available.
   b. Briefly state your career objective.
   c. If you are a recent graduate or are about to graduate, list your education first and then your employment history. Make sure items in these categories are listed in reverse chronological order, that is, from present to past. More experienced candidates might want to use a functional resumé.
   d. Write a cover letter to accompany your resumé that connects job requirements to your skills and experience.

6. To make your job search more successful, consider posting your resumé on the Web by using an online employment service.

8

SENTENCE STYLE

8

SENTENCE STYLE

21

LEARNING ABOUT SENTENCES, CLAUSES, AND PHRASES

21.1 Write sentences, clauses, and phrases.

21.2 Master sentence types.

21.1 Write sentences, clauses, and phrases.

21.1a Write sentences.

Writers express complete thoughts in **sentences** using subjects and verbs. A **subject** is the person, place, or thing that completes an action or that is described (*the sun*). A **verb** shows the reader what the subject is doing or helps describe the subject (*rises, is*).

The sun rises.   The sun is hot!

■ ■ ■ ■   ■ ■ ■ ■   **BASICLINK**   ■ ■ ■ ■   ■ ■ ■ ■
WWW

For more information on sentence structure, visit these sites:
http://webster.commnet.edu/grammar/fragments.htm
http://owl.english.purdue.edu/handouts/grammar/g_sentpr.html

■ ■   ■ ■   ■ ■   ■ ■   ■ ■   ■ ■   ■ ■   ■ ■   ■ ■   ■ ■   ■ ■   ■ ■

21.1b Write clauses.

A **clause** is a group of words with its own subject and verb. There are two kinds of clauses.

1. An **independent (main) clause** is the heart of a sentence; all sentences must contain at least one. An independent clause *can stand alone as a sentence* because it expresses a complete idea.

INDEPENDENT CLAUSES

The thunder boomed.

The waiter is polite.

The car sped along the highway.

Each of these independent clauses has a subject: *thunder, waiter, car.* Each has a verb: *boomed, is, sped.* Each expresses a complete thought. Therefore, each is a sentence.

361

2. A **dependent (subordinate) clause** also contains a subject and a verb. However, *it cannot stand alone as a sentence,* for it does not express a complete idea.

DEPENDENT CLAUSES

when the thunder boomed

although the waiter is polite

If you left these clauses as they are, your readers would ask: "What happened when the thunder boomed?" and "What about that polite waiter?" To answer these questions, you might join each dependent clause to an independent clause.

JOINING DEPENDENT AND INDEPENDENT CLAUSES

When the thunder boomed, the cat ran under the table.

Although the waiter is polite, he does not get big tips.

In each of these new sentences, the dependent clause (in italics) "depends" for its meaning on the complete idea (in the independent clause) to which it is attached. A dependent clause can be placed at the beginning, in the middle, or at the end of a sentence.

PLACING DEPENDENT CLAUSES IN SENTENCES

Although Maria is over fifty, she looks younger than her children.

Maria, *who is over fifty,* looks younger than her children.

Maria looks younger than her children *although she is over fifty.*

Regardless of their placement in the sentence, dependent clauses contain information that, though necessary, *is less important* than information in independent clauses.

21.1c Write phrases.

A **phrase** is a group of words without a subject and a verb. Like dependent clauses, phrases can't stand alone. Here are three examples:

PHRASES

while traveling in Canada

nervous and shy

with a loud screech

You can use phrases to communicate information less important than what you put into clauses. A phrase can be placed before, after, or in the middle of a clause.

PLACING PHRASES IN SENTENCES

While traveling in Canada, we saw a family of moose.

The young man, *nervous and shy,* approached his girlfriend's parents.

The red sports car turned the corner *with a loud screech.*

Writing Sentences, Clauses, and Phrases

Write a phrase, a dependent clause, and an independent clause containing the noun Panama. For example:

Phrase:	to Panama
Dependent clause:	when I went to Panama
Independent clause:	Panama is in Central America.

Then do the same for any five of the following nouns:

store	Matthew
movie	ocean
Sunday	caves
California	mirror
the Rocky Mountains	children

21.2 Master sentence types.

Sentences come in various types. Your purpose in writing a sentence helps you decide which type to use. Of course, you have to know how to begin and end a sentence.

1. To provide information, begin the sentence with a capital letter and end it with a period.

John opened the door.

2. To ask a question, begin the sentence with a capital letter and end it with a question mark.

Will you open the door, John?

3. To make a request or give a command or order, begin the sentence with a capital letter and end it with a period or an exclamation point.

Request:	Please open the door.
Command:	Open the door!

4. To emphasize a point or express a strong emotion, begin the sentence with a capital letter and end it with an exclamation point.

John screamed, "It's too hot in here!"

Using Various Sentence Types

Practice the four sentence types by writing four different kinds of sentences containing any three nouns in the list below. You should end up with twelve sentences in all.

zoo	painting	magazine	anger
bucket	classroom	Bible	time
visions	computer	baker	restaurant
witch	riding	Washington	letter

As an example, here are four sentences containing the noun window:

Provide information:	The window is open.
Ask a question:	Did you open the window?
Make a request:	Please close the window.
Emphasize a point:	I swear I didn't open the window!

Read two or three pages in a textbook other than this one. Then do the following:

1. *Find ten examples of independent clauses, ten examples of dependent clauses, and ten examples of phrases.*
2. *Find as many examples as you can of the four sentence types you just studied.*

MASTERING SENTENCE STRUCTURE

22.1 Avoid fragments.

A **sentence fragment** is a group of words—a phrase or a dependent clause—that is punctuated as if it were a sentence yet does not express a complete idea.

One way to spot fragments is to ask yourself if the sentence you have written contains a phrase or dependent clause without an independent clause.

Dependent clause fragment:	Since I was only fourteen.
Phrase fragment:	Near the large tree.

Fragments make your writing unclear and choppy. You can correct them in two ways.

1. Join the fragment to an independent clause that comes before or follows it.

Fragment:	Since I was only fourteen. I couldn't get a driver's license.
Revised:	Since I was only fourteen, I couldn't get a driver's license.

The fragment, introduced by the subordinating conjunction *since*, is a dependent clause; in the revision, it is joined to an independent clause.

Fragment:	The dog buried a bone. Near the large tree.
Revised:	The dog buried a bone near the large tree.

The fragment, a phrase, has been joined to the independent clause that comes before it.

2. Rewrite the fragment to add a subject or verb.

Fragment:	My neighborhood being a quiet place.
Revised:	My neighborhood is a quiet place.

Words ending in *-ing* can't serve as verbs by themselves. In the revision, *being* has been changed to the verb *is*.

Fragment:	The forest, the river, and the hills.
Revised:	I love the forest, the river, and the hills.

The addition of a subject and a verb has changed the fragment to a sentence.

Look for Conjunctions to Spot Fragments

To spot fragments, look for conjunctions that are *not* followed by complete ideas.

He shouted at us. *And* slammed the door!

She accepted the offer. *Because* she had no choice.

You can get rid of these fragments by writing

He shouted at us *and* slammed the door!

She accepted the offer *because* she had no choice.

Here are some other conjunctions that can introduce ideas that are not complete: *after, although, as, as if, because, before, but, even if, even though, since, though, unless, when, whenever, wherever, while.*

Other Fragment Signals

Other fragment signals are infinitives, relative pronouns, and *-ing* words that are *not* followed by complete ideas.

Infinitive:	The club met. *To elect* a new president.
Relative pronoun:	I lost the pen. *That* I bought today.
	He loved tacos. *Which* he ate often.
***-ing* word:**	*Swimming* quickly. He won the race.
	Love *meaning* that you are willing to sacrifice for another.

> **CAUTION!**
>
> Never use *being* as a verb. Instead, use a form of the verb *to be,* such as *am, was, have been, had been, will be, is, were, has been, are.*
>
> **Not:**   The technician being evaluated by a supervisor.
> **But:**   The technician was evaluated by a supervisor.

To revise these fragments, you might write

The club met to elect a new president.

I lost the pen that I bought today.

He loved tacos, which he ate often.

Swimming quickly, he won the race.

Love means that you are willing to sacrifice for another.

EXERCISE 22A

Eliminating Sentence Fragments

Rewrite the following paragraph to remove sentence fragments. Be sure you can explain the reasons for your corrections.

Brought to Europe from the New World. Potatoes seemed like the ideal crop. They were easy to grow and could be stored for long periods without spoiling. Rich in nutrients. Potatoes could be produced on a small piece of land to feed a family. By the mid-nineteenth century most of the people in Ireland depended on the potato for their livelihoods and their lives. In fact, much of Ireland's agricultural lands were given over to the growing of this one crop. Leaving the country vulnerable to a disastrous crop failure. Which finally came in 1845. In that year, a fungus, accidentally transported from America, wiped out the Irish potato crop. For the next five years, the fungus ravaged the potato fields. With more than 1 million people dying of starvation and its accompanying diseases. Another 1 million people were forced to flee Ireland. In order to escape what became known as "the great hunger." By the time the potato blight had run its course, the population of Ireland had declined twenty-five percent.

22.2 Avoid fused sentences.

A **fused sentence,** also called a **run-on,** occurs when you join two or more independent clauses without a conjunction or without correct punctuation. Here's an example of a fused sentence:

There were no other children around I spent my days hiking and swimming alone.

There are five ways to correct a fused sentence:

1. Add a period at the end of the first independent clause, and capitalize the first letter of the second.

There were no other children around. I spent my days hiking and swimming alone.

2. Place a semicolon between the two independent clauses.

There were no other children around; I spent my days hiking and swimming alone.

3. Place a comma and a coordinating conjunction between the two independent clauses. (You'll find more about coordinating conjunctions on page 454.)

There were no other children around, so I spent my days hiking and swimming alone.

4. Place a conjunctive adverb, such as *therefore* or *thus,* between the two sentences. A conjunctive adverb shows how the independent clauses it joins relate to each other.

There were no other children around; therefore, I spent my days hiking and swimming alone.

Be sure to place a semicolon immediately after the first independent clause. Place a comma after the conjunctive adverb.

Other Conjunctive Adverbs

consequently	indeed	nonetheless
furthermore	meanwhile	otherwise
hence	moreover	therefore
however	nevertheless	thus

5. Turn one independent clause into a dependent clause.

Because there were no other children around, I spent my days hiking and swimming alone.

22.3 Avoid comma splices.

A **comma splice** is similar to a fused sentence except that the comma splice connects two independent clauses with a comma alone.

I did not know she had a baby, I had not spoken with her in years.

You can correct comma splices the same way you correct fused sentences:

1. Change the comma to a period, and start a new sentence.
   I did not know she had a baby. I had not spoken with her in years.

2. Replace the comma with a semicolon.
   I did not know she had a baby; I had not spoken with her in years.

3. Add a coordinating conjunction.
   I did not know she had a baby, for I had not spoken with her in years.

4. Use a semicolon followed by a conjunctive adverb.
   I had not spoken with her in years; therefore, I did not know she had a baby.

5. Turn one independent clause into a dependent clause.
   I did not know she had a baby because I had not spoken with her in years.

EXERCISE 22B

Eliminating Fused Sentences and Comma Splices

Rewrite the following paragraph to eliminate fused sentences and comma splices. Be prepared to explain the reasons for your corrections.

In the early 1990s, Italian archaeologists working in Syria found a collection of approximately 15,000 inscribed clay tablets including government, commercial, and religious records these artifacts are thought to constitute the archives of a long-lost empire covering both Syria and Palestine. This hitherto undiscovered Canaanite civilization dates from about 2400 B.C., its capital city was called Ebla. The find may cast a great deal of light on biblical history interestingly, many of the place names mentioned in the clay tablets found at Ebla are also found in the Old Testament, including Sinai, Gaza, and Jerusalem place-names such as these were probably well known throughout the area, however, names of people, such as Ab-ra-mu (Abraham) and E-sa-um (Esau) also appear in the tablets, as does Is-ra-ilu (Israel) itself. Ebrum, a Canaanite hero and king, is also mentioned in the tablets, that scholars believe he may be Eber, the man from whom the Hebrews believed they were descended, is perhaps the most intriguing idea that has come from the discovery of this Bronze Age city.

CHAPTER WRAP-UP

Rewrite the following paragraphs to eliminate fragments, fused sentences, and comma splices:

The Greenhouse Effect

The *greenhouse effect* is a term. Describing the process by which the Earth's atmosphere traps heat. The sun's rays heat the surface and atmosphere of the Earth, in so doing they make possible photosynthesis. A process by which plants use light to convert carbon and water into carbohydrates. Essential to the life of plants.

Carbon dioxide is, in turn, excreted by plants, it is also produced by a variety of human activities—such as the burning of hydrocarbon fuels. Along with carbon dioxide, water vapor, and other waste products can accumulate in the atmosphere, this creates a kind of barrier to solar energy. Some of which would otherwise bounce off the earth's surface and escape through the atmosphere. If enough carbon dioxide and other materials accumulate. Scientists fear that our environment will become like a greenhouse. Covered by a barrier from which heat cannot escape. They are especially fearful that the more hydrocarbon pollutants we discharge into the atmosphere from factories, motor vehicles, and homes. The more formidable this barrier will become. That, in turn, will trap more heat in the earth's atmosphere, and on its surface the climate will get warmer. Causing catastrophic environmental changes such as flooding due to the melting of the polar caps.

COMBINING SENTENCES THROUGH COORDINATION AND SUBORDINATION

23.1 Use coordination to combine sentences.

23.2 Use subordination to combine sentences.

23.3 Avoid problems with coordination and subordination.

23.1 Use coordination to combine sentences.

When you **coordinate** parts of sentences, you use conjunctions such as *and, but, or, for, nor, so,* and *yet* to join words, phrases, and clauses of equal importance.

Maria *and* Varsha drove into the mountains.

Maria drove the car, *but* Varsha read the road map.

In the first example, two equally important nouns are joined by *and.* In the second, two independent (main) clauses are coordinated with *but.*

23.2 Use subordination to combine sentences.

When you **subordinate** certain words, phrases, or clauses, you make them less important than other parts of the sentence. Let's say you wrote the following sentence:

Maria drove the car while Varsha read the road map.

Maria drove the car is the independent (main) clause in this sentence; it can stand alone. *While Varsha read the road map* is a subordinate (dependent) clause; it cannot stand alone and depends for its meaning on what comes before. Therefore, it is less important than (subordinate to) the main clause.

Subordinate (dependent) clauses, which cannot stand alone, can be introduced by subordinating conjunctions such as *while, because, since, although,* and *unless* and by relative pronouns such as *that, which, who,* and *whom.* Here are four reasons to combine sentences and sentence parts through coordination and subordination:

1. To avoid fragments (see pages 365–366 for more about fragments)

Fragment: I can remember it. The day I got my first bike. Yellow and green. It was called a "Hi-Flyer."

Revised: I can remember the day *I got my first bike.* It was yellow and green, and *it was called a "Hi-Flyer."*

As revised, the first sentence uses subordination; the second, coordination.

2. To add variety to sentence openers (see pages 361–362 on using dependent clauses)

Lacks variety:	I will never forget the first time I drove a car. I was terrified. I had gotten my permit only two weeks before. I was afraid to get behind the wheel. I was with my cousin. She persuaded me to try.
Revised:	I will never forget the first time I drove a car *because I was terrified. Since I had obtained my learner's permit only two weeks before,* I was afraid to get behind the wheel, but *my cousin persuaded me to try.*

The first revised sentence uses subordination. The second uses both subordination *and* coordination. Combining helps the writer avoid beginning each sentence with *I.*

3. To avoid weak repetition (see pages 449 and 450 on using relative pronouns)

Repetitious:	The final section of the road led to a valley. The valley was cool, damp, and dark.
Revised:	The final section of the road led to a valley, *which was cool, damp, and dark.*

The second sentence is now subordinated to the first because the writer has used the relative pronoun *which.* As a result, *valley* is not repeated.

4. To correct choppiness

Choppy:	I love fast cars. I want to drive every one of them. Speed is my life. It's what I do best.
Revised:	I love fast cars. I want to drive every one of them *because speed is my life.* It's what I do best!

In the revision, subordination removes choppiness.

Choppy:	A hitchhiker walked my way. I stopped to talk with him. He said I couldn't get where I wanted to go. The bridge was out. He told me of another place I could see giant redwoods.
Revised:	I stopped to talk to a hitchhiker *who walked my way.* He said I couldn't get where I wanted to go *because the bridge was out,* but *he told me of another place I could see giant redwoods.*

In the revision, both coordination and subordination are used to remove choppiness.

23.3 Avoid problems with coordination and subordination.

23.3a Correct illogical and unnecessary coordination.

Use coordination only when the two ideas you are expressing are equal in importance. Otherwise, subordinate the less important idea to the more important one.

Illogical coordination:	The house was an A-frame, and snow slid off the roof easily.
Correct subordination:	*Because the house was an A-frame,* snow slid off the roof easily.
Illogical coordination:	The cold war ended, and the Soviet Union split up into several independent republics.
Correct subordination:	*After the cold war ended,* the Soviet Union split up into several independent republics.

In the correct versions, the less important ideas have been subordinated.

23.3b Do not subordinate major ideas.

Make sure that the idea you subordinate is not the major idea. Otherwise, your emphasis will be misplaced.

Illogical emphasis:	Having decided to join a gym, I had gained over thirty pounds.
Logical emphasis:	Having gained over thirty pounds, *I decided to join a gym.*
Illogical emphasis:	Latin, which had a significant influence on the formation of several modern languages, is studied in few schools.
Logical emphasis:	Although Latin is studied in few schools, *it had a significant influence on the formation of several modern languages.*

In each of these examples, the idea to be emphasized appears in the main clause, not the subordinate clause.

23.3c Correct excessive subordination.

Sometimes combining short sentences into longer, more fluid units causes writers to string together a long series of subordinate clauses. Doing so can make your writing cumbersome and hard to follow.

Excessive subordination:	In *The Woman Warrior,* Maxine Hong Kingston tells the story of the fate of her aunt who lived in a village in China in 1924 and who became pregnant by a man who was not her husband, thereby incurring the wrath of her neighbors, who ransacked the aunt's family's home and killed their farm animals.
Logical subordination:	In *The Woman Warrior,* Maxine Hong Kingston tells the story of an aunt who, living in a Chinese village in 1924, became pregnant by a man not her husband. As a result, this woman incurred the wrath of her neighbors, who ransacked her family's home and killed their farm animals.

The second version is clearer and easier to read. It replaces one long, awkward sentence with two that are more manageable.

The following paragraphs contain sentences that lack variety, are choppy, and are repetitious. Some even contain fragments. Rewrite the paragraphs by combining sentences.

1. The Stone Age is a period of prehistory. Believed to have begun in Africa about 2,500,000 years ago. It was a time when human beings and their humanoid ancestors fashioned weapons and tools out of stone and animal bone. It ended about 6000 B.C. At a time when people began to use metals in the manufacture of tools and other implements essential to their survival. The Stone Age is divided into three eras. These are the Paleolithic period, the Mesolithic period, and the Neolithic period. *Lith* is the root word for "stone." *Paleo* means "old." *Meso* means "middle." *Neo* means "new." Therefore, the three Stone Age periods are often referred to as the Old Stone Age, the Middle Stone Age, and the New Stone Age.

2. The Paleolithic period is by far the longest of the three Stone Age eras. It began about 2,500,000 years ago. Ending around 1300 B.C. when the last of the Ice Age glaciers receded. The Old Stone Age was characterized by the use of tools made chiefly of flint. Animal bones began to be used near the end of this period. In order to fashion tools and weapons such as needles and spearheads. The world was then populated by humanoid creatures such as Cro-Magnon man and Neanderthal man, who are the ancestors of *homo sapiens sapiens.* The scientific term for modern humans. Modern humans began to appear at the end of the Paleolithic era.

A sentence may contain a series of words, phrases, or clauses. Keep these elements parallel by putting them in the same grammatical form. Doing so makes the sentence smooth and easy to read; it can also make it powerful.

Abraham Lincoln used parallelism in his Gettysburg Address: "government *of the people, by the people, for the people* shall not perish from the earth." Each italicized item is a prepositional phrase, a preposition followed by a noun, so each uses the same structure. Here are other examples:

> *To err* is human, *to forgive* divine. (Alexander Pope)

Both items are infinitives, verbs preceded by the preposition *to*.

> *The evil that men do lives after them;*
> *The good is oft interred with their bones.* (William Shakespeare)

Two contrasting ideas are expressed in simple sentences.

> . . . for the support of this Declaration . . . we mutually pledge to each other *our Lives, our Fortunes, and our sacred Honor.* (Thomas Jefferson)

This list from the Declaration of Independence consists of three nouns, each preceded by a possessive pronoun.

> Let every nation know, whether it wishes us well or ill, that we shall *pay any price, bear any burden, meet any hardship, support any friend, oppose any foe* to assure the survival and the success of liberty. (John F. Kennedy)

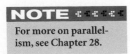

NOTE

For more on parallelism, see Chapter 28.

This quotation from the inaugural address uses a series of verb phrases.

THE BASICS OF TECHNOLOGY

PARALLELISM

Many word processors offer grammar and style checkers. To date, no such tool can match the expertise of a writer who has mastered the art of sentence structure for him- or herself. Therefore, rely on your own knowledge and abilities when it comes to editing your sentences for correct structure and, especially, for parallelism.

24.1 Maintain parallelism when using coordinating conjunctions.

Sentences that are not parallel can be wordy and awkward, and they usually lack emphasis. This problem sometimes occurs when sentence parts are incorrectly joined with the coordinating conjunctions *and* or *or*.

Not parallel: *The Catcher in the Rye* is interesting, well written, and it is popular with young readers.

Parallel: *The Catcher in the Rye* is interesting, well written, and popular with young readers.

In the original sentence, two items are adjectives; the third is an independent clause. In the revision, all are adjectives.

Not parallel: Many people get up early to jog along country lanes, to observe the wonder of nature, or just watching the sun come up.

Parallel: Many people get up early to jog along country lanes, to listen to the sounds of nature, or just to watch the sun come up.

In the original sentence, two items are infinitive phrases; the third is a participial phrase. In the revision, all are infinitive phrases.

24.2 Maintain parallelism when using correlative conjunctions.

Correlative conjunctions—such as *either . . . or, neither . . . nor, not only . . . but also, whether . . . or,* and *both . . . and*—always appear in pairs. What comes after the second correlative conjunction must be expressed in the same grammatical form as what comes after the first.

376 **CHAPTER 24** Parallelism

Not parallel:	Some defense experts argue that the attacks of September 11, 2001, were neither preventable nor were we able to foresee them.
Parallel:	Some defense experts argue that the attacks of September 11, 2001, were neither preventable nor foreseeable.

In the first version, an adjective follows the first correlative conjunction, but a main clause follows the second correlative conjunction. In the correct version, adjectives follow both the first and the second correlative conjunctions.

24.3 Maintain parallelism when using *than* or *as* to create comparisons.

As you should do with correlative conjunctions, express what comes after *than* or *as* in the same grammatical form as what comes before these words.

Not parallel:	I would rather spend the day at the dentist's office than listening to another one of his poems.
Parallel:	I would rather spend the day at the dentist's office than listen to another one of his poems.

In the first version, *than* is preceded by a phrase beginning with the verb *spend,* but it is followed by a participle, *listening.* In the correct version, both are simple verbs.

24.4 Maintain parallelism in lists.

Charges to a committee, procedures that students or employees must follow, characteristics of a group, and many other types of related items can be presented efficiently and clearly in lists. Indeed, information presented in a list is generally easier to read and remember than the same information presented in a block of text. However, items in a list must be expressed in parallel constructions.

Not parallel:	State University offers
	• Modern, well-equipped facilities.
	• An excellent faculty.
	• Degree programs that are varied and relevant.
Parallel:	State University offers
	• Modern, well-equipped facilities.
	• An excellent faculty.
	• Varied and relevant degree programs.

In the first version, the first two items are adjectives followed by nouns, but the third item contains a subordinate clause. In the correct version, all three items are adjectives followed by nouns.

■■■■   ■■■■   **BASICLINK**   ■■■■   ■■■■
WWW

To learn more about parallelism, visit this site:
http://leo.stcloudstate.edu/grammar/parallelism.html

■■ ■■ ■■ ■■ ■■ ■■   ■■ ■■ ■■ ■■ ■■ ■■

Rewrite the following paragraphs to correct problems with parallelism:

The African-American community has produced no more dedicated and articulate spokesperson, nor has a more influential figure represented that community, than W. E. B. Du Bois. Born in 1868, Du Bois graduated as the valedictorian of his otherwise all-White high school class, earned his BA at Fisk University in Nashville, and then it was on to Harvard University, where he earned a second bachelor's, a master's, and he was the first African American to earn a doctorate from that institution. Du Bois then started his long career as college professor and scholar, publishing several works on the problems Blacks faced in attaining social and political equality as well as doing well economically.

In his most famous work, *The Souls of Black Folks* (1903), Du Bois wrote: "The problem of the twentieth century is the problem of the color line—the relation of the darker to the lighter races of men in Asia and Africa, in America and the islands of the sea." Du Bois believed that Blacks had to lead "double lives"—one in which they put their faith in the promises of American democracy and then in the other one they were forced to face the reality of American racism. Therefore, he devoted his life to the attainment of racial equality, helping found the National Association for the Advancement of Colored People (NAACP), editing *Crisis* and *Phylon*, political journals influential in the Black community, writing several social and political studies as well as three autobiographies, and he also became a spokesman for Pan-Africanism, a movement that actively opposed the colonization of Africa.

25

USING MODIFIERS THAT MAKE SENSE

25.1 **Avoid dangling modifiers.**
25.2 **Avoid misplaced modifiers.**
25.3 **Avoid shifting or confusing modifiers.**
25.4 **Avoid split infinitives.**

Modifiers are words that describe or reveal something about other words. They act as adjectives or adverbs. *Adjectives* describe nouns and pronouns. *Adverbs* describe verbs, adjectives, and other adverbs. Regardless of whether modifiers are adjectives or adverbs, single words, phrases, or dependent clauses, they must always point clearly to the words they describe. (You can find more about phrases and clauses on pages 361–362.)

25.1 Avoid dangling modifiers.

Modifiers that do not point clearly to the words they describe make sentences illogical. This situation happens when a writer forgets to mention the word that a modifier is supposed to describe. Such a modifier is said to *dangle*—it has nothing to refer to. Suppose you wrote

Dangling: Walking across the field, the river came into view.

In this sentence, *walking across the field* seems to modify *the river,* but that's impossible. To correct such problems, you must add the word or words you forgot. To do so, however, you might have to rewrite the sentence.

Revised: Walking across the field, I saw the river.

In some cases, the word you forgot will have to be added to the modifier; in others, it will have to be put in the clause that follows the modifier.

Dangling: *After changing into my hospital gown,* the nurse told me to relax.

Revised: After I changed into my hospital gown, the nurse told me to relax.

Dangling: Before replacing a wall outlet, the electricity must be turned off.

Revised: Before replacing a wall outlet, you must turn off the electricity.

Avoiding Dangling Modifiers

Rewrite the sentences below to correct dangling modifiers:

1. By flossing your teeth daily, gum disease can be prevented.
2. Before engaging in strenuous aerobic exercise, warm-up activities are necessary.
3. Using a small amount of infected matter, serums can be prepared to inoculate people against infectious diseases.
4. Having applied a tourniquet, the bleeding from the victim's wounded arm was stopped.
5. Treated with penicillin, severe allergic reactions can occur.
6. After several years of abusing alcohol, liver disease is often one of the results.
7. Inhaling secondhand smoke, statistics show that the health risks can be significant.
8. Observing safe-sex practices or abstinence, the risks of contracting a sexually transmitted disease can be reduced or eliminated.
9. Following a strict low-fat diet, weight loss can become a reality.
10. Stung by wasps, bees, or other such insects, powerful toxins can cause severe, sometimes fatal, allergic reactions.

25.2 Avoid misplaced modifiers.

Place the modifier as close to the word it describes as you can. If you don't, your reader may have difficulty telling which word in the sentence you want to modify. Again, the results may be illogical or even funny.

Misplaced: *While still a boy,* my aunt and I went to the rodeo.

This sentence claims that your aunt was once a boy. A better version is

Revised: While still a boy, I went to the rodeo with my aunt.

Misplaced: My date invited me into the house *with a smile.*

Can a house wear a smile? Instead, try one of these revisions:

With a smile, my date invited me into the house.
Smiling, my date invited me into the house.

Here are other examples:

Misplaced: *To be cooked well,* you must steam vegetables.
Revised: *To cook vegetables well,* you must steam them.

The veggies should be cooked, not you.

| **Misplaced:** | Because John knew only English, he could not read a sign that he saw on a Mexican highway *written in Spanish.* |
| **Revised:** | Because John knew only English, he could not read a sign *written in Spanish* that he saw on a Mexican highway. |

The sign, not the highway, is written in Spanish.

Avoiding Misplaced Modifiers

Rewrite the following sentences to correct misplaced modifiers:

1. In the hotel cocktail lounge, guests could find a piano and a torch singer decorated in gold leaf.
2. They decided to build a house on an acre of land with three bedrooms.
3. Breaking down the door, the smoke that the firefighters encountered almost overwhelmed them.
4. Waking up on a rainy morning, the mountain trail we traveled seemed gloomy.
5. We were told to follow instructions for keeping ourselves safe from the police.

25.3 Avoid shifting or confusing modifiers.

25.3a Shifting modifiers.

In addition to being illogical, modifiers can be misleading if they are not placed just where they should be. Look at the placement of *only* in the following sentences:

> *Only* Sam worked in Phoenix for three years. (No one but Sam worked in Phoenix for three years.)
>
> Sam *only* worked in Phoenix for three years. (For three years Sam did nothing in Phoenix but work.)
>
> Sam worked *only* in Phoenix for three years. (Sam worked nowhere but in Phoenix for three years.)
>
> Sam worked in Phoenix for *only* three years. (Sam worked in Phoenix for no more than three years.)

As you see, the writer changed the meaning of the sentence just by shifting the position of one word. So make sure you place modifiers exactly where *you* want them.

25.3b Confusing modifiers.

Modifiers can cause confusion when they refer to words that come before and after them simultaneously. Consider this sentence:

Confusing: She claimed *yesterday* she saw a UFO.

Did the UFO appear to her yesterday? Or was yesterday when she claimed to have seen it? To answer this question, you need to change the position of the modifier.

Revised: Yesterday she claimed she saw a UFO.

Yesterday was the day she made the claim.

Revised: She claimed she saw a UFO yesterday.

Yesterday was the day she saw it.

■ ■ ■ ■   ■ ■ ■ ■   **BASICLINK**   ■ ■ ■ ■   ■ ■ ■ ■

WWW

For more information about using modifiers, visit these sites:

http://www.asu.edu/duas/wcenter/modifiers.html

http://www.uottawa.ca/academic/arts/writcent/hypergrammar/msplmod.html

■ ■   ■ ■   ■ ■   ■ ■   ■ ■   ■ ■   ■ ■   ■ ■   ■ ■   ■ ■   ■ ■   ■ ■

25.4 Avoid split infinitives.

In general, avoid split infinitives, which occur when a word comes between the infinitive marker *to* and the verb. In most cases, you can eliminate the intrusive word or place it after the verb.

Split infinitive: The police advised us to quickly move to higher ground.

Revised: The police advised us to move quickly to higher ground.

Split infinitive: The mechanic's recommendation was to completely overhaul the engine.

Revised: The mechanic's recommendation was to overhaul the engine.

In the second example, the word *completely* is redundant.

Exception

Trying to avoid a split infinitive can sometimes make your writing awkward. If that's the case, you would do better not to correct it.

Split infinitive:	The young couple was warned not to naively follow the advice of their new stockbroker.
Awkward correction:	The young couple was warned not to follow the advice naively of their new stockbroker.

CHAPTER WRAP-UP

Rewrite the following items to correct modifier problems and split infinitives.

1. Although born in Freiberg, Vienna is the city in which Sigmund Freud (1856–1939) spent most of his life.

2. After receiving his medical degree in 1881, his attention was turned to the study of psychiatry and nervous diseases.

3. Freud used hypnosis to often treat women suffering from hysteria as a young doctor.

4. In time, he developed a new field of medicine. Indeed, as the founder of psycho-analysis, psychology owes him a great deal.

5. A way to explore the unconscious mind, Freud believed that psychoanalysis could be used to reveal and, thereby, cope with our most hidden fears and desires.

6. By encouraging patients to express their deepest inhibitions, Freud's aim was to get them to deeply delve into their unconscious.

7. Drawing upon his research with female hysterics, the *Interpretation of Dreams* was written by Freud to explain how dreams express our unconscious desires.

8. For Freud, sources of sexuality could be found in the libido. If not satisfied, Freud believed that sexual desire would be imprisoned in the unconscious.

9. Expressed in dreams and nightmares, sometimes these repressed desires would cause a patient to terribly suffer from attacks of irrational fear, guilt, or other types of neuroses.

10. Though rejected by some of Freud's contemporaries, psychiatry continued to be influenced by his theories, and he remains an important figure in the history of medicine.

CORRECTING MIXED CONSTRUCTIONS AND FAULTY SHIFTS

26

Mixed constructions, which make your writing choppy and illogical, come in several forms. Essentially, all mixed constructions, including faulty shifts, violate the conventions of sentence construction.

26.1 Choose a logical subject—a noun or pronoun.

Sometimes writers begin sentences with a phrase or a subordinate clause that they incorrectly use as the subject of the sentence's main clause. This is called a predication problem. Review the following examples:

Illogical: By attending college will help me achieve my goals.

Logical: Attending college will help me achieve my goals.

In the first sentence, a prepositional phrase, *By attending college,* is being used as the subject. But only nouns or pronouns can act as subjects. In the second sentence, the preposition *by* has been dropped. The subject is *Attending,* which is a gerund, or a noun that names an activity.

Illogical: Just because she has not returned our call does not mean she is rude.

Logical: Her failure to return our call does not mean she is rude.

Just because she has not returned our call is a subordinate clause; it cannot be the subject of the main clause. In the second sentence, the subject is *failure;* the verb is *does . . . mean.*

Illogical: Because she was underweight worried the doctor.

Logical: The fact that she was underweight worried the doctor.

In this example, the subordinating conjunction *because* has been replaced by *The fact,* a noun (plus definite article) that acts as the subject.

26.2 Avoid contradictions.

As you edit, revise or remove any element that contradicts another element and, therefore, makes the sentence illogical.

Contradictory: She was intrigued by the *differences* that we *share* with the English.

Logical: She was intrigued by the *similarities* that we *share* with the English.

Contradictory: The young sea captain soon learned that Moll *didn't have no* money.

Logical: The young sea captain soon learned that Moll *didn't have any* money.

26.3 Revise sentences that connect main and subordinate elements with coordinating conjunctions.

Coordinating conjunctions (*and, but, or, for, nor, so, yet*) connect the same kinds of elements: nouns with nouns, adjectives with adjectives, main clauses with main clauses, and so on.

Illogical: He became very nervous, and even to the point of turning pale.

Logical: He became very nervous, even to the point of turning pale.

Logical: He became very nervous, and he even turned pale.

In the first sentence, the coordinating conjunction *and* connects a main clause with a phrase. In the second sentence, the *and* has been removed. In the third sentence, the phrase has been turned into a main clause; thus, the *and* now connects two main clauses. Both the second and third sentences are correct. (For more on coordination, see Chapter 23.)

26.4 Make sure that words relate logically to one another.

Sometimes writers connect parts of sentences in a way that expresses an unintended idea.

Illogical: Every morning, my father cooks, cleans, and walks the dog.

Logical: Every morning, my father cooks breakfast, cleans the kitchen, and walks the dog.

In the first sentence, the *dog* is being cooked, cleaned, and walked. In the second, it is clear that *breakfast* is being cooked, that the *kitchen* is being cleaned, and that only the *dog* is being walked.

26.5 Avoid *when* or *where* when defining unless the term is a time or place.

Illogical: Courtesy is when people show each other respect.

Logical: Courtesy is the practice of showing respect to others.

NOTE
A good way to begin a definition is with a noun. In the example to the left, the writer equates *courtesy* with the noun *practice* and then explains that practice.

Correcting Problems in Sentence Logic

Rewrite the following sentences to correct the problems in sentence logic:

1. Alvin Ailey founded the African-American dance troupe that bears his name. It has performed in several countries, including Senegal, Australia, China, and New York City's Metropolitan Opera House.
2. By originating in a Moscow orphanage in 1773, the Bolshoi Ballet gave its first performance in 1776.
3. Developing its own distinctive style of dance was when the Bolshoi Ballet started to become known in Russia.
4. With the rise of the Soviet Union in the 1920s and 1930s was the reason that the Bolshoi Ballet began to perform ballet celebrating the Communist movement.
5. Although I have heard that José Greco was born in Italy of Spanish and Italian parents, I don't have no idea where he learned to dance.
6. The polonaise is the national dance of Poland, and most people believe it is the polka.
7. What we saw while listening to Puccini's *La Bohème* on the car radio made us want to buy a CD of that opera.
8. A romantic dance in three-quarter time, the waltz is where two people glide elegantly across the floor to the beautiful music of composers such as Johann Strauss.
9. If choreographer Agnes De Mille were alive today, she would be turning over in her grave.
10. Just because the polka is popular in Poland doesn't mean it didn't originate in Hungary.

EXERCISE 26A

26.6 Avoid faulty shifts.

A **faulty shift** occurs when you change from one grammatical construction to another inappropriately. This mistake can make your writing inconsistent and even hard to read. You would create a faulty shift if you wrote

Shift: Laughter could be heard as we approached the Cheng house.

In this sentence, the subject has shifted needlessly from *laughter* to *we*. A more consistent version might read like this:

Revised: We could hear laughter as we approached the Cheng house.

Now the subject of both clauses is *we*.

The following sections discuss other kinds of shifts to avoid.

26.6a Avoid shifts in verb tense.

In the first sentence below the verb (*was*) is in the past tense; in the second sentence, the verb (*is*) is in the present tense.

Shift: He was at his desk. Anchorage Park, framed in the window behind him, is blanketed in fog.

Revised: He was at his desk. Anchorage Park, framed in the window behind him, was blanketed in fog.

Now both verbs are in the past tense. (You will find more about verb tenses in Chapter 34).

26.6b Avoid shifts in sentence type.

Different sentence types demand different patterns. (You can refresh your memory about sentence types by looking again at Chapter 21.)

Shift: I hope that you received my letter, and will you write back soon?

The first part of the sentence makes a statement; the second part asks a question.

Revised: I hope that you received my letter and that you will write back soon.

Both parts of this sentence make a statement.

Revised: Did you receive my letter, and will you write back soon?

Both parts of this sentence ask a question.

26.6c Avoid shifts in point of view.

Shift: If one studies hard, you can get an A in Professor Sullivan's class.

Revised: If you study hard, you can get an A in Professor Sullivan's class.

Revised: If a student studies hard, he or she can get an A in Professor Sullivan's class.

In the first item, the writer has shifted from the third-person pronoun *one* to the second-person pronoun *you*. The first revision corrects that problem by using the second-person pronoun *you* consistently. The second revision corrects the problem by using the third-person: *student* and *he or she*.

26.6d Avoid shifts from indirect to direct questions.

An indirect question states what someone else already asked. It is really a statement.

Shift: We argued about the role of the federal government in a democracy and was the right to bear arms absolute?

Revised: We argued about the role of the federal government in a democracy and whether the right to bear arms was absolute.

The first item shifts from a statement to a question. The second item contains two statements.

26.6e Avoid shifts from indirect to direct quotations.

An indirect quotation is a paraphrase of a statement, not its word-for-word re-creation.

Shift: The authorities advised us to lock all doors and windows, and residents should report any suspicious noises immediately.

Revised: The authorities advised us to lock all doors and windows and to report any suspicious noises immediately.

The first version begins with an indirect quotation but ends with a direct quotation. The revised version reports two indirect quotations.

Avoiding Faulty Shifts

EXERCISE 26B

Rewrite the following paragraph to correct faulty shifts. Be prepared to explain each of your changes.

Antonio Stradivarius (1644–1737) was the world's greatest violin maker. Born in Cremona, Italy, he studied under Nicholas Amati, a master craftsman, and was taught by Amati many of the secrets that make Cremona renowned for the manufacture of musical instruments. However, Stradivarius perfects the art of making stringed instruments. He made subtle modifications to their shapes, and a varnish with special qualities is applied at the end of the process. However, experts disagree about Stradivarius's materials and methods, but will we ever know why his instruments are of such high quality? Hundreds of his violins are still in existence, but can we say the same for his violas and cellos? No, they are very rare. Stradivarius continues making musical instruments deep into old age. He dies in his nineties, but his work was continued by his sons Francesco and Omobono.

■ ■ ■ ■   ■ ■ ■ ■   **B A S I C L I N K**   ■ ■ ■ ■   ■ ■ ■ ■

WWW

To practice recognizing faulty shifts, visit this site:

http://owl.english.purdue.edu/handouts/grammar/g_tensecEX1.html

■ ■   ■ ■   ■ ■   ■ ■   ■ ■   ■ ■   ■ ■   ■ ■   ■ ■   ■ ■   ■ ■   ■ ■

CHAPTER WRAP-UP

Rewrite the following sentences to correct logic problems and faulty shifts:

1. Because it was built in the first century makes the Roman Colosseum one of the world's oldest buildings.
2. When the Romans founded their civilization, they relied a great deal on what had been left by the Etruscans, whom they totally ignored.
3. The eucalyptus plant is the sole food of the koala bear, which feeds on other plants as necessary.
4. The car dealer advertised for a person to repair transmissions and two sales representatives.
5. Before dawn, we had washed, dressed, and eaten breakfast.
6. Etymology is where the history of words is traced.
7. The instructor lectured on Gresham's law, and then she tests us on it.
8. The Kiowas are nomads who once lived in the Black Hills, but they are forced out by the Sioux and then they move south, even as far as Mexico.
9. The young dancer nearly died in an apartment fire in which he lived.
10. Vaslov Nijinsky, a Ukrainian dancer and choreographer, is still considered one of the greatest ballet dancers since he died in 1950.

CREATING INTEREST BY VARYING SENTENCE PATTERNS

27

Variety—the spice of life, as the cliché goes—is no less important in writing than in any other activity. Indeed, varying sentence structure, length, and type will help you maintain your reader's interest and create emphasis, which is essential to forceful and effective writing.

27.1 Create interest by varying sentence structure.

In addition to containing a subject and verb, complete sentences can include adjectives, adverbs, prepositional phrases, and the like. However, no rule demands that a complete sentence begin with a subject followed by a verb. Interesting writing uses a variety of sentence patterns.

27.1a Begin with an adverb.

Adverbs describe verbs, adjectives, and other adverbs. They help explain when, why, where, or how.

> *Gradually,* the air became thinner, and the mountain climbers had difficulty breathing.
>
> *Near the summit,* they were forced to use bottled oxygen.

27.1b Begin with an infinitive.

An infinitive is the basic form of a verb preceded by the word *to.* Infinitives that act like nouns can make good sentence openers.

> *To outlive* one's children is a parent's nightmare.
>
> *To determine the guilt of a defendant* is the job of a jury, not of the newspapers.

27.1c Begin with a preposition or prepositional phrase.

Prepositions connect or show relationships between nouns or pronouns and the rest of a sentence. Prepositional phrases—which contain a preposition, a noun or pronoun, and any other words that modify the noun or pronoun—can be used to begin a sentence.

> *Without mastering biology,* a student might never be admitted to medical school.
>
> *On Mount Palomar,* which is close to San Diego, the California Institute of Technology operates one of the world's largest astronomical observatories.

27.1d Begin or end with a participle or participial phrase.

A participle is a verb turned into an adjective. Participles end in *-ed, -ing, -d, -t,* or *-n.* A participial phrase is a group of words containing a participle.

> *Found in all living things,* nucleic acids carry information that determines heredity.
>
> In 1884, Mark Twain published *The Adventures of Huckleberry Finn, considered one of the greatest novels in American literature* even to this day.

27.1e Begin with an adjective.

Adjectives, which modify nouns and pronouns, can be effective sentence openers.

> *Extinct,* the Hittite language was spoken more than 3,000 years ago in Asia Minor.
>
> *Different from other Western tongues,* Finnish, Hungarian, and Estonian are not members of the Indo-European language group.

27.1f Reverse the position of the subject and the verb.

Putting the verb before the subject varies the typical subject + verb + modifiers pattern.

> verb   subject
>
> In the foothills of the Guadeloupe Mountains *lie the Carlsbad Caverns,* one of the world's largest underground cave complexes.
>
> verb   subject
>
> Inside cells of higher organisms *is* a jellylike *substance* called cytoplasm, which surrounds the nucleus.

27.1g Use a colon.

Place a colon after an independent clause to introduce information that names or explains something in that clause.

> Oxygen is abundant on only one planet in the solar system: *Earth.*
>
> Five languages make up the Romance language subgroup: *French, Italian, Portuguese, Rumanian, and Spanish.*

In the first sentence, *Earth* names the *only planet.* In the second sentence, *French, Italian, Portuguese, Rumanian, and Spanish* name the *five languages.*

27.2 Create interest by varying sentence length.

A steady flow of sentences of the same length can put your readers to sleep. So, in general, try to vary the length of your sentences. A good way to do this is to combine short, choppy sentences by using coordination and subordination. Coordination allows you to combine ideas of equal weight into one sentence. Subordination allows you to emphasize one idea over another by expressing the less important one in a subordinate clause or in a phrase. (You can learn more about coordination and subordination in Chapter 23.)

27.2a Combine through coordination.

Choppy: In the second century B.C., Mongoloid peoples sailed across the Straits of Korea. They invaded Japan. They brought with them many ancient customs that survive in Japan to this day. They also introduced the Shinto religion into the islands of Japan. This religion is based on the worship of nature. It teaches that a divine presence fills the natural world.

Combined: In the second century B.C., Mongoloid peoples sailed across the Straits of Korea, and they invaded Japan. They brought with them many ancient customs that survive in Japan to this day, but they also introduced the Shinto religion into the islands of Japan. This religion is based on the worship of nature, for it teaches that a divine presence fills the natural world.

27.2b Combine through subordination.

Choppy: The Mohawk Indians lived on the East Coast. They were one of the five nations of the Iroquois confederacy. Three other members of the confederacy were the Cayuga, Oneida, and Onondaga nations. They inhabited what is now central New York State. The Senecas controlled the west. They lived near Lake Erie.

Combined: The Mohawk Indians, who lived on the East Coast, were one of the five nations of the Iroquois confederacy. While three members of the confederacy, the Cayuga, Oneida, and Onondaga, inhabited what is now central New York State, the Senecas controlled the west, living near Lake Erie.

27.3 Create interest by varying sentence type.

27.3a Use cumulative sentences.

Cumulative sentences begin with the main idea and then add clarifying informa-tion in the phrases and clauses that follow. The value of cumulative sentences is that they can convey a great deal of information in a logical, easy-to-follow unit. Here are two examples:

> The Roman satirist Seneca condemned the gladiatorial games, believing that they fostered greed, brutality, and poverty in a society that already contained too much of these commodities.

> In 1215, the English barons forced King John to sign the Magna Carta, a document forever limiting the power of the monarchy.

27.3b Use periodic sentences.

Unlike a cumulative sentence, a periodic sentence delays the completion of the main idea until the end of the sentence. As a result, a periodic sentence is a good way to create emphasis.

> In the thirteenth century, eastern Europe was terrorized by a fierce tribe of warrior horsemen from central Asia, the Mongols.

Notice that recasting this item as a cumulative sentence does not produce the same emphasis.

> In the thirteenth century, eastern Europe was terrorized by the Mongols, a fierce tribe of warrior horsemen from central Asia.

Here are two more examples of periodic sentences:

> In 1492, after the defeat of the last Moslem stronghold, the Iberian peninsula contained two new world powers, Spain and Portugal.

> In 1517, Martin Luther, a virtually unknown teacher of theology in Wittenberg, Germany, sparked an ecclesiastical revolution.

27.3c Use rhetorical questions.

Rhetorical questions—those to which the reader and the writer both know the answer and to which no response is expected—serve to create both variety and emphasis. Consider this example from a paragraph describing the effects of vio-lence on television, which ends with a rhetorical question:

> Many American children watch up to six hours of television every day. They see police dramas where shootings, murders, rapes, armed robbery, and other types of mayhem are regular fare. They have become addicted to the world of professional wrestling, which glorifies a world, albeit phoney, of brutality,

sadism, and sexism. And they seem to love martial arts movies, where cracking open an opponent's skull is seen as desirable behavior. Is it any wonder, then, that so many young children are using violence to resolve disagreements with siblings, friends, and schoolmates?

Rewrite the following paragraph by applying the techniques you learned above for varying sentence structure, length, and type. Feel free to delete or add words as necessary.

Archimedes of Syracuse

Archimedes was born in 287 B.C. in the Greek city of Syracuse. Syracuse is located in southeastern Sicily. He was a scientist, mathematician, and inventor. He also helped develop modern engineering methods. His discoveries in geometry and physics contributed greatly to the advancement of science. He found a way to measure the volume of a sphere. Some of his principles were adopted by practitioners of calculus, a branch of mathematics developed nearly 2,000 years after his death. Archimedes' principle is his most famous discovery. It is still used to calculate the weight of a body immersed in a liquid. Archimedes came upon this principle while taking a bath. He was so excited about his discovery that he sat up, jumped out of the tub, and shouted "Eureka!" This word is ancient Greek for "I have found it." However, he had neglected to put on his clothes. His most famous invention is Archimedes' screw. This device is still used to draw well water in some countries. Archimedes died during the Roman invasion of his city in 212 B.C. He was solving a knotty mathematical problem when a Roman soldier tried to arrest him. The soldier got angry when Archimedes refused to pay any attention until he had finished solving the problem. The soldier stabbed him.

WRITING IN A CLEAR AND EMPHATIC STYLE

28.1 Create clarity and emphasis by using strong verbs.

You can make your writing both interesting and emphatic by using strong verbs. When you choose verbs, try to avoid forms of the verb *to be* (*is, are, was, were, has been,* and so on). These kinds of verbs convey no action and usually serve only to make your writing wordy.

Not: The slowing of the economy was directly related to a sudden rise in interest rates.

But: A sudden rise in interest rates caused the economy to slow.

The second sentence is better than the first, but another alternative uses an even more active verb construction:

Better: A sudden rise in interest rates slowed economic growth.

An even more exciting choice of verbs might be

Better: When interest rates *surged,* they *retarded* economic growth.

Here is another example:

Not: Allied soldiers defeated the Nazis and moved inland.

But: Allied soldiers *routed* the Nazis and *pushed* inland.

As a rule, always choose a single verb over a verb phrase. The latter lacks energy.

Not	But	Not	But
have an argument	argue	give assistance	assist
make a decision	decide	be abusive to	abuse
offer advice	advise	conduct a test	test
create a plan	plan	confer an award	award
provide help	help	place emphasis on	emphasize

28.2 Create clarity and emphasis by using the active voice.

Sentences using the **active voice** contain subjects that are acting or that are being described. Sentences using the **passive voice** contain subjects that are being acted on. (You can learn more about active and passive voices in Chapter 34.)

There are four reasons to choose the active voice over the passive voice:

1. The active voice is more direct.

The passive voice usually requires more words than the active voice, for verbs in the passive voice come in two parts:

a. A helping verb—a form of *to be (is, are, was, were, will be)* or a form of *to have (has had, will have)*

b. A past participle

Active voice: The scientist completed the experiment.

In the active voice, the subject of the sentence, *scientist,* does the action. The verb is *completed.*

Passive voice: The experiment was completed by the scientist.

In the passive voice, the subject, *experiment,* receives the action. The verb is in two parts: the helping verb *was* and the past participle *completed.* The passive voice also adds the preposition *by,* lengthening the sentence even more.

2. The active voice usually produces a smoother and more natural sentence structure.

Active voice: Several students from my high school graduating class chose to enter the military rather than to attend college.

Passive voice: Entering the military rather than attending college was chosen by several students from my high school graduating class.

3. The passive voice can create problems with dangling or misplaced modifiers.

Active voice: Voting overwhelmingly for Proposition 227, Californians decreased support for bilingual education.

Passive voice: Voting overwhelmingly for Proposition 227, support for bilingual education was significantly decreased in California.

The modifier in the second sentence (*voting overwhelmingly for Proposition 227*) dangles: it should (logically) modify *Californians,* but it actually modifies *support. Support for bilingual education* did not vote; the *Californians* did.

4. The passive voice can result in forgetting to mention the doer of an action, thereby leaving out important information.

Passive voice:	The mayor was criticized for being insensitive to the problems of the poor.
Active voice:	The mayor's political opponents criticized her for being insensitive to the problems of the poor.
Active voice:	The newspaper editorial criticized the mayor for being insensitive to the problems of the poor.

The first sentence fails to tell us who was criticizing the mayor. Such an omission might be confusing, misleading, and, if intentional, even unethical. The reader is entitled to judge an action, statement, or opinion in relation to its source. Reread the two active-voice sentences; most readers would take the first far less seriously than the second because one's *political opponents* can hardly be considered impartial. On the other hand, a *newspaper*—which is supposed to be impartial— carries greater credibility.

Exceptions—When to Use the Passive Voice
The passive voice is appropriate in the following circumstances:

1. When the agent (doer of an action) is unknown or nonexistent

Not:	Someone abandoned an infant on the church steps.
But:	The infant was abandoned on the church steps.
Not:	No one can repair the computer.
But:	The computer cannot be repaired.

2. When the action is more important than the agent or when the agent is obvious

Not:	The government repealed the Eighteenth Amendment to the Constitution, the "prohibition amendment," in 1933, when it passed the Twenty-first Amendment.
But:	The Eighteenth Amendment to the Constitution, the "prohibition amendment," was repealed in 1933, when the Twenty-first Amendment was passed.

3. When using the passive voice makes the sentence more natural or shorter

Not:	The Turkish city of Istanbul once had the name Constantinople.
But:	The Turkish city of Istanbul was once called Constantinople.

Using the Active and Passive Voices

Rewrite the following items by changing the voice from active to passive or from passive to active.

1. During the early days of Ireland, beautiful metalwork and jewelry were created by the Celts.
2. Around 1000 B.C., iron was first smelted and used to create tools and utensils by many people of Asia and Europe.
3. Calling himself "Jack the Ripper," seven women were murdered by a man in London from August 7, 1888, to November 10, 1888.
4. In 1997, a filmmaker produced a movie version of Charles Dickens's novel *Great Expectations*.
5. At one time, people could see the jaguar in places as far apart as Louisiana and Uruguay. Today, however, one can find it living only in the rain forests of Central and South America.

28.3 Create clarity and emphasis through parallelism and repetition.

Parallelism is a way to connect facts and ideas in a sentence by expressing them in the same grammatical form, thereby giving them the same emphasis. For example, a writer might express an idea in a sequence of three or four nouns, three or four infinitives, three or four prepositional phrases, or three or four subordinate clauses. You can learn more about parallelism in Chapter 24. For now, read this excerpt from President Kennedy's inaugural address. The adjective phrases that are used to create parallelism appear in italics.

Let the word go forth from this time and place, to friend and foe alike, that the torch has been passed to a new generation of Americans—*born in this century, tempered by war, disciplined by a hard and bitter peace, proud of our ancient heritage*—and *unwilling to witness or permit* the slow undoing of those human rights to which this nation has always been committed.

Repeating important words and phrases can also create emphasis. (See another quotation from President Kennedy's inaugural address on page 374.) However, use this technique sparingly and carefully. Repeating the same words or using this technique too many times can make your writing boring and stiff, and it can destroy any natural emphasis.

Creating Clarity and Emphasis Through Parallelism

Rewrite the following items by using parallel structure:

1. Between 1933 and 1945, the Nazis maintained hundreds of death camps, where millions of political prisoners, homosexuals, Gypsies, and people of the Jewish faith were imprisoned.
2. The most notorious of these camps were Buchenwald and Dachau in Germany, and the Polish camps of Auschwitz and Treblinka.
3. During the years the Nazis held power in Europe, people from various countries were kept in these camps, and the Nazis tortured and executed millions of them.
4. The first step in the Nazi nightmare was an attempt to exterminate the Jewish people, but this genocide was to be extended to many other people, including Slavs and those living in Hungary.
5. The term *concentration camp* has been used to describe these camps, and the Russian slave labor camps of the Stalinist era are also known by this term.

28.4 Create emphasis by arranging ideas in ascending order of importance.

When writing a sentence containing several items, you can create emphasis by mentioning each item in order of importance. For example, Thomas Jefferson ends the Declaration of Independence by listing three things that he and his fellow signers are willing to sacrifice for the sake of liberty.

> And, for the support of this Declaration, with a firm reliance on protection of Divine Providence, we mutually pledge to each other our Lives, our Fortunes, and our sacred Honor.

Note that the most important of the three is their *sacred Honor.*

■ ■ ■ ■   ■ ■ ■ ■   **BASICLINK** ■ ■ ■ ■   ■ ■ ■ ■
WWW

For more information on arranging ideas, visit these sites:

http://www.uottawa.ca/academic/arts/writcent/hypergrammar/sntorder.html

http://www.inform.umd.edu/IAW/LanguageSkills/34emphasis.html

Rewrite the following to make them clearer and more emphatic by using the techniques you learned in this chapter:

1. The debate over the question of school vouchers has increased in intensity.
2. The addition of two new faculty positions at the college occurred last fall.
3. When the Romans launched an attack against the enemy's capital, they then made a plan to enter the city by digging a tunnel under its massive walls.
4. Emperor Franz Joseph of the Austro-Hungarian Empire suffered several personal losses: the suicide of his son Rudolph, the assassination of his wife Elizabeth, and his brother Maximilian, Emperor of Mexico, was killed in a revolution.
5. The Black Death came to Florence, Italy, in 1348, and many of the city's residents died from that disease.
6. In the Middle Ages, there was no help for people who got the plague. Physicians couldn't help them, there was no use giving them medicines, and no assistance came from the government.
7. In 1453, Constantinople was attacked and taken over by the Ottoman Turks.
8. The name of Constantinople was changed to Istanbul by the Ottoman Sultan Mehmed II.
9. Medieval women were often not allowed to work as laborers or to own businesses because the trade guilds, whose members were men, were able to get laws passed that would limit women's participation in the labor force.
10. However, some opportunities for profitable work were still available to women. For example, businesses were sometimes inherited by them upon the death of their husbands.

Sentence Basics Checklist

1. A **sentence** contains at least one **independent (main) clause.** An independent clause contains a subject and verb, and it expresses a complete idea. It can stand alone as a sentence. A **dependent (subordinate) clause** contains a subject and verb, but it does not express a complete idea and cannot stand alone as a sentence. A **phrase** does not contain a subject and a verb; it can appear before, after, or in the middle of a clause.

2. The punctuation mark with which you end a sentence depends on your purpose. A sentence that ends with a(n)
   a. Period provides information or makes a request.
   b. Question mark asks a question.
   c. Exclamation point expresses a command or strong emotion.

3. A **fragment** is a phrase or dependent clause that is punctuated as if it were a sentence, but it does not express a complete thought. To correct this error:
   a. Join the fragment to an independent (main) clause.
   b. Rewrite the fragment by adding a subject and a verb.

(Continued)

4 A **fused (run-on) sentence** connects independent clauses without a conjunction or correct punctuation. To correct this error:
   a. Add a period to the end of one clause and begin the second with a capital letter.
   b. Place a semicolon between the clauses.
   c. Place a comma and a coordinating conjunction between the clauses.
   d. Use a semicolon and a conjunctive adverb between the clauses.
   e. Make one independent clause a dependent clause.

5 A **comma splice** connects independent clauses with a comma. To correct this error, use the same methods you use to correct fused sentences.

6 **Coordination** combines words, phrases, clauses, and sentences to make them equal in importance. **Subordination** also combines elements but makes one less important than the other. Combining can help you avoid fragments and make your writing smoother.

7 Within a sentence, a series or list of words, phrases, and clauses should appear in the same grammatical form. This principle, called **parallelism**, will make your writing smooth and easy to read.

8 **Modifiers** should point clearly and directly to the words they describe. Dangling, misplaced, shifting, or confusing modifiers can make your writing unclear, illogical, or even unintentionally humorous.

9 Beginning writers should
   a. Make sure the subjects of sentences are nouns or pronouns.
   b. Make sure modifiers point clearly to the words they describe.
   c. Rewrite sentences that contain contradictions.
   d. Avoid connecting main and subordinate elements with coordinating conjunctions.
   e. Make certain that words in a sentence relate logically to one another.
   f. Avoid *when* or *where* when defining a term unless the term names a time or place.

10 A **faulty shift** occurs when you change patterns, tenses, persons, or types of sentences inappropriately. Such shifts make your writing hard to read.

11 As you revise your work, make sure to create interest by **varying sentence structure, length, and type**.

12 As you revise your writing, make sentences more emphatic by relying on **strong verbs**, using **repetition** and **parallelism**, and **arranging ideas in ascending order of importance**. In addition, keep sentences in the active voice except when
   a. The agent or subject is unknown or nonexistent.
   b. The action is more important than the agent.
   c. Using the passive makes the sentence more natural.

9

WORD CHOICE

9

WORD CHOICE

USING A DICTIONARY AND A THESAURUS

29.1 **Use a dictionary.**
29.2 **Use a thesaurus.**

If you are uncertain about the exact meaning of a word, look it up in a dictionary. If you want to use *synonyms* (words with similar meanings) to add variety to your writing, look for additional word choices in a thesaurus.

29.1 Use a dictionary.

In addition to providing the various definitions of a word, a **dictionary** contains information about the word's spelling, pronunciation, and origins. A dictionary also tells which part or parts of speech the word is used as and may offer sample sentences to show you how the word is used in various contexts. Synonyms are often included, as are antonyms, words that are opposite in meaning. Here is a sample dictionary entry:

> **rich** (rich) *adj.* [Old High German, *richi*] 1. owning much money or property; wealthy. 2. well-supplied (with); abounding (in). 3. valuable or costly. 4. full of choice ingredients, as butter, sugar, etc. 5. a) full and mellow: said of sounds. b) deep; vivid: said of colors. c) very fragrant. 6. abundant. 7. yielding in abundance, as soil. 8. [Colloquial] very amusing —*n.* **the rich:** wealthy people collectively. —**rich′ly** *adv.* —**rich′ness** *n.* (*Webster's New World Dictionary*)

What This Dictionary Entry Does

1. It gives the word's pronunciation in parentheses.
2. It tells us that *rich* is an adjective.
3. It explains that *rich* originated from *richi*, a word in a language known as Old High German.
4. It lists eight common meanings of the adjective *rich*.
5. It reveals the adverb and noun forms of the word.

CAUTION!

Always use a dictionary to double-check the meanings of words you find in a thesaurus. Words that are synonymous sometimes produce different meanings in different contexts. Let's say you write *My uncle was rich*. You might easily substitute *wealthy* or *affluent* for *rich*. But would *abundant, fertile,* or *gorgeous* convey the same meaning?

29.2 Use a thesaurus.

A **thesaurus** contains synonyms, words whose meanings are the same as or close to the meaning of the word you have in mind. It also lists antonyms. By making careful selections, you can increase the word choices at your fingertips. Here is a sample thesaurus entry:

> **rich,** *adj.* wealthy, affluent, opulent; fruitful, fertile, luxuriant; abundant, bountiful; sumptuous; gorgeous; sonorous, mellow. See MONEY, PRODUCTION. Antonyms, see POVERTY, INSUFFICIENCY. (*Roget's College Thesaurus*)

■■■■   ■■■■   **BASICLINK**   ■■■■   ■■■■
WWW

Try these sites for more information relating to word meanings, synonyms, and origins:

http://www.geocities.com/etymonline
http://www.m-w.com
http://www.bartleby.com/62

Chapter Wrap-Up

1. Look up the following eighteen words in a college dictionary. For each word, indicate what part(s) of speech it is, its origin(s), and its various meanings.

antecedent	impersonal	retrograde
bellicose	intellectual	stupefaction
conscience	motivation	temerity
diffusion	obscurity	ubiquitous
exposition	perspicacity	vitriolic
hierarchy	quantitative	whimsy

2. In a thesaurus, find three synonyms for each of the words in item 1. Use each synonym in a sentence. You should have fifty-four sentences when you complete this assignment. Remember that the meaning of a synonym might differ from that of the original word depending on the context in which it is used. So go back to the dictionary to double-check the meaning of the synonym you use.

USING EXACT LANGUAGE

Make sure you know exactly what a word or phrase means before you use it. Always rely on a college dictionary as the final authority on such matters. You can find more examples in the Glossary of Usage, which appears later in this chapter.

30.1 Distinguish between words that look or sound alike.

Read these three examples, which illustrate how easy it is to confuse words that are spelled or that sound alike:

New York City is *composed of* five boroughs, or counties.

New York City *comprises* five boroughs, or counties.

Composed of means "made of"; *comprises* means "includes or embraces." Don't write *is comprised of* when you mean *is composed of.*

The district attorney decided to *prosecute* the ex-governor for election fraud.

The Jews were *persecuted* in the Soviet Union as well as in Czarist Russia.

To prosecute means "to place on trial and to seek punishment for a wrongdoing." *To persecute* means "to oppress, harass, brutalize, or treat unfairly."

The lovers decided to be *discreet.*

The professor lectured on three *discrete* outcomes of the war.

Discreet means "cautious, careful, and quiet." *Discrete* means "separate, distinct, or not connected."

Distinguishing Between Words That Look or Sound Alike

Make sure you understand the distinction between the meanings of the following paired words. If necessary, consult a dictionary. Then write a sentence that uses each word correctly.

adolescence/adolescents
advise/advice
affect/effect
antidote/anecdote
counsel/council
emigrate/immigrate

fancy/fanciful
historic/historical
oral/aural
passed/past
precedence/precedent

30.2 Distinguish between words whose meanings are often confused or misused.

Many words and phrases are used incorrectly in daily conversation and even in writing. Here are some examples:

Not: The speaker *inferred* that the government might raise taxes.

But: The speaker *implied* that the government might raise taxes.

To imply means "to suggest." *To infer* means "to draw a conclusion from what is said or written." Speakers and writers imply; listeners and readers infer.

Not: His constant interrupting *aggravated* me.

But: His constant interrupting *annoyed* (or *irritated*) me.

To aggravate means "to make a bad situation worse." In most cases, *annoy* or *irritate* is a far more exact term.

Not: She wore a *fantastic* dress.

Not: She wore a *fabulous* dress.

But: She wore a *beautiful* dress.

The use of *fantastic* should be limited to discussions of *fantasy,* the portrayal of plots, settings, and characters that have no basis in reality. Similarly, *fabulous* refers to the literary genre known as the fable, stories in which animals take on human roles.

Not: The army was *decimated;* no one returned alive.

But: The army was *decimated,* but the remaining troops fought on to victory.

Decimated does not mean "destroyed." It means "reduced by 10 percent." Note the word's prefix, *deci-,* which means "ten" in Latin. Popularly, *decimate* often means "to severely weaken."

Distinguishing Between Words Whose Meanings Are Often Confused

Make sure you understand the distinction between the meanings of the following paired words. If necessary, consult a dictionary. Then write a sentence that uses each word correctly.

adulterate/(commit) adultery

amoral/immoral

apathetic/disinterested

atheist/agnostic

bimonthly/semimonthly

concave/convex

continuous/continual

eulogy/epitaph

famous/infamous

further/farther

healthy/healthful

incredible/incredulous

mad/angry

presently/currently

sympathy/empathy

unique/(very) different

verbal/oral

30.3 Use words appropriate to context: Connotation.

Words have denotations—their core, objective, or essential meanings. But many words also have **connotations**—the shades of or variations in meaning they suggest. For example, it is one thing to say, "I drank a glass of beer." It is quite another to say, "I guzzled a glass of beer." *To drink* is a fairly neutral term, meaning simply "to consume a liquid." *To guzzle,* on the other hand, suggests drinking quickly and without stopping. It has a negative connotation.

Whenever you consider connotations, keep your audience and purpose in mind. Let's say you are writing to members of the Veterans of Foreign Wars. It would be more effective to claim that increasing the U.S. defense budget at this time is unwise rather than to say that it is silly or immoral. Also consider your writing situation and your purpose. For example, you can explain that poor hygiene practices can result in offensive body odor, or you can say that not showering regularly will make a person stink. The former is softer; the latter, more direct and emphatic. Finally, avoid inflammatory language. It is unfair, and it often backfires because intelligent readers find it offensive. For instance, it is one thing to call the mayor a conniver; it is another to question his integrity. It is one thing to say that the government's policies make poor people slaves to the welfare system. It is quite another to say that such policies make poor people dependent on welfare. Here are some more examples:

Not: The guests *grazed* on the expensive caviar and other exotic appetizers.

But: The guests *enjoyed* the expensive caviar and other exotic appetizers.

Grazed is associated more with animals than with humans.

Not: The doctor *contrived* to break the news to us gently.

But: The doctor *tried* to break the news to us gently.

Contrived implies underhandedness, which is probably not what the writer of this sentence wished to convey.

Not: Because she was a single mother with a small income, Gloria had to be *stingy.*

But: Because she was a single mother with a small income, Gloria had to be *frugal.*

Stingy has a decidedly negative connotation, implying an unhealthy or unreasonable concern for money. *Frugal* has a more positive connotation. The single mother is to be admired for the care she must take with her limited funds.

EXERCISE 30C

Using Words Appropriate to Context

Read over the following pairs of words. Then, in a sentence or two, explain how one word in the pair differs in connotation from the other.

criticize/disparage	immorality/iniquity
defy/challenge	opposed/hostile
discuss/debate	praise/flattery
enemy/adversary	question/confront

30.4 Eliminate non-words.

Be sure that the words you use are actual words and not just incorrect, albeit common, variations of those words.

Not: After dinner, they ordered *expresso* and cream puffs.

But: After dinner, they ordered *espresso* and cream puffs.

Not: "Don't use excessive *verbage*," said the teacher.

But: "Don't use excessive *verbiage*," said the teacher.

Not: After World War I, the nation attempted to return to *normality.*

But: After World War I, the nation attempted to return to *normal.*

Not: The college instituted a plan that increased the number of students being *retented.*

But: The college instituted a plan that increased the number of students being *retained.*

EXERCISE 30D

Replacing Non-Words

Provide the correct alternative for the following non-words:

cohesivity

couragencss

hesitantness

indecisivity

indigentness

nuturate

pompousivity

proudful

sentimentalness

30.5 Use correct prefixes.

Make sure that the prefix you put before a word is the correct one for that word.

Not.	The news he brought us was *inimportant.*
But:	The news he brought us was *unimportant.*

Using Correct Prefixes

Rewrite the following with the correct prefixes.

imbitter

inhance

inpact

inpeach

instable

intangle

unconsequential

unconsiderate

unhospitable

untangible

EXERCISE 30E

30.6 Use words in keeping with their intended functions.

Use words according to their intended functions, which are determined by the parts of speech under which they are classified.

Not:	We had a *fun* time.
But:	We had an *enjoyable* time.

In the first sentence, the writer uses the word *fun* as an adjective to describe *time.* But *fun* is a noun, not an adjective.

Not:	She is a very *religion* woman.
But:	She is a very *religious* woman.

In the first sentence, the writer uses the word *religion* as an adjective to describe *woman*. But *religion* is a noun, not an adjective.

Not: The Ryans are in the market for a *use* car.

But: The Ryans are in the market for a *used* car.

The word *use* is a verb; the word needed here is an adjective, *used*.

Not: The children were *really* hungry.

But: The children were *very* hungry.

In formal writing, *really* should be replaced with *very*.

30.7 Review a glossary of usage.

The glossary that follows includes words commonly confused (such as *affect* and *effect*), words commonly misused (*lay*), and words that are nonstandard (such as *theirselves*). Review the list carefully. If you have a question about a word that's not listed here, check your dictionary.

a/an

A and *an* are indefinite articles because they point to something in a general way. *A* is used when the word that follows it begins with a consonant sound: *a horror movie, a house, a university, a year. An* is used when the word that follows it begins with a vowel sound: *an architect, an honor, an hour, an incredible experience.* Note that not all words that begin with vowels actually begin with vowel sounds and not all words that begin with consonants have initial consonant sounds.

accept/except

Accept is a verb meaning "to receive." (A community college will usually *accept* any applicant who has a high school diploma.) *Except* can be a preposition meaning "excluding." (My nephew likes all vegetables *except* lima beans.) It can also be a verb meaning "to exclude." (Her cousin was *excepted* from the wedding list.)

ad/advertisement

In formal writing, use the full word *advertisement*. (They read the *advertisement* with interest.)

adapt/adopt

Adapt is a verb that means "to adjust to or become accustomed to" and implies a modification of some sort. (In spite of their reservations, they easily *adapted* to their new situation.) *Adopt* is a verb that means "to take or to choose something voluntarily."

(They decided to *adopt* both children even though they already had ten. The department voted to *adopt* the textbook for all classes.)

adverse/averse
Adverse means "contrary," "hostile," or "unfavorable." (The jury delivered an *adverse* verdict to the defendant.) *Averse* means "being opposed." (None of the eleven members of the committee was *averse* to the chairperson's suggestions.)

advice/advise
Advice is a noun. (The value of good *advice* is not immediately recognized.) *Advise* is a verb. (The faculty member *advised* the student to drop the course.)

affect/effect
Affect is usually a verb meaning "to influence." (Automobile emissions can *affect* the earth's atmosphere.) *Effect* is usually a noun meaning "result." (The *effects* of global warming are difficult to determine.) *Effect* can also be a verb meaning "to bring about." (The antidepressants he was taking eventually *effected* a change in his personality.)

aggravate/irritate
Aggravate is a verb meaning "to make worse or more serious." (Her sciatica was *aggravated* by her sitting in a chair in front of a computer for more than four hours without a break.) In formal writing, avoid using it colloquially to mean "to annoy." Instead, use *irritate*. (He was *irritated* [not *aggravated*] by the loud music coming from the upstairs apartment.)

agree to/agree with
Agree to means "to give consent" or "to go along with." (She won't *agree to* her future mother-in-law's long guest list for the wedding.) *Agree with* means "to come to an understanding." (He *agreed with* his wife's plan to redecorate the living room.)

ain't
Ain't is nonstandard and should be avoided in formal writing. Instead, use *am not, are not,* or *is not.*

allowed/aloud
Allowed refers to having permission to do something. (Even though Carrie was only fourteen, her mother *allowed* her to go on a date.) *Aloud* refers to speaking in a normal tone and volume, as opposed to a whisper. (Talking *aloud* in the library was frowned upon.)

allude/refer	To *allude* is to mention something indirectly. (She *alluded* to his overdrawn bank account.) To *refer* is to mention something directly. (In his speech, he *referred* to his problem with alcohol.)
allusion/illusion	An *allusion* is an indirect reference. (The poet made an *allusion* to the Bible.) An *illusion* is a misleading image. (David Copperfield employs *illusions* in his magic tricks.)
alot/a lot/allot	A *lot* is the correct form; *alot* is a misspelling. *Allot* means to apportion. (He was *allotted* five acres of his parent's estate.
already/all ready	*Already* means "previously." (He planned to include a check in the envelope, but he had *already* sealed it.) *All ready* means "prepared." (They were *all ready* to leave when the rain started.)
alright/all right	The generally accepted spelling is *all right*. (The children were *all right*.) *Alright* is unacceptable in formal writing.
altogether/ all together	*Altogether* means "entirely." (The dancer was *altogether* brilliant in her performance.) *All together* means "gathered together." (The campaign workers were *all together* at the rally.)
ambiguous/ ambivalent	*Ambiguous* is an adjective meaning "doubtful" or "unclear." (The senator's answers to the reporter's questions were *ambiguous*.) *Ambivalent* is an adjective meaning "uncertain" or "having simultaneous and contradictory feelings." (His feelings about the candidate were *ambivalent*.)
among/between	Use *among* when dealing with more than two entities. (*Among* the candidates, he was the most popular.) Use *between* when dealing with only two entities. (Diane's choice was *between* dropping out of college at midterm and finishing the semester.)
amoral/immoral	*Amoral* means "being neither moral nor immoral" or "being beyond a code of morality." (Even though he had religious training, he was completely *amoral*.) *Immoral* means "lacking morality." (Genocide is *immoral*.)
amount/number	Use *amount* with quantities that cannot be counted. (The tornado left a large *amount* of damage in its wake.) Use *number* with those things that can be

counted. (There were a *number* of reasons why he did not want to attend the game.)

angry at/
angry with

To say that someone is *angry at* someone or someone's actions is nonstandard. Use *angry with* instead. (They were angry *with* [not *at*] John.)

ante-/anti-

The prefix *ante-* means "prior to" or "earlier than." (Cotton was king in the *ante*bellum South.) The prefix *anti-* means "against" or "opposed to." (Many Northerners were strong supporters of the *anti*slavery movement.)

anybody/anyone/
any body/any one

Written as one word, *anybody* and *anyone* are indefinite pronouns and are interchangeable. (Does *anyone* [*anybody*] want to go to the movies?) Written as two words (*any body* [adjective + noun] and *any one* [adjective + pronoun]), they refer to a single element or group. (Name *any one* of the Great Lakes. Name *any body* of water in Canada.)

anymore

Anymore is an adverb used primarily in negative situations. (She has told so many lies I can't believe her *anymore*.)

anyways/anywheres

Both are nonstandard and should not be used in formal writing. Use *anyway* or *anywhere*.

as/like

As is a subordinating conjunction. (*As* I told you yesterday, I can't make the meeting.) *Like* is a preposition and is followed only by a noun or noun phrase. (Charles looks *like* his father.)

awful/awfully

Do not use either word in place of the intensifier *very*.
Not: The committee looked *awfully* tired after sixteen hours of negotiations.
But: The committee looked *very* tired after sixteen hours of negotiations.

awhile/a while

Awhile is an adverb, so it cannot function as the object of a preposition, such as *for*. Therefore, you should not write "Stay *for awhile*." The form *a while* is a noun preceded by an article. Thus, you can say "Stay for *a while*." You can also say "Stay *awhile*."

backup/back up

Backup is a noun or adjective referring to something that serves as a substitute or support. (Don't forget to save your information on a *backup* disk.) *Back up* is a verb phrase. (Don't forget to *back up* the information. Be careful when you *back up* your car.)

bad/badly	*Bad* is an adjective; *badly* is an adverb. Use the adjective form after linking verbs (*be, is, are, was, were, appear, become, grow, seem, prove*) and after sense verbs (*feel, look, smell, sound, taste*). (I feel *bad* about missing your recital.) The adverb form modifies a verb or an adjective. (The Jets *badly* needed the victory to make the playoffs.)
being as/being that	Both forms are nonstandard. Use *because* instead.
beside/besides	*Beside* is a preposition meaning "next to." (They sat *beside* each other on the dais.) *Besides* is an adverb meaning "in addition." (*Besides* the Golden Globe, she won the Academy Award.) *Besides* is also a preposition meaning "other than." (The doctors decided something *besides* the food he ate was causing the nausea.)
between you and I/ between you and me	*Between you and I* is incorrect. *Between* is a preposition that requires the objective case (*me*). *I* is the subjective case.

Not: Just *between you and I*, I don't believe any part of his story.

But: Just *between you and me*, I don't believe any part of his story.

breath/breathe	*Breath* is a noun; *breathe* is a verb. (Take a deep *breath*, and then *breathe* at a normal rate.)
bring/take	Use *bring* when something is being brought to you. (He will *bring* me my lottery ticket before tonight's drawing.) Use *take* when something is being moved away. (*Take* these coffee cakes to the church bazaar.)
can/may	Use *can* to express an ability to do something. (Alice *can* act with the best of them.) Use *may* to express either permission or possibility. (No, you *may* not go to the movies tonight. You *may* pass the test, but only if you study hard.)
cannot	*Cannot* is preferred to *can not*.
capital/capitol	A *capital* is the official seat of government, as well as a crime calling for execution. (The *capital* of Texas is Austin. He was charged with a *capital* crime.) A *capitol* is a building in which a government meets. (The design of the state's *capitol* building is based on the *Capitol* in Washington.)

censor/censure	*Censor* as a verb means "to delete material considered offensive." (Some people believe the government should *censor* television programs.) *Censure* as a verb means "to reprimand" or "to condemn." (The senator was *censured* for accepting gifts.)
cite/site/sight	*Cite* means "to quote from or to refer to an authority." (When writing a research paper, you must *cite* all your sources.) *Site* means "a place." (The construction *site* is full of hazards.) *Sight* means "something that can be seen." (They enjoyed seeing the *sights* on their vacation.) *Sight* also means "the ability to see."
climatic/climactic	*Climatic* relates to the climate (weather). (The depletion of the ozone layer is causing *climatic* changes.) *Climactic* relates to a climax (the end of events). (In the *climactic* scene of the play, Sweeney Todd inadvertently kills his wife.)
coarse/course	*Coarse* is an adjective meaning "rough," "harsh," or "crude." (His language was too *coarse* for her sensibilities.) *Course* is a noun meaning "accustomed procedure" or "unit of study." (He needed to take an additional eight *courses* in his major in order to graduate.)
compare to/ compare with	*Compare to* relates to resemblances between dissimilar things. (He *compared* her radiant smile *to* a ray of sunlight.) *Compare with* relates to examining similar things to determine their similarities or their differences. (He *compared* the typed manuscript *with* the original handwritten one to see what changes the author had made.)
complement/ compliment	*Complement* is a verb meaning "to go with" or "to complete." It can also be a noun meaning "something that completes." (His flowered tie does not *complement* his checkered jacket.) *Compliment* is a verb meaning "to flatter." It can also be a noun that means a "flattering remark." (The paper's critic *complimented* her on her performance.)
conscience/ conscious	*Conscience* is a noun meaning "moral principles." (He was unable to sleep because his *conscience* bothered him.) *Conscious* is an adjective meaning "to be awake" or "to be aware." (Even though he had been hit on the head by the falling debris, he was still *conscious* of his surroundings.)

continual/ continuous	*Continual* implies occurring regularly or frequently. (The *continual* telemarketing calls interfered with her ability to concentrate.) *Continuous* means "uninterrupted." (The *continuous* car alarm kept the neighbors awake for over an hour.)
could care less/ couldn't care less	The correct version is *couldn't care less. Could care less* indicates there is some element of care left, which generally is not what is meant.
could have/ could of	*Could have* is the correct usage. *Could of* is incorrect.
council/counsel	A *council* is a group of people who meet to consult, deliberate, or discuss. (The faculty *council* makes recommendations about curricula to the administration.) *Counsel* means "to advise or to recommend." (Her lawyer *counseled* her about the next course of action in her lawsuit.)
desert/dessert	A *desert* is made up of sand. (They were stranded in the *desert*.) A *dessert* is something you eat after dinner. (After dinner, they had pecan pie for *dessert*.)
different from/ different than	The preferred form is *different from*. (Ebert's opinions of the movie were *different from* Roeper's.) *Different than* may be used to avoid an awkward construction. (Is your itinerary *different than* it was originally?)
disinterested/ uninterested	*Disinterested* means "impartial and free from bias." (Their boss was *disinterested* when discussing the reasons for each of the employee's complaints against the other.) *Uninterested* means "not interested." (He was *uninterested* in the outcome of the local school board election.)
e.g.	In formal writing, use *for example* or *for instance* rather than the Latin abbreviation *e.g.* (*exempli gratia*).
elicit/illicit	*Elicit* is a verb meaning "to bring out." (The reporter tried to *elicit* a response from the senator.) *Illicit* is an adjective meaning "unlawful." (The governor was accused of having an *illicit* affair.)
emigrate/ immigrate	*Emigrate* means "to leave one's country to go somewhere else." (The family next door to us *emigrated* from Latvia.) *Immigrate* means "to come

into a country." (Because of the fighting in their country, they *immigrated* to the United States.)

eminent/imminent *Eminent* means "outstanding" or "distinguished." (*The Allegory of Love* was written by the *eminent* scholar C. S. Lewis.) *Imminent* means "about to happen." (The president's news conference is *imminent.*)

etc./and etc. *Et cetera* (*etc.*) means "and the rest." *And etc.,* meaning "and and the rest," is redundant.

eventually/ ultimately *Eventually* means "at an unspecified time in the future." (The admiral knew they would *eventually* meet the enemy fleet.) *Ultimately* means "in the end" or "at the furthest extreme." (*Ultimately,* the dropping of the atom bomb ended the war.)

everybody/ everyone *Everybody* and *everyone* are singular pronouns meaning "every person." (Is *everybody* happy? Is *everyone* satisfied?)

everyplace/ everywhere *Everyplace* is informal; use *everywhere.*

explicit/implicit *Explicit* means "directly expressed or clearly defined." (The professor gave *explicit* directions abut the writing assignment.) *Implicit* means "implied or unstated." (The rules of the game were *implicit.*)

farther/further Once used interchangeably, *farther* is now preferred when referring to physical distance. (Lincoln Center is *farther* north than Columbus Circle.) *Further* is now used when referring to nonphysical distance. (We were told not to read any *further* in our textbook until after we had taken the examination.)

fewer/less *Fewer* refers to things that can be counted. (*Fewer* people showed up at the meeting than we expected.) *Less* refers to general amounts. (The new recipe calls for *less* sugar than did the old one.)

flaunt/flout *Flaunt* means "to display" (usually in a negative sense). (He *flaunted* his newfound wealth.) *Flout* means "to treat with contempt" or "to scoff at." (He *flouted* the rules of good manners.)

gonna/going to *Gonna* is a common misspelling based on pronunciation. The correct form is *going to.*

good/well

Good is an adjective. (Even though it is two weeks old, the fruit still looks *good*.) *Well* is an adverb. (Did you sleep *well*?) Both *well* and *good* can be used when referring to a state of health, but there are subtle differences. Therefore, *well* is preferred. (I feel *well* today.)

hanged/hung

Both words are the past tense of *hang*. *Hanged* refers to an execution. (Nazi war criminal Adolf Eichman was *hanged* in Israel after a trial.) For all other situations, use *hung*. (The decorator *hung* pictures on each side of the fireplace.)

hardly

Use *hardly* by itself instead of *can't hardly* and *not hardly*, which are considered double negatives.

Not: I can't hardly see the shoreline because of the fog.

But: I can hardly see the shoreline because of the fog.

has got/have got

Got is unnecessary in such constructions and should not be used.

Not: She *has got* three more days to prepare for her recital.

But: She *has* three more days to prepare for her recital.

heros/heroes

Heros refers to sandwiches. (We always have *heros* for dinner on Mondays.) *Heroes* refers to people. (Children often think of athletes as *heroes*.)

hopefully

Hopefully is an adverb that means "in a hopeful manner" and can modify a verb, an adjective, or another adverb. (They waited *hopefully* for their number to be drawn in the lottery.) *Hopefully* (meaning "I hope") is commonly used as a sentence modifier in speech and in informal writing, but it should be avoided in formal writing.

Not: *Hopefully, the guests will arrive on time.*

But: *I hope* the guests will arrive on time.

i.e.

In formal writing, use *that is* rather than the Latin abbreviation *i.e.* (*id est*).

in/into

In indicates location or condition. (The detective found the murder weapon hidden *in* the clock by the front door.) *Into* indicates movement or a change in condition. (Laura walked *into* the room and surprised everyone.)

ingenious/ ingenuous	*Ingenious* means "clever." (Sondheim's lyrics are *ingenious*.) *Ingenuous* means "naïve" or "frank." (He was *ingenuous* in his response to the situation.)
in regards to	Nonstandard for *as regards, in regard to,* or *regarding.*
irregardless/ regardless	*Irregardless* is nonstandard. *Regardless* is the accepted form. (They decided to buy a new car *regardless* of the cost.)
its/it's/its'	*Its* is the possessive pronoun. (The college will hold *its* graduation on Thursday.) *It's* is the contraction of *it is.* (Because storm clouds are rolling in, *it's* likely to rain before evening.) *Its'* is an error.
kind of/sort of	Use *somewhat* instead of *kind of* or *sort of.*

Not: Attack of the Clones was *kind of* disappointing.

But: Attack of the Clones was *somewhat* disappointing.

led/lead	*Led* is the past tense of the verb *lead.* (The performer *led* the audience in a sing a long.) *Lead* is a noun that refers to a metal. (Many older buildings are contaminated by *lead* paint.)
liable/libel	*Liable* means "responsible" or "legally obligated." It also relates to something unpleasant and is usually used with the word *to.* (Harold is *liable to* lose his court case.) *Libel* refers to writing something malicious about another person. (Harold sued the newspaper for *libel.*)
lie/lay	These two verbs cause numerous problems. Here are the troublesome tenses:

Present	Past	Present Participle	Past Participle
lie (*to recline*)	lay	lying	lain
lay (*to place*)	laid	laying	laid

Note that the past tense of *lie* is the same as the present tense of *lay. Lie* is an intransitive verb, meaning it doesn't take an object, while *lay* is a transitive verb, meaning it does take an object.

Not: Michael is so depressed that he *lays* in bed all day.

But: Michael is so depressed that he *lies* in bed all day.

	Not: The waiter *lay* the fork in the wrong place.
	But: The waiter *laid* the fork in the wrong place.
loath/loathe	*Loath* means "unwilling to do something contrary to one's way of thinking." (He was unusual; he was *loath* to cheat on his tax returns.) *Loathe* means "to dislike someone or something." (Susan *loathed* her brother-in-law's attitude toward women's liberation.)
loose/lose	*Loose* is an adjective meaning "not tight." (Amy prefers *loose* clothing when it is humid.) *Lose* is a verb meaning "to misplace" or "not to win." (I predict the team will *lose* on Sunday.)
lots/lots of	Avoid using in place of *many, much,* or *a lot.*
maybe/may be	*Maybe* is an adverb meaning "possibly." (Annie sings, "The sun will come out tomorrow," not, "*Maybe* the sun will come out tomorrow.") *May be* is a verb phrase. (There *may be* an easier solution, but I don't know what it is.)
may have/may of/ might have/might of	*May have* and *might have* are the correct forms. *May of* and *might of* are incorrect.
medium/media/ mediums	The singular form is *medium.* The plural form is *media* (or *mediums*).
off of/off	*Off of* is incorrect. Use *off.*
	Not: He jumped *off of* the bridge.
	But: He jumped *off* the bridge.
OK/O.K./okay	All three spellings are acceptable, but all should be avoided in formal writing.
passed/past	*Passed* is the past tense of the verb *pass.* (With help from a tutor, he *passed* the exam.) *Past* usually refers to a former time. (Alexis didn't consider her husband's *past* before she married him.)
percent/percentage	*Percent* is used with a specific number. (There is a 60 *percent* chance of rain tomorrow.) *Percentage* is used with a descriptive term such as *large* or *small,* not with a specific number. (A large *percentage* of the votes were not counted.)
personal/personnel	*Personal* refers to something that is private. (He received a letter marked "*Personal.*") *Personnel* generally refers to employees. (All the *personnel* had to wear identification badges.)

plus	*Plus* should not be used to join two independent clauses. **Not:** The rain helped clear the air; *plus,* it was good for the plants. **But:** The rain helped clear the air; *in addition,* it was good for the plants.
precede/proceed	*Precede* is a verb meaning "to go before." (In spelling, the letter *i* usually *precedes* the letter *e.*) *Proceed* is a verb meaning "to continue" or "to advance." (When you are finished with the first part of the test, you may *proceed* to the second part.)
principal/principle	*Principal* is a noun meaning "the head of a school or organization," "a sum of money," or "something of chief importance." (The *principal* closed the school at noon. He spent both the *principal* and the interest of his investment as soon as he received them. Dehydration is the *principal* cause of heat stroke.) *Principle* is a noun meaning "a basic truth, rule, doctrine, or assumption." (Religious *principles* are important to many people throughout the world.)
quite/quiet/quit	*Quite* is an adverb meaning "completely" or "positively." (She was *quite* happy with her promotion to associate professor.) *Quiet* is an adjective meaning "free from noise" or "calm." (The audience was so taken by her performance that they remained *quiet* for almost thirty seconds before breaking into thunderous applause.) *Quit* is a verb meaning "to leave (a job)." (He *quit* working at the bank.)
quote/quotation	*Quote* is a verb. Do not use it as a shortened form of the noun *quotation.* **Not:** He recited a long *quote* from Martin Luther King Jr.'s "I Have a Dream" speech. **But:** He recited a long *quotation* from Martin Luther King Jr.'s "I Have a Dream" speech.
raise/rise	*Raise* is a transitive verb meaning "*to elevate,*" "*to build,*" or "*to move to a higher position*" and takes a direct object. (The neighbors got together and *raised* a new barn to replace the one that had burned down.) *Rise* is an intransitive verb meaning "*to get up,*" "*to ascend,*" or "*to increase*" and does not take a direct object. (They decided to *rise* at 3 A.M. and go

fishing. She had to wait for the dough to *rise* before adding the candied fruit.)

real/really
Real is an adjective; *really* is an adverb. (The characters in *Monsters' Inc.* certainly looked *real*. She was hurt *really* badly in the building collapse.)

respectively/ respectfully
Respectively is an adverb meaning "singly, in the order designated." (He announced the winners *respectively*.) *Respectfully* is an adverb meaning "with respect." (He *respectfully* answered the questions asked by the judge.)

sensual/sensuous
Sensual relates to satisfying the physical, especially sexual, appetites. (Both of them found the movie to be highly *sensual*.) *Sensuous* relates to the senses. (They found the gently falling rain to be *sensuous*.)

set/sit
Set is a transitive verb meaning "to put or place" and takes a direct object. (*Set* the glass down carefully.) *Sit* means "to be seated" and and does not take a direct object. (*Sit* down and be quiet.)

shall/will
Shall is used for first-person questions requesting consent or an opinion. (*Shall* we leave?) *Will* is the future-tense helping verb for all persons: I, you, he, she, it, we, they will. (I *will* start listening when you start making sense.)

should have/ should of
Should have is the correct spelling. *Should of* is incorrect.

sometime/ some time/ sometimes
Sometime relates to an indefinite or unstated time. (As Mae West said, "Why don't you come up and see me *sometime*?") *Some time* relates to a span of time. (I will need *some time* to make up my mind.) *Sometimes* means "now and then." (I *sometimes* go to the movies on Monday nights.)

stationary/ stationery
Stationary means "remaining in one place." (The table is *stationary*; it cannot be moved.) *Stationery* refers to paper. (She wrote her letter on expensive *stationery*.)

suppose to/ supposed to
Supposed to is the correct spelling. *Suppose to* is incorrect.

than/then
Than is a conjunction used in comparisons. (Jodi and Bill arrived earlier *than* the other ticket buyers.)

	Then is an adverb denoting time. (Read the instructions; *then* assemble the bicycle.)
there/their/they're	*There* is an adverb specifying place. (Stand *there* if you want to see the president.) *Their* is a possessive pronoun. (*Their* house is on the corner.) *They're* is a contraction of *they are.* (*They're* too tired to stay awake.)
to/too/two	*To* is a preposition that also serves as an infinitive marker. (*To* vote, you have *to* register by going *to* city hall.) *Too* is an adverb meaning "also," "to an excessive degree," or "very." (Because the classroom was *too* cold, the professor canceled the lecture.) *Two* is a number. (The *two* of them decided to attend the reception.)
toward/towards	Both are acceptable, but *toward* is preferred. Whichever one you choose, use it consistently.
try to/try and	*Try to* is the correct form. *Try and* is incorrect. (Bob's mother should *try to* understand his problem.)
TV/television	In formal writing, use the full word *television.* (His favorite *television* show is *Law and Order.*)
unexceptionable/ unexceptional	*Unexceptionable* means "not open to criticism" or "beyond reproach." (Robert's handling of the situation was *unexceptionable.*) *Unexceptional* means "ordinary" or "commonplace." (The critics unanimously described the play as *unexceptional.*)
use to/used to	*Used to* is the correct spelling. *Use to* is incorrect.
wait for/wait on	*Wait for* means "to wait for someone or something." (We had to *wait* an hour for the plane.) *Wait on* relates to being served. (The hostess herself had to *wait on* us because she was short of help.)
wanna/want to	*Wanna* is a common misspelling based on pronunciation. The correct form is *want to.*
weather/whether	*Weather* relates to the condition of the atmosphere. (The *weather* outside is frightening.) *Whether* is a conjunction used to introduce the first of two or more alternatives. (*Whether* you decide to stay or to go is of no concern to me.)
who/which/that	*Who* is used to refer to people and to animals with names. (She is the woman *who* was captured on the surveillance tape. Rin Tin Tin and Lassie are the two dogs *who* had their own television shows.) *Which* is

used to refer only to things and to animals. (Those are my books, *which* need to be returned to the library by tomorrow. They captured the circus's black bear, *which* tried to break into the house.) *That* is used to refer to things and to most animals, and it also may be used to refer to a group or class of people. (A green Nissan was the car *that* ran the red light. Those are the people *that* signed the petition.)

who's/whose   *Who's* is a contraction of *who is.* (*Who's* going to the dance tonight?) *Whose* is a possessive pronoun. (*Whose* car are we taking to Atlantic City?)

would have/   *Would have* is the correct term. *Would of* is
would of   incorrect.

your/you're   *Your* is a possessive pronoun. (*Your* purse was found in the college center.) *You're* is a contraction of *you are.* (*You're* lucky that your money was not stolen.)

CHAPTER WRAP-UP

Rewrite the following paragraph to improve exactness:

The enthused crowd of students were huddled into the auditorium to hear a lecture from a speaker who had become infamous the world over. This was not the first time, however, that the college had invited a Nobel Prize lariat to speak. Indeed, the precedence had been set more than forty years before, when Enrico Fermi, the Italian physicist, had chatted to a packed house of science pupils on the pledge of the atom as a source of indefinite energy. This time, however, the discourse was meant for a far more diverse audience, for the current lecturer had received a reward in literature. Several of the students in the audience were inspiring young poets and novelists, and they listened with carefulness, as the speaker recalled the inceptions of her literary career. She persisted that the basic device for all blooming writers was a deep appreciation of the word, whether oral or verbal. Thus, she counciled the students to do as much reading, writing, and listening as probable. She also recommended that they continue to flock to academic lectures such as the one they were presently attending. She also encouraged them to observe both natural and human behavior in search of worldwide themes and queries they might discuss in their writing.

MAINTAINING APPROPRIATE TONE, STYLE, AND WORD CHOICE

31

31.1 Use tone appropriate to your subject.

Your subject determines your **tone**. Tone reveals the writer's attitude toward the subject. Let's say you want to write letters to the editor of a local newspaper on three different issues. Depending on your subject, you might use a humorous, a serious, or a mixed tone.

1. A **humorous tone** might be appropriate in a letter in which you poke fun at the city council's recent decision to require police officers to patrol on roller blades.

2. A **serious tone** might work in a letter explaining the dangers of lead poisoning to children.

3. A **mixed tone**—one that is serious and also pokes fun—might be effective in a letter responding to the government's explanation of why it must raise taxes.

Of course, tone is not as simple a concept as explained above and will vary widely from writer to writer, even when the subject is the same. However, these three classifications should help you choose the kind of tone appropriate to your subject.

31.2 Use style appropriate to your audience.

Your audience determines your **style**. Your audience is made up of the people who will read your writing. Once you have determined who your audience is, you can choose the level of language or the style that is appropriate to use with those readers. As explained in Chapter 3, there are, in general, three levels of language, or styles, to choose from:

1. **Informal.** You can use informal language when writing to yourself and to friends and acquaintances.

2. **Familiar.** You might want to use familiar language when writing to relatives or to the editor of a local or college newspaper or when composing short business memos to your colleagues at work.

3. **Formal.** This is the kind of language you should use when writing college essays; formal letters; or official business, technical, or government reports. Your audience for such writing will be instructors, classmates, business associates, and the like.

The rest of this chapter explains the kind of language you should avoid in formal writing, the kind of writing you should use to complete academic assignments.

31.2a Avoid *you* in formal writing.

Avoid the pronoun *you* and its various forms in formal writing unless you are addressing the reader directly. For example, if you write a letter to a friend with a drug problem, you might say

> If you continue abusing drugs, you will ruin your life.

However, if you are writing an essay that addresses a wide and varied audience—some of whom have no drug problem—you might say

> Drug abuse ruins lives.

EXERCISE 31A

Avoiding *You* in Formal Writing

Rewrite the following items without addressing the reader directly. In other words, do not use the pronoun you or any words formed from you, such as your or yourself.

1. You will find Yellowstone National Park in Wyoming, although you can visit parts of it in Montana and Idaho.
2. Because Yellowstone is located in the Rocky Mountains, some of its mountains rise above 10,000 feet. You can get excellent views of the park from several places, including Mount Washburn.
3. The Yellowstone River, which is nearly 700 miles long, cuts through what is known as the "Grand Canyon of the Yellowstone." You should not confuse this place with the better-known Grand Canyon of Arizona.
4. The Grand Canyon of the Yellowstone offers you spectacular views. Its volcanic rock walls of red, orange, yellow, and brown will appeal to your artistic side and fill you with awe.

31.2b Choose single-verb constructions.

Sometimes verbs can be combined with prepositions to form phrasal verbs. Using too many of these makes your writing less formal. In some instances, phrasal verbs can have more than one meaning. Therefore, try to use single, strong verbs in formal writing. Here are a few examples:

Phrasal Verb	More Formal Verb
bring up	raise, suggest
build up	strengthen, construct
check out	leave a hotel, examine
come up	rise, climb, appear
figure out	understand
find out	discover, learn
help out	assist
hold on to	grasp
let out	release
lie down	recline
look up	research, find
run up	accumulate
set up	create, establish
stand up for	support, defend, sponsor
stay around	linger, remain
take off	leave, rise, absent oneself
think about	consider
turn down	reject, lower
use up	exhaust
work out	exercise, solve

31.3 Use language that is idiomatic.

Many phrases in English take forms and convey meanings that are governed by convention (repeated use) and not by rules or even logic. For example, we *sit up* with a sick friend, but we *sit down* to eat dinner. In many instances, unidiomatic expressions result from using the wrong preposition in a phrase.

Unidiomatic: The Simpsons had dinner *over* our house.

Idiomatic: The Simpsons had dinner *at* our house.

Unidiomatic: In World War II, American volunteers led supply convoys to China *down* the Burma Road.

Idiomatic: In World War II, American volunteers led supply convoys to China *along* the Burma Road.

Here are some other examples:

Unidiomatic	Idiomatic
able of	able to
according with	according to
angry at	angry with
capable to	capable of
desirous to	desirous of
different than	different from
equal with	equal to
inferior than	inferior to
on the area	in the area
preferable than	preferable to
prior than	prior to
reason why is because	reason is that
sure and	sure to
try and	try to

31.4 Avoid illogical constructions.

When editing, read each sentence carefully to make sure that it conveys logical ideas.

1. Avoid using a preposition without considering its meaning.

Illogical: As leader of the Soviet Union, Gorbachev had many political problems *in which* he could not overcome.

Logical: As leader of the Soviet Union, Gorbachev had many political problems *that* he could not overcome.

Illogical: His lifestyle differs from mine *by* he is more active.

Logical: His lifestyle differs from mine *because* he is more active.

2. Avoid leaving out important words.

Illogical: She rushed *out* her house.

Revised: She rushed *out of* her house.

Illogical: Dancing the polka was *so* fun.

Revised: Dancing the polka was *so much* fun.

In the example above, the illogicality is that the adverb *so* modifies the noun *fun,* but only adjectives can modify nouns. In the revised version, the adjective *much* modifies *fun,* and the adverb *so* modifies *much.*

EXERCISE 31E

Using Formal, Idiomatic, and Logical Constructions

Rewrite the following sentences to make them more formal, idiomatic, and logical:

1. Running under the Channel Tunnel, trains now make the trip from London to Paris in less than three hours.
2. Paul Broca, a nineteenth-century physician, found out which part in the brain controls speech.
3. In the biography *His Holiness,* Carl Bernstein and Marco Politi talk about Pope John Paul II's role in the fall of communism in Eastern Europe.
4. Hundreds of years ago, the Maya built great cities in which one can still see these in Mexico.
5. As he reached Fort Ticonderoga, the colonial soldier came up to a British sentry, who asked him to say who he was.

31.5 Avoid slang, colloquialisms, and jargon in formal writing.

31.5a Avoid slang.

Slang is informal language. It might be appropriate in a relaxed conversation with friends, but slang is not standard English and should be avoided in college essays and reports. In fact, slang varies from group to group and changes over time. As a result, some readers may not recognize your particular brand of slang and get confused when they read it.

Slang:	I decided that I would be out of there before I got hassled.
Formal:	I decided to leave before I was harassed.
Slang:	They weren't into laying guilt trips on their kids.
Formal:	They tried not to make their children feel guilty.

31.5b Avoid colloquialisms.

Colloquial expressions appear in spoken conversations even among educated people. Some are used only in particular locales; others are common to the entire English-speaking world. Often, the meaning of a colloquial expression differs from the literal meaning of the words it contains.

Colloquial expressions are fine in informal or familiar writing, but they should be avoided in formal writing such as the kind used in academic assignments, business and technical reports, and other types of professional writing.

Colloquial:	After *working out,* Serena took a shower.
Formal:	After *exercising,* Serena took a shower.
Colloquial:	Cara is *pretty* tired.
Formal:	Cara is *very* tired.

31.5c Avoid jargon.

Jargon is language specific to a particular profession, discipline, or field of endeavor. Sometimes, such words can take on new meanings when removed from those contexts. For example, *bottom line* has come to mean "the essence or heart of a question or topic." But this phrase comes from the accounting profession in which the bottom line, being the last line of a ledger, indicates whether money has been earned or lost.

Jargon includes language to which special meanings have been attached. Using jargon with an audience that is well versed in the subject matter or discipline can help you save time and communicate specialized information quickly and effectively. However, using jargon with lay readers—those who are not expert in the discipline you are discussing—may rob your writing of its clarity and effectiveness, unless, of course, you define special terminology as you go along.

For example, a dentist might discuss the treatment for gum disease differently with a dental hygienist than he or she would with a patient. To the latter, the dentist might explain that annual office cleanings by a trained hygienist and daily brushing, flossing, and rinsing will be necessary to prevent further problems. When discussing the patient's condition with a dental hygienist, however, the dentist might express concern over the onset of gingivitis in the patient and prescribe a regimen of oral prophylaxis as well as home intervention to prevent the condition from developing into periodontitis.

Ask yourself these questions before you decide to use jargon in a particular piece of writing:

1. Is the audience familiar with such terminology? If not, can I conveniently insert definitions of these terms without interfering with the reader's train of thought?
2. Is jargon necessary to my purpose, or can I communicate effectively using nonspecialized language?

Sometimes writers use jargon simply to impress. Ironically, they often succeed only in confusing their readers. So, if the answer to either of the questions above is no, replace the jargon with language that is simpler and more common. The list below contains examples of unnecessary jargon and the clearer, simpler, and more common alternatives:

Jargon	Common Phrasing
The governor intends to interface with his constituents at the confab of agricultural exhibitors.	The governor intends to talk to people at the state fair.
Utilization of the inner lane is prohibited unless you are accelerating beyond slower-moving vehicles.	Keep right except to pass.
Expectorating on the pedestrian causeway is strictly prohibited.	Don't spit on the sidewalk.

31.6 Avoid clichés.

Clichés are expressions that lack freshness and emphasis because they have been overused. Clichés can be used in everyday spoken conversation without a problem, but they tend to make formal writing flat, uninteresting, and even unclear. Replace clichés whenever you can with fresher, more exciting, or more specific language.

Cliché: The teacher kept her students *on their toes.*

Revised: The teacher kept her students *alert and eager to learn.*

The following partial list will give you an idea of the kind of language you should look for and replace as you put freshness and originality into your writing.

Clichés

acid test	face the music	paid your dues
as good as done	fall on deaf ears	passed away
as the crow flies	fly like an eagle	picture-perfect
at all costs	foaming at the mouth	pure as snow
better half	going places	rest assured
bit the dust	green with envy	rite of passage
breaking my neck	grinning from ear to ear	sacred cow
broken record	healthy as a horse	short and sweet
clear as mud	hit the deck	sick as a dog
cold, hard facts	hit the sack	sink or swim
cool as a cucumber	hot potato	stone-cold sober
dark horse	keep your shirt on	stone's throw
dead as a doornail	ladder of success	strong as an ox
drunk as a skunk	like the plague	tighten our belts
early bird	little lady	to the point
easy for you to say	old hat	turn for the worse
edge of the seat	on your own	white as a ghost

Correcting for Slang, Colloquialisms, Jargon, and Clichés

Revise the following sentences to avoid problems such as those discussed in sections 31.5 and 31.6:

1. A stone's throw from the center of modern Athens is the ancient Acropolis.
2. In 480 B.C., the Persians invaded Athens and pretty much wasted every building in the Acropolis. In no time (by 467 B.C.), however, the Greeks had rebuilt the civic buildings and temples.
3. Off the coast of Ecuador, the Galápagos Islands consist of nine large islands and about fifty bits of land that seem to jump out of the Pacific Ocean. They have been called "the world's end" because most of them are rocky and desolate to the point of seeming weird.
4. However, in places where vegetation does grow, pesky flies and aggravating mosquitoes annoy anyone crazy enough to visit. In other areas of the Galápagos, the rocks are so sharp that they can cut a hiker's shoes to shreds.
5. Charles Darwin was the first scientist to visit the Galápagos Islands. While observing the local critters, he got the bright idea that something was funny about many of them.
6. Today, Darwin's theory is old hat, but when it was first published, it raised a few eyebrows, for it flew in the face of the creation theory of the universe as explained in religious texts.

31.7 Use concrete and specific language.

Words that are **concrete** point to something the reader has experienced or can experience through one or more of the five senses. Thus, things that are concrete are usually material. Abstract words name concepts, ideas, emotions, and other intangibles. Such things, while quite real, exist in the writer's mind or heart. Thus, readers find abstract language harder to grasp than concrete language. Note the difference between the two types of nouns in the following list:

Abstract	Concrete
affection	kiss, embrace
anger	shout
capital punishment	hanging
church	cathedral
happiness	laughter, smiles
pollution	smog
public transportation	city bus
rudeness	sneer
sadness	tears, sobbing
violence	punch, shot, fistfight

Specific words and phrases are far more descriptive and focused than those that are general. As you read the words and phrases in the table below, notice how much more effective the language becomes from left to right.

General	Less General	Specific
school	university	University of Minnesota
vegetable	legume	snap peas
television show	police drama	*Law and Order*
entertainer	rock star	Bruce Springsteen
fuel	gasoline	unleaded premium
fast food	hamburger	Big Mac
automobile	sport utility vehicle	Ford Explorer
computer software	Internet browser	Netscape Navigator

Using Concrete and Specific Language

Using language of your own choosing, rewrite the following sentences to make the language more concrete and specific:

1. He played a musical instrument with a band that appeared at outdoor public events.
2. Alicia is majoring in three different subjects, and she maintains a high grade point average.
3. The car raced along the road through the mountains and across the river.
4. Children in the day care center seemed to behave badly after having watched a cartoon that portrayed violent characters.
5. The crowd became fearful when the disaster struck.

EXERCISE 31D

31.8 Avoid sexist or biased language.

As you learned earlier, the language you choose affects your tone and your style. More important, it affects your credibility as a writer. Thus, it is important to replace sexist or biased language with more acceptable alternatives. Most people do try to avoid offensive language because of considerations related to common decency and because they know it will decrease the effectiveness of their writing and speech. Sometimes, however, we use language that is offensive to others without realizing that we are doing so. Therefore, it is important to pay attention to this concern when you edit your work.

31.8a Avoid gender-specific terms.

Unless you are referring to a specific individual whose gender you know, use gender-neutral terms.

Not	But	Not	But
chairman	chair, chairperson	policeman	police officer
clergyman	member of the clergy	postmaster	postal supervisor
comedienne	comedian	repairman	technician
congressman	representative	salesman	sales representative
fireman	firefighter	stewardess	flight attendant
manhole cover	utility cover	waitress	server
mankind	humankind	workman	worker
poetess	poet	workmanship	quality

Remember, too, that mentioning gender unnecessarily might be offensive. For example, refer to the *doctor,* not to the *woman doctor;* to the *stockbroker,* not to the *female stockbroker;* to the *nurse,* not to the *male nurse.*

31.8b Develop a sensitivity to biased language.

Words such as *bitch, Wop, Polack, darky,* and *fag* are obviously harmful, despicable, and rude. Never use such language. Also, stay away from clearly insulting terms such as *blind as a bat, spastic, fat,* and *stupid.*

In addition, however, sensitize yourself to other types of language, which, while not as obviously offensive, may disturb your readers or serve to depersonalize those it describes. For example, don't call someone a *diabetic* when referring to him or her as a *person with diabetes* is just as easy. Don't characterize someone as *handicapped* or *disabled;* instead, refer to him or her as *someone with a disability.* In addition, avoid stigmatizing people as *victims, targets,* or *sufferers* of a disease. Write *a person with AIDS,* not *an AIDS patient.* Refer to someone in a wheelchair as such, not as a *user of a wheelchair.*

In addition, do not mention a person's race, sex, sexual orientation, religion, or national origin unless such information is essential to the understanding of your message. Consider these examples:

Not: Although David's parents were born in Canton, he eats in Italian restaurants more often than in Chinese restaurants.

But: David eats in Italian restaurants more often than in Chinese restaurants.

Or: David can speak Cantonese because his parents, who were born in China, speak the language at home.

Not: Our electrician, who is gay, has never overcharged us.

But: Our electrician has never overcharged us.

Or: Our electrician lost two customers when they found out she is gay.

Finally, apply adjectives fairly and objectively. For example, writing that *the men were nervous, and the women were hysterical* can be construed as sexist.

Avoiding Sexist or Biased Language

Rewrite the following sentences to eliminate sexist or biased language:

1. The workmanship of the furniture was evident in the care the craftsman had taken in joining the corners of the drawers.
2. Although she is a cripple, Felicia still loves sports.
3. Whenever the Italian lady next door cooks meatballs, the smell drifts into our living room.
4. The child was revived by an Hispanic emergency medical technician and a black firewoman.

EXERCISE 31E

Rewrite the following sentences using what you have learned in this chapter:

1. When you go up to Washington, D.C., make sure to go by Arlington National Cemetery, which is right over the river, and have a look at the Tomb of the Unknown Soldier.
2. Also, have a peek at the Capitol Building, where congressmen introduce, debate, and pass legislation.
3. Diabetes gets its name from the Greek Aretaeus, an ancient doc, who used the word to describe an illness of which you get thirsty and have to pee a lot.
4. On the 1600s, doctors who checked out the urine of diabetics found that it was "sweet," or loaded with glucose sugar.
5. Today, we know that diabetes is caused from the body's inability to produce, or soak up, insulin, which controls the use of glucose.
6. Therefore, analyzing blood and urine samples for high levels of glucose has become the acid test for diabetes.
7. A diabetic can look healthy as a horse, but if the disease is not treated, he or she can lose appetite and throw up a lot.
8. In extreme cases, a victim of diabetes can become as sick as a dog and even croak.

CHAPTER WRAP-UP

32

MAKING YOUR WRITING CONCISE

32.1 Remove repeated words.
32.2 Remove unnecessary synonyms.
32.3 Avoid redundancies.
32.4 Remove labels and fillers.
32.5 Replace a long phrase with one word.
32.6 Be direct—remove constructions such as *it is* and *there was.*

Wordiness comes from using more words than you need to get your message across. Sometimes students become wordy simply to provide the number of words required by the assignment. Don't fall into that trap. Unnecessary words make your writing boring and sometimes confusing.

Wordiness is natural in the early stages of the writing process. In fact, many writers feel comfortable including more words than they need in rough drafts, just to make sure they have covered the topic. That's why it's best to correct wordiness when editing—*after* you have finished a few drafts.

Editing for wordiness doesn't mean that you should make your writing flat and uninteresting or that you should use short, choppy sentences. It means you should remove words that serve no purpose or that say the same things as other words you have used.

32.1 Remove repeated words.

Repeating a word in the same sentence or in a nearby sentence can cause wordiness. Edit your work carefully to avoid this problem.

Not: She is the best swimmer of the three Rumanian swimmers.

But: She is the best of the three Rumanian swimmers.

Not: The children love hockey. Hockey is the children's favorite sport.

But: The children love hockey; it is their favorite sport.

One easy way to eliminate wordiness is to use pronouns rather than repeat nouns. In the previous example, the pronoun *it* replaces the noun *hockey*, and the pronoun *their* replaces the noun *children's*.

32.2 Remove unnecessary synonyms.

Synonyms are words that mean the same as other words you have used. Don't use them unless they add new information.

Not: She threw away the broken stereo that doesn't work.
But: She threw away the broken stereo.

Not: He pays annual dues to his athletic club every year.
But: He pays annual dues to his athletic club.

Eliminating Repeated Words and Unnecessary Synonyms

Rewrite the following items by removing unnecessary words. Combine sentences if necessary.

1. A galvanometer is an instrument used in physics. This instrument measures electrical current in a circuit.
2. Direct electrical current flows in one direction. Its value remains the same and never changes.
3. A generator converts mechanical energy by changing it into electrical energy.
4. A voltmeter is a measuring device for determining the volts in either alternating or direct current.
5. The type of thermometer invented by David Gabriel Fahrenheit (1686–1737) was the alcohol thermometer. He also invented the type that uses mercury.
6. Fahrenheit also developed the Fahrenheit temperature scale, which is used to measure temperatures in the United States. On this scale, water boils at 212 degrees Fahrenheit and freezes at 32 degrees Fahrenheit.
7. Anders Celsius introduced another system for measuring temperatures. It is named the Celsius scale after its inventor.
8. The Kelvin scale is a way to measure absolute temperatures. Its starting point is absolute zero (−459.67 degrees Fahrenheit). Absolute zero, as defined in physics, is the point at which the motion of molecules essentially stops moving.

EXERCISE 32A

32.3 Avoid redundancies.

A **redundancy** occurs when you use two or more words that mean the same thing. It amounts to saying the same thing twice.

Not: They had never seen a dead corpse.
But: They had never seen a corpse.

All corpses are dead; therefore, *dead* is unnecessary.

Not: She spoke the honest truth.

But: She spoke the truth.

Describing truth as *honest* adds nothing to the meaning. After all, can truth be dishonest?

Common Redundancies

Wordy	Better
absolutely essential	essential
advance forward	advance
as of yet	yet
at this point in time	at this time
basic fundamentals	basics
both together	both
brilliant genius	genius
but yet	yet
combine together	combine
each and every dollar	every dollar
eleven P.M. at night	eleven P.M.
evil villain	villain
extremely overwhelming	overwhelming
free gift	gift
in my opinion, I believe	I believe
refer back to	refer to
rise up	rise
still continues	continues
still persists	persists
the reason is because	the reason is
the reason why	the reason
totally useless	useless
valuable asset	asset
very unique	unique
visible to the eye	visible

Eliminating Redundancies

Rewrite the following sentences to eliminate redundancies:

1. Although the art dealer claimed the painting of Audubon's woodpeckers was an authentic original, the buyer knew it was a total reproduction, for the signature of the artist's name was misspelled.
2. On September 1, 1939, Nazi armies advanced forward into Poland, an act of violent aggression that opened World War II in Europe.
3. The Black Death was a plague disease that swept over Europe during the fourteenth century, killing millions of the population's inhabitants.
4. The evil villain in Shakespeare's *Othello* is named Iago. Some scholars argue that the reason why Iago wishes to totally destroy Othello is that Iago is thoroughly consumed by jealousy.
5. It was absolutely essential for American intelligence to break Japan's secret code; otherwise, the U.S. Navy might have lost the naval Battle of Midway, an event that could have completely eliminated chances for an American victory in the Pacific.

32.4 Remove labels and fillers.

Labels are words that tell us what other words are. They are often useless.

Not: Jason is the kind of person who enjoys music.

But: Jason enjoys music.

Useless Labels

Wordy	Better
green in color	green
the month of July	July
the science of biology	biology
large in size	large
the French language	French
a friendly personality	friendly

CAUTION!

Forming an adjective by attaching *-like* or *-type* to a noun can make your writing wordy.

Not: The meal was served in a family-like style.

But: The meal was served family style.

Fillers are words that do little but distract readers. In the following sentences, fillers are in italics. They can be eliminated without any change in a sentence's meaning.

Not: The plant *that makes* Ford trucks needs mechanics *who are* skilled.

But: The Ford truck plant needs skilled mechanics.

Not: Many *of the people who* graduated from Monroe High School are politicians.

But: Many graduates of Monroe High School are politicians.

Common Fillers

Wordy	Better
people who work in a hospital	hospital workers
a person who paints houses	a house painter
a teacher who is dedicated to students	a dedicated teacher
try and see	try to **or** see
try to see	try to **or** see
the warehouse located in Dover	the Dover warehouse
I would like to thank you	Thank you

Removing Labels and Fillers

Rewrite the following sentences to remove labels and fillers:

1. Elizabeth Blackwell excelled at the practice of medicine. She was the first woman to earn a degree in medicine from a university located in the United States.
2. One has to learn a new alphabet if he or she wants to read the works of Maxim Gorky (1868–1939) in the original, for he wrote in the Russian language.
3. Although he is famous for his writing, Gorky is also remembered for his participation as a supporter of the Bolsheviks in the Russian revolutionary war.
4. Anyone who is a fan of Italian opera knows the story of *Tosca* by the composer Giacomo Puccini.
5. People who love the circus might enjoy Giuseppe Verdi's *Aida,* an opera in which elephants that come from Africa appear on the stage.
6. Many families that emigrated from China in the nineteenth century settled on the West Coast. Today, the state of California is home to many people who were born in America but who are of Asian descent.
7. The nations of Poland and Germany, which share a border, have not always been neighbors that are friendly.
8. The vocabulary of the art of opera evolved in Italy; as a result, operatic concepts and techniques have names in the Italian language.
9. In June 1944, when Allied landing craft and combat ships appeared off the coast of the province of Normandy, the Nazi commanders must have known that "Fortress Europa" would fall.
10. In an effort to try and make better diagnoses, doctors who examine patients are now using new types of technology such as magnetic resonance imaging (MRI).

EXERCISE 32C

32.5 Replace a long phrase with one word.

A group of words that acts as a verb, an adjective, or an adverb can often be replaced by a single word.

Not: Considering the fact that the bridge was under water, Rita had to turn back.

But: Because the bridge was under water, Rita had to turn back.

Common Wordy Phrases

Wordy	Better	Wordy	Better
arrive at an agreement	agree	during the course of	during
at the present time	now	gave approval to	approved
conduct a test	test	have an argument	argue
conduct an investigation	investigate	make an analysis of	analyze
due to the fact that	because	place emphasis on	emphasize

Replacing Long Phrases

Rewrite the following sentences to replace long phrases with one-word alternatives:

1. Using keywords is a good way to conduct a search on the Internet.
2. Both *Shindler's List* and *Life Is Beautiful* contain scenes in which Nazi guards conduct an examination of Jewish prisoners to determine who should stay alive.
3. Before World War II, most people could not go to college for the reason that they could not afford the tuition. After the war, however, the GI Bill made college more affordable for people who had served in the military.
4. Before the age of political primaries, bosses of political parties sat in rooms that were smoke filled and held discussions that decided who they would nominate for mayor, governor, or even president.
5. During the Great Depression of the 1930s, about one-third of the American labor force was in need of employment.
6. One reason the Japanese defeated the Russians in 1904 was that the Russian fleet had to travel a long distance away from its home port before engaging the Japanese navy.
7. The electron microscope can see much smaller objects than an ordinary microscope can see because it uses electrons, not light, to create the magnification of an image.
8. A popular song of the 1960s tells us that Andrew Jackson gave chase to the British on January 8, 1815. Jackson's victory had no effect on the outcome of the War of 1812 due to the fact that Britain and the United States had signed a peace treaty on December 14, 1814.

EXERCISE 32D

32.6 Be direct—remove constructions such as *it is* and *there was*.

Constructions such as *it is/was, there is/was,* and *there are/were* are often unnecessary. This is especially true when they appear before the subject and verb of a sentence.

Wordy: There were children playing in the yard.

The subject of the sentence is *children;* the verb is *were playing.* Why not start the sentence with these words?

Direct: Children were playing in the yard.

Being Direct

Rewrite the following sentences to make them more direct:

1. It was in 1928, while working on a treatment for influenza, that Sir Alexander Fleming discovered penicillin.
2. Fleming noticed that there was mold growing on one of his laboratory dishes, and he determined that it was this mold that had destroyed bacteria he was trying to grow.
3. It was decided by the Nobel Prize Committee in 1945 that Fleming should be honored for his medical research. There were two other scientists, Howard Florey and Ernst Chain, who shared the prize with Fleming because of their help in discovering penicillin.
4. It is because penicillin is effective against a wide variety of disease-causing bacteria that Fleming's work is so important.
5. There is one significant drawback to penicillin. It has been found that some people are allergic to the drug, but there is a simple test to determine whether a patient will react negatively.

Rewrite the following student essay to eliminate wordiness:

My family made a day trip to Sandy Hook seashore last summer. Getting ready for our day trip required so much preparation and so much work that I almost decided not to go and to stay home.

It was the night before that we made the decision to get an early start. That morning, of course, we overslept and got up later than we had hoped; the reason was because we had forgotten to reset the alarm the night before. I awoke from sleep at exactly 7:03 A.M. Rising up from the bed, I became anxious and nervous, for I was fully aware that the drive to the sea would be a difficult ordeal.

The drive was 200 miles in length, and if we didn't leave any time before 7:30 A.M., we would surely meet heavy, bumper-to-bumper traffic along the countrylike roads that we would have to take to get to the beach.

I rushed into the shower and completed my regular showering routine in three minutes flat. At the same time, I made a mental list in my mind of all the things we had to take: beach chairs, towels and blankets, suntan lotion, reading materials, books, magazines, and, of course, food and beverages—all the food and beverages we liked most.

As soon as I was dressed, I went down into the basement to find our cooler, which was very large in size. It is absolutely essential for the long day trips that our family enjoys taking. It was during the course of my search for the cooler that I knocked over four large boxes and the metal-type bed that is made of iron, nearly crushing my foot and seriously injuring myself.

Of course, as I was finishing the job of filling the cooler and loading up the car, my children proceeded to have an argument about who was to sit where in the car. My daughter shouted loudly that it was her turn to sit up in the front seat. That was the kind of discussion that took forever to resolve but we finally got going. When we were finally under way, however, my young son, who is five years old, decided that he would tell us he had to go to the bathroom. So we turned around and went back home. As you have probably guessed by now, we left a long time after 7:30 A.M. The roads were crowded with cars, and our trip to the seashore took about six hours to get there. By the time we arrived, it was time to return home again.

Word Choice Basics Checklist

1. Use a **dictionary** to check the meanings of words. Never use a word unless you are certain you know what it means. Use a **thesaurus** to find synonyms and antonyms. Always use a dictionary to check the meanings of words you find in the thesaurus.

2. As you edit and proofread your work, make sure you have not confused one word with another or that you have mistaken the meaning of a word.

3. Use a dictionary to check that the words you are using are appropriate to your **intended meaning** and to the verbal **context** you have created.

4. Use words according to their **intended functions**. For example, *automobile* can be used as a noun but also as an adjective, as in *automobile dealer*. However, the noun *fun* cannot be used as an adjective. Therefore, writing *we had a fun time* is incorrect.

5. Review the **glossary of usage** (pages 410–424) to help you remember the correct forms and meanings of words that are often confused.

6. Maintain a **tone** that is appropriate to your subject. Maintain a **style** that is appropriate to your audience.

7. As you revise, carefully review phrases and other constructions to make sure they are **logical** and **idiomatic**. Always **avoid *you*** in formal writing unless you are addressing the reader directly.

8. Write in formal language by avoiding **slang, colloquialisms,** and **jargon.** Make your language interesting by replacing **clichés** with vocabulary that is fresh. Also, rely on language that is concrete and specific as much as possible.

9. Never allow **biased** or **sexist language** to creep into your writing.

10. Eliminate **wordiness** during the editing process, *after* you have revised your paper several times.

11. Remove repeated words and unnecessary synonyms.

12. Avoid **redundancies,** words that say the same thing twice.

13. Remove **labels** and **fillers.**

14. Replace long phrases with single words.

15. Be direct. Try not to begin sentences with *It is, There are,* and similar constructions.

10

GRAMMAR

10 GRAMMAR

GRAMMAR

LEARNING PARTS OF SPEECH

To become an effective writer, you will have to analyze your work carefully. But first you should learn terms that will help you talk about your writing with your instructors and classmates. Doing so will also help you edit and revise your work. You don't need to memorize these terms, but you should know how they are used.

Words are classified as *nouns, pronouns, verbs, articles, adjectives, adverbs, prepositions,* and *conjunctions.* These are the **parts of speech.** Nouns or pronouns and verbs act as the basis of a sentence, but the others are also important.

33.1 Recognize nouns.

A **noun** names a person, place, or thing. There are two types of nouns: **common** and **proper.** Proper nouns name specific persons, places, and things; they are capitalized.

Types of Nouns

Common Nouns	Proper Nouns
woman	Eleanor
country	Nigeria
language	Japanese
lake	Lake Ontario
religion	Islam

NOTE
Watch for words that end in *-ing* and that stand for activities: *swimming, writing, talking, asking,* and *loving,* for example. They, too, are nouns.

Nouns act as subjects and objects. The **subject** of a sentence is a person, place, or thing that does an action or is described. In other words, if you ask,

447

NOTE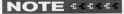

A sentence does not need an object, but it must have a subject. *The captain is ill,* for example, has no object.

"Who is doing something?" or "Who is being described?" your answer will be a subject.

NOUNS AS SUBJECTS

The *captain* gives orders. (The captain acts.)

The *captain* is ill. (The captain is described.)

The **object** of a sentence is a person, place, or thing that is receiving an action.

NOUNS AS OBJECTS

The captain saluted the *officers.*

The captain praised the *soldiers.*

Nouns are *singular* (one) or *plural* (more than one). To make *most* nouns plural, add *-s* or *-es* to the singular. For example, the plural of *captain* is *captains.* However, there are exceptions. Some nouns change their spelling (*mouse/mice*), and a few even use the same spelling in the plural as in the singular (*deer/deer*).

Noun Plurals

REGULAR NOUNS		EXCEPTIONS	
Singular	Plural	Singular	Plural
cat	cats	woman	women
vehicle	vehicles	child	children
compact disc	compact discs	louse	lice
injury	injuries	leaf	leaves

EXERCISE 33A

Using Nouns as Subjects and Objects

1. *Identify each noun as common* (cn) *or proper* (pn) *and as singular* (sing) *or plural* (pl):

husband _____   mechanic _____   doctor _____

running _____   Coca-Cola _____   hamburger _____

students _____   boats _____   flowers _____

America _____   sister _____   Spanish _____

Chicago _____   tractor _____   Mary Ann _____

2. *Reread what you learned about a sentence on pages 361–364. Then, on a separate piece of paper, write two sentences containing each noun in Exercise 33A1. In the first sentence, use the noun as a subject; in the second, use it as an object. For example:*

Subject: The *children* rode their bicycles.

Object: The parents carried their *children* home.

33.2 Recognize pronouns.

A **pronoun** replaces a noun; it, too, stands for a person, place, or thing. Like nouns, pronouns are singular or plural. For example, *I* is singular; *we*, plural.

Some pronouns act as subjects, some as objects, and some as words that show possession. Learn the following **personal pronouns:**

Personal Pronouns

Pronouns as subjects:	I, we, you, he, she, it, one, they, who
Pronouns as objects:	me, us, you, him, her, it, one, them, whom
Possessive pronouns:	my, mine, our, ours, your, yours, his, her, hers, its, their, theirs, whose

You can learn other types of pronouns in Chapter 36. For now, become familiar with **relative pronouns.** They introduce dependent (subordinate) clauses, which you read about on page 362. To refresh your memory, here are examples of dependent clauses that are introduced by the relative pronouns *that* and *who:*

She walked into a room *that was filled with flowers.*

Mr. Wilson, *who lives next door,* is a grouch.

Relative Pronouns

that	whichever	whom
whatever	who	whomever
which	whoever	whose

Using Pronouns as Subjects and Objects

Write fifteen sentences, each of which contains one of the personal pronouns listed in section 33.2. In sentences 1 to 5, use pronouns as subjects; in sentences 6 to 10, use pronouns as objects; in sentences 11 to 15, use pronouns to show possession (ownership). Here are some examples to get you started:

Subject: *I* called my family last night.

Object: Mother could not hear *me.*

Possession: *My* telephone is not working right.

33.3 Recognize verbs.

A **verb** shows what a subject does (action) or describes that subject.

The river *flooded* the town.

Flooded is a verb of action.

James *is* sick.

Is is a verb that describes.

You can learn more about verbs in Chapter 34.

> **NOTE**
>
> Words that end in *-ing* cannot act as verbs when they stand alone. They must be paired with helping verbs:
>
> My car *is being* towed!
> We *are seeing* a change in his attitude.
> She *was running* for the bus.

Identifying and Using Verbs

1. *Underline verbs in the following passages:*
   a. Let every nation know, whether it wishes us well or ill, that we shall pay any price, bear any burden, meet any hardship, support any friend, or oppose any foe to assure the survival and the success of liberty. (President John F. Kennedy, Inaugural Address)
   b. Poverty is being tired. I have always been tired. They told me at the hospital when the last baby came that I had chronic anemia caused from poor diet, a bad case of worms, and that I needed a corrective operation. I listened politely—the poor are always polite. The poor always listen. They don't say that there is no money for iron pills, or better food or worm medicine. The idea of an operation is frightening and costs so much that, if I had dared, I would have laughed. (Jo Goodwin Parker, "What Is Poverty?")
2. Reread pages 361–364, which explain the makeup of a sentence. Then, on a separate piece of paper, write ten sentences, each of which uses a different verb from the following list:

jump	paint	arrive	stand	leave
speak	play	eat	fight	read
ride	give	receive	drink	answer
load	hunt	fool	view	lead

Here are two examples to get you started:

I *received* a letter from Mary.

Our instructor *gave* Phil a book.

33.4 Recognize articles.

An **article** is a short word that comes before and points to a noun. The articles are *a, an,* and *the. The* points to a specific person, place, or thing.

The clock is on *the* mantel.

The elephant eats peanuts from *the* box.

A and *an* do not indicate something specific.

A clock tells time. (*Any* clock tells time.)

An elephant eats peanuts from *a* box. (*Any* elephant eats peanuts from *any* box.)

Identifying Nouns, Pronouns, Verbs, and Articles

EXERCISE 33D

In the passages that follow, write cn over common nouns, pn over proper nouns, pron over pronouns, v over verbs, and art over articles.

1. The Galesburg Marine Band marched past, men walking and their mouths blowing into their horns as they walked. (Carl Sandburg, "The Funeral of General Grant")
2. By walking, begging rides, both in wagons and in the cars, in some way, after a number of days, I reached the city of Richmond, Virginia. (Booker T. Washington, "Matriculating at Hampton")
3. Aunt Margaret came from Chicago, which consisted of the Loop, Marshall Field's, assorted priests and monsignors, and the black-and-white problem. (Mary McCarthy, "Uncle Myers")
4. At that moment she was a young girl standing on a wharf at Merry Point, Virginia, waiting for the Chesapeake Bay steamer with her father. . . . William Howard Taft was in the White House, Europe still drowsed in the dusk of the great century of peace, America was a young country, and the future stretched before it in beams of crystal sunlight. (Russell Baker, *Growing Up*)

33.5 Recognize adjectives.

NOTE ✦✦✦✦✦

When an adjective modifies a plural noun, the adjective does not become plural:

He purchased two *new* cars. (*Not:* He purchased two news cars.)

The jackets were *red.* (*Not:* The jackets were reds.)

An **adjective** tells the reader something about a person, place, or thing. In other words, it describes, or modifies, a noun or pronoun. An adjective answers questions such as "Which?" "What kind of?" and "How many?" Adjectives can come before the noun they modify.

The *angry* dog charges the fence.

We ate a *delicious* dinner.

However, an adjective that tells something about the subject of a sentence can come after a linking verb.

The food was *delicious.*

The dog is *angry.*

33.6 Recognize adverbs.

An **adverb** modifies, or tells something about, a verb, an adjective, or another adverb. Adverbs answer questions such as "Where?" "When?" "How?" "How much?" "How often?" and "To what extent?" Here are some examples:

Although the team played *well,* it lost the close match.

Well modifies the verb *played.*

Although the team played *well,* it lost the *extremely* close match.

Well modifies the verb *played; extremely* modifies the adjective *close.*

Although the team played *very well,* it lost the *extremely* close match.

Very modifies the adverb *well; well* modifies the verb *played; extremely* modifies the adjective *close.*

Adverbs

quickly	heavily	often	when
easily	lightly	never	where
effortlessly	thickly	seldom	now
merely	richly	sometime	just
truly	beautifully	ahead	beyond
happily	only	then	more
strongly	similarly	behind	less
silently	intensely	well	
loudly	usually	very	

You probably noticed that many adverbs end in -*ly*. But don't be fooled; many don't. Look at those in columns 3 and 4. In addition, some words that end in -*ly* can be adjectives—*early, orderly,* and *earthly,* for example.

Identifying and Using Adjectives and Adverbs

1. *Write adj over adjectives and adv over adverbs in the following paragraphs:*

a. One of my favorite approaches to a rocky seacoast is by a rough path through an evergreen forest that has its own peculiar enchantment. It is usually an early morning tide that takes me along that forest path, so that the light is still pale and fog drifts in from the sea beyond. (Rachel Carson, "Walking to the Seacoast")

b. I am the man in the middle; for where I stand determines where the middle is. I am compassionate; those less compassionate than I are "cold," and those more compassionate than I are "sentimental." I am steadfast; those less steadfast than I are "fickle," and those more steadfast than I are "stubborn." (Sydney I. Harris, "The Man in the Middle")

2. *On a separate piece of paper, write five sentences, each of which uses at least one adjective and one adverb from the following lists:*

Adjectives		Adverbs	
tired	favorite	very	warmly
bright	cold	truly	completely
beautiful	delicious	fully	thoroughly
calm	difficult	well	quickly
stormy	stubborn	loudly	seldom

33.7 Recognize prepositions.

A **preposition** comes before a noun or pronoun and shows how that word relates to other words in the sentence. When you join a preposition with a noun or pronoun, you create a phrase, one of the sentence parts discussed on page 362.

Prepositions

about	among	beyond	from	of	to
above	at	by	in	on	toward
across	before	despite	inside	out	under
after	behind	during	into	over	upon
against	below	for	near	through	with
along	between				

Prepositional Phrases

under the boardwalk	during her visit
for the children	at three o'clock
on the ledge	despite the traffic
in the room	between us
into his pocket	from the heart
over the bridge	through the valley
near the door	above the window

33.8 Recognize conjunctions.

A **conjunction** joins words or ideas. A **coordinating conjunction** joins words or ideas of the same importance. A **subordinating conjunction** joins ideas by showing that one is less important than the other.

Coordinating: A huge balloon sailed by, *and* the children screamed with joy.

Subordinating: *Because* a huge balloon sailed by, the children screamed with joy.

In the first sentence, the coordinating conjunction *and* joins two equally important ideas. In the second, the subordinating conjunction *because* introduces an idea that is now less important than what follows in the independent clause.

Remember what you read about independent and dependent (subordinate) clauses on pages 361–362. By using conjunctions to join independent clauses and dependent clauses, you can vary the way you organize sentences.

Coordinating Conjunctions

and	
but	
for	
nor	
or	
so	
yet	

Subordinating Conjunctions

after	in order to
although	since
as long as	unless
as soon as	until
as though	when
because	whenever
if	while

Identifying Prepositions and Conjunctions

Write prep *over prepositions and* conj *over conjunctions in this passage by William Least Heat Moon:*

The only shade along Arizona 87 lay under the bottomsides of rocks; the desert gives space then closes it up with the heat. To the east, in profile, rose the Superstition Mountains, an evil place, Pima and Maricopa Indians say, which brings on diabolic possession to those who enter. Somewhere, among the granite and greasewood was the Lost Dutchman gold mine. . . .

North of the Sycamore River, saguaro, ocotillo, paloverde, and cholla (cactus) surrendered the hills to pads of prickly pear the size of a man's head. The road climbed and the temperature dropped. At Payson, a mile high on the northern slope of the Mazatzal Mountains, I had to pull on a jacket. ("Arizona 87")

After reading the following paragraph, identify as many nouns, pronouns, verbs, articles, adjectives, adverbs, prepositions, and conjunctions as you can. Remember to distinguish between proper nouns and common nouns. Also, explain how nouns and pronouns are used: as subjects, as objects, or as words that show ownership.

The road into Saladsburg, Pennsylvania, takes several twists and turns until it comes to a small steel bridge and crosses on to Main Street in this sleepy village with a population of 250. In the center of town is Saladsburg's landmark: Cohick's Trading Post, home of Cohick's famous ice cream. The building is approximately 50 × 75 feet, or a total of about 3,750 square feet. Outside are two gas pumps and a reassuring sign: "If you treat your customers well, they will always come back." Once you get inside, you are confronted with a magnificent potpourri. On the front counter sits a wheel of aged sharp cheddar, from which customers may cut their own portions. As you stroll over the creaking old pine boards and down the narrow aisles, you encounter everything from buckshot to butter pecan ice cream. Other items range from hardware and agricultural supplies to dry goods, from sporting goods and hunting licenses to locally grown produce. The walls of the store are lined with animals that were shot or trapped and later stuffed: a porcupine, squirrels, several possum, a moose, and a rattlesnake. At the rear is a huge black bear mounted in a ferocious pose. (Nancy Boemo, "The Trading Post Is a Survivor")

34

MASTERING VERB FORMS AND TENSES

34.1 Know what a verb does.
34.2 Learn verb tenses.
34.3 Keep verb tenses consistent.
34.4 Use linking and helping verbs.
34.5 Learn the irregular verbs.
34.6 Learn to use the active and passive voices.
34.7 Become familiar with the four verb moods.

The essential elements of a sentence are a subject and a verb. In earlier chapters, you learned that a subject is a person, place, or thing (noun or pronoun) that acts, is acted upon, or is described. This chapter contains basic information about verbs and verb tenses.

34.1 Know what a verb does.

A **verb** (1) tells what the subject does, (2) tells what is done to the subject, or (3) describes the subject by connecting it with the words that follow.

1. A verb shows action by telling what the subject does.

   Shakespeare *wrote* poems and plays.
   She *ran* down the street.

2. A verb shows action by telling what is done to the subject.

   She *has been elected* class president.
   Math 105 *will be taught* next semester.

3. A verb describes the subject by connecting it with an adjective or with other words.

   Miriam *has been* ill.
   The car *weighed* 2,000 pounds.

Strengthen Your Writing with Vivid Verbs
Vivid verbs make your writing flow like a rapid stream. Dull verbs cause it to move without energy. Both sentences below are correct, but the second is stronger and more interesting.

   The glass *broke* as a rock *hit* the window.
   The glass *shattered* as a rock *smashed* the window.

34.2 Learn verb tenses.

The **tense** of a verb shows time. There are three basic tenses: *past, present,* and *future.*

34.2a Learn the present tense.

Verbs in the **present tense** tell readers about current facts or events—things happening right now. The present tense also shows habitual action, an action that occurs over and over again. Therefore, you can write

I walk the dog.　　**OR**　　I walk the dog every day.

Regular Verbs

All forms of regular verbs in the present tense are spelled alike *except one.*

Regular Verbs in Present Tense

Singular	Plural
I walk	We walk
You walk	You walk
He, she, it, one, anyone *walks*	They walk

The exception comes in third-person singular verbs, which end in -*s.* The third-person singular pronouns are *he, she, it, one, anybody, anyone, nobody, no one, someone, somebody.* A third-person singular subject can be a *singular* noun too. For example, the nouns *Charlene* and *horse* are singular and can act as subjects.

I *walk* every day.	He *walks* every day.
You *walk* every day.	No one *walks* every day.
We *walk* every day.	Charlene *walks* every day.
They *walk* every day.	My horse *walks* every day.

> **CAUTION!**
>
> Third-person singular verbs in the present tense end in -*s* even though their subjects are singular. Remember that, unlike plural nouns, plural verbs (those used with *we, you,* and *they*) do not end in -*s.*

Irregular Verbs

Irregular verbs are spelled differently in different tenses. (You will find a list of common irregular verbs on pages 463–464.) Be aware that the verb *to be* changes its spelling even in the present tense.

Present Tense of *To Be*

	Singular	Plural
	I am	We are
	You are	You are
	He/she/it/one is	They are

Using the Present Tense

The following paragraph uses the first-person singular pronoun, I. Rewrite the paragraph by substituting a third-person pronoun, he or she, for I. Then, add -s to each verb that needs it. Keep all verbs in the present tense.

I suffer from rheumatoid arthritis, a chronic disease afflicting millions of people. I often experience severe pain in the joints in my fingers, arms, and legs. Sometimes I become weak, and I seem to be burning up with high fevers. During these severe attacks, I lose all ambition and do little more than stay in bed and listen to music. I realize that my fingers are becoming twisted and deformed, another result of the disease. For relief from pain, I turn to aspirin and other anti-inflammatory drugs. I also engage in regular exercise to keep my joints and muscles as limber as possible. I know that my condition might persist for the rest of my life, but I continue to hope that a cure will be found soon.

34.2b Learn the past tense.

Verbs in the **past tense** tell your readers of actions that have been completed.

Regular Verbs

To form the past tense of a regular verb, add -*d* or -*ed* to the basic form of the verb.

PAST TENSE OF REGULAR VERBS

I *lived* in Michigan for two years.	They *recognized* their children.
Lincoln *freed* the slaves.	No one *answered* the phone.
She *repaired* the toaster.	James *traveled* to Mexico last year.
Someone *robbed* the store!	

Irregular Verbs

The past tense of irregular verbs is formed in various ways. That's why they're called irregular—they don't follow the rules. Consider the verb *to be,* for example.

Past Tense of *To Be*

	Singular	Plural
	I was	We were
	You were	You were
	He/she/it/one was	They were

You'll find a list of other irregular verbs on pages 463–464.

EXERCISE 34B

Using the Past Tense

The following short outline of the early history of Mexico uses regular verbs in the present tense. Rewrite the paragraph by putting these verbs in the past tense.

When the Spanish conquer Mexico at the beginning of the sixteenth century, they encounter several Native American peoples. The Spaniards marvel at what they discover. Cities of stone, complete with large buildings, religious and municipal complexes, paved streets, and even sports arenas appear all over Mexico. The Maya live in the southeastern part of the country. They rule over vast territories now in the modern Mexican states of Yucatan and Chiapas. The Aztecs dominate central Mexico. They construct their capital city on a tract of land surrounded by water. After the Spanish complete their conquest, they establish Mexico City, their capital and the current capital of Mexico, in the same spot.

34.2c Learn the future tense.

The **future tense** tells readers about events or facts that will occur or will be true at a later time. To form the future tense, place a **helping word** (or words) before the basic form of the verb.

James *will arrive* on the train tomorrow afternoon.

The verb is *arrive;* the helping word is *will.*

Sylvia *is going to study* Spanish next semester.

The verb is *to study;* the helping words are *is going.*

34.2d Learn the perfect tenses.

The **perfect tenses** combine *have, has,* or *had* with the past participle of a verb. To form the past participle of a regular verb, add *-d* or *-ed* to the basic form of the verb. The past participles of irregular verbs are listed on pages 463–464.

Present Perfect

Use the **present perfect** tense when you talk about an action that began in the past and is continuing in the present. Verbs in the present perfect use the helping word *have* in all cases except the third-person singular, which uses *has*.

I *have studied* piano for eight years now.

You *have* not *completed* the homework.

We *have run* in the marathon for the past six years.

The students *have begun* work on a research project.

She *has attended* all her classes so far this term.

The package *has been* mailed.

Someone *has turned on* the radio.

The committee *has elected* Francis chairperson.

Past Perfect

Use the **past perfect** tense when you talk about an action that happened in the past but that came before another event that also took place in the past. Verbs in the past perfect use the helping word *had,* the past tense of *have,* in all cases.

past perfect   past

She *had attended* all her classes before she *got* sick.

Had attended is the past perfect tense of the verb *attend;* it describes an action that happened before the subject got sick. *Got* is the simple past tense of the verb *get.*

past perfect   past

I *had studied* piano for eight years before I *played* in a concert.

Future Perfect

Use the **future perfect** to describe future events that will come before other events in the future. Verbs in the future perfect tense use the helping words *will have.*

By the time I reach my twentieth birthday, I *will have studied* piano for eight years.

This sentence means that the subject will practice the piano for eight years before turning twenty.

She *will have attended* all her classes this semester if she comes to school today.

You *will have completed* all the requirements for this course after you submit your term paper.

34.2e Learn the progressive tenses.

The **progressive tenses** combine a form of *to be* with the present participle, the *-ing* form of a verb. Progressive tenses show continuing action.

Present Progressive

I *am working* with him on the project.

The singer *is writing* new songs.

You *are dieting* to lose weight.

Past Progressive

I *was working* with him on the project.

The singer *was writing* new songs.

You *were dieting* to lose weight.

Future Progressive

I *will be working* with him on the project.

The singer *will be writing* new songs.

You *will be dieting* to lose weight.

Present Perfect Progressive

I *have been working* with him on the project.

The singer *has been writing* new songs.

Past Perfect Progressive

I *had been working* with him on the project.

The singer *had been writing* new songs.

> **NOTE** ≈≈≈≈≈
>
> If you are writing about a past event that occurred the day after another event, don't use the word *tomorrow* to show the passage of time. Instead, use expressions like *the next day* or *the following day.*
>
> **Not:** Every night, the bakers began work at 10:00 in order to have fresh bread tomorrow.
>
> **But:** Every night, the bakers began work at 10:00 in order to have fresh bread the next day.
>
> The first sentence is illogical; it tells us that the bread will be ready on the day after the sentence is being written!

34.3 Keep verb tenses consistent.

It is important to keep verb tenses consistent. Of course, you will sometimes have to shift from one tense to another, but be careful not to confuse your readers or to break the flow of your writing. First choose a controlling, or main, tense for your project; then switch to other tenses only when you need to describe actions that occurred or will occur *at other times.*

Let's say you write about how hard you find your college mathematics class. You choose the present as your controlling tense as you write this sentence:

I *spend* three hours a night on my math homework, and I still barely *pass* the quizzes my teacher *gives* us.

Spend, pass, and *gives* are in the present tense.

You can shift logically into the past if you decide to compare this course with the math you took in high school.

Back then I rarely *studied,* yet I *received* good grades.

Studied and *received* are in the past tense.

You might even make good use of the future tense.

Learning math *will help* me with the physics course I *will take* next year.

Will help and *will take* are both in the future tense.

However, you would not write

I *spend* three hours a night on my math homework, and I still barely *passed* the quizzes my teacher *will give* us.

Here the writer should not have switched tenses, for the three actions in the sentence are occurring at the same time. Therefore, switching tenses in this case is illogical and makes the sentence confusing.

■ ■ ■   ■ ■ ■ ■   **BASICLINK**   ■ ■ ■   ■ ■ ■
WWW

For additional help with verbs and verb forms, visit
http://webster.commnet.edu/grammar/verbs.htm

EXERCISE 34C

Keeping Verb Tenses Consistent

Rewrite the following paragraph to correct illogical shifts in verb tense:

Confucius, the Chinese philosopher, lived in the sixth century B.C. When he is only three years old, his father dies, and Confucius grows up in great poverty. At the time, government corruption was sapping China's strength and causing a decline in the people's well-being. Indeed, it leads to a decline in the general state of morality and, in turn, will even cause civil disorder. Confucius wants none of this, and he decided to become a teacher of the values and moral lessons he has read about in the literature and philosophy of the ancients. One of his most important teachings was that truly virtuous people had an obligation to teach by example. In fact, public officials, argues Confucius, are able to maintain order among those they govern only by pursuing an ethical and just life.

34.4 Use linking and helping verbs.

Some verbs do not show action. **Linking verbs** help describe a subject by connecting it to a noun or an adjective. Linking verbs include *be, am, is, are, was, were. Become, feel, grow, look, seem, smell,* and *sound* can also be linking verbs.

noun
They *were* police officers.

adj.
The little boy *seems* confused.

Helping verbs are used with other verbs to make specific time references and to create verb phrases. In fact, as you have seen, helping verbs are used with the future tense and with the perfect and progressive tenses. Helping verbs include *am, is, are, was, were, be, being,* and *been. Do, have, shall,* and *will* can also be helping verbs.

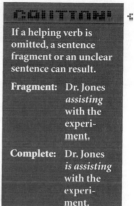

Dr. Jones *is assisting* with the experiment.

Compact discs *have replaced* record albums.

34.5 Learn the irregular verbs.

There are more than 300 irregular verbs in English. Their past tense is *not* formed by the addition of *-d* or *-ed* to the basic form of the verb. Note that the past participles of some of these verbs are also irregular.

Present	Past	Present Participle	Past Participle
arise	arose	arising	arisen
awake	awoke	awaking	awaked
beat	beat	beating	beaten
break	broke	breaking	broken
bring	brought	bringing	brought
catch	caught	catching	caught
choose	chose	choosing	chosen
cling	clung	clinging	clung
come	came	coming	come
dig	dug	digging	dug
do	did	doing	done
draw	drew	drawing	drawn
drive	drove	driving	driven
eat	ate	eating	eaten
fall	fell	falling	fallen
feel	felt	feeling	felt
fly	flew	flying	flown

(continued)

Present	Past	Present Participle	Past Participle
forgive	forgave	forgiving	forgiven
get	got	getting	got, gotten
give	gave	giving	given
go	went	going	gone
hold	held	holding	held
keep	kept	keeping	kept
know	knew	knowing	known
lay	laid	laying	laid
lead	led	leading	led
lie	lay	lying	lain
lose	lost	losing	lost
make	made	making	made
meet	met	meeting	met
ride	rode	riding	ridden
rise	rose	rising	risen
run	ran	running	run
see	saw	seeing	seen
send	sent	sending	sent
sit	sat	sitting	sat
speak	spoke	speaking	spoken
steal	stole	stealing	stolen
teach	taught	teaching	taught
tear	tore	tearing	torn
throw	threw	throwing	thrown
win	won	winning	won
write	wrote	writing	written

34.6 Learn to use the active and passive voices.

In the **active voice,** the subject of the sentence is the person or thing doing the action or being described. In the **passive voice,** the subject of the sentence is the person or thing being acted upon. The passive voice requires a two-part verb:

A helping verb—a form of the verb *to be* (*is, are, was, were, will be*) or a form of the verb *to have* (*has, had, will have*)

A past participle

Active voice: Massive earth movements created the Himalayan mountains about 50 million years ago.

The subject of the sentence, *movements,* does the action; the verb is *created.*

Passive voice: The Himalayan mountains were created by massive earth movements about 50 million years ago.

The subject of the sentence, *mountains,* receives the action. The verb is in two parts: the helping verb *were* and the past participle *created.*

The passive voice requires more words and is less direct than the active voice. For that reason, you should rely on the active voice in most cases. However, you can use the passive voice when the agent (person or thing that does an action) is unknown, obvious, or unimportant. You can also use the passive voice when there is no agent.

Agent unknown: The money *was stolen* this morning.
Agent obvious: Cures for AIDS *are being* actively *researched.*
Agent unimportant: An eighteenth-century burial ground *was discovered* during excavations for an office building.
No agent: Unfortunately, the common cold still *cannot be cured.*

34.7 Become familiar with the four verb moods.

Verbs have tenses (past, present, future, and so on) and voices (active and passive). They also have moods, which help convey the writer's intent.

The **indicative mood** conveys an action or information that the writer believes is true.

Tokyo *is* the capital of Japan.

Technological advances *have made* automobiles more fuel efficient.

The **subjunctive mood** reports actions that the writer knows are contrary to fact:

NOTE ⋅⋅⋅⋅⋅⋅

Sentences in the subjunctive convey information that the writer knows is not true, for *I am* not *rich,* and *Stalin is* not *alive.* Note also that, in the subjunctive, the present tense of the verb *to be* is *were,* not *am, are,* or *is,* as in the indicative mood.

Indicative:
I am
You are
He, she, it, one is
We are
You are
They are

Subjunctive:
I were
You were
He, she, it, one were
We were
You were
They were

If I *were* rich, I would buy a sports car.

If Stalin *were* alive today, he would be stunned to see the changes democracy has brought to Eastern Europe.

The subjunctive mood can also be used to communicate a desire.

I wish I *were* rich.

Professor Mendoza is such a good teacher that his students wish the semester *were not* over.

The **imperative mood** communicates a command or a request.

"Stop!" ordered the police officer.

Please return all books promptly.

The imperative is also used to give instructions or explain a process.

Turn on the computer.

Click on the program icon.

Open a new document.

NOTE ⋅⋅⋅⋅⋅⋅

In sentences using the imperative, the subject *you* is understood.

The **conditional mood** communicates information that could be true depending on the circumstances. Conditional statements usually begin with the word *if* or constructions that mean *if.*

If the college receives a National Science Foundation grant, we will be using a new chemistry lab next spring.

Had Hitler won the war, most Europeans would now be speaking German.

∴ CHAPTER WRAP-UP

Revise the following essay written by student MaryAnn Sullivan. It contains numerous verb errors, which have been added by the authors of this book. Be prepared to discuss the reasons for the changes you make.

The Journey Home

It was a cool, rainy morning in October, and the youth convention is coming to an end. Everyone said good-bye and started walking toward the waiting buses. We are leaving Biloxi, Mississippi, and all our new friends, whom we have made during our weeklong stay. As we boarded our buses, a depression fell over everyone because no one really wants to leave. It seemed as if the weather worsened as we head slowly toward New Orleans. The rain trickled down the bus windows, and small floods are forming in low-lying areas of the road.

It was 11 in the morning when we reached the airport, and it is already busy with early-morning travelers. The pace seems to quicken when we entered the terminal, as commuters hustle past us to catch their planes. A hurricane is heading toward New Orleans and the surrounding Gulf Coast, and the airlines wanted to get as many people out as they could before the storm hits with full force tomorrow. We were escorted to our seats on the airplane, and we all feel secure and somewhat happy that we were going home. Suddenly, I hear Mark yell, "The engine is on fire!" I couldn't believe what I have heard, and I looked out the window, only to see red and orange flames shoot out of the number one engine. Then the captain, in a very calm voice, announces, "Ladies and gentlemen, we will be delayed due to mechanical difficulties." Everyone looked at each other and slowly gathered their things. Then the stewardesses escort us once again, but this time it was off the plane to the waiting area.

Many of us were very tired from lack of sleep, and we try to relax while waiting for our flight to be called. About four hours had passed, and the storm was slowly approaching. We have all gathered around the phones to call our anxious parents and update them on what has happened. Those who had already talked with their parents stared aimlessly out the large tinted windows while sheets of rain pour down fiercely on them. Darkness had begun to fall and the wind has picked up significantly. Pieces of heavy debris were being kicked up like feathers and scattered over the runways.

After about five hours, we were told that we can board our plane again. We found our seats and prepare ourselves for the worst. The comfortable feeling we had before is gone and replaced by fear. The engines start, and we begin to move to our position on the runway. The sounds of the engines could hardly be heard over the pounding rain and howling wind. The tension in the air was thick, and silence falls over everyone as we begin our takeoff. The wind seems to guide us as we rocked from side to side, and a young woman in the back of the plane became hysterical and starts to scream. A small, blond boy in the front of the plane decided to break the tension by throwing his arms in the air, as if he were on a roller coaster, and yells, "This is fun!" This innocent outburst made some people laugh, but many others are still petrified and clung to their seats for dear life. The turbulence continues, rocking us to and fro, and we all just prayed that it will end. Suddenly, we broke above the cloud line, and the turbulence stopped. The airplane levels and the bumpy ride became a memory.

That horrible day took place almost five years ago, but my memory of it is as clear as if it has happened yesterday. Whenever I need to get on an airplane, I remembered everything that took place as the plane is fighting the weather to get into the air. It makes me nervous to remember that day, but it also made me realize that nothing can ever be as bad as that flight home. For many of us, that takeoff was the worst and longest five minutes of our lives, and most of us never forget it as long as we live.

MAINTAINING SUBJECT-VERB AGREEMENT

35.1 **Make verbs agree with subjects.**

When two words "agree," they are of the same number. That means that both are singular (one) or both are plural (more than one).

35.1 Make verbs agree with subjects.

A verb agrees with its subject in number. That is, if the subject is **singular** (one), the verb is singular; if the subject is **plural** (more than one), the verb is plural.

The *book is* on the table.

The subject of the sentence, *book,* is singular; therefore, the verb, *is,* is also singular.

The *books are* on the table.

The subject, *books,* is plural; therefore, the verb, *are,* is also plural.

You can have problems with agreement if you don't understand the number of the subject or if you choose the wrong word as the subject. Here are ten ways to avoid such problems:

1. Decide whether the subject is singular or plural. Most plural subjects, usually nouns, end in *-s* or *-es.*

	Singular	Plural
	building	buildings
	box	boxes

2. Don't be confused by words that come between a subject and a verb.

Not: The rivalry between the teams are fierce.

But: The rivalry between the teams is fierce.

The subject of the sentence is *rivalry*, not *teams*. Therefore, the sentence needs a singular verb, *is*. Between *the teams* is simply a phrase that describes *rivalry*.

> **CAUTION!**
>
> Form singular verbs by adding *-s* or *-es* to the simple form of the verb when *he, she, it,* or *one* (the third-person singular) is your subject.
>
> *he, she, it, one appears* (singular)
>
> but
>
> *they appear* (plural)

Not: The screams of the lost boy echoes in the cave.

But: The screams of the lost boy echo in the cave.

The subject of the sentence is *screams*, not *boy. Screams* is plural; the verb, *echo*, is also plural.

Spotting Words That Come Between Subjects and Verbs

Words that come between subjects and verbs can cause you to mistake the true subject. They often appear in phrases that begin with words such as these:

accompanied by	in addition to	of the
along with	including	plus
as well as	in front of	together with
besides	not to mention	with

Not: The patients, along with their doctor, is willing to speak about the new treatment.

But: The patients, along with their doctor, are willing to speak about the new treatment.

Not: Archimedes, as well as Plato, Aristotle, and Sophocles, have an important place in ancient Greek civilization.

But: Archimedes, as well as Plato, Aristotle, and Sophocles, has an important place in ancient Greek civilization.

3. Use a plural verb with subjects joined by *and*.

Carrie and Robert have decided to buy a house.

The subject, *Carrie and Robert*, is plural; the verb, *have decided*, must also be plural.

4. Use singular verbs with gerunds. A **gerund** is a noun that ends in *-ing* and names an activity. Here are some examples of gerunds: *swimming, eating, breathing, laughing, voting, understanding.*

Donating food and clothing to charity helps the less fortunate.

The subject is *donating*, not *food and clothing;* therefore, it takes a singular verb, *helps.*

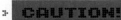

The verb is singular if both parts of the subject refer to the same person, place, or thing.

His one and only is his wife.

The subject, *one and only,* refers to the same person, so it is singular. The verb must also be singular.

5. Use singular verbs with subjects joined by *or, either . . . or,* or *neither . . . nor* if both subjects are singular.

By now, rain or snow has fallen in the mountains.

Each part of the subject, *rain* and *snow,* is singular; therefore, the verb is also singular. However, *if both subjects are plural,* use plural verbs.

Either his parents or his grandparents were born in Idaho.

Each part of the subject, *parents* and *grandparents,* is plural; therefore, the verb, *were born,* is also plural.

If one part of the subject is singular and the other is plural, the verb agrees with the one closest to it.

Neither the principal nor the teachers are here.

Neither the teachers nor the principal is here.

6. When a relative pronoun—*who, which,* or *that*—is a subject, make the verb agree with its antecedent, the word to which it refers.

Beloved is a novel about a woman who suffers the death of a child.

Who refers to *woman,* which is singular. Therefore, the verb, *suffers,* is singular.

People who suffer from diabetes can be helped.

Who refers to *people,* which is plural. Therefore the verb, *suffer,* is plural.

7. Use a singular verb when an indefinite pronoun, such as *any, each, every, either,* or *neither,* is the subject.

Not: Each of her sisters are a college graduate.

But: Each of her sisters is a college graduate.

Each, not *sisters,* is the subject. Therefore, the verb must also be singular.

Not: Either Roberto or Michael are calling.

But: Either Roberto or Michael is calling.

Roberto *or* Michael (either one, but not both) is calling; therefore, the verb must be singular.

Indefinite pronouns that end in *-one* or *-body* also take singular verbs. They include *anyone, anybody, everyone, everybody, none, no one, nobody, somebody,* and *someone.*

Everybody here knows my brother.

Everybody is singular; it takes the singular verb *knows.*

None of us has been invited.

The subject is *none,* not *us;* therefore, the verb, *has,* is singular.

Indefinite Pronouns

	-One Words	*-Body* Words
any	one	anybody
each	anyone	everybody
every	everyone	nobody
either	no one	somebody
neither	none	
	someone	

8. If a sentence begins with *there* or *here,* the subject comes after the verb; look for it there.

Here is the article we were searching for.

There are two answers to that question.

In the first sentence, the subject is *article,* not *here. Article* is singular; therefore, the verb must be *is.* In the second sentence, the subject is *answers,* not *there. Answers* is plural; therefore, the verb must be *are.*

9. If a subject follows the verb, read the whole sentence to find the subject before deciding whether the verb should be singular or plural.

In a stand by the front door are several umbrellas.

The subject of the sentence is *umbrellas,* not *stand* or *door;* therefore, the verb should be plural.

10. A collective noun, such as *company, family, class, community, troop,* or *committee,* names a group. Use a singular verb if *one* group is named. Use a plural verb if *more than one* group is named.

The class has voted to raise money for the United Way.

The subject, *class,* is one unit; therefore, the verb, *has voted,* is singular.

The committees have voted to write new by-laws.

The subject, *committees,* is more than one unit; therefore, the verb, *have voted,* is plural.

■■■■   ■■■■   **BASICLINK** ■■■■   ■■■■
WWW

To see additional examples of subject-verb agreement, visit
http://leo.stcloudstate.edu/grammar/subverag.html

■■ ■■ ■■ ■■ ■■ ■■ ■■ ■■ ■■ ■■ ■■ ■■

CHAPTER WRAP-UP

Rewrite the following selections to correct subject-verb agreement problems.

Ramayana

The *Ramayana*, an epic poem of the ancient Hindus, date back more than 2,000 years. According to literary historians, the poet Valmiki or some unknown writer are thought to have authored this long narrative. Ancient poems and songs, as well as tales from Hindu mythology, was collected and then combined into the *Ramayana*. Reading these tales and myths provide an insight into the development of Hindu thought. Here is expressed the value system and the cultural ideals of ancient India. Important to the action and meaning of the poem are a group of characters each of whom represent an ideal. For example, there is Dasa-ratha (the ideal king) and Sita (the ideal wife). However, at the center of the work stand Rama, the ideal prince who give the poem its name. By suffering pain and hardship, Rama become the symbol of endurance, sacrifice, and duty. These virtues, as well as a belief that people must behave according to the role life assigns them, forms the foundation of ancient Hindu thought.

Korea

The peninsula of Korea, which stretches into the sea some 600 miles, lie south of Manchuria. To the east is the Japanese islands. A nation that has been overrun by its larger and more powerful neighbors several times, Korea was split into two separate nations after the war of the early 1950s. Since that time, South Korea's economy, which follow the capitalistic model and enjoys the opportunities that come with free enterprise systems, have been growing steadily. In the north, on the other hand, the growth of industry and commerce have been stunted because of a repressive communist government. Indeed, visitors to the north notices immediately upon crossing the border that they have entered another, poorer country. People in the south has a great diversity of employment opportunities because of the many businesses and industries that have sprung up there in the last fifty years. For their counterparts in the north, on the other hand, a farm or fishing boat are the more likely employment venue. As a matter of fact, the standard of living for the typical South Korean make them one of the most prosperous of all people in the Pacific Rim.

LEARNING PRONOUN TYPES, CASES, AND REFERENCE

36.1 **Learn pronoun types.**
36.2 **Use pronoun cases correctly.**
36.3 **Check pronoun reference.**

Pronouns refer to and take the place of nouns.

The students are from Korea. *They* came here in 1992.

Africa is a large continent; *it* contains many countries.

By replacing nouns, pronouns help you avoid repetition. Without them, the sentences above might read

The students are from Korea. The students came here in 1992.

Africa is a large continent; Africa contains many countries.

36.1 Learn pronoun types.

The five types of pronouns are *personal, relative, indefinite, demonstrative,* and *reflexive.*

36.1a Learn the personal pronouns.

Personal pronouns can be used as subjects, objects, or possessives.

Subjects	Objects
I enrolled in Spanish 101.	Jacky praised *me.*
You missed dinner.	My mother likes *you.*
He came late.	Ms. Aroyo met *him.*
She had an appointment.	Professor Chen called *her.*
It was cold.	Vanessa ended *it.*
We got lost.	The family trusts *us.*
You are a large family.	The party includes *you.*
They took the train.	The music pleased *them.*

Possessives	
My check came.	The check is *mine.*
Your new car is here.	The new car is *yours.*
His dog is barking.	The dog is *his.*
Her class ended.	The class is *hers.*
Its roof is damaged.	
Our cameras are missing.	The cameras are *ours.*
Your rights are precious.	The rights are *yours.*
Their home is a ranch.	The home is *theirs.*

36.1b Learn the relative pronouns.

The **relative pronouns** connect groups of words to nouns or to other pronouns. *That* and *which* refer to animals, objects, or ideas. *Who, whoever, whom,* and *whomever* refer to people. *Whose* can be used in all cases.

The family enjoyed a pizza *that* Rinaldo cooked.

She studied Buddhism, *which* is a major world religion.

Andy spoke with students *who* majored in history.

The company *whose* employees were honored is Apex Lamp.

36.1c Learn the indefinite pronouns.

The **indefinite pronouns** listed below refer to people and things that are not named or are not specific.

any	everybody	nobody	some
anybody	everyone	no one	somebody
anyone	everything	one	someone
each	few		

Anybody can join the club.

Everyone has paid a dollar.

Angela told *no one* about the problem.

Somebody turned off the light.

36.1d Learn the demonstrative pronouns.

The **demonstrative pronouns**—*that, this, those, these*—refer to nouns that come *after* them.

Is *this* car rented?

Are *those* classes still open?

36.1e Learn the reflexive pronouns.

The **reflexive pronouns** end in -*self* or -*selves*. Use them when the subject of a sentence does something to itself.

I want to enjoy *myself.*

Andrew forgot *himself* and laughed out loud.

The cat scared *itself* when it looked into the mirror.

They give *themselves* no credit.

Pronouns ending in -*self* can also create emphasis.

I saw him take the money *myself.*

Alice *herself* has competed in the Olympics.

CAUTION!

Don't use *this* when you mean *the, a,* or *an.*

Not: As we marched onto the field, I felt this energy fill my body.

But: As we marched onto the field, I felt an energy fill my body.

CAUTION!

Don't write *ourselfs* for *ourselves.*
Don't write *theirselfs* or *themselfs* for *themselves.*
Don't write *hisself* for *himself.*

36.2 Use pronoun cases correctly.

The pronoun you choose depends on its use as a subject, complement, object, or possessive. These uses determine the pronoun's case.

36.2a Use pronouns as subjects.

Personal pronouns you can use as subjects are listed on page 473. You can also use indefinite and demonstrative pronouns as subjects.

Indefinite:	*Everyone* is here.
	Someone has stolen Peter's car.
	Anyone can join our team.
Demonstrative:	*That* is my coat.
	Those are Jeannine's parents.

Writers can get confused about which pronoun to use when a compound subject consists of a noun and a pronoun or more than one pronoun.

Not:	Angelo and me play basketball on Tuesdays.
But:	Angelo and I play basketball on Tuesdays.
Not:	Marjorie and her went swimming.
But:	Marjorie and she went swimming.

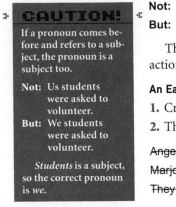

Not: They and us had dinner.

But: They and we had dinner.

These sentences demand subject pronouns, doers of actions.

An Easy Way to Select the Proper Subject Pronoun

1. Cross out the first part of the subject.

2. Then ask yourself if the new sentence makes sense.

~~Angelo and~~ me play basketball on Tuesdays. (?)

~~Marjorie and~~ her went swimming. (?)

~~They and~~ us had dinner. (?)

36.2b Use pronouns as complements.

Complements refer to subjects and are connected to them by such verbs as *is, are, was, have been,* and *will be.* Complement pronouns are the same as subject pronouns.

"It is *I* (not *me*)," Fino said as he knocked on the door.

An honest woman is *she* (not *her*) who speaks the truth.

It was *they* (not *them*) who taught us to love dogs.

36.2c Use pronouns as objects.

Direct Objects

Personal pronouns you can use as direct objects are listed on page 473. You can also use indefinite and demonstrative pronouns as objects. (Remember, objects receive action.)

Indefinite:	Betty likes *everyone.*
	Peter saw *no one* on the lake.
	Fran knows *somebody* who speaks Creole.
Demonstrative:	I heard *that* rumor yesterday.
	We bought *those* books in Chicago.

Compound Objects

Writers can get confused about which pronoun to use when the object contains a noun and a pronoun or more than one pronoun.

Not: Freddie challenged Angelo and I to a game.

Not: Evelyn called Sonia and she.

Not: The clerk overcharged both them and we.

The lists on page 473 show that *I, she,* and *we* are subjects—doers of action. In these three sentences, these words are used as objects—receivers of action.

But: Freddie challenged Angelo and *me* to a game.

But: Evelyn called Sonia and *her.*

But: The clerk overcharged both them and *us.*

An Easy Way to Select the Proper Object Pronoun

1. Cross out the first part of the object.

2. Then ask yourself whether the new sentence makes sense.

Freddie challenged ~~Angelo and~~ I to a game. (?)

Evelyn called ~~Sonia and~~ she. (?)

The clerk overcharged ~~both them and~~ we. (?)

Objects of Prepositions

A preposition comes before a noun or pronoun and shows how that word relates to the rest of the sentence. Pronouns that come after prepositions act as objects.

My sister called to *me* (not *I*) across the field.

Senator Mendoza spoke with *them* (not *they*) yesterday.

The dean wrote letters for Ida and *her* (not *she*).

36.2d Use pronouns as possessives.

Personal Pronouns as Possessives

Pronouns you can use as possessives appear on page 474. They show ownership or a relationship with a noun that follows. Some possessives come before the noun; others come after it.

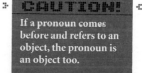

CAUTION!

If a pronoun comes before and refers to an object, the pronoun is an object too.

Not: They invited we students to dinner.

But: They invited us students to dinner.

In this example, *students* is a direct object, so the correct pronoun is *us.*

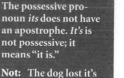

CAUTION!

The possessive pronoun *its* does not have an apostrophe. *It's* is not possessive; it means "it is."

Not: The dog lost it's leash.

But: The dog lost its leash.

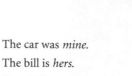

My mother is an officer.   The car was *mine.*

His brother is fifteen.   The bill is *hers.*

Our children just called.   The challenge is *ours!*

Their home was new.   The fault is *theirs.*

Indefinite Pronouns as Possessives

To make the indefinite pronouns on page 474 possessive, add -'s

> *Everyone's* right to vote is sacred.
>
> *No one's* children should go hungry.
>
> *Someone's* purse was found in the theater.

Possessive Pronouns with -*ing* Nouns

<table>
<tr>
<td>

CAUTION!

Don't confuse *their* with *they're* or *there*. *They're* means "they are"; *there* indicates a place.

Not: There house was small.

Not: They're house was small.

But: Their house was small.

</td>
<td>

Nouns ending in -*ing* describe activities: *swimming, crying, running, speaking, thinking,* and the like. Use possessive pronouns before such nouns.

> *My* (not *me*) moving out of the house was a mistake.
>
> I remember *our* (not *us*) pushing the car out of the mud.
>
> *Your* (not *you*) calling me unethical is hypocritical!
>
> *His* (not *him*) snoring disturbed us.
>
> *Their* (not *them*) coming home late angered her mother.

</td>
</tr>
</table>

36.2e   Avoid problems with *who, whom,* and *whose*.

> *Who* is a subject: *Who* are you?
>
> *Whom* is an object: *Whom* do you trust?
>
> *Whose* is possessive: *Whose* socks are these?

<table>
<tr>
<td>

CAUTION!

Never use *its', theirs', her's, hers', our's, ours', your's,* or *yours'*. These words do not exist.

</td>
<td>

Special problems can occur when *who* and *whom* come in the middle of a sentence.

> I met the woman *who* spoke to the class.
>
> I met the woman *whom* Professor Jones invited to class.

</td>
</tr>
</table>

Both of these sentences are correct. In the first example, *who* is the subject of the verb *spoke*. In the second, *whom* is the object of *invited*.

<table>
<tr>
<td>

CAUTION!

Don't confuse *whose* with *who's*. *Who's* means "who is."

Not: I met a man who's hair was blue.

But: I met a man whose hair was blue.

</td>
<td>

An Easy Way to Choose Between *Who* and *Whom*

1. Put brackets around the part of the sentence that follows *who* or *whom*.

> I met the woman who/whom [spoke to our class].
>
> I met the woman who/whom [Professor Jones invited to class].

</td>
</tr>
</table>

2. Decide whether the pronoun is the subject or object of the words in brackets.

3. If it's the subject, use *who;* if it's the object, use *whom.*

36.2f Use pronouns after *than* or *as.*

Use the correct pronoun after *than* or *as.*

> Joan is taller than I.
>
> She loved no other man as much as me.

An Easy Way to Select the Proper Pronoun After *Than* or *As*

1. Fill in information that will complete the thought.

> Jane is taller than I/me [am].
>
> She loved no other man as much as [she loved] I/me.

2. Decide whether a subject or object should be used.

> Jane is taller than I [am].
>
> She loved no other man as much as [she loved] me.

36.2g Avoid a special problem with *which.*

Don't write *in which* when you mean *which.*

> **Not:**   We knocked on the door, in which had just been painted.
>
> **But:**   We knocked on the door, which had just been painted.

Using Pronoun Cases Correctly

Rewrite the following sentences so that the pronouns are in the right case.

1. Benito Juarez is an important figure in Mexican history. It was him who led a successful revolution against the dictatorship of General Santa Anna in 1855.

2. After the revolution, it was Juarez whom proposed political and social reforms that influenced the writing of Mexico's constitution.

3. After French troops invaded Mexico in 1864 and installed Maximillian as emperor, Benito Juarez led his people in they're fight to regain there liberty.

4. Abraham Lincoln's speeches remain classics of American oratory. The speeches of Senator Stephen A. Douglas, the man Lincoln debated, are hardly remembered. Interestingly, most people who had heard Lincoln speak thought Douglas was far more eloquent than him.

5. From the beginning of his political career, Abraham Lincoln defended everyones right to self-government. Lincoln detested slavery. For he, owning slaves contradicted the very principle on which American democracy was founded.

EXERCISE 36A

(continued)

6. John Chavis (1763–1838), an African American who's family had been freed in the eighteenth century, worked in North Carolina to bring education to the children of slaves and to the children of poor white people alike.

7. John Chavis was murdered, some historians believe, because of him trying to improve the lives of black children.

8. Although he pursued the same goals as Harriet Tubman, Frederick Douglass, and other early African-American leaders, John Chavis is hardly as well known as them.

9. Harriet Tubman escaped from slavery in 1849, but before the Civil War began she returned to the South to help other slaves escape; these people included hers own parents.

10. Our professor asked we students to search the Internet for information on the Fugitive Slave Laws, the Underground Railroad, and the *North Star*, a newspaper edited by Frederick Douglass.

36.3 Check pronoun reference.

Pronouns must point to nouns clearly and directly. These rules will help you make sure that your pronoun references are correct:

1. Include the noun to which the pronoun points. If you forget to include the noun that a pronoun refers to, your writing will be unclear. In the first version below, the meaning of *which* is unclear; the sentence has no noun to which the pronoun can point. In the second version, *that* points to *fact*, a noun that comes before it.

Unclear: Americans are the most productive workers in the world, which is often forgotten.

Clear: Americans are the most productive workers in the world, a *fact* that is often forgotten.

Sometimes the best way to revise an unclear sentence of this kind is to drop the pronoun altogether. In the first version below, the pronoun *which* seems to refer to *collided;* but *collided* is a verb, and pronouns refer to nouns. In the second version, the sentence has been rewritten so that the pronoun is no longer needed.

Unclear: Two cars collided, which caused a traffic jam.

Clear: A collision of two cars caused a traffic jam.

2. Make sure the pronoun points to one noun only. Who was promoted— Jane or Flora?

Unclear: Jane was speaking with Flora when she learned she had been promoted.

Clear: Jane learned she had been promoted when she was speaking with Flora.

3. Don't hide the noun in another term. Most readers will know that *their* refers to Mexicans, but *Mexicans* is missing from the sentence. The first sentence should be revised.

Unclear:	Mexico's economy is expanding; their standard of living is rising.
Clear:	Mexico's economy is expanding; the Mexicans' standard of living is rising.

4. Avoid the use of *they, it,* or *this* without a clear antecedent, a word the pronoun can refer to.

Unclear:	They predict Stetson will win the election, but they are not always reliable.
Clear:	The polls predict Stetson will win the election, but they are not always reliable.

In the first version above, readers will not know what *they* refers to.

Unclear:	As Jerry approached the car, it could be seen that his luggage was missing.
Clear:	As Jerry approached the car, he could see that his luggage was missing.

In the first version above, *it* has no reference.

Unclear:	I saw a strange man near my house. This is why I called the police.
Clear:	I called the police because I saw a strange man near my house.

In the first version above, the pronoun has no clear reference. The easiest way to correct this sentence is to remove *this* by combining sentences.

Checking Pronoun Reference

Rewrite the following sentences to correct pronoun reference problems:

1. The way the media reports the news has a long-lasting effect, which is why journalists are said to write the rough drafts of history.
2. They were sure that Dewey would defeat Truman in the U.S. presidential election of 1948, but he surprised everyone.
3. In 1952, Eisenhower, the Republican candidate for president, claimed that President Truman's administration had mismanaged the Korean War, but he refuted the charges.

(continued)

EXERCISE 36B

4. Commissioned by the government to search for a water passage to the Pacific coast, Meriwether Lewis and William Clark explored the northwestern United States on a journey that lasted from 1804 to 1806. After his death in 1809, Clark assumed the responsibility of writing the report of their explorations.

5. They say that medical science will develop artificial substitutes for every organ in the human body.

6. The Italians are famous for their art. It is the birthplace of modern painting.

7. They think that the ancient Egyptian secret of making mummies will never be discovered.

8. Alaska is a natural wonderland, where they want to preserve the environment.

9. The Atlas Mountains, which are in northwest Africa, are rich in coal, oil, iron, and other resources. Governments in that part of the world find this very interesting.

10. They say in the history books that Atila the Hun did not destroy Rome in 452 A.D., which may have resulted from a lack of food and military supplies.

CHAPTER WRAP-UP

Rewrite the following student paragraphs to correct pronoun problems:

1. Rhonda and me work for the Ivyland Bus Company. Today we consider ourself sisters. However, when we were first hired, which was nearly five years ago, it was quite different. Our relationship got off to a rocky start. On our first day, this woman who heads the personnel department asked us to take a test. An employee that works in my department explained that the company just wanted to find out which jobs we could do best. Rhonda scored higher than me and was given the job I wanted, which made me jealous. In only one year, she became the supervisor of this large department, even though she had worked at Ivyland less time than them. I learned to respect Rhonda after seeing how well the people in her department and her got along. It is her to who I turn whenever I have problems at work. In fact, it was Rhonda that helped me get promoted last year, for which I will never forget her.

2. During a vacation to South Carolina's Seabrook Island, my family and me learned that their community had been devastated a few years earlier by Hurricane Andrew. This elderly gentleman whom had lived on the island all his life described the storm to my brother and I by claiming he had never seen anything like it. Early one morning they broadcast television reports showing how badly Andrew had hit Florida the day before. It was then that some of the old man's neighbors and him had begun to board up windows and gather food. But it was not possible to protect themself from a storm like Andrew. As a result, they decided to evacuate, which state officials had recommended all along. In the end, whole communities were destroyed. In one small town, people found shelter from the hurricane and it's destruction by sitting in there bathtubs under mattresses held over they're heads for protection.

MAINTAINING PRONOUN-ANTECEDENT AGREEMENT

37.1 **Make pronouns agree with their antecedents.**

37.2 Avoid sexist pronouns.

37.1 Make pronouns agree with their antecedents.

Just as a verb agrees with a subject, a pronoun agrees with its **antecedent,** the word to which the pronoun refers. An antecedent can be a noun or another pronoun. Here are four guidelines for pronoun-antecedent agreement:

1. Use singular pronouns to refer to singular antecedents; use plural pronouns to refer to plural antecedents.

The plate fell off the shelf, but it did not break.

The antecedent, *plate,* is singular; therefore, the pronoun, *it,* is also singular.

Some television commercials do not relate directly to the products they endorse.

The antecedent *commercials* is plural; therefore, the pronoun, *they,* must also be plural.

2. Use singular pronouns to refer to nouns joined by *or, either . . . or,* or *neither . . . nor* if both nouns are singular.

Neither she nor Dawn finished her research paper.

Each part of the antecedent, *she* and *Dawn,* is singular; therefore, the pronoun, *her,* is also singular.

Use plural pronouns if both nouns are plural.

Neither the tables nor the chairs could be repaired, so they were thrown out.

Each part of the antecedent, *tables* and *chairs,* is plural; therefore, the pronoun, *they,* is also plural.

In special cases, one noun may be singular and the other plural. In such instances, the pronoun agrees with the noun closest to it.

Neither the council members nor the mayor wished to compromise her position.

Neither the mayor nor the council members wished to compromise their position.

3. Use a singular or plural pronoun to refer to a collective noun depending on the sense of the noun.

The committee voted to revise its report.

In this case, *committee* means the group as a whole; therefore, the pronoun, *its,* is singular.

The committee debated whether to allow their families to attend the dinner.

Here, *committee* stands for several people who make up a group; therefore, the pronoun, *their,* is plural.

4. Use singular pronouns when you refer to indefinite pronouns, such as *neither, either, one, everyone,* and *everybody.* A list of such pronouns appears on page 474.

The men could not pay; neither had brought his wallet.

His refers to *neither,* which is singular.

EXERCISE 37A

Making Pronouns Agree with Their Antecedents

Rewrite the following paragraph to make all pronouns agree with their antecedents. Be prepared to discuss the reasons for your corrections.

Neither the lookout nor First Officer Murdoch knew what to expect as they watched the *Titanic* slowly veer away from the iceberg, but it soon became apparent that the great ship was in serious trouble. On orders from Captain Smith, the lifeboat crews reported to their stations, uncovered the boats, and swung it out, while the stewards ordered every passenger to put on their life jacket. At first, the women did not want to leave their husbands. However, as the downward angle of the ship increased, each decided they had no choice and stepped into a lifeboat. More than 1,500 passengers and crew lost their lives as the ship sank. Later the company that owned the *Titanic* was severely criticized, for they had not taken the proper precautions on the ship's first and only voyage.

37.2 Avoid sexist pronouns.

Sexist language can occur when an indefinite pronoun, such as *anyone, each, everyone,* and *somebody,* is the antecedent. It can also occur when a generic noun—a noun that is neither female nor male—is the antecedent.

37.2a Avoid sexism with indefinite pronouns.

Indefinite pronouns, such as *anybody, each, every, neither,* and *someone,* can be general in meaning and not refer to specific persons, places, or things. These pronouns are singular. Although writers sometimes use masculine pronouns—*he,* *his,* and *him*—to refer to indefinite pronouns, doing so offends many readers. Here are ways to avoid sexist language when using indefinite pronouns:

1. Use both masculine and feminine pronouns.

Sexist: Everyone should cast his vote on election day.

Revised: Everyone should cast his or her vote on election day.

The revision adds *her* to the sentence.

2. Replace the pronoun with *a, an,* or *the.*

Sexist: Each artist will complete his paintings in less than three months.

Revised: Each artist will complete the paintings in less than three months.

The revision substitutes *the* for *his.*

3. Replace the indefinite pronoun with a plural noun.

Sexist: Everyone should speak with his professor.

Revised: All students should speak with their professors.

In the revision, *students,* a plural noun, is referred to by *their,* which is neither masculine nor feminine.

37.2b Avoid sexism with generic nouns.

Generic nouns do not refer to a specific sex. Most nouns in English are generic. Exceptions include such words as *mother* and *father.* Use the methods described in section 37.2a to avoid sexist language when you use pronouns that refer to generic nouns, nouns that are neither male nor female.

1. Use both masculine and feminine pronouns.

Sexist: In some companies, the employee pays for his own medical insurance.

Revised: In some companies, the employee pays for his or her own medical insurance.

An employee may be either male or female; therefore, both masculine and feminine pronouns should be used.

2. Replace the pronoun with *a, an,* or *the.*

Sexist: A student must show her identification card at the library.

Revised: A student must show an identification card at the library.

3. Replace the singular noun with a plural noun.

Sexist: The police must read a person her rights when they arrest her.

Revised: The police must read people their rights when they arrest them.

EXERCISE 37B

Avoiding Sexist Pronouns

Rewrite the following paragraphs by using any of the methods for avoiding sexist pronouns.

1. Anyone who wants to be successful at college has to prepare himself adequately. First, he needs to learn how to study. Long hours of reading, writing, and other strenuous academic tasks await him, so he had better be organized. Taking careful and complete class notes will help him succeed in many demanding courses. Finally, he needs to know how to budget his time. Spending too many hours socializing and too few preparing for his classes may spell disaster for him.

2. A parent who believes her child is not as bright as the rest may be contributing to his failure in school. Unless a child has an exceptionally strong self-image, he will believe what his elders think about him. Too often, learning disabilities are mistaken for lack of intelligence, and the child is criticized for his inability to do simple math or to read his textbooks because he is "slow." This attitude is easily adopted by the youngster himself. A child with a hidden handicap such as dyslexia, for example, may start to believe that he is not as bright as his peers only because no one has identified and addressed his problem. His teacher may have her hands full with the problems of other students in her overcrowded classroom and may not be able to identify the reason that he doesn't do well in class because she has not been trained to recognize learning disabilities. Tragically, his parent might simply assume that her child is not as bright as most and, what's worse, will settle for average or below-average performance from him in school.

CHAPTER WRAP-UP

Rewrite the following student essay to correct pronoun-antecedent agreement problems and to eliminate sexist pronouns.

The Choice

A visit I paid to friends this spring has helped me make up my mind about the college I will attend next fall. My choice was between two schools a few hundred miles from home, each of which has an excellent reputation. Because I want to keep my grades high, I will be spending a great deal of time studying in my room or in the library. Therefore, the kind of social life offered by these campuses wasn't important, but I was eager to learn about each college's academic environment and about their typical student. In general, was he studious and willing to learn, or was he merely a "party animal," interested only in having a good time?

Neither of the two colleges I was considering was on break during the weekend I was able to borrow Dad's car, so I was in luck. However, I didn't have time to visit both, so I decided to go to the one north of my home, where my cousin and best friend, Bill, is attending. Another good friend, Mark, as well as a fellow I knew in the army, is also enrolled there. "Any one of them is able to show me around," I thought, "and they will give me an accurate picture of life on campus."

When I arrived, however, none of my friends was available to help. In fact, pledging a fraternity, making arrangements for a weekend ski trip, or trying to find a date for the next social seemed to have kept everyone so busy that they had little time for me.

Actually, their inability to help me was a blessing. I got to explore the campus and the town in which it is located, and I found that it was not for me. In fact, what I learned helped me decide that very weekend to attend the other college I was considering. For example, I learned that, whether male or female, the typical student at my friends' school is more interested in having fun than in learning. For him, any occasion   passing a math quiz, having a chance to do laundry, or watching the rain fall—is a good reason to party!

Visiting the library and poring over books is an activity foreign to the majority of students on this campus. I was in the library on Saturday morning; if anyone other than the reference librarian and a student worker were around, they were surely hard to find.

The party spirit is also evident in the small village two miles down the road, which exists only as a source of entertainment for the student body. There seem to be bars, taverns, video arcades, and expensive clothing boutiques on every street. Unfortunately, I was hard-pressed to find a bookstore, theater, or decent restaurant in the lot. As I left the campus Sunday night, I told my friend and my cousin that I wouldn't be going to school with them. To my amazement, neither Bill nor Mark was surprised, and since that day both have admitted that his ideas of college education are quite different from mine.

38

USING ADJECTIVES AND ADVERBS CORRECTLY

38.1 Learn to identify adjectives.
38.2 Learn to use participles.
38.3 Compare adjectives correctly.
38.4 Learn to identify adverbs.
38.5 Compare adverbs correctly.
38.6 Use adjectives and adverbs with sense verbs.

Adjectives and adverbs provide information about other words. Adjectives describe nouns and pronouns.

> The *bright yellow* lights on the *large suspension* bridge shone through a *thick* mist *hanging* over the *tired* city.

Adverbs describe verbs, adjectives, and other adverbs.

> *When* the doctor *finally* got *here,* she *slowly* removed the bandage from my *severely* burned hand and examined the wound *very carefully.*

Some words are both adjectives and adverbs, for example, *early, fast, hard, straight.*

Adjective:	The *early* train leaves at 6:00 A.M.
Adverb:	He arrived *early.*

38.1 Learn to identify adjectives.

Adjectives answer the questions "Which?" "What kind of?" and "How many?" Adjectives can come before nouns or can act as complements. **Complements** are words that describe subjects through linking verbs such as *is, are, was, have been,* and *will be.*

Before a noun:	The *rich* grocer sold his business.
	A *dark* cloud covered the sun.
As a complement:	Clarissa had been *rich.*
	The clouds were *dark.*

38.2 Learn to use participles.

Participles are adjectives formed from verbs. Participles end in *-d, -ed, -t, -en,* or *-ing.*

jump + ed = jumped
lose + t = lost

break + en = broken

roll + ing = rolling

Like other adjectives, participles can be used before or after the word they describe. They can also be connected to that word with linking verbs such as *are, was,* and *have been.*

A *rolling* stone gathers no moss.

Running, I tripped over your shoes.

The boy *walking* toward us is my brother.

The hikers are *lost.*

The students were *bored.*

CAUTION!

Use correct endings with participles.

Not:	He is use to us by now.
But:	He is used to us by now.
Not:	My aunt is not prejudice.
But:	My aunt is not prejudiced.
Not:	They drank ice tea with dinner.
But:	They drank iced tea with dinner.

38.3 Compare adjectives correctly.

Adjectives can be used to make comparisons. For example, if you compare three runners, you can say the first is *fast,* the second is *faster,* and the third is *fastest.* You can compare people or things with adjectives in three ways:

1. Add *-er* and *-est* to the basic form of single-syllable adjectives and adjectives that end in *-y.* Add *-er* when you are comparing *two* nouns or pronouns (comparative form). Add *-est* when you are comparing *more than two* (superlative form).

CAUTION!

With adjectives that end in *-y,* first change the *-y* to *-i; then* add *-er* or *-est.*

Basic form:	She is *young.*
Comparative form:	She is *younger* than I.
Superlative form:	She is the *youngest* of three sisters.

Basic	Comparative	Superlative
tall	taller	tallest
large	larger	largest
cold	colder	coldest
heavy	heavier	heaviest
busy	busier	busiest

Never add *-er* or *-est* when you use *more/most* or *less/least*.

Not: She is more faster than the other player.

But: She is faster than the other player.

2. Use *more/most, less/least.* Don't add *-er* or *-est* to adjectives of more than one syllable (with the exception of those ending in *-y*). Instead, use *more/most* or *less/least.*

Not: dangerous, dangerouser, dangerousest

But: dangerous, more dangerous, most dangerous

Basic	Comparative	Superlative
powerful	more powerful	most powerful
fattening	more fattening	most fattening
expensive	less expensive	least expensive

3. Change the spelling of **irregular adjectives.** Some adjectives don't fit the two methods just explained. They are irregular because they change their spellings (some even become new words) in the comparative and superlative forms.

Not: bad, badder, baddest

Not: bad, more bad, most bad

But: bad, worse, worst

Other Irregular Adjectives

Basic	Comparative	Superlative
many	more	most
little	less	least
good	better	best

EXERCISE 38A

Comparing Adjectives Correctly

On a separate piece of paper, rewrite the following sentences to correct adjective problems.

1. In area, Alaska is the larger of all fifty states in the United States.

2. According to the latest census, however, it has the most smallest population in the nation. In fact, it has even fewest inhabitants than Rhode Island, which is the smaller state in the country.

3. Locate in the northwest corner of North America, Alaska was first settled by people who traveled across the Bering Strait from Asia thousands of years ago.

4. The first Europeans in Alaska were Russians; they started one of the world's most earliest fur trades there.
5. The Russians sold Alaska to the United States in 1867, which seemed to some American politicians like one of the foolisher decisions the government had ever made. Few people thought Alaska was more valuabler than the $7 million it cost the United States.
6. They were wrong. Soon the territory experienced one of the greater gold rushes in history. By the turn of the century, people were flocking to Alaska pursuing their wilder dreams, in search of fortune and power.
7. Alaska's economy has always relied on the lumber, fishing, and mining industries. In 1968, however, oil and gas were discovered on the North Slope, raising great hopes for the economy and greatest fears for the environment.
8. The 1970s saw the opening of the Alaska pipeline, which carries oil from Prudhoe Bay to the port of Valdez. The discovery of oil has fired up the Alaska economy, creating many jobs. However, it also brought the worse environmental accident in U.S. history to Alaska's Prince William Sound.

38.4 Learn to identify adverbs.

Use adverbs—not adjectives—with verbs, adjectives, and other adverbs. **Adverbs** answer questions such as "When?" "Where?" "How?" "Why?" "Under what conditions?" and "To what extent?" Many adverbs—but not all—end in -*ly*. *Softly*, *fully*, and *quickly* are adverbs, but so are *well* and *very*.

Not:	She speaks soft and tender with children.
But:	She speaks softly and tenderly with children.
Not:	I did good on the last chemistry test.
But:	I did well on the last chemistry test.
Not:	The driver did not know how bad he was hurt.
But:	The driver did not know how badly he was hurt.

38.5 Compare adverbs correctly.

Like adjectives, adverbs can be used in comparisons. To compare adverbs that end in -*ly* (there are many of these), add *more/most* or *less/least* to the adverb.

Comparing Adverbs That End in -*ly*

Adverb	Comparative	Superlative
quickly	more quickly	most quickly
strangely	more strangely	most strangely
expertly	more expertly	most expertly
slowly	more slowly	most slowly

With adverbs that do not end in -*ly* (there are only a few of these), use the -*er* and -*est* endings or use *more/most* or *less/least*.

Comparing Adverbs That Do Not End in -*ly*.

Adverb	Comparative	Superlative
fast	faster	fastest
often	more often	most often

EXERCISE 38B

Using Adverbs Correctly

On a separate piece of paper, revise the following sentences to correct adverb problems.

1. In the Gettysburg Address, President Lincoln spoke brief and eloquent about the loss of American life in the Civil War. Although his speech contains only three paragraphs, it expresses his most deep held beliefs about this country, its people, and its government.
2. Nearly 50,000 soldiers from both the North and the South died in the four-day Battle of Gettysburg. Many thousands more were wounded bad. The men suffered terrible.
3. Five months after the battle, Lincoln went to Gettysburg to attend a ceremony dedicating the Civil War cemetery there. Some scholars believe he wrote his speech quick, on the back of an envelope, while traveling to Gettysburg on the train.
4. If that is true, we can only marvel at how easy Lincoln commanded words and how good he expressed his innermost feelings. Historians say that other speakers at the cemetery's dedication seemed to go on endless, for an hour or more. The president, on the other hand, spoke natural and sincere, for only a few minutes, but his speech is the one we remember and quote from most frequent.
5. Even today the Gettysburg Address communicates its message clear and powerful. And it sure serves as inspiration to all people who love liberty.

38.6 Use adjectives and adverbs with sense verbs.

Writers sometimes get confused when they use verbs such as *look, smell, sound, taste,* and *feel*, which relate to our physical senses. They might write

The taco didn't taste well.

But they really mean

The taco didn't taste good.

To avoid this problem, make sure you know what you are actually describing. In the example above, the taco—not the ability to taste—is being described. Because *taco* is a noun, an adjective, *good,* must be used. Here are more examples:

Not: I felt badly about the game.
But: I felt bad about the game.

The sentence above describes your feelings, not your sense of touch, so an adjective is needed.

Not: Miriam doesn't look well in brown.
But: Miriam doesn't look good in brown.

The sentence above describes Miriam's appearance, not her ability to see, so it calls for the adjective *good.*

Not: Miriam doesn't see good without glasses.
But: Miriam doesn't see well without glasses.

This sentence, on the other hand, describes Miriam's ability to see, so it calls for the adverb *well.*

CAUTION!

Using an adverb instead of an adjective can create a whole new meaning. Both of the following sentences are correct, but they have different meanings.

Adjective: Pete looked nervous.
Adverb: Pete looked nervously at the police officer.

The first sentence describes Pete; the second describes the way he looked at the officer.

Using Adjectives and Adverbs with Sense Verbs

Revise the following sentences to correct adjective and adverb problems. Write correct above items that need no revising.

1. The water in the pond smelled badly.
2. The politician looked fierce at his opponent.
3. No pie he bakes can taste well!
4. Chopin's music sounds sweetly.
5. The musicians looked tiredly.
6. That tie looks well on you.
7. I felt good about what she told me.
8. Our family felt badly about his leaving.
9. My parents looked around the house cautious.
10. The chicken in Ryan's Market always smells fresh.

EXERCISE 38C

On a separate piece of paper, rewrite the following student paragraphs to eliminate adjective and adverb problems.

1. Rowena felt bitterly about the fact that she hadn't been promoted. All along, her boss at the shoe store had told her she would be moving up soon and that customers liked her more better than any other salesperson. In fact, special training provide by the company was supposed to get her ready to become a supervisor. Then the promises of a promotion and raise seemed to get seriouser and seriouser. Rowena became even more surer that they were coming when the supervisor asked to speak with her. What a total disappointing meeting that was!

   When she was told that a raise was not possible because business was slowing down, Rowena's heart sank quick. To make matters worser, the supervisor explained that everyone's hours would have to be reduce. Of course, Rowena was complete depress, and she went home soonest than usual, looking a little sickly. Nonetheless, in her heart Rowena was certainly she would overcome this setback. She would apply herself more energetic than before. She would seek another job and show her new employers that she was the brighter, more hardworking salesperson they had ever known. That was ten years ago. Today Rowena owns her own shoe store!

2. Some people don't realize how easy their lives are until they meet someone least fortunate. I always used to complain that my life was hard. When our neighbors bought a new lawn mower, for example, I complained that we needed a new one, too, for cutting grass with that model would sure be more easier and faster than with ours. "Be thankful for what you have" was my parents' usually response.

   Then I met a school friend who looked differently from other students. Sometimes Divi wore clothes that were real old and out of style. He had emigrated from India a year before and was the only member of his family who spoke English fluent. As a result, he had an easiest time finding work than his father. In fact, among the three adults in his home who worked, he was the better provider. Of course, Divi sounded worried and tiredly whenever we talked; he was carrying a full academic load and worked hardly at a local bakery forty hours a week.

   After meeting Divi, I changed my attitude real quick. As far as I am concern, his life is definite more harder than mine. However, I still know many people whose lives are less demanding and stressfuller than mine. It's all a matter of perspective.

Parts of Speech

1 There are eight **parts of speech.**

 a. A **noun** names a person, place, or thing; it acts as a subject or an object.

 b. A **pronoun** takes the place of a noun.

 c. A **verb** shows action or helps describe a subject.

 d. The **articles**—*a, an,* and *the*—come before and point to nouns.

 e. An **adjective** modifies a noun or a pronoun.

 f. An **adverb** modifies a verb, an adjective, or another adverb.

 g. A **preposition** comes before a noun and shows how the noun relates to other words.

 h. A **conjunction** (coordinating or subordinating) joins words and ideas.

Verb Forms and Tenses

1 The **tense** of a verb shows time. There are three basic tenses: **past, present,** and **future.**

2 All forms of **regular verbs** in the present are spelled alike except the third-person singular, which ends in *-s.*

> **Not:** He/she/it/one run
>
> **But:** He/she/it/one runs.

3 The **irregular verb** *to be* changes its spelling in the present and the past tenses.

Present Tense

Singular	Plural
I am	We are
You are	You are
He/she/it/one is	They are

Past Tense

Singular	Plural
I was	We were
You were	You were
He/she/it/one was	They were

4 The **past tense** of a regular verb is formed by adding *-d* or *-ed.*

5. The **future tense** is formed by placing *will* or *am going to, is going to,* or *are going to* before a main verb.

6. The **perfect tenses** combine *has/have* (**present perfect**) or *had* (**past perfect**) with the **past participle.**

7. The **progressive tenses** combine a form of *to be* with the **present participle,** the *-ing* form of the verb.

8. You can keep verb tenses consistent by choosing one controlling tense and switching to others only when you describe actions that happen at other times.

9. **Linking verbs,** such as *be, am, were, become, feel, seem,* and *smell,* describe subjects by connecting them to nouns and adjectives. **Helping verbs** are used with other verbs to make specific time references and to create verb phrases.

10. **Irregular verbs** don't follow the rules that govern other verbs. Their past tenses have to be learned one by one.

11. The **passive voice** requires more words and is less direct than the **active voice.** Write in the **active voice** except when the agent is unknown, obvious, or unimportant.

12. The **indicative mood** of a verb conveys action or information that the writer believes is true. The **subjunctive mood** is used to convey information that is contrary to fact; it is also used to communicate a desire or wish. The **imperative mood** is used in commands and requests. The **conditional mood** conveys information that could be true depending on the circumstances. Conditional statements usually begin with the word *if* or with constructions that mean *if.*

Subject-Verb Agreement

1. Subjects agree with their verbs.
   a. Use singular (one) subjects with singular verbs; use plural (more than one) subjects with plural verbs. Most plural nouns end in *-s* or *-es.*
   b. Don't be confused by words that come between a subject and its verb.
   c. Use a plural verb with subjects joined by *and.*
   d. Use singular verbs with gerunds.
   e. Use singular verbs with subjects joined by *or, either . . . or,* or *neither . . . nor* if both subjects are singular. Use plural verbs if both are plural. If one subject is singular and the other plural, make the verb agree with the subject closer to it.
   f. If a pronoun such as *who, which,* or *that* is the subject of a verb, make the verb agree with that pronoun's antecedent.
   g. Use a singular verb if an indefinite pronoun such as *everyone* or *somebody* is the subject.
   h. If a sentence begins with *there* or *here,* look for the subject after the verb.
   i. If a subject follows a verb, read the entire sentence before you decide whether a singular or a plural verb is appropriate.

j. Use singular verbs with collective nouns if one group is named: use plural verbs if two or more groups are named.

Pronoun Types, Cases, and Reference

1. There are five types of pronouns: **personal, relative, indefinite, demonstrative,** and **reflexive.**

  a. **Personal** pronouns, such as *I, me,* and *my,* act as subjects, objects, and possessives.

  b. **Relative** pronouns, such as *that, which, who,* and *whom,* connect groups of words to nouns or other pronouns.

  c. **Indefinite** pronouns, such as *every, each,* and *someone,* refer to people or things that are not named or are not specific.

  d. **Demonstrative** pronouns, such as *that* and *those,* refer to nouns that follow.

  e. **Reflexive** pronouns, such as *herself* and *ourselves,* are used when a subject acts on itself. They also create emphasis.

2. Pronouns come in three cases. Depending on their purpose, they act as subjects, complements, objects, or possessives. Make sure you understand the pronoun's purpose before deciding on its case.

3. *Who, whom,* and *whose* can cause special problems. *Who* is subjective; *whom* is objective; *whose* is possessive. Don't confuse whose with the contraction *who's,* meaning "who is."

4. Choosing the correct pronoun after *than* or *as* depends on whether the pronoun is being used as a subject or an object.

5. Some beginning writers write *in which* when they mean *which.* Others write *this* when they mean *the, a,* or *an.* Don't fall into these traps.

6. Pronouns must refer, or point, to nouns clearly and directly. To check pronoun reference

  a. Make sure to include the noun to which the pronoun refers. This word should be the only noun to which the pronoun can point.

  b. Don't hide the noun in another term.

  c. Avoid using *it, they,* or *this* without a clear antecedent.

Pronoun-Antecedent Agreement

1. Pronouns agree with their antecedents.

  a. Use singular pronouns with singular antecedents, plural pronouns with plural antecedents.

  b. Use singular pronouns with nouns joined by *or, either . . . or,* or *neither . . . nor* if both nouns are singular; use plural pronouns if both nouns are plural. If one noun is singular and the other plural, make the pronoun agree with the noun closer to it.

c. Use a singular or plural pronoun to refer to a collective noun, depending on the sense of that noun.

d. Use singular pronouns to refer to *everyone, somebody,* and other indefinite pronouns.

2 Sexist pronouns can be avoided if you

a. Use both masculine and feminine pronouns.

b. Replace the pronoun with *a, an,* or *the.*

c. Replace a singular noun with a plural noun.

Adjectives and Adverbs

1 Adjectives modify (describe) nouns and pronouns. Adverbs modify verbs, adjectives, and adverbs. Participles are adjectives formed from verbs; they end in *-d, -ed, -t, -en,* or *-ing.*

2 Add *-er* when you compare *two* adjectives; add *-est* when you compare *more than two.*

3 In general, use *more/most* or *less/least* with adjectives of more than one syllable. Two-syllable words ending in *-y* are exceptions.

> **Not:** dangerous, dangerouser, dangerousest
>
> **But:** dangerous, more dangerous, most dangerous

4 Don't use *more/most* or *less/least* after you add *-er* or *-est* to an adjective.

> **Not:** more angrier/most angriest
>
> **But:** more angry/most angry
>
> **Or:** angrier/angriest

5 Don't use *more/most* with irregular adjectives.

> **Not:** I do more better at math than she.
>
> **But:** I do better at math than she.

6 When you compare adverbs:

a. Use *more/most* and *less/least* with adverbs ending in *-ly.*
They drove more carefully than we.
Of all the students, I am called on least frequently.

b. Add *-er* and *-est* to adverbs that do not end in *-ly,* or use *more/most* and *less/least.*
Sandra worked harder than the others.
Trains run less often on Sundays than on weekdays.

7 Before you decide to use an adjective or adverb with a verb of sense, such as *feel, taste,* and *look,* make sure you know what the sentence is actually describing.

11

PUNCTUATION, SPELLING, AND MECHANICS

11

PUNCTUATION, SPELLING, AND MECHANICS

MASTERING END PUNCTUATION

39.1 **Punctuate the four sentence patterns.**
39.2 **Use end punctuation with quotation marks.**

The punctuation mark used at the end of a sentence depends on the writer's purpose. A sentence can be declarative, interrogative, imperative, or exclamatory. Each of these four sentence patterns has its own end punctuation.

39.1 Punctuate the four sentence patterns.

1. A **declarative sentence** presents information. It ends with a period.

The Second World War ended in 1945.
Marilyn was on time for the audition.
Arturo bought a new car.

2. An **interrogative sentence** asks a question. It ends with a question mark.

Is there any more ice cream?
If the flight is delayed, when will we arrive in Omaha?

3. An **imperative sentence** gives an order, makes a request, or provides instruction. Use an exclamation point when the sentence gives an order. Otherwise, use a period to end an imperative sentence.

Get out of the way!
Please pass the mustard.
Turn right at the stop light, and drive up the hill.

> **CAUTION!**
> If an abbreviation appears at the end of a sentence, do not use a second period.
>
> Fred's job interview is scheduled for 10 a.m.

4. An **exclamatory sentence** expresses strong emotion. It ends with an exclamation point.

The accident victim gasped, "I can't breathe!"

Some exclamatory sentences have only one word.

Wow!   Stop!   Fire!

39.2 Use end punctuation with quotation marks.

1. **Periods** are always placed *inside* quotation marks.

According to former Speaker of the House Newt Gingrich, "The welfare state reduces the poor from citizens to clients."

2. **Question marks** and **exclamation points** are placed inside or outside quotation marks, depending on the sentence's meaning.

Inside: Robert asked me, "Have you read Thomas Sowell's *Inside American Education?*"

Don't end an *indirect* question with a question mark. An indirect question tells the reader what was asked in an earlier question.

Not:	He asked if I was ill?
But:	He asked if I was ill.

The part of the sentence in quotation marks is a question. However, the sentence itself is a statement; it tells what Robert asked. The question mark *applies only to the part that is quoted*, so it goes inside the quotation mark.

Outside: What did Martha mean when she said "I've bombed the Scholastic Aptitude Test"?

The part of the sentence in quotation marks is a statement. However, the sentence itself is a question. It asks what Martha meant. Therefore, the question mark *applies to the whole sentence*, so it goes outside the quotation mark.

CHAPTER WRAP-UP

Revise the following student paragraph to correct end punctuation.

An experience from which I learned a valuable lesson happened ten years ago. It was a beautiful Saturday when my grandfather bought me a new bike He called me to his room and said, "Before you take your new bike to go and play, I want to tell you something very important Don't lend your bike to anyone, especially strangers." When I heard his advice, I laughed and said, "Oh, don't worry, Grandpa, I won't." When I arrived at the park where my friends and I usually met to play together, they were all waiting to see my new bike One of the boys whom I didn't know so well walked toward me and said, "Can I borrow your bike for ten minutes" I said, "Yes" Then I gave it to him Two hours later I was still waiting, but he never came back Crying, I ran home and told my grandfather what had happened He looked at me with thunder in his eyes and screamed, "Didn't I warn you" Trembling, I ran to my room, closed the door, and began to sob In my mind, I kept thinking, "I hate that boy I hate that boy" From this experience I learned never to trust strangers and to listen to what older people tell me

MASTERING THE COMMA

When you speak, you can help make your meaning clear by pausing between words and phrases and by changing tone and pitch. Of course, these speaking clues are not available to you when you write, so you have to use punctuation marks to tell the reader *how* you want something to be read.

As you know, the period, question mark, and exclamation point are used to end sentences. Other marks of punctuation are used within sentences. The most common of these marks is the comma. It tells readers to pause briefly between words and groups of words, and it helps clarify meaning. Following are nine uses for the comma as well as a section on when *not* to use a comma.

40.1 Use commas with independent clauses and coordinating conjunctions.

An **independent clause** has a subject and a verb, and it expresses a complete idea. Use a comma between two independent clauses joined by a coordinating conjunction—*and, but, or, nor, for, yet,* or *so.*

> The hikers traveled for many hours, *and* they arrived tired.
>
> The legislature passed the bill, *but* the governor vetoed it.
>
> I have enough money, *for* I just got paid.
>
> Jeff had not eaten, *so* I offered him a sandwich.

NOTE

Place the comma *before* the coordinating conjunction, not after it.

Using Commas to Separate Independent Clauses

Each of the following items is a compound sentence that contains two independent clauses connected by a coordinating conjunction. Add commas in the right places.

1. Thomas Jefferson was opposed to the formation of political parties but he is credited as one of the founders of the party system in American politics.
2. Lech Walesa led the Solidarity labor movement in Poland and he became the first freely elected president of that nation.
3. Catherine the Great was born in Germany in 1729 yet she became one of Russia's greatest leaders.
4. Pegasus is the name given to the mythical winged horse and it is also the name of a constellation in the northern sky.
5. The Ndoki River is home to leopards, gorillas, elephants, and chimpanzees, some of which have never encountered human beings for the river is deep within the jungles of central Africa.

40.2 Use commas to set off introductory elements.

Use a comma to set off an introductory dependent clause, phrase, or word from an independent clause.

Introductory dependent clause:	*Because the state has budget problems,* many communities are faced with a loss of services.
Introductory phrase:	*Attempting to balance the budget,* the governor asked that the sales tax be increased.
Introductory word:	*However,* the legislature refused to go along with the increase.

Using Commas to Separate Introductory Elements

Place commas after introductory clauses, phrases, and words in the following sentences.

1. Second only to that of China India's population is now approaching one billion.
2. Created by the collision of a huge island with the Asian mainland more than 50 million years ago the Himalayas soar skyward over the northern frontiers of the Indian subcontinent.
3. When India won its independence from Britain in 1947 it was immediately partitioned into Hindu India and Muslim Pakistan, which consisted of two widely separated areas known as West Pakistan and East Pakistan (Bengal).
4. However because the Bengalis of East Pakistan believed that they were being denied the political and economic advantages enjoyed by West Pakistanis the Bengalis declared their independence in 1971 and established the independent nation of Bangladesh.
5. Having also been under British rule for several decades Burma, which is east of Bangladesh, received its independence in 1948.

40.3 Use commas to separate items in a series.

Use a comma to separate words, phrases, or clauses in a series.

Words: *People* magazine named Sean Connery, Mel Gibson, Mark Harmon, and Tom Cruise the "sexiest men alive."

Phrases: Western pioneers grew their own food, made their own clothing, and built their own homes.

Clauses: My father listens to classical music, I like jazz and bluegrass, and my sister loves rock.

> **NOTE** ◆◆◆◆◆
>
> You may leave out the comma before the final item in a series if you are sure readers will not misread the sentence. Whichever method you choose, be consistent.

Using Commas to Separate Items in a Series

Revise the following sentences by adding commas as necessary.

1. Although Buddhism was born in India in the sixth century B.C., it quickly spread to China Korea Japan and other parts of Asia.
2. Today, many countries have their social cultural religious and philosophical roots in the principles of Buddhism
3. Buddha, the founder of this major world religion, was named Siddhartha Gautama. Gautama is his family name Siddhartha is a name given to one who has reached a goal and Buddha means "the Enlightened One."
4. At age twenty-nine, Buddha, who was the son of a royal family, began to ponder human suffering illness and death. He gave up his life of wealth and power left his family and exiled himself from his kingdom.
5. Buddha wandered meditated and talked to others who were seeking a meaningful holy and ethical life. Soon he came to believe that human suffering results from the desire for pleasure and power that desire can and must be controlled and that the way to control desire is to follow the Noble Eightfold Path.
6. The Noble Eightfold Path consists of right views right intention right speech right action right work right effort right awareness and right concentration.

EXERCISE 40C

40.4 Use commas around nonessential elements.

Use commas around a word, phrase, or clause that adds information but is not essential to the meaning of the sentence.

Not essential: Chicago, *which is in Illinois,* was once destroyed by fire.

Which is in Illinois does not limit or change the meaning of Chicago; it only adds information about it.

Essential: The city *that I was born in* is Chicago.

That I was born in identifies the city you are writing about. Therefore, it is essential to the meaning of the sentence and should not be set off by commas.

Not essential: Aunt Jessie, *who learned to drive at thirteen,* wants to race stock cars.

Who learned to drive at thirteen simply tells us more about Aunt Jessie.

Essential: The woman *who drove us home* was Aunt Jessie.

Who drove us home limits the meaning of *woman* to a specific woman: Aunt Jessie. In other words, it identifies which woman *drove us home*.

An Easy Way to Decide Whether to Use Commas

If you can leave out the word, phrase, or clause without changing the meaning of the sentence, you can be sure you should use commas.

Word: Her husband, *Jim,* is an accountant.

Phrase: Jan Morrison, *our senior class president,* was given an academic scholarship.

Clause: My mother-in-law, *who is known for her love of children,* started the first day care center in Birmingham.

Try removing the words in italics. In each case, the meaning of the sentence does not change. Therefore, they should be set off by commas.

EXERCISE 40D

Using Commas Around Nonessential Elements

Add commas where necessary in the following items.

1. New York City originally called New Amsterdam was first settled by the Dutch.
2. The Taj Mahal a magnificent palace in India was built by a Mogul emperor.
3. Muhammad Ali born Cassius Marcellus Clay, Jr. is one of the world's best known and most respected professional athletes.
4. Michael Jordan probably the greatest player in professional basketball led the Chicago Bulls to several NBA championships.
5. The passenger pigeon a bird that was once very common has disappeared forever.

40.5 Use commas around nonrestrictive modifiers.

Nonrestrictive modifiers don't limit the meanings of the words they describe. **Restrictive modifiers,** on the other hand, limit the meanings of words they describe to a specific thing, place, individual, or group.

> **Nonrestrictive:**   Students, *who use the library free of charge,* must show their IDs.

Who use the library free of charge does not restrict the meaning of *students* to a particular group. It refers to all students.

> **Restrictive:**   Students *who study hard* should pass.

Here, *who study hard* is restrictive; this element limits the meaning of *students* to a particular group, those who study hard.

An Easy Way to Decide Whether to Use Commas
If the modifier can be removed without changing the meaning of the sentence, you can be sure you should use commas.

Using Commas to Separate Nonrestrictive Modifiers

Add commas where necessary in the following items. Write correct *for those items needing no additional commas.*

1. Women who rarely entered male-dominated professions before the 1970s are now becoming doctors, lawyers, and business executives in increasing numbers.
2. Women who work as hard as men at the same job should receive the same pay.
3. Joe DiMaggio who played baseball for New York in the 1950s was known as the "Yankee Clipper."
4. People who do not smoke and who are not overweight often qualify for reduced life insurance premiums.
5. Florida whose population continues to grow rapidly was once widely thought of only as a place to retire.

EXERCISE 40E

40.6 Use commas to set off sentence interrupters.

Sentence interrupters—including internal transitions, interjections, and words used in direct address—should be set off by commas.

> **Interrupter:**   He has reading problems, *they believe,* because he needs glasses.
>
> **Interrupter:**   Most people, *claims my father,* are worth knowing.

Transition:	For my family of seven, *on the other hand,* eating out is too expensive.
Interjection:	We walked for, *oh,* about two miles.
Word in direct address:	*Bob,* will this idea work?

Using Commas Around Sentence Interrupters

Add commas where they are needed in the following sentences.

1. The word *dinosaur* I have just read was coined by the British scientist Richard Owen. It comes from the Greek: *deinos* means "terrible," and *sauros* means "lizard."

2. The first reference to dinosaurs historians believe was made by Herodotus, the Greek historian, in the fifth century B.C.

3. Historians theorize that when Herodotus wrote about the bones of griffins, he was in fact describing the fossils of dinosaur bones and eggs that had been discovered in Asia. Griffins were mythological beasts—half lion and half eagle.

4. The Chinese dragon as a matter of fact may have its origins in the discovery of dinosaur bones. A Chinese manuscript dating from the third century A.D. makes reference to bones that may indeed be those of dinosaurs.

5. The dinosaurs became extinct claimed Luis and Walter Alvarez as a result of a gigantic meteorite's smashing into the earth 60 million years ago. Their extinction however was not a direct result of this catastrophe. The dinosaurs died the scientists speculated because the explosion sent up clouds of dust and ash, darkening the sky and in turn killing off vegetation on which the dinosaurs fed.

EXERCISE 40F

40.7 Use commas with names, degrees, titles, addresses, numbers, and dates.

Martin Luther King, Jr., was born in Atlanta, Georgia, and died in Memphis, Tennessee.

On July 12, 1991, Steven Cochran, M.D., using $25,000 that he borrowed from his parents, opened a practice at 198 Plaza Drive, Oklahoma City, Oklahoma.

Note that in numbers of four digits and longer (except years and street numbers), use commas to separate numbers into groups of three, starting from the right.

In 2004, the police issued 4,897 traffic summonses in our county.

Using Commas in Names, Degrees, Titles, Addresses, Numbers, and Dates

Add commas where they are needed in the following sentences.

1. The address of the White House is 1600 Pennsylvania Avenue Washington D.C.
2. Langston Hughes, an important African-American poet, was born in Joplin Missouri in 1902.
3. Union and Confederate soldiers fought the Battle of Antietam Creek, which is near Sharpsburg Maryland on September 17 1862. It was the single bloodiest day of the Civil War; the Union lost more than 2100 men, and the Confederacy lost 2700.
4. The Keck telescope is located on Maunu Kea Hawaii at a height of 13796 feet. It is the world's largest optical telescope.
5. Doris Dentum D.D.S. and Larry Lawsuit Esq. were married on July 15 1999.

40.8 Use commas to separate adjectives that describe the same noun.

When two or more adjectives come before a noun, you will have to decide whether or not to separate them with a comma. If you can insert *and* between two adjectives naturally, the adjectives should be separated by a comma. The adjectives in the following sentences are in italics.

They slept under a *warm, fluffy* quilt.

It would be perfectly natural to describe the quilt as *warm* and *fluffy*.

They slept on a *cold cement* floor.

These adjectives should not be separated by a comma; if you inserted *and* between them, the result would be an unnatural construction.

Using Commas to Separate Adjectives Before a Noun

Revise the following sentences by adding commas as necessary.

1. Mohammad, who lived in Mecca (a city in what is now Saudi Arabia) in the sixth century A.D., founded Islam, one of the world's largest most influential religions.
2. In A.D. 595, Mohammad married Khadijah, a beautiful resourceful widow who ran a well-known profitable caravan business and who helped him found his religion.
3. In A.D. 610, Mohammad heard Allah (God) calling him to prophesy, and he began teaching friends and family his innovative inspiring philosophy.

(continued)

4. However, his enemies in Mecca attacked his teachings and forced Mohammad and a group of devoted courageous followers to flee to Medina, an emigration now known as the Hegira.

5. After several military victories over his enemies, Mohammad returned with his followers to Mecca where they continued to spread the faith across North Africa and Asia, even to remote unknown lands such as Indonesia.

40.9 Use commas to make a sentence clearer.

As he was leaving, Tom said he would never return.

As he was leaving should be set off by a comma. Otherwise, readers might think, at least for a moment, that someone (*he*) was leaving Tom.

Sue claims Andrea is an expert gardener.

Sue, claims Andrea, is an expert gardener.

Both sentences are correct, but they mean different things. In the first, Sue claims Andrea is an expert gardener. In the second, Andrea claims Sue is the expert.

EXERCISE 40I

Using Commas to Make a Sentence Clearer

Add commas where they are needed in the following sentences.

1. In 1937 when the Japanese invaded China was in the middle of its own internal struggles, for the Nationalists led by Chiang Kai-Shek were fighting the Communists under Mao Tse-tung.

2. After divorcing his first wife Henry VIII of England married Anne Boleyn in 1533.

3. Believing the thirteen colonies were worth defending the British decided to use their overwhelming military power against the American rebels.

4. During the nineteenth century, when opposing armies fought their families and neighbors sometimes came out to watch the battle from nearby hillsides.

···· ···· **BASICLINK** ···· ····
WWW
For additional tips on using commas, visit
http://webster.commnet.edu/grammar/commas.htm

40.10 Learn when not to use a comma.

1. Do not use a comma to separate a subject and a verb.

Not: The Olympic champion, accepted the gold medal in fencing.

But: The Olympic champion accepted the gold medal in fencing.

Not: The city buried by the eruption of Mt. Vesuvius in 79 A.D., was Pompeii.

But: The city buried by the eruption of Mt. Vesuvius in 79 A.D. was Pompeii.

> **CAUTION!**
>
> As you learned earlier in this chapter, you should use *a pair of commas* when inserting a nonessential element between a subject and a verb.
>
> Eva Nescent, the girl he married, has a bubbly personality.

Don't fall into the trap of believing that a comma belongs after *79 A.D.* because you might pause at that spot when reading the sentence aloud. The subject of the sentence is *city;* the verb is *is. Buried by the eruption of Mt. Vesuvius in 79 A.D.* is simply a long adjective describing the *city.*

2. Do not use a comma to separate a verb and its direct object.

Not: The professor researched, the causes of the Whiskey Rebellion.

But: The professor researched the causes of the Whiskey Rebellion.

The verb is *researched;* the direct object is *causes.*

3. Do not place a comma *before* a clause that is introduced by a subordinate conjunction such as *after, although, because, if, since, unless, whenever, when,* and *while* unless it will make your writing clearer. You can learn more about subordinate conjunctions on page 454.

Not: Members of some ethnic groups resist assimilation, because they fear the loss of their cultural values.

But: Members of some ethnic groups resist assimilation because they fear the loss of their cultural values.

4. Do not place a comma *before* a prepositional phrase. Prepositional phrases begin with words such as *above, along, among, before, between, during, for, from, in, inside, into, over, through, to, upon,* and *with.* You can find a list of prepositions and prepositional phrases on pages 453–454.

Not: The city erected a new shelter, for homeless families.

But: The city erected a new shelter for homeless families.

Not: Marshall McLuhan (1911–1980), an expert in communications theory, became famous, during the 1960s.

But: Marshall McLuhan (1911–1980), an expert in communications theory, became famous during the 1960s.

5. Do not place a comma between two items joined by *and, but,* or *or* (unless they are main clauses).

Not: The mourners walked slowly, and wept bitterly as they followed the hearse.

But: The mourners walked slowly and wept bitterly as they followed the hearse.

EXERCISE 40J

Removing Incorrect Commas

Rewrite the following sentences by removing only the incorrect commas.

1. According to P. J. O'Rourke, "Giving money and power to government, is like giving whiskey and car keys to teenage boys."

2. The Maccabees, who are also referred to as the Hasmoneans, were a family of political and military leaders who fought against the Syrians, during the second, and first centuries B.C.

3. According to the law, you are not permitted to cast a ballot, unless you have registered to vote.

4. "All that is needed for evil to prevail, is for good men to do nothing," is a statement made by Edmund Burke, an eighteenth-century political philosopher.

CHAPTER WRAP-UP

Rewrite the following student paragraphs by adding or removing commas as needed. Be able to discuss the reasons for your changes.

1. When you first observe the Vietnam Memorial you are awestruck for words cannot describe the feeling. Nothing is spoken. You are overcome as you advance farther and farther along its length. It grows in size, from the first slab of marble which is only inches high, to the middle slab which measures nearly eleven feet, in height. The names of the fallen men and women, are carved, on a black cold lifeless wall. You reach out, and touch it ever so gently with your fingertips. The realization that 58,000 men and women lost their lives for their country, suddenly becomes too much to bear and a tear burns your skin as it races down your cheek. (Martin Burns, *The Wall*)

2. Growing up means a lot of "can'ts." You can't get mustard on your shirt. You can't giggle aloud or burp in a crowd. You can't walk in the rain, or step in a puddle you can't take the day off to pick up seashells on the beach and you can't take, your shirt off in the street to feel a warm breeze. You can't wish upon a star cross your heart walk atop a fence or hop along on one foot. You can't touch with innocence hug with warmth or kiss, a friend and you can't cry. Growing up means life is no longer simple, and not always good. Damn! I don't want to grow up. (Joseph Aliberti, *Growing Up*)

41

41.1 Use a semicolon between independent clauses.

41.2 Use a semicolon between independent clauses with a conjunctive adverb or transitional phrase.

41.3 Use a semicolon to separate items in a series when one or more items contain a comma.

As you learned in Chapter 40, the comma helps clarify meaning by telling readers to pause *briefly* between words and groups of words. The semicolon tells readers to pause a little longer; it is a stronger mark of punctuation than the comma. Semicolons are used primarily to separate clauses and phrases that are related and that receive equal emphasis.

41.1 Use a semicolon between independent clauses.

Place a semicolon between two independent clauses that are related and that are *not* connected by a coordinating conjunction.

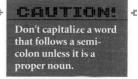

CAUTION!
Don't capitalize a word that follows a semicolon unless it is a proper noun.

The house was very old; it had been built in 1710.

The Scholastic Aptitude Test is widely used; each year more than a million students take it.

Using Semicolons to Separate Independent Clauses Not Joined by a Coordinating Conjunction

Each of the following sentences contains two independent clauses. Add semicolons in the right places.

1. In 1764, the British government passed the Sugar Act it required Americans to pay a tax on imported molasses.
2. When, in 1765, Parliament passed the Stamp Act, which taxed materials printed in America, the colonists complained bitterly they argued that the British were following a policy of "taxation without representation."

(continued)

3. British troops fired on a crowd of protesters in Boston in 1770 now known as the Boston Massacre, the incident resulted in the death of five colonists.

4. Three years later, several prominent citizens of Boston hosted a tea party at the expense of the British dressed as native Americans, they tossed a cargo of imported tea into the harbor to protest new importation taxes.

5. In 1774, the British passed the Intolerable Acts to punish the colonists their plans backfired when, in the First Continental Congress, the Americans recommended a boycott of all British goods.

6. Attempting to seize American arms at Lexington and Concord, Massachusetts, the British pushed the colonists to the brink of revolution meeting at the Second Continental Congress, the Americans established a continental army, led by George Washington.

7. On July 4, 1776, the American republic was born on that day representatives of the thirteen colonies approved the Declaration of Independence.

8. Today, Thomas Jefferson of Virginia is remembered as the Declaration's author nevertheless, credit for its contents must be given to other members of the Continental Congress as well.

41.2 Use a semicolon between independent clauses with a conjunctive adverb or transitional phrase.

A conjunctive adverb is used with a semicolon to connect two main (independent) clauses. It shows how the main clauses it connects relate to each other. A transitional phrase is a group of words that, like a conjunctive adverb, is used with a semicolon to connect two main clauses.

Conjunctive adverb:	Don't come late; *otherwise,* you will miss dinner.
	The prisoner hadn't eaten in three days; *nonetheless,* he refused the food a guard offered.
Transitional phrase:	In some schools, classes are small; *as a result,* teachers can give students individual attention.
	Eggplant is a popular vegetable; *as a matter of fact,* it is grown in many parts of the world.

CAUTION!
Use a comma after a conjunctive adverb or transitional phrase.

Here are some conjunctive adverbs and transitional phrases.

Conjunctive Adverbs	Transitional Phrases
accordingly	after all
consequently	all the same

finally	as a matter of fact
furthermore	as a result
however	even so
indeed	for example
moreover	for instance
nevertheless	in addition
otherwise	in fact
similarly	in other words
then	in reality
therefore	on the other hand
thus	to be specific

Using Semicolons Between Independent Clauses with a Conjunctive Adverb or Transitional Phrase

Each sentence below contains two independent clauses. Add semicolons and commas where they are needed.

1. The *Titanic* was designed to be unsinkable nevertheless it sank on its maiden voyage.
2. Tiring of his creation, Sir Arthur Canon Doyle killed Sherlock Holmes in what should have been his final adventure however in later stories he brought Holmes back to life.
3. Richard and John Plantagenet were medieval English kings as a matter of fact they were the sons of King Henry II.
4. John Ciardi is famous for his translation of Dante's *Divine Comedy* in addition his own poetry has received critical recognition.

EXERCISE 41B

41.3 Use a semicolon to separate items in a series when one or more items contain a comma.

At a recent seminar, we heard Reginald Mack, a district attorney, speak on victims' rights; Maria Mendoza, a professor of law, speak on the court system; and Olaf Christian, a police officer, speak on gun control.

This list contains three items, each beginning with a person's name. If the semicolons that now separate these items were replaced by commas, readers might have difficulty telling where one item ends and the next begins because each item already contains commas of its own.

Using Semicolons to Separate Items in a Series That Contains Commas

Each sentence below contains items in a series that has internal punctuation. Add semicolons where they are needed.

1. Around the turn of the century, Thomas Edison frequently went on camping trips with John Burroughs, the naturalist Henry Ford, the automobile manufacturer and Harvey Firestone, the rubber manufacturer.
2. When in Quebec City, be sure to visit the Citadel, an impressive fortress where one can see the changing of the guard the Rue de Notre Dame, the oldest street in the city dating from 1615 the Chateau Frontenac, an elegant hotel modeled on the chateaus of France and the Plains of Abraham, a battlefield where the British defeated the French in 1759 during the French and Indian War.
3. Shakespeare's plays fall into three categories: histories, such as *Henry IV* Parts I and II, *Henry V*, and *Richard III* comedies such as *Love's Labour's Lost, Twelfth Night,* and *As You Like It* and tragedies such as *Hamlet, King Lear,* and *Romeo and Juliet.*

Semicolons have been removed from this student essay. Correct it by putting in semicolons where necessary.

Many people have the misconception that poker is a game of great skill and know-how. This is not true. Poker consists of two things: luck of the draw and body language. The luck of the draw means you are stuck with whatever cards you are dealt you just have to make the best of it. However, this is only a minor part of the game body language is the most important part.

Body language can mean the difference between winning and losing. The guidelines are basically very simple: always keep your cool, even under the most stressful circumstances, and always look as if you have four aces, even when all you have is a pair of deuces.

Another thing to remember about body language is that the other players are using it too, usually without even knowing it. There are three types of players: the sloucher, the grinner, and the fidgeter. The sloucher will slouch low in his chair and keep his eyes constantly on his cards in reality he has nothing and will fold if the bet is raised. The grinner will sit comfortably in his chair, with his cards closed, and tap them on the table to throw off the other players' concentration in addition he will have a smug and confident grin on his face. But like the sloucher, he will have nothing in his hand he is bluffing.

The last type, the fidgeter, is the hardest to detect. He will casually look at the other players, looking for any of the aforementioned types of body language. He will move around in his chair, trying to get comfortable in addition he will frequently cough, sigh, or clear his throat. He is the most dangerous player of the three because he will lead you to believe that he has a terrible hand. This will give you a false sense of security and cause you to bet the house then he will strike with a superior hand and take your money. If you watch for the not-so-obvious telltale signs of the other players' positions, you will have no trouble winning however if all else fails . . . CHEAT! (Felix Shvartsman)

MASTERING THE COLON

42.1 Use a colon to separate independent clauses.

42.2 Use a colon to introduce information after an independent clause.

42.3 Use a colon to introduce a quotation.

42.4 Use a colon in the salutation of a business letter.

The colon is a mark of punctuation used inside a sentence to clarify meaning or create emphasis. The colon points to or introduces information that follows.

42.1 Use a colon to separate independent clauses.

Thomas Jefferson had a distinguished career in public service: he was the principal author of the Declaration of Independence, served as the third president of the United States, and founded the University of Virginia.

The second clause makes clear what the writer meant by *distinguished career in public service.*

42.2 Use a colon to introduce information after an independent clause.

Such information can be expressed in one word or phrase, or it may come in a list.

Goldie's Café serves my favorite dish: Hungarian goulash.

Hungarian goulash names the writer's favorite dish.

You will need two tools to assemble the wagon: a screwdriver and a wrench.

Screwdriver and *wrench* name the two tools.

Please do the following: Write your name at the top, mark your answers in the left column, and complete all fifty questions.

> **CAUTION!**
>
> Don't use a colon to separate direct objects or complements from verbs.
>
> **Not:** She carried: a saw, a hammer, and a drill.
> **But:** She carried a saw, a hammer, and a drill.
>
> *Carried* is the verb; *saw, hammer,* and *drill* are its direct objects.
>
> **Not:** He is: a good speller but a bad typist.
> **But:** He is a good speller but a bad typist.
>
> *Speller* and *typist* are complements of the verb *is.*

The colon introduces a list, which names things the reader is asked to do in the independent clause.

An Easy Way to Decide Whether to Use a Colon

Try substituting the word *namely* for a colon that introduces information after an independent clause. If the sentence still makes sense, the colon is correct. For example, one of the sentences above might read: *Goldie's Café serves my favorite dish, namely, Hungarian goulash.*

42.3 Use a colon to introduce a quotation.

The first amendment to the United States Constitution states: "Congress shall make no law respecting an establishment of religion, or prohibiting the free exercise thereof."

42.4 Use a colon in the salutation of a business letter.

Dear Professor Johnson:

:: CHAPTER WRAP-UP

Rewrite the following sentences by inserting or deleting colons.

1. We visited four Asian nations India, Pakistan, Nepal, and Sri Lanka.
2. My father took with him my stability and my security he disappeared when I was two years old.
3. Consider three important factors when purchasing a home location, location, and location.
4. Sports logos and emblems: have become status symbols among some young people.
5. A driver's license is not just a document it is a ticket to freedom.
6. In the past few years, computer technology has introduced several new terms to the language Internet, World Wide Web, e-mail, and FAQ.
7. The First World War gave birth to three new instruments of mass destruction the tank, the airplane, and poison gas.
8. In a way, Napoleon helped spread democracy across Europe his armies carried the ideals of the French Revolution to the countries they conquered.
9. The choir sang the minister's favorite song "Amazing Grace."
10. Expressing his faith in democracy, the speaker quoted Lincoln's Gettysburg Address "government of the people, by the people, for the people shall not perish from the earth."

MASTERING THE APOSTROPHE

Apostrophes show possession:

Richard's book

the teacher's desk

the store's merchandise

An apostrophe is also used to create special relationships between words. For example, you should use an apostrophe in *a night's sleep*, and in *two months' pay*. Strictly speaking, of course, *sleep* doesn't belong to the *night*, and the *pay* doesn't belong to the *months*. All the same, an apostrophe is required in such cases. Following are some rules for using apostrophes.

43.1 Use apostrophes with nouns.

1. Add -'s if the noun does not end in -s.

   Robert's license was taken away after he was arrested.

   The hospital's emergency room was crowded.

   The children's shoes were expensive.

>
> ✛ **CAUTION!** ✛
>
> If the pronunciation of a word with the added -'s seems awkward, some writers add only the apostrophe.
>
> Wallace Stevens' poetry is interesting.

2. Add -'s if the noun is singular and ends in -s.

   The bus's door jammed.

   James's book is missing.

3. Add only an apostrophe if the noun is plural and ends in -s.

   The mountains' peaks were not visible.

   The senior citizens' benefits were increased.

   The Greeks' plan was to enter Troy by hiding in a large wooden horse.

4. In a series of nouns, add -'s only to the last noun to show joint possession. Add -'s to *each* noun to show individual possession.

Joint: Groucho, Chico, and Harpo's films get high marks from movie fans.

                      Gary and Carol's divorce was final.

Individual: Angela's and Michael's study habits are different.

                      Boston's and San Francisco's waterfronts are very interesting, but I prefer Seattle's.

43.2 Use apostrophes in contractions.

Use the apostrophe in contractions to take the place of omitted letters or numbers.

Because it's raining, we can't go to the park.

It's = *it is;* can't = *cannot.*

He wouldn't have minded living in the '20s.

Wouldn't = *would not;* '20s = *1920s.*

43.3 Use apostrophes with abbreviations, numbers, and letters.

Add -'s to abbreviations that end in periods, to numbers used as numbers, and to letters used as letters to make them plural.

Bartenders check people's I.D.'s before serving them.

Carmen hit two 777's in a row on the slot machine.

Syed received three A's and two B's as final grades.

■ ■ ■ ■   ■ ■ ■ ■   **B A S I C L I N K**   ■ ■ ■ ■   ■ ■ ■ ■
WWW

For additional tips on using apostrophes, visit
http://owl.english.purdue.edu/handouts/grammar/g_apost.html

■ ■   ■ ■   ■ ■   ■ ■   ■ ■   ■ ■   ■ ■   ■ ■   ■ ■   ■ ■   ■ ■   ■ ■

Insert an apostrophe and/or -'s where needed in the following items.

1. The Abominable Snowman is a mythological creature, sightings of which have been reported in Nepal and other parts of Asia. However, stories of such "wild men" exist in many cultures. Canadas Sasquatch, Britains Grendel, and the United States own Bigfoot are just a few examples.
2. William F. Cody occupies an interesting place in Americas mythology. Today, hes known as Buffalo Bill.
3. Todays goat is often yesterdays hero.
4. The Greeks philosophy of government has influenced modern political thinkers.
5. Some of the Romans aqueducts carry water even to this day.
6. The pyramids builders were not slaves but paid laborers.
7. An agreement to disarm every ICBMs warhead was signed by representatives of the two nations.
8. Ama Ata Aidoo (1942–) is one of Ghanas most important novelists and poets. She studied at both the University of Ghana and Californias Stanford University.
9. Among South Africas eleven official languages are Zulu, Xhosa, Sesotha, Tsonga, Afrikaans, and English.
10. Louis Armstrongs lack of a formal education did not stop him from becoming one of the jazz worlds greatest stars.
11. Some people claim that loyalty to ones employer and pride in ones work have been replaced by apathy and carelessness.
12. C. S. Lewis works include the *Chronicles of Narnia,* a series of childrens books; *Out of the Silent Planet,* the first volume of the authors science fiction trilogy; and *The Screwtape Letters,* in which Lewis exposes the devils vanity and stupidity.
13. Women who dont get regular breast exams run a significant risk. Known as a mammogram, the test is a kind of X ray. Mammographys chief advantage is that it can detect tumors too small to feel.
14. The full title of Lewis Carrols most famous work is *Alices Adventures in Wonderland.*
15. In the 1300s, plague, flood, famine, and war destroyed much of Europes population.

44

MASTERING QUOTATION MARKS

Quotation marks enclose words, phrases, and sentences that are *directly* quoted. They also enclose titles of short poems, essays, short stories, and songs. Quotation marks are always used in pairs.

44.1 Use quotation marks for direct quotations.

> **CAUTION!**
>
> Don't put quotation marks around an *indirect* quotation.
>
> **Not:** She said that "she was going to the party."
>
> **But:** She said that she was going to the party.

Our college president said: "I am going to build a school the football team can be proud of."

Bertrand Russell wrote that three passions controlled his life: "the longing for love, the search for knowledge, and unbearable pity for the suffering of mankind."

44.2 Use single quotation marks to enclose a quotation within a quotation.

JoAnne said, "I told Jane, 'Don't swing on that branch,' but she ignored me and fell from the tree."

"I didn't believe Ralph when he claimed that 'the check is in the mail,' " Jerry said.

> **CAUTION!**
>
> Commas and periods are always placed *inside* quotation marks. Colons and semicolons are always placed *outside* quotation marks.
>
> Marianne Moore wrote the poem "Birds and Fishes"; Elizabeth Bishop wrote the poem "The Fish."

44.3 Use quotation marks in titles.

Use quotation marks around titles of articles (in magazines, journals, and newspapers), short poems, short stories, essays, songs, and episodes of television programs.

B. R. Jerman wrote an article called "Browning's Witless Duke."

It is about Robert Browning's poem "My Last Duchess."

She read Kate Chopin's "The Story of an Hour."

Michael Bolton wrote the hit song "We're Not Makin' Love Anymore."

"Who Shot J. R.?" was the most widely watched episode of *Dallas.*

Place quotation marks where they are needed in the following sentences.

1. One reason the Egyptians were able to develop a sophisticated system of farming, claimed my history professor, was the annual flooding of the Nile River, which deposited millions of tons of fertile silt on surrounding areas.

2. He loved the short stories of Eudora Welty, especially A Worn Path, Why I Live at the P.O., and The Wide Net.

3. In an article entitled Are Today's Suburbs Really Family Friendly? Karl Zinsmeister said: The best foundation for strong community life is regular personal contact among residents.

4. I wasn't sure what his response would be when I screamed Bill, you don't know what you're talking about, Annie said, but by that time I really didn't care.

5. Her favorite poem by Stephen Crane is War Is Kind.

45

MASTERING OTHER MARKS OF PUNCTUATION

45.1 Use ellipses and brackets.

An **ellipsis** is three spaced periods (. . .) that indicate you have removed words from a direct quotation.

> According to one critic, "the director was not allowed . . . to edit the film's final version."

The original quotation read: "The director was not allowed by the studio to edit the film's final version." When using an ellipsis in this way, be careful not to change the meaning of the original statement. Also, be certain that the remaining parts of the quotation read smoothly and do not contain any grammatical breakdowns.

If you omit the final part of a quotation, add a period before the ellipsis.

> When announcing his candidacy for president in 1968, Senator Robert Kennedy said: "I run not to oppose any man but to propose new policies. I run because I feel that our nation is on a perilous course, and I feel obliged to do all that I can. For these are not ordinary times. . . ."

Brackets ([/]) are used around words you have inserted within a direct quotation.

> According to one critic, "the director [Spike Lee] was not allowed by the studio to edit the film's final version."

45.2 Use dashes.

The **dash** is typed as two hyphens (--) with no space before or after them.

1. Use a dash to set off material that needs emphasis.

> Cats are very friendly and affectionate pets—when they want to be.
>
> The languages that Andrea studied—all three of which required that she learn new alphabets—were Arabic, Hebrew, and Russian.

2. Use a dash to clarify an idea. (In formal prose, use a colon.)

> You have a choice—obey the rules or get kicked out.

3. Use a dash to separate a list from an independent clause at the start or end of a sentence.

> *Star Wars, The Empire Strikes Back,* and *Return of the Jedi*—these are his favorite movies.
>
> Mayonnaise contains three ingredients—egg yolks, vegetable oil, and vinegar.

45.3 Use parentheses.

Words that appear within **parentheses** interrupt the flow of the sentence, but the interruption is less forceful than it is when dashes are used.

1. Use parentheses to set off words that emphasize or specify.

> Modern life (especially for the young) is filled with anxieties and questions.
>
> His cars (Lincolns, LTDs, and Cadillacs) always cost more than he could afford.

2. Use parentheses to set off explanatory sentences within sentences.

> Hell's Canyon (it is well named) is not a good place to go camping.

Note that the first word of a parenthetical sentence within a sentence is not capitalized unless that word is a proper noun or adjective.

3. Use parentheses to enclose brief definitions.

> We placed an anemometer (an instrument to measure wind speed) on the roof.

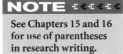

NOTE

See Chapters 15 and 16 for use of parentheses in research writing.

4. Use parentheses to enclose numbers or letters before items in a list.

> Before leaving, she (1) canceled the newspaper delivery, (2) asked the post office to hold her mail, and (3) set the timer on the living room lights.

Correct errors in ellipses, brackets, dashes, and parentheses in the following paragraph.

A Christmas Carol, Oliver Twist, and *Great Expectations* these were three of the novels written by Charles Dickens that were Dorothy's favorites. Being the romantic she was, however, her favorite one of all of Dickens's novels was *A Tale of Two Cities.* The two cities were Paris and London, and the story takes place during the French Revolution. The book's opening line, "It was the best of times, it was the worst of times," is now considered a classic. The novel's main characters are Dr. Manette, his daughter Lucie, Charles Darnay, and Sydney Carton. At the end of the novel, Carton, who resembles Darnay, sacrifices himself by taking Darnay's place on the scaffold and utters the famous words: "It is a far, far better thing that I do, than I have ever done; it is a far, far better rest that I go to, than I have ever known."

:: CHAPTER WRAP-UP

46

IMPROVING YOUR SPELLING

Most experienced writers don't worry unnecessarily about spelling in the early stages of writing. They correct spelling and other mechanical problems as they edit and proofread.

46.1 Use *i* before *e* except after *c*.
46.2 Add an ending to a word that ends in -*y*.
46.3 Add -*able*, -*ed*, or -*ing* to a word that ends in a consonant.
46.4 Make nouns plural.
46.5 Spell irregular nouns correctly.
46.6 Spell contractions correctly.
46.7 Spell frequently misspelled words correctly.

Nonetheless, spelling is important. In view of all the work that goes into writing a paper, you owe it to yourself to be careful. Above all, be honest with yourself. If you aren't absolutely sure that you have spelled a word correctly, look it up in the dictionary. Of course, you may have a little trouble finding it if you aren't sure how it begins. But stick with it; your hard work will pay off.

The best way to improve spelling is to read a lot and be attentive to new or difficult words. You might even want to keep a list of such words in a notebook or journal or on the blank pages of this book. In the meantime, here are some hints to help you improve your spelling.

46.1 Use *i* before *e* except after *c*.

CAUTION!

Don't expect a computer spell checker to catch all errors. For example, it won't help you spell proper nouns, nor will it help if you have confused such words as *their* and *there* or *to*, *two*, and *too*. And a spell checker won't catch typing errors such as writing *fun* when you mean *fan*.

Keep *i* before *e* except after *c* or when it sounds like *ay*, as in *neighbor* and *weigh*.

i **before** *e*:	achieve, believe, friend, mischief, relieve, tries, siege
After *c*:	ceiling, deceive, perceive, receive
Sounded like *ay*:	neighbor, sleigh, weigh, vein
Exceptions:	ancient, conscience, counterfeit, either, foreign, leisure, seize, weird

EXERCISE 46A

Using *ie* or *ei*

Insert the missing letters—either ie or ei—in the following words:

retr____ve   gr ____ f   sl ____ gh   f ____ ld   c ____ ling

anc ____ nt   n ____ ce   perc ____ ve   n ____ ther   s ____ ze

w ____ ght   v ____ n   f ____ nd   w ____ ld   bel ____ ve

46.2 Add an ending to a word that ends in -y.

When adding an ending to a word that ends in *-y*, first change the *-y* to *-i* if the *-y* comes after a consonant (that is, any letter except *a, e, i, o, u*).

cry + ed = cried   beauty + ful = beautiful

fly + er = flier   penny + less = penniless

try + es = tries   happy + ness = happiness

But keep the *-y* if it comes after a vowel (*a, e, i, o, u*).

delay + ed = delayed   monkey + s = monkeys

And always keep the final *-y* in a word when you add *-ing:*

cry + ing = crying   defy + ing = defying

EXERCISE 46B

Adding Endings to Words That End in -y

Add the endings shown to the words in the following list:

play + ful = _____   rely + ed = _____   enjoy + ed = _____

marry + ing = _____   qualify + es = _____   horrify + es = _____

relay + ed = _____   comply + ed = _____   pry + es = _____

lay + ing = _____   sturdy + er = _____   reply + ing = _____

pity + ful = _____   mercy + less = _____   lovely + ness = _____

deny + es = _____   fry + ed = _____   vary + ed = _____

try + ing = _____   fly + er = _____   buy + ing = _____

apply + ed = _____   marry + es = _____   carry + es = _____

(continued)

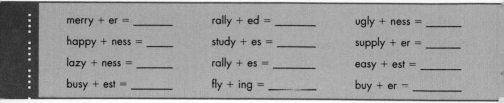

merry + er = _____   rally + ed = _____   ugly + ness = _____

happy + ness = _____   study + es = _____   supply + er = _____

lazy + ness = _____   rally + es = _____   easy + est = _____

busy + est = _____   fly + ing = _____   buy + er = _____

46.3 Add -able, -ed, or -ing to a word that ends in a consonant.

When you add -able, -ed, or -ing to a word that ends in a consonant, you often double that consonant.

hop + ing = hopping   hope + ing = hoping
scar + ed = scarred   **BUT**   scare + ed = scared

If the final -e in a word is not pronounced, drop that -e when you add an ending that begins with a vowel.

wave + ing = waving   fame + ous = famous
remove + able = removable

But keep the -e when you add an ending that begins with a consonant.

love + less = loveless   **Exceptions:**   awe + ful = awful
pave + ment = pavement   true + ly = truly
time + ly = timely   die + ing = dying

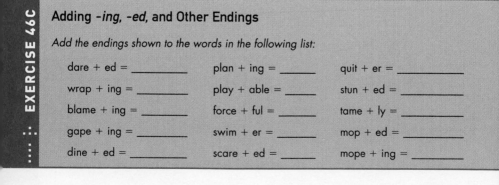

EXERCISE 46C

Adding -ing, -ed, and Other Endings

Add the endings shown to the words in the following list:

dare + ed = _____   plan + ing = _____   quit + er = _____

wrap + ing = _____   play + able = _____   stun + ed = _____

blame + ing = _____   force + ful = _____   tame + ly = _____

gape + ing = _____   swim + er = _____   mop + ed = _____

dine + ed = _____   scare + ed = _____   mope + ing = _____

46.4 Make nouns plural.

1. In general, add -s or -es.

automobile/automobiles   bench/benches
bank/banks   class/classes

2. Form the plural of an abbreviation that is written without periods by adding -s.

CDs   BTUs
PIAs   VCRs

3. If a noun ends in a -y that follows a consonant, change the -y to -i and add -es. This rule does not apply to proper names, however.

country/countries   party/parties
glory/glories   the three Marys

4. If the y follows a vowel, just add -s.

attorney/attorneys   monkey/monkeys
day/days

5. In general, if a word ends in -f, or -fe, change the ending to -v and add -es.

knife/knives   **Exceptions:**   roof/roofs
wife/wives   belief/beliefs
half/halves

6. Add -s to some words that end in -o, -es to others.

piano/pianos   tomato/tomatoes
solo/solos

> **CAUTION!**
>
> The plural of *hero* is *heros* or *heroes*.
>
> heros = long sandwiches
> heroes = brave people

When in doubt about -os and -oes endings—or any others—check the dictionary.

7. To form the plural of a term consisting of two or more words, whether or not they are joined by hyphens, add -s or -es to the first noun in the group.

attorneys general
sisters-in-law
attorneys-at-law
editors-in-chief

46.5 Spell irregular nouns correctly.

Irregular nouns don't follow the above rules. Some change their spellings in the plural.

    child/children
    woman/women
    tooth/teeth
    ox/oxen

Some are spelled the same in the plural as in the singular.

    deer/deer
    fish/fish

Check the dictionary if you have doubts about how to spell such plurals.

EXERCISE 46D

Forming Plurals

Write the plurals of the following words:

earring _____   donkey _____

room _____   journey _____

gentleman _____   duty _____

officer _____   company _____

mother-in-law _____ chef _____

wife _____   sheep _____

belief _____   cargo _____

self _____   cupful _____

city _____   county _____

library _____   story _____

series _____   leaf _____

doctor of medicine _____   shelf _____

46.6 Spell contractions correctly.

Contractions join two words into one with an apostrophe.

can + not = can't   it + is = it's

will + not = won't   they + are = they're

An Easy Way to Decide How to Spell Contractions
Just remember that, with the exception of *won't*, the apostrophe takes the place of an omitted letter or letters.

CAUTION!

In contractions made with *not*, the apostrophe comes between the *n* and the *t*.

Not	But
could'nt	couldn't
should'nt	shouldn't
are'nt	aren't
were'nt	weren't

46.7 Spell frequently misspelled words correctly.

46.7a Misspellings caused by mispronunciations

Failing to pronounce words correctly often leads to misspellings. Here are some examples:

almost *not* almos	irrelevant *not* irrevalent	perspiration *not* persperation
athletics *not* athaletics	laboratory *not* labratory	
candidate *not* cannidate	length *not* lenth	prescription *not* perscription
constant *not* constent	library *not* liberry	
department *not* departmen	lightning *not* lightening	probably *not* probly
	mathematics *not* mathmatics	publicly *not* publically
disastrous *not* disasterous	mischievous *not* mischievious *or* mischefous	September *not* Setember
drowned *not* drownded		specific *not* pecific
February *not* Febuary		strength *not* strenth
height *not* heighth	October *not* Ottober	
interest *not* intrest		

46.7b Other frequently misspelled words

absence

absent

accommodate

acquaintance

acquire

aggravate

alcohol

all right *not* alright

analyze

apart *not* a part

argument *not* arguement

assistance

attention

beginning

belief

believe

benefit

benefited

between

calendar *not* calender

changeable *not* changable

coming *not* comming

condemn *not* condem

conscience

conscious

convenience *not* convience

deer *not* deers

definite *not* definate

dependent *not* dependant

develop *not* develope

don't *not* do'nt

embarrassed *not* embarased

environment *not* enviroment

equipment *not* equiptment

escape *not* excape

example

exercise

existence *not* existance

explanation *not* explaination

foreign

forty *not* fourty

fourth

government *not* goverment

grammar *not* grammer

happiness *not* hapiness

however *not* how ever

imaginary

immediately

knives *not* knifes

license *not* lisence

magnificent

maintenance *not* maintainence

marriage *not* marrige

mature

necessary *not* necessery

occasionally

occur

occurred

occurrence

paid *not* payed

parallel *not* parellel

perform *not* preform

personal

personnel

precede

preferred *not* prefered

proceed *not* procede

recede *not* receed

refer

referring

separate *not* seperate

sophomore *not* sophmore

succeed

surrender

terrible

terror

their

there

they're

tragedy *not* tradgedy

truly *not* truely

until *not* untill

usually *not* usualy

vacuum *not* vacum

valuable *not* valueable

·· ·· ·   ·· ·· ·   BASICLINK   ·· ·· ·   ·· ·· ·

WWW

To look at an extensive list of commonly misspelled or misused words, visit
http://www.wsu.edu/~brians/errors/

·· ·· ·· ·· ·· ·· ·· ·· ·· ·· ·· ··

Revise the following student paragraphs to correct errors in spelling:

1. When people become alcaholics, they surender to a substence as powerful as any narcotic, and thier lives take on tradgic dimensions. From the day they get hooked, thier lives slowly fall a part. They begin to lose freinds and family, they become isolated from nieghbors, and they aleinate co-workers. My cousin is an esample; he is totaly controled by alcahol. Almos every member of our family has tryed to help him, but he has disregaurded our warninges and has even become angry with his mother. His moods are so changable and he is so easily irritated that he has been forgoten by the people who were once closest to him.

2. Cocaine destroyes the body and the mind. Over the course of her addiction, a classmate of mine has lost fourty-five pounds. She is only twenty-seven, but she looks like a sixty-five-year-old, having aged prematurly because of lack of nutreints in her deit. She had been homeless untill only recently. When she first left homo, she lived in a box under an anceint tree. Then she learnd she qualifyed for public assistents and, fortuntly, was able to move into a one-bedroom apartment in an old building owned by the county goverment.

3. Okra is a plant with stickey green pods that is used in soups and stews. When okra is fryed, its stickeyness decreases, but I have never liked it. In fact, I hate okra; its just too slimey. It constently slides off your fork while you're triing to eat it. One Thanksgiving, as twenty-one of us sat a round the table, Grandma placed a giant bowl of okra between the two turkies we had carved. Unfortunly, it looked edible, even tastey. Upon puting it into my mouth, how ever, I felt as if I had swallowed a huge glob of mucous, and I just could'nt eat any more. I spit it out all most immediatly. That was the first and last time I even considered eating this snail-like substence.

47

USING THE HYPHEN

Listed below are four general rules for using the hyphen. Remember, however, to check the dictionary whenever you have doubts about whether a hyphen belongs in a word.

47.1 Use hyphens to join words that work together to describe a noun.

47.2 Use hyphens to connect prefixes to capitalized words.

47.3 Use hyphens to connect prefixes such as *all-*, *ex-*, *pro-*, and *self-*.

47.4 Use hyphens with numbers from twenty-one to ninety-nine.

47.1 Use hyphens to join words that work together to describe a noun.

Note that the words are hyphenated when they come before, but not when they follow, the noun.

Hyphen	No Hyphen
a six-room house	a house with six rooms
a fire-prevention class	a class on fire prevention
a well-kept garden	a garden that is well kept
opening-night jitters	jitters on opening night
a six-inch diameter	a diameter of six inches
the Dallas-Houston bus	the bus between Dallas and Houston

47.2 Use hyphens to connect prefixes to capitalized words.

pre-Columbian
un-American
pro-Canadian
pre-Civil War

47.3 Use hyphens to connect prefixes such as *all-*, *ex-*, *pro-*, and *self-*.

all-knowing

ex-mayor

pro-family

self-doubt

In most cases, however, prefixes are attached to words without hyphens.

antifreeze

prenatal

midyear

nonbinding

ongoing

postoperative

untidy

47.4 Use hyphens with numbers from twenty-one to ninety-nine.

Fifty-five students enrolled in Professor Ryan's class.

CHAPTER WRAP-UP

Rewrite the following sentences by inserting or removing hyphens as needed:

1. Early nineteenth century America gave rise to many reform-movements aimed at improving society.
2. Abraham Lincoln was born in a one room cabin in Kentucky in 1809.
3. In the late 1940s, the Marshall Plan provided economic aid to post war Europe.
4. As the USS *Constitution* sailed from its berth in Boston Harbor, a twenty one gun salute was heard in the distance.
5. Bob Hope once played Jimmy Walker, the ex mayor of New-York City, in a movie.
6. Mark Twain once served as the editor in chief of a small newspaper in Virginia City, Nevada.
7. Robert Redford got his start in acting doing off Broadway plays and playing bit parts in television-dramas.
8. Ansel Adams (1902–1984) is famous for his black and white photographs of American wilderness landscapes.

48

MASTERING THE RULES OF CAPITALIZATION

Like checking spelling, correcting mechanical problems should be done when you edit and proofread your writing. Rules that govern mechanics are important, and you should follow them carefully.

Following are a few rules to help you with capitalization. If you are unsure about capitalizing a word, refer to a dictionary.

48.1 Capitalize the first word of a sentence.

Cold air blew through the broken window.
When he was a child, he was afraid of the dark.

48.2 Capitalize proper nouns.

Proper nouns (which name *specific* places, persons, and things) should be capitalized; common nouns should not.

Proper nouns	Common nouns
Asia	a continent
the Baltic Sea	a sea, the sea
Composition 101	a writing course
Governor Chan	the governor
Grand Canyon National Park	a national park, the park
Hope College	a college, the college
Independence Day	a holiday

the Indian Ocean	an ocean, the ocean
the Library of Congress	the library
Professor Del Vecchio	my accounting professor
the Renaissance	the sixteenth century
the Secret Service	a federal agency or bureau
the United States Army	an army, the army
the Washington Monument	a tall monument, the monument

48.3 Capitalize proper adjectives.

Capitalize proper adjectives, those made from proper nouns.

the Spanish language	Jamaican rum
French toast	Norway maple
a German shepherd	Japanese beetles
Rocky Mountain spotted fever	a Labrador retriever

48.4 Capitalize a title before a name.

Capitalize a title when it immediately precedes a person's name; do not capitalize a title when it is used alone.

Professor Pat Graber	a professor
Dr. Stephen Winters	a doctor
General Tommy Franks	a general
Ms. Mary Jones	a woman

48.5 Capitalize abbreviations made from capitalized words.

EPA (Environmental Protection Agency)
FBI (Federal Bureau of Investigation)
NASA (National Aeronautics and Space Administration)
UNESCO (United Nations Educational, Scientific, and Cultural Organization)
WHO (World Health Organization)

Some abbreviations are capitalized even though the words they replace are not.

RBI (runs batted in)	RAM (random access memory)
MS (manuscript)	ATM (automated teller machine)
CD (compact disk)	MPV (multipurpose vehicle)

48.6 Capitalize calendar items: days of the week, months, and special days.

Do not capitalize seasons.

Monday	spring
November	summer
Thanksgiving	fall
Hanukkah	winter

48.7 Capitalize major words in a title.

Capitalize nouns, verbs, adjectives, and adverbs, but do not capitalize articles (*a, an, the*), prepositions, or conjunctions of fewer than five letters unless they begin the title.

A Midsummer Night's Dream	*Gone with the Wind*
"The Fall of the House of Usher"	*The Confessions of St. Augustine*
The Color Purple	*A Tale of a Tub*
Romeo and Juliet	

48.8 Capitalize the pronoun *I*.

Do so even when *I* is part of a contraction.

I'm going to the store, but I don't know what I'll buy.

48.9 Capitalize a section of the country or world.

Capitalize *north, south, east,* or *west* when they indicate a region, but not when they indicate a direction.

The North and the South fought the American Civil War.

Will peace ever come to the Middle East?

They drove south on Route 245.

My sister lives about two miles east of here.

48.10 Capitalize brand names.

Do not capitalize the generic terms.

Band-Aid	bandage
Coke	cola
Jeep	four-wheel-drive vehicle
Kleenex	tissues
Scotch tape	adhesive tape
Xerox machine	photocopier

Correct errors in capitalization in the following sentences:

1. In the last days of his run for the president of the united states, bob dole completed a ninety-six-hour Campaign Marathon.
2. When i was in Washington, d.c., i visited the smithsonian institution, the jefferson memorial, and arlington national cemetery.
3. The Professor knew both greek and latin, but she never studied hebrew.
4. I donate to many Charities, but i make most of my contributions to the aspca and the american cancer society.
5. The start of the Semester always seems to arrive too fast; this year, Fall classes begin Wednesday, august 29.
6. We decided to see *minority report*, spielberg's new film, which most Critics praised.
7. Adriana put two energizer batteries into the toy corvette that was a part of her collection of barbie dolls.
8. It was dress-down Friday at the united way office where i work, so i decided to wear my levis, a wrangler shirt, and my nikes.

49

LEARNING TO ABBREVIATE WORDS, PHRASES, AND TITLES

The use of abbreviations will vary depending on the type of writing you are doing—academic, business, scientific, or research. Certain standard abbreviations are acceptable in all types of writing. Such abbreviations include initialisms and acronyms. (For more on initialisms and acronyms, see sections 49.2 and 49.3.) Other standard abbreviations that may appear in all types of writing include the following:

a.m. or A.M.	B.A., M.A., Ph.D.
p.m. or P.M.	MD., DD.
B.C. or B.C.E.	Mrs., Ms., Mr.
A.D. or C.E.	mph

NOTE
B.C.E. stands for "before the Common Era" and C.E. stands for "Common Era."

While not acceptable in formal writing, other abbreviations are acceptable in forms, research papers, reports, and statistic sheets:

Mar.	ft. (foot)
Apr.	no. (number)
Aug.	mo. (month)
Sept.	p. (page)
Oct.	pp. (pages)

Most of the writing you will do for your college courses will require you to observe the rules that follow for using abbreviations.

49.1 Use periods with single-word abbreviations.

Abbreviations of single words usually take periods.

vols.	volumes
Jan.	January
Mr.	Mister

49.2 Write initialisms without periods.

Initialisms are abbreviations made from the first letter of each word of a string of words.

IRS	Internal Revenue Service
GDP	Gross Domestic Product
URL	Uniform Resource Locator
FBI	Federal Bureau of Investigation
ATM	Automated Teller Machine

Initialisms are usually written without periods.

Use initialisms when you believe your audience will already be familiar with the names or terms for which they stand. However, if you think an initialism (such as GDP) will not be readily familiar to your reader, spell out the full term, followed by the initialism in parentheses. In later references, you can use the initials alone: for example, "The program Aid to Families with Dependent Children (AFDC) has been replaced with the program Temporary Assistance for Needy Families (TANF)."

49.3 Write acronyms without periods.

Acronyms are words formed from the first letters of a string of words.

NOW	National Organization for Women
AIDS	Acquired Immune Deficiency Syndrome
LASER	Light Amplification by Stimulated Emission of Radiation
RADAR	RAdio Detecting And Ranging
SCUBA	Self-Contained Underwater Breathing Apparatus
SONAR	SOund NAvigation Ranging

Acronyms that have become accepted as words do not need periods. Note that certain acronyms, such as *laser, radar, scuba,* and *sonar,* now appear in lowercase.

49.4 Use capitals consistently.

1. Be consistent in capitalizing abbreviations, acronyms, and initialisms.
2. Capitalize the abbreviations of words only if they are normally capitalized when written out in full.
3. Capitalize initialisms.

49.5 Avoid abbreviations for titles, but use them for degrees.

NOTE ✦✦✦✦✦✦

When referring to the president of the United States, the word *president* is often capitalized.

Use the spelled-out form of a title in formal prose.

Not: The sen. urged the pres. to sign the bill.

But: The senator urged the president to sign the bill.

49.5a Use the abbreviation for the title in the inside address in a letter.

President	President Bush	Pres. George W. Bush
Professor	Professor Kelly	Prof. John Kelly
Reverend	Reverend Stephens	Rev. Alice Stephens

49.5b Use abbreviations for academic degrees.

Ph.D.   MS   MA   BA   BS

49.5c Place academic titles before a name and academic degrees after, but do not use both at the same time.

Not: Dr. Donald Winn, Ph.D.

But: Dr. Donald Winn

Or: Donald Winn, Ph.D.

49.6 Use familiar abbreviations.

Use technical abbreviations in governmental, military, scientific, and technical writing when your audience will be familiar with the terms.

ADP (automatic data processing)
APR (annual percentage rate)
CAD (computer-aided design)
CRT (cathode-ray tube)
GHz (gigahertz)
MHz (megahertz)
VDT (video display terminal)
VHF (very high frequency)

However, when writing for a general audience, write out the technical term the first time, followed by the abbreviation in parentheses. In later references, you can use the abbreviation alone: guaranteed annual wage (GAW).

■ ■ ■ ■ ■ ■ ■ ■ **B A S I C L I N K** ■ ■ ■ ■ ■ ■ ■ ■

WWW

For a glossary of computer-oriented abbreviations and acronyms, go to
http://www.comadvantage.com/babel.html

■ ■

49.7 Avoid abbreviations with dates.

In most writing, dates are not abbreviated. Write out the days of the week and the months of the year.

Not: The biggest-grossing movie of the year opened the last Fri. of Sept.

But: The biggest-grossing movie of the year opened the last Friday of September.

49.8 Use abbreviations for weights and measures.

When the terms for measures and weights appear with numbers, use abbreviations.

50 min.	2 tsps.	12 oz.	5 hrs.
12 g.	29 km	65 mph	22 mpg

However, when the terms for weights and measures appear without numbers, write them out in full.

Not: He bought the car for its looks, not for the mpg it gets.

But: He bought the car for its looks, not for the miles per gallon it gets.

49.9 Use abbreviations for temperature and time.

Abbreviations for temperature and time are acceptable in all types of writing.

32 B.C.	1492 A.D.	3:30 A.M.	68°F
71 B.C.E.	1066 C.E.	2:17 P.M.	10°C

The abbreviations B.C., B.C.E. (before the Common Era), and C.E. (Common Era) appear *after* the date. A.D. appears *before* the date. All are capitalized.

49.10 Avoid abbreviations with most place-names.

Generally, in formal writing, place-names are not abbreviated, except in addresses, lists, specialized subject areas, and bibliographical references. However, a few abbreviations are acceptable.

U.K.	U.S. (or USA)	U.S.S.R.
D.C.	Mt. (Mt. Fuji)	St. (St. Louis)

Spell out the various terms used with street names, except in addresses.

alley	boulevard	highway	place	route
avenue	circle	parkway	road	turnpike

In addresses, use abbreviations for the terms noted above. The standard postal abbreviations for them are as follows:

Aly.	Blvd.	Hwy.	Pl.	Rte.
Ave.	Cir.	Pkwy.	Rd.	Tpke.

In addresses, use standard postal abbreviations, without periods, for the states.

State	Abbreviation	State	Abbreviation
Alabama	AL	Kentucky	KY
Alaska	AK	Louisiana	LA
Arizona	AZ	Maine	ME
Arkansas	AR	Maryland	MD
California	CA	Massachusetts	MA
Colorado	CO	Michigan	MI
Connecticut	CT	Minnesota	MN
Delaware	DE	Mississippi	MS
District of Columbia	DC	Missouri	MO
Florida	FL	Montana	MT
Georgia	GA	Nebraska	NE
Hawaii	HI	Nevada	NV
Idaho	ID	New Hampshire	NH
Illinois	IL	New Jersey	NJ
Indiana	IN	New Mexico	NM
Iowa	IA	New York	NY
Kansas	KS	North Carolina	NC

State	Abbreviation	State	Abbreviation
North Dakota	ND	Texas	TX
Ohio	OH	Utah	UT
Oklahoma	OK	Vermont	VT
Oregon	OR	Virginia	VA
Pennsylvania	PA	Washington	WA
Rhode Island	RI	West Virginia	WV
South Carolina	SC	Wisconsin	WI
South Dakota	SD	Wyoming	WY
Tennessee	TN		

49.11 Use abbreviations for common Latin expressions.

Use abbreviations for commonly used Latin expressions.

i.e. (*id est*—that is)
e.g. (*exempli gratia*—for example)
et al. (*et alii*—and others)
etc. (*et cetera*—and so on)
cf. (*confer*—compare)
N.B. (*nota bene*—note well)

49.12 Use abbreviations in bibliographical citations.

Use appropriate abbreviations for elements of books in parenthetical citations, endnotes, and footnotes.

p.	pp.	vol.	vols.
ch.	bk.	sec.	

However, the words should be written out when used in the text of your writing.

Not: After reading the last ch., Carrie Diane put the bk. away.

But: After reading the last chapter, Carrie Diane put the book away.

49.13 Avoid symbols in formal writing.

In general, avoid using symbols as abbreviations in your academic writing. Certain symbols, however, are acceptable. For example, you can use the dollar sign ($) if it is followed by an amount, but avoid using both the dollar sign and the word *dollar.*

Not: The dealer's price for the used car was $3,000 dollars.

But: The dealer's price for the used car was $3,000.

Or: The dealer's price for the used car was 3,000 dollars.

Avoid using the ampersand (&) in your writing unless it is part of a title or a name.

A&E   *Road & Track*   Lord & Taylor   *House & Garden*

:: CHAPTER WRAP-UP ::

Rewrite those sentences that contain errors in the use of abbreviations. If the sentence is correct, write correct.

1. This yr. the fourth of July falls on a Thurs., but since we have to go to work on Fri., we will try to end our celebration by 11 p.m.

2. The Roman emperor Claudius lived from B.C. 10 to a.d. 54.

3. By 2:00 p.m. the temperature had reached 97°F.

4. Dr. Rita Huddy, Ph.D, Michael's prof., asked him to read ch. 9 (over 78 pp. long) in his psych. textbook.

5. For their school outing in Mar. the students went to Washington, d.c., where they visited the Smithsonian Ins. and the headquarters of the F.B.I.

6. John Ashcroft, the atty. gen. of the US, was appointed by Pres. Bush.

7. Kevin is working on his ph.d. in sociology at nyu.

8. The senior sen. from NJ has been undergoing a congressional investigation.

USING NUMBERS AND ITALICS CORRECTLY

50.1   **Use the correct form of numbers.**
50.2   **Use italics correctly.**

50.1 Use the correct form of numbers.

1. Write out one- or two-digit numbers. Use numerals for all others. You can combine numerals with *million, billion,* and so on.

   The club welcomed *thirty-seven* new members.

   The librarian purchased only *118* books during the year.

   Foreign tourists added *$4.7* billion to Canada's economy this year.

2. Never begin a sentence with a numeral. Write out a number that begins a sentence, or rewrite the sentence so that the numeral appears later.

   One hundred seventy people attended the fund-raiser.

   The fund-raiser attracted *170* people.

3. Use numerals for dates, exact times of the day, sums of money, scores of games, addresses, volume and page numbers, miles per hour, and numbers used as numbers.

   He was born on *November 29, 1941,* at *6:15* in the morning.

   The book actually cost me *$17.38,* so I lost *50 cents* on the deal.

   They won the game by a score of *8* to *3.*

   She lives at *903* Summit Street.

   I found the information in volume *2,* page *403.*

   He was going *78 mph* in a *55-mph* zone.

   I saw her at the ice rink, practicing figure *8s.*

50.2 Use italics correctly.

Italics is a style of type in which the letters slant to the right. If you don't have a typewriter or computer that creates italics, just underline the words that would appear in italics.

1. Use italics to emphasize a word or phrase.

   The speaker said, "The United States owes its lenders 4 trillion dollars. Now *that's* a deficit."

2. Use italics to indicate a word or letter is being used as a word or letter.

   The word *separate* contains two *e*'s and two *a*'s.

3. Use italics to indicate the title of a book, a magazine, a journal, a play, a film, an opera, a television series, a long poem, or a newspaper and the name of a ship, an airplane, a spaceship, or a work of art.

The Stand (novel)	*Vanity Fair* (magazine)
The Waste Land (long poem)	*Lancet* (journal)
New York Times (newspaper)	*The Crucible* (play)
Lusitania (ship)	*Minority Report* (movie)
Spirit of St. Louis (plane)	*Rigoletto* (opera)
Challenger (spaceship)	*60 Minutes* (television series)
Sunflowers (work of art)	

:: CHAPTER WRAP-UP

Correct the errors in the use of numbers and italics in the following paragraph:

Mark had always enjoyed writing and had received straight A's in his English classes during his 4 years of high school. As a result, his teacher during his senior year, Dr. Richard Horton, had suggested he major in English. At least once a week, Dr. Horton wrote a quotation on the blackboard. The one Mark remembered the most was by Richard Marius, a professor at Harvard University, from his book "A Writer's Companion." In fact, he even memorized it. It went like this: "Writing is hard work, and although it may become easier with practice it is seldom easy. Most of us have to write and rewrite to write anything well. We try to write well so people will read our work. Readers . . . will seldom struggle to understand difficult writing unless someone . . . forces them to do so." And Dr. Horton had forced Mark to write and rewrite each paper up to 6 times. Thus Mark decided to major in English when he began his 1st year of college.

End Punctuation

1. **Declarative sentences** present information. They end in periods.
2. **Interrogative sentences** ask questions. They end in question marks.
3. **Imperative sentences** that give orders end in exclamation points. Those that make requests or give instructions end in periods.
4. **Exclamatory sentences** express strong emotion and end with exclamation points.
5. Place periods *within* quotation marks; place question marks and exclamation points *inside or outside* quotation marks, depending on the sentence's meaning.

Commas

Use commas

1.
   a. Between independent clauses joined by coordinating conjunctions: *and, but, or, nor, for, so, yet.*
   b. Between introductory words, phrases, or clauses and the main clauses that follow.
   c. Between items in a series.
   d. Around words that add information but are not essential to the sentence's meaning.
   e. Around nonrestrictive modifiers (describers). Nonrestrictive modifiers don't limit the meaning of the words they describe.
   f. Around sentence interrupters, including internal transitions, interjections, and words used in direct address.
   g. With academic degrees, addresses, numbers, and dates.
   h. Between adjectives if *and* could naturally be inserted between them.
   i. In any part of a sentence when doing so will make the sentence clearer and easier to understand.

2. Do not use commas
   a. To separate a subject and a verb.
   b. To separate a verb and its direct object.
   c. Before a clause that is introduced by a subordinate conjunction such as *after, although, because, if, since, unless, whenever, when,* and *while.*
   d. Before prepositional phrases, which begin with words such as *by, for, in, into, of, to,* and *with.*
   e. Between two items joined by *and, but,* or *or,* unless these items are main clauses.

Semicolons

Use a semicolon

1. Between two independent clauses that are related but not connected with a coordinating conjunction.

(continued)

2 Between independent clauses joined by a conjunctive adverb or transitional phrase.

3 Between items in a series when some or all of those items contain commas.

Colons
Use a colon

1 Between independent clauses when the second clause clarifies or explains the first.

2 After an independent clause to introduce information naming something in that clause.

3 To introduce a quotation.

4 After the salutation in a business letter.

Apostrophes

1 Use an apostrophe
   a. To show possession.
   b. To form contractions.
   c. With abbreviations, numbers, and letters.

Quotation marks

1 Use double quotation marks to
   a. Enclose the *exact* words of a speaker or a text.
   b. Enclose titles of short works such as articles, poems, short stories, songs, and television episodes.

2 Use single quotation marks to enclose a quotation within a quotation.

Other Marks of Punctuation

1 Use an ellipsis to show that you have removed words from a direct quotation.

2 Use brackets to enclose material you have added within a direct quotation.

3 Use a dash to
   a. Set off material that is emphasized.
   b. Clarify an idea.
   c. Separate a list from an independent clause.

4 Use parentheses to
   a. Set off words that emphasize or specify.
   b. Set off an explanatory sentence within a sentence.
   c. Enclose a brief definition.
   d. Enclose numbers or letters before items in a list.

Spelling

1 If you aren't sure that a word is spelled correctly, look it up in the dictionary. Never rely on a computer spell checker to catch all errors.

2 Following these rules can help improve your spelling:

   a. Keep *i* before *e* except after *c* or when it sounds like *ay*, as in *neighbor* and *weigh*.

   b. When you add an ending to a word that ends in *-y*, first change the *-y* to *-i* if the *-y* comes after a consonant.

   c. When you add *-able*, *-ed*, or *-ing* to a word that ends in a consonant, usually double that consonant.

   d. If the final *-e* in a word is not pronounced, drop that *-e* when you add an ending beginning with a vowel.

   e. In general, add *-s* or *-es* to make nouns plural. But keep in mind the rules on page 529.

   f. To form the plural of a term consisting of more than one word, add *-s* or *-es* to the first noun in the term.

   g. Learn to spell irregular nouns.

3 Contractions join two words into one with an apostrophe.

4 Frequently misspelled words (listed on page 532) need to be reviewed often.

Hyphens

1

   a. Join words that work together to describe the nouns that follow them.

   b. Connect prefixes to capitalized words.

   c. Connect prefixes such as *all-*, *ex-*, and *self-* to the words they modify.

   d. Appear in numbers from twenty-one through ninety-nine.

Capitalization

1 Capitalize

   a. The first word of a sentence.

   b. Proper nouns (names of specific places, persons, and things) and proper adjectives (adjectives made from proper nouns).

   c. A title used before a person's name.

   d. Abbreviations made from capitalized words.

   e. Months, days of the week, and holidays.

   f. Major words in a title.

   g. The pronoun *I*.

   h. A section of the country or world.

   i. Brand names.

Abbreviations

1 Be consistent in punctuating abbreviations.

2 Be consistent in capitalizing abbreviations, initialisms, and acronyms.

   a. Capitalize abbreviations of words that are normally capitalized when written out in full.

(continued)

b. Don't capitalize abbreviations of words not normally capitalized when written out in full.

c. Capitalize initialisms.

d. Use the appropriate abbreviations for titles, degrees, and names.

e. Place academic titles or degrees either before or after a name, but not both.

f. Use appropriate technical abbreviations in governmental, military, professional, scientific, and technical writing.

g. Use appropriate abbreviations for organizations and agencies.

h. Use appropriate abbreviations for dates.

i. Use appropriate abbreviations for weights and measures.

j. Use appropriate abbreviations for temperature and time.

k. Use appropriate abbreviations for place-names.

l. Use the correct abbreviations for commonly used Latin expressions.

m. Use appropriate abbreviations for elements of books in parenthetical citations, endnotes, and footnotes.

n. Avoid using symbols as abbreviations in academic writing.

Numbers and Italics

1 ⋮ Use numbers correctly.

a. Write out one- or two-digit numbers. Use numerals for others.

b. Never begin a sentence with a numeral.

c. Use numerals for dates, sums of money, scores of games, addresses, volume and page numbers, exact times of the day, miles per hour, and numbers used as numbers.

2 ⋮ Use italics to

a. Emphasize a word or phrase.

b. Show that a word or letter is being used as a word or letter.

c. Indicate the title of a book, a magazine, a play, a film, an opera, a television series, a long poem, or a newspaper and the name of a ship, an airplane, a spaceship, or a work of art.

12

12

A GUIDE FOR ESL WRITERS

12 A GUIDE FOR ESL WRITERS

MASTERING ARTICLES AND PLURALS OF NOUNS

51.1 **Master articles.**
51.2 **Use plurals correctly.**

51.1 Master articles.

1. Use *a* or *an* for general reference. When you use *a* or *an*, you mean "any."

My friend ordered a salad.

This is the same as saying "any salad."

Our hiking club saw *an* eagle.

This is the same as saying "any eagle."

Use *the* when you mean a particular person, place, or thing, which the reader can point to. When you use *the,* you mean "the one."

The child wanted to ride *the* elephant.

This sentence refers to a particular child and a particular elephant.

2. Place *a* or *an* before singular nouns only.

a desk		desks
a building	BUT	buildings
an animal		animals
an orange		oranges

Place *the* before singular or plural nouns.

the computer	the computers
the woman	the women

3. Place *a* or *an* before nouns that can be counted. Don't use *a* or *an* before nouns that can't be counted or nouns that stand for abstractions.

Count Nouns	Noncount Nouns
I ate *a sandwich*.	I breathe *oxygen*.
You drive *a tractor*.	You drive heavy *equipment*.
Jason was *a hero*.	Jason had *courage*.
He has *a dog*.	He condemns *violence*.
She read *a poem*.	She wrote *poetry*.
We heard *a song*.	We listened to *music*.
The children rode *a pony*.	They studied *mathematics*.
They went to *a movie*.	They manufactured *clothing*.

Some nouns can be both count and noncount.

Count Nouns	Noncount Nouns
a (particular) hope	hope
a (head of) cauliflower	cauliflower
a (glass of) beer	beer
a (cup of) coffee	coffee
a (corner) pharmacy	pharmacy (study of drugs)
a (kind of) medicine	medicine (study of healing)
a (particular) sport	sports
a (lump of) sugar	sugar
a (particular) fish	fish

4. Place *a* before consonant sounds; place *an* before vowel sounds.

CONSONANT SOUNDS

The immigrants faced *a* wall of alienation.

We spoke to *a* priest, *a* minister, and *a* rabbi.

VOWEL SOUNDS

I have *an* appetite for *an* orange.

They flew to *an* island in *an* airplane.

EXCEPTIONS

Words beginning with a silent *h* take *an*.

an hour, *an* honor.

When *u* at the beginning of a word is pronounced like *you*, the article is *a*.

a university, a union, a unicycle, a unicorn.

5. If an adjective comes before a noun, follow these rules:

Place *a* before adjectives that begin with consonant sounds.

an island		a big island
an angle	BUT	a right angle
an office		a small office

Place *an* before adjectives that begin with vowel sounds.

a woman		an intelligent woman
a child	BUT	an eager child
a dog		an angry dog

6. In most cases, don't use articles with abstract nouns such as words that name attitudes, diseases, emotions, holidays, languages, philosophies, religions, sports, and studies.

Alfonso despises laziness.

Always avoid sexism and racism!

She suffered from tuberculosis.

Jealousy is destructive.

I love Thanksgiving.

The students learned Korean.

Some ancient Greeks practiced stoicism.

Jan has read much about Buddhism.

Andrea loves to play soccer.

Denise finds economics interesting.

7. Don't use *the* when referring to all members of a group or to something in general.

Doctors have to have years of special training.

Trees and other green plants give off oxygen.

Ice and snow cover much of Antarctica.

8. Don't use articles with these types of proper nouns:

PEOPLE, REAL OR FICTIONAL

Dr. Bergin, Ms. Ancona, Professor Luke, Wonder Woman, Zeus

COUNTRIES, CONTINENTS, STATES, PROVINCES, CITIES, TOWNS, ISLANDS

Panama, Africa, Wyoming, Ontario, Denver, Milltown, Sardinia

PARKS

Yellowstone National Park, Lincoln Commons, Central Park

MOUNTAINS

Pikes Peak, Mount Etna

LAKES, PONDS, OTHER SMALL BODIES OF WATER

Lake Huron, Lake Victoria, Scutter's Pond

NAMES OF POLITICAL OR RELIGIOUS LEADERS

President Lincoln, King Hussein, Pope John Paul II

9. Use articles with these types of proper nouns:

REGIONS OF A COUNTRY OR OF THE WORLD

the Middle East, the Southwest, the Yukon

MOUNTAIN RANGES

the Sierra Nevadas, the Himalayas, the Pyrenees

GROUPS OF ISLANDS

the British Isles, the Hawaiian Islands

LARGE BODIES OF WATER

the Gulf of Mexico, the Indian Ocean, the Mediterranean Sea

NAMES OF CERTAIN NATIONS

the United States of America, the United Kingdom, the Empire of Japan, the People's Republic of China

WARS

the American Revolution, the Franco-Prussian War, the Boxer Rebellion, the First World War (*but* World War I)

BUILDINGS, CANALS, BRIDGES

the Taj Mahal, the Erie Canal, the Golden Gate Bridge

TITLES OF POLITICAL AND RELIGIOUS LEADERS

the president of the United States, the king of Jordan, the pope, the Dalai Lama

For more on articles, see section 33.4.

51.2 Use plurals correctly.

1. Form the plurals of **regular nouns** by adding -*s* or -*es*.

Singular	Plural
school	schools
college	colleges
university	universities

NOTE

If a word ends in -*y*, first change the *y* to *i*, and then add -*es*.

The plurals of **irregular nouns** are formed in ways other than by adding -*s* or -*es*.

Singular	Plural
child	children
woman	women
deer	deer

2. Be alert to noncount nouns. They are always singular.

Not: The equipments were outdated.
But: The equipment was outdated.

Not: The furnitures are on sale.
But: The furniture is on sale.

Not: I had to do my homeworks.
But: I had to do my homework.

Not: I was not good in maths.
But: I was not good in math.

3. Use plural nouns immediately after adjectives such as *a few, many, most,* and *some* and after pronouns such as *these* and *those.*

Not: A few customer entered the store.
But: A few customers entered the store.

Not: Many car were double-parked.
But: Many cars were double-parked.

Not: Most police officer work hard.

But: Most police officers work hard.

Not: Some bear have been seen in these mountains.

But: Some bears have been seen in these mountains.

Not: These apple are sweet.

But: These apples are sweet.

Not: Those pear are juicy.

But: Those pears are juicy.

4. Use plural nouns after adjective phrases introduced by *one of the.*

Not: A Porsche is one of the most expensive car.

But: A Porsche is one of the most expensive cars.

Not: She is one of the best student.

But: She is one of the best students.

5. Use *many* and *many of* with plural count nouns. Use *much* and *much of* with noncount nouns, which are singular.

Plural Count Noun

Not: Much of the students admired Professor Richards.

But: Many of the students admired Professor Richards.

Singular Noncount Noun

Not: Many courage was shown during the battle.

But: Much courage was shown during the battle.

6. Use *a few* with plural count nouns; use *a little* with noncount nouns, which are singular.

Plural Count Noun

We listened to a few songs.

Singular Noncount Noun

A little singing does the heart good.

7. Use *all, a lot of, most of,* or *more* with plural count nouns and with noncount nouns, which are singular.

Plural Count Nouns

All steelworkers wear hard hats.

A lot of people like pizza.

Most of the soldiers were tired.

More volunteers are needed.

Singular Noncount Nouns

All homework is due on Tuesday.

My class has read a lot of poetry.

She earned most of her wealth by working hard.

Mozart wrote more music than we thought.

8. Use singular, not plural, nouns after *much* and *much of.*

Not:	Much bloods has been shed for liberty.
But:	Much blood has been shed for liberty.

Not:	Much of the flours was used to make bread.
But:	Much of the flour was used to make bread.

9. Use the adjectives *this* and *that* with singular nouns; use *these* and *those* with plural nouns.

Not:	This gardeners works hard.
But:	This gardener works hard.
Or:	These gardeners work hard.

10. In some languages, plural nouns take plural adjectives. *This is not true in English. In English, never make adjectives plural.*

Not:	The bests students received awards.
But:	The best students received awards.

Not:	The chocolate chips cookies were fattening.
But:	The chocolate chip cookies were fattening.

Not:	The people were angries.
But:	The people were angry.

11. Use singular, not plural, nouns after phrases such as *a kind of, a type of, a sort of, a style of.*

Patricia practices a type of Buddhism.

This experimental car uses a new kind of fuel.

My father likes a style of opera made famous in Italy.

12. Use plural nouns after phrases such as *kinds of, types of, sorts of, styles of.*

I like the types of books they read.

What sorts of people did she invite?

For more on plural nouns, see sections 46.4 and 46.5.

> **NOTE**
> *Any* can be used with singular *and* plural nouns.
>
> **Singular:** Any car parked illegally will be towed.
> **Plural:** We didn't meet any movie stars.

> **NOTE**
> This rule applies even when a noun acts as an adjective.
>
> **Not:** He is a movies director.
> **But:** He is a movie director.

> **NOTE**
> Noncount nouns are always singular.
>
> I like his style of journalism.
>
> They studied three styles of journalism.

52

52.1 Follow regular word order for declarative sentences.
52.2 Follow inverted word order for questions.
52.3 Use *it* and *there* as subjects.
52.4 Avoid using pronouns to repeat subjects and direct objects.

52.1 Follow regular word order for declarative sentences.

Declarative sentences convey information. In most cases, follow regular word-order patterns for declarative sentences. Here are two patterns you can use to write such sentences:

DECLARATIVE SENTENCE = SUBJECT + VERB + DIRECT OBJECT

Not: My lunch the dog ate.
But: The dog ate my lunch.

Not: Everything I said she believed.
But: She believed everything I said.

DECLARATIVE SENTENCE = SUBJECT + VERB + MODIFIERS

Not: The children in the garden played.
But: The children played in the garden.

Not: The horse to the top of the hill ran.
But: The horse ran to the top of the hill.

Use regular, not inverted, word order when you introduce a subordinate clause with *where, when, how,* or *why.*

Not: I did not know where was I going.
But: I did not know where I was going.

Not: Sharon wondered how was she going to solve her problem.
But: Sharon wondered how she was going to solve her problem.

Not: The professor asked why was my essay late.
But: The professor asked why my essay was late.

52.2 Follow inverted word order for questions.

In general, use inverted word order in questions. That is, put the verb before the subject. Here are three common patterns to use for questions:

QUESTION = VERB + SUBJECT

Not:	You are hungry?
But:	Are you hungry?

Not:	What he has done?
But:	What has he done?

In this question, the pronoun *What* is a direct object; nevertheless, the word order is still inverted.

Not:	Where they are?
But:	Where are they?

This question begins with the adverb *Where.* As with all questions, however, the word order is inverted.

Not:	How old the child is?
But:	How old is the child?

This question begins with the modifier *How old;* again, the word order is inverted.

QUESTION = HELPING VERB + SUBJECT + MAIN VERB

If a helping verb is needed, place the helping verb first, then the subject, then the main verb.

Not:	You are going to class?
But:	Are you going to class?

Not:	You will be on time?
But:	Will you be on time?

QUESTION IN PAST TENSE = WERE/WAS/DID/HAD + SUBJECT + PAST PARTICIPLE

To ask some questions in the past tense, you may have to add a helping verb. Follow this pattern:

1. Begin with one of these helping verbs:

   Was or *were* (past tense of *be*)

   Did (past tense of *do*)

   Had (past tense of *have*)

2. Follow with the subject.

3. Add the past participle. (Past participles of regular verbs end in *-d, -ed, -en, -n,* and *-t.* The participles of irregular verbs are explained in Chapter 34.)

Not: You received an award?

But: Did you receive an award?

Not: Janet visited Poland before seeing Hungary?

But: Had Janet visited Poland before seeing Hungary?

52.3 Use *it* and *there* as subjects.

Add words such as *it* and *there* when they are needed as subjects.

Not: Was raining very hard.

But: It was raining very hard.

Not: Sometimes takes 15 minutes to find a parking spot.

But: Sometimes it takes 15 minutes to find a parking spot.

52.4 Avoid using pronouns to repeat subjects and direct objects.

52.4a Do not use a pronoun to repeat the subject of a sentence.

Not: Our neighbors they helped us.

But: Our neighbors helped us.

Not: English it can be a difficult language.

But: English can be a difficult language.

Not: Studying with friends that helps me learn better.

But: Studying with friends helps me learn better.

52.4b Avoid using pronouns to repeat direct objects.

Not: The teacher we asked him what would be on the test.

But: We asked the teacher what would be on the test.

Not: Doctors treated the child we brought her to the clinic.

But: Doctors treated the child we brought to the clinic.

MASTERING VERBS AND SUBJECT-VERB AGREEMENT

53

53.1 **Master special problems with verbs.**
53.2 **Master subject-verb agreement.**

53.1 Master special problems with verbs.

1. Include helping verbs as needed. **Helping verbs** are used to create special tenses. Always include a helping verb before the main verb when you form the following tenses.

PRESENT PROGRESSIVE TENSE

The magician *is practicing* several tricks before the show.

The helping verb is *is;* the main verb is *practicing.*

PRESENT PERFECT TENSE

The magician *has practiced* several tricks before the show.

The helping verb is *has;* the main verb is *practiced.*

PAST PERFECT TENSE

The magician *had practiced* several tricks before the show.

The helping verb is *had;* the main verb is *practiced.*

FUTURE TENSE

The magician *will practice* several tricks before the show.

The helping verb is *will;* the main verb is *practice.*

2. Learn to use modals. A **modal** is a type of helping verb. Unlike other helping verbs, however, modals cannot act as main verbs. They are used before main verbs to create special meaning. In the following sentences, modals are in italics.

She *can* learn to operate the fax machine quickly.

Tom *did* arrive on time despite the traffic jam.

You *must* promise not to reveal the secret to anyone.

If the mayor *will* supply the equipment, the town council *will* approve the plan.

The students *would* register for his course if it met later in the day.

If you qualify, you *should* enter the contest.

Modals

can	do	may	shall	will
could	does	might	should	would
	did	must		

> **CAUTION!**
>
> Do not add *-ed* to verbs that come after modals.
>
> **Not:** I could not opened the door.
> **But:** I could not open the door.

3. Combine gerunds and infinitives correctly with verbs. A **gerund** is an *-ing* noun formed from a verb; it stands for an activity.

Hiking is my favorite sport.

I love *running* through the fields.

An **infinitive** is the basic form of a verb preceded by *to.* Infinitives act as nouns, adjectives, or adverbs.

Noun: *To eat* well is *to live* well.
Adjective: Shoppers often make lists of things *to buy.*
Adverb: I stopped at a small hotel *to rest.*

Here are some important things to remember when you combine gerunds and infinitives with verbs:

a. Some verbs take both gerunds and infinitives with no change in meaning.

Infinitive: I love to swim in the ocean.
Gerund: I love swimming in the ocean.

Other verbs mean one thing when they are combined with gerunds and something else when they are combined with infinitives.

Infinitive: Jane forgot to buy a birthday card for her aunt.
Gerund: Jane forgot buying a birthday card for her aunt.

In the first sentence, Jane did not buy a card. In the second, she bought a card but forgot that she had done so.

b. Some verbs can be used with gerunds but not with infinitives. In general, these are **transitive verbs**—that is, verbs that take direct objects.

Not: I imagined to be rich.
But: I imagined being rich.

Other Verbs to Use with Gerunds but Not with Infinitives

admit	deny	endure	practice	reject
approve	discuss	finish	prevent	suggest
avoid	disprove	give up	recall	understand
consider	dispute	know	recommend	

c. Some verbs can be used with infinitives but not with gerunds. These can be **transitive verbs,** which take direct objects, or **intransitive verbs,** which do not take direct objects.

TRANSITIVE VERBS

Not: I want taking the bus.

But: I want to take the bus.

INTRANSITIVE VERBS

Not: I happened meeting him at the station.

But: I happened to meet him at the station.

Other Verbs to Use with Infinitives but Not with Gerunds

agree	demand	long	refuse
arrange	desire	plan	say
ask	expect	pledge	swear
decline	have	promise	vow

4. Learn how to combine verbs with particles. **Particles** are adverbs or prepositions that change a verb's meaning. For example, the verb *to look* means simply "to see"; on the other hand, *to look ahead* means "to plan or to predict." Here are some important things to keep in mind when you work with particles:

Some verbs can be separated from their particles. For example, you can write:

He threw out the old newspaper.

or

He threw the old newspaper out.

Some verbs, however, cannot be separated from their particles. Here are two examples:

Not: She goes often out.

But: She goes out often.

Not: Theresa carried her plan out.

But: Theresa carried out her plan.

Other Verbs You Should Not Separate from Their Particles

act on	lie down	run out of	take care of
come upon	look after	see to	think about
dream about	look to	sit up	think up
dream up	put up with	sit up with	wonder about
grow up	run around	stay up with	work at

For more on verbs, see section 33.3 and Chapter 34.

53.2 Master subject–verb agreement.

1. Use singular verbs, which end in -*s*, with indefinite pronouns. Indefinite pronouns are in italics in the following sentences.

Anything goes.

Every student takes English.

Everybody gets paid on Friday.

Neither woman has called.

Nobody is home.

Someone is knocking.

Something tells me I am in trouble.

Other Indefinite Pronouns

any	each	no one	some
anybody	everyone	nothing	somebody
anyone	everything	one	

2. Make verbs in subordinate clauses agree with the nouns those clauses modify. Subordinate clauses can begin with pronouns such as *that, which, who,* and *whom.*

Not: The car that *interest* you has been sold.

But: The car that *interests* you has been sold.

That refers to *car,* a singular noun; therefore, the verb following *that* must be singular.

Not: The Great Smoky Mountains, which *is* in North Carolina and Tennessee, are beautiful.

But: The Great Smoky Mountains, which *are* in North Carolina and Tennessee, are beautiful.

Which refers to *Mountains,* a plural noun; therefore, the verb following *which* should be plural.

Not: My sister, who *love* math, is an engineer.

But: My sister, who *loves* math, is an engineer.

Who refers to *sister,* a singular noun; therefore, the verb following *who* should be singular.

For more on subject-verb agreement, see Chapter 35.

54.1   **Master adjectives.**
54.2   **Master adverbs.**
54.3   **Master participles.**

54.1 Master adjectives.

1. When you use a noun as an adjective, make sure it is singular even if the noun it describes is plural.

Not: She works in a toys factory.

But: She works in a toy factory.

Not: Whenever she goes *foods* shopping, she always buys vegetables.

But: Whenever she goes *food* shopping, she always buys vegetables.

2. Follow these general guidelines to position adjectives before a noun.

PLACE THE ADJECTIVE BEFORE, NOT AFTER, THE NOUN

the red dress   the dress red

NOT

a terrible storm   a storm terrible

PLACE ADJECTIVES OF COLOR BEFORE THOSE THAT DESCRIBE MATERIALS

the red wooden barn   the red mahogany desk

the yellow woolen blanket   a green clay vase

PLACE ADJECTIVES OF AGE BEFORE ADJECTIVES OF COLOR

the old red wooden barn   an ancient green clay vase

the new yellow woolen blanket   the new red convertible

a secondhand red mahogany desk an old brown dog

PLACE ADJECTIVES OF SIZE, WEIGHT, AND SHAPE BEFORE THOSE OF AGE

a big old wooden barn   the sleek new red convertible

the big old yellow blanket   a fat old brown dog

a heavy ancient vase

PLACE ADJECTIVES OF QUALITY OR CONDITION BEFORE THOSE OF SIZE, WEIGHT, AND SHAPE

a charming big old barn　　　　　the beautiful sleek convertible

the elegant big yellow blanket　　a friendly fat old dog

an unusual heavy clay vase

PLACE ADJECTIVES FORMED FROM NOUNS NEXT TO THE NOUNS THEY MODIFY

the old Italian painting　　　　　the ancient church steeple

long-necked Canada geese　　　a round kitchen table

The Order of Adjectives

Use this quick guide to check the placement of adjectives before a noun:

1. Article
2. Adjective of quantity
3. Adjective of quality or condition
4. Adjective of size, weight, or shape
5. Adjective of age
6. Adjective of color
7. Adjective of material
8. Adjective formed from a noun
9. Noun

For more on adjectives, see sections 33.5, 38.1, 38.3, and 38.6.

54.2 Master adverbs.

Do not place adverbs between verbs and their direct objects.

Not:　He wrote quickly a note to his parents.

But:　He quickly wrote a note to his parents.

Or:　He wrote a note to his parents quickly.

Or:　Quickly, he wrote a note to his parents.

The verb is *wrote;* the direct object is *note.*

Not:　He liked usually hamburgers for lunch.

But:　He usually liked hamburgers for lunch.

Or:　Usually, he liked hamburgers for lunch.

The verb is *liked;* the direct object is *hamburgers.*

For more on adverbs, see sections 33.6, 38.4, 38.5, and 38.6.

54.3 Master participles.

Participles are adjectives made from verbs. Present participles end in *-ing*. Past participles of regular verbs end in *-d, -ed, -en, -n,* and *-t.* (You will find a list of the past participles of irregular verbs on pages 463–464.)

1. Use **present participles** to show action or to describe a noun or pronoun; use **past participles** to show what is done to a noun or pronoun.

Present participle: The comedian's jokes were *insulting.*

The participle describes the jokes.

Past participle: *Insulted,* the audience walked out.

The participle explains what was done to the audience.

Present participle: The *driving* rain entered the house.

The participle describes the rain.

Past participle: *Driven* by strong winds, the rain entered the house.

The participle explains what was done to the rain.

Present participle: The teacher found Philip *frustrating.*

The participle describes Philip.

Past participle: *Frustrated* by Philip, the teacher asked him to leave.

The participle explains what was done to the teacher.

Past participle: The teacher found Philip *frustrated* by the math problem.

The participle describes Philip's state of mind or condition.

2. Participles are adjectives. To avoid confusing them with nouns and verbs, always include participial endings.

Not: I like ice tea.
But: I like iced tea.

Not: I bought a use car.
But: I bought a used car.

For more on participles, see section 38.2.

55.1 Avoid inappropriate substitutions.

55.1a Do not substitute nouns for verbs.

Not: They don't cooperation.
But: They don't cooperate.

Not: Please advice me about this problem.
But: Please advise me about this problem.

Not: He success when everyone else failures.
But: He succeeds when everyone else fails.

55.1b Do not substitute nouns for adjectives.

Not: The room was too crowd.
But: The room was too crowded.

Not: They used life worms for bait.
But: They used live worms for bait.

55.2 Learn to use indirect objects.

Indirect objects are nouns or pronouns *to which* or *for which* an action is done.

The carpenter built Fred a bookcase.

Mary wrote me a letter.

In these sentences, *Fred* and *me* are indirect objects; *bookcase* and *letter* are direct objects.

Some verbs require the preposition *to* or *for* before indirect objects.

Not: I want to explain you a process.
But: I want to explain a process to you.

Not: The author dedicated them the book.
But: The author dedicated the book to them.

Not: Peter translated the teacher an Arabic poem.

But: Peter translated an Arabic poem for the teacher.

Strictly speaking, an indirect object used with a preposition is called an **object of a preposition.**

Some verbs do not require prepositions with indirect objects. Whether to use prepositions depends on where the indirect object appears. Don't use a preposition if the indirect object comes immediately after the verb.

Not: I wrote to you a letter.

But: I wrote you a letter.

Not: They offered to Jack a soda.

But: They offered Jack a soda.

Not: We cooked for Mom dinner on her birthday.

But: We cooked Mom dinner on her birthday.

Do use a preposition, however, if the indirect object comes immediately after the direct object.

I wrote a letter to you.

They offered a soda to Jack.

We cooked dinner for Mom on her birthday.

55.3 Learn the prepositions that belong in idioms.

Use the correct prepositions to form idiomatic expressions.

abide by a rule	*aware of*
according to	*bored by (with)* the show
accuse of a crime	*complain about* (not *complain with*)
adapt to a situation	*conform to* the rules
afraid of the dog	*cooperate with* the authorities
agree on a plan of action	*disappointed in (by)* a person
agree to a change	*disappointed in (with)* a thing
agree with the professor	*familiar with*
alternatives to (not *alternatives for*)	*fired from* her job
angry with his father	*get in* a car
argue about (not *argue on*)	*get on* a bus (boat, plane, train)
arrive at the airport (not *arrive to*)	*impatient with* a person

inferior to	*proud of*
jealous of her boyfriend	*relate to*
just in time	*run up (down)* the stairs
listen to the instructions	*scared by* the thunder
live in a house (city)	*similar to*
live on a street	*sit at* a table
look at a book (not *look to*)	*sit in* a chair
march in a parade (not *march on*)	*superior to*
married to a doctor (not *married with*)	*tired of* his job
oblivious to one's surroundings	*wait for* the bus
on many occasions	*wait in (on)* line
opposed to	*wait on* the customers
park in a driveway	*walk on* the sidewalk (not *walk in*)
park on a street	*work on* a project (not *work in*)
part with an item	*write about* the accident

■ ■ ■ ■   ■ ■ ■ ■   **B A S I C L I N K**   ■ ■ ■ ■   ■ ■ ■ ■

WWW

For students whose first language is not English, the following Web site might provide helpful hints for addressing academic audiences:

http://owl.english.purdue.edu/handouts/esl/eslaudience.html

■ ■   ■ ■   ■ ■   ■ ■   ■ ■   ■ ■   ■ ■   ■ ■   ■ ■   ■ ■   ■ ■   ■ ■

Checklist for ESL Writers

1 ⁞ Master articles.
   a. Use *a* or *an* for general reference, *the* for specific reference.
   b. Place *a* or *an* before singular nouns only.
   c. Use *a* or *an* before count nouns, not before noncount nouns.
   d. Place *a* before consonant sounds, *an* before vowel sounds.
   e. In most cases, don't use articles before abstract nouns.
   f. Don't use *the* when referring to members of a group or to something in general.
   g. Don't use articles with proper nouns that name people; countries, continents, states, provinces, cities, or islands; parks; mountains; small bodies of water; and political or religious leaders.
   h. Use articles with proper nouns that name regions; mountain ranges; groups of islands; large bodies of water; certain nations; wars; buildings, canals, and bridges; and titles of political or religious leaders.

2 ⁞ Use plurals correctly.
   a. Form the plurals of regular nouns by adding *-s* or *-es*.
   b. Be alert to noncount nouns, which are always singular.
   c. Use plural nouns immediately after adjectives such as *a few, many, most,* and *some* and after pronouns such as *these* and *those*.
   d. Use plural nouns after adjective phrases introduced by *one of the.*
   e. Use *many* and *many of* with plural count nouns. Use *much* and *much of* with noncount nouns, which are singular.
   f. Use *a few* with plural count nouns; use *a little* with noncount nouns, which are singular.
   g. Use *all, a lot of, most of,* or *more* with plural count nouns and with noncount nouns, which are singular.
   h. Use singular, not plural, nouns after *much* and *much of.*
   i. Use *this* and *that* with singular nouns; use *these* and *those* with plural nouns.
   j. Do not make adjectives plural, even when they describe plural nouns.
   k. Use singular, not plural, nouns after phrases such as *a kind of, a type of, a sort of,* or *a style of.*
   l. Use plural nouns after phrases such as *kinds of, types of, sorts of,* or *styles of.*

3 ⁞ Master sentence structure.
   a. In most cases, follow regular word order for declarative sentences.
   b. In general, use inverted word order for questions.
   c. Use regular, not inverted, word order when introducing a subordinate clause beginning with *where, when, how,* or *why.*
   d. Add words such as *it* and *there* when they are needed as subjects.
   e. Do not use a pronoun to repeat the subject of a sentence.
   f. Do not use a pronoun to repeat a direct object.

CREDITS

INDEX

Correction Symbols for Common Problems

abr	correct faulty abbreviation	49.1–13	ref	check pronoun reference	36.3
add	add information		red	eliminate redundancy	32.3
adj/adv	use correct adjective/adverb	38.1–6	rep	correct repetitious language	23.2, 32.1
agr	correct subject-verb or pronoun-antecedent agreement	35.1, 37.1, 53.2	run-on	correct run-on sentence (see "fused sentence")	22.2
art	insert or correct article	51.1	sent log	correct sentence logic	26.1–2, 26.5, 31.4
awk	correct awkward phrasing		sexist	avoid sexist language	31.8, 37.2
cap	capitalize correctly (upper/lowercase)	48.1–10	shift	correct faulty shift	25.3, 26.6
case	use correct pronoun case	36.2	slang	inappropriate use of slang	31.5
cliché	eliminate overused expression	31.6	sp	correct spelling	46.1–7
coh	improve paragraph coherence	4.5	ss	revise sentence structure	22.1–3
			style	use appropriate style	31.2
coord	correct coordination problem	23.3, 24.1, 26.3	tense	use correct verb tense	34.2–3
			tr	transpose	
cs	eliminate comma splice	22.3	trans	add a transition	4.5
dev	develop paragraph or idea more fully	5.1–2	ts	add/revise topic sentence	4.3, 5.2
			unity	improve paragraph unity	
dm	correct dangling modifier	25.1	var	vary sentence types	27.3
doc	correct documentation problem	15.1–3, 16.1–2, 17.1–2	vb	use correct verb form	34.2–7
			wc	check word choice	30.1–7
frag	correct sentence fragment	22.1	wdy	eliminate wordiness	32.1–6
fs	correct fused sentence	22.2	∀	insert an apostrophe	43.1–3
hyph	add hyphen	47.1–4	[/]	insert brackets	45.1
ital	underline or set in italics	50.2	:	insert a colon	42.1–4
jarg	eliminate inappropriate jargon	31.5	∧	insert a comma	40.1–9
			no ∧	omit unnecessary comma	40.10
lc	lowercase letter needed	48.1–10	—	insert a dash	45.2
log	correct problem with logic	6.8	...	insert an ellipsis	45.1
mm	correct misplaced modifier	25.2	!	insert an exclamation point	39.1
mod	correct modification	25.1–3	-	insert a hyphen	47.1–4
ms	correct manuscript form	5.5, 15.4, 16.3, 17.3	(/)	insert parentheses	45.3
			?	insert a question mark	39.1
num	use correct form of number	50.1	"/"	insert quotation marks	44.1–3
//ism	correct parallelism	24.1–4	⊙	insert a period	39.1–2
pl	plural	51.2	¶	start a new paragraph	4.1
para	correct problem with paraphrase	13.4	no ¶	do not start a new paragraph	4.1
			#	insert a space	
pass	change to active voice	28.2	⌒	close up space	
quote	correct problem with quotation	13.4	∧	insert	
			ℐ	delete	
			??	unclear	

CONTENTS

4 ▷ **Master special problems with verbs.**
    a. Include helping verbs as needed.
    b. Learn to use modals to create special meanings.
    c. Learn to use gerunds and infinitives with verbs. Some verbs take both
        gerunds and infinitives with no change in meaning. Others mean one
        thing when used with gerunds and another thing when used with
        infinitives. Some verbs can be used only with gerunds; others, only with
        infinitives.

5 ▷ **Master subject-verb agreement.**
    a. Use singular verbs that end in -s with indefinite pronouns.
    b. Make verbs in subordinate clauses agree with the nouns those
        clauses modify.

6 ▷ **Master adjectives and adverbs.**
    a. When using a noun as an adjective, make sure it is singular even though
        the noun it describes is plural.
    b. Follow this order for placing adjectives before a noun:
    article; adjective of quantity; adjective of quality or condition; adjective of size,
    weight, or shape; adjective of age; adjective of color; adjective of material;
    adjective formed from a noun; noun
    c. Do not place adverbs between verbs and their direct objects.

7 ▷ **Master participles.**
    a. Use present participles to show action or to describe a noun or pronoun; use
        past participles to show what is done to a noun or pronoun.
    b. Always include participial endings.

8 ▷ **Use words correctly.**

Do not substitute nouns for verbs or for adjectives.

Learn to use prepositions with indirect objects.
    a. Don't use a preposition if the indirect object comes immediately after the
        verb.
    b. Do use a preposition if the indirect object comes immediately after the direct
        object.

Review the list of idiomatic expressions, and remember the correct preposition to
use in each expression.